OXFORD WORLD'S

WASPS AND OTI

ARISTOPHANES (*c*.450–385) was the most important poet oɪ Uɪu
Comedy, the exuberant, satirical, and often obscene form of festival
drama which flourished during the heyday of classical Athenian culture in the fifth century BC. Much of his career fell within the years
of the prolonged Peloponnesian War between Athens and Sparta
(431–404); three of his plays, *Acharnians* (425), *Peace* (421), and
Lysistrata (411), draw on the war, though in highly fantastic fashion,
for inspiration. The earlier part of his career was dominated by issues
from the city's democratic politics and by scurrilous treatment of the
demagogue Kleon, especially in *Knights* (424) and, more obliquely, in
his comedy on the law courts, *Wasps* (422). But Aristophanes also
showed a leaning towards cultural themes: hence his caricature of the
philosopher Sokrates in *Clouds* (423), and later his burlesque of materials
from the tragic stage in both *Women at the Thesmophoria* (411) and
Frogs (405). A vein of sheer absurdity and dreamlike wish-fulfilment
runs through his work, reaching a kind of *ne plus ultra* in the cosmic
triumph of Peisetairos, the man-bird-god, in *Birds* (414). His last two
surviving plays, *Assembly-Women* (*c*.393) and *Wealth* (388), partly represent a change of direction for the genre, moving away from a biting,
uninhibited ethos towards the gentler humour of character and situation
which was eventually to generate the New Comedy of Menander.

STEPHEN HALLIWELL is Wardlaw Professor of Greek Emeritus at
the University of St Andrews. He has taught in the universities of
Oxford, London, Cambridge, and Birmingham, and held visiting
professorships in Belgium, Canada, Italy, and the USA. His extensive
publications on Greek literature, philosophy, and culture include two
prize-winning books: *Greek Laughter: A Study of Cultural Psychology
from Homer to Early Christianity* (2008, winner of the Criticos Prize
2008), and *The Aesthetics of Mimesis: Ancient Texts and Modern
Problems* (2002, winner of the Premio Europeo d'Estetica, 2008). His
book *Between Ecstasy and Truth* was published by OUP in 2011. He is
a Fellow of both the British Academy and the Royal Society of
Edinburgh.

OXFORD WORLD'S CLASSICS

*For over 100 years Oxford World's Classics have brought
readers closer to the world's great literature. Now with over 700
titles—from the 4,000-year-old myths of Mesopotamia to the
twentieth century's greatest novels—the series makes available
lesser-known as well as celebrated writing.*

*The pocket-sized hardbacks of the early years contained
introductions by Virginia Woolf, T. S. Eliot, Graham Greene,
and other literary figures which enriched the experience of reading.
Today the series is recognized for its fine scholarship and
reliability in texts that span world literature, drama and poetry,
religion, philosophy, and politics. Each edition includes perceptive
commentary and essential background information to meet the
changing needs of readers.*

OXFORD WORLD'S CLASSICS

ARISTOPHANES

Wasps and Other Plays

Translated with an Introduction and Notes by
STEPHEN HALLIWELL

OXFORD
UNIVERSITY PRESS

OXFORD

UNIVERSITY PRESS

Great Clarendon Street, Oxford, OX2 6DP,
United Kingdom

Oxford University Press is a department of the University of Oxford.
It furthers the University's objective of excellence in research, scholarship,
and education by publishing worldwide. Oxford is a registered trade mark of
Oxford University Press in the UK and in certain other countries

© Stephen Halliwell 2022
First Published in 2022, as *Aristophanes: Acharnians, Knights, Wasps, Peace*
First published as an Oxford World's Classics paperback 2024

The moral rights of the author have been asserted

All rights reserved. No part of this publication may be reproduced, stored in
a retrieval system, or transmitted, in any form or by any means, without the
prior permission in writing of Oxford University Press, or as expressly permitted
by law, by licence or under terms agreed with the appropriate reprographics
rights organization. Enquiries concerning reproduction outside the scope of the
above should be sent to the Rights Department, Oxford University Press, at the
address above

You must not circulate this work in any other form
and you must impose this same condition on any acquirer

Published in the United States of America by Oxford University Press
198 Madison Avenue, New York, NY 10016, United States of America

British Library Cataloguing in Publication Data

Data available

Library of Congress Control Number: 2023948075

ISBN 978-0-19-890022-1

Printed and bound in the UK by
Clays Ltd, Elcograf S.p.A.

Links to third party websites are provided by Oxford in good faith and
for information only. Oxford disclaims any responsibility for the materials
contained in any third party website referenced in this work.

PREFACE

THIS is the third and final volume of my verse translation of the eleven surviving plays of Aristophanes. The first volume, containing *Birds*, *Lysistrata*, *Assembly-Women*, and *Wealth*, was published in Oxford World's Classics in 1998 as *Aristophanes: Birds and Other Plays*; the second, containing *Clouds*, *Women at the Thesmophoria*, and *Frogs*, as well as selected fragments from the lost plays, appeared in the same series as *Aristophanes: Frogs and Other Plays* in 2016. My approach as translator has remained consistent across all three volumes; it is explained in further detail in the section of the general Introduction on 'Translating Aristophanes'. In short, I have tried to combine a high degree of historical accuracy, not least for the sake of university and school students, with sufficient fluency and vigour to engage the interest of modern readers. The desire to preserve as much as possible of the extraordinarily rich texture of Aristophanes' plays—texts unparalleled in their range of reference to the political, social, and cultural life of classical Athens—is also reflected in the provision of fuller annotation than is to be found in most other versions. Reading Aristophanes requires a constant imaginative effort, but one informed by historical understanding.

The substance of the general Introduction remains much the same as in the previous volumes, though I have made numerous revisions and additions of detail. The Introductions to individual plays attempt to develop critical perspectives of my own on major issues of interpretation which continue to be the subject of keen debate among modern scholars. It is worth repeating that in the vexed matter of the spelling of ancient Greek names I have sacrificed perfect consistency to a workable compromise: while I largely avoid Latinized forms, I have sometimes kept familiar English spellings where not to do so might seem precious, and/or where their pronunciation assists the rhythms of the translation. Almost all dates are BC; the main exceptions are to be found in the part of the Introduction entitled 'Aristophanes and Posterity'. The Index of Names contains only certain people, places, and institutions mentioned multiple times in the texts of the plays; technical terms relating to theatrical performance are explained in the sections of the general Introduction entitled

'Formality and Performance' and 'Stage Directions'. Marginal numerals in the translation refer to the standard lineation of the Greek text (following the editions specified in the Select Bibliography).

S.H.

St Andrews
October 2020

CONTENTS

INTRODUCTION

Aristophanes' Career in Context

THE ELEVEN extant plays of Aristophanes are not only the earliest surviving comedies in the history of Western theatre, they are actually the first fully fledged comic dramas which we possess from any culture in the world. They represent a phase of Greek comedy to which ancient scholars eventually attached the chronological label 'Old' Comedy, in order to indicate its remoteness from the later phase of the genre's history which they termed 'New' Comedy.[1] While the roots of Old Comedy lay partly in the improvised practices of archaic folk festivity (see below), it had its heyday in the theatrical festivals of Athens in the middle and second half of the fifth century, so that it belongs unequivocally to the matrix of what we now call classical Athenian culture. Its distinctive ethos, as we see in the plays of Aristophanes himself and can corroborate from the numerous available fragments of the work of other poets of Old Comedy, is quintessentially zany, fantastic, scurrilous, and larger-than-life. In that spirit, its treatment of both character and action flaunts a basic disregard for dramatic consistency, plausibility, or coherence; it is permeated by a comic mentality which is physically reductive, i.e. preoccupied with the impulses of the 'lower body' (in Bakhtinian terms), and crudely cynical. All this is in sharp contrast to New Comedy, which flourished in the time of Menander and others during the later fourth and third centuries, and is marked by semi-realistic if somewhat stylized characterization, neatly integrated plots, benign sentimentality, and an underlying tolerance of human foibles. New Comedy is the ancestor, via the Roman reworking of Greek plays by Plautus, Terence, and others (and later, in turn, via the vernacular adaptation of Roman comedy itself in the Renaissance), of the broad spectrum of European comedy of manners and situation comedy. But if New Comedy has a lineage which visibly continues right the way up to modern sitcom, this makes it all the more significant that, in most

---

[1] On the intermediate category of so-called 'Middle' Comedy, a term which broadly describes plays of the first half of the fourth century, see the Introductions to *Assembly-Women* and *Wealth* in my *Aristophanes: Birds and Other Plays* (Oxford, 1998).

respects, it is a world apart from what Aristophanes would have recognized as comic theatre.[2] To appreciate Aristophanes on his own terms, therefore, we may need to suspend some of our standard expectations of dramatic comedy.

The history of ancient Greek comedy was, in its larger trajectory, a process of slow but irreversible evolution from 'Old' to 'New'. At the micro level of individual plays, however, the process was hardly a linear, let alone a teleologically driven, progression. Between around 480 and 300, probably more than one thousand comedies were staged at the official Athenian dramatic festivals, the City Dionysia and the Lenaia (see below). Since the overwhelming majority of those plays are lost (leaving us, though, with thousands of fragments to stimulate and tantalize the imagination), we naturally cannot chart the entire development of the genre in detail. But we can be sure that it was a matter of perpetual theatrical experimentation and (re-)invention, teeming with dramatic forms and features which even in principle could not be fitted into a single schema of historical change. This must have been especially true of the prime period of Old Comedy in the later decades of the fifth century, the period to which nine of Aristophanes' eleven extant plays belong.

In a career which stretched from 427 to the mid-380s, Aristophanes wrote more than forty plays for the Athenian theatre. The eleven which remain demonstrate that his favoured mode of humour involves exuberance, irreverence, and indecency carried to absurdist extremes and mediated through a repertoire of dramatic techniques which revel in the topsy-turvy mixing and jumbling of categories (mythical and actual, human and animal, male and female, abstract and concrete, real and pretended, public and private) as well as in the creative manipulation of many disparate registers of language and poetic form. To attune ourselves to Aristophanes' comic world at a distance of two-and-a-half millennia, we need to open our minds to a multifaceted genre in which vulgarity and sophistication, far-fetched extravagance and down-to-earth grossness, constantly rub shoulders. But we also need a historical framework of understanding, without which the cultural specificity of Old Comedy will elude us.

---

[2] For some further points of contrast between the legacy of Old and New Comedy, see 'Aristophanes and Posterity', below.

At the time of Aristophanes' birth (probably between 450 and 445), comedy had been part of the official programme at the City (or Great) Dionysia festival, celebrated in late March or early April each year, for close to two generations (since 487/6, to be precise). It was added to the schedule of the Lenaia (late January), another but lesser festival of Dionysos, not long before 440, when Aristophanes was a boy (but could already have attended the theatre: see below). By the second half of the fifth century, plays included in these festivals, both comedies and tragedies, were performed by professional actors (though chorus-members were citizen amateurs)[3] at technically high standards of production worthy of major state-organized events. At a much earlier stage, Attic comedy had emerged from a long prehistory in a range of improvised and popular entertainments performed by 'volunteers'. That last term, evidently denoting enthusiastic amateurs, is Aristotle's (*Poetics* 4.1449a2) in a passage where he also picks out, as the most prominent forerunner of the dramatic genre of comedy, the semi-ritualized but boisterous celebrations which he calls *phallika*, 'phallic processions/songs' (4.1449a10–13). As it happens, Aristophanes himself incorporates a phallic procession into one of his surviving plays, at *Acharnians* 241–79, where we can catch something of the heady atmosphere of festive ceremonial, bawdy revels, and personal scurrility which might have marked such occasions.[4] The setting at this point in the play is the protagonist Dikaiopolis's celebration, with carefree and egotistical hedonism, of the Rural Dionysia, a local festival held in the various demes (or villages) of Attika. The scene is in one sense a symbol of Old Comedy's own Dionysiac spirit, but the fact that Aristophanes can dramatize a phallic procession of this type in a somewhat parodic fashion is itself a sign, albeit a nicely ambiguous one, of how far Athenian comedy had acquired an artistic status above and beyond its earthy origins. Beginning from the sub-literary level of folk 'mummery' and

---

[3] Pseudo-Xenophon, *Constitution of the Athenians* 1.13, seems to suggest that chorus-members would receive some financial payment, but this still would not have put them in the same professional bracket as the major actors.

[4] A comparable example is the Eleusinian procession in the parodos of *Frogs* (316–459), which refers to a mixture of earnestness and mirth at 389–90 and culminates in a representation of communal, festive abuse at 416–30: choral satire is particularly well adapted for evoking the spirit of collective, ritualized exhilaration of this kind. Cf. S. Halliwell, *Greek Laughter: A Study of Cultural Psychology from Homer to Early Christianity* (Cambridge, 2008), 206–14.

festival sideshows, comedy had by the mid-fifth century developed into a poetic and theatrical genre that was able to sustain a coexistence alongside tragedy at two major civic festivals. In the Rural Dionysia scene of *Acharnians*, we see Aristophanes taking a wry glance at Old Comedy's local roots from, so to speak, his elevated position in a state-sponsored dramatic competition. This is a case, as quite commonly in Aristophanes, of comedy looking at itself in its own (distorting) mirror.

Aristophanes reveals an awareness of the history and traditions of his genre above all in the parabasis of *Knights* (514–44),[5] where he (comically) recalls and appraises a trio of important predecessors: Magnes, whose highly successful career went back close to the official beginnings of comedy at the City Dionysia (he was already a leading figure in the 470s); Kratinos,[6] whose early plays were staged in the mid-450s but who was still active at this time and actually competing against *Knights* in 424; and Krates, whose career fell largely in the 440s, and perhaps the early 430s, at a time when Aristophanes is likely to have attended the theatre as a boy. Although the vignettes of these three figures are coloured and embroidered with fictional freedom, they do give us some valuable hints about those aspects of the development of fifth-century comedy which might have seemed salient to a playwright of Aristophanes' generation. The passage highlights, for one thing, the visual and musico-choreographic elements which had become so fundamental to comedy's theatrical style, and in which it is reasonable to accept that Magnes had been a pioneer.[7] It mentions also the urbane type of wit supposedly characteristic of Krates, whose plays may well have been notable for a less scurrilous seam of humour than was practised by most of his contemporaries.[8] Yet above all it foregrounds, and burlesques as mock-heroic, the satirical power of Kratinos, who had dominated the comic theatre of the 440s and

---

[5] On the general nature of the parabasis as a performative convention, see 'Formality and Performance', below.

[6] For Kratinos, see the Index of Names.

[7] It is not insignificant for Aristophanes himself that Magnes' titles include *Birds* and *Frogs*.

[8] At *Poetics* 5.1449b7–9, Aristotle claims that Krates was the first comic poet at Athens to abandon the 'iambic mode'—i.e. scurrilous personal satire—and to concentrate on coherent plot-construction. The few surviving fragments of Krates' work are at any rate compatible with the thesis that he tended to avoid the satire of named individuals that was so basic to the genre in general.

430s (winning a total of nine first prizes) and had specialized in vehement topical ridicule whose targets included Athens' greatest politician, none other than Perikles. For all its rhetorical contrivance, then, this part of *Knights* conveys an underlying artistic self-consciousness which recognizes a whole array of comic resources—the flamboyantly theatrical, the linguistically clever, and the satirically hard-hitting—made available by the history of the genre in Athens.

The ostensible purpose of Aristophanes' comments on some of his predecessors in *Knights* is to explain why he had not taken personal charge of the staging of his own plays prior to that date (424). The explanation offered takes the form of emphasizing, with the colourful elaboration already mentioned, what a complicated and hazardous business it was to produce a comedy in front of a mass festival audience of Athenians. It is plausible that this was the chief reason why Aristophanes, who may have been as young as 18 when his first play (*Banqueters*) was staged in 427, turned in the early years of his career to the services of a specialist producer/director, Kallistratos (who possibly had qualifications as an actor too). Since Old Comedy employed a chorus of twenty-four dancers (compared to fifteen in tragedy), who needed months of vocal and choreographic training for their substantial and intricate routines,[9] the duties of the producer (*didaskalos*, lit. '(chorus-)trainer') must have been onerous. Inexperience alone makes Aristophanes' early use of Kallistratos understandable; but the fact that several of his later plays as well were produced by others (see the Chronology), including Philonides (an actor-playwright himself), suggests that the technical sophistication of theatrical production was by this date becoming increasingly demanding and entailed professionalized skills in the rehearsal and staging of plays which not all poets felt comfortable assuming. The old convention of the combined poet-producer, which appears to have been the norm for both tragedy and comedy in the first half of the fifth century, was by now on the wane.

It would be fascinating if we could reconstruct in more precise terms how the career of a young playwright was launched in classical Athens. Unfortunately our evidence hardly allows us to do this in much detail, but in Aristophanes' case we do have tantalizing glimpses

---

[9] See below, 'Formality and Performance', for details of the chorus's main contributions to Old Comedy.

of some relevant conditions. *Clouds* 528 refers, in connection with the production of the earlier play *Banqueters* (see above), to a group of people whom the author finds it 'a pleasure to mention': we are prob-ably entitled to infer that these were backers or patrons, people of influence who helped to promote his entry into the official world of festival drama.[10] In this same passage Aristophanes talks of himself as an 'unmarried girl' whose baby had to be 'exposed' (i.e. abandoned) and was taken up by 'another girl'. The reality behind this ironically coy imagery is best interpreted as a situation in which a gifted but inexperienced new playwright needed extensive support in, first, applying to the relevant magistrate (Archon) for permission to have his plays staged at state festivals, and, secondly, in turning those plays into successful, large-scale performances before an audience of many thousands. Aristophanes is nonetheless likely to have had some practical involvement in theatrical rehearsals for his early plays, and *Knights* 541–4 (with its analogy to a hierarchy of functions on board a ship) suggests that he was steadily acquiring familiarity with the arts of production during the period 427–4.

As for the ability to write complex *texts* suitable for production, Aristophanes must have benefited both from a particularly thorough version of the education in poetry and music which was available to well-to-do Athenian sons,[11] and from many experiences, starting in his boyhood (see *Clouds* 539, *Peace* 50, 766, for the presence of boys in the theatre), as a spectator of plays himself, and later perhaps as a choreut or chorus-member.[12] But it is also possible that the pre-parations for, and even the early phases of, his career involved some element of poetic collaboration (of the kind known from other theat-rical traditions, including Elizabethan-Jacobean England). The phe-nomenon of collaboration is, at any rate, apparently assumed at *Wasps*

[10] On the official procedures involved in having a play selected for performance, see 'Old Comedy and Dionysiac Festivity', below.

[11] See esp. Plato, *Protagoras* 325d–6c, for a description of this education, with Aristophanes' own *Clouds* 961–72 for a partly travestied reflection of traditional musico-poetic schooling.

[12] We know from the famous Pronomos vase, on which the choreuts are all beardless, that adolescents or very young men could be members of satyr-play choruses: see e.g. pl. 8 in E. Csapo and W. J. Slater, *The Context of Ancient Drama* (Ann Arbor, 1995). Those age-groups are also likely to have been able to perform in comic choruses: cf. the beardless figures in the illustration in J. Rusten (ed.), *The Birth of Comedy* (Baltimore, 2011), 430.

1018–20, where there is a reference to secret assistance supposedly given by Aristophanes himself to other poets. This is another parabatic claim that is no doubt skewed by the rhetorical bragging expected of comic poets, but it does receive some support from other pieces of available evidence.[13] No one can now be confident about the practical circumstances of Aristophanes' 'apprenticeship' in the early to mid-420s, but given the nature of Athenian theatrical culture it is a reasonable supposition that they were many-stranded.

If a sense of comedy's rich theatrical history, as we saw in the parabasis of *Knights*, was one factor which shaped Aristophanes' early development as a dramatist, another factor, albeit of a more ambiguous kind for a satirist, must have been his awareness of belonging to the largest and most self-confident polis in Greece. Aristophanes grew up at a time when Athens was close to the zenith of its power and authority in the Greek world, during an era of political and cultural life presided over by Perikles as the city's most influential politician. Under Perikles' leadership the 440s and 430s saw, among much else, the building of the Parthenon as a monument to the imperial dominance and wealth of Athens, and the establishment of the city as a cosmopolitan centre which attracted artists, intellectuals, traders, tourists, and others from all round the Mediterranean and even beyond. It was in large part, however, Athens' very success as the head of a notional 'alliance'[14] of Greek cities, though gradually transformed into a de facto empire, which caused a steady deterioration in relations with her main rival, and leader of an alternative power-bloc, Sparta. Conflict came to a head in 431 with the outbreak of hostilities which were to run, with only short interruptions, till Athens' final defeat in 404, and which we now know (following Thucydides' conception of its historical significance) as the Peloponnesian War. Most of Aristophanes' career, including probably some three-quarters of his output, fell within the years of the war, as can readily be seen from the details of his surviving plays given in the Chronology.[15]

---

[13] See my article, 'Authorial Collaboration in the Athenian Comic Theatre', *Greek, Roman, and Byzantine Studies*, 30 (1989), 515–28. Cf. n. 16 below.

[14] The so-called Delian League, founded in 478–7 in the aftermath of the second Persian invasion: see Thucydides 1.96–7.

[15] For the chronology of the lost plays, together with a selection of fragments from them, see the Appendix to my *Aristophanes: Frogs and Other Plays* (Oxford, 2016).

Aristophanes lived, then, through the period in which Athenian imperial hegemony was challenged and eventually defeated by Sparta and her allies, though the last part of his career, in the early years of the fourth century (to which *Assembly-Women* and *Wealth* belong), saw the rebuilding of Athens' position and the emergence of new power relations between the leading Greek city-states. Old Comedy of the kind practised by Aristophanes had been formed in most essential respects in the generation before him, not least under the influence of Kratinos's politically topical mode of satire (see above). It is no coincidence that the comic spirit running through Aristophanes' work presupposes, in the exuberance of its various freedoms, the democratic and cultural self-confidence which had been established in Athens between around 470 and 430 on the basis of the city's imperial power and the economic prosperity flowing from it. Equally, however, many of Aristophanes' plays were produced at a time when this self-confidence was being tested and threatened in a war which came to assume unprecedented proportions. Although we cannot precisely correlate the themes and emphases of Aristophanes' entire oeuvre with the upheavals of the war years, we can at any rate see that without this context much that we find in his plays would not have taken the form that it does. The war itself became a recurrent starting-point for his plots: three of the extant works (*Acharnians*, *Peace*, *Lysistrata*) are in that basic sense 'war-plays', though it is important in each case to recognize how very selective, and even unreal, Aristophanes' comic treatment of the war actually is. Other features of Athens' particular historical situation find their echoes in the playwright's choice of subjects, among them the workings of the democratic Assembly (*Acharnians*, *Assembly-Women*), the system of law-courts (*Wasps*), and the city's demagogic or 'populist' leadership in the years after Perikles' death (*Knights*), as well as the officialdom of Athenian imperialism (*Birds*). Even so, it is difficult to chart a consistent relationship between Aristophanes' themes and the shifting currents of Athenian politics and society, especially once sufficient allowance is made for the uneven representation of the different phases of his career in the plays available to us.

The concentration of surviving works from the 420s probably leaves us with a rather unbalanced impression of the playwright's total output, but it is nonetheless far from accidental. This was an intense stretch of Aristophanes' career: between 427 and the end of the decade he wrote a comedy for each of the major festivals, the City Dionysia and the Lenaia, in most years, and won several first prizes. As a result he became established, alongside his close contemporary Eupolis,[16] as outstanding among a new generation of comic dramatists. During these years he acquired an especially pungent satirical style which owed something to his most successful predecessor, Kratinos. While several playwrights in the 420s fell under the influence of Kratinos, it was Aristophanes who made particularly distinctive use of this influence by vigorously lampooning Kleon, the most prominent and potent politician in the city in the post-Periklean era (Thucydides 3.36.6 called Kleon the 'most aggressive' but also 'most persuasive' of the city's leaders). Although Kleon himself may not have been an explicit target in one of Aristophanes' earliest comedies, *Babylonians*, in 426, it was that play which provoked him into taking the unusual step of making an official complaint before the Council about the poet's treatment of Athens' relations with her allies. The gravamen of his complaint was, it seems, that highly sensitive elements in those relations had been mocked in front of an audience containing ambassadors from the allied cities at the City Dionysia. But the fact that our chief evidence for this controversy comes from Aristophanes himself, in two remarkable passages of metatheatre in *Acharnians* (377–82, 502–8), is doubly pertinent: both because we need to allow for comic distortion of the details, and because the poet is not afraid to advertise the incident for his own purposes, which hardly suggests it had done him great harm.[17] If, moreover, *Wasps* 1284–91 refers (colourfully) to the same episode, which not all scholars accept, then while Kleon may have tried to extract from Aristophanes an undertaking to avoid embarrassing the city in front of allied ambassadors, there is nothing whatever to support the traditional idea that he formally 'prosecuted' the playwright. In this same

---

[16] Aristophanes' only reference in his surviving plays to Eupolis (whose career ran from 429 to *c.*412) is at *Clouds* 553–7, which accuses him of plagiarism. Eupolis himself subsequently claimed (fr. 89) that he had helped Aristophanes write *Knights*. While we are undoubtedly dealing in such cases with the give-and-take of comic rivalry, so that individual details may be pure fiction, it is hard to see how such humour could operate if collaboration was not sometimes practised. Cf. n. 13 above.

[17] For further discussion of the clash with Kleon, see my Introduction to *Acharnians*, with Halliwell, *Greek Laughter*, 248–9; for other views, see the items by Sommerstein and Storey in the Bibliography, under 'Aristophanes' Career'. For what we do and do not know about *Babylonians*, see my *Frogs and Other Plays*, 237–8.

passage of *Wasps*, we should notice, Aristophanes feels able to boast that he had the last laugh. Certainly Aristophanes was free to satirize Kleon personally, and he made the most of that freedom with his elaborately and scabrously allegorical attack on the politician in *Knights*. In the long run, the controversy over *Babylonians*, whatever exactly it involved, may even have helped to lend some kudos to the young playwright in the early years of his career.

Despite his quasi-political clash with Kleon, the extent to which Aristophanes' choice of satirical topics and targets can be interpreted as politically motivated in a thoroughgoing sense remains a keenly disputed issue to which I shall return later in this Introduction (see 'Satire and Seriousness'). But it is worth pointing out here that the 420s witnessed a configuration of factors in Aristophanes' career—not only in terms of his recurrent concern with aspects of war and democracy, but also in his almost obsessive interest in one particular politician—which was not subsequently sustained. After the Peace of Nikias in 421, which ended the first phase of the Peloponnesian War, Aristophanes' work appears to have deliberately moved in a rather different direction. Although we cannot take entirely at face value the account he gives of this change at *Clouds* 545–62 (a passage revised a number of years after the first performance in 423), it is not meaningless that he there mocks his rivals for continuing to write plays about individual politicians, and boasts, with flamboyant aplomb, about his own perpetual search for comic originality. That passage is entertainingly tendentious, in the usual manner of the poet's pronouncements in the parabasis, but beneath its rhetoric there is a claim which does seem to be borne out by our other evidence for his career. In particular, after 420 Aristophanes appears never again to have devoted a play to a single political figure,[18] in the way in which, for example, Plato comicus did on several occasions (with his *Peisandros*, *Hyperbolos*, and *Kleophon*), or Eupolis seems to have done once more around 415, when his *Baptai* ('*Bathers*') made Alkibiades its major butt. On the other hand, Aristophanes turned repeatedly after this date to mythological burlesque (some ten titles at least apparently belong in this category), but also to themes that were literary or broadly cultural in comic character (*Women at the*

---

[18] This includes *Triphales*, which was once thought to have been about Alkibiades (cf. note on *Acharnians* 716); our slight evidence does nothing to support that hypothesis.

Thesmophoria and *Frogs* being salient cases in point). Of course substantial political elements of a kind do appear in some of his post-420 plays, though in the two most obvious cases, *Lysistrata* and *Assembly-Women* (which were written almost twenty years apart), the world of politics is transmuted into the extreme fantasy of 'women on top' plots, and there is relatively limited direct satire of real individuals or specific contemporary issues. So we do have some grounds for supposing that in the rather intense early years of his career—the years to which all the plays in the present volume belong—Aristophanes indulged his appetite for bitingly political work to the point where he felt he had sated it on the divisive figure of Kleon (who died in 422),[19] and that thereafter he sought to break new ground in the open-ended possibilities of Old Comedy.

Old Comedy and Dionysiac Festivity

Comedy, like tragedy, was not available all year round at Athens in regular theatrical performances; it was staged only at a small number of festivals, of which the two main ones, the Lenaia and the City or Great Dionysia, have already been mentioned. The Lenaia took place in mid-winter, the City Dionysia in late winter or early spring; but plays for both were selected by major magistrates (Archons: see Index of Names) months in advance. In submitting what was presumably an outline and/or provisional extracts, the poet was officially 'requesting a chorus' (cf. *Knights* 513), and in choosing a play the Archon 'granted a chorus', even though the costs of the twenty-four-man chorus, unlike the fees of the individual actors, were defrayed not by the state but by a *chorêgos* (see *Peace* 1022), a kind of sponsor or impresario appointed for the purpose on criteria of personal wealth. The long period between selection and performance involved not only rehearsals and the making of costumes (including masks), but also completion and revision of the text. Traces of ongoing revision can be seen, for example, in the case of *Knights*, where gibes about Kleon's 'stolen' victory at Pylos (54–7, etc.) cannot have been inserted

---

[19] In addition to the parabasis of *Clouds* cited in my text above, note the suggestion at *Wasps* 62–3 that Aristophanes intends to move away from his satirical preoccupation with Kleon: the suggestion is, as it turns out, partly disingenuous (see my Introduction to *Wasps*), but it nonetheless underlines that leaving old themes behind was an *idea* which made sense to Aristophanes.

before around early September 425, or in that of *Frogs*, where references to the death of Sophokles (76–9, 787), who died some months
later than Euripides, probably represent a fairly late addition to the
text. The case of *Peace*, staged at the Dionysia 421, is particularly
intriguing in this regard. When Aristophanes was originally
awarded a chorus for that festival, there was no direct prospect of
peace with Sparta. But negotiations opened in late summer or early
winter 422, proceeded through the course of that winter, and led
to a peace treaty which was signed, as Thucydides tells us (5.20.1),
immediately after the City Dionysia. Aristophanes was writing, revis-
ing, and rehearsing the play, in other words, during a period when the
prospects of an actual peace, as opposed to his comedy's fantasy version, were gradually turning from possibility to reality.

The fact of a festival context is crucially important for the nature of
Old Comedy. The Greek word *kômôdia* means 'revel-song'. A *kômos*,
which might easily form part of a larger festival framework, typically
consisted of an exuberantly celebratory, alcohol-fuelled procession
accompanied by song and dance.[20] The ethos of the *kômos* as a cultural practice can be sensed at many points in Aristophanes' plays,
but perhaps especially in the rumbustious endings of works like
Acharnians, *Wasps*, *Peace*, and *Birds*: it is no accident that in such
cases the opportunity for a *kômos* arises from, or becomes in some
way associated with, a symposium (*Wasps*), a drinking contest (*Acharnians*), or a wedding (*Peace*, *Birds*). The generic vitality and freedom of
comedy stemmed, as we earlier saw Aristotle suggesting, from the
improvisatory spirit of such practices as phallic processional-songs.
The *kômos* was a kindred phenomenon, a mobile, high-spirited revel
that lent itself to play-acting and uninhibited self-expression: it is telling that Dikaipolis addresses the phallic personification Phales as
'fellow-reveller' within the context of his phallic song at *Acharnians*
264. The greater cultural 'respectability' which comedy had achieved
by 487–6, when it was first given official status alongside tragedy in the
City Dionysia, must have reflected a perception of increasingly ambitious standards—poetic, dramatic, and theatrical—on the part of the

---

[20] In addition to *Acharnians* 264 (see the text above), there are references to various
forms of *kômos* at e.g. *Acharnians* 980 (the metaphor of drunken War gate-crashing a
symposium, smashing the furniture, etc.), *Wasps* 1025 (where 'cruise round' translates a
unique Greek verb literally meaning 'to revel round'), *Clouds* 606 (Dionysos), *Women at
the Thesmophoria* 988, and *Frogs* 218.

genre's practitioners and audiences. But this elevation to the rank of state-organized festival performance did not erase the underlying comic impulse towards carnivalesque absurdity, indecency, and vulgarity, all of which preserved vestigial traces of the genre's 'folk' origins.

That tragedies and comedies were performed during the same Dionysiac festivals, even sometimes on the same day,[21] itself epitomizes the double-headed nature of Athenian festivity. These festivals were both deeply serious, as events affirming the collective identity and communal activity of the democratic polis, and yet at the same time opportunities for a kind of liberated and liberating licence. We can observe these opposed yet complementary forces particularly clearly in the case of the City Dionysia. This festival, which usually lasted for five or six days, was an occasion in part for an exceptionally ostentatious display of Athenian pride and self-confidence. Visitors from all over the Greek world were present, including, as earlier mentioned, ambassadors from Athens' allied cities, who brought with them the tribute that embodied their subservience to Athenian hegemony.[22] The festival's framework, like that of many others, was provided by ceremonial processions, prayers, sacrifices, and rituals, and among its oldest elements was the performance of dithyrambs, choral hymns to Dionysos. In addition, the Dionysia contained important public proclamations, such as the bestowal of honorific crowns on public benefactors. Yet amidst all this solemnity there was also an air of abandon and 'play', with a heady release from quotidian routine. Much civic business, including that of the courts, was suspended for the festival's duration, and prisoners were bailed from the city's prisons. Feasting and revelling of various kinds took place, and it was this side of the festivities which accounted for the celebratory, *kômos*-conducive traditions from which comedy itself came into existence. If the serious dimension of the Dionysia was typified by ceremonies involving the city's war-orphans in the theatre itself,[23]

---

[21] Although the details of the festival arrangements varied at different dates, *Birds* 789 shows that tragedies and comedies were performed on the same day at the date of that play (414).

[22] Aristophanes mentions these aspects of the City Dionysia when making a contrast with the Lenaia at *Acharnians* 502–8.

[23] The orphans were presented with suits of armour in the theatre, and some were given front seats for the dramatic performances: see Isokrates, *On the Peace* 82, Aischines, *Against Ktesiphon* 154.

comedy's capacity to invert civic seriousness is equally typified by a scene such as *Peace* 1270 ff., set in the context of a rustic wedding, where the idea of preparing the young for the acceptance of patriotic-military values is exposed to the scorn of a protagonist bent on festive self-gratification.

The two features of Aristophanes' plays, and of Old Comedy more generally, which most conspicuously express this hedonistic aspect of the Dionysia are an element of 'obscenity' (i.e. a freedom to treat sexual topics with shame-free explicitness)[24] and an extreme satirical licence (i.e. a freedom to ridicule practically anyone and anything). Both features could be loosely covered by the Greek term *aischrologia*, 'speaking what is shameful' (or, more pithily, 'filthy talk'). Comedy, that is to say, acted out a temporary escape from the norms of shame and inhibition which were an essential element in Athenian and Greek social mores. Sexual explicitness, mirroring the traditional practice of phallic songs, was built into the very fabric of comic performances in the shape of the phallus standardly worn by the actors and affording, together with their padded buttocks and belly, great scope for physical grotesqueness (cf. 'Stage Directions', below). It was further developed in frequent verbal and physical bawdy (including scatological crudity), such as Dikaiopolis's appearance with a pair of prostitutes at the end of *Acharnians* (1198 ff.), the antics between Philokleon and a prostitute at *Wasps* 1341–77, the extended series of sexual jokes about Harvest and Festivity at *Peace* 847–904, or the preposterously priapic frustrations of Kinesias at *Lysistrata* 845–98. The extent of this facet of Old Comedy should be read as a direct index of Dionysiac festivity and even of a kind of collective psychological regression—a sign of the genre's charter to throw off the inhibitions on sexual language and action which normally prevailed in the public sphere.

The same is broadly true of comedy's satirical freedom, which gave it a special privilege to lampoon and denigrate even the most prominent of citizens, including not only leading politicians such as Perikles and Kleon but also the city's major military officers, the generals, during their tenure of office. (See further in 'Satire and Seriousness', below.) While the making of certain serious allegations in public

---

[24] The term 'obscenity' calls for careful handling in relation to Greek conceptual categories, but it need not be dispensed with altogether: for further discussion of this issue, see Halliwell, *Greek Laughter*, 219–25.

life—such as that of being a 'shield-discarder' or military deserter—was prohibited by law, and would in any case have brought with it the direct risk of political or legal reprisals, comedy appears to have enjoyed a largely unlimited licence to ridicule and abuse, traditionally exempted as it was from the conditions applying to other types of public speech. This generalization is not substantially undermined by the fact that on rare occasions comedy's special freedoms generated political tensions, as when Kleon reacted adversely to Aristophanes' *Babylonians* in 426 (see the previous section), and even produced attempts, always short-lived, to impose formal limits on what comic poets were permitted to say. The extreme autonomy which comedy had acquired by the mid-fifth century both reflected and required a buoyant Athenian culture to sustain it. In a longer historical overview we can see that the indulgence allowed to comic poets by Athenian democracy in the fifth century was an extraordinary experiment which gradually gave way, in the fourth, to a narrower spectrum of entertainment, eventually yielding the urbane inoffensiveness of New Comedy.

I have already emphasized that Old Comedy was performed in the same cultural and theatrical context as tragedy. The two genres shared many basic dramatic conventions: the combination of actors and chorus, the use of masks, multiple role-playing by actors, and many of the same metres and verse-forms. It is plausible to suppose that comic poets were influenced by the desire to produce plays that could match tragedy for poetic and dramatic quality (note, for instance, Aristophanes' parabatic boasts about his 'mighty art' of language and thought at *Peace* 749–50), while at the same time providing a theatrical experience that was in ethos the polar opposite of tragedy. We cannot now confidently reconstruct the lines of comedy's relationship to tragedy before the time of Aristophanes, though the fragments of earlier plays suggest that none of Aristophanes' predecessors manifested quite his degree of interest in the detailed parody and burlesquing of tragic materials. This would help to explain why Kratinos, who seems himself to have turned more readily to epic and lyric poetry for parodic possibilities, made one of his characters refer to someone as a 'Euripid-aristophanizer' (fr. 342), thereby gibing at Aristophanes' particular penchant for converting Euripidean plays and motifs into a source of richly comic effects. This penchant is well illustrated for us in the surviving plays: by *Acharnians* 393–488 (where Dikaiopolis visits Euripides to acquire a tragic costume, which is then used for the extended *Telephos* parody at 496 ff.); by Trygaios's appropriation of the role of Bellerophon, and the replacement of Pegasos by a dung-beetle, at *Peace* 62–176; by the whole of *Women at the Thesmophoria* (where Euripides resorts to acting out parts of his own plays, especially *Helen* and *Andromeda*, in a metatheatrical attempt to rescue his captured Kinsman); and by the virtuoso contest between Aischylos and Euripides in the second half of *Frogs*.

Aristophanes was certainly not alone in exploiting the capacity of comedy to operate as a kind of creative parasite on tragedy, drawing nourishment for itself from the other genre's life-blood.[25] But he does appear to have made a distinctive trait out of a type of humour which relies on an astute feeling for destabilizing shifts between the disparate voices of the two genres. The modern reader of his plays needs to bear this constantly in mind, since it is so often basic both to Aristophanes' shaping of situations and to the fine texture of his writing. Aristophanes could count on his original audiences' extensive familiarity with tragedy (which is not the same thing as a precise recollection of individual passages) and their corresponding ability to follow the stylistic twists and turns of parody. This is demonstrated not just by sustained paratragedy of the kind mentioned above but, in a sense, even more tellingly by his habit of allowing the language and tone of tragedy to infect virtually any context with a sudden, 'spontaneous' switch of register.[26] A characteristic instance of this kind occurs at the point in *Acharnians* where Dikaiopolis is so overjoyed at the sight of a Boiotian eel (a gourmet food hard to obtain during the war) that his culinary relish is translated into the mock-tragic language of, first, a scene of reunion, but later, when the eel is taken away to be cooked, a funerary context:

> O my beloved, for whom I've pined so long,
> You're back! (885–6)
> ...
> Now carry her off. [*To the eel*] Not even once I'm dead
> Could I bear to be without you...beetroot-wrapped. (893–4)

[25] On the relationship of Old Comedy in general to tragedy, see M. Farmer, *Tragedy on the Comic Stage* (New York, 2017), 11–113.

[26] I treat the concept of 'paratragedy' as embracing a multiplicity of ways in which tragic language is playfully quoted, echoed, adapted, distorted, and manipulated by Aristophanes; it is not reducible to the single comic function of derision. See my Introduction to *Women at the Thesmophoria* in *Frogs and Other Plays*.

Another instance, more intricately woven into the fabric of its context, is the climactic point in *Knights* (1232–52) where Paphlagon, whose final downfall has been confirmed by oracular revelations (a leitmotif of the play), expresses his grief like a doomed tragic figure, as well as picturing himself—with metatheatrical self-consciousness—as needing the *ekkuklêma* (see 'Stage Directions', below) for his removal from the stage:

> Alas, what the god foretold has been fulfilled!
> Wheel back inside this godforsaken man. (1248–9)

That such lines occur in a passage which also contains vulgarities (even a primary linguistic obscenity, 1242) associated with the Sausage-Seller only underlines how far Aristophanic paratragedy can thrive on anomalies of register.

There is no limit to the subtle variations that can be played, even in miniature, on this comic technique. Near the start of *Clouds*, there is a moment where Strepsiades, gloomily checking his list of debts and creditors in the middle of the night, drops into a short tragic phrase (linguistically unmistakable in the Greek as a departure from ordinary Attic) for just half a line, before returning to an entry in his financial records:

> 'What burden next was mine'—after Pasias' loan?
> Three minas, chariot base and wheels: Ameinias. (30–1)

The effect is so brief that the audience has to catch the effect instantaneously—or miss it altogether. A final example illustrates one more nuance on the spectrum of comic tone which Aristophanes can achieve by this play with abrupt shifts of poetic register. In *Assembly-Women* Blepyros inserts two (doctored) lines from Aischylos when lamenting the loss of his Assembly pay:

> O alack alas!
> 'Antilochos, lament your fill for me
> And not for my—three obols. The loss is mine.'
> [*Normal voice*] But what was happening there, to make this throng
> Turn up in such good time? (*Assembly-Women* 391–5)

Without warning, we have to adjust to the old Athenian's partial and fleeting adoption of the voice of Achilles, from Aischylos' *Myrmidons*, lamenting the death of his companion Patroklos; and then to switch back to his ordinary citizen voice and his curiosity about the abnormally large numbers that had turned up for a meeting of the Assembly. Literary historians continue to argue about just how close a knowledge of specific tragic sources Aristophanes assumed in his audience. What is beyond doubt is that he looks for, and comically titillates, a finely tuned ear for the detailed incongruities of tragic and comic timbres in juxtaposition. That he was able to do so tells us something about the hybrid cultural atmosphere of Athenian festival theatre, where the two genres coexisted yet embodied starkly opposed ranges of poetic and imaginative experience.

The Dynamics of Fantasy

Although it is hazardous to generalize about Old Comedy on the basis of just eleven complete plays out of the many hundreds staged at Athens in the course of the fifth century, our appreciation of Aristophanes' comic artistry—an artistry which encompasses the entire gamut of modes of humour (satire, parody, caricature, burlesque, bawdy, farce, irony, wit, nonsense)—can benefit from a critical perspective which sets the specifics of individual works against the backcloth of generic characteristics. In this and the following section I explore in turn both sides of a central feature (and paradox) of the genre: its combination of imaginative fluidity with theatrical formality.

The imaginative fluidity of Old Comedy derives from its unrestricted freedom to construct dramatic worlds out of whatever material it chooses. Unlike tragedy, which with rare exceptions such as Aischylos' *Persians* (based on the battle of Salamis) was confined to myths of what might be called 'heroic sufferings' (Aischines 3.153), comedy could and did take its subjects from virtually any and every conceivable domain. The stuff of actual Athenian life, both high and low, public and private; figures and events from earlier Greek history; the stories of myth, fable, and folktale; life on Olympos and in Hades; the subject-matter and styles of other genres of poetry, including epic, tragedy, and lyric—all these (and more) were used, in assorted and unpredictable ways, to create the scenarios of comedy, though more often than not (in fact always, in our eleven plays) within the notional timeframe of 'the present' from the point of view of author and audience. Athenians attending the theatre to watch tragedies could have clearly anticipated the kinds of plots they would be likely to see. The same people turning up for *comic* performances in the fifth century would have had no way (other, of course, than tip-offs from cast members) of knowing what sort of scenario they were about to watch in any given case:[27] hence, indeed, the typical element of mystery at the start of an Aristophanic play, sometimes turned into active 'teasing' of the audience (esp. *Wasps* 54–87, *Peace* 43–8) or more generally foregrounded by the ridiculous oddities and uncertainties of openings such as those of *Women at the Thesmophoria* and *Frogs*. A comic audience's expectations would have been limited only by, on the one hand, awareness of certain formal theatrical conventions (see 'Formality and Performance'), and, on the other, familiarity with the genre's established spirit of scurrility and indecency whose context I sketched in the previous section.

At the heart of Aristophanes' and Old Comedy's unpredictability lie the workings of fantasy: the unfettered manipulation of situations and ideas in ways which conform not to realistic probability but to special imaginative rubrics invented afresh in each work. All eleven of Aristophanes' plays start, at least approximately, in 'the present' of the audience, and most of them (the two exceptions being *Birds* and *Frogs*) are notionally located in Athens itself (with a lengthy excursion to Olympos along the way in *Peace*). But in every case the comedy takes us into a parallel universe in which the course of the plot follows its own rules, or, rather, breaks the rules of normality in its own peculiar manner. Aristophanes is particularly fond of beginning a play in a relatively (and misleadingly) down-to-earth setting, from which a fantastic leap of imagination can then take off all the more piquantly. In *Acharnians*, we hear the rambling musings of a war-weary peasant farmer, isolated from his rural home and troubled about life in general; in *Clouds* it is the burden of his unpayable debts which keeps Strepsiades awake in the middle of the night; in *Knights*, *Wasps*, and *Peace* we are given the point of view of a pair of slaves (or a single slave in *Wealth*) engaged in onerous domestic tasks, though with early hints of something out of the ordinary in each case;

---

[27] Spectators of tragedy could attend the 'preview' or proagon at which tragedians gave some sort of advance announcement of their forthcoming plays: see Plato, *Symposium* 194a, with Csapo and Slater, *The Context of Ancient Drama*, 105, 109–10. But we have no evidence for a comic proagon; cf. M. Revermann, *Comic Business* (Oxford, 2006), 169–71. See the Appendix in *Frogs and Other Plays*, 248–9, on Aristophanes' lost play *Proagon*.

in *Birds* we meet a pair of old men stumbling around, lost, in the countryside, and in *Women at the Thesmophoria* another pair looking for a particular house in Athens itself; in both *Lysistrata* and *Assembly-Women* a woman is impatiently, and a little mysteriously, waiting for other women to turn up in an Athenian street. Even in *Frogs*, where the identity, as well as the ludicrous costume, of the god Dionysos plunges us immediately into something blatantly bizarre (and made all the more dramatically teasing by his slave's metatheatrical banter), the sight of a baggage-carrying donkey is ironically compatible with a perfectly ordinary journey.[28]

Yet any first impressions of a banal, down-to-earth setting at the start of an Aristophanic play are always a foil to the transformative powers of comic fantasy. The means and process of transformation can be sudden or gradual, outlandish or subtle. At one extreme, comedy can rewrite myth (with which it shares certain features: see below) in its own image. This is conspicuously so in *Peace*, where Trygaios reinvents himself as a would-be Bellerophon intending to ride up to Olympos, but on a dung-beetle instead of the winged horse Pegasos; in *Birds*, where Peisetairos will pass through animal metamorphosis and, as a new bird-deity, dethrone Zeus himself as master of the cosmos; in *Frogs*, where Dionysos emulates his half-brother Herakles by undertaking a journey down to Hades (but to recover a dead tragic poet, not to capture the hell-hound Kerberos); and in *Wealth*, where Chremylos brings home the god of wealth Ploutos, cured of his former blindness, to live in his own house. Towards the other, non-mythical end of the spectrum of Aristophanic fantasy we might place *Clouds*, in which Strepsiades' hopeless inadequacy for intellectual education and his decision to send his son Pheidippides to be taught by Sokrates do not, when stated in those bare terms, enter the realms of the impossible, though the comic flesh put on that skeleton—including the strange involvement of cloud-deities and Strepsiades' eventual burning-down of Sokrates' Thinking Institute—certainly removes everything onto an absurdist plane. Similarly within the bounds of

---

[28] The start of *Frogs* may have further comic layers as well: it is likely to have triggered thoughts in at least some spectators of the mythological episode in which Hephaistos was brought back on a donkey to Olympos by Dionysos; see e.g. T. H. Carpenter, *Art and Myth in Ancient Greece* (London, 1991), ills. 2–15 (various). Aristophanes' scenario (with Xanthias for Hephaistos, and Hades rather than Olympos as destination) ironically inverts the myth in question.

the physically possible yet utterly *outré* is *Wasps*, where a semi-plausible addiction to jury service on Philokleon's part is only the starting-point for a trajectory that includes imprisonment in his own house and the child-like pretence of hearing domestic (and 'animal') court cases at home.

In between those two ends of the spectrum, other plays distribute themselves with individually varying mixtures of real-world and imaginative elements. *Acharnians* hinges on a weird, quasi-magical moment (the sudden appearance of Amphitheos as a divinely sanctioned peace-envoy) which takes place at a meeting of the city's Assembly but opens up Dikaiopolis's opportunity for a 'private' peace with Sparta—a peace somehow lived out, cocoon-like, within Athens itself. *Knights* belongs in a category of its own, since it follows through a grotesque allegory of the democratic citizen-body of Athens as a slobbering old man and the city's politicians as his 'slaves', while also contaminating the allegory, so to speak, with the figure of the Sausage-Seller as a new politician equipped to take populist demagoguery to an even lower level of shameless vulgarity. Two of Aristophanes' 'women plays', *Lysistrata* and *Assembly-Women*, pursue a different sort of fantasy by inverting the gender norms of contemporary Athens in relation to the structures of political power; yet these works display contrasts at least as large as their affinities: within the impossible framework of a panhellenic women's uprising, *Lysistrata* exploits an almost-plausible sexual psychology to puncture male egos and force men to end the war (but with the promise of a return to the status quo in other respects), while *Assembly-Women* uses the plot-device of a political coup carried out by women in male disguise, and then the setting-up of a grotesque system of sexual 'communism', to change the structures of Athenian society on a permanent basis.

In two further plays the engine of fantasy is driven by a rampant confusion and interpenetration of 'art' and 'life', complete with copious use of metatheatre. *Women at the Thesmophoria* couples together two nonsensical hypotheses: one, that the women of Athens collectively (and in the secrecy of their annual Thesmophoria festival) plot 'revenge'—even to the point of a vote of condemnation to death!—against the tragic poet Euripides for the (supposedly negative) way he depicts female characters in his plays; the other, that Euripides himself schemes to undermine the women's plans by disguising an ageing, boorishly misogynistic Kinsman as a woman and getting him to infiltrate the women's gathering on the Akropolis. The resulting scenario, carried to an ultra-absurdist level when Euripides tries to rescue the unmasked Kinsman by acting out scenes from his own plays, is a comically doubled (if not tripled) case of 'life imitating art'. *Frogs* stretches the parameters of fantasy even further by collapsing the space between the domains of gods and humans, as well as that between life on earth and the afterlife in Hades, into a compound comic universe in which the god of theatre, Dionysos, can visit Hades to bring back a tragic playwright from the dead. Since Dionysos himself is characterized as both a lover of tragedy and yet an archetypally comic buffoon, he provides a perfect vehicle for one of Aristophanes' favourite modes of humour, the anomalous intermingling of these two dramatic genres—a mode sustained with immense poetic virtuosity in the contest between Aischylos and Euripides in the second half of the play.

To gain a more detailed sense of some of the operations of Aristophanic fantasy, let us consider the almost Beckettesque opening of one of his plays, *Birds*.[29] The work starts in an unspecified rural setting (probably indicated, but only sketchily, in the original staging) where two elderly Athenians, their age and apparently rather ordinary social status indicated by their masks and costumes, are staggering around with birds on their wrists and with a variety of baggage and paraphernalia. They appear bewildered and lost, and so too, though with more amusement, might an audience be. For what are these old men doing? Their baggage probably suggests a long journey, perhaps even 'emigration', as well as the possibility of a sacrifice. But why are they using chained birds for orientation? As soon as Euelpides tells us that these are birds bought from a named Athenian market-trader, Philokrates (14), yet purchased with a view to finding Tereus, mythological Thracian king (15–16), we are confronted with a binary frame of reference that is quintessentially Aristophanic. The spectators are required not only to accept simultaneously, but also to allow to merge into one another, the real-life logic of the contemporary polis, where birds are for sale every day on market stalls, and the outer reaches of Greek myth, in which metamorphosis from man to bird is possible. We are invited, in other words, into a comic world which both is and

---

[29] For Aristophanes and Samuel Beckett, cf. n. 120 below.

is not continuous with the Athens of the audience. Various threads of connection can always be traced between the dramatic plane of fantasy and the contemporary viewpoint of the audience, but they are threads which every play, in its own way, takes it upon itself to tangle and tie in knots.

The inner workings of this comic world are revealed more fully when Euelpides turns to the audience at 27 ff. (a metatheatrical gesture itself characteristic of Aristophanes' handling of opening scenes: compare *Knights*, *Wasps*, and *Peace*) to 'explain' the situation. Euelpides and Peisetairos are ageing Athenians looking for an escape from the oppressive reality of the city, especially its culture of litigation. That they are so old and yet prepared to turn to such a far-fetched means of release from their frustrations is itself ludicrously off the scale of improbability. Aristophanes repeatedly and paradoxically associates the transformations effected by comic fantasy with elderly male protagonists who become symbols of prodigious daring and/or rejuvenation: this is a feature of *Acharnians*, *Knights*, *Wasps*, *Peace*, *Wealth*, as well as, more ambiguously, of the Kinsman's gender-transformation in *Women at the Thesmophoria*. Moreover, the two old men in *Birds* do not speak as consistent individuals with whom reasonably predictable dealings would be possible, but as figures whose voices continually shift tone and level—now reflecting elements of social reality (concern over debts, etc.: compare *Clouds*), now engaging in the artificial joke exchanges of a comic double-act (e.g. 54–60), and generally displaying a capacity to tolerate incongruity in themselves as well as around them.

This quality of comically free-floating personality, familiar from the routines of stand-up comedians and clowns (and compare the very start of *Frogs* for precisely that kind of joke routine), is a hallmark of Aristophanic characterization and can best be described as quasi-improvisatory. It leaves the impression that, to invert a principle of Aristotle's, the figures often say what the playwright wants and not what (in realistic terms) the situation plausibly calls for.[30] It is the unrestricted reach of Aristophanic fantasy which gives rise to this

---

[30] Cf. Aristotle, *Poetics* 16.1454b34–5: the principle applies, of course, to the serious genres of epic and tragedy. It would be instructive to see how far the practices of Aristophanic characterization could be read as the inverse of Aristotle's own principles of characterization in *Poetics* ch. 15.

malleability of persona (as likewise of plot), so that many of the leading characters in the plays are constructed more by aggregation than
by integration: they are, so to speak, constantly reinvented—and/or
appear constantly to reinvent themselves—as the plots which are
their vehicles unfold. We cannot coherently connect the downtrod-
den, war-weary Dikaiopolis who sits alone on the Pnyx at the start of
Acharnians, or the more generally world-weary Peisetairos who stumbles around with his friend at the start of *Birds*, with the comically
'heroic' figures we are presented with at the end of these two plays,
the first having ironically become the toast of an Athens within which
he somehow lives out his own one-man city, the other having
achieved—as human, animal, god rolled into one—the ultimate status of being a new Zeus. Not every Aristophanic protagonist traces an
unequivocal trajectory from dejection to elation: the crazy antics of
Philokleon at the end of *Wasps* leave his prospects, if one can put it
that way, somewhat uncertain; Euripides achieves a truce, but no better, in *Women at the Thesmophoria*; Strepsiades in *Clouds* can even
count as a kind of failure.[31] But every plot follows a course which
requires its audience to abandon normal modes of sense-making and
to recalibrate its standards of dramatic understanding according to
the unpredictable demands of comic flights of fancy.

If comic fantasy has what can be called a narrative logic, it is of a
special type which shares certain characteristics with both mythology,
from which, as already noted, it often borrows (and distorts) its
materials, and dreaming (which happens to play an explicit role in the
opening scene of *Wasps*).[32] In all three realms, the impossible becomes
not only thinkable but capable of attainment. The mundane impedi-
ments which have to be faced in the real social world can be imaginatively ignored in the interests of some grand (and/or crazy) goal,

---

[31] Strepsiades is ultimately left with the pleasure of revenge, but that does nothing to
mitigate the outright failure of his original impulse to escape his creditors: see my
Introduction to the play in *Frogs and Other Plays*.

[32] The dreams recounted by the two slaves at *Wasps* 13 ff. exhibit, in miniature, characteristic elements of Aristophanic comedy itself: narrative discontinuity, the blurring of
identities, and confusion of categories (especially human and animal); I discuss some of
the details of this passage in 'Translating Aristophanes' below. The rival dreams (an alternative to oracular prophecy) of Paphlagon and the Sausage-Seller at *Knights* 1090–95
contain motifs akin to larger themes of the play. Note also that the grounding fantasy of
Birds, i.e. the idea of humans achieving winged flight, is associated with dreams at Plato,
Theaitetos 158b.

whether this involves—to oversimplify—an engagement with deep-rooted cultural anxieties (myth), the enactment of basic fears and desires (dreaming), or the pleasure derived from allowing the imagination to blur and dissolve the normally accepted categories of experience (comic fantasy). Equally, and for much the same reason, myth, dreams, and Aristophanic comedy all share a tendency towards dislocation, discontinuity, and the temporal telescoping of events, so that selective attention to key moments overrides the need for sequentially detailed cohesion. Finally, these three modes of thought commonly generate concrete, sensuous, or personified representation of abstract and general ideas. In Aristophanes' case, we find, for instance, the eponymous chorus of *Clouds*, emblematic (at first sight, anyway) of the nebulous notions 'worshipped' by other-worldly intellectuals like Sokrates; the chef-like figure of War, with his destructive (pestle and) mortar, at *Peace* 236 ff., as well as Peace herself, the statuesquely symbolic female, in the same play; the caricature of the Athenian people as a semi-senile householder, Demos, in *Knights*; the girl Princess in *Birds*, incarnation of the cosmic power which passes from Zeus to Peisetairos; Reconciliation, sexually incarnating the territorial terms of a peace treaty, at *Lysistrata* 1114 ff.; the seedy, castanet-playing, prostitute-like 'Muse' of Euripides in *Frogs* (1305 ff.), supposed embodiment of the tragedian's low-grade lyrics; and the blind god Wealth, in the play of the same name, whose entry into a house is tantamount to its acquisition of material prosperity.[33] Realization of the impossible, narrative discontinuity, and concrete embodiment of the abstract are recurrent, defining features of Aristophanic fantasy which lend its creations an air of comic mythologization and dreamlike transcendence of the ordinary.

I have already stressed how the figures who inhabit this fantasy world tend, though with many gradations, towards a semi-improvised, aggregative form of behaviour. But there is another component of Aristophanic characterization which deserves to be highlighted: the adventurous energy and self-assertive proclivities of his protagonists.[34] This is a phenomenon which critics have often analysed in terms of wish-fulfilment. On this reading, individual characters act

[33] The image of a domestic visit from Wealth, as a metaphor for prosperity, occurs in a fragment of the sixth-century iambic poet Hipponax (fr. 36 *IEG*).

[34] It is no coincidence, in view of my previous paragraph, that these are features, respectively, of many myths and dreams.

out strong psychological cravings, whether for material goods, power, sexual gratification, or a more generalized relief from the problems and pressures of reality. It is easy to find a prima facie justification in the surviving plays for this type of analysis. Aristophanic protagonists often display a larger-than-life vitality which leads to the breaching of boundaries and the transgression of norms, whether those of social status (e.g. with the peasant-farmers Dikaiopolis in *Acharnians* and Trygaios in *Peace*, or the vulgar Sausage-Seller in *Knights*, all of whom discover an improbable political prowess), of age (as with the elderly males of *Acharnians*, *Wasps*, *Peace*, and *Birds*, who experience a rejuvenation in their vigour, sexuality, capacities of persuasion, etc.), of law (as with Strepsiades' attempt in *Clouds* to refuse to pay his debts, or with Philokleon's shameless criminality in the later part of *Wasps*), of gender (as with the activist female protagonists of *Lysistrata* and *Assembly-Women*), of 'biology' (as with the semi-metamorphosed Peisetairos in *Birds*), of religion (as with Peisetairos again, who can even threaten a goddess with rape, *Birds* 1253–6, but also the Zeus-defying Trygaios in *Peace*), and, finally, of death itself (as with Dionysos's recovery of a dead poet from Hades in *Frogs*, though there we have of course the comic complication that the agent is a god).

Yet wish-fulfilment in its most egotistical form is a far from invariable trait of these figures. In most plays the action of the main character(s) involves the exercise of a radical, problem-solving ingenuity, whether individual or collective; and in every case but one (the exception is *Clouds*) the end result is the satisfaction of fundamental desires or the harmonization of previously conflicting forces. In the broadest terms, a redistribution of power is a central aim and/or accomplishment in *Knights*, *Birds*, *Lysistrata*, and *Assembly-Women*, though in all of these except *Knights*[35] it is coupled with some variety of sexual reward, which is also an achievement of the protagonists of *Acharnians*, *Wasps* (briefly and ambiguously, at any rate: 1341 ff.), and *Peace*. The attainment of wealth, or an escape from the conditions which curb or diminish it, is the primary aim that drives the protagonists of *Clouds* (where, however, it becomes converted into an immoral need for rhetorical prowess) and *Wealth*; it is also a benefit that accrues to

---

[35] Even there we have the sexual symbolism/incarnation of the personified Peace Treaties at 1390 ff.

Dikaiopolis in *Acharnians* and to almost everyone (via utopian 'communism') in *Assembly-Women*. The desire for peace, with the wider potential for prosperity (including wealth and sexual fertility) which it represents and presumptively creates, is the driving motivation of the protagonists of *Acharnians*, *Peace*, and *Lysistrata*; it also plays a subordinate part in *Knights* (1388 ff.) and *Birds*. *Women at the Thesmophoria* and *Frogs* are less easy to categorize in such basic terms, but both certainly fantasize a solution to difficulties and conflicts: the former resolves (or perhaps dissolves) the male/female and poetry/life tensions between Euripides and the city's women, while *Frogs* celebrates a triumphant finale that ostensibly equates Athenian 'salvation' with the recovery, via Aischylos, of ancestral wisdom, strength, and peace.

As even that schematic survey of the plays indicates, the model of comic fantasy as wish-fulfilment needs to be qualified by a recognition of the complexities and peculiarities of individual figures and their situations. Although bold self-assertion is a recurrent characteristic, Aristophanic protagonists are certainly not uniform manifestations of a Freudian id or of purely selfish instincts. Peisetairos in *Birds* comes closest to this status: his original desire, shared with Euelpides, for a decadently sybaritic life (128–42) is ultimately fulfilled in a blaze of cosmic glory in which, as already mentioned, Zeus-like power and sexual potency coalesce. Philokleon in *Wasps* is Peisetairos's nearest neighbour in terms of a craving for pleasure without responsibility, and this is equally true of him both in his role as juryman (where, however, his pleasure is shown to be delusional) and in the rechannelled energies of the later scenes: what he loses by way of supposed power over others in the courts he makes up for in the rampant, irrepressible sensuality of his new social life, even though he ends the play, as he started it, not in possession of any secure source of gratification, only in a state that others count as 'madness'. But other protagonists, with the exception of Strepsiades in *Clouds*, whose immoral ambitions remain finally unfulfilled, are impelled by mixed impulses.

This is true even of Euripides in *Women at the Thesmophoria*. While he acts at first purely to save himself from the vengeful wrath of the city's women (whom he takes, ludicrously, to be threatening his very life, 76–84), he finds himself having to assume the role of rescuer to his Kinsman, now a 'hostage' of the women, during the second half of the play, and he is eventually prepared to offer the women a 'truce', albeit on comically ironic as well as self-interested terms (1160–9). In *Acharnians* Dikaiopolis initially wants the city as a whole to make peace; the fantasy of his alternative one-man peace treaty stems from a thwarted political desire, not from sheer selfishness, though he does display plenty of the latter when it comes to safeguarding the exclusive privileges which he finds himself, in dream-like fashion, enjoying. What Dikaiopolis originally craved is what Trygaios actually brings about in *Peace*, with the help of the chorus of farmers whose class he belongs to: both the internal dynamics of the plot and the contemporary background of an imminent peace treaty between Athens and Sparta make the protagonist's achievement, like his marriage to Harvest, an emblem of something more-than-individual, albeit focused sharply on the protagonist's ebullient (self-)satisfaction in relation to the appetites for food and sex.

In the case of *Lysistrata*, *Assembly-Women*, and *Wealth* the concerns of the main character for some kind of communal good are unequivocal. Chremylos, in *Wealth*, is troubled by a decline in moral behaviour and social justice; what he goes on to accomplish is restored prosperity not just for himself but for all 'decent' people. Lysistrata and Praxagora are patently motivated by the interests not only of women but of all Athenians, and even, in the case of Lysistrata's panhellenic plan, the whole of Greece. Lysistrata cunningly controls the libido of both women and men, restricting the former in order to arouse the latter; she does so for the sake of the higher goals of peace and marital concord. Praxagora goes further still, organizing a female seizure of power in pursuit of permanent utopia (as she sees it) for the entire polis. Different again is the Sausage-Seller of *Knights*, whose initial role as the ne plus ultra in socio-political grossness (a role foisted on him by others: an unusual pattern)[36] is subsequently overtaken by the function of becoming 'saviour' of the democracy, though some ambiguity between those two things lingers right to the end of the play. Finally, even the 'effeminately' sensualist Dionysos of *Frogs*, for whom the idea of bringing back Euripides from the dead has a quasi-physical intensity (52–66) and is presented as an obsessive need of his

---

[36] The nearest parallel is *Women at the Thesmophoria*, where Euripides tries to enlist Agathon's services and then falls back on those of his Kinsman: here the pattern neatly fits Euripides' status as the playwright who tries to script the drama of his own life.

own theatre-loving personality, turns out, in a typically late twist to the plot, to have a public-spirited interest in resurrecting from Hades a poet who can help (once again) to 'save' the city (1419). Whether the ending of *Frogs* (or of any other Aristophanic comedy) is given any compelling plausibility in terms of the good of the city as a whole remains a matter for debate. But there is no doubt that the final stretch of the work at any rate broadens the god of drama's horizons beyond a desire for something that is his alone to enjoy.

Aristophanic protagonists, then, typically possess a determination, inventiveness, and confidence which make them suitable agents for the achievement of fantastic ends, but their specific motivations vary considerably and can mutate in the course of a play without any regard for plausible consistency of character. Furthermore, the success and hedonistic rewards which usually come their way are not necessarily accompanied by outright self-centredness: to judge by the eleven plays we have, protagonists are, or aspire to be, 'saviours' (of one kind or another) as often as they are egotists, even if comedy is only too happy to blur and destabilize a distinction of that kind. One important implication of these claims is that there are no straightforward conclusions to be drawn about the relationship between the protagonists of Old Comedy and the allegiances of the mass audiences which gathered for the Dionysiac festivals at Athens. In the past, critics have too often attempted to detect or construct correlations between Aristophanes' choice of characters and particular sections of Athenian society, especially the smallholder farmers who made up a substantial portion of the demos or citizen body. Sociological hypotheses have led to dubious critical judgements about the intrinsically 'sympathetic' nature of certain protagonists and their behaviour. But there are too many variables in the configurations of plot and protagonist to yield useful generalizations of this kind; each case needs considering on its merits. Needless to say, no hermeneutic paradigm based on an alignment of social position or outlook between audience and characters can readily encompass *Lysistrata* and *Assembly-Women*: even if we allow for the presence of some women in the audience (see below under 'Stage Directions' for this controversial issue), the great majority of spectators were certainly men. Nor, for different but comparable reasons, can such a model do justice to *Women at the Thesmophoria* and *Frogs*: most Athenians were neither tragic poets like Euripides nor gods! Questions of audience sympathy obviously extend beyond the single factor of the protagonist's identity. In *Women at the Thesmophoria*, there is the asymmetrical pairing of Euripides and his Kinsman to reckon with; notwithstanding their collaboration, they are evidently chalk and cheese in social and cultural terms, a consideration which blocks any easy 'sympathy' reading. In *Frogs*, the second half of the play sets up a poetic polarization between Aischylos and Euripides, setting the split loyalties of Dionysos oscillating in the middle. But at the level of protagonists alone, even before further factors are taken into account, it is impossible to apply some sort of consistent formula for how spectators might have responded to the characters on-stage.

That point holds up even in the case of certain recurrent 'types'. Dikaiopolis in *Acharnians* and Trygaios in *Peace* both belong to the same broad class of peasant-farmers, yet the question of how 'sympathetic' either of them might have been to an Athenian audience at large cannot be treated independently of the specific way they are contextualized within their plots (and fantasies). Dikaiopolis's war-weariness and nostalgia for the countryside, far from making him self-evidently sympathetic to an Athenian audience, are linked to the (exaggerated) premise that he is a loner in a city that has no general desire for peace; and this is only reinforced by the fact that the bellicose chorus of charcoal-burners belongs just as much as he does to the rural population of Attika. The contrast with *Peace*, where an antipathy to war and a yearning for a 'return to the land' are the very things which form a bond between protagonist and chorus, could hardly be greater. Strepsiades in *Clouds* is also from a rural background, but both his utter immorality and the (comically) distinctive nature of his marriage to an aristocratic woman give his case a peculiar slant. In *Knights*, on the other hand, the 'hero' or saviour of the democracy is a Sausage-Seller who can only represent a class of low urban workers, if he represents anything at all, yet he finds himself in a political pact with the chorus of (putatively) wealthy cavalrymen. Protagonist and chorus represent an anti-Kleon alliance, but that hardly provides an easy way of reckoning the play's relationship to its audience: it is a basic presupposition of the comedy that Paphlagon only succeeds as a politician because the demos or citizen body as a whole is so easily duped by him, and the demos necessarily includes a majority of the play's own spectators. In the case of *Birds*, it is arguable that the protagonist is sociologically somewhat indeterminate, though

conceivably thought of at one point (33, which gives a hint of aristocratic ancestry) as from a well-to-do family which has fallen on hard
times.[37] But Peisetairos's salient features at the outset are old age and
disillusionment with Athenian litigiousness; it is hard to see that this
makes him easily identifiable in terms of social background or status.
These examples bear out the difficulty of assimilating Aristophanic
protagonists to a uniform model. They also indicate the danger of
assuming that the heterogeneous fantasies in which those protagonists become involved are designed to yield any one simple kind of
satisfaction for the large, mixed audiences of Athenian citizens who
watched the plays.[38]

Formality and Performance

Old Comedy is remarkable, as we have seen, for its festive freedom
and the plasticity of its plots and protagonists. But it was also, and just
as significantly, a genre which exhibited a high degree of theatrical
formality and structural patterning—more so, perhaps surprisingly,
even than tragedy. The origins of this formality have been often but
inconclusively investigated. For our purposes it is enough to be aware
that the fragments of Old Comedy show that the main types of structure found in Aristophanes' surviving plays (and detailed below) were
well established before his time and were the common property of
comic poets in the second half of the fifth century. That is not, however, to suggest that the formality of the genre was static; Aristophanes'
own works clearly show otherwise. Continual experiment with dramatic form was an important aspect of the evolution of Attic comedy,
including the phase of so-called Middle Comedy represented by the
last two extant Aristophanic plays, *Assembly-Women* and *Wealth*.

The formal conventions and structures to be discussed in this section have to be tracked by modern readers on the printed page.[39] But
it is essential to remember that for Aristophanes and his audience
they were integral to their performed presentation through verbal/

---

[37] It is possible that costume was used to mark him as a rustic, but if so the text gives
no clue to this. His companion Euelpides is apparently given a rural deme at 496 (but a
different one at 645!).

[38] On the size of fifth-century theatre audiences, see n. 94 below.

[39] My translation explicitly labels the major formal sections of each play (parodos,
agon, parabasis), in order to keep the reader alert to this aspect of comic theatricality.

rhythmical shape, musical ethos, and visual reinforcement (especially dance). To understand something of the vividly animated theatricality of these elements, we need to know that comedy, like tragedy, used three principal 'modes' of poetic performance or delivery:[40] first, the spoken verses of the iambic trimeter, a metre whose flexible rhythms can admit a large range of registers (from the colloquial to the high-flown); secondly, longer verses (tetrameters, in both iambic and other rhythms),[41] which were chanted or declaimed, often by the chorus-leader, to the accompaniment of the double pipes (*auloi*, plural of *aulos*)[42] and are now customarily bracketed together, with a term borrowed from music, as the 'recitative' mode; and, finally, full song (in Greek, *melos*), again accompanied by the *aulos*, in lyric sections (sung by the chorus or sometimes by individual characters) which make use of a wide selection of rhythms but are frequently constructed in matching strophic pairs (strophe + antistrophe). Of these modes, the first and second depend on stichic metres—that is, those involving the repetition of regular 'lines'—whereas lyric sections comprise units of varying length and complexity. Choral song was supported and enhanced by choreography; the same was true with some cases of recitative as well.

In our surviving fifth-century tragedies the recitative mode is put to more limited use than in comedy, being predominantly limited to (part of) the entrance, or parodos, of the chorus in certain plays.[43] For the most part, tragedy is constructed from scenes of iambic speech/dialogue, alternating with the lyric songs or odes of the chorus (and sometimes the solo singing, monody, of characters).[44] Old Comedy too employs iambic speech and free-standing choral songs, but it also makes much more extensive use than tragedy of recitative, which it

---

[40] Cf. my further comments on these modes in 'Translating Aristophanes', below. Comedy also very occasionally admits short portions of prose, such as the Herald's announcements at *Acharnians* 43, 61, 123, the chorus-leader's exclamation at *Knights* 941, the ritual formulae at *Peace* 433–4, the proclamation at *Women at the Thesmophoria* 295–311 (the longest passage of prose in the extant plays), and several interrupted utterances by the Decree-Seller and Inspector at *Birds* 1035–50.

[41] See further in nn. 83–4.

[42] On the *aulos*, cf. also the later section 'Stage Directions'.

[43] It is ironic, therefore, that the development of musical recitative in early Italian opera was influenced by the belief that much of ancient tragedy was musically declaimed in a style halfway between speech and song; cf. C. V. Palisca, *Humanism in Italian Renaissance Thought* (New Haven, 1985), 408–33.

[44] Cf. *Frogs* 1330–63 for a pointed parody of Euripidean monody.

incorporates into large-scale structures of a strongly formal, often symmetrical, type. This is all part-and-parcel of comedy's interest in a theatrically flamboyant and showy style of entertainment which maximizes the resources of both actors and singers/dancers. In this connection it is helpful to keep in mind two attributes of the comic chorus which differentiate it from the tragic variety: first, its size, twenty-four dancers as opposed to tragedy's fifteen (originally twelve); secondly, its characteristically colourful and elaborate costuming, often involving animal-forms (wasps, birds, frogs, etc.) or the distinctive accoutrements of special groups such as the charcoal-burners of *Acharnians*, the cavalry of *Knights* (who make their entry 'riding' in some form or other),[45] the farmers of *Peace* (who carry shovels, crowbars, and ropes), or the old men (carrying logs and a brazier) and old women (carrying buckets of water) in *Lysistrata*. These features contribute to, and can be illuminated by, the three major formal units or sequences of Old Comedy—the parodos, agon, and parabasis—which now need to be considered in turn and which serve as primary building blocks in the dramatic architecture of most of Aristophanes' surviving works.

The parodos is the section of a play where the chorus makes its first appearance in the *orchêstra* ('dancing-floor': see 'Stage Directions', below). Aristophanes typically treats this as a high-profile event in its own right: he organizes the parodos, which we know was a formalized convention long before his time, in such a way as to create both theatrical spectacle and a specific intervention in the dramatic circumstances. The chorus's movements in the parodos are choreographed to represent a particular kind of action, condition, or mood, ranging from the aggression of the charcoal-burners in *Acharnians* or the cavalry attack in *Knights* to the (temporarily) pathetic sluggishness of the old jurors in *Wasps*,[46] from the earthy robustness of the farmers in *Peace* to the ethereally 'floating' remoteness of the cloud-deities in

---

[45] An Athenian vase of *c.*530 shows a comic chorus with cavalry men riding piggy-back on others wearing horse-masks: see e.g. the illustration in Rusten, *Birth of Comedy*, 57. Some such arrangement is one possibility in the case of *Knights* itself; another is perhaps the use of hobbyhorses of some kind, though we cannot rule out that the act of riding was evoked simply by dance steps. I assume that real horses were not an option.

[46] After the warning of the jurors' stinging waspishness at 223 ff., the parodos brings a humorous defeat of expectations; but in a second reversal, 404 ff. subsequently functions as a kind of deferred or postponed parodos of the chorus qua wasps.

Clouds. In *Lysistrata*, the use of a divided chorus of old men and old women allows the parodos to foreground a confrontation between the gendered points of view of the two groups, though it anticipates the future course of the plot by making the men far more ineffectual than their female counterparts. Especially intriguing, but also problematic, is the case of *Frogs*, which has two quite separate choruses—the eponymous frog-chorus itself and the chorus of initiates in the underworld—and therefore arguably two parodoi (at 209 ff. and 316 ff.). Some scholars have believed that the frog-chorus is never actually visible (there is nothing in the text which proves that it is) but is only heard singing offstage: if so, 209 ff. will be a kind of 'false' or virtual parodos. But those who, like myself, believe that the frog-chorus hopped around the *orchêstra* (presumably with amphibian costume to match its dance steps), in a way fully in keeping with the genre's traditions of animal choruses, will infer that Aristophanes has exploited the theatrical impact of a choral parodos twice over in this play.

No two parodoi are identical in form (the two in *Frogs*, just mentioned, are radically different in scale and structure). In fact, there is legitimate disagreement about how strictly to delimit the parodos of a comedy. In the *Poetics* (12.1452b22–3), Aristotle defines the parodos of a play—he is discussing tragedy but his definition is equally applicable to comedy—simply, but less than decisively, as 'the first complete utterance' of the chorus; he also indicates (1452b19–20) that it directly follows the prologue. Some scholars, insisting on a moment of entrance, would say that *Women at the Thesmophoria* does not even have a parodos, on the grounds that the text suggests that the women of the chorus enter silently as a crowd (by or at line 295) and then sing as a foregathered group (at 312 ff.); by that criterion, *Assembly-Women* is more anomalous still.[47] These are technical variations, however, adapted to the plot requirements of the works in which they occur. They need not affect our general perception of the parodos in Aristophanes as the point in a comedy at which the presentation of the scenario is expanded by the introduction of the musico-choreographic resources of the chorus.

[47] Paradoxically, the chorus takes up its formation and delivers its first lines at *Assembly-Women* 285 ff. precisely to prepare for its *exit* (to the Assembly) at 311; it will return at 478 ff.

Flexibly understood,[48] each parodos can make use, for its specific needs, of two of the three poetic modes explained above, i.e. recitative and song, moulded in such a way as to shape the dramatic interaction between chorus and characters. Overall, recitative metres preponderate, since they lend themselves best to the depiction of group movement with a clear 'direction of travel', but the parodos of *Clouds* is an instance which tellingly starts in lyric mode (275 ff.) because of the indefinite manner—drifting across the sky, as it were—in which the cloud-deities gradually make their way onto the scene. The kind of impetus which can be enacted by recitative metres is well illustrated in *Knights*, where the chorus's entry comes in response to the request from one of Demos's slaves (i.e. allegorical politicians qua 'servants of the people') for assistance in the fight against Paphlagon (242–6). Trochaic rhythms are employed here to convey the mimicry of a galloping cavalry attack (247 ff.). Whether piggy-back on pantomime horses or in some other fashion (see n. 45), the dancers manoeuvre themselves in quasi-equestrian formation, circling round, cornering, and eventually assaulting Paphlagon with, among other conspicuous gestures, kicks to his (comically padded) belly (273). The sight of cavalry drill would have been familiar to Athenians from training grounds in the city, but this parodos is a burlesque version of the practice which comically intermingles the idea of equestrian exercises with motifs of crude brawling, wrestling imagery, and political polemics.[49] Taken as a whole, from 247 to 302, the parodos of *Knights* constitutes a gradual crescendo of verbal and physical hostility: the effect of the horsemen's onslaught is to embolden the Sausage-Seller, who gradually takes over the momentum of the campaign against Paphlagon.

The ingenuity with which Aristophanes constructs and varies his parodoi is well brought out by *Birds*. Here the chorus's entry is unusually preceded, or initiated, by the appearance of four extra dancers in specially ostentatious bird-costumes on the roof of the stage building, the *skênê* (267–93). Aristophanes teases the audience at this point, raising the possibility that the whole chorus may enter

---

[48] Scholars differ in their understanding of the extent/limit of the parodos in particular cases: its length as marked in my translations is sometimes fuller than others would take it to be.

[49] See my Introduction to *Knights* on different layers of significance in the play's allegory.

individually on the roof, i.e. 'in the air'. (I believe that the roof was also used as part of a long tease about the choral entry in *Clouds*, at 275 ff.; there the joke is on the bemused Strepsiades, not on the audience.) But at *Birds* 294, as the human characters look into the sky for further birds, the real chorus suddenly enters at ground level in a flurry of running, wing-flapping, and screaming cries. All this multiform ornithological commotion is going on for sixteen lines (294–309) before the chorus-leader starts to chant, in recitative, on behalf of the group. Uniquely as far as the surviving plays go (but there were precedents and parallels in lost works), the twenty-four dancers are individually costumed to represent different species. Unlike the pre-announced cavalry attack in *Knights*, this parodos initially projects a riot of colour, movement, and sound, and it is a crucial part of the comic effect that only gradually, at least to the humans themselves, does it become apparent that the birds are collecting with menacing intentions. Also, whereas in *Knights* the chorus's hostility is a burlesque version of an obvious model—real-life cavalry manoeuvres—the birds' aggression incongruously endows the animal-chorus with a type of behaviour not naturally characteristic of it. At any rate, it seems likely, in view of the military language later in the encounter at 352 ff., that the parodos of *Birds* made use of choreography which included not only feathery agitation but also movements and gestures reminiscent of warfare. Here, as elsewhere in the play, the comedy engenders a deliberate confusion of the avian and the human.

After the preliminary scene-setting provided by the prologue of a comedy, the parodos usually carries with it a lavish expansion of the play's scenario through a rich array of poetry, dance, and music. It sets up an interplay, whether of alliance or hostility, between characters and chorus—or even within the chorus itself, as we have already noted in the case of *Lysistrata*. With some notable exceptions (Trygaios's summoning of his fellow farmers in *Peace* is one such; another is the procession of Eleusinian initiates at *Frogs* 316 ff.) the parodos often prepares for or sets up a scene of confrontation, which brings us to the second of the three major theatrical conventions with which we are concerned in this section. This is the agon, the 'contest' or 'debate'. Formal competition was a near-pervasive feature of Greek culture: the term *agôn* was applied to the adversarial contexts of law-court trials, debates in political assemblies, athletic events, military conflicts, as well as dramatic competitions themselves. Although military associations regularly attach themselves to the larger setting of a comic agon, it is the first of these areas—the sphere of verbal and argumentative contests—which lends the convention its predominant tone of acrimonious dialectic. Moreover, the agon not only provides the framework for a specific dramatic clash. It also allows for the opening up of general issues—political, educational, artistic, etc.—which go beyond the immediate situation in the play.

In its full form, the agon is a substantially symmetrical structure,[50] each half of which comprises (i) a lyric section, in which the chorus elaborates on its expectations of the speaker; (ii) a long stretch of recitative, introduced by an exhortation to the participants by the chorus, and containing arguments from the speaker(s); (iii) a climactic conclusion and tail-piece to the recitative, consisting of shorter lines and more rapid rhythm—a kind of accelerando flourish. This is the form which occurs, for example, at *Knights* 756–942, *Clouds* 949–1104, *Wasps* 526–724, *Lysistrata* 476–607, *Frogs* 895–1098. The symmetry of the full agon thus constitutes a combination of song and declamation, technically known as a syzygy, which we shall shortly meet again in the parabasis and whose main components can be set out in diagrammatic form as in Table 1.[51]

The importance of this symmetry is that it represents the fusing of poetry, music, and (for the lyrics) dance into a theatrical design which in performance would be simultaneously aural and visual. Although

TABLE 1. *Symmetrical structure of the Aristophanic agon*

	First Half	Second Half
SONG/ DANCE	(1) strophe: choral expectations	(1) antistrophe
RECITATIVE	(2) arguments (introduced by choral exhortation)	(2) counter-arguments (with second exhortation)
	(3) accelerando conclusion	(3) accelerando conclusion

[50] The agon proper is sometimes preceded by a preparatory recitative or pre-contest (e.g. *Clouds* 889–948, *Lysistrata* 467–75): this can be left aside for present purposes.

[51] The technical terms normally used for the components are: ode/antode (songs); epirrhema/antepirrhema (arguments); katakeleusmos/antikatakeleusmos (exhortations); pnigos/antipnigos (conclusions).

the parodos and the agon both use a combination of song and recitative, it is easy to see why the agon but not the parodos should be usually symmetrical. Where the parodos forms a dynamic juncture, connecting the prologue to what follows (often the agon itself) and moving the action forward into a new phase, the agon supplies a framework in which the issues of a conflict can be squarely faced up to and, more often than not, resolved by the victory of one side over the other. Theatrical patterns mirror dramatic functions.

Just as in the case of the parodos, however, the precise deployment and function of the agon vary from play to play. It is sometimes suggested that the norm is a single complete agon occurring in the first half of the drama, i.e. before the main parabasis (on which, see below), and producing an outcome whose consequences are then explored after the parabasis, typically through a sequence of 'intruder scenes' in which the protagonist has to deal with unwanted visitors. But, as with so many aspects of Old Comedy, talk of norms can be misplaced: the scheme just indicated is found in only two of the surviving works, *Wasps* (with a delayed parabasis) and *Birds*, though in a third, *Lysistrata*, there is something close to it.[52] *Frogs*, by contrast, has an agon in the second half of the play, for it is only there that a contest between Aischylos and Euripides (an element not anticipated in the earlier scenes) can be staged. Both *Knights* and *Clouds* actually contain two full agons.[53] In *Knights*, whose first agon contains an unusual doubling of strophes in both its lyric sections (303–32, 382–406), this reflects the fact that the plot consists of a sustained, serial conflict between the Sausage-Seller and Paphlagon which is not settled until the latter's final defeat at 1263. In *Clouds*, on the other hand, the second agon—between father and son (1345–1451)—serves a comically ironic function by marking the reversal which Strepsiades suffers when Pheidippides turns against him the very sophistic education which he had originally so much wanted his son to acquire.

Several plays (*Peace*, *Assembly-Women*, and *Wealth*), on the other hand, possess only a half-agon, where formality of structure is retained but without the symmetry. In *Peace* (582–656) this scaling

---

[52] The victory won by the women at *Lysistrata* 607 is only over the Commissioner; resolution of the larger male/female conflict has to wait till much later in the play.

[53] Passages such as *Wasps* 334–402 and *Birds* 327–99 are also sometimes counted as preliminary agons: what is certainly germane is that these passages display, on a smaller scale, the theatrical symmetry which gives the agon its distinctive shape.

down arises from the fact that the situation calls for no antagonistic debate (protagonist and chorus are in harmony; Peace has already been extracted from her cave) and some of the formal components of an agon can instead be adapted to serve the purposes of an explanation by Hermes of how Peace came to be absent from Greece in the first place. In *Assembly-Women* and *Wealth*, on the other hand, the use of a half-agon is probably a symptom of the overall decline in large-scale theatrical formality, with the concomitant diminution of the chorus's role, during the period of Middle Comedy. In *Women at the Thesmophoria*, the function of an agon is fulfilled by an exchange of speeches—contra and pro Euripides—between the women and the disguised Kinsman at 372–573; but the last section of that scene, at 520–73, formally approximates to another half-agon. Finally, Aristophanes' earliest surviving play, *Acharnians*, has no formal agon at all, even though it does involve a scene of quasi-forensic confrontation in which Dikaiopolis has to defend himself against the chorus's aggressive allegation of treason. Here the omission of a structured agon is motivated by the need to give the protagonist a parody of the great speech of self-defence made by Telephos in Euripides' play of that name; some of the characteristic dialectic of an agon is then displaced onto the following scene, where, after a temporary division within the chorus (557–65), we get a face-to-face showdown between Dikaiopolis and the general Lamachos.[54] There are other variables too in Aristophanes' manipulation of the agon, such as the difference between genuinely two-sided debates (e.g. *Clouds*, *Wasps*) and those heavily dominated by one of the parties to a conflict (e.g. *Birds* and *Lysistrata*). But enough has been said already to indicate that the agon is a structure of elaborate theatrical formality, yet at the same time a dramatic unit which can be tailored in diverse ways to suit the particular details of any plot in which it finds a place.

Whereas the agon, like the parodos, is always causally integrated into the plot, the last of the major formal sequences of Old Comedy, the parabasis, functions above all as a set-piece performative 'event' in its own right. The parabasis (English stress parábasis, plural parábases, Greek plural *parabaseis*) has often been thought to be a very

---

[54] Given the responsion between strophe and antistrophe at *Acharnians* 489–96 and 566–71, the whole of 489–625 can be regarded as a formally unique sequence which replaces a symmetrical agon but keeps something of the spirit of one.

old constituent of the genre; given its conspicuous use of direct audience-address, there are various theories about whether it might originally have been placed at the beginning or end of a play. In the surviving comedies it is typically positioned somewhere towards the middle of the plot, the limiting cases being *Clouds* (510 ff.), where only a third of the play precedes it, and *Wasps* (1009 ff.), where it occurs two-thirds of the way through the work. The term parabasis means 'stepping forward',[55] or, more literally, 'stepping aside' (i.e. from the dramatic action of the play): it is a performance routine in which the chorus, normally alone on-stage,[56] addresses itself directly to the audience, sometimes on behalf of the playwright (see below); we might legitimately call it 'paratheatrical' as well as metatheatrical in character. The full form of the routine is introduced by a short linking comment (song or recitative) on the preceding scene, continues with the parabasis proper (a substantial recitative section of audience-address, sometimes called the 'anapaests', though that is not always the actual metre of the section),[57] and is completed by a symmetrical pattern or syzygy—song and recitative; matching song and recitative—which parallels that of an agon. The structure is thus as indicated in Table 2.

TABLE 2. *Formal structure of the Aristophanic parabasis*

SONG/ RECITATIVE	Linking comment, usually addressed by the chorus to departing character(s)
RECITATIVE	Parabasis proper ('anapaests'), addressed by the chorus to audience
SONG	Strophe (typically a prayer/hymn)
RECITATIVE	Declamation ('epirrhema'), usually delivered in the chorus's dramatic identity
SONG	Antistrophe
RECITATIVE	Matching declamation ('antepirrhema')

[55] See the cognate verb, in the relevant sense, at *Acharnians* 629, *Knights* 508, *Peace* 735, *Women at the Thesmophoria* 785; the noun parabasis itself does not occur in Aristophanes' surviving plays.

[56] *Women at the Thesmophoria* 785–845 is an exception: the Kinsman is on-stage too, trapped at the altar of the Thesmophoreion.

[57] For the term 'anapaests', see my note on *Acharnians* 627.

This full form is found, with only small variations, in *Acharnians*, *Knights*, *Clouds*, *Wasps*, and *Birds*. *Peace*, *Lysistrata*, *Women at the Thesmophoria* (the only parabasis without songs), and *Frogs*[58] all have reduced or reorganized parabases, while by the time of *Assembly-Women* and *Wealth* the convention has become entirely dispensable. This distribution tends to suggest that the parabasis exercised a declining appeal for poets and audiences in the later years of the fifth century and beyond. That inference is reinforced by the parallel disappearance of 'second parabases'. The works which have a second parabasis—usually a reduced version of the main parabatic form—are *Knights*, *Clouds*, *Wasps*, *Peace*, all from the 420s, and *Birds* of 414. But in the last five surviving plays of Aristophanes the only remaining trace of this phenomenon is the section of audience-address at *Assembly-Women* 1154–62.

Unlike the parodos and agon, where the choral element is interwoven with the world of the dramatic characters, the parabasis is an exclusively choral presentation which exploits to the full the vocal, choreographic, and visual aspects of the dancers. But that general observation fails to do justice to a remarkable fact about the parabasis, namely its fluctuations and flexibility of 'voice'. There are three fundamental voices which can be adopted, in part or whole, by the chorus of a parabasis. The first is (ostensibly) that of the poet himself: this can be expressed in either the first person singular, as though the playwright were actually speaking (*Clouds* 518–62, all the more interesting for being a partly revised version which reacts to the poor reception of the play at its first production), or the third person singular, with the chorus(-leader) 'reporting' a message from the poet (*Acharnians*, *Knights*, *Wasps*, and *Peace*); at *Acharnians* 659–64 and *Peace* 754–74, however, there is a striking switch from third to first person within the same passage. The second voice is that of the chorus's dramatic identity, and this is the usual point of view from which they deliver the symmetrical series or syzygy of songs and recitatives (the last four parts in Table 2), as we see from all the surviving parabases, including those in reduced form, except for *Peace* and *Frogs*. But here too there are variations of emphasis: in *Acharnians*, for example, one song reminds us of the chorus's primary status as

---

[58] For an additional peculiarity of *Frogs*, see my notes on lines 354–71 and 674 of that work in *Frogs and Other Plays*.

charcoal-burners (665–75), but what follows represents the stand-point of old men in general. The third voice or persona sometimes assumed in the parabasis—as the songs in *Peace* (775 ff.) and the whole of *Frogs* 674–737[59] demonstrate—is that of a comic, dramatic, or festival chorus pure and simple, without more specific markers of identity.

The availability of these different voices and frames of reference, often juxtaposed within a single parabasis, yields a particularly rich vehicle of poetry, humour, and thematic imagery. Indeed, the length of the parabasis, together with the fact that it never concretely affects the action of the play, makes it—unlike either the parodos or the agon—a strikingly free-standing form in its own right, which is the main reason why it has been the subject of so much speculation regarding its origins and purposes. Aristophanes' plays from the 420s suggest that the independence and internal complexity of the para-basis gave it, at that stage of comedy's history, special attractions for both playwrights and audiences. One of the most interesting of these attractions can be described as a kind of theatrical self-consciousness, to which I drew attention in a previous section when discussing the parabasis of *Knights* (see 'Aristophanes' Career in Context'). It is a related point that the parabases of the early plays are used to build up an extravagantly rhetorical portrait of the poet's own character, standing, and ambitions, as well as the supposed shortcomings of his rivals.[60]

Perhaps Aristophanes' most virtuoso effort in this respect is the section of *Wasps* (1030 ff.) where he depicts himself as a new Herakles fighting against the terrifying monstrosity of the politician Kleon. The theatrical appeal of this passage seems to be vouched for by the fact that Aristophanes repeated these lines, almost verbatim, the fol-lowing year in *Peace* (752 ff.)—the only such wholesale repetition of a passage in the extant plays. I shall have more to say in the next

---

[59] The case of *Frogs* is slightly complicated by two factors: first, the section of 'advice' (686 ff.) is implicitly reminiscent of the convention of the poet's own parabatic voice, though it does not make direct appeal to the latter; secondly, the references to 'sacred' choruses (674, 686) might be thought to resonate with the chorus's identity as Eleusinian initiates, though the parabasis as a whole makes this an optional association.

[60] The fragments of other poets' works from roughly this period show that comic boasting and the denigration of rivals were found in their works too, though with some differences from Aristophanes: see A. H. Sommerstein, *Talking about Laughter* (Oxford, 2009), 116–35.

section about the nature of such Aristophanic bravado and boasting, but there is no doubt at all that in the earlier part of his career he was able to exploit very effectively the potential of the parabasis for ostensibly extra-dramatic self-promotion. On the other hand, it is this particular feature of the parabasis which appears to have faded rather rapidly after the 420s, so that in *Birds*, *Lysistrata*, and *Women at the Thesmophoria* the chorus remains in its dramatic identity throughout this section of the play.[61] Given the more general evidence, already noted, for a decline in the parabasis during the later fifth century, it is a reasonable hypothesis that the intricacies of the form, which had once provided such elaborate scope for musico-poetic, comic, and choreographic flourishes, had come to seem too cumbersome and old-fashioned for the evolving tastes of dramatists and their public.[62]

I stressed at the outset of this section that we should not allow the technical analysis of compositional forms in Old Comedy to conceal their primarily theatrical character as structures in which meaning, rhythm, music, and dance all came together in a performative synthesis. The parodos, agon, and parabasis helped Aristophanes, as they did other poets, to give shape to his plays in ways which engaged with, yet constantly modified (and sometimes defeated), the expectations of his audience. Understanding something about these structural components enables us to form an idea of an important interface between convention and creativity, continuity and change, in the generic practices of Old Comedy.

Satire and Seriousness

The overwhelming impression created by Aristophanic humour is of an imaginative world that is unlimitedly fluid, grotesque, and absurd in its possibilities of both action and character. Despite this, scholars and critics have long been interested in seeking, and have often claimed to discover, a layer of 'serious' intent and meaning in the

---

[61] *Frogs* (cf. n. 59) revives the tradition of parabatic 'advice', but not with overt reference to the supposed views or standing of the poet himself.

[62] It is often suggested that the diminution in choral elements (including the parabasis) visible by the time of *Assembly-Women* and *Wealth* was a result of Athens' impoverishment in the Peloponnesian War. Although economic factors may have played a part, I would prefer to look in the first instance for an explanation in terms of theatrical and dramatic evolution.

playwright's work. It is not hard to see what has stimulated and sustained such interest, though much harder to agree about the conclusions it leads to. While fantasy is the dominant mode of Old Comedy,
the materials on which fantasy operates its techniques of invention
and distortion are frequently drawn from the contemporary social
and political world of Athens. It is, at root, the interplay (and tension)
between fantasy and reality which has given rise to sharply contrasting judgements of Aristophanes' dramatic aims and values.

For a long time after the Renaissance the extremes of disagreement
in this area were posed chiefly in moral terms, with Aristophanes
regarded as either a shamelessly indiscriminate jester or an edifyingly
didactic chastiser of reprobates. The play most often treated as a test-
case in this debate was *Clouds*, where the key question was whether
Aristophanes had wantonly attacked the blameless Sokrates or had
used the figure of the philosopher as a means of exposing the subversive fraudulence of very different types of intellectuals, especially the
so-called Sophists. In eighteenth-century England, when an ideal of
benevolent humour was widely espoused, the case of *Clouds* was cited
so regularly in this connection that one literary historian has suggested that the period made the issue 'its peculiar property, by infinite
repetition'.[63] Unsurprisingly, given the ethical aesthetics of the time,
the standard reaction is exemplified by Joseph Addison, who saw
Clouds as a prominent illustration of satire's 'poisoned darts, which
not only inflict a wound but make it incurable'.[64] After all, had not
Clouds allegedly contributed to the eventual condemnation and death
of Sokrates? (I shall return below to this vexed point.)

From the early nineteenth century, however, the focus of debate
over Aristophanic satire shifted markedly towards the arena of politics. The central questions, which have tended to dominate scholarship
on the playwright ever since, became: was Aristophanes a committed,
purposeful satirist in his treatment of individual leaders and the
workings of democracy? and, if so, where did he stand on the spectrum of available political affiliations in late fifth-century Athens? It
was first in Germany, and subsequently elsewhere, that the basic
interpretative positions were staked out, with the philosopher Hegel,

---

[63] S. M. Tave, *The Amiable Humorist* (Chicago, 1960), 23. For an earlier attack on
Clouds, by the puritan William Prynne, see n. 113 below.
[64] *The Spectator*, 23 (March 27, 1711).

among others, advancing a view of Aristophanes as a patriotically motivated teacher, and the translator Droysen delineating the opposing idea of the pure entertainer. For most of the last hundred and fifty years the majority view has been that Aristophanes *was* in some degree committed to expressing and conveying political judgements in his comedies, especially through the use of satirical ridicule and critique. But there has been much less agreement about exactly what those judgements were, or from what kind of general stance they were delivered.[65]

The stance most commonly ascribed to Aristophanes has been that of a political 'conservative', which is to be defined in this context principally as a matter of opposition to the 'radical' democracy of the later fifth century and a nostalgic hankering after an earlier, supposedly more moderate era of Athenian politics.[66] But there have been many variations on this conservative model: arguments have been advanced for Aristophanes as hostile to the principle of democracy per se, Aristophanes as 'true' democrat (opposed only to the populist abuse of power by demagogues), Aristophanes as champion of the supposedly traditionalist class of smallholder peasant-farmers—and other positions besides. There is insufficient space here to examine each of these possibilities, but one objection to all categorical formulations of Aristophanes' putative political values is that they inevitably tend to simplify a whole mass of comically and dramatically variegated material which by its very nature might be thought to destabilize the possibility of a consistent reading. Some specific issues raised by the kinds of views mentioned above are pursued further in my Introductions to individual plays: Aristophanes' treatment of Athens' policies and conduct in the Peloponnesian War, at various stages of its history, in the Introductions to *Acharnians*, *Peace*, and *Lysistrata*; his complex relationship to the politician Kleon in the Introduction to *Knights*; and his depiction of one of the main

---

[65] For changing views of Aristophanes' politics in anglophone scholarship since the nineteenth century, see P. Walsh, 'A Study in Reception: The British Debates over Aristophanes' Politics and Influence', *Classical Receptions Journal*, 1 (2009), 55–72.

[66] Aristophanes has also frequently been regarded as a 'cultural' conservative in matters of education, poetry, and music, despite the fact that his boasts about his own dramatic artistry stress originality and innovation (*Clouds* 545–8, *Wasps* 1053–9). See my Introductions to *Clouds* and *Frogs* in *Frogs and Other Plays* for objections to simplified inferences about the poet's own views on topics such as these.

institutions of Athenian democracy, its law–court system, in the
Introduction to *Wasps*. What I attempt in the remainder of this section is to outline some reasons for exercising great caution about the
feasibility of deducing Aristophanes' personal allegiances from his
comedies.

The plays of Aristophanes contain such unrestrained and often
seemingly brutal satirical elements precisely because they belong
to a special genre of festival theatre. As explained earlier ('Old
Comedy and Dionysiac Festivity'), Old Comedy enjoyed a peculiar
freedom to break the taboos and contravene the norms which obtained
in the Athenian social world at large, a freedom which manifests itself
in sexual obscenity as well as (and often at the same time as) vituperative mockery. This freedom stemmed partly from archaic folk practices of scurrilous jesting and inebriated celebration of the kind which
Aristophanes himself twice incorporates in his surviving plays.[67]
What is so telling about this side of comedy is the 'irresponsibility' of
its licence to ridicule, to lampoon, and to vilify. Despite some prima
facie suggestions to the contrary (see 'Aristophanes' Career in
Context' on the case of *Babylonians*), the playwrights of the genre
were essentially exempted from any need to justify or answer for their
choice of satirical targets. Unlike the personal abusiveness which
undoubtedly played a part in the rivalries of Athenian politics, comedy was not usually constrained by the threat of legal reprisals, nor by
the pressures involved in persuading an audience to take a practical
decision (other than the judges' voting of a prize to the best comedy)
on a particular occasion. These differences are culturally and psychologically fundamental; without them it would be impossible to understand why classical Athens allowed comedy a type and degree of
liberty (of speech and thought) which was not available in other
contexts of public life. The result of the special conditions in which
Old Comedy thrived is that Aristophanic satire often lambasts its
targets—both individual and institutional—with a free abandon which
it is intrinsically hard to cash out in the currency of genuinely authorial
commitments.

In the case of many 'victims' of satire, comic prominence should be
taken less as a reflection of scandalous notoriety than, paradoxically,

---

[67] See 'Aristophanes' Career in Context', above, for the phallic song at *Acharnians*
263 ff., with n. 4 on the Eleusinian mockery at *Frogs* 416 ff.

an index of these individuals' possession of status and power in the city. This is most obviously true of leading politicians, generals, and office-holders (Perikles, Kleon, Hyperbolos, Lamachos, etc.), and despite the limitations of our evidence we can be confident that this was true of many of the lesser targets as well. Kleonymos, for example, is set up as an obese glutton, a military coward, and thoroughly detestable in each of the first six of Aristophanes' surviving plays, from *Acharnians* to *Birds*. It would be easy to jump to the conclusion that he must have been a blatantly risible figure, and yet we know that he was politically active at a high level (proposing decrees in the Assembly on several occasions) and we have some reason to connect him with Kleon's circle in the mid-420s.[68] Similarly, the Kinesias who appears as both a vacuous poetaster and a physical freak at *Birds* 1372 ff. and elsewhere was very probably a much more significant figure, both culturally (as composer and chorus-trainer) and even politically, than we would ever guess from a literal-minded reading of his profile in Aristophanes. Naturally, not all butts of satire were eminent or influential, but like many later satirists Aristophanes did not waste much of his fire on utter social misfits or outcasts. Aristophanic derision has an overtly debasing and degrading thrust, and therefore an inbuilt tendency to direct itself against targets whose public standing permits a satisfying disparity between accepted realities outside the theatre and the grotesque reductiveness of comedy itself. In this respect Old Comedy's mockery of human beings is parallel to its burlesque presentation of the gods. Most scholars would not now try to infer Aristophanes' personal religious attitudes, nor prevailing currents of religious feeling in Athens, from the treatment of Hermes in *Peace*, *Birds*, or *Wealth*, of Iris and Poseidon in *Birds*, or of Dionysos in *Frogs*. For comparable reasons, we should be highly circumspect about translating his satire of individual Athenians into a personal set of political and social convictions.

At this point we need to take into account a seemingly obvious consideration. This is the commonly stated orthodoxy that comic playwrights *did* possess, in their parabases (and occasionally elsewhere too), the means to communicate to their audiences the specific perspective from which they observed and judged the life of the polis. It is on the basis of parabatic passages where the chorus can speak either

---

[68] See the Index of Names for further references to Kleonymos.

in the voice of the poet or on his behalf (see 'Formality and Performance', above) that Aristophanes has commonly been regarded as a professedly engagé dramatist. In *Acharnians* (633 ff.), for example, the chorus explains that Aristophanes believes himself to have been responsible for many benefits to the democracy, especially by bringing to its attention in his recent play *Babylonians* (see above, 'Aristophanes' Career in Context') the deceitful flattery used by foreign ambassadors when addressing the Assembly in Athens. The poet is not afraid, claims the chorus, to speak out in the interests of truth and justice, and thereby to serve his people as adviser and teacher (645–58). In a similar vein, the chorus of *Wasps* reports Aristophanes' boast that he has not indulged in petty ridicule of ordinary people but has deployed his satire against the biggest of targets, namely the politician Kleon, here allegorically described as a monster whom it requires Heraklean powers to overcome (1029–35, cf. *Peace* 751–8). Aristophanes, the chorus insists, has fought and continues to fight on behalf of the Athenian people (*Wasps* 1037). The comic playwright, on this reading, is himself a committed political agent with a determinate political agenda.

It is naive, however, to suppose that any such parabatic claims offer us the direct, authentic, and unfiltered voice of the poet himself. The parabasis, though always standing outside the progress of the dramatic action, is nonetheless a fully comic construction in its own right. Its elaborate formality (rhythmical, musical, and choreographic), as discussed in the last section, lends it the status of a highly stylized theatrical event. Moreover, the 'voice' of the poet in which the first part of the parabasis is sometimes delivered is a conventional fiction, an opportunity for comedy to ape and burlesque the postures of public discourse which were familiar to Athenian audiences from the political Assembly, the adversarial contests of the law-courts, and other democratic institutions.[69] When Aristophanes 'speaks' to the city in his parabases, whether in the first or third person, he can always be seen to be making use of a more-or-less parodic rhetoric by *feigning*, not actually fulfilling, the role of adviser and teacher to his fellow citizens.

---

[69] Public oratory is burlesqued in a different way by being made the mode of discourse in which even *women* speak at their own festival meetings, *Women at the Thesmophoria* 372–519.

Of the two examples mentioned above, *Acharnians* provides a ripe instance of mock-rhetoric in two modes, both that of self-defence (Aristophanes is replying to the complaint made against him by Kleon after the staging of *Babylonians*) and that of political advice. What gives the game away, above all, are the ludicrous claims at 643 ff.: first, that representatives of allied cities will now hurry to Athens with their annual tribute in order to have a chance to see Aristophanes himself (as though he were a panhellenic celebrity); and then, more preposterously still, that even the king of Persia is said to have remarked on the essential value of the poet to the Athenian war-effort (and this in a play whose protagonist has made a private peace treaty!). In *Wasps*, similarly, Aristophanes' depiction of himself as a quasi-Heraklean enemy of Kleon is an exercise in extravagantly hyperbolical bluster, the spirit of which matches the comically outrageous terms (briefly anticipated at 35–6) in which Kleon is transformed into a physically repulsive compound of dog, seal, camel, and more besides. Finally, and very tellingly, the trite boast of fighting for the people (1037) is a transparently rhetorical cliché, and as such was twice satirized earlier in the play—ironically through the mouth of Philokleon himself (593), and head-on by his son (667)—as a populist hallmark of slick, exploitative orators (593).

In short, there is nothing authoritative about anything said in the poet's name in a parabasis, since the poet's voice is part of, not a detached commentary on, the theatrically artificial and fantastically inflated world of each play.[70] Indeed, the kind of argument I have been criticizing could profitably be stood on its head: it is precisely the air of *mock*-seriousness, the posturing rhetoric, and the pretence of didactic influence found in some parabases which reinforce the grounds for supposing that Old Comedy is a perpetual creator of illusions and fabrications about itself as about everything else.

Even in the case of the one surviving parabasis, that of *Frogs*, where there is an apparent linkage to a political decision subsequently taken by the Athenians, caution is in order about relationships of cause and effect. The proposal that Athens should restore citizen rights to some

---

[70] The same is true of *Acharnians* 497–500, where Dikaiopolis prefaces his 'defence speech' with some remarks about comedy itself: to treat this as programmatic of the author's own stance, as has often been done, is to tear it out of the context of parody and metatheatre in which it is teasingly embedded.

of its disenfranchised citizens if they fight in the fleet (686–702)—a proposal, it is worth noting, advanced by the chorus of initiates, not in the name of the poet as such—is one that must have been already under consideration in certain quarters in the period 406–405.[71] Athens had a manpower shortage in the later years of the Peloponnesian War: hence the enfranchisement of slaves who fought at the battle of Arginousai, as this same passage of *Frogs* mentions. When the Athenians did in fact restore rights to some disenfranchised citizens in the final months of 405, as a result of the decree of Patrokleides (and after their disastrous naval defeat at the battle of Aigospotamoi), this must have been because it had by then attracted the support of a sufficiently large body of opinion in the city, not directly because of Aristophanes' comedy. At most, the parabasis of *Frogs* was echoing and, as it were, cheering on a sentiment that had already been conceived by some Athenians, not independently advocating a new political initiative. That Aristophanes chose to include this material in his play probably tells us something about a growing mood in the city. But its place in the intricate web of threads which make up the total fabric of *Frogs* should not be exaggerated. Nor does it provide anything like a template for comedy's general relationship to the processes of real political decision-making.

To return to the broader issue of satirical purpose in Aristophanes, it is practically inevitable that a form of comedy predicated on the licence to abuse, denigrate, and lampoon should sometimes give the impression of embodying politically committed positions. In most social contexts, forthright mockery is a weapon of aggression, superiority, or contempt. But Athenian democracy had allowed comic drama to develop, however riskily, as a festively 'protected' opportunity for scurrility-without-responsibility. (The point applies to the treatment of religion as well: nowhere outside comedy could a god like Dionysos be treated as a complete buffoon, as happens in *Frogs*.) From at least the time of Kratinos, in the generation before Aristophanes, poets had exploited this opportunity to subject leading politicians, generals, and other office-holders, as well as a range of lesser individuals, to the force of collective laughter. If we ask why this should have been so, it is impossible to avoid a culturally speculative

---

[71] On the political/military context at the date of *Frogs*, see my Introduction to the play in *Frogs and Other Plays*.

model of explanation. Two factors of fundamental importance were stressed in my earlier section on 'Old Comedy and Dionysiac Festivity': one, the sub-literary 'folk' roots of this variety of comic satire in old traditions of popular revelry; the other, the flourishing of Old Comedy during the period when Athenian democracy was actually most buoyant and prosperous (as well as confidently 'imperialist') and therefore most comfortable about allowing elements of its world to be exposed to ridicule within a temporary framework of festivity. We are probably dealing, in other words, with a type of collective celebration which was pre-democratic in origin, 'sub-democratic' in its psychological appeal to anti-authoritarian irreverence, and yet functionally democratic by virtue of its incorporation in the city's festive calendar.[72]

We need to remind ourselves here of a cultural paradox and puzzle. Dionysiac festivals at Athens were thought equally suitable settings for the performance of both tragedy and comedy: for experiencing (or, at any rate, imagining) life in both its darkest and its most absurd forms. These were occasions when, on the one hand, the city distributed marks and awards of honour to pre-eminent citizens, but also when carnivalesque pleasures of ritual mockery and licensed obscenity were prominent in the shape of masked revellers on wagons or floats who processed through the city hurling ribald abuse at one another and at the watching crowds.[73] It is as if the heady atmosphere of Dionysiac festivals was thought simultaneously appropriate for the opposing extremes of solemn, civic earnestness *and* disruptive, topsy-turvy play. More interestingly still, the recipients of honorific and satirical attention were in some cases the very same people: this might be so, for example, with the city's generals, who were sometimes granted rights of front seating (*prohedria*) in the theatre[74] but who might then find themselves, as Kleon and others did, the object of vilification in the very plays they were watching. Satirical mockery may, in a psychologically subtle way, have temporarily counterbalanced and inverted

[72] For a fuller statement of this view of the genre's cultural psychology, see Halliwell, *Greek Laughter*, 243–63.

[73] See Halliwell, *Greek Laughter*, 177–81.

[74] See *Knights* 575, 702–4.

the possession of public power or esteem, but it is hard to believe that it could have been allowed to negate or cancel out those things.[75]

Nor does our other evidence, if assessed sensitively, encourage belief in comedy's potency as a direct influence on currents of public opinion in classical Athens. The case of Aristophanes' seemingly stormy relationship with the leading politician Kleon has been touched on more than once already. Whatever its other implications, it provides no cogent evidence that comedy could make a significant difference to the practicalities of democratic politics. On the contrary, it might be thought to throw into relief the asymmetry between 'real' and 'comic' politics. When, in the parabasis of *Clouds* (549–50), Aristophanes boasts that in *Knights* he had struck Kleon 'hard in the belly' and 'knocked him flat' (as if in an all-in wrestling contest) but had then moved on to other subject-matter for his subsequent plays (itself a claim, we should note, that is hard to square with serious political commitment), this is a self-evident piece of pseudo-political arrogance. If anything, Kleon's power and prestige in Athens had actually *risen*—as testified by his repeated election to generalships in 424–423 and 423–422—during the very period when Aristophanes' lampooning of him was at its most comically scabrous. Aristophanes' own words betray the paradox: he had supposedly knocked Kleon down when he was, in fact, 'at his height' or most powerful (*Clouds* 549).

Nor does another famous case, the treatment of Sokrates in *Clouds*, point in a different direction. Here appeal is often made to two passages in Plato's *Apology* (18c–19c) which many have taken to provide testimony, albeit written some thirty years after the play's staging, that *Clouds* had contributed to the accumulation of hostility towards Sokrates which eventually (almost a quarter-century later) led to the philosopher's trial and execution. But contrary to what is usually claimed, it is far from clear that Plato means these passages to suggest that *Clouds* itself had been a genuine causal factor in the dissemination of negative perceptions of the philosopher. On a more nuanced reading, the *Apology* uses the example of *Clouds* as a pointed illustration

---

[75] Our only fifth-century observation on the satirical practices of Old Comedy is the claim in pseudo-Xenophon (the so-called 'Old Oligarch'), *Constitution of the Athenians* 2.18, that the targets of comedy are largely 'the rich, noble, or powerful', not members of the common people: although this passage is hardly a precise formulation, it at least leaves the impression that comedy did not *change* anything in Athenian society.

of just how ludicrous the distortions of his life and character could become: Sokrates actually contrasts comic 'nonsense' with the 'animus and malice' shown by his real-life enemies and accusers.[76] We know, moreover, that at its first performance in 423 (when Plato himself was a very young child) *Clouds* had been something of a flop with the audience, as we learn from the play's revised parabasis (524–6) and as *Wasps* 1043–50 underscores, though not without a touch of humorous conceitedness in both cases. This weakens even further any argument that might be constructed about the comedy's supposed influence on Athenian attitudes to Sokrates in the late fifth century.

Because comic performances were limited to two main festivals in the year (though with some additional opportunity for smaller productions in local deme theatres),[77] they were not sufficiently integrated into the all-year-round processes of social and political life to impinge on the latter in any regular or sustained way. This is not to say, however, that comedy was simply 'innocent fun'; doubting our capacity to discern a consistent agenda in Aristophanes' work does not entail jumping to the opposite extreme of regarding comic satire as light-hearted or frivolous. The genre's unfettered freedom of speech permitted it to voice feelings of disgruntlement, exasperation, and cynicism which no doubt partially reflected the underside of political consciousness in the city. But we will be prone to considerable self-deception if we think that we now have much chance of picking our way through its distortions, absurdities, contradictions, and outrageous transformations of life, and coming out at the end with a coherent, steady sense of the playwright's own point of view. All humour tends to some extent towards the dissolution of sense, and the characteristic modes of Old Comedy do so to an exceptional degree. Aristophanes' theatrical strength lies in his multifarious talent for manipulating images and ideas into surprising yet dramatically satisfying scenarios. But anyone who looks to him for clear or deep insights into the forces at play in Athenian society is likely to be ultimately disappointed.

[76] For further discussion of the references to *Clouds* in Plato's *Apology*, see my Introduction to the play in *Frogs and Other Plays*.

[77] See Rusten, *The Birth of Comedy*, 126–31, for inscriptional evidence on performances in deme theatres. Plato, *Republic* 5.475d, refers to theatre addicts who try to go to as many local dramatic performances as they can.

Translating Aristophanes

The translator of Aristophanes is confronted by challenges more varied and formidable than those posed by any other ancient author. There are three main sources of difficulty. First, Aristophanic verse encompasses many different linguistic registers; it frequently achieves its distinctive effects by piquant or incongruous shifts between these. As well as echoing and parodying other genres of Greek poetry—epic, lyric, and above all tragedy[78]—the stylistic range of Old Comedy constantly moves backwards and forwards between the colloquial and the elevated, the informal and the technical, the delicate and the gross. Secondly, large areas of Aristophanic humour are inextricably tied up with verbal details of imagery, puns, coinages, and other kinds of word-play, many of which are hard if not impossible to preserve in modern translation. Finally, Old Comedy is saturated with historically specific references to people, places, institutions, and assorted paraphernalia. These sometimes created problems even for postclassical Greek readers in antiquity[79] and they continue to form a barrier to appreciation for those who are not extensively familiar with fifth-century Athenian culture. The conjunction of these various factors means that issues of fidelity of the sort which affect all fields of translation arise in an acute form with Aristophanes' work: the expectation of comic fluency and the desirability of historical accuracy make competing and often irreconcilable demands.

Translations are intrinsically ambivalent constructions. On the one hand, they implicitly invite us—and the more so the greater the cultural distance between their originals and ourselves—to extend our experience beyond the bounds of what is immediately available within our own language and its associated thought-world. On the other, they inevitably engage in some degree of assimilation by the very act of transference into the translator's/reader's language. Translators strive, according to their inclinations and purposes, either to strike a balance between these contrasting implications, or else to accentuate one at the expense of the other. In the case of comic texts, the temptation to prefer assimilation and modernization over the acknowledgement and savouring of historical distance is very considerable, for the simple reason that readers of

---

[78] Cf. 'Old Comedy and Dionysiac Festivity', above.

[79] For one example, see my discussion of Plutarch in 'Aristophanes and Posterity', below.

comedy readily expect to be amused, and amusement is by nature a relatively spontaneous response which does not normally require a special effort of imagination or understanding. But the present translation tries, in the main, to resist this temptation, on the assumption that readers of Aristophanes should be looking for something other than a ready-made entertainment of a kind straightforwardly equivalent to, and interchangeable with, the products of their own culture.

My translation has accordingly been guided by the conviction that, while it is desirable to make Aristophanes as accessible as possible, accessibility must involve access *to* something that is not our own, rather than a modern substitute for it. The comic pleasures which can still be obtained from these plays depend on the willingness of readers to participate in a well-informed experience of a historically peculiar, even alien, mode of drama. What I have tried to provide are versions which approximate as closely to the original texture of Aristophanic poetry, and to the proclivities of Aristophanic humour, as is compatible with reasonable fluency in modern English. This means, for one thing, that I have generally retained as much as possible of the historical fabric of names, references, and allusions, so that readers will not at any rate be badly misled about the salient features, real and fictional, of Aristophanes' dramatic universe. It also and equally importantly means that I have chosen not to translate the plays into prose, since that would involve, in my judgement, too great (and comfortable) an assimilation to the dominant medium of comic drama in our own world, with a corresponding loss of the poetic forms which are so integral to the nature of Old Comedy. Here as elsewhere, however, some compromise is appropriate, as will become clear from further explanation of the verse-forms I have adopted.[80]

In an earlier section of this Introduction, 'Formality and Performance', I described Aristophanes' use of the three basic modes of poetic delivery: speech (in iambic trimeters); chanted 'recitative' (in longer lines of various rhythms), musically accompanied by the double *aulos*; and sung lyrics (in often complex metrical units), also with musical accompaniment. These three modes pose distinct challenges to a translator. The spoken iambic trimeters call for treatment which maintains a sense of tight verse structure while allowing for easy variation in phrasing

---

[80] In the case of oracles, which use dactylic hexameters (the metre of epic) in Greek, I have attempted something loosely approximating to accentual hexameters, with an inevitable degree of rhythmical licence: see esp. *Knights* 1015 ff., *Peace* 1063 ff., *Birds* 967 ff., *Lysistrata* 770 ff.

(including division between speakers, a particular source of verbal give-
and-take in Aristophanes)[81] and for a wide spectrum of registers and
effects, including the colloquial,[82] though the latter is not quite as dominant a voice as many modern translators of Aristophanes have made it.
Here I have adopted a five-beat line (with a little stretch for some Greek
proper names) which represents a version of blank verse, the so-called
English 'iambic pentameter', in maximally supple form, not least with
frequent substitution of anapaests, i.e. two light syllables before a stressed
syllable, for iambs, i.e. one light followed by one stressed. This has three
advantages to recommend it: first, it is not too far in metrical shape from
the Greek iambic trimeter (making allowance for the difference between
the quantitative rhythms of Greek verse and the dynamic stress-patterns
of English);[83] secondly, it has a combination of regularity with flexibility
which can cope with the gamut of styles employed, echoed, and parodied by Aristophanes in the spoken parts of his plays; thirdly, it
has a historical embeddedness in English verse (particularly in the practice of dramatic and satiric poets) which stretches back to the sixteenth
century and which ought to make it conveniently familiar to readers.
Unlike some other modern versions, my translations keep line-by-line
step with the Greek text, which has the additional advantage of making
it simple for readers to identify passages cited with the standard line
numbers in secondary literature.

   The recitative sections of Aristophanes' comedies use longer lines
(tetrameters) of iambic, trochaic, and anapaestic type, and occasionally other rhythms too (e.g. cretics at *Wasps* 1275 ff.).[84] It is scarcely

---

[81] For token examples from the plays in this volume, see *Acharnians* 45–6, *Knights*
1160–1, *Wasps* 851, *Peace* 198. The maximum splitting of a line between speakers (six
separate utterances) is found at *Wealth* 393. For similar effects in a different metre, see
the sustained play with 'echoes' at *Women at the Thesmophoria* 1078–96.

[82] See Aristotle's well-known remark that 'the iambic trimeter, more than any other
metre, has the rhythm of speech: an indication of this is that we speak many trimeters in
conversation with one another' (*Poetics* 4.1449a24–7; cf. 22.1459a12, *Rhetoric* 3.8,
1408b33–5).

[83] If Greek iambics were assimilated to a stress-patterned metre, the result would be
six main 'beats' in the line, as opposed to the five of blank verse. It is thus important to
notice the difference between standard terminology for Greek and English metres. An
English iambic 'trimeter' would have *three* beats, a 'tetrameter' four, etc.; for Greek units,
'-meter' denotes a metron, which roughly corresponds to a pair of feet, hence two beats,
in English rhythms. Cf. n. 84.

[84] In the Greek context, 'tetrameter' denotes four metra, which roughly correspond to
either seven or eight English feet/beats; thus a Greek iambic tetrameter is approximately
twice as long as the English line so-called (as e.g. in Marvell's 'To his Coy Mistress').

feasible to match all these rhythms with their nearest English equivalents. Trochaic rhythms in Greek typically had a springy quality, but it is hard to capture this consistently by English trochees, which cut too much against the grain of the language and tend to sound laboriously mannered. Even so, I have sometimes rendered shorter passages of Aristophanes' trochaic tetrameters as English trochaics (in lines of *eight* stresses): examples in this volume are the agitated entry of the aggressive charcoal-burners at *Acharnians* 204–40 (the chorus-leader's lines), the symmetrical ('epirrhematic') sections of the parabasis in both *Acharnians* (676–91, 703–18) and *Knights* (565–80, 595–610), and the chorus-leader's rustic musings in the equivalent sections of the second parabasis in *Peace* (1140–58, 1172–90, with half-lines at the end of each section). In some other cases, however, and especially where trochaic tetrameters are employed for extended periods, I have capitulated by converting them into eight-stress *iambic* lines: examples include the confrontation between Bdelykleon and the wasp chorus at *Wasps* 415–525, and the recitative section of the half-agon at *Peace* 601–50.

Anapaests are even harder to sustain without either awkwardness or a rolling Gilbertian manner that palls when kept up for the length of passages in which this metre occurs in Aristophanes. The attempt by Swinburne to translate part of the parabasis of *Birds* (anapaestic tetrameters) into an English equivalent (anapaestic heptameters) shows that even a practised versifier is stretched to carry off the exercise without making a reader stumble;[85] and I give my reasons in 'Aristophanes and Posterity' (below) for thinking it advisable to avoid endowing Aristophanes with the genial spirit of Gilbert and Sullivan. In the present volume, therefore, I have dispensed with regular anapaestic rhythms altogether.[86] Some anapaestic colouring can be kept, however, by the type of longer line which I use to translate most of Aristophanes' tetrameters: namely, a flexible version (allowing variable numbers of unstressed syllables) of the iambic heptameter (or, in its strictest form, the 'fourteener'), i.e. an iambic line with seven main

---

[85] Swinburne's version was first published in the *Athenaeum*, 30 October 1880, then in his *Studies in Song* (London, 1880), 67–74; see *The Poems of Algernon Charles Swinburne*, v (London, 1904), 41–5. Smoother anapaests such as those of B. B. Rogers have the drawback of tending to become more monotonous.

[86] For a short example in a previous volume (*Birds and Other Plays*), see *Birds* 209–22, where anapaests well suit the Hoopoe's excited summons to his nightingale wife.

stresses.[87] The English heptameter has enough fluency to accommodate the numerous kinds of material found in Aristophanes' Greek tetrameters, and enough declamatory formality to convey something of the slightly raised, stylized tone of the passages in question. Examples in the present volume include the main section of parabatic recitative in all four plays: *Acharnians* 626–64, *Knights* 507–50, *Wasps* 1015–59, and *Peace* 729–74, with a 'tail' of shorter lines in every case. There are also occasional runs of shorter lines, e.g. the iambic dimeters at *Knights* 367–81, 441–56 (giving a snappy tit-for-tat pattern to the exchange of coarse abuse between Paphlagon and the Sausage-Seller), or the anapaestic dimeters at *Peace* 82–101, 154–72 (part of Trygaios's skyward ride on his dung-beetle) and 974–1015 (Trygaios's pseudo-solemn prayer to Peace), which I have rendered with iambic tetrameters in the English sense, i.e. four-beat lines.

Finally, the sung lyrics. Here it would be pointless to follow B. B. Rogers and several of his Victorian predecessors in aiming for anything like a consistent correlation with Greek rhythms, since too many of the latter, even when turned into stress metres, would make no recognizable pattern to a modern ear. In some passages, however, part of the rhythmical ethos can be captured in at least an approximate manner, either by the 'shape' and length of metrical phrases or, occasionally, by some of their dominant rhythms. My general strategy in this area has been to employ a fluid free-verse technique. Aristophanic lyrics, which can involve characters as well as chorus, vary greatly in style and tone both within and between plays. Some are relatively prosaic in diction and sentiment but are given a perky song-and-dance tautness by their rhythms: the mocking vignettes of various undesirables who will not have access to Dikaiopolis's agora, at *Acharnians* 836–59, is a case in point; another is the quasi-anecdotal pair of swipes at Kleon (the only time he is mentioned by name in the play) at *Knights* 973–96. Others are integrated into stage action in various ways: see e.g. the stark contrast between the wounded Lamachos and the inebriated Dikaiopolis at *Acharnians* 1190–1233, the concerned communication between the chorus and Philokleon at

---

[87] The English metre is sometimes divided into alternating lines of four and three stresses, as in Coleridge's *Rhyme of the Ancient Mariner*. My treatment of the end of heptameters allows both 'masculine' (final syllable stressed) and 'feminine' (final syllable unstressed) cadences. The same is true of my occasional longer trochaic lines.

Wasps 273–345,[88] or the choreographed rope-pulling (to excavate the goddess's statue) at *Peace* 459–72, 486–99. The spectrum of Aristophanic lyrics reaches all the way, in fact, from ditties of smutty vulgarity and outright obscenity (including the phallic song at *Acharnians* 264–79) to pseudo-exercises in high-register lyric, as at *Peace* 775–818, where adapted motifs from Stesichoros are bathetically undermined by crude abuse of named individuals. While it is impossible to mirror all this in modern English, translation of the lyrics calls for maximum pliancy in both formal and linguistic terms.[89] In reading the lyrics, readers in turn need to stretch their imaginations and cultivate a sense of what must have been contributed by the lost music and choreography.

I referred at the start of this section to three main categories of difficulty facing any translator of Aristophanes. The problem of mixed and unexpectedly shifting stylistic registers—above all, the typical Aristophanic juxtapositioning of 'high' and 'low'—is ubiquitous. In coming to terms with it I have made use, where appropriate, of parodically archaizing language, added stage directions (see the next section) that signal changes of tone, and quotation marks to prompt the reader's aural imagination. In the case of puns and word-play, one is partly at the mercy of luck in terms of the latent potential of English. Four brief examples from near the start of *Wasps*, a passage replete with intricate verbal humour, can usefully illustrate the problem. The dream recounted by Xanthias at lines 15–19 depends in Greek on the fact that the same noun can mean either a serpent (which can be seized by a swooping eagle) or a military shield (which can be discarded by a runaway coward like Kleonymos): there is simply no equivalent word in English, so I have adopted the next-best option of building a kind of explanation into the joke, even though this reduces the neatness with which the Greek conveys the sense of displacement so characteristic of dreams. Shortly after this, Sosias reports that his own dream concerns the whole 'ship' of the city, thereby evoking the old idea of the 'ship of state'; in asking to hear about the dream, Xanthias

---

[88] This sequence is affected by the reordering of lines followed in my translation; see the note on *Wasps* 290.

[89] One resource I have abstained from, however, is the structural use of rhyme, despite its appeal to some other Aristophanic translators. I have never been quite able to convince myself that it serves a desirable purpose in this context.

changes by just one letter a word meaning the 'nature' (of the matter) to one meaning the 'keel' of a boat (29): I am not the first translator to seize eagerly on the near-enough equivalent, 'the hull of the matter'. The intricately imagistic dream which Sosias proceeds to recount partly depends on the difference of accent, and no more, between two words spelt *dêmos* and meaning respectively 'the people' (i.e. the citizenry) and animal 'fat' (40–1): once again, no ready-made equivalence is available, so that some sort of additional elaboration is called for if the spirit of the pun is to be conveyed. Finally, the continuation of Sosias's dream represents Alkibiades as having a lisp (as he is indeed supposed to have had) which makes him pronounce *r* as *l*, in the present case thus converting a word for 'raven' into one for 'flatterer' or 'hanger-on' (42–9). A translator is entitled to despair over this kind of challenge; compromise is inescapable, and my own solution (a play on 'raven' and 'craven') is purchased at the price of partly blurring the nature of the lisp.[90]

Things are at any rate easier with the third source of difficulty mentioned earlier, namely the plethora of topical references (to people, places, institutions, etc.) in Aristophanes' plays. For reasons already explained, a historically focused translation such as mine has no choice but to preserve as many of these references as possible, since they are an essential part of the fabric of the work in relation to their time and place. Such references bring with them, of course, the need for explanatory annotation.

Two further matters, both involving stylistic choices (one small-scale, one larger), are worth brief comment to conclude this section: they concern oaths and dialects. The use of oaths is commonplace in Aristophanes' plays; the main reason for this is undoubtedly that they were a general feature of real Attic speech at all social and cultural levels. Many of them, such as the commonest of all ('by Zeus'), functioned as little more than expletives or exclamations. Others lend varying degrees of intensification or emotional colour to their utterances. And some have further significance, for example as markers of

---

[90] It is worth adding that if there are good and bad puns, we have no hope of judging which of Aristophanes' would have struck his audiences as more or less successful; to make such judgements, which are anyway notoriously subjective, requires an intimate, instinctive feel for a spoken language. Nor should we overlook the possibility that some puns are metacomically funny in virtue of *deliberate* 'feebleness' (see my note on *Acharnians* 808).

female speech[91] or as the basis of local comic effect. In the latter category belong the Sausage-Seller's oath by Hermes at *Knights* 297 to support his insistence that he knows how to steal (Hermes himself being, among other things, a notional 'god of thieves'); the same character's idiosyncratic oath by the various thrashings and blows he received in his rough upbringing as a butcher's boy (411–12); Paphlagon's self-regarding oath by his (i.e. Kleon's) triumph at Pylos (*Knights* 702); Aristophanes' authorial oath by Dionysos, god of theatre, in his bold claims for the quality of his work (*Wasps* 1046); and Hermes' oath by Earth at *Peace* 188, which is doubly comic both as an oath on the lips of a god[92] and as one which ironically conveys his exasperation with the presence of a human being on Olympos. To translate each and every oath literally would lead to an excessively arch effect in English. But to omit most of them would be to lose both a distinctive trait of Athenian speech patterns and a source of much verbal pointing of comic dialogue. I have decided, therefore, to keep a fair proportion of oaths, especially those which are pointedly expressive in one way or another.

In the case of dialects, however, I have diverged from the practice of most earlier translators by declining to employ a systematic differentiation of speech patterns in the case of characters depicted as speaking dialects other than Attic (principally, the Megarian and Boiotian in *Acharnians*, and Lampito in *Lysistrata*). This is for the simple but fundamental reason that no appropriate equivalent, making even vaguely similar sense in both linguistic and cultural terms, is readily available. Athenians must have heard other Greek dialects spoken on many occasions, in the streets of their own city as well as elsewhere; the dialects as such were not intrinsically amusing, and indeed a passage in Plato (*Laws* 1.642c) shows that Greeks could in principle enjoy the sound of dialects other than their own. In particular, to give the three characters mentioned above a 'funny accent' is not the point. Many translators in the past have made Lampito speak Scots, but this is, and always was, unsuitable in a version which can be

[91] The only instance of this, I think, in the plays in the present volume is the Breadseller's oath at *Wasps* 1396: see my note there. For other examples, see the notes on *Women at the Thesmophoria* 254, 383, 594 in *Frogs and Other Plays*.

[92] For other comic cases of a god swearing an oath, see Poseidon's oath by himself (!) at *Birds* 1614 and Dionysos's partly stifled cries to Apollo and Poseidon (which he then tries to pretend were quotations from poetry) at *Frogs* 659 and 664.

read as well in Scotland as anywhere else. Other translators have opted for a dialectal element which can be perceived, from the point of view of the implicit readership or audience, as markedly rustic or backward; in America, this usually means a hill-billy variety of speech. But such a strategy is certainly inapt for Lampito, and probably for the two characters in *Acharnians* too, since we have no reason to suppose that Athenians perceived the relevant dialects in this light. I have therefore eschewed the use of an overtly dialectal presentation of these figures, allowing the comic features of their behaviour to come across, as in the original, by other means.[93] A different strategy is called for with characters who actually mangle Greek, as with Pseudartabas, the (pseudo-)Persian ambassador, at *Acharnians* 100–4, the Persian Datis in the supposed snatch of song at *Peace* 291, the Triballian god at *Birds* 1615 ff., or, most extensively, the Skythian Archer at *Women at the Thesmophoria* 1001 ff.: the deformed 'barbarian' speech of the latter should remind us, by contrast, that every other slave in Aristophanes speaks just as good Attic as do all the citizen characters.

Stage Directions

The Theatre of Dionysos in Athens, on the SE slope of the Akropolis, was the location for the dramatic performances at both the City Dionysia and, almost certainly, the Lenaia too (cf. 'Aristophanes' Career', above). The details of its fifth-century form are contentious, since the archaeological remains are mostly of much later date and literary evidence is scanty. But in recent years there has been an emergent consensus that the area for the audience's wooden benches on the hillside, and therefore the size of the audience, was smaller in the late fifth century than previously supposed. Many scholars now believe that Aristophanes' comedies would have been watched by some 5,000–7,000 spectators (including a certain number of non-

---

[93] There is no real alternative to giving him a strongly yet indeterminately pidginized form of English. But even here Aristophanes is playing subtle language games: the Skythian's egregious errors still fit the verse rhythms flawlessly, and part of their effect depends less on their morphological or grammatical faults per se than on the extreme clash of speech registers which they set up with the poetry of Euripidean tragedy.

Athenians at the Dionysia, fewer at the Lenaia).[94] That is still, however, a substantial proportion of the citizen body, representing
approximately the same scale of attendance as at (larger) political
Assembly meetings.[95] In addition to front-row seating (*prohedria*) for
various dignitaries, including generals (*Knights* 575, 702–4), we know
that a special area of seating was reserved for members of the Council
(five hundred in total, if all attended), a fact exploited for the purposes of an obscene joke at *Birds* 794 and for some physical interaction with the audience at *Peace* 882–908.

On the question of whether women attended the theatre in the
fifth century, scholarly opinion remains divided. Our main evidence,
if it can be called that, comes from Aristophanes' own plays and is
open to conflicting interpretations. A joke at *Peace* 966–7 about how
Athenian women or wives failed to get any of the barley (also a slang
term for 'penis') which has been thrown into the audience is compatible in principle with both the absence of women and their confinement to a small area at the back. Another sexual joke, at *Women at the
Thesmophoria* 395–7, is premised on the idea that wives are at home
(and perhaps committing adultery) while their husbands are in the
theatre; exactly the same comic premise is present at *Birds* 793–6.
Such jokes, needless to say, provide no solid basis on which to erect
sociological generalizations. Some weight might be placed on the
fact that in various Aristophanic passages where the audience is
addressed or described, women go unmentioned: *Peace* 50–3, stress-
ing different age-groups of males, is a telling instance. But such
silence might reflect a rhetorical convention more than a simple
physical fact. Since we have explicit references from the fourth century to women in the theatre,[96] it is difficult to rule out altogether
their possible presence in the fifth. But it remains judicious to

---

[94] See e.g. Revermann, *Comic Business*, 168–9, D. K. Roselli, *Theater of the People:
Spectators and Society in Ancient Athens* (Austin, 2011), 64–75 (arguing for additional
spectators outside the official seating area). For the wooden benches on which most spectators sat, cf. *Women at the Thesmophoria* 395, though there may have been stone seating
for dignitaries at the front.

[95] For the scale of Assembly attendance, see M. G. Hansen, *The Athenian Democracy
in the Age of Demosthenes* (Oxford, 1991), 130–2.

[96] The earliest of these is Plato, *Gorgias* 502d (possibly composed *c*.385, but with a
fifth-century dramatic setting); considerably later are Plato, *Laws* 2.658d, 7.817c, and
probably later still, Alexis fr. 42 (referring to a section of seating at the back for foreign
women).

suppose that very few if any women would normally have been spectators at fifth-century comedies.

The main components of the Theatre of Dionysos as a perform-ance space in Aristophanes' time were a substantial, probably wooden stage building (*skênê*), and, in front of it, a large area, possibly recti-linear and elongated (trapezoidal) rather than circular in shape (as it was later to be), known as the *orchêstra* (lit. 'dancing-floor') and used by both actors and chorus. The dimensions of the *orchêstra* were per-haps of the order of some twenty metres in diameter and eight in depth, and to either side of it was an entrance/exit (*eisodos*, pl. *eiso-doi*)[97] for the performers; it probably had a low altar at its centre, which comes into play at moments such as *Peace* 942 ff. and *Women at the Thesmophoria* 689 ff. The stage building had a main central door (which could change its identity in the course of a play: see *Acharnians* and *Peace* in this volume), an accessible roof (e.g. *Acharnians* 262 ff., *Wasps* 136 ff., *Birds* 267 ff., *Lysistrata* 829 ff.), windows (cf. *Wasps* 156 ff., 317 ff., *Assembly-Women* 884 ff.), and, when required (e.g. *Acharnians*, *Peace*, *Clouds*), a second door.[98] It is possible that there was a low wooden stage in front of the stage building, connected to the *orchêstra* by two or three steps;[99] if so, it did nothing to impede the physical interaction between characters and chorus which is often evident in Old Comedy, for example in the confrontational parodoi of plays such as *Knights* (247 ff.) and *Birds* (352 ff.). Also available, though employed by Aristophanes almost entirely for the purposes of para-tragedy, were the *mêchanê* ('machine'), a sort of crane which sus-pended characters in simulated flight (see Trygaios on his dung-beetle at *Peace* 82 ff., with metatheatrical address to the crane-operator at 174, Sokrates' aerial entry at *Clouds* 219 ff., Iris at *Birds* 1199 ff.),

[97] *Eisodos* is Aristophanes' own term at *Clouds* 326, *Birds* 296; the term *parodos* (whose correct application denotes the chorus's entry: see 'Formality and Performance', above), though common in modern books, is post-classical usage for a theatrical side entry/exit.

[98] There has in fact been a lot of debate among modern scholars about how many doors are employed in certain plays; the issue can be safely ignored by readers of a translation.

[99] An Athenian vase from Aristophanes' lifetime shows such a stage (see Csapo and Slater, *The Context of Ancient Drama*, pl. 4B, with their discussion on 64–5), though we cannot be certain that it represents arrangements in the Theatre of Dionysos. Some scholars take certain verbal references in Aristophanes to moving up/down (e.g. *Wasps* 1341, which I interpret differently) to presuppose a raised stage, but this too is uncer-tain. I have agnostically refrained from adopting the hypothesis of a stage in my stage directions.

and the *ekkuklêma* or wheeled platform, which represented interior scenes (Euripides' house at *Acharnians* 407–79, the cave from which the statue is excavated at *Peace* 431 ff., Agathon's house at *Women at the Thesmophoria* 101–265).[100]

Most comedies were performed by three main actors, taking more than one role each when necessary but occasionally supplemented by a fourth and even fifth actor for smaller parts; mute parts were additional. Masks, typically exaggerated and often grotesquely so, were always worn. All roles were played by males, and this probably held even for silent female figures such as the two prostitutes who accompany Dikaiopolis at *Acharnians* 1198 ff., the pair of Peace Treaties at *Knights* 1390 ff., Dardanis the pipe-girl at *Wasps* 1326 ff., Harvest and Festivity at *Peace* 523 ff., Peisetairos's bride Princess at the end of *Birds* (1720 ff.), Reconciliation at *Lysistrata* 1114 ff., and Euripides' Muse at *Frogs* 1308 ff. Even when such roles were notionally 'naked', as with the Peace Treaties, Dardanis, and Reconciliation, the body stockings which formed a standard part of comic actors' costumes would simply be designed to represent bare flesh and the appropriate anatomical externals.[101] A body stocking also allowed for the padding of the actor's belly and rump, which seems to have been a frequent means of augmenting the general sense of corporeal grotesqueness projected by Old Comedy. A visible phallus was a conventional appendage for male characters; it could be more or less prominent, more or less comically 'activated' (cf. the playwright's somewhat disingenuous comments on this point at *Clouds* 537–9): instances in the present volume of visible play with it include *Acharnians* 156 ff., 591, *Knights* 26, *Wasps* 936 ff., 1342 ff., *Peace* 877 ff., though none of these moments matches the hyperbolically phallic humour of Kinesias's priapism at *Lysistrata* 845 ff. (cf. 832). Those three grotesque accoutrements of the comic performer—distorted mask, padding, and phallus—must have created for spectators a pervasive, inescapable

---

[100] There is also a parodic reference to tragedy's use of the *ekkuklêma* at *Knights* 1249, but it is unlikely that the device is actually in operation there.

[101] Body stockings are regularly depicted in fourth-century vase-paintings of comic actors from Magna Graecia: see the illustrations in Rusten, *The Birth of Comedy*, 434–54. They are also conspicuous on the important Athenian vase widely known as the 'Getty Birds' (formerly but no longer in the Getty Museum): see Rusten, *The Birth of Comedy*, ill. 72A, Csapo and Slater, *The Context of Ancient Drama*, pl. 5, Revermann, *Comic Business*, pl. 8, O. Taplin, *Comic Angels* (Oxford, 1993), pl. 24.28.

aura of vulgarity carried to an absurdist extreme, ensuring that the action of a play was always visually suspended in a kind of misshapen world of its own.

The chorus, as mentioned in previous sections, consisted of twenty-four singers/dancers, including a chorus-leader who spoke and declaimed certain sections solo, especially when in dialogue with individual actors.[102] Many of the choral dance sections took symmetrical strophic form, involving the musically and rhythmically matching pairing of strophe and antistrophe, as indicated in the margins of my translation. Musical accompaniment was provided by a piper, whose instrument was a pair of *auloi* or reed-pipes (akin to oboes). Comedy sometimes draws the piper temporarily into the sphere of the dramatic action, as with the sounds of Prokne at *Birds* 209 ff., Euripides' use of Teredon as part of his ruse at *Women at the Thesmophoria* 1176 ff., or the old hag's address to the player at *Assembly-Women* 890–2.[103]

When the plays of Aristophanes were written down, they contained, like virtually all ancient dramatic texts, no stage directions. We are therefore left to make our own inferences about the kind of staging which they could or would have been given, guiding ourselves, wherever possible, by other sources of information about the Athenian theatre. So the reader of this, as of any other, translation of Aristophanes (or of Greek tragedy) should keep in mind that all stage directions are a matter of interpretation, not independent fact, even though a fair number of them can be established uncontroversially and more still can be persuasively justified from clues in the text. Readers should themselves cultivate the habit of picturing the realization of the script in an open-air theatrical space, and by a cast of grotesquely attired players, of the kind described above, though always remembering that the honed skills of professional actors were needed to do justice to the extraordinarily rich comic poetry of plays such as those of Aristophanes.

---

[102] We cannot always be confident whether particular choral utterances were collective or the leader's alone, but I have tried to follow a reasonably consistent practice of attribution in this respect.

[103] Additional musicians are sometimes involved: see e.g. the Theban pipers at *Acharnians* 862; a Spartan 'bagpiper' has often been posited at *Lysistrata* 1242, but the reference is probably to the ordinary piper.

Aristophanes and Posterity

The works of Aristophanes have often aroused the curiosity of writers, readers, and audiences of comedy, but they have rarely influenced the later history of the genre to an appreciable extent. The fundamental reason for this state of affairs lies in two kinds of difficulty: the difficulty of understanding, and, until recently at any rate, ethical difficulty. The former arises from linguistic challenges (colloquial idioms, stylistic parodies, an immense range of imagery), topical references (to people, places, objects, and institutions), and imaginative exoticism. Ethical difficulty, though no longer a prevalent issue for modern readers, stemmed historically from Old Comedy's scurrilous and even seemingly vicious personal satire, its irreverence in the treatment of religion, and a degree of obscenity, visual as well as verbal, not paralleled elsewhere in ancient literature: all three of these elements have regularly troubled readers committed to the long-dominant, indeed orthodox, view of comedy as a morally edifying genre (see below). Yet these two sets of features, when seen from a different angle, can also be regarded as a large part of what makes Aristophanes' plays special and therefore absorbing for anyone interested in the history of comic theatre. The story of 'Aristophanes and Posterity', of which this section can provide only a thumbnail sketch, is consequently a matter of rather delicately balanced considerations, in which factors of attraction and repulsion have often operated side by side.

Old Comedy was so closely tied to the society and culture of fifth-century Athens that it could never have been expected to have a fully sustained afterlife even in the ancient world. Unlike the New Comedy of Menander and other playwrights in the late fourth and early third centuries, which was transported to Rome about a century later by Plautus, Terence, and others, and was subsequently to be a fertile ground for the development of theatrical comedy in the Renaissance and beyond, Old Comedy's dominant traits do not lend themselves to easy imitation or emulation in different cultural contexts. Until recently it was thought likely that no Aristophanic play ever received a performance after the poet's own lifetime. Serious doubt has recently been cast on that claim, since vase-painting has given us near-certain evidence for the transference of some Old Comedies to the theatres of fourth-century Magna Graecia (South Italy and Sicily). The most compelling single item of such evidence is a South

Italian depiction of the moment from *Women at the Thesmophoria* where, in parody of Euripides' lost play *Telephos*, the Kinsman threatens Mika's 'baby', in reality a wineskin, with a sword.[104] In this particular instance it is germane that we are dealing with a play built around the (fictionalized) tragedian Euripides, whose works themselves received productions in the Greek theatres of South Italy and Sicily. But it remains hard to imagine how, without considerable adaptation at any rate, some of Aristophanes' other comedies could have been transplanted to cities where their detailed references to Athenian phenomena would not have been fully intelligible. So there is no good reason to suppose that Old Comedy's performance-life was much extended in this way.

For the rest of Graeco-Roman antiquity the plays of Aristophanes were to be known only as texts, and then mostly to very small numbers of the highly educated. The survival of eleven plays (out of more than forty) to the age of printing was, as with many other works of ancient literature, the result of a long and complex process, part cultural and part accidental. *Clouds*, for example, was preserved largely because of the lasting fascination of its central character, Sokrates, and a similar factor may have obtained in the cases of *Women at the Thesmophoria* and *Frogs*, in both of which Euripides, the most popular tragedian throughout antiquity, is so prominent.[105] It was for very different reasons, however, that *Wealth* not only survived but became established as the most commonly read of Aristophanes' works in antiquity and the Byzantine period. *Wealth* was valued as the least taxing, both historically and linguistically, of the poet's plays, but also for the apparently clear-cut morality of its plot, in which wealth is supposedly redistributed exclusively to the just. The second of those factors—the litmus test of moral edification—became increasingly active during the medieval centuries when pagan literature was

---

[104] The vase (Würzburg, Antikensammlung, H5697) is illustrated in e.g. Taplin, *Comic Angels*, pl. 11.4, Revermann, *Comic Business*, pl. 2, R. Green and E. Handley, *Images of the Greek Theatre* (London, 1995), ill. 27, and as the frontispiece to C. Austin and S. D. Olson, *Aristophanes* Thesmophoriazusae (Oxford, 2004).

[105] But the case of *Women at the Thesmophoria* also illustrates the importance of chance: the play survived the Middle Ages in only a single manuscript; if that one copy had been destroyed at any point between around 1000 and 1500, the play would now be on our list of lost works.

subjected to judgement, though hardly ever it seems to censorship, in the light of Christian values.

Clearly, though, such criteria were not consistently applied. If they had been, works such as *Knights*, with its dense texture of contemporary political allegory (as well as its unrelentingly scabrous tone), or *Wasps*, with its detailed technical references to the Athenian judicial system, would not have been preserved and copied. In instances like these it is tempting to suppose, though impossible to show, that survival partly depended upon the interests of certain readers, especially scholars, in precisely this rich element of historical allusiveness. Be that as it may, it was *Wealth*, *Clouds*, and *Frogs* which eventually became standard 'set texts' in the schools of Byzantium. Equally, and not accidentally, the three 'women plays', *Lysistrata*, *Women at the Thesmophoria*, and *Assembly-Women*, all of which contain a great deal of sexually explicit humour, were the least studied of the eleven during the Byzantine centuries.

Among ancient readers of Aristophanes probably belong the Roman authors of poems in the genre of *satura*, 'satire'. By the time of Horace, whose own *Satires* were composed in the 30s BC, the idea had acquired some currency that fifth-century Athenian Comedy was a precursor of, or partial model for, Roman satire. Horace refers to this idea at the beginning of *Satires* 1.4, where he claims that Lucilius, the creator of the Latin genre of verse satire, was heavily indebted to the Old Comedy of Kratinos, Eupolis, and Aristophanes.[106] The connection, according to Horace, takes the form of a shared concern for the public chastisement of vice and crime. Horace's claim, which exemplifies a view of Aristophanic satire which has had a long history (see 'Satire and Seriousness', above), can best be interpreted as a mock-formal, and somewhat tongue-in-cheek, arrogation of Greek pedigree for his own literary genre. But the view itself became a kind of academic orthodoxy, represented, for example, in the statement by Quintilian, rhetorician and educationalist of the late first century AD, that Old Comedy had been 'pre-eminent in the persecution of vice' (*in insectandis vitiis praecipua*, 10.1.65).

The fullest critical reaction we possess from an individual ancient reader of Aristophanes is that of Plutarch, philosopher and polymathic littérateur, in the later first and early second century AD. It

---

[106] Horace, *Satires* 1.4.1–6; cf. 1.10.16–17, Persius, *Satires* 1.123–4.

is a hostile reaction. Plutarch complains of Aristophanes' vulgarity, linguistic artificiality, confusions of tone, failures of consistent characterization, and acrid malice; in all respects he compares him unfavourably with Menander.[107] Plutarch's points suggest nothing so much as a chasm of taste between his own rather dry, academic leanings and the earthy scurrilities which had evidently appealed to a common Athenian sensibility (and need?) in the Dionysiac festivities of the classical period. It is an interesting index of the special status of Old Comedy within its own culture that even so well-informed an antiquarian as Plutarch is essentially nonplussed about its original significance.[108]

A greater and more creatively fruitful insight into the genre's qualities can be traced in the Greek writer of comic dialogues, Lucian (second century AD), whose own combination of fantasy and satire self-consciously owes something to Aristophanic precedent. Lucian's writing is, however, much blander, less sharply contemporary, and more reliant on generalized, stereotypical images of human vice. For that very reason, Lucian himself was to exercise greater influence than Aristophanes on the classicism of the Renaissance.[109] While Lucian's works were quite widely translated into several European languages in the sixteenth century, the plays of Aristophanes were very rarely tackled in this context. The contrast with the Roman poets of New Comedy is even starker. The works of Plautus and Terence dominated both the theory and the practice of comedy in the Renaissance. They supplied scenarios, characters, and themes which could be so much more easily staged, imitated, and adapted than the peculiarities of the Aristophanic imagination, whose grotesque contortions were so much harder to reconcile with the prevailing notion of comedy as a supposedly instructive 'mirror of life'.

---

[107] Plutarch, *Moralia* 853–4. For a fuller analysis of this text, together with an account of Plutarch's attitudes to Old Comedy more generally, see Anna Peterson, *Laughter on the Fringes: The Reception of Old Comedy in the Imperial Greek World* (New York, 2019), 25–51.

[108] This did not stop Plutarch from citing Aristophanes, in his *Lives* and elsewhere, as though his plays were a straightforwardly reliable source of historical information.

[109] For an overview of Lucian's relationship to Aristophanes, see E. Bowie, 'The Ups and Downs of Aristophanic Travel', in E. Hall and A. Wrigley (eds.), *Aristophanes in Performance 421 BC–AD 2007* (London, 2007), 32–51, at 34–9, with the appendix of quotations at 43–9. For Lucian's own influence, see C. Robinson, *Lucian and His Influence in Europe* (London, 1979).

That situation was to hold good throughout the various phases of neoclassical drama, right up to the eighteenth century. For the whole of this period Aristophanes was a 'name' to be brandished in various contexts, the prime example of this, as mentioned earlier (see 'Satire and Seriousness'), being the repeated indictment of *Clouds* by puritans and moralists concerned about uncontrolled or malicious laughter. But the reading of Aristophanes, in any language, was the preserve of a few. In the sixteenth century, Erasmus's wide knowledge of the author emerges from the frequency with which he cites him in his *Adages* and elsewhere. In England, where Erasmus's friend Thomas More made Aristophanes one of the authors available in his Utopia, we know that Ben Jonson possessed two editions of Aristophanes and read at least some of the plays in the original; Jonson's own works, both his plays and his notebook *Timber*, contain references to Aristophanes and Old Comedy. Jonson was undoubtedly intrigued by the ancient playwright, and occasionally indebted to him: perhaps the best instance is the mock-trial of the dogs, an idea taken from *Wasps*, in Act V of *The Staple of News*. Yet even Jonson was nonetheless typical in knowing Lucian better than he knew Aristophanes, and modern claims about Aristophanic influence on his work have sometimes been exaggerated.[110]

Later creative writers to have exhibited a fascination with Aristophanes include Racine, whose only comedy, *Les Plaideurs* (1668), adapts its basic scenario and several motifs from *Wasps*, blending these with the style of commedia dell'arte characters to produce a result (as Racine acknowledged in the Preface) rather remote from the dominant Terentian model of comedy at the time; and Goethe, who read a good deal of Aristophanes at more than one point in his life and staged a loose imitation of *Birds*, as the basis for a satire on German literary culture, at Weimar in 1780. Productions of Aristophanes had, up to this date, been even more of a rarity than translations. In England, to which my attention here is largely confined, we know for certain only of two before the nineteenth century, both of them in sixteenth-century Cambridge. The first, at St John's College in 1536, was almost inevitably of *Wealth*, which was likewise

---

[110] On Jonson's relationship to Aristophanes, see the synopsis by R. S. Miola, 'Aristophanes in England, 1500–1660', in S. D. Olson (ed.), *Ancient Comedy and Reception: Essays in Honor of Jeffrey Henderson* (Berlin, 2014), 479–502, at 495–502.

later to be the first play to be translated into English (by Thomas Randolph, adopted son of Ben Jonson).[111] The second, *Peace*, produced at the newly founded Trinity College in 1546, seems at first sight an odd choice, until we note the involvement in it of John Dee, later notorious as an astrologer at the courts of Elizabeth and James I. The one recorded fact about the production is that Trygaios's ascent to heaven on his dung-beetle was effected illusionistically, a fact which points to Dee's familiarity with continental techniques of stage-machinery and an interest in recreating the ancient use of the 'machine' or crane, *mêchanê*, which is not only used but metatheatrically joked about in *Peace* itself (174: see 'Stage Directions', above). It is likely that the whole production was built around Dee's aspiration to merge modern theatrical technology with antiquarian experimentation.[112]

Not long after those late Renaissance productions, the chances of staging any Aristophanic comedy in England must have diminished steadily, first under the pressure of puritanical attitudes to the theatre,[113] and later because of the eighteenth century's predominant favouring of benign, humane laughter over more ribald, indecent varieties of humour. The eighteenth century was not a propitious time for the appreciation of Old Comedy. It is rather revealing that the title of 'the English Aristophanes' or 'the modern Aristophanes' was sometimes given to a dramatist of farces, Samuel Foote, who had very probably never read a word of his supposed model. Even practising satirists such as Swift and Pope ostensibly repudiated comparison with Aristophanes.[114] It was hard anywhere in Europe, in fact, to provide a publicly respectable justification of Aristophanic comedy at

[111] Randolph's version may itself have been acted in Cambridge at some point before 1628: for this possibility, within the general context of performances of classical plays in this period, see B. R. Smith, *Ancient Scripts and Modern Experience on the English Stage 1500–1700* (Princeton, 1988), 168–77.

[112] For one brief discussion, see P. French, *John Dee: The World of an Elizabethan Magus* (London, 1972), 24.

[113] One of the largest of puritan tracts on the stage, William Prynne's *Histriomastix*, refers to Aristophanes as 'that scurrilous, carping comedian . . . [who] personally traduced and abused virtuous Socrates' (1633 edn., p. 121).

[114] See the ironic couplet in Swift's 'A Letter to the Rev. Dr. Sheridan', 5–6 ('But as to comic Aristophanes, / The rogue's too bawdy and too prophane is'), and Pope's 'Epistle to Henry Cromwell', 102–4.

this date, given the still strong sway of neoclassical canons of taste and decorum.

A more far-reaching interest in Aristophanes starts to develop only in the later eighteenth century, and builds up during the nineteenth, with the growth of a more historically informed attempt to understand Old Comedy in its original cultural context. There was certainly no instant or total change of attitudes in this period, for in England, at least, the Victorian age saw a continuing concern over the moral dangers of too close a familiarity with the playwright: it is not surprising, for example, that the scholar who remarked that *Lysistrata* 'turns upon a proposal so gross, that we shall not insult our readers with it' subsequently published perhaps the most heavily bowdlerized translations of Aristophanes ever produced.[115]

Yet around this same time there are signs of a potential change of climate. In 1820, for example, Shelley wrote a savage satire, entitled *Oedipus Tyrannus, or Swellfoot the Tyrant*, on the contemporary royal cause célèbre of George IV's attempted divorce of Queen Caroline. Shelley, living in Italy at the time, was partly inspired by Aristophanic precedents: the work's animal chorus (of pigs) and its scurrilous and grossly fantastic political allegory, as well as a number of smaller details (such as compound Greek names: Wellington is Laoktonos, 'People-Slayer'), are undoubtedly reminiscent of Aristophanes, whom we know that Shelley had recently been reading.[116] Shelley's experimental work, which owed much to the radical traditions of English visual satire, is hardly part of a trend; nor was it successful (only seven copies were sold before a threat of prosecution led to its withdrawal). But it is nonetheless a harbinger of new possibilities opened up by Romanticism's more 'liberated' attitudes to ancient Greece.

In the course of the nineteenth century there was a growing recognition in some quarters that Old Comedy, like so much else from antiquity, could not be instinctively appreciated from a standpoint of modern taste. By 1871 John Addington Symonds was able to write: 'The time has come at which any writer on Greek literature, if not

---

[115] The scholar was Thomas Mitchell: the quotation is from an anonymously signed review in *Quarterly Review*, 9 (1813), 139–61, at 142. Even Mitchell had a sense of new priorities: on the preceding page he had warned against coming to the plays 'with English feelings and English ideas'; but he just could not practise what he preached.

[116] See F. L. Jones (ed.), *The Letters of Percy Bysshe Shelley*, ii (London, 1964), 468.

content to pass Aristophanes by in silence, must view him as he is.'
Symonds warned that ordinary canons of comedy were of no use in
interpreting the author; he described the plays as 'Dionysiac day-
dreams', utterly alien to the expectations bred by Christian ideas,
both ethical and religious.[117] Whatever reservations one might have
about details of Symonds' essay, its direction of thought is clear and
incisive. It represents an appeal for a fresh, informed, and unmoralis-
tic appraisal of Aristophanes and his genre. The work of such an
appraisal had, in fact, been underway for some time. We can
find a major contribution to it in George Grote's great *History of
Greece*, which started to appear in 1846, where amazement is
expressed at the traditional tendency to treat the freely inventive
materials of Old Comedy as though they could be made the basis of
either historically or morally secure inferences. Like Symonds,
though in rather more scholarly fashion, Grote perceived a cultural
distance which could only be bridged by a careful combination of
information and imagination; and in this fundamental respect he was
concerned to create a framework of interpretation which holds good
to this day.

Certain aspects of Aristophanes' work remained inescapably problematic, of course, for most nineteenth-century readers. In particular,
the obscenity of Old Comedy continued to be bowdlerized[118] or tamed
in both translations and productions (which, as with Greek tragedy,
became increasingly common from the 1880s onwards). Aubrey
Beardsley's priapic illustrations to *Lysistrata*, produced in 1896, are
an exception that proves the rule: they were printed in a small limited
edition 'for private distribution', and confiscations of copies by the
police, on grounds of obscenity, are recorded in England as late as
1966. At the same time the late Victorian period fostered the curious
idea, which still has some currency, that the light operettas of Gilbert
and Sullivan were close in spirit to Aristophanic comedy. Although
Gilbert was undoubtedly influenced by a few Aristophanic motifs,
and more especially by the rhythmical translations of the plays which

---

[117] Symonds' essay originally appeared in *The Westminster Review*, 39 (1871), 291–322,
and was reprinted in *Studies of the Greek Poets*, 1st ser., vol. 2 (London, 1873), ch. 18.

[118] For a contrast between English and continental practices in this respect, see
K. J. Dover, 'Expurgation of Greek Literature', in his *The Greeks and Their Legacy*
(Oxford, 1988), 270–86.

had become standard in the nineteenth century,[119] the gulf between the two forms of drama, and between their cultural dynamics, makes any attempt to assimilate them a historically very questionable enterprise. To turn the earthy, profane brio of Aristophanes into the arch tweeness of Gilbert is to emasculate the former's energy.

Despite the temptation to take excessive self-satisfaction in modern standards of sophisticated reading, it is reasonable to claim that the twentieth century saw a steady improvement in our understanding of Aristophanic comedy and the (reconstructed) nature of Old Comedy as a theatrical genre. Scholarship has made enormous progress in the interpretation of Athenian culture as a whole in the classical period, and resulting benefit has accrued to our grasp of the city's politics, social life, festivals, and theatrical resources, among much else. While older controversies over Aristophanes' point-of-view as an observer and satirist of his world have continued to elicit polarized disagreement, criticism of the plays more generally has learnt to take their theatricality and their Dionysiac background into account, at every level, much more successfully than was the case in earlier periods. These developments have strengthened a critical rehabilitation which was already well underway when George Bernard Shaw felt able repeatedly to include Aristophanes in a 'great tradition' of comedy, and of theatre tout court. An escape from (in historical terms) the unduly moralistic concerns of neoclassicism has of course been facilitated by wider patterns of change in ethical and social attitudes. Where he previously appeared dangerously licentious (though his power to shock has certainly not yet been lost), Aristophanes has come to appear enjoyably bawdy and scurrilous to democratic audiences which flatter themselves that they are peculiarly well attuned to his outspokenness and licentiousness.

There is, however, a subtle risk of misunderstanding lurking here. Classical Athens was not a 'liberated' society in (our) sexual, social, and ethical terms. To grasp the special nature of Old Comedy, we need a historically circumspect approach to the plays, not a reliance on peculiarly modern intuitions or assumptions. There may be a price to pay in other respects too. Twentieth-century translators of Aristophanes eschewed the somewhat mannered verse which had

---

[119] Gilbertian verbal mannerisms were in turn influential on the widely known translations by B. B. Rogers, published (in their final forms) between 1902 and 1915.

been the norm with their predecessors; but the predominant use of either prose or free verse has arguably tended to erase a sense of the playwright's distinctive combination of formality with invention, virtuosity with vulgarity (see 'Translating Aristophanes', above). Here as elsewhere one might be wise to conclude that there is something too multifarious about Aristophanes and his genre to be wholly or comfortably encompassed by our own cultural responses.

The first commercial (as opposed to university and school) stagings of Aristophanic plays go back to the first decade of the twentieth century, when at least two productions of *Lysistrata* were put on in London. They were, naturally, still far from faithful to the sexual details of the original, and it was not until the 1990s that productions appeared, such as the one directed by Peter Hall in London in 1993 (with its attempt to recapture the spirit of the original phallic and padded costumes), of which this was no longer true. It is arguable that appreciation of Aristophanic humour, in principle at least, has benefited from the pluralism of modern styles of entertainment: to some extent a contemporary audience is disposed to find in his work elements of, say, stand-up comedy, farce, pantomime, cabaret, topical satire, variety or vaudeville shows, and even theatre of the Absurd,[120] all synthesized into a rich theatrical kaleidoscope. Similarly, it is possible to find recent works which, whether coincidentally or not, have a broadly Aristophanic ethos. Tom Stoppard's *Jumpers* (1972) is a case in point, with its central philosophical character, its quasi-animal chorus, its dialectical verbal wit, and its pervasive mixture of fantasy and reality.

Direct influence, on the other hand, was no more common in the twentieth century than in the past. T. S. Eliot's *Sweeney Agonistes*, drafted in 1924 and subtitled 'Fragments of an Aristophanic Melodrama', is a peculiar hybrid of music-hall routines combined with ritualistic overtones derived from theories of comedy's origins propagated by the 'Cambridge School' of anthropologists: echoes of

---

[120] There are, at any rate, passages in Samuel Beckett which remind one subtly of Aristophanes: compare, for example, the combination of suggested suicide, sexual humour, and exaggerated politeness in *Waiting for Godot* (*Samuel Beckett: The Complete Dramatic Works* (London, 1986), 18–19) with the prologue to *Knights*, where similar routines all occur; for another instance, see note 7 to my Introduction to *Peace*. A short comparison of *Waiting for Godot* and *Birds* is offered by C. Segal, 'Aristophanes and Beckett', in A. Bierl and P. von Möllendorff (eds.), *Orchestra: Drama, Mythos, Bühne* (Stuttgart, 1994), 235–8.

the comedies are few, and the so-called agon, with its rather morbid blurring of life and death, is remote from the Aristophanic form whose name it borrows (see 'Formality and Performance', above). At a rather different point on the comic spectrum, Tony Harrison's *The Common Chorus* (first published in 1988), a version of *Lysistrata* set in the women's anti-nuclear peace camp at Greenham Common, contains obscenities which remarkably outdo even the original. The piece is extensively related to its Greek model, but the view of both war and sexuality it projects is grimmer and more disturbing than anything to be found in Aristophanes' play.

I have tried in this final section of my Introduction, albeit in a highly selective manner, to convey some sense of the fluctuating responses to Aristophanes' work between antiquity and the present. For the post-Renaissance period I have concentrated largely on anglophone examples, partly for obvious reasons of convenience and partly because in certain respects these represent a more complicated, often contradictory, set of attitudes than were sometimes found on the continent.[121] But one overarching point, which I stress in conclusion, could have been made just as well by reference to other European countries. Aristophanes has never been central to literary or artistic forms of (neo)classicism, yet his peripheral status in this respect has always been counterpoised by an underlying recognition of his importance as the sole survivor of an extraordinary phenomenon of classical Athens. It is not hard to see here a two-sided moral: if Old Comedy has proved to be largely inimitable, and therefore an elusive model for classicizing writers and artists, that is for precisely the same reasons as those which tied it so intimately to its original time and place. But since understanding the past must embrace the experience of what is unlike as well as what is like ourselves, the plays of Aristophanes will always remain rewarding material for anyone who wishes to come seriously to terms with the history of theatre, the possibilities of comedy, and the relationship between both these things and the culture of democracy.

---

[121] Outside Greece itself, at any rate, where Aristophanic revivals have sometimes carried a special political charge: see Gonda A. H. van Steen, *Venom in Verse: Aristophanes in Modern Greece* (Princeton, 2000).

NOTE ON THE TRANSLATION

In accordance with the principles explained in the general Introduction, 'Translating Aristophanes', my translation follows the structure of the Greek text closely: for the editions on which the translations are based, see the Bibliography. However, because the marginal numbers in the translation refer to the standard modern numeration of the Greek text, and since this numeration is sometimes (mostly in lyric passages) slightly anomalous, readers should be warned that the sequence occasionally does not match exactly the printed lines of the translation itself. For consistency of reference, line numbers in the General Introduction, the Introductions to individual plays, and the Index of Names refer to the strict Greek numeration. However, line numbers as given in the lemmata to Explanatory Notes have, where necessary, been slightly adjusted for the convenience of the user of the translation.

SELECT BIBLIOGRAPHY

THESE suggestions for further reading are reluctantly restricted to items written in, or translated into, English; preference has also been given to more recent and more accessible publications. I have tried, nonetheless, to give guidance to a reasonably wide range of publications, suitably flagged so that readers can follow up as much or as little as suits their interests. References to works which contain untranslated Greek have been minimized but not altogether excluded. Full publication details of books are given only at the first citation.

General Works

All aspects of Aristophanes' plays and their genre are covered by a comprehensive reference-work:

Sommerstein, A. H. (ed.), *Encyclopedia of Greek Comedy*, 3 vols. (New York, 2019).

An exceptionally stimulating overview of Greek (and Roman) comedy is provided by:

Lowe, N. J., *Comedy* (*Greece & Rome* New Surveys in the Classics, no. 37: Cambridge, 2007).

Two concise introductions to Greek Comedy:

Handley, E. W., 'Comedy', in P. E. Easterling and B. M. W. Knox (eds.), *The Cambridge History of Classical Literature*, i. *Greek Literature* (Cambridge, 1985), 355–425.

Rusten, J., 'A Short History of Athenian Comedy', in J. Rusten (ed.), *The Birth of Comedy: Texts, Documents, and Art from Athenian Comic Competitions, 486–280* (Baltimore, 2011), 16–38.

Three up-to-date sets of essays whose coverage includes Old Comedy are:

Dobrov, G. W. (ed.), *Brill's Companion to the Study of Greek Comedy* (Leiden, 2010).

Fontaine, M., and Scafuro, A. C. (eds.), *The Oxford Handbook of Greek and Roman Comedy* (New York, 2014).

Revermann, M. (ed.), *The Cambridge Companion to Greek Comedy* (Cambridge, 2014).

Among the best general books on Aristophanes are the following (the last of which is the least introductory):

Cartledge, P., *Aristophanes and His Theatre of the Absurd* (London, 1990).
Dover, K. J., *Aristophanic Comedy* (Berkeley and Los Angeles, 1972).
MacDowell, D. M., *Aristophanes and Athens* (Oxford, 1995).
Robson, J., *Aristophanes: An Introduction* (London, 2009).
Silk, M. S., *Aristophanes and the Definition of Comedy* (Oxford, 2000).

For four other books which contain thought-provoking ideas but are more free-wheeling, see:

McLeish, K., *The Theatre of Aristophanes* (London, 1980).
Reckford, K., *Aristophanes' Old-and-New Comedy* (Chapel Hill, NC, 1987).
Ruffell, I. A., *Politics and Anti-Realism in Athenian Old Comedy* (Oxford, 2011).
Whitman, C. H., *Aristophanes and the Comic Hero* (Cambridge, Mass., 1964).

A standard collection of essays, several of which are cited separately below, is:

Segal, E. (ed.), *Oxford Readings in Aristophanes* (Oxford, 1996).

A good deal of Aristophanic material is interestingly analysed, sometimes in technical detail, in:

Sommerstein, A. H., *Talking about Laughter and Other Studies in Greek Comedy* (Oxford, 2009).

Old Comedy is set within one (rather sweeping) vision of the history of comedy by:

Segal, E., *The Death of Comedy* (Cambridge, Mass., 2001).

Individual Aspects of Aristophanic Comedy

On the origins and prehistory of comedy, see the conspectus of literary and visual evidence in:

Rusten, 'Proto-Comedy', in Rusten (ed.), *The Birth of Comedy*, 45–58.

Various literary techniques are lucidly discussed in:

Harriott, R., *Aristophanes Poet and Dramatist* (London, 1986).

A vigorous discussion of all the plays, whose thematic focus is indicated by its title, is:

Bowie, A. M., *Aristophanes: Myth, Ritual and Comedy* (Cambridge, 1993).

On Old Comedy's use of traditional elements of 'sub-literary' entertainment, see:

Murphy, C. T., 'Popular Comedy in Aristophanes', *American Journal of Philology*, 93 (1972), 169–89.

The fundamental but slippery subject of humour receives fresh attention in:

P. Swallow and E. Hall (eds.), *Aristophanic Humour: Theory and Practice* (London, 2020).

Some basic physical aspects of Aristophanic humour are dealt with by:

Dobrov, G., 'The Dawn of Farce: Aristophanes', in J. Redmond (ed.), *Farce* (Themes in Drama 10, Cambridge, 1988), 15–31.
Kaimio, M., 'Comic Violence in Aristophanes', *Arctos*, 24 (1990), 47–72.
MacDowell, D. M., 'Clowning and Slapstick in Aristophanes', in Redmond (ed.), *Farce*, 1–13.

A sensitive discussion of the discontinuities of Aristophanic characterization in terms of 'imagist' logic is presented in:

Silk, M., 'The People of Aristophanes', in C. B. R. Pelling (ed.), *Characterization and Individuality in Greek Literature* (Oxford, 1990), 150–73; repr. (without Greek) in Segal (ed.), *Oxford Readings*, 229–51.

For discontinuities in the personae adopted by Aristophanic choruses, see:

Henderson, J., 'The Comic Chorus and the Demagogue', in R. Gagné and M. G. Hopman (eds.), *Choral Mediations in Greek Tragedy*, 278–96.

Aristophanes' own (mostly parabatic) statements about his poetic values are examined, sometimes too literal-mindedly, in:

Bremer, J. M., 'Aristophanes on His Own Poetry', in J. M. Bremer and E. W. Handley (eds.), *Aristophane* (Vandoeuvres-Geneva, 1993) 125–65.

The rhetoric of Aristophanic self-presentation (chiefly in the parabasis) is also treated from various angles in:

Goldhill, S., *The Poet's Voice* (Cambridge, 1991), 188–205.
Hubbard, T., *The Mask of Comedy: Aristophanes and the Intertextual Parabasis* (Ithaca, NY, 1991).
Murray, R. J., 'Aristophanic Protest', *Hermes*, 115 (1987), 146–54.

A radical case for Aristophanes as a kind of 'literary critic' more con-cerned for highly educated *readers* than mass audiences is made by:

Wright, M., *The Comedian as Critic* (London, 2012).

Some suggestive remarks on deceptiveness, both in Aristophanes' presentation of himself and in his characters, are offered by:

Heath, M., 'Some Deceptions in Aristophanes', *Papers of the Leeds International Latin Seminar*, 6 (1990), 229–40.
Salingar, L., 'The Trickster in Classical Comedy', in *Shakespeare and the Traditions of Comedy* (Cambridge, 1974), 88–104.

A detailed but often naive use of Aristophanes as sociological evi-dence is made by:

Ehrenberg, V., *The People of Aristophanes* (2nd edn., Oxford, 1951).

For those interested in details of Aristophanic language, it is impossible to avoid works which require knowledge of Greek. Two illuminating articles are:

Dover, K. J., 'The Style of Aristophanes', in his *Greek and the Greeks* (Oxford, 1987), 224–36.
———, 'Language and Character in Aristophanes', *Greek and the Greeks*, 237–48.

Essential for advanced study of the plays within a sociolinguistic framework is:

Willi, A., *The Languages of Aristophanes* (Oxford, 2003).

Aristophanic obscenity receives a full analysis (though marred by errors), whose introductory chapters are partly accessible without knowledge of Greek, in:

Henderson, J., *The Maculate Muse: Obscene Language in Attic Comedy* (New Haven, 1975; repr. with addenda: New York, 1991).

On the same subject in relation to Aristophanic humour more gener-ally see:

Robson, J., *Humour, Obscenity and Aristophanes* (Tübingen, 2006).

For surprise as a defining feature of Aristophanic comic technique on various levels (verbal, thematic, theatrical), see:

Kanellakis, D., *Aristophanes and the Poetics of Surprise* (Berlin, 2020).

Aristophanes' Career

A range of views on the problems of Aristophanes' early career, especially his use of others to produce his plays, are taken by:

Halliwell, S., 'Aristophanes' Apprenticeship', *Classical Quarterly*, 30 (1980), 33–45; repr. with Greek translated in Segal (ed.), *Oxford Readings*, 98–116.
MacDowell, D. M., 'Aristophanes and Kallistratos', *Classical Quarterly*, 32 (1982), 21–6.
Slater, N. W., 'Aristophanes' Apprenticeship Again', *Greek, Roman, and Byzantine Studies*, 30 (1989), 67–82.

A broader (but partly technical) argument for collaboration between comic poets is put by:

Halliwell, S., 'Authorial Collaboration in the Athenian Comic Theatre', *Greek, Roman, and Byzantine Studies*, 30 (1989), 515–28.

Aristophanes' relationships with his rivals, especially Kratinos and Eupolis, are examined in:

Bakola, E., *Cratinus and the Art of Comedy* (Oxford, 2010), 16–29.
Biles, Z. P., *Aristophanes and the Poetics of Competition* (Cambridge, 2011).
Heath, M., 'Aristophanes and His Rivals', *Greece & Rome*, 37 (1990), 143–58.
Storey, I. C., *Eupolis Poet of Old Comedy* (Oxford, 2003), 278–300.

On the poets of Old Comedy in their own right, there is a rich collection of essays in:

Harvey, D., and Wilkins, J. (eds.), *Aristophanes and His Rivals: Studies in Athenian Old Comedy* (London, 2000).

The difficulties of reconstructing Aristophanes' clash with Kleon after *Babylonians* (and perhaps at a later date as well) are discussed, with conclusions different from mine, in:

Sommerstein, A. H., 'Harassing the Satirist: The Alleged Attempts to Prosecute Aristophanes', in I. Sluiter and R. M. Rosen (eds.), *Free Speech in Classical Antiquity* (Leiden, 2004), 145–74.
Storey, I. C., '*Wasps* 1284–91 and the Portrait of Kleon in *Wasps*', *Scholia* 4 (1995), 3–23.

Festivals and Festivity

The outstanding work on festivals, audiences, actors, etc., but containing untranslated Greek and rather technical for the general reader, is:

Pickard-Cambridge, A. W., *Dramatic Festivals of Athens*, 2nd edn., rev. J. Gould and D. M. Lewis (Oxford, 1968; repr. with addenda, 1988).

Much of the same ground is more accessibly covered by an excellent sourcebook in translation:

Csapo, E., and Slater, W. J., *The Context of Ancient Drama* (Ann Arbor, 1995).

The relevant documentary evidence is also presented in translation by:

Rusten (ed.), *The Birth of Comedy*, 93–132.

On the proto-comic spirit of Dionysiac festivity at Athens, including phallic processions and songs, see:

Csapo, E., 'The Earliest Phase of "Comic" Choral Entertainments in Athens: The Dionysian Pompe and the "Birth" of Comedy', in S. Chronopoulos and C. Orth (eds.), *Fragmente einer Geschichte der griechischen Komödie / Fragmentary History of Greek Comedy* (Heidelberg, 2015), 66–108.

On the composition of theatre audiences, see (with some caution on details):

Roselli, D. K., *Theater of the People: Spectators and Society in Ancient Athens* (Austin, 2011).

For comedy's festive status, and effective exemption from legal and other norms of decency, see:

Halliwell, S., 'Comic Satire and Freedom of Speech in Classical Athens', *Journal of Hellenic Studies*, 111 (1991), 48–70.
———, *Greek Laughter: A Study of Cultural Psychology from Homer to Early Christianity* (Cambridge, 2008), 206–14, 243–63.

The general place of dramatic festivals in the culture of Athens is explored by:

Osborne, R., 'Competitive Festivals and the Polis: A Context for Dramatic Festivals at Athens', in A. H. Sommerstein et al. (eds.), *Tragedy Comedy and the Polis* (Bari, 1993), 21–38.

That the City Dionysia, the oldest dramatic festival, was of democratic (not Peisistratid) origin, and represented a celebration of civic freedoms, is argued by:

Connor, W. R., 'City Dionysia and Athenian Democracy', *Classica et Medievalia*, 40 (1989), 7–32.

The relationship between tragedy and comedy is shrewdly explored by:

Taplin, O., 'Fifth-Century Tragedy and Comedy: A *Synkrisis*', *Journal of Hellenic Studies*, 106 (1986), 163–74, repr. with Greek translated in Segal (ed.), *Oxford Readings*, 9–28.

For the application to Aristophanes of the idea of 'carnivalesque' laughter as developed by the Russian theorist Mikhail Bakhtin, see (but with caution about his simplified view of comic poets as 'conservatives'):

Edwards, A. T., 'Historicizing the Popular Grotesque: Bakhtin's *Rabelais* and Attic Old Comedy', in R. Scodel (ed.), *Theater and Society in the Classical World* (Ann Arbor, Mich., 1993), 89–117.

Formality and Performance

The three modes of dramatic poetry (speech, recitative, song) are technically analysed in:

Pickard-Cambridge, *Dramatic Festivals*, 156–67.

Formal structures are discussed, with schematic analyses of the plays, by:

Pickard-Cambridge, A. W., *Dithyramb Tragedy and Comedy*, 2nd edn. rev. T. B. L. Webster (Oxford, 1962), 194–229.

On the genre's formal conventions, see also:

Dover, *Aristophanic Comedy*, 49–53, 66–8.
Harriot, *Aristophanes Poet and Dramatist*, esp. chs. 2–3.

For the entry of the chorus (*parodos*) as manifesting Aristophanes' creative adaptation of formal conventions, see:

Zimmermann, B., 'The *Parodoi* of the Aristophanic Comedies', *Studi Italiani di Filologia Classica*, 2 (1984), 13–24; repr. with Greek translated in Segal (ed.), *Oxford Readings*, 182–93.

The parabasis (see also under 'Aspects of Aristophanic Comedy', above) is analysed in detail, though from contrasting angles, in:

Hubbard, *The Mask of Comedy*.
Sifakis, G., *Parabasis and Animal Choruses* (London, 1971).

A typology of Aristophanic plots in terms of narrative patterns and functional elements akin to those of folktale is attempted by:

Sifakis, G. M., 'The Structure of Aristophanic Comedy', *Journal of Hellenic Studies*, 112 (1992), 123–42.

Satire

Thought-provoking surveys of the issues and controversies in this area are presented by:

Carey, C., 'Comic Ridicule and Democracy', in R. Osborne and S. Hornblower (eds.), *Ritual, Finance, Politics: Athenian Democratic Accounts Presented to David Lewis* (Oxford, 1994), 69–83.

Pelling, C., '"You Cannot Be Serious": Approaching Aristophanes', in *Literary Texts and the Greek Historian* (London, 2000), 123–40.

Storey, I. C., 'Poets, Politicians, and Perverts: Personal Humour in Aristophanes', *Classics Ireland*, 5 (1998) 85–134. [Online at http://www.ucd.ie/cai/classics-ireland/1998/ClassIre98.html.]

A much-cited older work, spirited but actually rather muddled, is:

Gomme, A. W., 'Aristophanes and Politics', *Classical Review*, 52 (1938), 97–109; repr. in his *More Essays in Greek History and Literature* (London, 1962), 70–91.

There is an influential but dogmatic reading of Aristophanes as a committed political conservative in:

Croix, G. E. M. de Ste., *The Origins of the Peloponnesian War* (London, 1972), appendix XXIX, 355–71; repr., in abridged form with Greek translated, in Segal (ed.), *Oxford Readings*, 42–64.

For a critique of de Ste. Croix, see:

Pritchard, D., 'Aristophanes and de Ste. Croix: The Value of Old Comedy as Evidence for Athenian Popular Culture', *Antichthon*, 46 (2012), 14–51.

Aristophanes' multifarious dealings with Athenian politics have been dissected most recently in:

Rosen, R. M., and Foley, H. P. (eds.), *Aristophanes and Politics: New Studies* (Leiden, 2020).

The views of scholars hesitant (in various ways) about the possibility of inferring the poet's own political and social values from his plays are represented by:

Chapman, G. A. H., 'Aristophanes and History', *Acta Classica*, 21 (1978), 59–69.

Halliwell, S., 'Aristophanic Satire', *Yearbook of English Studies*, 14 (1984), 6–20; repr. in C. Rawson (ed.), *English Satire and the Satiric Tradition* (Oxford, 1984), 6–20.

Heath, M., *Political Comedy in Aristophanes* (Göttingen, 1987).

Lewis, D. M., 'Aristophanes and Politics', in *Selected Papers in Greek and Near Eastern History* (Cambridge, 1997), 173–86.

Redfield, J., 'Drama and Community: Aristophanes and Some of His Rivals', in J. J. Winkler and F. I. Zeitlin (eds.), *Nothing to Do with Dionysos?* (Princeton, 1990), 214–335.

Van Steen, G., 'Politics and Aristophanes: Watchword "Caution!"', in M. McDonald and J. M. Walton (eds.), *Cambridge Companion to Greek and Roman Theatre* (Cambridge, 2007), 108–23.

A reading of comedy as embodying the power of the democracy to humble individuals, and remind elite leaders of the sovereignty of the people, is developed by:

Henderson, J., 'The *Dêmos* and the Comic Competition', in Winkler and Zeitlin (eds.), *Nothing to Do with Dionysos?*, 271–313; repr. with abridgements in Segal (ed.), *Oxford Readings*, 65–97.

——, 'Comic Hero versus Political Élite', in Sommerstein et al. (eds.), *Tragedy Comedy and the Polis*, 307–19.

For a perspective on how attitudes to Aristophanes' politics have evolved in anglophone scholarship since the nineteenth century, see:

Walsh, P., 'A Study in Reception: The British Debates over Aristophanes' Politics and Influence', *Classical Receptions Journal*, 1 (2009), 55–72.

For the relationship of comic satire to larger Greek conceptions of laughter, see:

Halliwell, *Greek Laughter*, 215–63.

Arguments against the idea of Old Comedy as either a reliable reflector of, or a potent influence on, the currents of Athenian publicity are put by:

Halliwell, S., 'Comedy and Publicity in the Society of the Polis', in Sommerstein et al. (eds.), *Tragedy Comedy and the Polis*, 321–40.

For an old but strikingly negative case on the question of influence, see also:

Stow, H. L., 'Aristophanes' Influence on Public Opinion', *Classical Journal*, 38 (1942), 83–92.

Old Comedy's satirical and obscene connections with the earlier, semi-dramatic genre of iambos are investigated by:

Rosen, R. M., *Old Comedy and the Iambographic Tradition* (Atlanta, 1988).

Translating Aristophanes

For discussion of the problems, and the history of attempts to tackle them, see:

Dover, *Aristophanic Comedy*, 230–7.
Halliwell, S., 'Aristophanes', in O. Classe (ed.), *Encyclopedia of Literary Translation* (London, 1998), vol. 1, 77–8.
Robson, *Aristophanes*, ch. 10.
———, 'Transposing Aristophanes: The Theory and Practice of Translating Aristophanic Lyric', *Greece & Rome*, 59 (2012), 214–44.
Silk, M., 'Translating/Transposing Aristophanes', in E. Hall and A. Wrigley (eds.), *Aristophanes in Performance 421 BC–AD 2007* (Oxford, 2007), 287–308.
Sommerstein, A. H., 'On Translating Aristophanes: Ends and Means', *Greece & Rome*, 20 (1973), 140–54.
Walton, J. M., *Found in Translation: Greek Drama in English* (Cambridge, 2006), 145–61, 253–67.

A challenging treatment of Aristophanic lyrics, arguing that their strength lies in the subtle exploitation of a 'low', popular idiom, is offered by:

Silk, M., 'Aristophanes as a Lyric Poet', in J. Henderson (ed.), *Aristophanes: Essays in Interpretation* (*Yale Classical Studies*, 26, Cambridge, 1980), 99–151.

Stage Directions

On the Theatre of Dionysos and other performance-related matters, see:

Csapo and Slater, *The Context of Ancient Drama*, 79–81.
Rusten (ed.), *The Birth of Comedy*, 399–433.

The most substantial work on Aristophanic comedy in relation to its original theatrical context is:

Revermann, M., *Comic Business: Theatricality, Dramatic Technique, and Performance Contexts of Aristophanic Comedy* (Oxford, 2006).

A lively reading of all the plays as performance texts is undertaken by:

Slater, N. W., *Spectator Politics: Metatheatre and Performance in Aristophanes* (Philadelphia, 2002).

Some distinctively comic features of theatricality are analysed with insight by:

Lowe, N. J., 'Greek Stagecraft and Aristophanes', in Redmond (ed.), *Farce*, 33–52.
———, 'Aristophanic Spacecraft', in L. Kozak and J. Rich (eds.), *Playing around Aristophanes* (Oxford, 2006), 48–64.

Other useful works on theatrical matters include:

Compton-Engle, G., *Costume in the Comedies of Aristophanes* (Cambridge, 2015).
Dover, K. J., 'The Skene in Aristophanes', *Proceedings of the Cambridge Philological Society* 12 (1966), 2–17; repr. in *Greek and the Greeks*, 249–66.
Dover, K. J., 'Portrait-Masks in Aristophanes', *Greek and the Greeks*, 266–78.
Handley, E. W., 'Aristophanes and His Theatre', in Bremer and Handley (eds.), *Aristophane*, 97–123.

A well-illustrated book for the general reader is:

Green, R., and Handley, E., *Images of the Greek Theatre* (London, 1995), esp. chs. 4–5.

Aristophanes and Posterity

A miscellaneous collection of essays in this area is:

Walsh, P. (ed.), *Brill's Companion to the Reception of Aristophanes* (Leiden, 2016).

For selective observations on the evidence for post-classical knowledge of Aristophanes in antiquity, see:

Dover, *Aristophanic Comedy*, 221–9.
Sommerstein, A. H., 'Aristophanes in Antiquity', in D. Barrett and A. H. Sommerstein (trans.), *Aristophanes: The Knights etc.* (Harmondsworth, 1978), 9–20.

Evidence for fourth-century restaging of Aristophanes and other Old Comedy in Magna Graecia is presented and illustrated in:

Austin, C., and Olson, S. D. (eds.), *Aristophanes* Thesmophoriazusae (Oxford, 2004), lxxv–lxxvii.
Taplin, O., *Comic Angels* (Oxford, 1993).

————, 'Do the "Phlyax" Vases Have Bearings on Athenian Comedy and the Polis?', in Sommerstein et al. (eds.), *Tragedy Comedy and the Polis*, 527–44.

A lively summary of certain aspects of the reception of Aristophanes' plays, especially from the point of view of translation, can be found in:

Griffith, M., *Aristophanes' Frogs* (New York, 2013), 220–57.

An informative set of studies on the performance history of several of Aristophanes' plays is:

Hall and Wrigley (eds.), *Aristophanes in Performance*.

There are also numerous essays on the reception of Aristophanes' plays in:

Olson, S. D. (ed.), *Ancient Comedy and Reception: Essays in Honor of Jeffrey Henderson* (Berlin, 2014).

For a small selection of further items which illustrate striking aspects of Aristophanes' reception and influence, see:

Atkins, S., 'Goethe, Aristophanes, and the Classical Walpurgisnacht', *Comparative Literature*, 6 (1954), 64–78.

Gross, N., 'Racine's Debt to Aristophanes', *Comparative Literature*, 17 (1965), 209–24.

O'Sullivan, N., 'Aristophanes and Wagner', *Antike und Abendland*, 36 (1990), 67–81.

Schork, R. J., 'Aristophanes and Joyce', *International Journal of the Classical Tradition*, 2 (1996), 399–413.

Segal, E., 'Aristophanes and Beckett', in A. Bierl and P. von Möllendorff (eds.), *Orchestra: Drama, Mythos, Bühne* (Stuttgart, 1994), 235–8.

Van Steen, G. A. H., *Venom in Verse: Aristophanes in Modern Greece* (Princeton, 2000).

Acharnians

My translation is based, with a few small exceptions, on the Greek text edited (with full commentary) by:

Olson, S. D., *Aristophanes* Acharnians (Oxford, 2002).

An edition with facing translation and notes is provided by:

Sommerstein, A. H., *Aristophanes* Acharnians (Warminster, 1981), with addenda in the same author's *Aristophanes* Wealth (Warminster, 2001), 225–37.

The following is a selection of interesting articles on the play:

Carey, C., 'The Purpose of Aristophanes' *Acharnians*', *Rheinisches Museum*, 136 (1993), 254–63.

Compton-Engle, G. L., 'From Country to City: The Persona of Dicaeopolis in Aristophanes' *Acharnians*', *The Classical Journal*, 94 (1999), 359–73.

Fisher, N. R. E., 'Multiple Personalities and Dionysiac Festivals: Dicaeopolis in Aristophanes' *Acharnians*', *Greece & Rome*, 40 (1993), 31–47.

Foley, H. P., 'Tragedy and Politics in Aristophanes' *Acharnians*', *Journal of Hellenic Studies*, 108 (1988), 33–47.

Pelling, *Literary Texts and the Greek Historian*, 141–63.

Knights

In producing my translation, I have made use of the Greek text in both of the following editions, though I have sometimes exercised my independent textual judgement (including the attribution of lines to speakers):

Neil, R. A., *The* Knights *of Aristophanes* (Cambridge, 1901).

Wilson, N. G., *Aristophanis Fabulae*, vol. 1 (Oxford, 2007).

An edition with facing translation and notes is provided by:

Sommerstein, A. H., *Aristophanes* Knights (Warminster, 1981), with addenda in the same author's *Aristophanes* Wealth (Warminster, 2001), 238–49.

Various approaches to the play are represented by:

Brock, R. W., 'The Double Plot in Aristophanes's *Knights*', *Greek Roman & Byzantine Studies*, 27 (1986), 15–27.

Hall, E., 'The Boys from Cydathenaeum: Aristophanes versus Cleon Again', in D. Allen et al. (eds.), *How to Do Things with History: New Approaches to Ancient Greece* (Oxford, 2018), 339–63.

Osborne, R., 'Politics and Laughter: The Case of Aristophanes' *Knights*', in Rosen and Foley (eds.), *Aristophanes and Politics*, 24–44.

Rhodes, P. J., 'The "Assembly" at the End of Aristophanes' *Knights*', in E. M. Harris et al. (eds.), *Law and Drama in Ancient Greece* (London, 2010), 158–68.

Rosen, in Dobrov (ed.), *Brill's Companion to the Study of Greek Comedy*, 245–55.

Wasps

My translation is based, with a few small exceptions, on the Greek text edited by:

Biles, Z. P., and Olson, S. D., *Aristophanes* Wasps (Oxford, 2015).

An edition with facing translation and notes is provided by:

Sommerstein, A. H., *Aristophanes* Wasps (Warminster, 1983), with addenda in the same author's *Aristophanes* Wealth (Warminster, 2001), 264–72.

A selection of items dealing with various aspects of the play:

Biles, Z. P., 'Thucydides' Cleon and the Poetics of Politics in Aristophanes' *Wasps*', *Classical Philology*, 111 (2016), 117–38.
Farmer, M., *Tragedy on the Comic Stage* (New York, 2017), 117–54.
Kidd, S. E., *Nonsense and Meaning in Ancient Greek Comedy* (Cambridge, 2014), 71–7.
Konstan, D., '*Wasps*', in *Greek Comedy and Ideology* (New York, 1995), 15–28.
Olson, S. D., 'Politics and Poetry in Aristophanes' *Wasps*', *Transactions of the American Philological Association*, 126 (1996), 129–50.
Pütz, B., *The Symposium and Komos in Aristophanes*, 2nd edn. (Warminster, 2007), 83–103.
Ruffell, I., 'Stop Making Sense: The Politics of Aristophanic Madness', *Illinois Classical Studies*, 43 (2018), 326–50.

Peace

My translation is based, with a few small exceptions, on the version of the Greek text (with full commentary) edited by:

Olson, S. D., *Aristophanes* Peace (Oxford, 1998).

An edition with facing translation and notes is provided by:

Sommerstein, A. H., *Aristophanes* Peace, 2nd edn. (Warminster, 1990), with addenda in the same author's *Aristophanes* Wealth (Warminster, 2001), 273–83.

For an introductory guide to the play, see:

Storey, I. C., *Aristophanes:* Peace (London, 2019).

The following is a diverse selection of items on the play:

Hall, E., 'Casting the Role of Trygaeus in Aristophanes' *Peace*', in *The Theatrical Cast of Athens* (Oxford, 2006), 321–52.
McGlew, J. F., 'Identity and Ideology: The Farmer Chorus of Aristophanes' *Peace*', *Syllecta Classica*, 12 (2001), 74–97.
Sulprizio, C., 'You Can't Go Home Again: War, Women, and Domesticity in Aristophanes' *Peace*', *Ramus*, 42 (2013), 44–63.

Tordoff, R., 'Excrement, Sacrifice, Commensality: The Ophresiology of Aristophanes' *Peace*', *Ramus*, 44 (2011), 167–98.

Walin, D., 'An Aristophanic Slave: *Peace* 819–1126', *Classical Quarterly*, 59 (2009), 30–45.

Wilkins, J., *The Boastful Chef: The Discourse of Food in Ancient Greek Comedy* (Oxford, 2000), 134–50.

Further Reading in Oxford World's Classics

Aristophanes, *Birds and Other Plays*, ed. Stephen Halliwell.

—— *Frogs and Other Plays*, ed. Stephen Halliwell.

Artemidorus, *The Interpretation of Dreams*, ed. Peter Thonemann, trans. Martin Hammond.

Plautus, *Four Comedies: The Braggart Soldier; The Brothers Menaechmus; The Haunted House; The Pot of Gold James*, ed. Erich Segal.

Sophocles, *Antigone and other Tragedies: Antigone, Deianeira, Electra*, ed. Oliver Taplin.

Xenophon, *Estate Management and Symposium*, ed. Emily Baragwanath, trans. Anthony Verity.

A CHRONOLOGY OF ARISTOPHANES

This chronology contains the dates of *(a)* Aristophanes' surviving plays (as well as a few of his lost works), *(b)* certain prominent events mentioned in the plays themselves, and *(c)* a small selection of other important events in Athenian/Greek history.

*c.*525   Birth of Aischylos, tragic playwright.

514   Assassination of Hipparchos, brother of the Athenian tyrant Hippias, by Harmodios and Aristogeiton (the so-called 'tyrannicides').

510   Expulsion (with Spartan help) of the Athenian tyrant Hippias.

508   Kleomenes, Spartan king, occupies Athenian Akropolis but is forced to withdraw.

Kleisthenes' democratic reforms of Athenian politics, including creation of demes.

*c.*496   Birth of Sophokles, tragic playwright.

490   First Persian invasion of Greece, under Dareios. Battle of Marathon.

486   Comic drama introduced into the official programme of the City Dionysia festival (spring).

480–479   Second Persian invasion of Greece, under Xerxes. Battles of Artemision, Thermopylai, Salamis, and Plataia.

*c.*480   Birth of Euripides, tragic playwright.

478   Founding of Delian League of Greek states against Persia under Athenian leadership; subsequently evolves into de facto Athenian empire.

472   Aischylos' *Persians*.

469   Birth of Sokrates, Athenian philosopher.

467   Aischylos' *Seven against Thebes*.

462   Further democratic reforms at Athens, promoted by Ephialtes and Perikles.

458   Aischylos' *Oresteia* trilogy.

456   Death of Aischylos.

*c.*455   Birth of Thucydides, Athenian historian.

Athenian system of democratic law courts strengthened; on Perikles' proposal, payment for jurors instituted.

451 Athenian citizenship law (requiring both parents to be Athenian) introduced by Perikles.

c.450 Birth of Alkibiades, controversial Athenian aristocrat.

450–445 Birth of Aristophanes.

447 Building of Parthenon starts: financed by Athenian imperial revenues; completed in late 430s. Cult statue of Athena Polias designed by sculptor Pheidias.

446–445 Thirty-year peace treaty concluded between Athens and Sparta.

c.440 Comic drama introduced into official programme of the Lenaia festival (mid-winter).

438 Euripides' *Telephos*.

c.432 Megarian decree passed by Athenians, on Perikles' proposal, prohibiting Megarian trade/business with Athens and her allies.

431 Thirty-year peace collapses: friction between Athenian and Spartan spheres of influence erupts into major conflict ('Peloponnesian War', spanning 431–404).

First of annual series of Spartan invasions of Attika, to damage crops and property.

430–429 Major outbreak of plague at Athens. Death of Perikles.

Ascendancy of Kleon as democratic leader: he proposes increase in rate of jury pay.

428 Euripides' *Hippolytos*.

427 Aristophanes' first play, *Daitales* (*Banqueters*), festival unknown, probably placed second; produced by either Kallistratos or Philonides.

Gorgias, Sicilian rhetorician, visits Athens.

c.427 Birth of Plato, Athenian philosopher.

426 Aristophanes' *Babylonians* (Dionysia), produced by Kallistratos, probably first prize: leads to official backlash from Kleon.

425 Aristophanes' *Acharnians* (Lenaia), first prize; produced by Kallistratos.

Athenian capture of Spartans on island of Sphakteria near Pylos; military kudos for Kleon.

424 Aristophanes' *Knights* (Lenaia), first prize.

424–423 Kleon elected as one of Athens' ten generals.

423   Aristophanes' *Clouds*, first version (Dionysia), third place.

423–422 Kleon reelected as general.

422   Aristophanes' *Wasps* (Lenaia), probably second place behind
       another Aristophanic play, *Proagon*: one of the two plays was
       produced by Philonides.

       Death of Kleon at battle of Amphipolis.

421   Aristophanes' *Peace* (Dionysia), second place.

       Peace of Nikias signed between Athens and Sparta.

419–417 Gradual breakdown of peace, and renewal of outright war,
       between Athens and Sparta.

*c.*416 Ostracism of Hyperbolos, leading Athenian 'demagogue'.

415   Athens sends major expedition to Sicily; scandalous mutilation of
       herms takes place on eve of fleet's departure. Alkibiades, accused of
       parodying the Eleusinian Mysteries, flees into exile.

414   Aristophanes' *Birds* (Dionysia), second place; produced by
       Kallistratos.

413   Sparta occupies fort at Dekeleia in N Attika.

       Sicilian expedition ends in catastrophic defeat.

413–412 Athenian Council (*Boulê*) temporarily replaced by group of
       Commissioners (*Probouloi*).

412   Euripides' *Andromeda* and *Helen*.

       Defection of Miletos and other cities from Athenian empire.

411   Aristophanes' *Lysistrata* (Lenaia, probably), result unknown;
       produced by Kallistratos.

       Oligarchic coup at Athens, led by Peisandros and others (the Four
       Hundred).

       Aristophanes' *Women at the Thesmophoria* (Dionysia, probably),
       result unknown.

410   Democracy restored at Athens.

408   Aristophanes' *Wealth* I.

407–406 Return of Alkibiades to Athens, later followed by his second
       exile.

406   Athenian victory in naval battle at Arginousai, followed by trial and
       execution of several generals.

       Deaths of Euripides and Sophokles.

405   Aristophanes' *Frogs* (Lenaia), first prize; produced by Philonides.

Athenian defeat in battle of Aigospotamoi; effective destruction of the city's military capacities.

404 Final surrender of Athens to Sparta; Spartans destroy city's Long Walls and impose rule of Thirty Tyrants.

403 Expulsion of the Thirty from Athens; restoration of democracy.

c.400 Agyrrhios proposes introduction of pay for attendance at Athenian Assembly.

399 Sokrates executed on charges of impiety and corrupting the young.

396–395 Athens and Thebes form anti-Spartan league, later joined by Korinth and Argos.

395 Athens begins rebuilding its Long Walls.

394 Battle of Knidos: Spartan fleet destroyed by Persian fleet under Athenian leadership.

c.393 Aristophanes' *Assembly-Women* (festival and result unknown).

388 Aristophanes' *Wealth* II (surviving version); festival unknown, possibly first prize.

c.387 Plato opens philosophical school, the Academy.

c.385 Death of Aristophanes.

ACHARNIANS

INTRODUCTION

ACHARNIANS is Aristophanes' earliest surviving comedy, and therefore the earliest complete comic drama in Western culture.[1] The play, which won first prize at the Lenaia of 425, has numerous features which were to become hallmarks of the poet's repertoire: among them, a coarse and egotistical protagonist, a plot which hinges round the realization of dreamlike fantasy, a trenchantly cynical attitude to contemporary Athenian politics, a substantial element of (Euripidean) paratragedy, and, intersecting with the latter, a penchant for metatheatre which in the present case goes as far as to produce, at certain points, a teasing confusion between protagonist and playwright. Since *Acharnians* is built around one man's determination to escape from the hardships of the Peloponnesian War, a great deal of modern writing on the play has converged on claims of its putative political agenda, understanding it as a *pièce à thèse* which advances a serious critique of Athens' responsibility for the outbreak of hostilities and for continuing to prosecute the war aggressively even in the face of Spartan overtures for peace.[2] But the exuberant absurdity and the outlandish exaggerations of Aristophanic comedy always place fundamental obstacles in the way of stable, let alone didactic, readings. The political dimension of *Acharnians* is far from easy to interpret as the expression of a coherent stance on the part of the playwright. Before we succumb to the temptation to extract from *Acharnians* a meaningful view of the politics of war in the mid-420s, we need first to grapple with the multiple challenges presented by the work's boldly experimental style of comic theatre.

For the purposes of theatrical orientation in the mind's eye (a capacity we need to cultivate in order to turn ourselves from readers into imaginary spectators in the Theatre of Dionysos), it is worth starting with some basic points about the play's supple dramaturgy of

---

[1] See the Chronology for basic details of Aristophanes' early career, with my *Aristophanes: Frogs and Other Plays* (World's Classics, 2016), 235–54, for what we know of his lost plays.

[2] Such views already existed in antiquity: in the main ancient Hypothesis (i.e. plot summary) transmitted with the play, *Acharnians* is described as belonging to those works which 'in every way urge the cause of peace'.

place and time. The opening scene (1–203) is situated on the Pnyx hill, the location of meetings of the Athenian Assembly. In the course of this scene, indeed over a mere forty-five lines (129–75) and in the time it takes for the envoy Theoros to report back to the Assembly on his mission to Thrace, the peculiar character Amphitheos is able to make a return trip to Sparta in order to obtain a personal peace treaty for Dikaiopolis (a treaty, we should notice, for which the protagonist does not specify even a single condition: 130–2). That temporal compression is part-and-parcel of the magical fantasy of the protagonist's private peace itself. Once that peace is acquired, Dikaiopolis returns to his remote rural deme, later identified as Cholleidai (see 406), to hold a family-centred version of the Rural Dionysia (202, 237 ff.), a festival celebrated in December and therefore earlier in the Athenian year than the Lenaia festival at which *Acharnians* itself was staged. Dikaiopolis is pursued in his deme by the chorus of bellicose Acharnian charcoal-burners: they originally pursued Amphitheos on his way back from Sparta (176–85) but then switched their pursuit, in a typically comic ellipsis (i.e. without any realistic explanation), to the protagonist himself. In order to defend himself against the chorus, Dikaiopolis visits the house of the tragedian Euripides (393 ff.), whose location is not specified in any way, in search of a suitable 'costume'— and a temporary shift from comic to 'tragic' status—in which to perform his verbal self-defence before the Acharnians.

That plot detour is of a kind without close parallel elsewhere in the surviving plays, but its spirit of dramatic freedom is nonetheless quintessentially Aristophanic. When Dikaiopolis eventually delivers his defence speech to the chorus, he is notionally standing outside his own house, since that is where he had placed the butcher's block behind which he stands (358–67). At the same time, the speech is in certain respects redolent of one addressed to the Athenian Assembly, as though Dikaipolis can now play the role of public orator which was certainly not open to him, as a 'little man' from rural Attika, in the earlier Assembly scene itself, where he was limited to heckling from the sidelines. When he is subsequently confronted by the *miles gloriosus* figure of Lamachos (572 ff.), who appears instantaneously when summoned by half the chorus, it is redundant to ask exactly where the action might be imagined as occurring: what matters here is rather the sense of a comically engineered inversion of the normal power relations between a prominent military officer and an 'ordinary' individual citizen. That inversion will be carried further in the second half of the play.

After the parabasis, a different kind of layered dramaturgy comes into action. The scene is now set, after more compression of dramatic time, in Dikaiopolis's private agora or marketplace. Its location, in keeping with the overarching fantasy of a one-man peace with Sparta and her allies, cannot be rationally situated in the reality of Athens. It represents a kind of comically cocooned substitute for the city's own Agora. It is visited by non-Athenian traders (the Megarian and Boiotian) who once had access to that market but have it no longer; in that sense, it is a return to pre-war trading conditions. But it can also be entered by informers, i.e. citizens maliciously on the lookout for opportunities to spot contraband goods and profit from legally exposing them (817 ff., 910 ff.), as well as by a selection of Athenian characters, most of whom try to obtain a share in Dikaiopolis's peace—i.e. in comically tangible terms, some of his peace-wine[3]—either for themselves or, in the case of slaves, for the masters who have sent them. In two further twists of the kind of 'parallel world' logic of the comic fantasy, Dikaiopolis is presented, notwithstanding his withdrawal from Athens qua city at war, as a figure who nonetheless—indeed, for that very reason!—acquires a privileged position within the city: he participates in a drinking competition (announced by the Herald at 1000–2) which forms part of the Choes festival (celebrated around late February, early March, thus *later* than the Lenaia; contrast the Rural Dionysia, as noted above); and he receives a special invitation to a party with the Priest of Dionysos (actually present in the front row of the theatre) at 1085 ff., from which he will return in a state of sexual and alcoholic bliss in the closing lines of the play, brandishing his prize from the drinking competition (1203, 1225). Dikaiopolis is, therefore, somehow successfully (re)integrated into the very city from whose wartime conditions he has escaped; the city is, so to speak, turned inside out for him. Some of the ironies that arise from this double-sided dramatic situation are touched on in the chorus's songs: at 836–59 the chorus envisages Dikaiopolis finding it easy to avoid all the disagreeable people one might meet in the real Agora; at 971–6 they equate his mercantile advantages with the

---

[3] The play repeatedly exploits the fact that the Greek noun for 'peace treaty' literally means 'libations (of wine)'; cf. my note on *Acharnians* 187.

utopian happiness of the Golden Age; and at 1037–9 they re-emphasize the personal and selfish status of the rewards he reaps from his new marketplace.

One thing thrown into relief by my outline of *Acharnians'* dramaturgy of place and time is how the comic fantasy unfolds in ways which allow Dikaiopolis both to exempt himself from reality and at the same time to manipulate aspects of reality for his own purposes. This structural and imaginative paradox is enacted as a kind of projection of the protagonist's own will, albeit initially enabled by the go-between services of Amphitheos in his trio of brief appearances at 45–58, 129–32, 175–203. After the disillusionment and resentment voiced by Dikaiopolis as a powerless 'nobody' in the play's opening scene (both before and during the Assembly meeting), he finds himself able to overcome the opposition of others and to mould everything effortlessly to his own desires. To a degree matched (and even outdone) only by Peisetairos in *Birds*, the main dramatic trajectory of *Acharnians* is a process of transformation by means of pure wishfulfilment. Action and protagonist are mutually defining. Any interpretation of the play, including its politics, must therefore rest on an interpretation of the protagonist himself.

Dikaiopolis, like many Aristophanic characters, is a bundle of only loosely connected features. He starts the play as a disgruntled rustic who has found it hard to adjust to the urban confinement (including its monetary economy, 34–6) which has been forced on him, as on other members of the rural population of Attika, by the Periklean wartime strategy of vacating the countryside during annual Spartan incursions.[4] Whether his glee at the (alleged) humiliation of Kleon in lines 5–8 refers to a scene in comedy or a genuine political event, it prompts us to think of Dikaiopolis as remote from the more urbanized classes who seem to have supplied much of the democratic support for Kleon as the most powerful figure in Athens of the mid-420s. But it is striking that Dikaiopolis's disillusionment with Athens' war policies actually has very little to say about the influence of the politicians who dominate and shape debate in the Assembly, despite the early mention of them at line 38. The Assembly scene turns out to be

---

[4] See Thucydides 2.18–23 for details of the first of these invasions in summer 431; further invasions took place in 430, 428, 427, and (after *Acharnians*) 425, but were halted after the Athenians' capture of Spartan troops at Pylos later in 425 (see the Introduction to *Knights*).

preoccupied with corrupt ambassadors and envoys, not regular politicians; Dikaiopolis's set-piece defence speech focuses on the outbreak of the war, not its more recent conduct, and Perikles is therefore the one figure it targets (530); and Kleon will be mentioned later in the play only in two passages, to be discussed in detail below, where Dikaiopolis momentarily impersonates the playwright (377, 502).[5] One thing this means is that Dikaiopolis is never given anything that sounds like a politically informed view of where things now stand with the war or a persuasive conception of how peace might be negotiated with Sparta. The core of his yearning for peace in the prologue, and for much of the Assembly scene too, is more of a generalized 'anti-establishment' resentment about the workings of the city's political institutions than a specific stance on individual policy options. His initial mentality is, above all, that of a discontented old peasant farmer deprived of the simple pleasures of his pre-war existence; and this helps prepare the way for the fact that in the second half of the play the benefits of peace which he both pursues and receives are overwhelmingly those of his bodily appetites for food, drink, and sex.

There is, accordingly, an inescapable irony in the protagonist's very name, which means 'just city' and is adapted from a unique Pindaric epithet.[6] The Aristophanic Dikaiopolis is neither just nor Pindaric; he is self-centred and vulgar. By the time his name is announced at 406 (and the announcement is a comic moment in its own right), we have become familiar with his blunt disgruntlement and earthy coarseness, especially in his heckling interventions during the Assembly scene and in his phallic song for the Rural Dionysia at 263–79. What is more, already in the play's prologue the impression is unmistakably created that there is simply no general, let alone majority, 'movement' for peace in Athens at this time (17–39). Dikaiopolis may put the primary blame for this on the Prytaneis' control of Assembly business, but the Prytaneis represent a committee of the Council whose membership rotates on a monthly basis and which

---

[5] Kleon is also mentioned twice by the chorus at 300 and 659; see my notes on the lines in question.

[6] See Pindar, *Pythian* 8.22, where the word is predicated of the island Aigina; it may have appealed to Aristophanes partly because of his own connection with that island (see my note on *Acharnians* 652–4).

represents, broadly speaking, a cross-section of Athenian citizens.[7] Right from the outset, in other words, Dikaiopolis is set up as a loner at odds with most of his fellow-citizens; he does not purport to speak on behalf of a group (note here a sharp contrast with Trygaios in *Peace*), and this in itself limits the extent to which we might imagine him as a magnet for political sympathy from an Athenian theatre audience in the circumstances of early 425. We might, perhaps, allow scope for a sort of visceral, sub-political sympathy with his sheer longing for peace, especially among certain portions of the displaced population of rural Attika.[8] Such instinctive sympathy might even have hardened into a degree of more consciously political agreement about the central contention of Dikaiopolis's defence speech to the Acharnians, namely that Athens should never have allowed itself to be drawn into the present war with Sparta in the first place. But leaving aside for a moment the complications introduced by the intricately parodic fabric of that speech, it is hard to deny that once Dikaiopolis's private peace has been secured he behaves as a hyper-egotistical individual who might attract comic indulgence but cannot coherently be regarded as symbolic of the values of a 'just city'. This extreme individualism is built into the sheer fantasy of a personal peace with Sparta and is translated into the full-blooded sensuality of the second half of the play, where food, drink, and sex are his exclusive priorities. In short, Dikaiopolis is not a protagonist designed to carry the weight of a sustained political critique in relation to the realities of Athens' military situation in 425.[9]

---

[7] At *Knights* 667–72, for what it is worth, we have a picture of the Council rejecting 'with one voice' a suggestion of peace negotiations from (ironically!) Kleon; the context is comically distorted, but it may reflect the possibility that the Council could sometimes reflect popular opinion with a force which individual politicians could not override.

[8] The qualification '*certain* portions' is vital: the chorus itself belongs, like Dikaiopolis, to a rural deme, yet the Acharnians are supporters of a bellicose attitude towards Sparta; Thucydides 2.21.2–3 confirms that this was true for the actual Acharnians in the context of the first Spartan invasion of Attika in 431. For the general distress caused by displacement from countryside to city at the start of the war, see Thucydides 2.14 and 16. Cf. my note on *Knights* 792–3.

[9] Numerous aspects of the contemporary situation go wholly unmentioned in the play, among them the activities of the general Demosthenes in NW Greece, the Athenians' use of their fleet to make raids on the Peloponnese, and the presence of an Athenian force in Sicily (since 427); for the latter, see my note on *Acharnians* 602–6 (which says nothing about military operations as such). In this connection, it is worth pointing out that part of the magical fantasy of the peace which Amphitheos obtains for Dikaiopolis is the sheer idea of the Spartans' own immediate and seemingly unconditional willingness to offer a thirty-year peace at this stage of the war!

It might be objected, however, that the argument just sketched fails to reckon with the remarkable way in which at two points in the course of Dikaiopolis's self-defence against the belligerent Acharnian chorus and their accusation that he is a 'traitor' to his country (290) his voice ventriloquizes the viewpoint of the playwright himself. These two passages are indeed remarkable; they have no clear parallel elsewhere in Aristophanes' surviving plays.[10] The first occurs at 377–82, where, after expressing concern for the likely hostility to his peace treaty on the part of both rural and older Athenian citizens (two groups to which he himself supposedly belongs!), Dikaiopolis refers to:

> What I suffered myself at Kleon's hands last year
> Because of my comedy . . . ,

and proceeds to describe being badly roughed up in the Council by Kleon. Ancient scholars tell us that this is a reference to Kleon's adverse reaction to Aristophanes' *Babylonians*, staged at the Dionysia of 426. A further reference to the same events occurs at *Acharnians* 502–8, where, after anticipatory hints at 442 and 497 (the speech is metatheatrically addressed to the 'spectators', rather than the Acharnians) and 499 (the character's self-identification as 'a wine-song poet'), Dikaiopolis defiantly states:

> And this time Kleon can't slander me with the charge
> Of defaming the city with visitors in our midst.
> We're on our own, the Lenaia is just for us . . . .

The most we can safely infer from these passages about the events of the previous year is that Kleon had used his political muscle to intimidate Aristophanes after the performance of *Babylonians* by making some kind of official complaint in the Council; and the complaint seems to have centred on the idea that in a critical wartime situation the city's reputation in the eyes of its allies had been damaged by the staging of a play which mocked various aspects of Athens'

---

[10] This fact has sometimes given rise to the speculation that Aristophanes may himself have acted the part of Dikaiopolis; but this is too much of an ad hoc hypothesis which lacks any independent evidence and in any case does not really explain the intricate metatheatre of the passages in question.

relationship with those allies and the workings of the city's politics in general.[11]

But why, to return to the immediate issue, should Aristophanes contrive a momentary identification (or fusion) of protagonist with playwright in these two passages if not to give Dikaiopolis's defence of his peace treaty a kind of authorial endorsement? The inference may seem straightforward, but it is not so. For one thing, the temporary switch into the persona of the author involves experimental use of a technique which, while unusual for an individual character, is common with Aristophanic choruses; in fact, the very same thing happens at *Acharnians* 659–64 itself, and very probably with reference to the same clash in the previous year between the poet and Kleon. More fundamentally, neither of the passages in question allows the equation, Dikaiopolis = Aristophanes, to be firmly established; both of them create a temporary ambiguity, a kind of 'double take', and by the time of the second passage Dikaiopolis has put on the ragged costume of a Euripidean hero, the disguised Telephos, and is delivering a speech which is parodically rich in echoes of the latter's own coded duplicity in a mythological scenario.[12] If Aristophanes had wanted to address his audience 'through' his character in unmistakably authorial terms and in order to advance an unambiguous political message, he could easily have produced something much more transparent and intelligible than the comically intricate layering of personae and voices which he has actually created. The authorial intrusion, if we can call it that, is best understood as a piquant piece of self-advertisement on the poet's part—even cashing in, as it were, on the publicity that he may have acquired from being singled out for hostile attention by the powerful Kleon after the Dionysia of 426 but having survived to tell the tale. As regards immediate dramatic impact, Aristophanes is less concerned to employ Dikaiopolis as a politically didactic mouthpiece than to turn him into a figure in a game of multiple and shifting identities.

---

[11] See the general Introduction, 'Aristophanes' Career in Context', for some further discussion of *Babylonians*, together with my *Frogs and Other Plays*, pp. 237–8, for what little is really known about the contents of the play. Cf. also *Wasps* 1284–91 for what may be a further retrospective 'account' of the clash with Kleon over *Babylonians*.

[12] Cf. n. 13 below.

That game was anticipated at 440–4, where Dikaiopolis, requesting the costume of the tragic hero Telephos from Euripides, had told
the tragedian:

> I need to seem a beggar for just today,   440
> To *be* myself but not to *appear* to be;
> The spectators need to know just who I am,
> But I need to make the chorus look like boobies
> And use my crafty speech to give them the finger!

This passage is a teasingly disorientating exercise in metatheatre, a
toying with the essential theatrical act of role-playing. A comic character is addressing a tragic playwright, (absurdly) requesting part of
the latter's theatrical repertoire in order to adopt a persona that will
help him deal with the Acharnians who form the chorus of the comedy. But in this very passage, at 440–1, he is also 'quoting' from
Euripides' *Telephos* itself; this is, in fact, one of a series of parodic
adaptations of the words and plot of the latter in the first half of
Acharnians.[13] 'Life' (Dikaiopolis's supposedly real predicament) is
collapsed into theatre, and a hybrid comico-tragic theatre at that.[14]
The metatheatrical layering, or confusion, cannot be converted into
fully coherent sense: in rational terms, Euripides knows nothing
about Dikaiopolis other than his name, and it is not a theatrical
'chorus' (443, cf. the same point earlier at 416) but a group of
Acharnian demesmen whom Dikaiopolis needs to deceive—although,
to add a further twist of comic irony, deception hardly seems a perfect
description for a situation in which the Acharnians are standing
watching the whole encounter with Euripides! The 'myself' of 441
cannot be simply equated, as some scholars have wished, with
Aristophanes himself, even if the earlier fusion of protagonist and
playwright at 377–82 might trigger a fleeting sense of ambiguity on
the part of spectators: if such a simplified reading were followed

---

[13] Lines 440–1 are a close quotation of Euripides fr. 698. The two main parodic uses
of Euripides' *Telephos* (for which, see my note on *Acharnians* 430) are in Dikaiopolis's
taking of a coal-scuttle as 'hostage' at 331 ff., and his defence-speech at 497 ff.: see the
notes on these passages for further details, with C. Collard et al., *Euripides: Selected
Fragmentary Plays*, vol. 1 (London, 1995), pp. 17–52, for all the relevant evidence on
Euripides' play.

[14] Aristophanes exploits a kindred kind of metatheatricality on a much larger scale,
and with some further use of Euripides' *Telephos*, in *Women at the Thesmophoria*: see my
Introduction to that later comedy in *Frogs and Other Plays*, pp. 94–5.

through, it would also require lines 416–17 to imply that Aristophanes himself faces 'death' if Dikaiopolis's forthcoming speech is not a success! Finally, at 444 Dikaiopolis—fully 'in character', we might think, given all his earlier coarseness and scurrility—presents the aim of his intended disguise not as a matter of genuinely political persuasion but as a means of enacting an encoded insult: saying, in effect, 'up yours!' to his opponents.

That last detail sends us back to the larger question of the politics of *Acharnians* and to a decisive final point on this issue. If, as so much modern criticism contends, the play conveys an authorially underwritten viewpoint, what exactly would this viewpoint amount to? From the original Assembly scene we might extract the idea that there is considerable resistance, especially on the part of a privileged military-political 'establishment' of paid ambassadors, generals, etc., to seeking peace with Sparta, though the status of the Acharnian chorus equally warrants the inference that such resistance is widely shared by large sections of Athenian citizens in general. So far so good, but hardly a didactically powerful insight. From Dikaiopolis's own 'Telephos' speech at 497–556 we could even more easily extract a 'thesis', albeit one self-evidently contaminated by the story of 'a pair of Aspasia's whores' (527): namely, that Athens itself was primarily responsible for allowing the war to break out in the first place. But, once again, that in itself was hardly a novel observation, nor, six years into the war, a belief which could make much material difference; it does not provide any concrete or realistic basis for negotiating peace in 425.[15] To this we can now add a consideration which clinches the sceptical case against reading *Acharnians* as a meaningful 'plea for peace'. If that was Aristophanes' agenda, we would inevitably expect to find some confirmation and reinforcement of it in the one place where sustained discourse in the poet's (ostensible) voice was possible, namely the parabasis. But what do we actually find in the parabasis of *Acharnians*? First—and this is generally overlooked—no

---

[15] The idea that the Megarian decree (see my note on *Acharnians* 530–4) was the critical factor in the outbreak of war corresponds to Thucydides' account (1.139.1) of the Spartans' demands (and the response of some Athenians) in 431. It subsequently became a standard view for many: cf. the retrospective comment of Andocides 3.8, where the war is said to have been 'on account of the Megarians'. But that does not vindicate the extensively comic details of Dikaiopolis's narrative, which also, significantly, differs from the role of the Megarian decree in Hermes' (even more absurd) account at *Peace* 609 (see my note there).

attempt whatever is made to underline the earlier metatheatrical play with the 'Dikaiopolis = Aristophanes' equation: on the contrary, at the start of the parabasis, the identity of character and playwright are kept explicitly apart (626–33). Secondly, and even more tellingly, after the chorus has presented Aristophanes' defence of his previous play *Babylonians* (as, broadly speaking, a satirical exposé of how democracy can be exploited by corrupt rhetoric) and has trumpeted the poet's status as 'a good adviser' to the city (651), what does it go on to say about his relationship to the war as such? Only that the king of Persia supposedly remarked that the city in possession of this adviser will thereby *win* the war (651), and, equally, that the Spartans' demands for the return of Aigina—a reference which may be histor- ically imprecise[16]—are no more than a ploy to get possession of Aristophanes for themselves (652–4)! In so far as there is any direct reference to the current possibility of peace negotiations with Sparta, the chorus actually assert, on Aristophanes' behalf, that they should *not* be pursued (655). The parabasis of *Acharnians*, in short, flies entirely in the face of any attempt to interpret the play as the vehicle of a coherent 'message' about making peace.

The argument just presented does not amount, it must be empha- sized, to claiming that *Acharnians* is not a 'political' play or that it does not, like much of Aristophanes' work, contain satirically tren- chant treatment of many aspects of contemporary Athenian politics. What it does insist on, however, is the gap between trenchant satire and coherent, authorially endorsed didacticism. *Acharnians* is not a quasi-Brechtian *Lehrstück*, let alone a piece of agitprop. The critical approach I am adopting might be complemented, from a slightly dif- ferent angle, by the proposition that Aristophanic comedy, here as often elsewhere, thrives far more on negative, even destructive, ridi- cule than on constructive suggestions for political change. This fea- ture of *Acharnians* is well illustrated by the treatment of the military figure Lamachos. He is first mentioned in the play, briefly and in the plural (hence 'warlike Lamachos-types'; cf. 1071), at 270, where Dikaiopolis's 'phallic song' is celebrating escape from the whole world of war. Already here, Lamachos's name, which literally means 'bellicose', readily serves the satirical characterization of self-profiting

---

[16] It is far from certain that this Spartan demand had the kind of recent prominence which Aristophanes' text implies: see my note on 652–4.

militarism. There can be little doubt that the etymology of the name helps to explain why *Acharnians* spotlights Lamachos rather than many other available individuals with military connections.[17] But the name happened to be appropriate. The historical Lamachos was a major and experienced military leader: his career as a high-ranking officer goes back at least to the mid-430s, he was elected general on more than one occasion (including 425-4, just a few months after the staging of *Acharnians* itself), and he remained prominent in military service until his death in 414 during the ill-fated Athenian expedition to Sicily of which he was one of the chief commanders. Lamachos was also a member of the same official 'tribe' as the Acharnians (568), which is part of the motivation of one half of the chorus (the chorus's views having become polarized at this juncture, 557 ff.) for summoning him to deal with the peace-making Dikaiopolis.

In the scene which follows that appeal, and again in the two later parts of the play where he reappears, Lamachos is depicted as pompously vainglorious (with weapons which symbolically match his sense of self-importance: see esp. 574–92, 964–5), violently bellicose (paradigmatically at 620–2), and someone who seeks office for personal (monetary) gain, though this last allegation, as made at 595–619, rapidly melts from a specific point about Lamachos into an effusive set of gibes at paid office-holders in general. There is little or nothing here that can yield historically secure inferences about Lamachos, except perhaps that he represented, in Athenian terms, a developing type of military 'professional'. Those who held military office were by definition involved in the activities of war; we have no strong evidence to suppose that Lamachos himself pursued a particular agenda in relation to the war in the mid-420s, and, if he did, *Acharnians* gives us no specific indications of what it might have entailed. Much more fundamental is the fact that Lamachos is set up as a target who, in the fantasies of comic theatre, can be insulted and humiliated from a perspective which represents the cynical, hard-done-by viewpoint of the ordinary citizen serving as a 'stalwart soldier-man' in the ranks (596). *Acharnians* subjects Lamachos to satirical humiliation in the complementary forms of gross contempt from Dikaiopolis (the physical and sexual gibes at 584–6 and 591–2

---

[17] Among other wordplay, line 1080 involves an untranslatable compound adj., *polemolamachaïkos*, 'war-Lamach-istic'. Cf. also my note on *Peace* 304.

set the tone) and a narrative which sees him compelled to endure a harsh winter campaign while others enjoy the sensual pleasures of festivity (1073–1142) and then made the victim of relatively minor but ignominious injuries of a kind which strip him of all official and professional dignity (1174–1226). False grandeur, even 'heroism' (see 575 and the echo at 578), is deflated by comedy's own special weapons.

There is no definitive criterion by which to assess the purport or potential impact of satirical mockery such as that of Lamachos. But it remains clear that Lamachos's career was unaffected by *Acharnians* and it would be naive to suppose that Aristophanes could ever have expected things to be otherwise: whatever animus, authorial or otherwise, may conceivably have informed the comic treatment of the man (but even speculation is beside the point), Lamachos evidently possessed military experience and ability which virtually everyone would have admitted that the city needed. Once again, in coming to terms with the extreme techniques of Aristophanic satire we must distinguish between pursuit of a specific political agenda, which there is no evidence to show was ever a real option for Old Comedy, and comic theatre's vigorous exploitation of its special freedom for public derision within the conventions of Dionysiac festivity.[18]

Dionysiac festivity did not just provide the framing occasion for the performance of *Acharnians*; it is also internalized into the plot structure and comic dynamics of the work. As we saw earlier when tracing the play's dramaturgy of space and time, Dikaiopolis's first act, once in possession of the 'wine' of peace, is to return to his rural deme and celebrate the Rural Dionysia. Later on, the admiration he (paradoxically) attracts as a one-man city-at-peace brings him a special invitation to a dinner and symposium with the Priest of Dionysos Eleuthereus (who was in fact sitting in the front row in the theatre itself);[19] and his acceptance of that invitation is combined with his success in winning the drinking contest, part of the Dionysiac festival of the Choes, announced by the herald at 1000–2. We have, therefore, a character whose escape from war takes him into a multiple series of Dionysiac contexts, so that *Acharnians* and its protagonist are, as it

---

[18] See further in the general Introduction, 'Satire and Seriousness'.

[19] See the metatheatrical appeal to the Priest at *Frogs* 297 by none other than the character Dionysos himself!

were, matching phenomena of Dionysiac festivity. Dikaiopolis's first words, when he smells the wine of the thirty-year peace treaty brought for him by Amphitheos, are indeed an exclamatory reference to such festivity, 'Dionysiac bliss!' (195).

The spirit of such festivity, as enacted by Dikaiopolis at any rate, combines a sense of (temporary) escape from life's problems in general, but especially war, with a desire for unlimited gratification of bodily appetites, pushed by Dikaiopolis, in his phallic song at 263–79, to the extreme of imagining himself raping the female slave of a neighbour. But all this is given a peculiar, if not ironic, twist by its fusion with the solitary status of Dikaiopolis. Whereas Athens' actual Dionysiac festivals, including the one at which *Acharnians* itself was performed, were expressions of shared religious and social celebration, Dikaiopolis turns the Dionysiac into a gratification of his own egotism. As the chorus observe at 1037, peace brings the protagonist a pleasure he has no intention of sharing. They make that remark at the end of the short scene with the partially blind Attic farmer Derketes. It is an uncertain (and unnecessary) hypothesis to suppose that Derketes was a known individual and that the audience will have been aware of something which made him deserving of the short shrift he gets from Dikaiopolis. In particular, the inference that Derketes was readily identifiable as a strong advocate of the war, and therefore an implicit hypocrite in seeking peace from Dikaiopolis, receives no shred of support from the text. It is true that Derketes' white costume (picked up by Dikaiopolis at 1024) might prompt the inference—which a good comic actor could easily amplify—that he is a fraud, employing a fake pathos (the loss of his pair of oxen and the damage done to his eyes by weeping over this loss) in an attempt to deceive Dikaiopolis. But whether or not we are attracted by that reading, it is perfectly simple to see the basis of the scene, duly confirmed by the chorus's comment, as proof of the protagonist's brusque refusal to share his peace with anyone, since, as he indicates in the following scene, where he makes a single exception for a *woman* (cf. 1062), he has not abandoned his conviction that Athenian citizens are collectively responsible for allowing and sustaining the war against Sparta.

This opens up a larger critical issue which deserves, in conclusion, some attention here. Too much has been made in modern scholarship on Aristophanic comedy of the assumption that the protagonist of a play needs to be strongly and transparently 'sympathetic', that is, capable of arousing consistent approval, perhaps even a kind of identification, on the part of a majority of spectators. Such an assumption is rarely if ever thought in need of justification, and yet its application to the surviving plays generates numerous problems.[20] The most basic objection to the assumption can be stated bluntly: a protagonist needs, certainly, to be the focus and vehicle of a comically satisfying experience, but why should comic satisfaction be reduced to the requirement of consistent alignment with the character or conduct of the protagonist? In Dikaiopolis's case, in fact, notwithstanding the scope for (some) spectators to share his initial longing for peace (see above), it is built into his dramatic persona that he *cannot* straightforwardly and consistently be 'sympathetic' to a large number of Athenians (the Acharnians, let us not forget, originally wanted to stone him to death as a traitor!),[21] for the fundamental reason that, in the world of the comic fiction, he is explicitly at odds with Athenians in general.[22] Yet there is no mystery about how this could, at the same time, be comically satisfying to an Athenian theatre audience: comic satisfaction arises from the working out of the character's story in the total fabric of the play, not from directly imagining what one would think of such a person (an impossibility, after all) in real life.[23] The essential object of comic pleasure is the whole play, not the character in his own right. And that pleasure has a multiplicity of strands whose complexity offers a far more sophisticated range of theatrical experience than the receipt of a 'message' from the playwright.

---

[20] For further discussion of this point, see the general Introduction, 'The Dynamics of Fantasy'.

[21] Cf. the curious passage at Plato, *Laws* 12.955c, where the death penalty is prescribed for anyone who makes a 'private' peace.

[22] If Dikaiopolis makes a kind of exception for the Priest of Dionysos by accepting the invitation to his party, that is because the invitation (i) gives him an opportunity for the further gratification of his appetites, and, in any case, (ii) is a characteristically Aristophanic dramatic non sequitur designed to create an exuberantly triumphalist ending to the play.

[23] It is worth recalling here the distinction drawn by Sokrates at Plato, *Republic* 10.606c, between a spectator's relaxed enjoyment of a comic character's 'bad' behaviour and the kind of values that would come into operation in real life; for the Freudian affinities of this passage, see my book *Greek Laughter* (Cambridge, 2008), 255–6.

ACHARNIANS

Speaking Characters

DIKAIOPOLIS: an elderly Athenian peasant farmer
HERALD: a functionary who makes public announcements
AMPHITHEOS: an Athenian of allegedly divine ancestry
AMBASSADOR: spokesman of an Athenian embassy returned from
   Persia
PSEUDARTABAS: official representative ('Eye') of the king of Persia
THEOROS: an Athenian envoy, reporting from king Sitalkes of
   Thrace
CHORUS: of old men, charcoal burners from the outlying Attic
   deme of Acharnai
LEADER: of the CHORUS
DAUGHTER: of DIKAIOPOLIS
SLAVE: of EURIPIDES
EURIPIDES: tragic playwright
LAMACHOS: an Athenian military officer
MEGARIAN: a visiting market trader
DAUGHTERS: of the MEGARIAN
INFORMER: an Athenian citizen who exploits the legal system for
   personal gain
BOIOTIAN: a visiting market trader
NIKARCHOS: another informer
SLAVE: of LAMACHOS
DERKETES: an Athenian farmer
SLAVE: of an Athenian bridegroom
SLAVE: of the Priest of Dionysos

Silent Characters

PRYTANEIS: members of the steering committee of the Council
SKYTHIAN ARCHERS: armed (slave) attendants of the PRYTANEIS
AMBASSADORS: members of an Athenian embassy to Persia

EUNUCHS: (fake) Persians accompanying PSEUDARTABAS

THRACIANS: light-armed barbarian troops, brought back from Thrace by THEOROS

SLAVES (including XANTHIAS): of DIKAIOPOLIS

WIFE: of DIKAIOPOLIS

HISMENIAS: slave of the BOIOTIAN

PIPE-PLAYERS: Theban musicians, accompanying the BOIOTIAN

CHILDREN: of DIKAIOPOLIS

BRIDESMAID: accompanying the bridegroom's SLAVE

PROSTITUTES: in attendance on DIKAIOPOLIS at the end of the play

[*The stage building contains two doors, whose identities will emerge (and change) as the play progresses. In front of it stand some benches: the setting, we soon learn, is the Pnyx, the Athenian hill on which the Athenian Assembly is due to meet early in the day. A decrepit elderly character, in peasant garb and carrying a stick and a food bag, wanders on from one of the* eisodoi *and sits down on the ground: after becoming increasingly restless, he starts to reminisce anecdotally, while intermittently acknowledging the presence of an audience.*]

DIKAIOPOLIS [*sighing*]. So many gnawing cares my heart has suffered!
  I've had scant pleasures; yes, scant. [*On his fingers*] Well, *four* in
      fact.
  Yet my pains are as many as grains in a heap of sand.
  [*Pondering*] Let's see: which pleasure provided *delectation*?
  I know a sight that thrilled my heart with joy:
  That pile of money that Kleon was made to vomit!
  I beamed with delight at that and I love the Knights
  For that deed of theirs: it's 'worthy indeed of Hellas'.*
  But I had to suffer, in turn, a *tragic* pain
  When I waited all agog for some Aischylos   10
  But the herald cried: 'Bring in your chorus, Theognis'.*
  Just imagine what a blow that struck my heart!
  Never mind; there was pleasure again when after Moschos
  Dexitheos entered to sing a Boiotian song.*
  This year I nearly died, and went cross-eyed,
  When Chairis slunk into view to play an old tune.*
  But never before, ever since I started to wash,
  Has the sting of soap in my eyes caused such distress
  As things right now. [*Gesturing*] The Assembly's scheduled to meet,
  Yet here, at dawn, the Pnyx is quite deserted,   20
  While those in the Agora chatter then run pell-mell
  To escape the crimson rope that would force them here.*
  No sign of the Prytaneis either.* They'll turn up late,
  And then you can just imagine the way they'll jostle
  And scramble with one another to sit at the front
  When they all surge in at once. As for making *peace*—
  They couldn't care less about that. 'O city! O city!'*
  It's always *me* who's first to arrive for the meeting
  And sit myself down here. Then while I'm alone,

I groan and yawn and fidget and let out farts,   30
Feel bored, draw doodles, pluck my beard, count coins,
While gazing out to the fields, full of longing for peace
And loathing for urban life.* I *pine* for my deme,
Which never in all my life shouted 'Buy your coals!',
Nor oil or vinegar either—such cries weren't known.
The deme was self-sufficient; no rasping vendors.
Well, today I've come along with a firm resolve:
To barrack, to heckle, to jeer the public speakers*
Every time they talk about anything other than peace.

[*A group of* PRYTANEIS *rush on from the side, scrambling for places on the benches; they are followed by a number of* SKYTHIAN ARCHERS.]

Look! Here come the Prytaneis now—almost mid-day!   40
And didn't I say? *Exactly* what I predicted:
They're jostling, one and all, for a front-row seat.

[*Formal Assembly proceedings commence.*]

HERALD. Step inside the perimeter!
Step inside, to stand within the sacred ground.*

[*A further figure runs in, breathless and late, from one of the* eisodoi.]

AMPHITHEOS. Has anyone spoken yet?
HERALD [*formally*].   Who wishes to speak?
AMPHITHEOS. I do.
HERALD.   Your name?
AMPHITHEOS.   Amphitheos.
HERALD.   What, not human?*
AMPHITHEOS [*pompously*]. Immortal I am. Demeter's child
    Amphitheos
  Was fathered by Triptolemos. His son, Keleos,
  Took Phainarete, my grandmother, in marriage,
  And she produced Lykinos—as a result   50
  My ancestry's divine: to *me* the gods
  Have given the task of making peace with Sparta.
  But though immortal I need . . . my travel expenses:
  The Prytaneis are blocking my claim.
HERALD.   Quick, Archers!

[SKYTHIAN ARCHERS *step forward and forcibly bundle* AMPHITHEOS
to one side.]

AMPHITHEOS. Triptolemos and Keleos, come to help me!
DIKAIOPOLIS [*jumping up*]. You Prytaneis are wronging the whole
    Assembly,
    Removing a man who had such good intentions
    Of making peace and hanging up our shields.
HERALD. Sit down, keep quiet!
DIKAIOPOLIS.   I swear by Apollo I won't,
    Unless you Prytaneis put peace on the agenda.   60
HERALD [*ignoring* DIKAIOPOLIS]. Ambassadors from the Persian
    king!*

[A *group of* AMBASSADORS *enter with an air of self-importance and
perhaps wearing some elements of Persian dress.*]

DIKAIOPOLIS [*heckling*]. The Persian king! Ambassadors make
    me sick,
    With all their peacocks* and all their swindling tricks!
HERALD. Keep quiet!
DIKAIOPOLIS.   How shocking! What Persian posers they are!*
AMBASSADOR [*formally*]. You sent our mission to visit the Great
    King's court,
    Our official rate of pay two drachmas a day,
    When Euthymenes was Archon.*
DIKAIOPOLIS.   Woe, those drachmas!
AMBASSADOR. We toiled our way across the Kaÿstrian plain,
    A long meandering route in wagons with awnings,
    Reclining in cushioned luxury all the way.*   70
    We almost *perished*.
DIKAIOPOLIS.   Oh yes! While *I* was safe
    Reclining in rubbish right next to the city walls!*
AMBASSADOR. We found ourselves, as guests, compelled to drink
    From crystal goblets and cups of solid gold
    A fine and unmixed wine.*
DIKAIOPOLIS.   O stalwart city,
    Just hear the contempt the ambassadors feel for you!
AMBASSADOR. You see, the barbarians only count as *men*
    The people who eat and drink on the grandest scale.

DIKAIOPOLIS. For *us* it's cock-sucking types with buggered arses!*

AMBASSADOR. It took three years to reach the royal palace.   80
But the king, with his army, had left to ease himself:
He was shitting for eight whole months on the Golden Mountains.*

DIKAIOPOLIS. And when did he manage to close his arsehole up?

AMBASSADOR. He waited until full moon, then went back home.
His hospitality stretched to serving banquets
Of whole baked oxen, fresh from the oven.

DIKAIOPOLIS.   What nonsense!
Who ever saw oven-baked oxen? A total hoax!*

AMBASSADOR. I swear by Zeus he served us up a bird
Three times Kleonymos' size—its name was guller.*

DIKAIOPOLIS. So that's how you gulled away two drachmas a day!   90

AMBASSADOR. We've now returned, Pseudartabas here with us,
The Eye of the Persian king.*

DIKAIOPOLIS.   If only a raven
Would peck out your very own eye, ambassador fraud!

HERALD. Come forward, the Eye of the king!

[*Enter* PSEUDARTABAS, *a supposedly Persian official with large painted
eyes on his mask, and two supposed Persian* EUNUCHS *whose lower faces
are swathed in clothing.*]

DIKAIOPOLIS [*to* PSEUDARTABAS].   Lord Herakles!
You look, by the gods, just like a warship's prow.*
Are you rounding a headland, looking for somewhere to dock?
I suppose that's a leather flap round your lower eye too.*

AMBASSADOR [*to* PSEUDARTABAS]. Come, tell us the message the
    king of Persia wants
To deliver, Pseudartabas, to the people of Athens.

PSEUDARTABAS. Iarta mane xarxas apissona satra.*   100

AMBASSADOR. Do you all grasp what he's saying?

DIKAIOPOLIS.   I certainly don't!

AMBASSADOR. He says the king intends to send you gold.

[*To* PSEUDARTABAS] Reiterate, in a loud clear voice: *the gold*.

PSEUDARTABAS. No getty goldy, gapey-arsed Ionee.*

DIKAIOPOLIS. Well, I'll be damned! That's clear enough.

AMBASSADOR.   What is?

DIKAIOPOLIS. He says Ionians' *arses* gape like mouths
If they think barbarian gold will come their way.

AMBASSADOR. Not at all—it's *bars* of gold he's talking about.

DIKAIOPOLIS. What bars are those? You're a monstrous charlatan.

[*Pushing forward*] Get out of my way! I'll test this fellow
    myself.   110

[*To* PSEUDARTABAS] Right, tell me straight, and look my fist in the
    face—

    Or I'll pummel you into purple dye from Sardis:*

    Does the Great King mean to send us gold or not?

      [PSEUDARTABAS *nods upwards*]*

    So, the whole idea's a sham by these envoys here? [PSEUDARTABAS
    and EUNUCHS *nod*]

    I say, that's a very *Greek* nod these men just gave—

    They surely must be natives from these parts.

[*In what follows,* DIKAIOPOLIS *'unmasks' the* EUNUCHS *by removing
the swathing round their faces to reveal their beardless chins.*]

    Well, as for the first of this pair of eunuchs here,

    I've got it: it's *Kleisthenes*, Sibyrtios' son!*

    'O you whose hot-willed arse is shaven clean . . .

    Is *this* the kind of beard you have, o ape,'*   120

    When you come disguised as a eunuch in this costume?

    Now, who's this other one here? Not, surely, Straton?*

HERALD. Silence! Sit down!

    The Council invites the king of Persia's Eye

    To dine in the Prytaneion.*

      [*The* AMBASSADORS *and* EUNUCHS *leave the Assembly.*]

DIKAIOPOLIS.   It makes me choke!

    Am I going to waste my time by idling here,

    While *they* receive unlimited food and drink?

[*Thinking*] I've a plan, instead, for something big and bold.

    But where's Amphitheos got to?

AMPHITHEOS [*jumping forward*].   Here I am!

DIKAIOPOLIS. I want you to take eight drachmas as expenses   130

    And make peace-terms with Sparta *for me alone*,

    Along with my little kiddies and wedded wife.

[AMPHITHEOS *takes the money from* DIKAIOPOLIS *and rushes off by
the opposite* eisodos *from the one used by the* AMBASSADORS.]

[*To* PRYTANEIS] You lot can stick with embassies, you fools!

HERALD. Theoros, envoy from Sitalkes.*

THEOROS [*stepping forward*].   Present.

DIKAIOPOLIS. Another charlatan's being invited to speak.

THEOROS. Our mission in Thrace would never have lasted so
    long—

DIKAIOPOLIS. I'm sure it wouldn't, if your pay hadn't been so
    large!

THEOROS. —If the whole of Thrace had not been covered in snow
    And all the rivers frozen—

DIKAIOPOLIS.   Ah, that was the time
    When frigid Theognis was having a play performed!*   140

THEOROS. I was with Sitalkes drinking throughout this time.
    He showed himself *prodigiously* fond of Athens,
    A lover, no less, of you all: on his walls he wrote
    Graffiti, 'I fancy handsome Athenian men!'*
    His son, whom we'd already made a citizen here,
    Loved Apatouria sausages for his life
    And begged his father assist 'my homeland true'.*
    Sitalkes solemnly swore he'd send assistance
    With an army so large the Athenians would exclaim,
    'Phenomenal numbers of locusts are coming this way!'*   150

DIKAIOPOLIS. I'll be damned if a single word of this report
    Contains any truth—except, that is, for locusts!

THEOROS. As it is, it's the fiercest tribe in all of Thrace
    He's sent to help us.

DIKAIOPOLIS [*peering round*]. I think I can see what's coming!

HERALD. Come forward, the Thracian troops Theoros has brought.

[*Enter from one side a group of* THRACIANS, *carrying small shields and
                javelins and wearing obtrusive phalluses.*]

DIKAIOPOLIS. What on earth's this riff-raff?

THEOROS.   Odomantian troops.*

DIKAIOPOLIS. Odomantian trash! Just tell me what's going on here.
    Who's peeled the fig-leaves back around their pricks?*

THEOROS. These men, if paid two drachmas each a day,
    Will rampage, Thracian style, across Boiotia.*   160

DIKAIOPOLIS. Two drachmas for *them*—this bunch with foreskins
    peeled?

That's bound to vex the top decks of our rowers,
The city-saving throng.*

[*The* THRACIANS *snatch* DIKAIOPOLIS's *food bag from him.*]

I'm under attack!
An Odomantian raid has plundered my garlic.
Throw me back my garlic at once!
THEOROS [*to* DIKAIOPOLIS].   You nasty lout,
Get back! They're garlic-primed like fighting cocks.*
DIKAIOPOLIS. How could you, Prytaneis, just watch me suffer
In my very homeland, and at barbarians' hands?
I now forbid the Assembly to continue
Discussing the pay of Thracians. I have to tell you   170
There's been an omen—I've felt a drop of rain!*
HERALD. The Thracians must leave and return in two days' time.
The Prytaneis declare the Assembly closed.

[*Exit* THRACIANS, THEOROS, PRYTANEIS, *and* HERALD; *stage-hands
remove the benches on which the* PRYTANEIS *had been seated.*]

DIKAIOPOLIS. What a wretch I am! I've lost my garlic paste.*
But wait—here's Amphitheos returned from Sparta.

[AMPHITHEOS *runs back on from the side on which he exited: he is now
carrying three wineskins but looking back over his shoulder with breathless
concern.*]

Good to see you, Amphitheos.
AMPHITHEOS.   Not till I can stop!
I need to escape a group of Acharnian men.
DIKAIOPOLIS. But what's the matter?
AMPHITHEOS.   I was bringing peace for you
As fast as I could. [*Pointing back*] Some old men got the scent—
Acharnians, hard old fellows, gnarled like oak,   180
Relentless, Marathon veterans,* tough old timbers.
The pack of them shrieked at me, 'You filthy traitor!
You're bringing a treaty, when all our vines are axed?'*
They started to gather up stones inside their cloaks.
I started to run. They started to chase and shout.
DIKAIOPOLIS. Who cares if they shout! But have you got the treaty?
AMPHITHEOS. Yes, here it is—three vintages to taste.*

This one will last five years. Here, take a taste.
DIKAIOPOLIS [*sniffing*]. Bhhh, yuck!
AMPHITHEOS.   What's wrong?
DIKAIOPOLIS.   Don't like this
    one at all:
It's got a smell of pitch and naval planning.*   190
AMPHITHEOS. Well, try a taste of this ten-year version instead.
DIKAIOPOLIS [*sniffing*]. But this one smells of endless embassies
    And grinding our allies down—it's very acidic!
AMPHITHEOS. Well, here's the last—a thirty-year treaty, no less,
    Which covers land and sea.
DIKAIOPOLIS.   Dionysiac bliss!
What a lovely bouquet! Ambrosia, nectar too!
And not a whiff of soldiers' three-day rations.*
[*Drinks*] The taste in your mouth says: 'Travel wherever you want!'
Yes, *this* is for me—libations and heavy drinking!
I don't give a toss for all these Acharnian folk.   200
I'm getting free of war and all its woes.
I'll go and hold the Rural Dionysia.*
AMPHITHEOS. While *I'll* clear off, to escape the Acharnians here.

[*As* AMPHITHEOS *runs off into one of the wings,* DIKAIOPOLIS *exits into the stage building, one of whose doors now becomes identified as his house, notionally located in the Attic countryside. Shortly afterwards, the Acharnian* CHORUS *enters from the opposite side: they are carrying stones in their cloaks, and their movements are choreographed to accentuate geriatric decrepitude. In what follows, strophe and antistrophe consist of the* LEADER'*s chanted instructions and the* CHORUS'*s sung lyrics.*]

[PARODOS: 204–40]

LEADER. *This* way, quickly, one and all! Keep chasing him.   *Strophe*
    Be sure to ask
Every single passer-by his whereabouts. Our city calls.
Catch this man we must. [*To the audience*] Please, people, give us
    information now,
Any of you who know which route he took, this man who's
    brought the treaty.
CHORUS.   All in vain: fled and gone. Woe is me! I feel my years.   210
        Different then, back in my youth. Used to carry bags of coals,

Sprinted on Phaÿllos' heels.* Different story in those
    days:
This bringer of peace, pursued by me,
Would never have easily shaken me off.

LEADER. Now because decrepitude has made my shins   *Antistrophe*
    too stiff to run,
Weighing Lakrateides down with heavy legs to match his years,   220
Vanished the one we chased! But still we must pursue. He mustn't
    escape,
Scoffing away at folk he simply thinks are old Acharnian men.

CHORUS.   Father Zeus, and all the gods: peace he's made* with
       deadly foes,
The very ones with whom the war for all our land must
      be redoubled.
I won't relent until I pierce straight through them like a
      stake,   230
Sharp and painful, right to the hilt.
No longer will they trample my vines.

LEADER. Onwards, no delay, we've got to seek the man, look high
    and low,
Chase him to the ends of earth, pursue him till we corner him,
Pelt him with these stones of mine, yes pelt and pelt until I drop.

[DIKAIOPOLIS *'s booming voice is heard from inside the door of his house.*]

DIKAIOPOLIS. Keep ritual silence! Keep ritual silence!
LEADER [*to* CHORUS]. Hold your tongues, the lot of you! Did you
    hear his ritual call, my men?
He's the very man we seek. Step back this way, each one of you,
Out of sight. The man intends, it seems, to come and sacrifice.   240

[*As the* CHORUS *moves to the sides of the* orchêstra *to make itself incon-
spicuous,* DIKAIOPOLIS *enters from his house to organize the procession
for his Rural Dionysia: he is accompanied by a pair of* SLAVES *(one of
them* XANTHIAS*) holding between them a large phallic pole, as well as by
his* DAUGHTER *and* WIFE, *who carry the other objects mentioned in
the text.*]

DIKAIOPOLIS. Ritual silence! Ritual silence!
[*To his* DAUGHTER] Let the basket-girl step forward just a little.*

Let Xanthias erect the phallic pole.
Put down the basket, daughter—let's begin.
DAUGHTER. Please pass me, mother, the soup-jug over here,
To allow me to pour some soup on the sacred cake.
DIKAIOPOLIS. Well what a fine thing it is, Lord Dionysos,
For me to give you pleasure with this procession,
Then after I've sacrificed with all my household
I'll hold your rural festival in style   250
And be free from military service. May my treaty
Turn out for the best for its thirty-year duration!
Come, daughter, carry the basket with classy poise
But maintain a haughty look. How happy the man
Who'll take you in wedlock, begetting weasel-children
As good as you at farting when daybreak's near!
Move forward now, but take great care in the crowds*
That no one slyly filches your golden necklace.
Next, Xanthias, you two must hold erect
The phallus right behind the basket-girl.   260
I'll take up the rear and sing the phallic song.*
You, wife, stand on the roof to watch. Advance!

[DIKAIOPOLIS's WIFE *exits into the stage building and shortly after-*
wards re-appears on the roof.]

DIKAIOPOLIS [*singing*]. Phales, companion of the Bacchic god,
                    Fellow-reveller, night-stalker, adulterer, boy-lover:
                    Gladly I hail you, returned to my deme in this sixth year,*
                    With a peace treaty all of my own and escape from
                        trouble,
                    From war and warlike Lamachos-types!*   270
                    Much nicer now by far, O Phales, Phales,
                    To catch a ripe young girl who's stealing wood,
                    A Thracian slave from a neighbour's rocky land,
                    Then wrestle her to the ground and . . . squeeze out her
                        grape-pip!
                    O Phales, Phales!
                    If you drink with us, your hangover cure
                    Will be a dish of *peace* tomorrow morning.
                    Our shields will hang above the fire, unused.

[*At a signal from the* LEADER, *the* CHORUS *launches an assault on*
DIKAIOPOLIS, *pelting him with the stones wrapped in their cloaks. In
the choreographed skirmish that follows, the rest of* DIKAIOPOLIS*'s
household escape back into the stage building.*]

CHORUS.   This is the man, the very man!   280
                 Pelt him, pelt him, pelt him, pelt him,
                 Strike him, strike the filthy wretch!
                 Pelt him more, pelt him more!

[*In both the strophe and antistrophe (at 335 ff.)* DIKAIOPOLIS *chants in
recitative metres and the* CHORUS *responds in song, while the subsequent
exchanges with the* LEADER *are entirely in recitative.*]

DIKAIOPOLIS. Heavens above! What's going on here?   *Strophe*
          You're going to smash our cooking pot!
CHORUS. It's *you* we'll smash with stones, you filthy wretch.
DIKAIOPOLIS. What's the reason for this assault, I ask you,
          esteemed Acharnian elders?
CHORUS.   You need to ask? What shamelessness and vileness you
                    display:
                 Betrayer of your fatherland, solitary peace-maker,   290
                 You nonetheless dare to look me in the eye.
DIKAIOPOLIS. Shouldn't you learn the reasons why I made this
          peace? Give me a hearing.
CHORUS.   What, listen to *you*! You're doomed. We'll bury you
                    with these stones.
DIKAIOPOLIS. *Please* don't, till you've listened to me. I beg you,
          show restraint, my friends.
CHORUS.   Don't expect restraint from me. I have no interest in
                    your pleas.
                 I loathe you even more than I do Kleon, the man   300
                 I'll cut into leather soles for the Knights to wear.*

LEADER. Save your breath. I'm not prepared to listen to lengthy
          speeches here.
     You're the man who's come to terms with Sparta. Now expect
          revenge!
DIKAIOPOLIS. Won't you please just put aside the Spartans for a
          little while?

What you need to hear is whether my reasons for this peace were
    sound.
LEADER. Justification can't be found for making peace with people who
    Can't be trusted to show respect for religion or keep their sacred oaths.*
DIKAIOPOLIS. *My* conviction, though, is this: the Spartans, whom
    we love to blame,
Aren't the only source of all the problems that afflict our lives. 310
LEADER. What, you scoundrel! Not the source? You have the neck
    to say these things
Brazenly and to our faces? Shouldn't I kill you on the spot?
DIKAIOPOLIS. Aren't the *only* source, I said. I'd now go even
    further still:
Many examples I could cite where they're the ones who suffer
    some wrong.
LEADER. Scarcely can my ears believe your terrible, heart-
    confounding words.
Dare you actually make a speech that advocates our enemies' case?
DIKAIOPOLIS. Put me to the test, then; if I'm wrong and can't
    convince you all,
Over a butcher's block I'll hold my head while speaking—that's
    my offer.*
LEADER [*to* CHORUS]. Tell me, members of my deme, why spare
    him from these stones of ours?
Tear the man to pieces now, let's turn him into blood-red rags. 320
DIKAIOPOLIS. Black and fiery coals of anger seethe away inside you all.
    Won't you listen at all to me, O men of proud Acharnian stock?
LEADER. *No*, we'll never listen to you.
DIKAIOPOLIS.   I'm doomed to become your
    victim then.
LEADER. Rather be destroyed, I would, than listen to you.
DIKAIOPOLIS.   Please
    change your minds!
LEADER. Imminent death awaits you now.
DIKAIOPOLIS.   No choice, it seems, but tit
    for tat.
Death's the fate to be inflicted on your dearest loved ones too.
Hostages of yours I've taken—now's the time to slit their throats.

[DIKAIOPOLIS *rushes into his house, leaving the* CHORUS *perplexed.*]

LEADER [*to* CHORUS]. Tell me, tell me, fellow demesmen, what's
     this threat he's brandishing?
     What's the danger now we face, Acharnians one and all, from him?
     What's inside his house—a kidnapped child of ours, or something
     else?   330

[DIKAIOPOLIS *returns with a charcoal-basket and a sword: treating the*
     former as his hostage, he threatens to 'kill' it.]

DIKAIOPOLIS [*defiantly*]. Pelt me then with stones, if that's your
     wish, but *I* will kill this child.*
     Now we'll soon find out how much you care about your charcoal kin.
LEADER. Utter destruction faces us—this charcoal-basket's from
     my deme!
     No, hold back, don't execute this plan of yours! Please change
     your mind.

[*The stand-off is now concluded with a further song in which the* CHORUS
is forced to prove, with elaborate gyrations, that they have dropped their
stones, while DIKAIOPOLIS *eventually puts down his sword.*]

DIKAIOPOLIS. Shriek and shout as much as you like,   *Antistrophe*
     I'm going to kill him—I just won't listen.
CHORUS. Show mercy on me, I'm as old as you—and a charcoal-lover!
DIKAIOPOLIS. *Now* our roles have been reversed. You refused to
     listen to me just now.
CHORUS.   Make your speech then, if you'd like, explain to us
                 Just what your partiality for the Spartans is.
                 This sweet little charcoal-basket I'll never betray.   340
DIKAIOPOLIS. *First* get rid of those stones of yours, please tip them
     out here on the ground.
CHORUS [*dropping stones*]. There, they're on the ground. Now *you*
     put down your sword.
DIKAIOPOLIS. Hmm, I'm still concerned more stones are hidden
     away inside your cloaks.
CHORUS.   My cloak's been emptied thoroughly. Don't you see it
                 shaken?
                 No more excuses from you, just put down your weapon.
                 My cloak's been shaken out with all this twirling.

DIKAIOPOLIS. You were bound, I knew it, to stop your hue and cry.

[*Pointing to basket*] This charcoal from Parnes was only a whisker
   from death,
  All because, what's more, of its demesmen's crazy antics.*
  But out of fear the basket shat thick coal-dust   350
  All over me, like a cuttle-fish squirting its ink!
  It's a terrible thing when a nasty burst of anger
  Makes people resort to aggressive and noisy acts
  And refuse to listen to balanced exchanges of views,
  Even though I offered to speak with my head on a block
  While making the points about Sparta I want to put forward.
  'And yet I have no wish to lose my life.'*

CHORUS.   Deliver your speech, bring out the block,   *Strophe*
            Set it up here outside.
            Explain then, wretched man,   360
            The big idea you've got.
            I'm longing now to hear
            What thoughts are in your mind.

LEADER. Well, stick to the rules you made yourself for this trial:
  Bring your chopping block here and set about making your case.

[DIKAIOPOLIS *enters his house and soon re-appears with a large butcher's
    block: he stands behind it with his head up against the top of it.*]

DIKAIOPOLIS. There it is for you all to see—my butcher's block.
  Here stands the tiny man who will make his speech.
  I've no intention, by Zeus, of taking cover;
  I'll say what I truly think in defence of Sparta.
  And yet—I'm really afraid! Our country folk   370
  Like nothing more, I know, than when a speaker
  Heaps praise on them and on the city itself,
  No matter how bogus he is or whether it's true.
  That's how they fail to know they're being swindled.
  I'm also aware how the minds of our old men
  Think all that matters is using their votes to hurt.
  What I suffered myself at Kleon's hands last year
  Because of my comedy, *that* I won't quickly forget.*
  He dragged me brusquely into the Council chamber;
  He slandered me, bad-mouthed me with packs of lies,   380
  Like a deafening torrent he soaked me with his abuse.

I was nearly destroyed by the flood of filth he produced.
So before I make my speech, allow me please
To find a costume that rouses maximum pity.

CHORUS.   What's all this twisting, crafty guile   *Antistrophe*
              To engineer delay?
              You can fetch, for all I care,
              From Hieronymos
              A dark, thick, bushy-haired
              Helmet of Hades!*   390

LEADER. You'd better divulge your Sisyphean ruses.*
    This contest won't allow for any excuses.
DIKAIOPOLIS [*melodramatically*]. The time has come for all my
    strength of soul—
    I'd better be off to the house of Euripides!

[DIKAIOPOLIS *approaches the second door of the stage building, which
now becomes identified as the house of the tragedian* EURIPIDES. *He
knocks on the door.*]

    Slave, open!
SLAVE [*opening door*]. Who's this?
DIKAIOPOLIS.   Is Euripides at home?
SLAVE. Not at home yet home as well, if you understand.*
DIKAIOPOLIS. What, both at home yet not?
SLAVE.   Correct, old man.
    His intellect's outside collecting verses,
    So it's not at home, yet *he's* inside on a couch
    Composing a tragedy.
DIKAIOPOLIS.   Happy Euripides,   400
    When his slave can answer questions with such finesse!
    Would you call him out?
SLAVE.   Impossible! [*Shuts door*]
DIKAIOPOLIS.   Nevertheless—
    I'm not prepared to leave. I'll bang on the door.
    Euripides! Euripi*diddles*!
    Please answer the door, if you've ever done so before.*
    It's Dikaiopolis, deme Cholleidai, calling.*

    [EURIPIDES *appears at a window in the stage building.*]

EURIPIDES [*brusquely*]. I'm busy now.
DIKAIOPOLIS. Please use the trolley.*
EURIPIDES.   Impossible.
DIKAIOPOLIS.   Nevertheless.
EURIPIDES. Very well, I'll use the trolley—but need my feet up.

[EURIPIDES' *house door opens and the tragic trolley rolls out with the poet*
dressed in rags and reclining on a couch, surrounded by a variety of theatrical
props, costumes, and masks. In the background stands his SLAVE. *For much*
of what follows, EURIPIDES *attempts, with increasing difficulty, to main-*
tain a loftily poetic manner in the face of DIKAIOPOLIS's *rustic tenacity.*]

DIKAIOPOLIS. Euripides—
EURIPIDES [*poetically*].   Thou sayest?
DIKAIOPOLIS.   Composing with feet up   410
    Must be the reason your characters turn out lame!*
    But why are you wearing these pitiful tragic rags?
    No wonder all your characters turn out beggars!
    I beseech you by your knees, Euripides,
    Please give me a rag from that very old play of yours.
    I need to deliver a long speech to the chorus;
    The penalty's death if I don't deliver it well.
EURIPIDES. Which tatters are those? [*Picking up a mask*] The ones
    this Oineus wore—
    Ill-fated, agéd figure—when playing his role?*
DIKAIOPOLIS [*trying to remember*]. Not Oineus, no. Someone more
    pitiful still.   420
EURIPIDES. Blind Phoinix's rags?
DIKAIOPOLIS.   No, Phoinix isn't the one.
    Someone more pitiful still than even Phoinix.*
EURIPIDES [*loftily*]. What rended garments doth this man request?
    You mean the beggar Philoktetes' rags?*
DIKAIOPOLIS. No, someone *much* more beggarly than him too.
EURIPIDES. Well would you like the filthy set of robes
[*Pointing*] This lame Bellerophon was costumed in?*
DIKAIOPOLIS. Not Bellerophon. The person I have in mind
    Was lame, a beggar, a blather, and clever at speaking.
EURIPIDES. It's Mysian Telephos!
DIKAIOPOLIS.   Yes, Telephos!*   430
    I beg you, give me the strips of cloth he wore.

EURIPIDES. Slave, give him the ragged weeds of Telephos.

[*The* SLAVE *rummages among various piles of ragged costumes lying on the floor round* EURIPIDES' *couch.*]

They're lying on top of the rags worn by Thyestes,
Next to Ino's.* There they are. [*To* DIKAIOPOLIS] Here, take
them now.

[DIKAIOPOLIS *inspects the rags then pulls them over his countryman's clothing.*]

DIKAIOPOLIS [*quasi-tragically*]. O Zeus, whose vision penetrates all
things,
May my costume make me as pitiful as can be.
[*Informally*] Euripides, since you've already done one favour,
Please give me the other things that go with the rags.
I'd like the Mysian cap to put on my head.*
I need to seem a beggar for just today,   440
To *be* myself but not to *appear* to be;*
[*Gesturing*] The audience needs to know just who I am,
But I need to make the chorus look like boobies
And use my crafty speech to give them the finger!*
EURIPIDES. It's yours: you scheme so subtly with your guile.
DIKAIOPOLIS. So kind! 'And for Telephos my silent wishes.'*
[*Puts on cap*] Oh good, I feel a surge of crafty language.
But I still require a beggar's staff to carry.
EURIPIDES [*handing him one*]. Take this—then leave this stone
abode of mine.
DIKAIOPOLIS [*melodramatically*]. My heart, you see me driven from
this palace—   450
[*craftily*] Even though I need more props. Resolve to be
Relentless in your demands. Euripides,
Please give me a little basket burnt by a lamp.*
EURIPIDES. Why lack you, wretched man, this wicker object?
DIKAIOPOLIS. No lack is mine—I'd like it all the same.
EURIPIDES [*handing the basket*]. Thou vexest me; depart now from
my palace.
DIKAIOPOLIS. I wish you all prosperity . . . like your mother!*

EURIPIDES. Please go away.

DIKAIOPOLIS.   But just one more request:
  I'd like the little cup with the broken rim.

EURIPIDES. Well take it, then get lost! [*Loftily*] You trouble my
    palace.   460

DIKAIOPOLIS. But you still don't seem to know your own defects.*
  Please, sweetest Euripides—the very last thing:
  I need a tiny pot that's bunged with a sponge.*

EURIPIDES. You'll deprive me, fellow, of everything from my play.
  Just take the pot and go.

DIKAIOPOLIS.   I'm leaving now.
[*Pausing*] And yet, alas—without one final prop
  I'm doomed. Please listen, sweetest Euripides,
  If I get what I need, I'll disappear for good.
  Just give me scraps of greens to put in the basket.

EURIPIDES. You'll finish me off! Here then. My plays have
    vanished!*   470

DIKAIOPOLIS. I'll leave you alone. I'm going. I know I'm trouble,
  'Though I didn't think the chieftains so detest me.'*
[*Turning back*] Oh no, it's all gone wrong! I quite forgot
  The thing on which my whole success depends.
  Euripi*diddles*, O sweetest, dearest friend,
  I swear I'm prepared to die if I ask any more—
  Except for one, just one, just one more thing.
  Please give me a bunch of herbs from maternal stock!*

EURIPIDES. This man's outrageous! Fasten the palace doors!

[*The trolley is wheeled back inside, taking* EURIPIDES *and his* SLAVE
with it.]

DIKAIOPOLIS [*portentously*]. O heart, you must advance without the
    herbs.   480
  Do you know how great a contest now awaits you
  As you ready yourself to make the case for Sparta?
  Advance, my heart! See here the starting line.
  Press on with Euripides' words inside your belly.
  I know your strength. Come then, my suffering heart,
  Go to that place and put your head on the block
  As you make the speech that states your true convictions.
  Be bold. Come! On your way! Bravo, my heart!*

[*As* DIKAIOPOLIS *makes his way back to the chopping block and gets back into position to make his speech, the* CHORUS *sing and dance in eager expectation.*]

CHORUS.   What will you do? What say? Be sure   *Strophe*   490
               You're shameless, hard as iron as well,
               To stick out your neck for the city to chop
               When you contradict the views of all.
               The man lacks fear. So be it.
               You made the choice—so speak.

DIKAIOPOLIS. Please feel no grudge towards me, you spectators,
    If I stand before Athenians as a beggar
    To speak, a wine-song poet, about the city.*
    For even the wine-song knows what's right and wrong.   500
    What I say will cause offence, but still it's right,*
    And this time Kleon can't slander me with the charge
    Of defaming the city with visitors in our midst.*
    We're on our own, the Lenaia is just for us,
    It's too early in the year for visitors yet;
    The tribute and our allies haven't arrived.
    We're on our own, like grain without the husks—
    The metics I count as bran mixed in with us.*
    To be clear, I hate the Spartans with a passion,
    And I hope the god whose shrine's at Tainaron   510
    Will send an earthquake, smashing all their homes!*
    My lovely vines have been cut down like yours.*
    But, all you friends now gathered to hear my words,
    Why do we blame the Spartans for these things?
    Some men of *ours*—and I don't mean the city;
    Remember this, it's not the city I mean—
    Some nasty little men, like dodgy coins,
    Worthless, ill-stamped, half-foreign into the bargain,
    Denounced the cloaks Megarians tried to sell us,
    The cucumbers as well, the little hares,   520
    The piglets and the garlic, chunks of salt, . . .
    Megarian goods were seized and then resold.*
    At first these petty affairs were purely local,
    But then young men, while on a Megarian trip,
    Got wildly drunk and stole a whore, Simaitha.

So then the Megarians, like fighting cocks,
Stole in reprisal two of Aspasia's whores.*
And that was the start of war for all of Greece,
A war about three women...who do blow jobs!
After that, Olympian Perikles showed his wrath,   530
With lightning and with thunder churning Greece,
Proposing laws that read like drinking songs,
That Megarians 'must be banned from Attic soil,
From Athens' markets, from sea and mainland too'.*
So then the Megarians, beginning to starve,
Requested Sparta to get the decree reversed,
The one on account of women who do blow jobs!
They asked us several times but we wouldn't shift;
And that was when the clash of shields began.
Someone will say, 'The Spartans shouldn't have acted'.*   540
Well suppose some Spartan had sailed in a little barque
And denounced and sold a puppy from Seriphos,
Would you sit inert in your homes? I hardly think so!*
On the contrary, you'd launch without delay
Three hundred ships; the mood in the city would teem
With clamour of troops and hubbub round trierarchs,
Crews' wages being paid, ships' emblems gilded,
The echoing porticoes where rations are measured,
With wineskins, oar-thongs, storage jars being bought,
Abundance of garlic and olives and onions in nets,   550
Plus garlands, sprats, pipe-girls—black eyes as well!*
The docks would resound with the noise of blades being planed,
Ships' bolts being hammered, and oars being fixed in place,
Pipe-playing, the shouts of boatswains, and other signals.
I know for sure you'd act like that: 'So if
We think that Telephos shouldn't', we've got no sense.*

[DIKAIOPOLIS, *confident of the effect of his speech, moves away from
behind the chopping block. The* CHORUS *temporarily splits into divided
factions.*]

CHORUS^A. I can't believe my ears, you filthy scoundrel!
    You dare, a beggar, to speak of Athens like this?
    And you think informers merit such harsh abuse?
CHORUS^B. But by Poseidon he's justified! His claims   560

Are totally right—not a word of his was false.
CHORUS^A. Well even so, was it up to *him* to say this?
[*Advancing menacingly*] I don't intend to let him escape scot-free.
CHORUS^B [*blocking the way*]. Hey you, get back! If you try to land a
    blow,
  You'll find yourself knocked back with instant force.

CHORUS^A.   O Lamachos, whose eyes flash lightning,   *Antistrophe*
        Bring help at once, dire-crested hero,
        O Lamachos, our friend, our tribesman!*
        Or anyone else, taxiarch or general
        Or expert in siege warfare, bring us help   570
        Without delay! I face a struggle!

[*With sound and fury,* LAMACHOS *enters from one of the* eisodoi: *he is
wearing a helmet with both a triple horsehair crest and additional plumes,
and he carries a shield with the image of a Gorgon's head emblazoned
on it.*]

LAMACHOS [*portentously*]. Whence reached my ears the sound of
    warlike cries?
  Where needs my help? Where must I carry the fight?
  Who's woken my Gorgon up inside her shield-case?*
DIKAIOPOLIS [*ironically*]. O hero Lamachos, such crests and tactics!
CHORUS^A. O Lamachos, this man has spent much time
  Besmirching all our city with his abuse.*
LAMACHOS [*to* DIKAIOPOLIS]. You dare, a beggar, to speak like this
    in public?
DIKAIOPOLIS. O hero Lamachos, show understanding,
  If I spoke and chattered away though just a beggar.
LAMACHOS. What was it you said? Admit it.
DIKAIOPOLIS.   I don't now know.   580
  The sight of your weapons is making me faint with fear.
  I beg you, move that bogey shield away.
LAMACHOS [*doing so*]. There you are.
DIKAIOPOLIS.   Well place it face-down on the
    ground.
LAMACHOS. As you say.
DIKAIOPOLIS.   Then give me that feather off your helmet.
LAMACHOS. Here's the plume you want.

DIKAIOPOLIS. Now hold me by the head.

[DIKAIOPOLIS *leans forward over the upturned shield and starts to push the feather into his mouth.*]

I need to vomit—your crests just make me puke!
LAMACHOS. Hey, stop! You mustn't vomit on my plume.
It's a special plume—
DIKAIOPOLIS. Of what? Yes, do explain
Which bird it's from. A braggart-buzzard, maybe?
LAMACHOS [*drawing his sword*]. You'll pay with your life.
DIKAIOPOLIS. No, please
don't, Lamachos! 590
This isn't a trial of strength. But *if* you're strong
[*Gesturing with phallus*] Why not peel back my foreskin, well-
armed man!*
LAMACHOS. You dare, a beggar, to speak of a general like this?*
DIKAIOPOLIS. Who says I'm a beggar?
LAMACHOS. Well who exactly *are* you?
DIKAIOPOLIS. An upright citizen, not an office-chaser,
Since war broke out, a stalwart soldier-man,
While *you*, since war broke out, have creamed your pay.
LAMACHOS. They elected me.
DIKAIOPOLIS. Who did? Three cuckoos I bet!*
That's why in disgust I made my own peace treaty.
I watched old grey-haired men serve in the ranks 600
While younger men like you avoided action,*
Some earning up in Thrace three drachmas a day—
Teisamenos, Phainippos, and similar rogues—
While others were envoys among the Chaonians,
The likes of Geres and Theodoros, sheer frauds,
And others in Sicily, making pure fools of us all.*
LAMACHOS. They were all elected.
DIKAIOPOLIS. But what's the reason why
It's people like you who always contrive to get paid
[*Pointing to* CHORUS] But none of these older men? Marilades,*
Have you served on a single embassy, old man? 610
He hasn't, despite his soundness and hard work.
And what of the rest of you, with your hearts of oak?
Have you been to Persia or to the Chaonians?

It's always Koisyra's son and Lamachos,*
The sort of men who never repay their debts
And are shunned by their former friends like dirty water
That people slop out in the street at the end of the day.

LAMACHOS. Democracy! Can you tolerate speech like this?

DIKAIOPOLIS. Well it tolerates *you* and the pay you receive for
    office!

LAMACHOS [*belligerently*]. I'll continue to fight our Peloponnesian
    foes.*   620
I'll never give up the war. I'll wreak great havoc
With ships and troops—I'll battle with all my might! [*Exits*]

DIKAIOPOLIS. While *I'll* send heralds to tell the Peloponnesians,
The Megarians and Boiotians too, that they
Can come and trade with me, not Lamachos!

[*As* DIKAIOPOLIS *exits into his house, the* CHORUS *moves into formation
in the* orchêstra *to deliver the parabasis.*]

[PARABASIS: 626–718]

LEADER. This fellow's won the argument! The people are
    persuaded
His peace is just. Let's shed our cloaks and tackle the anapaests.*
Ever since our trainer has been in charge of preparing comic
    plays,
He's never stepped forward to tell the spectators how very skilful
    he is.*
But now that his enemies slander him, and the fickle Athenians
    listen,   630
On the grounds that he mocks this city of ours and does the
    demos down,
He needs to answer this charge before you volatile people of
    Athens.
Our poet claims there are many good things for which you ought
    to thank him.
He's stopped you being deceived by tricks employed by visiting
    speakers,
The way you swallow their flattering words with gullible, gawping
    faces.
In the past you used to be deceived by our allied cities' envoys.

They would start by calling you 'violet-wreathed': as soon as
    someone said this,
Their mention of wreaths would make you sit up on the tips of
    your pert little buttocks.
Or if such flattering speakers called this city of Athens
    'gleaming',*
They achieved their goal with that single word—a description
    fit for whitebait!   640
By stopping such things the poet claims he's done you a wealth of
    good.
He also exposed the way democracy worked in the allied cities.*
In consequence, these cities now will rush to bring you tribute,
Because they want to come and see the best of comic poets,
The one who had the courage to tell the Athenians only what's
    right.*
In fact, the poet's boldness now has earned him world-wide fame,
To the point where the king of Persia asked a Spartan embassy
Not just which side in the war possessed the greatest fleet of ships
But which was the one this comic poet assailed with most abuse,
Since *they* were the ones who must have been improved by such
    reproach   650
And would easily win the war, he said, with such a good adviser.
That's the reason why the Spartans now are proposing peace to
    you
And asking you to return Aigina: it's not because they care
About the island itself, they want to steal this *poet* from you!*
Don't let him go—his plays will always show what's right and
    wrong.
He claims he'll teach you many good things and help to make you
    happy.
He'll never flatter, nor bribe you with pay, nor dupe you with his
    words,
Nor resort to tricks, nor spray you with praise, but only teach
    what's best.
        So Kleon can use his machinations
        And scheme against me all he likes.*   660
        What's good is on my side, what's right
        Will be my ally. I'll never be found
        To be, like him, where the city's concerned,

A coward and...gaping arsehole!

CHORUS.   Come hither, Muse, with flaring might of fire,   *Strophe*
           Come full of ardour, Acharnian Muse!
           Just like a spark of flame that leaps
           From charcoals of oak,
           Aroused by vigorous fanning,
           When the fish are lying there, ready for roasting,   670
           And gleaming-crowned Thasian sauce is stirred,
           And barley-cakes are kneaded—
           With blazing force like that, come, Muse,
           And bring a song of rustic ardour
           To me your fellow-demesman.

LEADER. Old as we are, yes ancient even, we have a complaint we
      wish to make.
   Rightful rewards are now withheld for naval victories *we* once
      won.
   Nourishing care for our old age is not forthcoming; you let us
      suffer.
   Old men find themselves dragged into court on trumped-up legal
      charges,
   Made the butts of mockery aimed at them by youthful
      orators,   680
   Treated as worthless, just like worn-out pipes that no one plays
      any more,*
   Nothing to keep them on their feet except their walking-sticks,
      that's all.
   Muttering in forlorn senility, there we stand before the court,
   Blind to our surroundings, with judicial mist upon our eyes.
   Then the young man, full of zeal to do the work of advocate,*
   Quickly strikes his older victim, using words like sling-thrown
      stones.
   Next he hauls him up for questions, placing numerous verbal
      traps,
   Tearing him, an old Tithonos, into shreds with harassing ploys.*
   Feebleness of age befuddles him; by the end his guilt is fixed.
   Then he's left to sob and weep profusely and to tell his
      friends: 690
   'All I'd saved to buy a coffin has now been lost to pay my fine.'

CHORUS. How can it make sense to destroy an old   *Antistrophe*
    man like this,
        A white-haired figure yet tested in court,
        Despite the toils he's undertaken,
        All the hot and manly sweat
        He's wiped away in profusion,
        A man who served the city with valour at Marathon?
        Well, when we served at Marathon, *we* did the charging,
        But now at the hands of lousy people
        It's we who are charged in court   700
        And convicted into the bargain.
        What Marpsias will contest this?*

LEADER. *Where's* the sense, I ask again, when a stooped old man like
    Thucydides
  Gets destroyed when he finds himself entangled with a Skythian
    brute,
  Namely this loquacious advocate, Kephisodemos' son?*
  How I welled with pity for him and wiped the tears that drenched
    my face,
  Watching such an elderly fellow get harassed by one from archer's
    stock.
  Long ago, when in his prime, Thucydides—I swear on oath—
  Wouldn't have been intimidated by even Artachaias himself.*
  Ten times over he could have defeated Euathlos in a wrestling
    bout,   710
  Thirty thousand archers he could have defeated in a shouting
    match,
  Not to mention shooting an arrow much further than his father's
    kin.*
  Now that you refuse to let old men sleep peacefully in their beds,
  Vote at least to keep apart the cases that come into court:
  When a defendant's old, assign an advocate who's old and
    toothless;
  Let the young have Kleinias' son with his gaping arse and
    prattling tongue.*
  Legal penalties in the future should follow this age-related rule:
  Banish the old by means of the old, the young by the young—
    that's only fair.

[*As the* CHORUS *moves back to the sides of the* orchêstra, DIKAIOPOLIS
*enters from his house. He is carrying a large whip and several other objects;
he proceeds to distribute the latter on the ground to mark out a private
market—his personal substitute for Athens' Agora—in front of his house.*]

DIKAIOPOLIS. These objects mark the boundaries of my market:
   All Peloponnesian folk can come and trade,   720
   And all Megarians and Boiotians too,
   Provided they sell to *me*, not Lamachos.
   The market officials to keep good order here*
   Will be this triple whip of toughest leather. [*Cracks it with relish*]
   Informers are strictly forbidden to enter here
   Or anyone else whose purpose is to grass.*
   I'll fetch the stele on which my treaty's written
   And set it up in my market for all to see.

[DIKAIOPOLIS *puts his whip on the ground and goes back into his house.
From one of the wings enters the* MEGARIAN *with his two small* DAUGH-
TERS. *The* MEGARIAN *carries a sack from which he will produce various
items of disguise for the girls.*]

MEGARIAN. Agora of Athens, dear to Megarians, greetings!
   By the god of friendship, I've missed you like my mother.   730
   But come, you poor little girls of a wretched father,
   Step over here to see if there's food to be found.
   Now listen and pay attention with all your . . . stomach.
   Do you want to be sold, or prefer to starve to death?
DAUGHTERS [*squealing*]. Be sold! Be sold!
MEGARIAN. That's my view too. But who would be so mad
   As to purchase such a blatant burden as you?
   Nonetheless I've got a Megarian trick to play:
   I'll dress you up as piglets I'm bringing to market.*
   Here, fit these piglet hooves on your hands and feet.   740
   Be sure to look like stock from a very good sow;
   In Hermes' name, if you go back home unsold
   There's nothing for you but miserable starvation.
   Here, tie on these snouts as well around you heads,
   Then come and get inside this sack of mine. [*They do so*]
   Make sure you grunt and squeal authentically

And sound like piglets picked for the Mystery rites.*
I'll summon Dikaiopolis, if he's around.
[*Shouting*] Dikaiopolis, do you want to buy some pigs?
DIKAIOPOLIS [*entering*]. What, someone from Megara?
MEGARIAN.   Yes, we've
    come to trade.   750
DIKAIOPOLIS. How are things by you?
MEGARIAN [*shrugging*].   We sit round the fire and starve.
DIKAIOPOLIS [*ironically*]. By Zeus, sounds nice—provided there's
    music as well!
    What else are Megarians doing these days?
MEGARIAN.   Not much.
    When I left the place to make my journey here,
    The Commissioners were taking steps to ensure
    That the city would quickly meet with sheer disaster.*
DIKAIOPOLIS. Oh well, that means your troubles will end!
MEGARIAN.   No doubt.
DIKAIOPOLIS. What other Megarian news? The price of grain?
MEGARIAN. Sky high by us—as high as the gods in the clouds.
DIKAIOPOLIS. Have you got any salt?
MEGARIAN.   But Athens controls it all.   760
DIKAIOPOLIS. No garlic either?
MEGARIAN.   Garlic! Same old story.
    Whenever your people invade, you're like field mice
    And dig up the heads of garlic with stakes of wood.*
DIKAIOPOLIS. Then what have you brought?
MEGARIAN.   I've piglets for Mystery
    rites.
DIKAIOPOLIS. Sounds promising. Show me.
MEGARIAN.   Look, they're really lovely.

[*The* MEGARIAN *opens his sack and reveals one of his* DAUGHTERS *in her
                    piglet 'disguise'.*]

    You can feel this one, if you want; it's fat and lovely.
DIKAIOPOLIS [*startled*]. What on earth is this?
MEGARIAN.   A piglet, I swear by Zeus.
DIKAIOPOLIS. What kind of piglet is this?
MEGARIAN.   The Megarian kind.
    Don't you really think it's a piglet?

DIKAIOPOLIS.   I certainly don't!

MEGARIAN [*feigning outrage*]. Just listen to how distrustful this man
    is!   770
  He denies that this is a piglet. In that case,
  I'm ready to wager a bag of thyme-flavoured salt*
  That this is what every Greek counts as a piglet.

DIKAIOPOLIS. But it's clearly a human child.

MEGARIAN.   By Diokles,*
  She's mine of course. Who else's would she be?
  Would you like to hear the sound of her voice?

DIKAIOPOLIS.   By heaven,
  I certainly would.

MEGARIAN [*to* DAUGHTER[A]]. Make a sound then, quickly, piglet!
  Won't you do as you're told? Still silent, damn your head!
  I'll take you home, by Hermes, that's what I'll do.

DAUGHTER[A]. Oink! Oink!   780

MEGARIAN. Are you satisfied it's a pig?

DIKAIOPOLIS [*looking closely*].   Well now I am.
  But when she grows up, she'll become a furry pussy!*

MEGARIAN. Within five years, for sure, she'll be like her mother.

[*At this point the* MEGARIAN'*s other* DAUGHTER *emerges from the sack.*
    DIKAIOPOLIS *turns his attention to her.*]

DIKAIOPOLIS. Well *this* one here's not fit for sacrifice.

MEGARIAN. But what do you mean by that?

DIKAIOPOLIS.   She needs a tail.*

MEGARIAN. That's because she's young. But when she's a full-
  grown sow
  She'll possess a tail that's big and fat and red.
  If you want to rear her, she's the piglet for you.

DIKAIOPOLIS [*examining her*]. Her cunt's akin, I see, to the other
  one's too.

MEGARIAN. That's because her mother's the same—and her father
  as well.   790
  But if she's fattened and grows a layer of hair,
  She'll be fit to dedicate to Aphrodite.

DIKAIOPOLIS. No piglet is sacrificed to Aphrodite.

MEGARIAN. What? She's the *only* goddess these things are for!
  What's more, these piglets' flesh will be delicious

If you pierce it through with a spit that's long and straight.

DIKAIOPOLIS. Are they old enough to be reared without their mother?

MEGARIAN. By Poseidon, yes—without their father as well.

DIKAIOPOLIS. What exactly does this one eat?

MEGARIAN. Whatever you give her.
But ask her yourself.

DIKAIOPOLIS. Hey, piglet, piglet!

DAUGHTER^B. Oink! 800

DIKAIOPOLIS. Would you like to nibble some chickpeas?

DAUGHTER^B. Oink! Oink!
Oink!

DIKAIOPOLIS. What else then? Maybe dried figs too?

DAUGHTER^B. Oink! Oink!

DIKAIOPOLIS [*to* MEGARIAN]. And what about you yourself?
The same?

MEGARIAN. Oink! Oink!

DIKAIOPOLIS. How shrill your shrieks when you hear the mention
of figs!

[*Calling into house*] Let someone bring a basket of figs out here
For these little piglets.

[*A* SLAVE *comes out of* DIKAIOPOLIS's *house and throws dried figs to the*
DAUGHTERS, *who proceed to eat them ravenously.*]

Well, will they eat them? Crikey!
What a furious chomping noise, in Herakles' name!
Where *do* these beasts come from? [*Cornily*] From a *gorge*, it
seems!*

MEGARIAN. But they didn't gorge down every one of the figs you
gave them.
I managed to snatch this one from them for myself. [*Gulps it
down*] 810

DIKAIOPOLIS. By Zeus, what a pair of charming creatures they are.
Tell me what's the price of these little piglets of yours.

MEGARIAN. Well, this one here will cost a bunch of garlic.
The other is yours for a single pound of salt.

DIKAIOPOLIS. I'll buy them. Just wait here. [*Into house*]

MEGARIAN. I certainly will.
By Hermes god of traders, I'd like to sell
My wife like this, and my very own mother as well!

[*Enter, from one of the* eisodoi, *a prowling* INFORMER: *he looks around suspiciously and spots the* MEGARIAN, *whom he immediately confronts.*]

INFORMER. Hey, *who* are you?
MEGARIAN.   A Megarian seller of pigs.
INFORMER. Then I'll go and report these little piglets of yours
    As enemy goods—and you as well.
MEGARIAN.   Not again!   820
    This is how our woes began in the very first place.*

[*The* MEGARIAN *starts to take evasive action.*]

INFORMER. Don't try your Megarian tricks! Give me that sack.
MEGARIAN. Dikaiopolis! Come quickly! I'm being denounced.

[DIKAIOPOLIS *re-emerges from his house, bringing with him garlic and salt. He picks up his whip, previously designated as his 'market officials' (723), and confronts the* INFORMER *both verbally and physically.*]

DIKAIOPOLIS. Who by? Who dares to denounce you? Market
    officials,
    Your job's to keep informers out of this place. [*Cracks whip*]
[*To* INFORMER] You're bringing things to light... with no wick in
    your lamp?*
INFORMER. Am I not to denounce our enemies?
DIKAIOPOLIS.   At your cost!
    You'd better run fast and go and inform elsewhere.

[*As* DIKAIOPOLIS *is on the point of assaulting him with his whip, the* INFORMER *runs away in the direction from which he had entered.*]

MEGARIAN. What a plague of people like this you've got in Athens.
DIKAIOPOLIS. Don't worry, Megarian. Here's the price for your
    piglets: 830
    You can take the garlic and salt agreed before. [*Hands them over*]
    Farewell!
MEGARIAN [*gloomily*]. Fare *well*? That's not how Megarians live.
DIKAIOPOLIS. My mistake—I'll keep the wish for myself instead!
MEGARIAN [*to* DAUGHTERS]. My little piglets, even without your
    father
    Keep dipping your bread into salt, if anyone offers.*

[*The* MEGARIAN *departs on the side from which he entered, while* DIKAI-
OPOLIS *goes back into his house, taking the* DAUGHTERS *with him. The*
CHORUS *comes forward to sing.*]

CHORUS.   This fellow's life is happy! Did you hear the way his plans
     Are working out with full success? He'll sit in his
       marketplace
     And reap rewards for all his trade. And if some Ktesias*
     Or any other informer enters there, they'll soon regret
       it!   840

     No other trader will undercut your prices and do you down.
     No Prepis will be in the crowds and rub his sodomized
       arse against you.
     No need to jostle Kleonymos. You'll stroll in a shining
       cloak
     And won't encounter Hyperbolos with his numerous
       legal threats.*

     There's someone else who won't approach and accost
       you in the market:
     Kratinos, whose hair is always cropped in slick
       adulterer's style,
     A new Artemon (but even worse), a man whose plays
       are sloppy,   850
     And one whose armpits stink like the goats his father
       used to tend.*

     And another thing: you won't be mocked by the nasty
       upstart Pauson,
     Nor Lysistratos, a man who puts his deme Cholargos to
       shame,*
     The one deep-dyed in wicked tricks, who's always cold
       and hungry
     For every one of the thirty days of every single month!

[*As the* CHORUS *moves back to the sides of the* orchêstra, *a* BOIOTIAN
trader enters from the same eisodos *previously used by the* MEGARIAN.
Behind him walks his slave, HISMENIAS: *between them they are carrying
a variety of objects on a shoulder-pole and in baskets. He is also accompanied by (two?) Theban* PIPE-PLAYERS.]

BOIOTIAN [*removing a bag*]. Let Herakles be my witness, my
    shoulder's wrecked!   860
  Take care with the pennyroyal, Hismenias.
  You pipers, who've come all the way from Thebes,
  Give a blast of tune— [*ironically*] perhaps 'The old dog's arsehole'.

[*The* PIPE-PLAYERS *start to emit disagreeably rasping sounds from their
instruments. The noise brings* DIKAIOPOLIS *back out of his house.*]

DIKAIOPOLIS. What the hell's this racket? Some blasted wasps at
    my door!
  How on earth has this godforsaken swarm got here?
  They make a droning rumble as bad as Chairis.* [*The piping stops*]
BOIOTIAN. By Iolaos, my friend, you've done a favour.*
  They've been blasting away behind me ever since Thebes;
  They've made the pennyroyal shed its leaves!
  But if you'd like, you can purchase some of my wares: 870
  I've birdies and beasties of every conceivable kind.
DIKAIOPOLIS. Hello, my fine Boiotian gourmandizer!
  What goods have you got?
BOIOTIAN.   Boiotian delicacies:
  Origanum, pennyroyal, rush-mats, lamp-wicks,
  Ducks, jackdaws, francolins, and coots as well,
  Plovers, dabchicks—
DIKAIOPOLIS.   You're like a gust of wind
  That's swept great clouds of birds to my marketplace!
BOIOTIAN. There's more besides—I've also geese, hares, foxes,
  Mole rats, hedgehogs, cats, and even badgers,
  Martens, otters, and eels from lake Kopaïs.*   880
DIKAIOPOLIS [*mock-poetically*]. O thou who bringest fish of pure
    delight,
  Allow me to address these eels of yours.
BOIOTIAN [*likewise*]. Oldest of lake Kopaïs's fifty daughters,
  Come hither, bestow your favours on this stranger.

[*The* BOIOTIAN *produces an eel from one of his baskets.* DIKAIOPOLIS
*takes hold of it with relish: his address to it is heavily coloured by poetic
formality.*]

DIKAIOPOLIS. O my beloved, for whom I've pined so long,
  You're back! You were missed by the wine-song's choruses,*

And we know that Morychos always loved you too.*
[*Calling*] Slaves, bring me out the brazier and the bellows.

[SLAVES *come out of the house, bringing the requested objects; they are followed by* CHILDREN *of* DIKAIOPOLIS, *who proceeds to show them the eel.*]

Behold, my children, this finest lady eel,
Who's returned, so badly missed, in this sixth year.*   890
Address her fondly, offspring of mine, while I
Provide a charcoal fire for our visitor's sake.

[DIKAIOPOLIS *shows one of the* SLAVES *how he expects the eel to be grilled, then motions for the brazier to be taken back into the house.*]

[*Solemnly*] Now carry her off. [*To the eel*] Not even once I'm dead
    Could I bear to be without you . . . beetroot-wrapped.*
BOIOTIAN. But how do you intend to pay me for it?
DIKAIOPOLIS. It can count as the market tax you need to pay me.
    But tell me which other goods of yours are for sale.
BOIOTIAN. I'm selling whatever you see.
DIKAIOPOLIS.   And what are your prices?
    Or are you prepared to barter for goods of mine?
BOIOTIAN. I'll only take what we don't have in Boiotia.   900
DIKAIOPOLIS. In that case why not take some Phaleron whitebait*
    Or pottery ware?
BOIOTIAN.   But we've got those things back home.
    Give me goods we don't possess but are plentiful here.
DIKAIOPOLIS. I've got it then—you can take an informer home!
    You can take it wrapped like a pot.
BOIOTIAN [*naively?*].   Well, by the twins,*
    That would certainly represent a profit for me,
    As good as taking a monkey that's full of mischief!
DIKAIOPOLIS. But look, here comes Nikarchos on the prowl.*
BOIOTIAN. He's not very tall.
DIKAIOPOLIS.   But evil from top to toe!

[NIKARCHOS *enters from one side; he makes a beeline for the* BOIOTIAN'*s goods and quickly rifles through them.*]

NIKARCHOS. Who owns these goods I see?

BOIOTIAN.   They belong to me.   910
   They've come from Thebes, Zeus be my witness!
NIKARCHOS.   Well then
   I intend to report them as enemy goods.
BOIOTIAN.   What's wrong
   To make you wage a war against my birdies?
NIKARCHOS. I'm denouncing *you* as well.
BOIOTIAN.   What harm have I done you?
NIKARCHOS. I'll explain for the sake of those around us here:
   You're smuggling lamp-wicks in from enemy lands.
DIKAIOPOLIS. You're exposing contraband goods because of a
   lamp-wick?*
NIKARCHOS [*pompously*]. This wick could be used to ignite our
   naval dockyards.
DIKAIOPOLIS. A single wick?
NIKARCHOS.   Indeed.
DIKAIOPOLIS.   Exactly how?
NIKARCHOS [*fantasizing*]. A Boiotian might attach it to a
   cockroach,   920
   Then light it and let it sail into the dockyard
   By means of a sluice, once a big north wind was blowing.
   As soon as fire made contact with the ships,
   They'd blaze alight at once.
DIKAIOPOLIS.   You damnable wretch,
   They'd blaze alight from a wick on a cockroach boat?*

[DIKAIOPOLIS *starts to assault* NIKARCHOS. *In the noisy struggle
that follows, the latter is gradually tied and bundled up like an item of
merchandise.*]

NIKARCHOS. I call for a witness!
DIKAIOPOLIS [*to a* SLAVE].   Do something to close his mouth!
[*To another* SLAVE] Give me some straw—I need to package
   him up
   And carry him like a pot, to avoid any breakage.

[*The* CHORUS *dances round the scene as the action proceeds; the whole
exchange with* DIKAIOPOLIS *is sung. Once the* INFORMER *has been fully
tied up, the* SLAVES *will help* DIKAIOPOLIS *to hang him upside down
from the* BOIOTIAN'*s shoulder-pole.*]

CHORUS. Tie up the merchandise all tight, old chap, for   *Strophe*
         our visitor here.
         Make sure it's safe for him to carry without any risk. 930
DIKAIOPOLIS. I'll take good care of this. It's still producing a
   jabbering noise.
  [*Striking*] It sounds like a pot that's cracked, a piece of junk.
CHORUS. What use will it be to him?
DIKAIOPOLIS. A multi-purpose vessel:
         A mixing-bowl for trouble, a mortar for lawsuits, a base
           for a lamp
         To expose corruption of magistrates, and a cup to stir
           things up!*

CHORUS. But how could anyone trust a vessel like this   *Antistrophe*
         to use at home?
         It continues to make an alarming amount of worrying
           noise.   940
DIKAIOPOLIS. The package is now secure, don't worry. There's no
   way it could break,
         Provided he's hung by his feet, head down, like this.*
CHORUS [*to* BOIOTIAN]. It's ready for you to carry.
BOIOTIAN. I'm going to reap a profit!
CHORUS. Well off you go, good friend, enjoy your harvest! Carry
         this man
         And take him wherever you want—an informer for all
           occasions!   950

DIKAIOPOLIS. That was quite a struggle to get the wretch tied up.
   So there's your pot, Boiotian, you're welcome to take it.
BOIOTIAN. Get your shoulder under this pole, Hismenias.
DIKAIOPOLIS. Just take great care as you carry him home with you.
   You're taking something foul, but it can't be helped.
   If you make a profit by taking this package away,
   You'll prosper, since there's plenty where this came from!

[*The* BOIOTIAN *and* HISMENIAS *depart with the packaged* INFORMER
on their shoulder-pole; the PIPE-PLAYERS *follow them off.* DIKAIOPO-
LIS, *with the help of his* SLAVES, *starts arranging for the Boiotian goods
he has obtained to be taken indoors. He is interrupted by the arrival of*
LAMACHOS's SLAVE *from one of the* eisodoi.]

SLAVE. Dikaiopolis!

DIKAIOPOLIS.   Well, what are you yelling for now?

SLAVE. I've been sent by Lamachos to give you a drachma   960
    In return for thrushes to celebrate the Choes,
    And a further three drachmas to buy a Kopaïc eel.*

DIKAIOPOLIS. What Lamachos is this who wants an eel?

SLAVE [*portentously*]. The fearsome one with an awesome Gorgon
        shield,
    On whose head there shake three large and shadowed crests.*

DIKAIOPOLIS. No chance I'd sell him an eel if he gave me his shield!
    His shaking crests deserve no more than salt-fish.*
    If he offers more bluster, I'll call the market officials.*

[LAMACHOS's SLAVE *exits empty-handed, while* DIKAIOPOLIS *glee-
fully returns to the task of taking all the Boiotian merchandise into
his house.*]

    I'll gather up all these goods that are now my own.
    Back inside 'on the wings of thrushes and blackbirds' I go.* [*Exits
        with* SLAVES]   970

CHORUS.   Did you see, all Athens, this shrewd and   *Strophe*
                hyper-wise man?
            His peace has brought him merchandise for further
                business,
            With useful domestic objects and food to gulp down
                warm.
            All the good things of life come to him of their own
                accord.*
            Never again will I welcome War inside my house,
            Or let him recline alongside me and sing the
                Harmodios song
            At a drinking party.* He's proved a drunken vandal!
            He came on a revel to those who enjoyed a nice
                life,   980
            Wrought utter havoc, smashed furniture, spilt the wine,
            Kept fighting despite repeated requests to stop,
            'Recline and drink, here take this cup of friendship.'
            This made him behave even worse. He set fire to the
                vine-poles

And violently spilt the wine from the vines we had
    tended.*

[DIKAIOPOLIS *appears briefly outside his house door to drop feathers
    from the birds he is cooking.*]

He's all aflutter for dinner! His pride is so   *Antistrophe*
    high!
These feathers he's dropped outside are proof of his
    lifestyle.
[*Dreamily*] O Reconciliation—companion of lovely Kypris and the
    gorgeous Graces—
Your face has a beauty I failed to notice before.   990
How I wish that Eros might join you and me in
    marriage,
Like the painted Eros I've seen with a garland of
    blossoms.*
No doubt you think I'm just a decrepit old man.
But I'm sure if I held you I'd manage to make it three
    times:*
The first time to lay out a lengthy row of grapevines,
Alongside that to plant young shoots of fig-trees,
And third, plant a cutting of vine-branch, old though
    I be.
All round my plot I'd bed down olive trees,
Getting oil that I'd rub on us both at the start of each
    month.*

[*A* HERALD *enters from one of the* eisodoi; *as he makes his announce-
    ment,* DIKAIOPOLIS *appears at his house door to listen.*]

HERALD. Attention please, you throngs! By ancestral custom   1000
    It's time, when the trumpet sounds, to drink from our wine-jugs.
    For the first to finish, a skin of . . . Ktesiphon.*
DIKAIOPOLIS [*calling in*]. My slaves, and all you women, no time for
    slacking!
    Get working! Take your cue from the herald's words!
    Get boiling, roasting, and turning the meat. Cook the hare
    Till it's thoroughly done. Prepare the garlands for feasting.
    I need some spits: I'll prepare the thrushes myself.

[SLAVES *come out of the house with braziers, etc. (compare 888 ff.) and a scene of busy cooking ensues.*]

CHORUS.	I envy your good planning, or rather good feasting.	*Strophe*
	It's on display before our eyes.	1010
DIKAIOPOLIS.	Just wait till you see the thrushes thoroughly roasted!	
CHORUS.	I suspect you're right about that as well!	
DIKAIOPOLIS.	Keep stirring the charcoal fire.	
CHORUS.	Did you hear how like a chef, with culinary fancy talk, He's ministering to his needs?	

[*Enter* DERKETES, *a farmer, wearing a white garment and walking in a way which betrays poor eyesight. Throughout the conversation which follows,* DIKAIOPOLIS *continues to monitor the cooking of the food.*]

DERKETES. O woe is me!
DIKAIOPOLIS.   By Herakles, who's this now?
DERKETES. An unhappy man.
DIKAIOPOLIS.   You can keep all that for yourself!
DERKETES. My dearest friend, you're the only one with a
    treaty,   1020
  So measure me out some peace—maybe just five years?
DIKAIOPOLIS. What's happened to you?
DERKETES.   I'm ruined: I've lost two oxen.
DIKAIOPOLIS. How come?
DERKETES.   The Boiotians stole them from me in Phyle.*
DIKAIOPOLIS [*sarcastically*]. A terrible fate! So why are you dressed
    in white?*
DERKETES. What's more, by Zeus, these oxen were my source
  Of endless dung.
DIKAIOPOLIS.   Then what do you want from me?
DERKETES. I've ruined my eyesight weeping for my oxen.
  If you care at all about Derketes of Phyle,*
[*Gesturing*] Anoint my eyes with the balm of peace at once.
DIKAIOPOLIS. I'm sorry, poor thing, I'm not a public doctor.*   1030
DERKETES. Please help, I beg you; I need to recover my oxen.
DIKAIOPOLIS. Can't help. Go and take your tears to Pittalos.*
DERKETES. I implore you, give me a single drop of peace:

Just put it inside this tube of reed I've brought.

DIKAIOPOLIS. Not even the tiniest droplet! Go and get lost!

DERKETES. Alas, alas, for my pair of working oxen. [*Trudges off*]

CHORUS.   This man's discovered a life of pleasure   *Antistrophe*
                         through peace.
                 He's no intention of sharing it.

DIKAIOPOLIS. Baste the sausage with honey. Keep grilling the
          cuttle-fish.   1040

CHORUS.   Did you hear his booming orders?

DIKAIOPOLIS. Keep roasting the strips of eel.

CHORUS.   You'll kill me with hunger, your neighbours too! The
                         smell's so strong
                 As you issue your instructions.

DIKAIOPOLIS [*inspecting*]. Keep roasting everything here to a nice
          brown finish.

[*Enter a* SLAVE *sent by an Athenian bridegroom: he carries some meat and
is accompanied by the* BRIDESMAID, *who carries an empty perfume bottle.*]

SLAVE. Dikaiopolis!

DIKAIOPOLIS.   And *now* who have we here?

SLAVE. A bridegroom's sent me here with meat for you
     From his wedding feast.

DIKAIOPOLIS.   Very kind, whoever he is!   1050

SLAVE. In return for the meat, and to keep him from military
          service,
     Since he wants to stay at home and keep on fucking,
     He asks for a cupful of peace in this perfume bottle.

DIKAIOPOLIS. Away, away with this meat! You can keep it all.
     I wouldn't pour out any peace for a thousand drachmas.
     But who's this woman who's with you?

SLAVE.   She's the bridesmaid:
     She's bringing a private message for you from the bride.

DIKAIOPOLIS. Right, what's this message of yours?

          [*The* BRIDESMAID *whispers in his ear.*]

                                        Good heavens, how funny
     To hear such a firm request from the bride herself:
     She wants the bridegroom's prick to remain at home!   1060

Bring out my wine of peace: she alone will have some,
Since she's a woman and not to blame for the war.

[*One of* DIKAIOPOLIS*'s* SLAVES *goes into the house and returns with a
jug of wine.* DIKAIOPOLIS *takes the perfume bottle from the bridegroom's*
SLAVE, *gives it to the* BRIDESMAID, *and pours some of the peace-wine
into it.*]

DIKAIOPOLIS. Hold up the perfume bottle like this, woman.
   Do you know what needs to be done? Instruct the bride
   That when they're enlisting troops to go on campaign,
   She should rub this wine on her husband's prick at night.

[*The* BRIDESMAID *and bridegroom's* SLAVE *depart.* DIKAIOPOLIS *proceeds to give instructions for his participation in the drinking competition
announced at 1000–2.*]

Take my peace-wine back inside. Bring out a ladle:
   I need it to pour some wine into the jugs.
LEADER [*paratragically*]. Lo, here comes one whose anxious
      eyebrows show
   He hastens hither to bring some grim report.   1070

[*While* DIKAIOPOLIS *is pouring out wine, the* HERALD *enters from one
side with great urgency: at his call,* LAMACHOS *appears from the stage
building's second door, which at this point takes on the identity of the
general's house. The tone is mock-grandiose.*]

HERALD. O toils and battles and Lamachos-es a plenty!*
LAMACHOS. Who clamours around my bronze-accoutred palace?
HERALD. The generals send you orders to leave today
   And go on campaign with all your tactics and crests.
   Your task's to wait in the snow and guard the passes:*
   For while the Choes and Chutroi were taking place,*
   Reports arrived of raiders from Boiotia. [*Exits*]
LAMACHOS. Alas! So many generals, yet so worthless!
   Outrageous I should miss the festival!
DIKAIOPOLIS [*mocking*]. Alas! Campaigns for warrior
      Lamachos!   1080
LAMACHOS. What a wretched life! And *you* now dare to mock me?
DIKAIOPOLIS. Do you want to fight, you monster? I've got more
   feathers!*

LAMACHOS. O woe! What a grievous message the herald brought
me!

DIKAIOPOLIS [*ironically*]. O woe! What message for *me* is this
runner bringing?

[*A* SLAVE *sent by the Priest of Dionysos comes running on from an
eisodos.*]

SLAVE. Dikaiopolis!

DIKAIOPOLIS. What is it?

SLAVE. Come quickly to dinner.
Bring along a basket of food and your wine-jug too.*
The Priest of Dionysos invites you to come.
You need to dash; you're holding up the dinner.
The preparations are fully complete for the meal:
The couches, tables, cushions, the rugs for draping, 1090
The garlands, perfume, nibbles—the prostitutes too;
The biscuits, cakes, the sesame loaves, the crispbreads,
The gorgeous dancing girls (Harmodios' type).*
Please hurry along.

LAMACHOS [*self-pityingly*]. My godforsaken life!

DIKAIOPOLIS. With a Gorgon on your shield, what else to expect?
[*To* SLAVES] Prepare to lock my house, and pack my dinner.

[*In what follows, the* SLAVES *of* LAMACHOS *and* DIKAIOPOLIS *rush in
and out of their masters' houses, on parallel tracks as it were, bringing out
various objects in accordance with their instructions.*]

LAMACHOS. Hey slave, bring out my soldier's knapsack for me.

DIKAIOPOLIS. Hey slave, bring out my dinner basket for me.

LAMACHOS. Bring out thyme-flavoured salt and onions too.*

DIKAIOPOLIS. And *I'll* have slices of fish—I can't stand
onions! 1100

LAMACHOS. Bring me a fig-leaf stuffed with rotting salt-fish.*

DIKAIOPOLIS. For me to cook, a fig-leaf full of beef-fat.*

LAMACHOS. Bring me the feathers to fasten on my helmet.

DIKAIOPOLIS. For me it's slices of dove and thrush-breast too.

LAMACHOS. How nice and white this ostrich feather looks.

DIKAIOPOLIS. How nice and brown this piece of dove-meat looks.

LAMACHOS. Just stop your scoffing, fellow, towards my weapons.

DIKAIOPOLIS. Just stop your envy, fellow, towards my thrush-breast.

LAMACHOS. Bring out the case that holds my triple crest.

DIKAIOPOLIS. Bring out the bowl with all my hare-meat in it.   1110

LAMACHOS. Have moths devoured the hairs of all my crests?

DIKAIOPOLIS. Shall I devour jugged hare before my dinner?

LAMACHOS. Stop saying things to me, impertinent fellow!

DIKAIOPOLIS. I *wasn't*—my slave and I were disagreeing.
[*To* SLAVE] Do you want to bet, with Lamachos to decide,
   What's more delicious, grasshoppers or roasted thrushes?

LAMACHOS. Such gross insults!

DIKAIOPOLIS [*to* SLAVE].   He clearly thinks grasshoppers.

LAMACHOS. Slave, take my spear from the wall and bring it out.

DIKAIOPOLIS. Slave, fetch my well-cooked sausage and bring
   it out.

LAMACHOS. Come, let me take the spear out from its case.   1120
   Here, slave, take hold of one end.

DIKAIOPOLIS.   Slave, hold the spit.

LAMACHOS. Bring out the frame on which my shield stands up.

DIKAIOPOLIS. Bring out the loaves which help to fill me up.

LAMACHOS [*pompously*]. Bring out my round and Gorgon-coated
   shield.

DIKAIOPOLIS. Pass me the round and cheese-encrusted cake.

LAMACHOS. Who can deny that this is sheer derision?

DIKAIOPOLIS. Who can deny flat cakes like this taste good?

LAMACHOS. Slave, polish my shield with oil: I see reflected
   An old man soon to face a cowardice charge.*

DIKAIOPOLIS. Pour on the honey. The old man standing here   1130
   Tells bugaboo Lamachos to go to hell.

LAMACHOS. Slave, fetch out here my breastplate for the war.

DIKAIOPOLIS. Slave, bring a wine-jug out to stiffen my spirit.

LAMACHOS. I'll fit this tight before I face the foe.

DIKAIOPOLIS. And I'll get tight when drinking at the party.*

LAMACHOS. Slave, tie my bedding securely in my shield.

DIKAIOPOLIS. Slave, pack the dinner securely in my basket.

LAMACHOS. I'll carry my military knapsack on my own.

DIKAIOPOLIS. I'll carry my cloak myself—I'm sauntering off.

LAMACHOS. Slave, pick up my shield and start to walk ahead.   1140
   It's snowing. Oh no! Such winter woes await me.

DIKAIOPOLIS. Pick up my dinner. Some heavy drinking awaits
   me.

[DIKAIOPOLIS *and* LAMACHOS *depart by opposite* eisodoi, *each accompanied by a* SLAVE *who carries their respective belongings. The* CHORUS *moves into formation.*]

[SECOND PARABASIS: 1143–73]

LEADER.   Farewell to both on your expeditions!
           How different the paths you're taking:
           For one, a night of garlanded drinking,
[*To* LAMACHOS] But for *you* keeping guard in the freezing cold,
           While the other falls gently asleep
           Alongside a gorgeous young girl
           While having his what-not massaged.

CHORUS.   Antimachos son of Spittle, foul poetaster,* *Strophe* 1150
           Let's put it bluntly: Zeus wipe him off the earth!
           As Lenaia *chorêgos* he sent poor me home unfed.
           So I'd like to watch when he's waiting for squid to be
               roasted,
           And it's sizzling, fresh from the sea, and ready to land
           On his table—but just as he reaches for it
           May a dog come and snatch it away!   1160

           May that first mishap be matched by   *Antistrophe*
               a second at night.
           While walking home with a fever, after a horse-ride,
           May a drunken Orestes deliver a blow to his head
           In a frenzied mugging. Then seeking a stone in the dark
           May he pick up a freshly laid turd! When he charges
               ahead   1170
           With this glistening missile, may his throw hit…Kratinos!*

[*From the* eisodos *by which* LAMACHOS *had departed, his* SLAVE *now re-enters. His demeanour is parodically redolent of a messenger bringing fateful news in tragedy.*]

SLAVE.   O attendants in the house of Lamachos,
          Heat up abundant water in a pot.
          Get bandages ready, together with a salve,
          And some pieces of wool to wrap around his ankle.

He was wounded by a stake while jumping a ditch,
Then twisted his ankle badly, quite out of joint,
And smashed his head on a rock as he fell to the ground,   1180
Thereby awaking the Gorgon on his shield.
When a braggart-buzzard's big feather fell from his helmet*
Onto the rocks, he exclaimed a grim lament:
'O gleaming eye of the sun, for the final time
I behold the light—my life now nears its end.'
These words just spoken, he fell in a ditch of water,
Then pulled himself out and confronted his troops running
      scared
As he drove back the raiders and warded them off with his spear.*
But here's the man himself. Open up the door!

[*A* SLAVE *appears from* LAMACHOS's *house with the medical supplies requested, just as* LAMACHOS *himself staggers on stage in a bedraggled state. A few moments later,* DIKAIOPOLIS *enters from the opposite* eiso-dos, *supported by a pair of naked* PROSTITUTES *and carrying his empty wine-jug; in his delirious state he does not notice* LAMACHOS *till 1205. The following exchange, to 1225, is mostly in sung form.*]

LAMACHOS. Aaaaaaaaaaaaaaargh! Aaaaaaaaaaaaaaargh!   1190
            Grievous, bone-chilling woes! O wretched me!
            I perish, smitten by an enemy spear.
            Yet even more distress I'd suffer
            If Dikaiopolis, seeing me wounded,
            Guffawed at my misfortune.
DIKAIOPOLIS. Aaaaaaaaaaaaaaargh! Aaaaaaaaaaaaaaargh!
            What gorgeous tits! So firm and quince-like!
            Give me sensuous kisses, my twin treasures,   1200
            With open mouths and sexy tonguing.
            I was first to drink my wine-jug dry.*
LAMACHOS. The wretched fate of my catastrophe!
            The stabs of pain from my wounds!
DIKAIOPOLIS. Ha! Ha! O greetings, Lamach-horsey!
LAMACHOS. Grievous my plight! Woeful my plight!
DIKAIOPOLIS [*to* PROSTITUTES]. Oo-oo, why these kisses? Oo-oo,
      why these nibbles?
LAMACHOS. O woe is me, for my doom-laden charge.   1210

DIKAIOPOLIS. Did someone try to *charge* you for wine at the
Choes?*

LAMACHOS. O god of healing, save me!

DIKAIOPOLIS. You've got the wrong god for the festival today!

LAMACHOS. Hold up my leg, hold up my leg—what pain!
Support me on your arms, o friends!

DIKAIOPOLIS. Hold up my prick, the two of you together.
Support it in your hands, my dears!

LAMACHOS. I'm feeling dizzy; my head struck a rock.
My eyesight's dark.

DIKAIOPOLIS. I want to go to bed with a large erection   1220
And fuck in the dark.

LAMACHOS. Take me off to Pittalos' surgery.*
Lift me with healing hands.

DIKAIOPOLIS. Take me to the judges. Where's the King Archon?
Give me the wineskin I've won.*

[*As* LAMACHOS's SLAVES *carry him off by one* eisodos, DIKAIOPOLIS
*approaches the front row of the audience, where someone hands him his
victor's wineskin, before swaggering off on the opposite side with the help
of the* PROSTITUTES *and followed by the cheering* CHORUS. *The final
lines of the play are chanted in recitative.*]

LAMACHOS. A spear has pierced right through my bones and
wracks my body with pain.

DIKAIOPOLIS. You see my empty wine-jug here. All hail the
brilliant victor!*

LEADER. All hail the brilliant victor, since that's what you ask, old
man!

DIKAIOPOLIS. What's more, I poured the wine unmixed and
drained it in one draught.*

LEADER. All hail the brilliant victor! Good fellow, now claim your
wineskin prize.   1230

DIKAIOPOLIS. Then follow me chanting endlessly, 'All hail the
brilliant victor!'

LEADER. We'll follow indeed in celebration, to hail the brilliant victor.
All hail the brilliant victor, and the wineskin that he
carries!

[*Exit all.*]

KNIGHTS

INTRODUCTION

EVEN by Aristophanic standards, *Knights* is a work of comic extremes. It presents a remorseless satire of populist democratic politics in the Athens of the 420s, focusing in glaring close-up on the supposedly most shameless exponent of such populism, Kleon, who is here allegorized (and therefore fictionalized) as an unspeakably nasty Paphlagonian slave. The work's satirical themes naturally have a strong resonance for modern readers preoccupied with populism in their own political world. There are, however, fundamental difficulties in the way of establishing a steady historical perspective on the comedy's wildly hyperbolic dynamics. For one thing, *Knights* has the densest linguistic texture of all the surviving plays of Aristophanes, a texture clotted with elaborate metaphor and imagery—from domains including those of food, leather-working, sailing, wrestling, and sex— and with large numbers of comic coinages, to an extent which makes sustained reading or hearing highly demanding. But those demands must, in part, have existed for the original audience as well. *Knights'* relentless concern with the (alleged) vulgarity, corruption, and viciousness of contemporary Athenian politics is embedded in a text of challengingly sophisticated detail—one of the reasons why, in the parabasis of *Clouds*, Aristophanes could refer back to *Knights* as an exemplification of his commitment to comic values of originality and cleverness.[1] Despite its subject-matter, *Knights* employs blatantly colloquial crudity (in particular, the primary anatomical, scatological, and sexual obscenities) in relatively few places. Instead, most of its depiction of the debasement of political life by unscrupulous competition for populist success is paradoxically embodied in a linguistic fabric of intricate poetic inventiveness, a fact impossible to convey successfully in a modern translation. The resulting disparity— between, so to speak, the satirical headlines and the poetic small print, or between the idea of foul-mouthed coarseness and its conversion into verbal creativity—necessarily complicates our attempts to attune

---

[1] See *Clouds* 545–50, though the passage is itself comically disingenuous in claiming that *Knights* had 'knocked Kleon flat' by a satirical blow to the 'belly' (a wrestling image): Kleon's political dominance was unaffected by Aristophanes' play.

ourselves to the comedy's tone and ethos. However trenchant the
satire, the work in its totality is anything but simple.

A further complication of the work's extravagantly satirical nature
arises from a consideration which, to some degree, affects all conceptions of political populism, our own included. If populism is a bad
thing, is that the fault of politicians or the people—or both? *Knights*
brings this question starkly into the foreground by making the
Athenian demos (the collective citizen body) into a personified character, old man Demos.[2] The play starts, and most of it is set, outside
Demos's own house, with the politicians as his 'slaves' locked in devious rivalry for his favour and desperate to avoid punishment at
his hands. This allegorical framework, which was not original with
Aristophanes but is sustained by him with exceptional imaginative
intensity, has built into it the double-edged nature of populism in
a democratic context, particularly a direct democracy of the Athenian
type. At the level of democratic discourse, the model of master and
servants is seemingly clear-cut. But in a comic version of an Athenian
household, slaves can all too easily be imagined as scheming figures
with access to the resources of the domestic economy—the food,
drink, and clothing which the householder needs for basic sustenance
and well-being—and consequently as having scope for manipulative
and dishonest power, not least theft. *Knights* makes much of the
ambiguities of the master-and-servants allegory of democracy, though
it also 'contaminates' it by allowing the status of politicians to
oscillate between that of slaves and common tradesmen (the latter
symbolic both of social vulgarity and of the reduction of politics to
the level of disreputable financial machinations). But does the play
yield a coherent satirical critique of who really holds power in contemporary Athenian democracy? As we shall see, Aristophanes goes
out of his way to make a conundrum out of the question whether
Demos is a dupe of the politicians or someone ultimately capable
of imposing his own will on them. I shall return to that conundrum
at the end of this Introduction, but we should bear in mind
throughout that it is asking a great deal of an individual comedy,
and especially one which revels in so many kinds of exaggeration

---

[2] Demos did exist in Athens as a (rare) personal name: see *W*. 98, with Plato, *Gorgias*
481d–e for a punning comparison between one such individual and populist democratic
politics.

and excess, to solve a problem which may be inescapable in all forms of democracy.

The plot-structure of *Knights* is more subtle than may appear at first sight. The way in which it weaves together its various strands will repay careful analysis. The core of the play consists of a series of aggressive and vituperative confrontations between (servile/political) rivals for the favour of Demos, the allegorized people of Athens. But on closer inspection the basis and development of the contest contain a number of significant convolutions. We start with a domestic scenario involving the resentment of a pair of Demos's slaves (who may have flickering allegorical associations with actual political figures but are not consistently allegorized)[3] over the vile 'new' Paphlagonian slave (whose trade is that of a 'tanner', thereby making him an unmistakable allegory of the leading politician Kleon) who is Demos's current favourite and exploits that position to manipulate his master. After the pair of slaves have despairingly considered running away or even killing themselves, they discover a powerful piece of information, that Paphlagon has been keeping secret an oracle which predicts his own eventual downfall to one whose trade is even lower on the social scale than his own, namely a sausage-seller. The Sausage-Seller, however (whose 'actual' name will not be revealed for more than another thousand lines), soon turns out to be a low-grade Athenian citizen, not a slave—a fact which introduces an element of comic instability into the play's allegorical terms of reference and allows the idea of competition between politicians from ill-bred commercial backgrounds to predominate over, though never entirely to erase, the 'household slaves' scenario for much of the work. As for the oracular information itself, Aristophanes keeps it in the picture just long enough for the Sausage-Seller to be persuaded that there is divine encouragement (with a promise of greatness) for his entry into political life, but then suppresses it altogether until it can return with comically special force at the final stage of Paphlagon's downfall (see below).

If the initial allegory of *Knights* has, with a characteristically Aristophanic blurring of dramatic frames, been already compromised

---

[3] There has been a longstanding but inconclusive scholarly debate on the relation of the two slaves to the generals Demosthenes and Nikias: see, in brief, my notes on *Knights* 55 and 358.

in the play's prologue, a further step in that direction is taken with the theatrical entrance (i.e. the parodos) of the chorus which gives the work its title. The parodos is always a theatrically fundamental moment in the establishment of an Aristophanic comedy's 'world'. In the present case, the Knights, i.e. the Athenian cavalry corps (but the term 'Knights' is too hallowed by longstanding convention to be dispensed with), have no place at all within the framework of the domestic allegory. As a distinctive component of Athens' military forces, as well as representatives of a socio-economic stratum of the citizenry, the Knights belong to the literal world of Athenian society and politics. As such, they are appealed to as allies in the campaign to back the Sausage-Seller as a new rival to Paphlagon qua dominant demagogue, or 'leader of the people', on the current Athenian political scene. (I leave aside for now the blatant anomaly that in pursuit of their hatred for Paphlagon-Kleon the Knights are supposedly happy to support a demagogue even 'worse' than him.) In fact, the chorus's entrance, which is given a theatrically flamboyant flourish[4] by being staged as an equestrian manoeuvre (though one which sets up something more like a mugging of Paphlagon), serves to push the original allegory into the background for some time. We are now faced with a level of satirical significance that deals, however grotesquely and hyperbolically, with central factors in Athenian politics: individual figures competing for influence and power; their groups of supporters; the citizenry as a collective entity; and the institutions (Council, Assembly, law-courts) in which relations between leaders and people work themselves out.

It is this orientation which is maintained until the appearance of Demos from his house around halfway through the play. The action up to that point is organized in the following sequence: first, the parodos itself (242–302), already noted, where physical violence against Paphlagon is coupled with a slanging match that broaches many of the motifs of political invective which will run through the comedy as a whole; second, the first of the play's two agons or set-piece debates

---

[4] It remains uncertain how, if at all, the chorus's horses were represented: certainly not by real animals, but that leaves several possibilities open: some choreuts costumed as horses and others 'riding' on their backs (for this, see the black-figure vase illustrated in e.g. Rusten, *The Birth of Comedy*, 57); some form of hobbyhorses; costuming of all the choreuts with a mixture of human and equine features; or simply the use of choreographed movements to mimic horse-riding.

(303–460), which is 'rigged' to give an increasingly self-confident Sausage-Seller an advantage (he and Paphlagon speak equal numbers of lines in the first half, but the Sausage-Seller has half as many again as his rival in the second); third, a short scene (461–97) in which Paphlagon accuses his opponents of a conspiracy and exits to report the matter to the Council, soon followed by the Sausage-Seller, who is now prepared for a contest that is compared both to a wrestling bout and to a cock-fight; fourth, and after the 'interval' of the parabasis, a scene (611–82) in which the Sausage-Seller returns to recount how he got the better of Paphlagon in the Council by turning his own rhetorical techniques against him, in this case effectively bribing the Councillors with the promise of cheap and even free food, something which interests them much more than matters of war and peace; fifth, the scene (691–755) in which, after the return of a now furious Paphlagon and yet another exchange of over-the-top abuse, the old man Demos himself, 'the people' personified, at last makes his appearance (728), brought out of his house by the noisy wrangling outside his door.

Demos's entry simultaneously reactivates the original domestic allegory *and* shifts the institutional setting of the political conflict on the 'literal' level from the Council to the Assembly, whose meeting (see 746–51) notionally and loosely takes place in the play's second agon (756–942).[5] Although Aristophanes, as we have seen, is happy to allow allegorical and non-allegorical levels of meaning to coexist without being neatly aligned, this central juncture in the play nonetheless introduces a new element which helps to hold the two together. This is the motif, which we know belonged to contemporary democratic discourse, of being a passionate 'lover' of the city and/or its people.[6] Paphlagon introduces this as soon as Demos comes out of his house ('It's my fondness, Demos, for you—because I'm your lover', 732) and the Sausage-Seller, as with so much else, echoes it at once ('I'm a rival of his to be your lover', 733). This erotic metaphor helps to produce an overlap between the domestic allegory, where it

---

[5] 'Notionally', because the text makes no reference to the actual procedures of an Assembly meeting: contrast this with the various procedural and related details incorporated in the Assembly meeting at *A*. 43–173 or in the women's rehearsal for the Assembly at *AW* 128–240.

[6] See note on *Knights* 732, including the matching motif of accusing one's enemies of unpatriotically 'hating' the city or people.

resonates with the idea of pandering flatteringly to all of Demos's needs (and, equally, aiming to be his 'favourite' slave), and the recognizable realm of contemporary political rhetoric, where it functions as a rhetorically florid way of affirming pure devotion to the best interests of the people and city.

The implications of the 'love(r) of the people' motif remain fundamental to the remainder of the play, right up to the point in the final scene at which the Sausage-Seller gets the by then reformed Demos to recognize that in future he must *repudiate*, as a deceptive ploy, any such affirmations made by individual politicians (1340–9). In the second agon (756–942), and beyond, the motif is translated, on the allegorical level, into the two rivals' comically reductive concern to offer Demos the best creature comforts (comfortable cushions, new footwear, tasty food). The second agon is dominated even more markedly than the first by the Sausage-Seller; he has almost exactly twice as many lines as his rival. But the debate also involves a double pivot in the movement of the plot. Towards the end of its first half, Demos explicitly rebuts Paphlagon's protestations of love for him and expresses for the first time his belief that Paphlagon has deceived him (821–2): the tide has started to turn. Shortly before this, there has been another significant twist in the thematics of the contest. Increasingly under pressure from his opponent, Paphlagon makes an appeal to oracles which, he claims, promise future panhellenic rule for Demos, i.e. an even larger and more emphatic empire for Athens (797 ff.). The Sausage-Seller retorts a few lines later, in a way which is hard to interpret precisely, that Paphlagon's use of oracles helps to create divisions among Athenian citizens (818).[7]

Mention had been made in the prologue of Paphlagon's penchant for oracles (61); it was when sent to steal these from him (109–11) that one of the slaves had discovered the one particular oracle which Paphlagon was keeping secret because of its reference to his own downfall (116 ff.). But it is not till this point in the second agon that Paphlagon employs an appeal to oracles as a political tactic. That prepares the way, however, for the next stage of the contest, dominated precisely by the politics of oracles, and beyond that, after a further

---

[7] That Kleon could be seen as a divisive figure (cf. the dream at *Wasps* 39–41) is an inference difficult to avoid; but that might be true of any leader in challenging times: compare the bitterly divided reactions to the consequences of Perikles' war policy in 431 and later at Thucydides 2.21.3–22.1, 59.1–3, 65.1–2.

deferral (to see which rival can supply Demos with the best food), the existence of the 'downfall' oracle itself will eventually play a climactic role in the resolution of the contest. The double-sided theme of oracles—representing both a supposed weapon in Paphlagon's armoury and a source of 'information' pointing to his downfall—is thus woven into the plot of *Knights* with a sort of comically teasing irregularity: it is broached in the prologue, then suppressed (or left hanging) for over half the play, before moving right into the foreground of the contest in the sustained exchange of oracles at 997–1110 (a scene prompted by Paphlagon's desperation at 960 ff. but hammering some of the final nails into his coffin), until, after the tying together of other strands, the 'downfall' oracle itself is fulfilled in a moment of conclusive revelation and dénouement at 1229–52. In these latter lines, despite being already defeated by his rival, and stripped of the appurtenances of his former stewardship (the ring of Demos, 947 ff., and the wreath which signifies his prominence as a speaker in the Assembly, 1227–8, 1250), Paphlagon nonetheless needs to satisfy himself that the conditions of his private oracle have been truly fulfilled. As he poses a series of questions to the Sausage-Seller (about two stages of his education, his trade, and its location), his speech contains clear paratragic markers, including three adaptations of lines from Euripides. For modern readers, the scene may be reminiscent of Oedipus's fateful interrogation of the herdsman at Sophokles, *Oedipus Tyrannus* 1121–85, though there is no reason to suppose that Aristophanes had that scene particularly in mind; he could easily have known other tragedies too in which an oracle's fulfilment was established through a sequence of questions.

I shall return in due course to the subject of oracles as one satirical theme among many in *Knights*; my comments above have drawn attention to the double role of oracles in the plot design of the play. As a final observation on this design, it needs to be emphasized that right up to the end of the scene in which Paphlagon recognizes his own downfall there is no real warning of the extra, surprising twist which is still to be given to the plot after the second parabasis.[8] Ever since the prologue, it has been a premise of the action that Paphlagon can

---

[8] Retrospectively one can see Demos's request to the Sausage-Seller to 're-educate' him at 1099 as a kind of clue as to what is to come; but a spectator would need to be near-clairvoyant to infer from this momentary hint what lies in store in the play's final scene.

and will be overcome only by someone even 'more disgusting' (134) than himself. The Sausage-Seller fits this bill not just in virtue of his extremely low-grade occupation but also because, as the action unfolds, he shows himself fully equipped to match and then outdo all the vulgar and vile traits of Paphlagon. This makes it, on one level, transparently ironic when, immediately after being confirmed as Demos's new steward and favourite, the Sausage-Seller exits the stage before the second parabasis with these lines:

> I promise, Demos, I'll be your faithful servant.
> You'll soon agree you've never seen anyone else
> Who's done more public good for the city of Gawpers.
>
> (1261–3)

Everything here is only too obviously an echo and *reprise* of Paphlagon's own demagogic ploys and deceptions, off-set by the characteristically Aristophanic joke-technique of a piece of self-betraying derision in the replacement of 'Athenians' by 'Gawpers' (i.e. gullible democratic audiences).

Right up to this point, then, the audience has no way of anticipating what will happen in the final scene (1316–1408), where it turns out that the Sausage-Seller, or Agorakritos as he is now revealed to be (1257), is no longer to be the latest in an ever-declining series of demagogues, but instead a kind of redeemer of Demos who has restored him to his pristine 'self' (defined by the glory days of the Persian Wars, especially the Athenian victory at Marathon: 1334) and has ensured that he will never again yield naively to the flattery of corrupt politicians. *Knights* is one of three surviving Aristophanic plays which end with a kind of sting in the tail or a 'reversal' (what Aristotle's *Poetics* later calls a *peripeteia*) in the direction of the plot: the others are *Clouds*, where Strepsiades suddenly decides on revenge against Sokrates, and *Frogs*, where Dionysos decides to take back Aischylos from Hades instead of, as he originally intended, Euripides.[9] But anyone inclined to assume that this final scene convincingly resolves all the issues raised by the play is in danger of succumbing to a comic illusion. I have already noted the deep irony that Agorakritos now makes Demos repudiate the very same type of demagogic blandishments

---

[9] See *C.* 1464 ff. and *F.* 1467 ff., with my Introductions to both plays in *Frogs and Other Plays* for discussion of the difficulty of making simple sense of either ending. For the Aristotelian term *peripeteia*, see esp. *Poetics* 11.1452a22–9.

that the Sausage-Seller himself had used as recently as the end of the previous scene (see 1261–3 with 1340–9). It is a related irony that the reformed figure of Demos is celebrated by the chorus in terms which elsewhere in Aristophanes are themselves exposed as tropes of rhetorical trickery.[10] A further anomaly is that Demos is now presented, in certain respects, less as a representative of the general 'demotic' citizenry than a parodic version of an old-fashioned but rich Athenian: he wears the sort of cicada-brooch in his hair (1331) that Thucydides specifically tells us was a fad of some wealthy citizens, and he is given a slave to walk round carrying a folding chair for him (1384–6), both details redolent of a luxurious life-style. On top of this, the finale offers a farrago of ideas—reducing the system of public pay; ensuring that sailors are paid on time; preventing individuals from evading military service; weaning young men off rhetoric and politics and instead sending them off to hunt; bringing about peace—which animate the spirit of 'back to the good old days' but hardly amount to a politically meaningful agenda in the circumstances of the mid-420s.

Any view of the conclusion of *Knights* depends ultimately, however, on a reading of the play as a whole. Having provided above a synopsis of the work's plot-construction, I want now to examine in a little more detail the main satirical threads, many of them touched on already, which run through the fabric of the work and lend it the character of a relentless assault on the current democratic politics of populism. These threads are connected, and frequently tangled, in a variety of ways. By attempting to separate them out analytically, with brief comments on what is at stake under each heading, it will be possible to appreciate not just how densely packed Aristophanes makes the satirical texture of *Knights*, but also how satire is itself a manipulative mode of comedy which often depends on creating an overall impression that conceals its underlying intricacies.

Base Origins

Within the allegorization of politicians as slaves, Paphlagon is called 'new(ly purchased)' (2); the motif recurs at 43–4. This

---

[10] See the adjectives in line 1329 with my note on *Acharnians* 637–9, where the same words are mocked by Dikaiopolis as belonging to the repertoire of deceptive rhetorical flattery to which the Athenian demos all too easily falls victim.

detail, which self-evidently conveys the idea of Kleon as an upstart, blurs into the more pervasive image of Paphlagon as a (citizen) tanner (44, 47, and passim), which is itself aligned with a satirically inflected narrative of Athenian politics as on a downward decline into an era of 'tradesmen' politicians—products of the Agora (e.g. 181, 218, 293–7, 636, 1245 ff.)—whose nadir will be the political leadership of a sausage-seller (129–44). We know that this narrative became eventually well established in some quarters: it is spelt out, for instance, in the Aristotelian *Constitution of the Athenians*, ch. 28 (whose sources may have included comedy itself), where the death of Perikles is claimed to have marked a turning-point, with democratic leaders now being taken for the first time from people 'not well-regarded among respectable [i.e. wealthier] citizens'.[11] There is little doubt that the last quarter of the fifth century did see the emergence of a number of prominent politicians who were not members of the traditional aristocracy. But the picture was not simple, in part because aristocratic credentials and commercial wealth were not mutually exclusive, and in part because we have scanty information about the financial resources of most Athenian politicians prior to the Peloponnesian War. For our purposes it is enough to note that Kleon himself did in fact have inherited wealth and status. Kleon's father, Kleainetos, was involved in high-status cultural activity in 460–459,[12] presumably employing the profits of the family's tanning business. It is even conceivable, as asserted by some ancient scholars, that Kleon was originally one of the cavalry himself but withdrew from the group as a result of some sort of dispute. *Knights*' picture of Paphlagon is, therefore, an exercise in the crude distortion of social and economic facts for the purposes of satirical stereotyping: Old Comedy revels in grotesque exaggeration; it is the very reverse of a reliable historical source of information. It is worth adding that Thucydides' famous contrast between Perikles and his successors makes nothing at all of the latter's supposedly inferior social background; indeed, his prime exhibit of the errors made by those successors, the Sicilian expedition

---

[11] Kleon's career in fact overlapped with that of Perikles (a fact suppressed by Thucydides), though by how much we cannot say: Perikles is mocked as under attack from 'fiery/fierce Kleon' in the comic poet Hermippos fr. 47 (from *c.*430?).

[12] See my note on *Knights* 574–5.

of 415–413, was a venture strongly associated with Alkibiades, a blue-blood aristocrat.[13]

Flattery and Deception

Paphlagon is an adept flatterer of Demos, winning him over (for his own corrupt purposes) by tending solicitously to the old man's needs (while cheating him behind his back): the point is introduced emphatically at 46–54 and is kept in view throughout, not least in the allegorical form of providing Demos with food, drink, and creature comforts. All such behaviour is treated as fundamentally deceptive: the language and imagery of deception, including the gullibility of Demos (e.g. 62, 396, 1115–17), abound (e.g. 48, 633, 809, 1103, 1224). The political idiom, as noted above, of proclaiming oneself a passionate 'lover' of the city/people also belongs here (but see below). This whole dimension of the play represents, at its most cynical, the core critique of populism: individual politicians aim to gratify the wishes of 'the people', replacing well-founded policy with crude appeals to the lowest form of (economic) self-interest which serve at the same time to mask their own ambitions.[14] *Knights* was created at a time when such judgements of contemporary democracy had some currency. Thucydides appeals to a related idea of populism when he contrasts what he deems to have been the patrician skills of Perikles, who was even prepared to contradict the views of the majority, with the tendency of his successors, in their rivalry for political supremacy, to pander to the pleasure of the demos in every way (2.65.8–10). But Thucydides also provides a key piece of evidence that any view of Kleon as an out-and-out populist is likely to be a simplification: in the notorious Mytilenean debate of 427, Kleon is shown doing precisely what Thucydides had identified as a feature of Perikles' leadership, i.e. resisting a large wave of opinion in the Assembly (and, indeed, being defeated in the second debate). The speech put in Kleon's mouth by Thucydides on this occasion actually begins with a resounding

---

[13] See Thucydides 2.65.10–13; there is also no aspersion on Kleon's social background, despite the historian's evident animus towards him, in the comments on him at 3.36.6, 4.21.3, 4.28.5, 5.16.1.

[14] This is the same populist model as characterized by Socrates at Plato, *Gorgias* 502d–3a. Note also the idea of the demagogue as 'flatterer of the people' at Aristotle, *Politics* 5.11, 1313b40–1; cf. n. 35 below.

criticism of democracy, as 'incapable of ruling over others', and proceeds to make other trenchant complaints about tendencies of democratic decision-making.[15] It is true that in this same context there is
a hint of a populist streak in Kleon's statement of preference for
'ordinary' over 'sophisticated' citizens in the making of democratic
decisions (3.37.3). But even that is not a decisive difference between
the Thucydidean depiction of Perikles and Kleon,[16] to which we must
add the important fact that in Thucydides it is Perikles himself who
makes most prominent use of the trope of being a 'lover' of the city.[17]

Stridency and Slander

Knights depicts Paphlagon/Kleon as having 'the voice of a deafening
torrent' (137), a 'loathsome voice' (218). 'Strident shouts' (274) are
alleged to be his characteristic mode of public utterance, and verbs of
yelling, shrieking, etc. are prominent in the contest (e.g. 256, 285–7,
304–11, 628, 863, 1018; cf. *Peace* 313–14). The Paphlagonian identity
is itself resonant in this regard, since it puns on a verb, *paphlazein*
(used in line 919), which means 'bluster' and 'splutter'. But the point
is evidently not just a matter of volume or cacophony: it is a marker,
rather, of nasty aggressiveness. Paphlagon's repulsive voice is the
instrument with which, in particular, he 'slanders' others. His 'slanderous ways' are mentioned near the start of the play (7) and referred
to frequently in what follows (45, 64, 288, 486–96); the Sausage-
Seller, aiming to beat his opponent at his own game, resorts to the
same technique (711, cf. 810). The Greek terminology in question
(noun *diabolê*, verb *diaballein*) can cover a number of things, but it
centres on aggressive denigration and ad hominem rhetorical attacks,
including false accusations. In a sense, almost the entire contest
between Paphlagon and the Sausage-Seller involves the tone and
ethos of 'slander' at its most extreme, especially in the form of vicious
abuse and mud-slinging (delivered, moreover, at a comically heightened shouting pitch): it is this, more than anything else, which gives

---

[15] See Thucydides 3.37, where Kleon also ruthlessly calls the Athenian empire a 'tyranny', exactly as the Thucydidean Perikles does (2.63.2), and further resembles the latter
in asserting his own steadfastness of views (3.38.1, cf. Perikles at 2.61.2).

[16] See Thucydides 2.43.1, where Perikles hints that Athenians in general know certain
things just as well as politicians who might make lengthy speeches on the subject.

[17] Thucydides 2.43.1 (of citizens in general), 60.5 (of Perikles himself).

Knights its scabrous atmosphere of personal invective between the (would-be) leaders of the demos.

It is very likely that the real Kleon was perceived, by his critics at any rate, as a practised exponent of a style of rhetoric and politics marked by slanderous tendencies: Thucydides makes Kleon's opponent in the Mytilenean debate, Diodotos, imply this point (3.42.2), his own description of Kleon as the 'most aggressive' of politicians (3.36.6) points in the same direction, and he explicitly cites slander as a hallmark of Kleon's both during the Pylos episode (4.27.4) and when recording his death (5.16.1).[18] Aristophanes may have felt himself the personal victim of this slanderous style, if the references to Kleon's attack on him after *Babylonians* in 426 are authentic in this respect.[19] It would certainly be preposterous to doubt that the historical Kleon cultivated a rhetorical vehemence which included direct attacks on rivals and opponents. We know, moreover, that with the passage of time this factor coloured his lasting reputation. But when the Aristotelian *Constitution of the Athenians* (28.3), written almost a century after Kleon's death, describes him as having been the first ever Athenian politician who 'shouted and engaged in abuse' in the Assembly, can we possibly believe that? Hardly. Violently ad hominem rhetoric was an age-old resource of Greek rhetoric: this is spectacularly illustrated by the earliest surviving image of public debate in Greek culture, in the first book of the *Iliad*, where Achilles in particular resorts to savage character-assassination of Agamemnon (esp. 1.225–31). This part of the rhetorical spectrum was not a constant in all times and places; Kleon may have resorted to it more than most. But we know that acoustic conditions in the Assembly, typically with an audience of some thousands and with ample scope for heckling (cf. *Acharnians* 38),[20] could not have been coped with by anyone lacking a robust voice ('shouting' is what your enemies call it). Moreover, Thucydides, despite his animosity, was forced to admit that Kleon was an accomplished orator who could command impressive powers

---

[18] Note, however, that Thucydides does not regard such things as peculiar to Kleon: see e.g. 2.65.11, where he attributes slanderous rivalries to political leaders in Athens at the time of the Sicilian expedition of 415–413.

[19] See *Acharnians* 380, 502, and cf. 630, with my Introduction to that play.

[20] For noise levels in the Assembly, note Thucydides' account of heckling and shouting in the Pylos debate at 4.28.1–3; cf. the general characterization of noise in various public gatherings at Plato, *Republic* 6.492b.

of persuasion.[21] *Knights*, on the other hand, satirically exaggerates and distorts matters by making Paphlagon's cacophonous slanderousness an invariable and irredeemably vile trait, debasing it to something which will be confined in future to slanging-matches with prostitutes in the 'red light' district near the city's gates (1400). Satire easily shades into grotesque caricature.

Intimidation and Agitation

Paphlagon/Kleon is a fearsome figure: he intimidates other politicians (66) and both rich and poor are scared of him (223–4). This goes together with the larger impression of someone who constantly churns or stirs things up, creating a sense of upheaval and agitation: see e.g. 363, 692, and 864–7, the latter with an elaborate simile of eel-fishers who stir up the mud at the bottom of water to catch their prey. We might also include here the idea of whipping up a sense of political urgency by accusing others of 'conspiracy': this is the first thing Paphlagon does at his entry (236–8), and the motif recurs with some frequency (257, 452, 475–9, 628, 862–3). But fear of political conspiracy was a common if not constant factor in Athenian politics (and in many other Greek cities as well), all the more so during a major war with Sparta, itself an oligarchic state and a supporter of oligarchies elsewhere; a few years later, *Wasps* 487–507 depicts conspiracy theories (aimed there at individuals and therefore citing 'tyranny') as a sort of current neurosis. The war would indeed in the long run produce two (short-lived) oligarchic revolutions in Athens, in 411–410 and 404–403. We have no way of knowing whether the historical Kleon strongly exploited fear of political conspiracy; for what it is worth, Thucydides 3.37.2 makes Kleon stress the *opposite*, i.e. the lack of such suspicions in Athenian society. But if he did, it seems likely that he was partly responding to a heightened level of war-time anxiety in this regard.

---

[21] When Thucydides describes Kleon as the 'most persuasive' orator of his time at 3.36.6, the combination with 'most aggressive' makes interpretation delicate, but it is certain at least that Kleon is being treated as someone who could do more than simply shout abuse; Thucydides repeats the description 'most persuasive' at 4.21.3, and it is therefore all the more telling that *Knights* itself incorporates the same perception in passing (629).

Venality

Paphlagon is financially corrupt through-and-through: a kleptocrat. Taking bribes is his universal practice (402–3), whether from his political rivals (66) or from Athens' allied cities (e.g. 802, 1197; but both 438 and 834 may be absurd inversions of the 'truth'); equally, he accuses others of bribery (442–3) and, when under pressure, *offers* bribes himself (439, cf. 472–3). He is likewise characterized, in sweeping terms, as a thief or robber (e.g. 137, 205, 248, 1218–26); he himself makes the same charge against his rival (435–6). We have no way of knowing how much financial corruption really existed among politicians and officials in classical Athens, but the *idea* and suspicion of venality was a common element in the competitive discourse of democratic politics and in the (cynical) assumptions of observers.[22] While making Paphlagon the embodiment of corruption, *Knights* nonetheless plays with the idea that such things are part-and-parcel of political life (e.g. 176, 1127, 1147). When Thucydides claims that Perikles was 'transparently incorruptible' (2.65.8), he clearly means this to be highly exceptional; even so, the historian may have deliberately suppressed charges to the contrary, if the separate evidence of Plato, *Gorgias* 516a and Plutarch, *Perikles* 32.2 can be trusted. We can legitimately doubt whether *Knights* conveys a seriously credible suggestion that Kleon was mired in more corruption than others: its pervasive imputation of venality is an inescapable concomitant of its depiction of political power.[23]

Jury Pay

The initial description of Paphlagon's ceaseless pandering to Demos's comforts includes an allegorical reference to the former's winning of popularity by proposing that the courts should sometimes be allowed to close early, though without reducing the jurors' daily rate of state pay (*misthos*), three obols. Later passages reinforce this picture of the

---

[22] For examples of the assumption that politicians or office-holders engage in financial corruption, see Thucydides 2.65.7 (political leaders after Perikles were motivated by personal gain), Euripides, *Suppliants* 415, Lysias 19.49, Xenophon, *Memorabilia* 2.6.24, Hypereides, *Demosthenes* 25. Thucydides 3.38.2 makes Kleon brandish a general suggestion of corruption on the part of other speakers.

[23] Compare *Wasps* 665–7 for the idea that all populist politicians are venal; note also *Wasps* 554.

populist symbiosis between Paphlagon/Kleon and the substantial
body of Athenians (six thousand of them) who were registered annually on the roster of jurors or dikasts: see 255–6, 798–800, 804–7,
904–5, 1019. We know that Kleon himself had proposed the increase
of dikastic pay from two to three obols in 425, just the year before
Knights. Lines 805–7 in particular suggest that this could be perceived, or perhaps had actually been advanced, as a means of helping
to compensate many poorer citizens for the loss of livelihood they had
incurred because of the pressure to leave the land and live within the
city walls during the early years of the Peloponnesian War.[24] But there
is a larger point to bear in mind. The scale of the Athenian legal system, as developed in the middle of the fifth century, required large
numbers of citizens to be prepared to serve as jurors; this would
hardly have been feasible without dikastic pay, which was introduced
on the proposal of Perikles in the 450s or possibly even 460s. In the
circumstances of war, the increase in jury pay must have made sense
as a way of maintaining the system as well as providing some financial
support to a large number of ordinary citizens. But its connection
with Kleon gave a handle to those who took the view that he was
manipulating the matter for his own benefit by creating a quid pro
quo relationship with Athenian jurors, turning the latter into the core
of his political 'base'. *Knights* reflects that view and *Wasps* will move it
into the very centre of its satirical perspective, converting Kleon into
the sole protector of jurors as a kind of social class (which they were
not). But it remains hard to see that the system of dikastic pay actually
gave Kleon any concrete advantage over other politicians in specific
situations. We should note that *Knights* 1352 implies that justifying
expenditure of the city's wealth on 'state pay' was not something
exclusive to Kleon.

Oracles

My earlier analysis of the plot-structure of *Knights* has already traced
the theme of oracles in its double function as (i) a resource exploited
by Paphlagon to manipulate the beliefs and hopes of Demos (especially

---

[24] See the Introduction to *Acharnians* for this aspect of the war. By the time of *Knights*,
some displaced Athenians had returned to their rural properties, but many had not (as
Knights 805 itself indicates); compare *Peace* for a fundamental and symbolic sense that
only ending the war would allow a full return to the countryside.

61, 110, 797 ff., 818, 961 ff., 997 ff.), and (ii) a dramatic device by which to mark both the expectation and the eventual realization of Paphlagon's downfall (125 ff., 1229 ff.). Only (i) is relevant to the question of how far Aristophanes' satirical designs respond to, or how far they invent and distort, features of the historical figure of Kleon. Here the 'facts' are easy to state. First, we know that oracles were appealed to by various politicians (and others) on various occasions in this period.[25] Secondly, we have no independent evidence whatever that Kleon used this practice more than others (or even at all); indeed if Kleon had really possessed a large collection of oracles in the way that Paphlagon does (997 ff.), we might have expected Thucydides to make something of this. As it is, we may suspect ludicrous fiction here, with assimilation of Paphlagon to a professional oracle-collector. And it is at least plausible that Aristophanes chose to make so much of point (i) above because of the comic counterpoint it allowed him to create with point (ii).

War

Paphlagon is depicted at 794–6 as resolutely set against peace with Sparta. This is implicitly connected with the Pylos affair (see below). We know from Thucydides (4.21–2) that it was Kleon who spearheaded the Assembly's rejection of a peace offer from Sparta in 425 after the capture of the latter's troops on Sphakteria, and we have little choice but to assume Kleon's centrality in the rejection of further Spartan embassies later in 425–4 (Thucydides 4.41.3–4). Thucydides evidently saw Kleon as the main obstacle to peace in the later 420s: he makes this point when recording Kleon's death at 5.16.1. But apart from the one passage cited above, *Knights* actually makes rather little of the theme of war. There is a nice moment of irony at 668–9 when Paphlagon feigns interest in peace negotiations as a desperate ploy to keep the Council on his side. But the larger presuppositions of this passage are revealing. The Council are more interested in the price of sprats than in war and peace; 'let war

[25] Thucydides attests popular interest in oracles at e.g. 2.8.2, 2.21.3, 2.54.2–5, and 5.26.3; he nowhere links this point to Kleon. The Athenian Assembly sometimes consulted Delphi, though its replies were always subject to the deliberation and decision-making powers of the Assembly itself (cf. the famous case at Herodotos 7.142–3), a fact which underlies the oracle scene of *Knights* itself (997 ff.).

continue!' they cry with one voice. Ludicrous though the scenario is, the reality at this date was that majority opinion in Athens was prepared to sustain the war until Sparta was willing to make further concessions. *Knights* itself does not seem to anticipate an imminent end to the war (see 579 and 805). There is insufficient satirical scope to make Kleon's attitude to war a central component in the demonization of his allegorical persona, Paphlagon.

Pylos

Kleon's success in playing a military part in the capture of almost three hundred Spartan troops (including one hundred and twenty Spartiates, i.e. full Spartan citizens) on the island of Sphakteria, close to the harbour of Pylos (in the SW Peloponnese), in summer 425, is mentioned more than a dozen times in the course of *Knights* (54–7, 76, 355, 392–4, 469, 702, 742–3, 846, 1005, 1053, 1058–60, 1167, 1172, 1201). This event, which marked an important change in Athenian fortunes in the war, clearly impinged at an early stage on Aristophanes' composition of his play, though he had probably been granted a chorus, and must therefore have had something like an outline of the plot to show the Archon, prior to its occurrence.[26] Thucydides provides a very full account of the whole episode, though one hostile to Kleon in its composite of the following claims: first, that Kleon was pressurized by the Assembly into accepting a special military command at Pylos when he did not really want it; second, that even so Kleon promised to resolve the situation within twenty days; third, that Kleon succeeded in keeping his 'mad' promise, even if, Thucydides would have us believe, the primary responsibility for the capture of the Spartans lay with the general Demosthenes, who was on site throughout.[27] Reading between the lines, it is easy to see two competing views of Kleon's involvement in the Pylos campaign: the first (occluded by Thucydides), that it was a bold and brilliant

---

[26] *A.* 300–1 (see n. there) is often taken to indicate that Aristophanes was already planning *Knights* in early 425, but that is not a necessary inference from that passage. For the process of being 'granted a chorus', see the general Introduction, 'Old Comedy and Dionysiac Festivity'.

[27] See Thucydides 4.3–23 for the original military circumstances, and 26–41 for Kleon's involvement and the capture of the Spartans; Kleon's promise is called 'mad', retrospectively, at 39.3.

intervention, one which must have helped to bring about Kleon's election, just a few months after *Knights*, as a full general for the following year, 424–3 (as well as in each of the following two years), and which was long remembered as an outstanding achievement;[28] the other, that it was a piece of pure luck as far as Kleon's own initiative was concerned. *Knights'* satirical use of the Pylos episode tellingly betrays something of its two-sided significance: from the outset, it makes the episode an example of Paphlagon's 'theft' of something for which the real credit belonged to others, but at the same time it confirms that Kleon had in fact received great acclaim for the success and was able to exploit it to bolster his leading position in Athenian politics. In this instance, then, the satirist cannot denigrate his target without acknowledging the prima facie prestige achieved by him—a point that applies also to the awards Kleon had received as a result of the Pylos campaign, i.e. front-row seats in the theatre and elsewhere (702, cf. 575) and 'dining rights' in the Prytaneion (281, 709, 1404, with related allusions at 167, 535, 766).[29]

Imperialism

Paphlagon is said to show an intense, even excessive, interest in the collection of tribute from Athens' allied cities (312, 1071). Tribute was the single largest part of the city's income and was more important than ever in the circumstances of a very expensive war. The Thucydidean Perikles draws attention to this aspect of Athens' finances at the start of the war (2.13.2–3), and had Perikles lived beyond 429 he would have had to address the acute pressure placed on this source of income by the costs of war. What is more, that same passage of Thucydides shows Perikles warning the Athenians to 'keep a tight grip' on her allies, which fits with the metaphor of empire as 'tyranny' employed by him elsewhere in Thucydides.[30] In these respects, Kleon seems to have stayed close to the position adopted by

[28] A litigant at Demosthenes 40.25 (dating from *c.*347) can still expect a jury to remember the capture of Spartans at Pylos as a glorious achievement of Kleon's.

[29] The Athenians had recently passed a general decree to codify official dining rights for various groups of people, including victors in the Olympic and other games and the descendants of the tyrannicides, Harmodios and Aristogeiton (see n. on 977–9), but we do not know how many generals received such awards (cf. the hyperbole of 575).

[30] See n. 15 above.

Perikles. Kleon was almost certainly behind a major reassessment (and increase) of the allies' tribute contributions in 425–4; the proposer, one Thoudippos, was probably his son-in-law.[31] The lines of *Knights* cited above may glancingly reflect a concern in some quarters that Kleon was too uncompromising in his dealings with the allies; note here also the reference to 'battering' one particular ally, Miletos, in line 361 (though the point of the passage is obscure). Kleon certainly went to an extreme in 427 by proposing the execution of all adult males in Mytilene after its unsuccessful revolt from Athens (Thucydides 3.36.6); but that proposal, narrowly defeated in a second vote, is nowhere mentioned in *Knights*, nor, one should note, is it overtly criticized by Thucydides.[32] Imperialist brutality is certainly not a central target of the play, nor of any other part of Aristophanes' work:[33] however appalling it seems to us, such brutality was probably too acceptable to too many Athenians, at any rate when Athens' own survival was at stake in all-out war, to provide a solid basis for sustained satire.[34]

Even the selective unpicking of *Knights*' thematic threads I have undertaken above exposes something of the play's complex satirical entanglements. One final observation will underline that point. In the lyric exchange between Demos and the chorus which takes place while the two demagogic rivals are offstage fetching the best 'food' they can offer their master to secure his favour (1111–50), an idea emerges which is sharply at odds with most of the play up to this juncture. The idea is that perhaps Demos is not purely the victim of the demagogues' calculating duplicity; perhaps there is something more going on behind his ostensible gullibility. Demos's claim that he constantly monitors the city's leaders and brings them crashing down when they abuse their position as his servants is not, in fact,

[31] Full details in R. Osborne and P. J. Rhodes, *Greek Historical Inscriptions 478–404 BC* (Oxford, 2017), 308–22.

[32] The reference to taking a bribe from Mytilene in line 834 may conceivably be an *ironic* allusion to events of 427, but that interpretation is by no means secure.

[33] Note the telling detail that at *Birds* 186 Aristophanes allows Peisetairos to make a joke about the way that Athens had starved Melos into submission (and then executed many of its citizens) in 415.

[34] Cf. the case of Skione (see note on *Wasps* 210), which defected from alliance with Athens just two days after ratification of a truce between Athens and Sparta in 423 (Thucydides 4.122.6): Kleon persuaded the Athenians to vote for the killing of all Skione's (male) citizens, though this was only carried out in 421, sometime after Kleon's own death (Thucydides 5.32.1).

altogether implausible: it was an inescapable institutional fact about Athenian democracy, as Perikles, Kleon, and others periodically discovered, that it was indeed the votes of the people, in Assembly and Council, that had the decisive say on the city's policies. Although the final scene of *Knights* will make Demos admit, after all, his former naivety (1337–55), the lyric exchange in question does enough to spell out an assumption that was already lurking within the master-slave image itself: that populism is a double-edged phenomenon which permits no definitive answer to the conundrum of where power resides in the workings of Athenian democracy.[35] *Knights* allows Aristophanes both to mock and to redeem Demos, while embedding this ambiguity in a play which starts from the premise that democracy is going from bad to worse (128–43) yet manages to conclude by conjuring up a hazy fantasy of 'back to the good old days' (though no thanks, it should be noticed, to the cavalry chorus, who nowhere develop an intelligible politics of their own). In the end, all we can safely say is that Aristophanic comedy, as so often, likes having things both ways.

[35] Cf. Aristotle's (negative) evaluation of radical democracy at *Politics* 4.4, 1292a4–37, where power resides in the hands of the majority as a quasi-tyrannical 'despot' in its collective capacity, while demagogues manipulate the system as 'flatterers' (cf. n. 14 above) to the people. On the ambiguities of democracy, note Thucydides' ironic remark on how, after the debacle of the Sicilian expedition in 413, the Athenians turned against the politicians who had been supporters of the venture, 'as if they had not themselves voted for it' (8.1.1).

KNIGHTS

Speaking Characters

SLAVE[A]: of DEMOS
SLAVE[B]: of DEMOS
SAUSAGE-SELLER: a low-status Athenian; retrospectively called
Agorakritos (1257)
PAPHLAGON: a 'new' slave of DEMOS and caricature of the
politician Kleon
CHORUS: of young Athenian cavalrymen
LEADER: of the CHORUS
DEMOS: personification of the Athenian citizen body

Silent Characters

BOY: a young slave for the rejuvenated DEMOS (1385 ff.)
PEACE TREATIES: a pair of female personifications

[*The stage building, with a single door, represents the house of* DEMOS; *a harvest branch (see n. on 729) hangs on or next to the door. After sounds of some kind of physical beating offstage,* SLAVE^A *enters, clutching his back and ribs, soon followed by* SLAVE^B.]

SLAVE^A. Ouch! Ouch! What terrible pain I'm in! Ouch! Ouch!
　I hope this vile new Paphlagonian slave,*
　With all his schemes, will be blasted by the gods!
　Ever since he found his way into the house,
　He's made sure the other slaves get constant beatings.
SLAVE^B. No Paphlagonian merits a nastier end,
　With all his slanderous habits.
SLAVE^A. 　　　　　　　　　　Poor wretch, how are you?
SLAVE^B. In the same bad state as you.
SLAVE^A. 　　　　　　　　　　　　Then come over here.
　Let's perform a mournful tune like a pair of *auloi*:*
[*Miming together*] Mu-mu, mu-mu, mu-mu, mu-mu, mu-mu.　　10
[*Reflecting*] Why whine like this in vain? What we need to find
　Is a means of escape for us both, not a reason for crying.
SLAVE^B. Well what do you have in mind?
SLAVE^A. 　　　　　　　　　　　You say.
SLAVE^B. 　　　　　　　　　　　　　　No, you.
　I'm happy for you to go first.
SLAVE^A. 　　　　　　　　　I simply refuse.
　Explain your own idea, then I'll tell mine.
　'If only thou couldst say what I must say!'*
SLAVE^B. But I've got no spunk. If only I myself
　Could state the point in fancy Euripidese.
SLAVE^A. No no! No chopping herbs with me. I just won't have it.*
　I want a way to give our master the slip.　　　　　　20
SLAVE^B. Then follow my lead and say after me 'let's do'.
SLAVE^A. All right, I'll say it: let's do.
SLAVE^B. 　　　　　　　　　　Now add on the end
　The words 'a bunk'.
SLAVE^A. 　　　　　A bunk.
SLAVE^B. 　　　　　　　　　That's right—very good.
　Imagine now you're wanking: keep repeating
　'Let's do' then 'a bunk'; and keep on getting faster.
SLAVE^A [*holding his phallus*]. Let's do—a bunk. Let's do a bunk.

SLAVE^B.   That's it!
Well isn't it nice?
SLAVE^A.   Not half! I'm just afraid
There's an omen here for the skin on my back.
SLAVE^B.   Why's that?
SLAVE^A. Since when you wank the skin gets peeled away!
SLAVE^B [*despairing*]. The very best thing for the pair of us right
    now   30
Is to supplicate a statue of some god.*
SLAVE^A. A statue! You really believe the gods exist?*
SLAVE^B. I certainly do!
SLAVE^A.   What kind of proof do you have?
SLAVE^B. I'm godforsaken myself! Doesn't that make sense?
SLAVE^A. I take your point. Perhaps we should rethink.
Shall I let the audience know what's happening here?
SLAVE^B. That's not a bad idea. Let's add a request:
They should make it clear to us by the look on their faces
If they like the lines we speak and the plot of the play.
SLAVE^A. I'll tell them then. [*To audience*] You see, we have
    a master   40
Who's rustic-tempered, bean-chewing, choleric too.
He's Demos and lives on the Pnyx.* A grumpy old man
Who's almost deaf. At the start of the present month
He bought a new slave, a Paphlagonian tanner,*
A wheeler-dealer addicted to slanderous malice.
This slave worked out the old man's character traits.
Like a Paphlo-tanner he fawned away on our master:
He wheedled, cajoled, and flattered him, utterly duped him
With measly off-cuts of leather and words like this:
'After judging a single law-case go to the baths',   50
'Let me feed you whatever you want', 'Have your three
    obols pay',*
'Shall I serve you a special meal?'—then he'd snatch away
What another of us had cooked and give it the master
As though a treat of his own. Just the other day
When I'd kneaded a cake at Pylos from Spartan flour,*
He used his wiliest cunning to sneak and filch it
And served what *I'd* prepared as though *he'd* made it.
He scares off the other slaves and won't allow us

To tend to the master. At meals he stands with a whip
And frightens away the rest of the...politicians.*   60
He chants oracles too: the old man laps them up.*
When he sees he's made the master a drooling fool,
His art has been perfected: he slanders the others
With downright lies, then the rest of us get a real lashing.
As Paphlagon makes his way round the household slaves
He issues demands, intimidates, pockets big bribes:
'D'you see how Hylas gets whipped on account of me?*
If you don't all grease my palm, you'll be finished today.'
So we all pay up. Otherwise, we get trampled over
By the old man himself and shit ourselves umpteen times.   70
[*To* SLAVE[B]] You and I, old chap, need to do some hasty thinking
   About the best path to take. Who can help us out?
SLAVE[B]. As you said, it's best to 'do a bunk', old chap.
SLAVE[A]. But we can't escape this Paphlagon's attention.
   He observes the world from a height, as he stands with one leg
   In Pylos, the other one planted in the Assembly.
   When he stands with legs astride on such a scale,
   His arsehole's right among the Chaonians,
   His hands in Aitolia, his mind in Klopidai.*
SLAVE[B]. The best thing, then, for us is death.
SLAVE[A].   Think hard   80
   What the manliest way of facing death would be.
SLAVE[B] [*pondering*]. Right: how, well how, would be the manliest
      way?
   The perfect choice for us is to drink bull's blood:
   It's preferable to die like Themistokles.*
SLAVE[A]. No, better to toast a good spirit with unmixed wine: *
   That way we might conceive an excellent plan.
SLAVE[B]. 'Unmixed', just listen! You're always obsessed with drink.
   How on earth could anyone drunk conceive good plans?
SLAVE[A]. Is that what you think! You water-spout-gusher of
      nonsense!
   You dare to abuse wine's intellectual powers?   90
   What else can match the productive force of wine?
   Don't you see? When people drink wine, they think of themselves
   Getting rich, achieving their goals, succeeding in court,
   Being happy with life and helping all their friends.

[*Urgently*] Bring me out, as quick as you can, a jug of wine:
  I'd like to moisten my mind and say something clever.
SLAVE^B. Oh no, you'll do us great harm with all your drinking.
SLAVE^A. On the contrary. Bring me the jug, while I recline.*
  If I get myself quite drunk, I'll spray the place
  With numerous plans, ideas, and shafts of insight.   100

[SLAVE^A *lies on the ground, adopting the posture of a reclining symposiast,*
while SLAVE^B *goes into the stage building before returning shortly after-*
wards with a jug of wine and a metal cup.]

SLAVE^B. What a stroke of luck I managed to steal this wine
  Without getting caught inside.
SLAVE^A.   What's Paphlagon doing?
SLAVE^B. The creep's been licking up confiscated goods.*
  He's snoring away, blind drunk, on a pile of leather.
SLAVE^A. Come on then, slosh me out a nice big cup
  To drink my toast.
SLAVE^B [*pouring*]. Here, take it, toast your good spirit.
SLAVE^A. Drain, drain this draught for the spirit of Pramnian wine.*
    [*Drinks*]
[*Animated*] Good spirit, this plan's inspired by you, not me.
SLAVE^B. What is it? Please tell me.
SLAVE^A.   Go quickly back inside
  And steal all Paphlagon's oracles from the house   110
  While he's still asleep.
SLAVE^B.   Okay. But I'm rather afraid
  What's waiting for me in there is a very *bad* spirit! [*Exits*]
SLAVE^A [*slyly*]. Let me bring this jug itself up to my lips:
  I'd like to moisten my mind and say something clever. [*Drinks*
    again]
SLAVE^B [*returning*]. How loudly Paphlagon farts and snores in his
    sleep!
  The noise allowed me to filch this oracle here,
  The one he tried to keep secret.
SLAVE^A.   What skill you possess!
  Give it here, let me read.* [*Takes scroll*] Meanwhile, pour out
    for me
  Another large cup. Let me see, what have we here? [*Reads*]

O oracles! Quick, quick, give me the cup to drink.   120
SLAVE^B. Here you are. Well, what does it say?
SLAVE^A [*drinks*].   Pour out another.
SLAVE^B [*naively*]. You mean the oracle says 'Pour out another'?
SLAVE^A. O Bakis!*
SLAVE^B.   What is it?
SLAVE^A.   Quick, give me the cup to drink.
SLAVE^B. Well Bakis's oracle obviously needed this cup!
SLAVE^A. Vile Paphlagon! No wonder you kept this secret.
  You dreaded predictions about *yourself*.
SLAVE^B.   Which ones?
SLAVE^A. It's stated here that he's doomed to meet his end.
SLAVE^B. But how?
SLAVE^A.   The oracle states in direct terms
  That first of all there'll be a seller of flax
  Who'll be the leader in running the city's affairs.*   130
SLAVE^B. So that's one tradesman. What comes next? Read more.
SLAVE^A. The second one after him is a seller of sheep.*
SLAVE^B. A pair of tradesmen then. What's that one's fate?
SLAVE^A. His power will last till a more disgusting man
  Comes to take his place; that marks the other one's doom.
  It's the Paphlagonian tanner who takes his place—
  A robber who shrieks with the voice of a deafening torrent.*
SLAVE^B. So the seller of sheep was fated, according to this,
  To be destroyed by a tanner?
SLAVE^A.   That's right.
SLAVE^B.   Oh no!
  So where could one more tradesman be somehow found?   140
SLAVE^A. There's one more here—his trade will really astound
    you.
SLAVE^B. Please tell me who it is.
SLAVE^A.   Shall I say?
SLAVE^B.   You must.
SLAVE^A. The scourge of the tanner will be . . . a sausage-seller!
SLAVE^B. A *sausage*-seller? Poseidon, what kind of trade!
  We really need this man, so where will we find him?
SLAVE^A. Let's go and search.
SLAVE^B [*pointing*].   But I see him approaching here!
  By luck he's on his way to market.

[*The* SAUSAGE-SELLER *enters from one of the* eisodoi: *he is carrying a folding table, culinary equipment, and various pieces of meat. The two* SLAVES *turn eagerly towards him.*]

SLAVE^A.   All hail,
    O sausage-seller! Come over here, dear friend,
    Be the city's god-sent saviour, and ours as well.
SAUSAGE-SELLER. What's that then? What do you want?
SLAVE^A.   Come here
        to learn   150
    The really great good fortune that's yours to enjoy.
SLAVE^B. Right, make him put down his table, and then explain
    How the oracle from the god relates to him.
    I'll go and watch in case Paphlagon should wake. [*Exits into house*]
SLAVE^A. Look, please put down your equipment on the ground.
    Then kiss your lips in worship to earth and gods.
SAUSAGE-SELLER. There. What's this for?
SLAVE^A [*effusively*].   O blesséd and prosperous
        one,
    O nobody now, tomorrow a very great man,
    O mighty lord of Athens, the happiest city.
SAUSAGE-SELLER [*bewildered*]. Just leave me alone, old chap, to
        wash my tripe   160
    And sell my sausages. Please stop making fun.
SLAVE^A. You idiot, tripe indeed! Look over here.
[*Pointing at audience*] Do you see these throngs of people in rows?
SAUSAGE-SELLER.   I do.
SLAVE^A. You yourself will be commander of all these,
    Of the Agora too, the harbours, as well as the Pnyx.
    You'll walk all over the Council, constrain the generals,
    Lock people up—suck cocks in the Prytaneion!*
SAUSAGE-SELLER. What, me?
SLAVE^A.   Yes you! And there's more for you to see.
    Climb up on top of this table of yours right here.

[*The* SAUSAGE-SELLER *unfolds his tradesman's table and climbs onto it, peering into the distance in response to* SLAVE^A's *directions.*]

[*Gesturing*] Now turn your gaze on the islands spread all round.   170
SAUSAGE-SELLER. I see them.

SLAVE[A].   And the ports and merchant ships?
SAUSAGE-SELLER. Those too.
SLAVE[A].   Then isn't this great good fortune
    for you?
[*Pointing*] Now turn your right eye there towards Karia,
    Turn the other this way towards Carthage in the distance.*
SAUSAGE-SELLER. How happy I'll be if my eyes get twisted apart!
SLAVE[A]. No fear. All this is for you to make a profit.
[*Brandishing scroll*] Your destiny, this oracle here predicts,
    Is to be the greatest man.
SAUSAGE-SELLER.   But how, please tell me,
    Can a sausage-seller like me become a real man?
SLAVE[A]. It's this very thing that marks you out for greatness—   180
    Your lack of breeding, your trade, your shameless life.
SAUSAGE-SELLER. But I don't believe I deserve to wield great power.
SLAVE[A]. Oh dear, what makes you doubt yourself like that?
    You seem to know something *good* about yourself.
    You're surely not from superior stock?
SAUSAGE-SELLER.   Ye gods,
    I'm entirely from the basest stock.
SLAVE[A].   That's lucky!
    That fits you perfectly for political life.
SAUSAGE-SELLER. But I haven't had anything like real education;
    I can barely read and write, and very badly.*
SLAVE[A]. But even badly counts as a drawback here!   190
    Political leadership no longer belongs
    To cultured men with decent character too.
    It's for someone ignorant and vile to boot.
    Don't pass up the chance the gods are offering you.
SAUSAGE-SELLER. Well what does the oracle say?
SLAVE[A].   It's written in words
    That form a complex riddle deep in meaning.
[*Chanting*] '*Should* the time come when a crooked-clawed leathery
    eagle
    Grasps in its jaws a blood-drinking idiot serpent,
    Then is the garlic-brine sauce of the Paphlagonians doomed,
    While on the tripe-selling tribe bestoweth a god greatest glory,   200
    Only excepting they make their choice to sell sausage instead.'
SAUSAGE-SELLER. Well what's this got to do with me? Explain.

SLAVE^A [*pointing*]. The leathery eagle is Paphlagon in here.

SAUSAGE-SELLER. But what are his crooked claws?

SLAVE^A.   It surely means
 He uses his crooked hands to grasp and steal.

SAUSAGE-SELLER. But what's the serpent about?

SLAVE^A.   It couldn't be clearer!
 A serpent is something long, and so is a sausage.
 Moreover, both sausage and serpent drink up much blood.
 So he says the serpent will conquer the leathery eagle
 'Only excepting' he finds himself melted by words.   210

SAUSAGE-SELLER. The oracle's teasing me. I fail to see
 How *I* could serve the people as its steward.*

SLAVE^A. The simplest task! Just do what you already do:
 Chop everything up as you would for sausage meat.
 Make sure you keep the people on your side
 By keeping them sweet with the lingo of a cook.
 You've everything else a demagogue needs to have:
 A loathsome voice, bad breeding, vulgar manners.
 You're fully equipped to enter political life,
 And the oracles all agree, including Delphi.   220
 So garland yourself and toast your guardian Dimwit,*
 Then resolve to defeat the man.

SAUSAGE-SELLER.   But who will be
 My *allies*? The rich are all afraid of him,
 While the hordes of poor are scared right down to their bowels.

SLAVE^A. But you've got a thousand horsemen, all fine fellows,*
 Who hate his guts and will rally to serve your cause.
 All citizens of superior type will help,
 [*Pointing*] And every spectator here who's clever as well.
 And *I'll* help too, and the god will lend support.
 No need to worry: his mask doesn't look like him!   230
 The mask-makers were so afraid of him
 They wouldn't produce a likeness.* Even so
 He'll be recognized with ease. Spectators are clever!

SLAVE^B [*calling from inside*]. Oh no! Big trouble ahead! Paphlagon's
 coming out!

[PAPHLAGON *comes storming out of* DEMOS*'s house: he is simultan-*
eously vulgar-looking (perhaps with some elements of a tanner's dress)

and monstrously uncouth; he is also wearing a garland. He delivers his lines at a stridently menacing pitch. The SAUSAGE-SELLER *will quickly take fright before being persuaded to join the fight against him.*]

PAPHLAGON. I swear by all the gods you two will suffer!
　　You've long conspired together against the people.
　　[*Seeing drinking cup*] Aha, what have we here—a Chalkidian cup?
　　You must be inciting Chalkis to raise a revolt.*
　　You're doomed, you're about to die, you loathsome pair.
SLAVE[A]. Hey you, don't run away now, please come back here!　　240
　　Fine sausage-seller, you mustn't betray our plan.

[*The metre now changes to chanted recitative as* SLAVE[A] *calls on the* CHORUS *of horsemen to come to their assistance. The* CHORUS *enters in cavalry formation and with a choreographic representation of riding manoeuvres. What follows involves a stylized evocation of both a military assault and a wrestling fight:* PAPHLAGON *is encircled by the others and struck on his body, not least his theatrically padded belly.*]

[PARODOS: 242–302]

　　Men of the cavalry, come to our aid! It's critical now. I call on
　　　　Simon,
　　Panaitios as well: lead round your forces here towards the right.*
　　[*To* SAUSAGE-SELLER] Support is near. Maintain defence and wheel
　　　　back round in this direction.
　　A dust-cloud makes it clear they're close and on the point of
　　　　making a charge.
　　Maintain defence, pursue the man, and try to make him turn in
　　　　flight.
LEADER. Come, strike and strike the vicious thug, the scourge of all
　　　　our cavalry ranks!
　　He's a farmer of taxes, a gaping chasm of greed, a truly rapacious
　　　　Charybdis.*
　　He's vicious, he's vicious, that's what he is: I'll keep repeating this
　　　　very word,
　　Since he himself repeats his viciousness, every moment of every
　　　　day.　　250
　　Strike him, chase him! Keep on causing consternation throughout
　　　　his mind.

Show that you loathe him, the way that we do, to the pit of your
    stomach. Cry out in attack.
Be careful he doesn't just give you the slip, for he knows some
    special routes to take,
The ones that Eukrates slipped down to make his money from
    trading bran!*

PAPHLAGON. I call upon all ageing jurors, clansmen of the three-
    obol fee,*
The ones I feed by bringing noisy charges to court, whether right
    or wrong:
I summon you, come and help me now—I'm under attack from
    conspirators.

LEADER. And rightly so, for stuffing your mouth from public funds
    when not in office,
And squeezing magistrates up for review as if you were squeezing
    figs in your hand,*
To find out which aren't ready to pick, and which are nice and
    ripe to bite.   260
Your eyes are peeled for citizens who appear naive as bleating sheep,
The sort of person who's rich, good-hearted, but terrified of
    public affairs.
Whenever you spot someone who wants a quiet life and is easily
    duped,
You drag him back here from the Chersonese, use slanderous lies
    like a wrestler's trip,*
Then twist his shoulder to pin him down and stand with your foot
    right on his belly.

PAPHLAGON [*to* CHORUS]. Are you too joining in this assault? But
    you're the reason I'm being attacked:
It was my intention to recommend we honour you on the
    Akropolis
With a monument to celebrate the manly courage you've shown in
    war.*

LEADER. What a total fraud! A leathery cheat! Did you see how far
    he's prepared to go?
He treats us like senile old men and aims to bamboozle us with his
    tricks.   270
[*Pointing*] Well, if he moves in that direction, our blows will stop
    him in his tracks;

If he tries to sneak away back here, he'll find my leg right in his
    face.

PAPHLAGON. O city! O people of Athens! What beasts these are
    who kick me in the belly.

SAUSAGE-SELLER. Are these your usual strident shrieks when
    forcing your will on the city at large?

PAPHLAGON. My shouts will deal with *you*, at least—they're bound
    to make you flee in terror.

LEADER. Well if your shouts defeat this man, we grant the victory
    will be yours.

But if he outdoes your shamelessness, then *we're* the ones who'll
    claim the credit.

PAPHLAGON. I wish to make a legal move against this man. My
    claim is this:

He sends supplies to the Spartans' ships—a sausage stew to feed
    their crews!

SAUSAGE-SELLER. By Zeus I'll bring a counter-charge: when he
    darts inside the Prytaneion   280

His stomach is empty, but when he darts out he's managed to
    stuff it quite full with food.

SLAVE[A]. By Zeus that's right! He breaks the rules by taking out
    bread and meat with him,

And slices of fish as well—a thing that even Perikles never was
    granted.*

PAPHLAGON.   The pair of you are about to die.

SAUSAGE-SELLER. I'll shriek and shout three times as loud.

PAPHLAGON.   I'll shout and bawl you into submission.

SAUSAGE-SELLER. I'll shriek and screech you into submission.

PAPHLAGON.   I'll slander you if you serve as general.

SAUSAGE-SELLER. I'll flog you the way I would flog a dog.

PAPHLAGON.   I'll trap you with my fraudulent tricks.   290

SAUSAGE-SELLER. I'll block the paths you intend to take.

PAPHLAGON.   Look me in the eye without a blink.

SAUSAGE-SELLER. I too was reared in the marketplace.

PAPHLAGON.   I'll rip you apart if you make any noise.

SAUSAGE-SELLER. I'll turn you to shit if you shout and scream.

PAPHLAGON.   I freely admit I'm a thief, but you don't.

SAUSAGE-SELLER. Not true, by Hermes god of the market!
            I perjure myself in broad daylight.*

PAPHLAGON.   Your clever retorts are modelled on mine.
              I'm about to report to the Prytaneis   300
              That you've failed to pay the legal tithe
              On the sacred tripe in your possession.*

              [AGON I: 303–460]

CHORUS.   You loathsome, odious shrieker! Your brashness   *Strophe*ᵃ
              Pervades the earth, pervades the Assembly:
              It fills our tax affairs and legal system,
              You churner of mud who've spattered your filth
              Everywhere in this city of ours.   310
              You've deafened Athens with all your yelling
              Like a lookout for tunny, high up on the rocks, with his
                  sight set on...tribute!*

PAPHLAGON. I recognize now what's going on here: you've been
      stitching it up for quite some time.

SAUSAGE-SELLER. If *you* don't know about stitching shoes, then
      I don't know about sausage production!

   You used to take thin cuts of leather from ox-hides of the poorest
      kind

   Then make a crooked sale to country folk who thought the leather
      was thick

   But found within a day it had big holes when used for the soles of
      shoes.

SLAVEᴬ. By Zeus he did just that to me and managed to make me
      a laughing stock

   When my fellow-demesmen and all my friends saw the terrible
      state my feet were in: 320

   Before I was anywhere near to home, I was swimming inside the
      boots I'd bought.

CHORUS.   Did you not display from the very start   *Strophe*ᵇ
              The shamelessness of all politicians?
              That's what you rely on when plucking the fruit from
                  rich foreigners.
              It's you in charge, while Hippodamos's son looks on in
                  tears.*
              But now there's another man who's appeared
              Even viler than you, which makes me rejoice:

He'll end your career and, for all to see, he'll outdo
you   330
In vicious behaviour and brazenness
And a bag of bamboozling tricks.

LEADER. O you who were reared in the only place from which men
   rise these days,
  Now demonstrate that it counts for nothing to have a good
  upbringing.
SAUSAGE-SELLER. Well, listen, I'll tell you just how bad a citizen
   this man is.
PAPHLAGON. Can't I speak first?
SAUSAGE-SELLER.   You certainly can't. I'm just as base
   as you.
SLAVE[A]. And if he argues with that, just add your ancestry's utterly
   base.
PAPHLAGON. Can't I speak first?
SAUSAGE-SELLER.   No you can't.
PAPHLAGON.   Yes I can.
SAUSAGE-SELLER.   By Poseidon,
   you certainly can't.
  I'll stand my ground and fight you out to ensure I speak before you.
PAPHLAGON. Outrageous! I'll explode with rage.
SAUSAGE-SELLER.   But I won't allow
   you to do so.   340
SLAVE[A]. Oh do allow him, by all the gods—I'd like to see him
   explode!
PAPHLAGON. What gives you confidence to speak in defiance of my
   pronouncements?
SAUSAGE-SELLER. Because I too can make a speech—as well as
   a spicy sauce!
PAPHLAGON. What *you*, make speeches! I'm sure that if some
   urgent issue cropped up,
  You'd make as good a job of it as you'd handle a piece of raw meat.
  Do you know what I think has happened to you? It's
  a commonplace delusion.
  Suppose you've made a competent speech in the trivial trial of a metic.*
  You needed to learn your words all night and to mutter them in
  the street;

You drank just water and bored your friends by making them hear
   you rehearse.

Yet now you believe you're an expert speaker. You idiot, what
   a delusion! 350

SAUSAGE-SELLER. Well what's the drink that *you've* imbibed to
   strike the city dumb

When it's overcome by your violent tongue, and no one else can
   speak?

PAPHLAGON. You can't compare me with anyone else. Just hear
   what I'm able to do:

On a stomach full of hot tunny fish and a jug of unmixed wine,

I'll well and truly shaft the generals who held command
   at Pylos.*

SAUSAGE-SELLER. I'll go one better: I'll make a dish of cow's
   stomach and tripe of pig,

I'll funnel it down, then drink the broth, and with my unwashed
   hands

I'll strangle all the politicians and unnerve Nikias.*

SLAVE^A. I liked the rest of the points you made; I've just got one
   concern:

You intend to siphon off for yourself the broth of public
   affairs. 360

PAPHLAGON. Well you won't devour Milesian bass then batter
   Miletos itself.*

SAUSAGE-SELLER. But I'll feed myself on ribs of beef then acquire
   some mining leases.*

PAPHLAGON. But *I'll* rush into the Council chamber and cause
   a great commotion.

SAUSAGE-SELLER. But *I'll* stuff meat right up your arse as I would
   with a sausage skin.

PAPHLAGON. I'll fold you double, your bum sticking up, and drag
   you into the street.

SLAVE^A. In Poseidon's name, if you do that to him, you'll have to
   drag me too.

PAPHLAGON.   I'm itching to fasten you in the stocks.*

SAUSAGE-SELLER. I'll have you in court on a cowardice charge.*

PAPHLAGON.   I'll have your skin stretched out for tanning.

SAUSAGE-SELLER. I'll flay you and make a bag for thieving. 370

PAPHLAGON.   I'll peg you out on the ground like leather.

SAUSAGE-SELLER. I'll turn you into a pile of mincemeat.

PAPHLAGON. I'll pluck every single eyelash of yours.

SAUSAGE-SELLER. I'll slice your gullet out of your neck.

SLAVE[A]. And yes, by Zeus, let's thrust a peg,
The way that expert butchers do,
Right into his mouth, then open it wide,
Pull out that nasty tongue of his
And take an extremely careful look
Inside the gaping orifice   380
Of his... arsehole, to check for pimples!*

CHORUS. So there really is something hotter than   *Antistrophe*[a]
fire!
There are speeches more shameless than shameless
ones!
The business in hand is not easy or slight:
[*To* SAUSAGE-SELLER] Attack him! Confuse him! Don't slacken
your efforts.
You've now got him tight in your grip.
If you use your assault to soften him up,
You'll find he's a coward.* I know all too well what
he's like.   390

SAUSAGE-SELLER. That's what he's been throughout his life yet
nevertheless he seemed to many
To be a stalwart man by reaping a harvest where others had sown
the seed.
But the plentiful crop he gathered together and brought to
Athens from foreign fields
He's now placed under lock and key, and plans to sell for personal
gain.*

PAPHLAGON. I've got no fear of all you people so long as the
Council's where I thrive
And while old Demos sits in his place with a drooling look on that
face of his.

CHORUS. It's the same old shamelessness we know.   *Antistrophe*[b]
Not the slightest change in his complexion.
[*To* PAPHLAGON] If I don't hate your guts, may I lie as a fleece on
Kratinos's bed   400

And train as a chorus-member for a tragedy by
  Morsimos!*
O you who, at every conceivable chance,
Come to rest like a bee where bribery blossoms,
May you throw up each mouthful you found it so easy
  to swallow!*
This alone would give me cause to sing
'Drink, drink for this happy event!'

LEADER. And Oulios, I'm sure of it, that aged ogler of wheat,*
  Would cry aloud in pure delight and sing a Bacchic ode.
PAPHLAGON. You'll never outdo my shamelessness, no matter how
  hard you try.
  If you do, may I never take part again in the worship of Zeus
    Agoraios!*   410
SAUSAGE-SELLER. I swear by all the thrashings I've had on
    numerous occasions
  Ever since my childhood, and by the blows I've had from
    butchers' knives,
  I *will* outdo these vices of yours. Otherwise my life's been wasted
  In feeding myself to this bulky size on food others threw on the
    floor.
PAPHLAGON. From food on the floor, like a dog, you mean? How
    then, you miserable wretch,
  If you live on the food of a dog, can you hope to contend with
    a dog-faced baboon?*
SAUSAGE-SELLER. What's more, by Zeus, I've mischievous tricks
    I learnt when still a boy.
  I used to deceive the butchers then by saying this sort of thing:
  'Look over there, lads, don't you see? A swallow! It must be
    spring.'
  Then while they stood and were looking away, I'd filch some meat
    from them.   420
SLAVE^A. You're a clever piece of meat yourself! I admire your skilful
    foresight:
  There's a proverb, 'eat nettles before spring comes'; you did the
    same with thieving!
SAUSAGE-SELLER. And most of the time I was undetected. But if
    ever anyone noticed,

I'd hide the meat between my buttocks and deny by the gods that
    I had it.

When one of the politicians saw me behaving like this, he
    declared,

'The future of this boy is certain: he'll be the people's steward!'*

SLAVE^A. A flash of insight on his part! But it's clear what his reason
    was:

You'd committed theft then perjury too … and your arse had
    room for meat.

PAPHLAGON. I'll stop this brash behaviour of yours—in fact, of the
    pair of you.

I'll blast against you with vigorous force like a swooping, powerful
    wind.   430

I'll churn up earth and sea together, and spread confusion
    between them.

SAUSAGE-SELLER. I'll trim my sausages, just like sails, then let my
    vessel proceed

Across the waves, with the wind behind, and bid you go to hell!

SLAVE^A. I'll lend a hand by watching out for leaks inside the hold.

PAPHLAGON. In Demeter's name, you won't escape scot-free for all
    those talents

You stole from the people of Athens.

SLAVE^A [*to* SAUSAGE-SELLER].   Watch out! Now slacken that
    rope on the sail.

There's a big north-easterly wind ahead, and it's threatening
    litigation.

SAUSAGE-SELLER. You made ten talents yourself, I know, when
    Potidaia surrendered.*

PAPHLAGON [*wheedling*]. I'll give you ten percent of that, if you
    promise to say no more.

SLAVE^A. This man would happily take a bribe. [*To* SAUSAGE-
    SELLER] Now slacken off the reefing.   440
                 The wind is starting to die down now.

PAPHLAGON.   You'll face four charges of bribery,
                 Each one with a hundred-talent fine.*

SAUSAGE-SELLER. And you'll face twenty for dodging service,
                 And more than a thousand for theft.

PAPHLAGON.   I allege your ancestors were those
                 Who polluted the goddess's shrine itself.*

SAUSAGE-SELLER. I allege your very own grandfather
    Was a bodyguard—
PAPHLAGON.   What's that? Explain.
SAUSAGE-SELLER. Of the mistress of whips, Hippias' wife.*
PAPHLAGON.   You're a trickster, you!
SAUSAGE-SELLER.   And you're a crook.   450
SLAVE^A.   Keep hitting him hard.
PAPHLAGON.   Aargh! Aargh! Stop that!
    These conspirators are beating me up.
SLAVE^A.   Deliver the hardest blows you can.
    Aim punches and kicks to stomach and gut:
    Make sure the whole of his ample belly
    Gets thoroughly pummelled and punished.
LEADER [*to* SAUSAGE-SELLER]. O noblest hunk of meat, whose
    spirit is bravest of all men,
  The god-sent saviour of the city and all its citizens too,
  What a skilful, agile job you made of assaulting this man with
    words.
  If only our praise of you could match the pleasure we currently
    feel!   460

[*The agon over, the dialogue returns to unaccompanied speech.*]

PAPHLAGON. In Demeter's name, don't think I wasn't aware
    Of the fabrication of all your plans. I knew
  All the fixing and gluing together of what you're up to.
SAUSAGE-SELLER. And *I'm* aware of your own dealings in Argos.
[*To* SLAVE^A] He's using friendship with Argos as just a pretext;
    Behind the scenes he's plotting with Sparta against her.*
SLAVE^A [*to* SAUSAGE-SELLER]. But can't you match that carpentry
    talk of his?
SAUSAGE-SELLER. I also know what all his welding's for:
    He's forging metal to clamp the prisoners here.*
SLAVE^A. Bravo! Give him blacksmith terms for his talk of
    gluing.   470
SAUSAGE-SELLER. There are men on the other side too who are
    working with him.
[*To* PAPHLAGON] Don't think that bribing me with silver or gold
    Nor sending your friends to see me you'll buy my silence

And stop me reporting the truth to the people of Athens.

PAPHLAGON. I'm going to go and report to the Council at once
To tell them how you're all conspiring now:
I'll reveal your nighttime plottings against the city,
Conspiratorial plans with the Persian king,
And cheesy schemes involving Boiotian affairs.* [*Starts to leave*]

SAUSAGE-SELLER [*sarcastically*]. Do tell us how sales of cheese are
in Boiotia.   480

PAPHLAGON. In Herakles' name, I'll stretch your hide for tanning!
[*Exits*]

SLAVE^A [*to* SAUSAGE-SELLER]. It's urgent, tell us the best idea
you've got.
You'll surely think of a plan, in view of the way
You hid that meat, as you told us, up your buttocks.
You'd better dash straight away to the Council chamber:
Paphlagon will rush there himself and slander us all,
Yelling out his lies at the highest pitch of his voice.

SAUSAGE-SELLER. I'm off at once. But first, there's just one thing:
I'll leave my tripe and knives with you for now. [*Hands over his
equipment*]

SLAVE^A. Here, take this oil and rub it all over your neck: 490
When you wrestle with him, you'll slip from his slanderous holds.

SAUSAGE-SELLER. Good advice—just like a professional wrestling
coach!

SLAVE^A. And pop this garlic into your mouth.

SAUSAGE-SELLER.   What for?

SLAVE^A. To prime yourself, old chum, like a fighting cock.*
Now hurry along.

SAUSAGE-SELLER. I will.

SLAVE^A.   And don't forget
To bite, to slander, to snap off his comb with your teeth,
And be sure to gobble his wattles before you return.

[*The* SAUSAGE-SELLER *rushes off by the same* eisodos *by which*
PAPHLAGON *exited.* SLAVE^A *goes back inside the house of* DEMOS, *as the*
CHORUS *moves into formation to perform the parabasis.*]

[PARABASIS: 498–610]

CHORUS.   May your journey prosper! May your success

Fulfil my hopes and bring you protection
From Zeus Agoraios.* And after winning   500
May you come back to us
Bestrewn with garlands.
[*To audience*] But *you* should now attend to us
As we start the anapaest section.*

LEADER. If ever in the distant past a comic producer had tried
To make us step before you here and speak these lines to the
theatre,*
He wouldn't have found it easy. But now this poet deserves this
favour,
Because he hates the people we hate and dares to speak what's
right,*   510
And nobly wages campaign against the whirlwind monster
Typhos.*
There's something he says that many of you have puzzled about
and approached him
To press him on why he hasn't requested a chorus before on his
own.*
He's asked us now to explain this matter. The fellow would like
you to know
This practice of his wasn't empty-headed. The reason, instead,
was just this:
He thinks that being a comic playwright's the hardest thing in the
world.
Mistress Comedy's hard to seduce: many try, but she gratifies few.
He's also long been aware that you spectators have changeable
tastes;
You abandon poets you used to like once old age overtakes them.
Our playwright knows what Magnes suffered when all his hair
turned grey.*   520
His trophies showed how often he'd won a victory over his rivals.
He filled the theatre with numerous sounds: plucking lyre-strings,
flapping his wings,
Acting Lydian, buzzing like fig-flies, dressed in costume dyed
frog-green.
Yet even so, when in old age, he ceased to be judged good
enough;

He was booed offstage in his elderly state, on the grounds that
  he'd lost all his bite.
Our playwright also recalls Kratinos, who used to be buoyed up
By a flood of praise that carried him like a river across the plains.
With sweeping force he tore from their roots oak trees and
  planes—and his rivals!
The only song at drinking parties was 'Bribe-goddess, fig-wood-
  besandalled'
And 'Builders of fine-wrought hymns'.* That's how he flourished
  when in his prime.   530
But now you observe him yourselves in his dotage and feel no pity
  for him:
He's like a lyre whose pegs have slipped, whose strings have lost
  their tension,
Whose joints are coming apart. He stumbles around in a senile state,
Like wretched Konnos, his garland withered, and plagued by
  deadly thirst.*
Yet his former victories merit a place in the Prytaneion . . . for
  drinks!*
He should stop writing drivel, just watch plays instead, scrubbed
  clean in a seat at the front.
Then there's Krates too, who had to endure such harsh rough
  treatment from you.*
The meal he served in those plays of his was prepared at slight
  expense;
He kneaded such witty ideas for you with a mouth whose humour
  was dry.
Yet he barely withstood the theatrical test, and his work was
  sometimes a flop.   540
So failures like these made our poet afraid. Moreover, he reached
  the conclusion
One ought to serve as a rower at first before taking command of
  the rudders,
Then move to the post of bow-officer next and learn to interpret
  the winds,
Then finally steer a ship of his own.* For all these different
  reasons,
Since our playwright was modest and didn't jump in feet first
  with plays full of rubbish,

Please raise a great splash of applause for him, with a sound like
   oars in the waves,
        The finest clamour to suit the Lenaia,
        So our poet may go home happy today,
        His aims successfully achieved,
        With a brightly gleaming forehead!*   550

CHORUS.   O equestrian lord Poseidon,   *Strophe*
        Who thrills in the thud of bronze-shod hoofs
        And the whinnying sounds of horses,
        As well as swift and dark-prowed ships,
        Triremes with state-paid crews,
        And the contests of adolescents
        Winning glory in chariot races
        (And sometimes crashing as well),
        Come here to our chorus, O god of the golden trident,
        O guardian of dolphins with your Sounion shrine, 560
        O son of Kronos, worshipped at Geraistos,
        Adored by Phormion,
        And Athens' favourite among the gods
        In the present situation.*

LEADER. Now's the time we'd like to offer a speech of praise for our
   ancestors.
Stalwart men they were who did their country and the peplos
   proud.*
Whether the fight took place on land or in formations of ships at
   sea,
Everywhere they proved the victors, adorning the city with high
   renown.
Never when sight of enemy forces faced them did they spend
   their time
Counting the numbers ranged against them; resolute their spirit
   remained.   570
Anyone in mid-battle who fell from his horse and hit his shoulder
   hard
Wouldn't admit he'd fallen at all; he brushed it off and got back on.
Persevere and carry the fight—*that* was what they always did.
Nor did earlier generals ask Kleainetos for dining rights;

These days, though, unless they get front theatre seats and grub
    as well,*

Fighting's not for them. Yet we, your horsemen, happily serve the
    city,

Nobly and without reward defending her and our native gods.

Furthermore, we ask for nothing—well, maybe just one little
    thing:

Should this war give way to peace and all our toils come to an end,

Don't resent the way we grow long hair or live in pampered
    style.*   580

CHORUS.   O Pallas, protectress of our citadel,   *Antistrophe*
                This holiest of all lands,
                This city supreme in war and in poets
                And in the mighty reach of its power,
                Is yours to watch over:
                Come hither to us and bring with you
                The goddess who in war's campaigns
                Is our constant helper,
                Nike, companion of choruses,*
                Who sides with us against our foes.   590
                Come, then, appear before us.
                These men of the chorus implore you
                To use every means to help them win,
                Now more than ever before.

LEADER. Now's the time, with inside knowledge, we'd like to praise
    our horses too.

They deserve a eulogy, for many the struggles they've shared with us,

Carrying us through thick and thin in raids and battles we've had
    to fight.

Nevertheless our favourite thing is more than all their feats on land.

Once they leapt with manly strength aboard the equestrian
    transport ships;*

Soldiers' cups they'd bought already, and some had garlic and
    onions too.   600

Soon they started to take the oars exactly as we humans do.

Striking the water hard they neighed their cries, 'Whe-hey',
    'Who'll start to row?'

'*Harder*! harder!', 'What's the matter?', 'Onwards now, you
    branded horse'.*
Once we'd got to Korinth, they jumped ashore, and then the
    youngest ones
Started to dig their beds with their hooves and went in search of
    food as well.
Crabs were what they ate instead of Persian clover, the usual stuff;
Crabs not only that crawled ashore, but some they even caught
    from the sea.
Watching this, Theoros claimed he heard a Korinthian crab
    exclaim:
'Woe betide me, lord Poseidon, if every hiding place is blocked—
Neither on land nor in the sea will I ever escape the cavalry
    corps!'*   610

[*As the parabasis finishes, the* SAUSAGE-SELLER *reappears from the side
on which he left, now displaying an air of triumph and self-confidence.*]

LEADER. Our dearest friend, who embodies such youthful vigour,
    We've worried about you greatly in your absence.
    But now you've come back here all safe and sound,
    Report to us the outcome of your contest.
SAUSAGE-SELLER. My news is clear—I was victor in the Council!

CHORUS.   Appropriate, then, for all to whoop in triumph!   *Strophe*
               O bringer of good tidings, though your deeds
               Are even mightier than your words,
               Recount the whole story in detail.
               I don't hesitate to say   620
               I'd make a lengthy journey
               To hear your account. So speak, we urge you,
               With resolute confidence.
               We all feel delight in your presence.

SAUSAGE-SELLER [*self-preeningly*]. Indeed I have a narrative well
    worth telling.
    As soon as I'd hurried from here, hot on his heels,
    In the Council chamber he broke into thunderous words,
    Making monstrous threats against the cavalry corps,

Hurling verbal rocks and shouting 'conspirators!'
With huge persuasiveness.* As the Council listened,
It swallowed complete the lies and nonsense he spoke;   630
They all looked mustard and angrily knitted their brows.
When I saw how receptive they were to what was said,
How easily duped by his piles of balderdash,
I said to myself, 'Come now, deceitful demons,
Flapdoodle, Bamboozle, and Fakery to boot,
And you the Agora, where I was trained as a boy,
Bestow on me now real brashness, a fluent tongue,
A shameless voice.' As these thoughts occurred to me,
Some bugger let out a fart to the right of me.*
I kissed my lips in worship and with my backside   640
Knocked wide the gate* and stretching wide my mouth
I cried aloud: 'O Council, I bring good news
And want to be the first to report it to you.
Ever since we found ourselves plunged into war,
I've never seen small fry sell so cheaply here.'*
At once a look of bliss spread over their faces;
They wanted to crown me as bringer of joyous news.
I told them, but made it top secret for themselves,
That in order to purchase small fry for an obol
They should seize all bowls at once from the potters' shops.   650
They burst into loud applause and gawped with amazement.
But Paphlagon, deeply suspicious, and knowing too well
The kinds of speeches the Council likes to hear,
Came forward with a proposal: 'It seems to me
That to celebrate the news that's been reported
We should sacrifice to Athena a hundred cattle.'*
This made the Council switch attention to *him*.
When I saw that I was losing to his bullshit,
I went one better, *two* hundred cattle I said,
And suggested honouring Artemis the Huntress   660
With a sacrifice of a thousand goats tomorrow,
If the price of sprats should fall to a hundred per obol.
This made the Council fixated on me once again.
When he heard my words, he panicked and started to rant.
The Prytaneis got the archers to have him removed,*
While the Councillors stood and cheered about the sprats.

He pleaded with them to let him have more time:
'I want you to hear a message the Spartans have sent
With a herald; he's come to raise the question of peace.'*
But with one voice they all cried in response: 670
'So *now* they're interested in peace? Because
They've seen how cheaply small fry sells round here!
We have no need of peace—let war continue!'
They shrieked for the Prytaneis to end the meeting,
Then started to jump across the wooden fence.*
I beat them to it and bought the coriander
And all the onions too on sale in the market,
Then gave them out as relish to go with the sprats,
As if doing a popular favour amidst the shortage!
They cheered me to the skies, every one of them hollered   680
'Hurrah!'. So I've come back here having bought the Council
For just a trifling amount of coriander.

CHORUS.   Complete success is yours! The mark of a   *Antistrophe*
                   winner!
            That vicious man has met his match, someone
            Endowed with even greater vices,
            Elaborate tricks,
            And wheedling words.
            But be sure to compete this well
            In the contests still to come.
            In us you've got loyal allies:
            You've known that all along.   690

SAUSAGE-SELLER. Look, here comes Paphlagon himself again,
    Like a surging wave that's about to crash and churn.
    He's hoping to swallow me up. Gorblimey, what brashness!

[PAPHLAGON *rushes back on in a furious rage.*]

PAPHLAGON. If I don't annihilate you by making use
    Of all my habitual lies, may I split into pieces!
SAUSAGE-SELLER [*laughing*]. What delightful threats, hilarious
    puffs of bluster!
[*Dancing*] I jig with contempt for you, I crow at your nonsense.

PAPHLAGON. In Demeter's name, if I don't devour you whole,
  To get rid of you from this land, my life is over!
SAUSAGE-SELLER. I can say the same if I fail to drink your
  blood,   700
  Even if I burst apart while swilling you down!
PAPHLAGON. I'll destroy you, I swear by the seating I won for
  Pylos.*
SAUSAGE-SELLER. The seating! I'll soon make sure I see you removed
  From your front-row seat and left to watch from the back.
PAPHLAGON. I swear by heaven I'll have you tied in the stocks.*
SAUSAGE-SELLER. So irascible! [*Ironically*] What kind of food can
  I give you?
  What bread would you like—a *bag*uette of money perhaps?
PAPHLAGON. I'll tear your entrails out with these nails of mine.
SAUSAGE-SELLER. I'll claw from your guts your Prytaneion food.
PAPHLAGON. I'll drag you before the demos to get you punished. 710
SAUSAGE-SELLER. I'll drag you there myself and tell bigger lies.
PAPHLAGON. The people won't believe you at all, you wretch.
  But I can dupe them myself as much as I want.
SAUSAGE-SELLER. How convinced you are that the demos is in your
  pocket.
PAPHLAGON. That's because I know the pap that gives them
  pleasure.
SAUSAGE-SELLER. You feed them slyly just like nurses do.
  You chew the food and put a small piece in their mouth
  While taking three times as much for yourself to swallow.
PAPHLAGON. By Zeus, I possess a special skill with which
  To make the demos expand and shrink at will.   720
SAUSAGE-SELLER. I too can play that trick—but with my arsehole!
PAPHLAGON. You won't get away with reviling me in the Council.
  Let's go before the demos.
SAUSAGE-SELLER.   I've no objection.
  Go straight ahead—let's not delay any longer.

[*The two characters jostle one another as they approach* DEMOS*'s house:
  they start knocking on the door and calling out with urgency.*]

PAPHLAGON. O Demos, come out at once.
SAUSAGE-SELLER.   Yes please, old father,

Come out.

PAPHLAGON.   O Demos, on whom I dote so fondly,
Come out: you need to see how I'm being abused.

[*The door opens and* DEMOS, *an old man in shabby rustic clothing, enters.*]

DEMOS [*testily*]. Who's making all this racket? Away from my door!
You've completely ripped to pieces my harvest branch.*
[*Seeing* PAPHLAGON] Who's harming you, Paphlagon?
PAPHLAGON.   It's for
your sake.   730
This fellow and these young men are beating me.
DEMOS.   Why?
PAPHLAGON. It's my fondness, Demos, for you—because I'm your
lover.*
DEMOS [*to* SAUSAGE-SELLER]. Who are *you?*
SAUSAGE-SELLER.   I'm a rival of his to be
your lover.
I've long been in love with you and want to serve you.
Many other superior people feel the same.*
But our way's been blocked by *him*. And that's because
You're like those boys who acquire a crowd of lovers.
The superior ones are the people you won't accept;
Yet you give yourself to lamp-sellers,* menders of shoes,
Shoe-makers, and sellers of leather of every kind.   740
PAPHLAGON. That's because I treat Demos well.
SAUSAGE-SELLER.   Oh yes? Say how.
PAPHLAGON. By sneakily winning a race with the generals at Pylos:
I sailed there and brought the captured Spartans back.*
SAUSAGE-SELLER [*ironically*]. But *I*, while strolling around, slipped
into a workshop
And filched a pot of soup that another was boiling.
PAPHLAGON. Well then, convene an Assembly meeting at once,
O Demos, in order to learn which one of us two
Is more loyal to you: you must choose which one you'll befriend.
SAUSAGE-SELLER. Yes yes, you must choose between us—but not
on the Pnyx.
DEMOS. There's nowhere else I'm prepared to hold a session.   750
Proceed! You need to go to the Pnyx for the meeting.

SAUSAGE-SELLER. Oh wretched me, I'm doomed! I know the old man
   Is completely shrewd when he's here inside his house,
   But once he takes his seat on top of that rock
   He gawps like an idiot munching on dried figs!

[*The scene supposedly changes to the Pnyx:* DEMOS *sits himself on
a nearby piece of rock. Throughout what follows,* PAPHLAGON *and the*
SAUSAGE-SELLER *act out their competition for* DEMOS's *favour with
physical gestures as well as verbal tit-for-tat.*]

[AGON II: 756–942]

CHORUS.   Time now to slacken the ropes and let out your   *Strophe*
           sails to full extent,
           To bear a warlike temperament, use words like deadly
              weapons
           With which to overwhelm your foe. The man has
              slippery tricks
           And knows how to find a cunning way out when in an
              intractable spot.
           So be sure you blast against him now like a strong and
              vigorous wind.   760

LEADER. But take precautions: before he has a chance to launch an
   attack,
  Swing up your dolphin-weights and bring your boat aside the ship.*
PAPHLAGON. To mistress Athena, who cares for our city, I make my
   opening prayer:
   If the evidence shows that the people of Athens have always found
     me to be
   The finest man after Lysikles . . . and Kynna and Salabaccho,*
   May I dine as now in the Prytaneion, although I don't deserve it.
   But if I hate you, Demos, and fail to stand alone to defend you,
   May I be wiped out and sawn in two and cut into leather yoke-straps.
SAUSAGE-SELLER. If *I* don't love and adore you, Demos, then cut
   me too into pieces
   And boil me in mincemeat. If that's not enough to make you trust
     what I say,   770
   May I be mashed up on this table of mine in a garlic paste with
     cheese

Or dragged by a meat-hook fixed to my balls to the Kerameikos
   graveyard.*

PAPHLAGON. But how could a citizen love you more, O Demos,
   than I do?

To start with, on the Council I maximized the public wealth:

I extracted taxes by numerous means—with torture, strangling,
   blackmail.

No individual mattered to me, just doing you popular favours.

SAUSAGE-SELLER. That's no big deal, I assure you, Demos. I'll do
   the same for you.

I'll snatch the bread that belongs to others and serve it on your
   plate.

And I'd like to explain he has no love nor loyalty either for you;

If he does, that's simply because he desires to warm himself at
   your fire.   780

Ever since on Marathon's plain your swordplay saved us from the
   Persians,

And your triumph there gave politicians great scope to sing your
   praises,

This man has never shown any concern that you sit on this hard
   rock here,

Whereas *I* have stitched this cushion for you. [*Producing it*] Stand
   up, then sit back down

On its nice soft base, to protect those buttocks that rowed in the
   Salamis ships.*

DEMOS. Delightful! What's your name? You must descend from
   Harmodios.*

This deed of yours shows noble breeding and true love of the
   people.

PAPHLAGON. For just these measly flattering scraps you've
   switched allegiance to him!

SAUSAGE-SELLER. But you yourself caught him in your nets with
   much smaller bait than this.

PAPHLAGON [*to* DEMOS]. You've never seen a man who protected
   the people better than me   790

Or who loves you more: on that I'm prepared to wager my head
   itself!

SAUSAGE-SELLER. If you love him so much, how come you've
   watched him living in shantytowns,

In the tiniest nooks and crannies, for seven years now, without any
    pity?*
Instead you squeeze him and steal his honey. When
    Archeptolemos brought
An offer of peace, you threw it away.* And you send peace
    embassies packing
With a great big kick up the arse for them, to drive them out of
    the city.

PAPHLAGON. But my aim is to make him rule all Greece. The
    oracles state quite clearly
He'll do his jury service one day in Arkadia, paid five obols,
If he bides his time. But till that day, I'll nourish and care
    for him,
Finding means fair or foul to ensure that he gets his daily three
    obols as juror.*   800

SAUSAGE-SELLER. It was never your plan to extend his rule as far as
    Arkadia.
Your aim was to steal and take big bribes from our allied cities,
    while *he*
Would be blinded by the fog of war to the villainy you were
    committing,
But would still be forced to hang on your words to earn his jury
    pay.*
If ever Demos returns to the fields and lives a life of peace,
Restored by eating porridge and by his fondness for olive cakes,
He'll recognize what you cheated him of with a life of earning
    state pay.*
He'll come for you then, an acrid rustic, and look for a way to
    condemn you.
You know that could happen and that's why you dupe him and try
    to confuse him with dreams.*

PAPHLAGON. How scandalous to hear you say these things and
    slander me   810
To Demos and the Athenians, when I've done the city more good
Than Themistokles ever did for it—by Demeter, I swear I have!

SAUSAGE-SELLER. 'O city of Argos, hark at his words!'* You
    compete with Themistokles?
He made our city a brimming vessel when he'd found it less than
    full,

And kneaded the new Peiraieus harbour as barley cake for its
    lunch,*
And served it up new kinds of fish while keeping the old ones too.
But *you* have turned Athenians into citizens with small minds,
Creating factions, chanting oracles—pseudo-Themistokles!*
Yet *he* was exiled from this land, while *you* can gorge yourself.

PAPHLAGON. How scandalous for me to be abused by him like
    this   820
Because of my love for you!

DEMOS.   Shut up! Enough of your filthy brawling.
You've kept me in the dark for far too long about your swindles.

SAUSAGE-SELLER. He's thoroughly vile, my mighty Demos, his
    villainy knows no bounds.

                        While you're distracted, he picks the stalks
                        From magistrates who are under review*
                        And swallows them down, while with both hands
                        He guzzles the public funds.

PAPHLAGON.   I'll get you for this! I'll convict you in court
                        Of stealing thirty thousand drachmas.*

SAUSAGE-SELLER. Why thrash your oars with all this splashing,   830
                        When you've been exposed as thoroughly vile
                        To the people of Athens? I'll prove as well,
                        By Demeter I will, and upon my life,
                        That you took a bribe from Mytilene
                        Of more than forty minas.*

CHORUS.   O you who've shown yourself to be a boon   *Antistrophe*
                for all mankind,
            I envy you your fluent tongue. If you carry the
                onslaught forward,
            You'll be the greatest of all Greeks and you alone will
                hold
            Control of the city's affairs, while ruling our allies with
                a trident
            You'll brandish with force and use to make large profits
                for yourself.   840

LEADER. Don't let your opponent escape—you've got him gripped
    in a winning lock.

You'll easily finish him off with the strength that you have in those
    ribs of yours.
PAPHLAGON. That's not the stage we've reached, good sirs, I swear
    by Poseidon's name.
You're ignoring the fact that *I've* achieved a feat of huge
    proportions
Which enables me to gag the mouth of every one of my foes,
So long as the shields brought back from Pylos are there for all
    to see.*
SAUSAGE-SELLER. Just hold it there, with that mention of shields:
    I've got your neck in a lock.
If you love the people as much as you say, you shouldn't have
    made a point
Of allowing the shields to be displayed with their handles still
    intact.
See, Demos, this is a ploy of his, in case you ever should wish   850
To punish this man with a proper beating; he's found a way to
    prevent it.
You can see the crowd of young leather-sellers who always stand
    around him.
Well, next to them in the market are the sellers of honey and cheese.
These groups have formed themselves into a single gang of his.
So if you start to snort with anger and toy with ostracism,*
They'd use the cover of night to go and grab those shields from
    the wall,
Then rush to block all access to the barley-market stoa.*
DEMOS. How terrible! Do they really have their handles? Oh you
    blackguard!
You've cheated me for far too long with sneaky machinations.
PAPHLAGON. I beg you, sir, don't let yourself be swayed by what he
    said.   860
You mustn't suppose you'll ever discover a better friend than me.
I alone put a stop to conspirators' plans. No group can ever
    evade me
If it plots against the city's interests: I always cry foul at once.
SAUSAGE-SELLER. Of course, because you're just the same as those
    who fish for eels.
When the surface of the lake is still, they find there's nothing to
    catch.

But if they stir the mud at the bottom and make the water murky,
That's when they catch. And you do too, when you agitate the city.
Just tell me this: although you sell so many pieces of leather,
Did you ever give a piece to him to provide the soles for boots,
Since you say you love him?

DEMOS.   He certainly didn't, I swear by Apollo
    he didn't!   870

SAUSAGE-SELLER [*to* DEMOS]. You see then what he's really like?
    But look how different I am:
I've bought a pair of boots for you—[*producing them*] and here's
    a gift of them.

DEMOS. Of all the men I know, I judge you kindest to the people;
You show the greatest loyalty to the city . . . and my toes!

PAPHLAGON. How scandalous that a pair of boots should sway you
    quite so much,
And make you forget the many things I did for you in the past.
I put a stop to men being fucked, throwing Grypos out of the city.*

SAUSAGE-SELLER. How scandalous that you should exercise an
    arsehole watch
And put a stop to men being fucked! Your only motivation
Was rivalry, in case they then turned into public speakers.*   880
Meanwhile you saw old Demos here was living without a tunic
Yet you never thought that he deserved a sleeved one he could
    wear
In the middle of winter. [*Producing a garment*] But *I*, however,
    have got this present for you.

DEMOS. A masterstroke of thought—and one Themistokles never
    had!
I must admit Peiraieus harbour was quite a clever idea.*
But this new tunic of mine is just as good an invention as that.

PAPHLAGON. This is bad for me, you're damaging me with all your
    monkey tricks.

SAUSAGE-SELLER. But I'm like a man at a drinking party who
    needs to have a shit
And borrows somebody's slippers: I'm only using your own
    methods.

PAPHLAGON. You'll never outdo me with toadying tricks. [*Removes
    his cloak*] I'll drape this cloak of mine   890
Around his shoulders as well. Bad luck for *you*, vile wretch!

DEMOS.   Oh yuck!
  Get away from me and go to hell, with your nasty stink of leather!
SAUSAGE-SELLER. That's why he tried to put it on you, to choke
    you with the smell.
  He used a plot like this before. Can you recall the time
  That silphium stalks became so cheap?*
DEMOS.   Of course, I remember it well.
SAUSAGE-SELLER. Well that was his doing. He made quite sure the
    plant would be that cheap
  So all of you would buy it and eat it, then in the courts next day
  The jurors would fart so noxiously they'd knock out one another.
DEMOS. Poseidon! I've heard that story before—a Koprian man
    once told me.*
SAUSAGE-SELLER. You must have all turned yellowy-brown when
    farted on like that.   900
DEMOS. We did, by Zeus! The trick belonged to a man with
    light-brown hair.*
PAPHLAGON. Buffoonish jokes like these, you scoundrel, are
    making me alarmed.
SAUSAGE-SELLER. Athena herself instructed me to defeat you with
    my humbug.
PAPHLAGON. You *won't* defeat me. I promise you, Demos, I'll make
    it easy for you
  To slurp a dish of public pay without earning it at all.
SAUSAGE-SELLER [*to* DEMOS]. But *I've* got something else for you:
    a pot of soothing ointment
  To rub all over those little sores that plague you on your shins.
PAPHLAGON. But *I'll* pluck all your grey hairs out and make you
    young again.
SAUSAGE-SELLER. Look, here's the tail of a hare for you to wipe
    your poor old eyes.
PAPHLAGON. After blowing your nose you can wipe your hand, old
    Demos, on my head.   910
SAUSAGE-SELLER. No, wipe it on mine.
PAPHLAGON.   I insist on mine.
[*To* SAUSAGE-SELLER] I'll make you have to fund a warship
                And spend a fortune of your own.
                You'll be assigned an ancient vessel:
                The expenditure will never end,

	Repairs will be a constant need;
	I'll do whatever it takes to ensure
	That the sails are rotting away.*
SAUSAGE-SELLER.	His bluster's bubbling. Stop him at once.
	He's boiling over. We need to remove 920
	Some wood from under the pot, then skim
	His threats from the scum on top.
PAPHLAGON.	I'll make you pay a heavy price:
	You'll be hard-pressed by property tax.*
	I'll make damned sure you get enrolled
	On the registers of the rich.
SAUSAGE-SELLER.	I'll now dispense with threats myself
	But pronounce this curse on you instead.
	Imagine a frying-pan full of squid
	That's sizzling away on the fire;* 930
	And you're getting ready to put a proposal
	About Miletos*—and make a profit,
	A talent no less, if you win the vote—
	But you're eager to fill yourself up first
	With some of that squid before you rush
	To attend the Assembly meeting.
	Before you've managed to eat, your client
	Turns up, and in your eagerness
	To get the talent you gulp the squid...
	And choke to death as you do so! 940

LEADER. How wonderful—by Zeus, Apollo, Demeter!

[*The agon complete, the argument returns to unaccompanied speech.*]

DEMOS. That's my view too, and it's patent in all respects
   This man's an outstanding citizen of the kind
   The low-cost masses have missed for a very long time.
   But you, Paphlagon, have riled me with fake love.
   So give me back my ring*—you'll no longer be
   My household steward.
PAPHLAGON [*removing ring*]. Here then. But mark my words,
   If you don't allow me to be your steward, another
   Far *worse* than me will come to take my place.   950

DEMOS [*inspecting*]. But this ring here is not the one I gave you.
    The picture on the seal is not the same.
    Are my eyes at fault?
SAUSAGE-SELLER.   Let me see, what picture was yours?
DEMOS. A roasted fig-leaf stuffed with *masses* of dripping.*
SAUSAGE-SELLER. No sign of that.
DEMOS.   No fig-leaf? What does it show?
SAUSAGE-SELLER. A big-mouthed gull on a rock addressing the
    masses.
DEMOS. Ugh! How disgusting!
SAUSAGE-SELLER.   What's wrong?
DEMOS.   Get it out of my sight!
    It's not my ring he had but Kleonymos' ring.*
    Take this one of mine instead and be my steward.
PAPHLAGON. But please don't do this yet, I beg you, master,   960
    Until you've heard these oracles of mine.
SAUSAGE-SELLER. And mine as well.
PAPHLAGON.   But if you listen to *him*,
    You'll be flayed for a leather bottle.
SAUSAGE-SELLER.   Well, listen to *him*
    And you'll have your foreskin stripped to your bushy hair.*
PAPHLAGON [*to* DEMOS]. My oracles state you're destined to be
    ruler
    Over every part of Greece, and crowned with roses.
SAUSAGE-SELLER. But mine assert that wearing a purple robe
    With spangly threads, and a diadem too, you'll ride
    A golden chariot in pursuit of... justice!*
DEMOS [*to* SAUSAGE-SELLER]. Well go and fetch your oracles, so
    that he   970
    Can hear what they say.
SAUSAGE-SELLER.   I will.
DEMOS.   And you go too.
PAPHLAGON. All right.
SAUSAGE-SELLER.   All right, by Zeus! Without delay.

[*The two characters, jostling with one another, rush into the house of*
DEMOS, *from which they will shortly reappear with numerous oracle
scrolls in their arms. In their absence, the* CHORUS *comes forward to
perform a song.*]

CHORUS.   Joyous the dawn of that day will be,   *Strophe*
            For those of us alive at present
            And people of the future too,
            When Kleon meets his destruction!*
            I heard some older men, however—
            The kind who show their nasty traits
            When seeing the lists of trials forthcoming—
            Once arguing about the man   980
            And saying that if he'd never risen
            To prominence in the city, we'd lack
            Two truly useful implements:
            The pestle and stirring ladle!

            And here's another object of wonder: *Antistrophe*
            His swinish lack of culture.
            One hears it claimed about him,
            By those who went to school with him,
            That the Dorian mode exclusively
            Was often the way he tuned his lyre;   990
            He refused to learn any other.
            This made his music teacher
            Get angry and have him expelled:
            'There's no other music this boy
            Is capable of learning
            Than . . . calling the tune for himself!'*

PAPHLAGON. Look, here's what you asked me for—I could have
      brought more.
SAUSAGE-SELLER. I'm shitting beneath the weight—and could
      have brought more.
DEMOS. What are *these*?
PAPHLAGON.   My oracles.
DEMOS.   All of them?
PAPHLAGON.   You're amazed,
      But by Zeus I've got a whole box full of these things.   1000
SAUSAGE-SELLER. Well I've got several *houses* crammed with
      them.
DEMOS. Right then, what's the source of these oracles of yours?
PAPHLAGON. My oracles come from Bakis.*
DEMOS.   And whose are yours?

SAUSAGE-SELLER. They come from Glanis—an older brother of
   Bakis.

DEMOS. And what's their subject?

PAPHLAGON.   Athens, and also Pylos,
   And you, and me—well, every conceivable thing.

DEMOS. And yours, what are *they* about?

SAUSAGE-SELLER.   Well, Athens, and soup,
   The Spartans, and freshly pickled mackerel too,
   The people who cheat when measuring grain in the market,
   And you, and me—and *he* can bite his prick!   1010

DEMOS. Right then, I want you both to read them out,
   Not least the one about me I like so much
   That says I'll become an eagle in the clouds.*

PAPHLAGON. Then listen and pay the closest attention to me.

[*Chanting*] '*Mark* thou, Erechtheus' son, the oracular path which
      Apollo
   Screeched from his innermost shrine by means of his venerable
      tripods.
   Keep and preserve, he bids you, the sacred, jag-toothed dog,
   Him who protects you with teeth all bared and with deafening
      barking.
   He is the source of state pay, and will otherwise meet his
      destruction.
   Many the jackdaws who hate him and raucously caw for his
      downfall.'*   1020

DEMOS. By Demeter, I haven't a clue what all that means!
   Erechtheus, jackdaws, dog—what on earth's the link?

PAPHLAGON. The dog is *me*—because I bark to protect you.
   And Phoibos says you should cherish me as your dog.*

SAUSAGE-SELLER. That's not what the oracle says. This dog of yours
   Likes to nibble and bite out bits of the oracle texts.
   I've got the truth myself about this dog.

DEMOS. Recite it then. But first I'll pick up a stone
   In case the canine oracle tries to bite me.

SAUSAGE-SELLER [*chanting*]. '*Mark* you, Erechtheus' son, the dog
      Kerberos, trader of slaves.*   1030
   Fawner he is with his tail, but he bides his time till you're dining.
   Then he'll consume all your savoury treats, while you gawp
      somewhere else.

Into the kitchen he'll creep and in dog-like fashion unnoticed
　　All of your dishes by night he'll lick clean—and the islands as
　　　　well.'*
DEMOS.　By Poseidon, I like this one much better, O Glanis!
PAPHLAGON.　Please listen again, old sir, then choose between us.
[*Chanting*] '*Know* there's a woman who'll bring forth a lion in holiest
　　Athens.
　　He is the one who will fight for the people 'gainst numerous
　　　　gnats,
　　Lion-like standing astride his cubs. And him thou must
　　　　safeguard,
　　Building a wall made of wood and great towers constructed from
　　　　iron.'*　　　　　　　　　　　　　　　　　　　　　　　　　1040
[*Speaking*] Do you know what it means?
DEMOS.　　　　　　　　　　　　　By Apollo, I certainly don't!
PAPHLAGON.　The god was clearly instructing you to protect me,
　　Since I'm the one who serves as a lion for you.
DEMOS.　But how did you keep your leonine traits a secret?*
SAUSAGE-SELLER.　There's a crucial thing he's choosing not to
　　explain—
　　The point of this special wall of iron and wood
　　Where Loxias instructed you to keep him.*
DEMOS.　Then what was meant by the god?
SAUSAGE-SELLER.　　　　　　　　　　　　He gave instructions
　　To lock this man in a five-hole pillory frame!*
DEMOS.　I think this oracle's soon to be fulfilled.　　　　　　　1050

[*From 1051 to 1060* PAPHLAGON *and the* SAUSAGE-SELLER *not only
chant extracts from their oracles but assimilate their own advice to* DEMOS
to the same metrical and linguistic form.]

PAPHLAGON.　Don't lend belief to these things, for the crows are
　　croaking with envy.
　　'Ever the grasping hawk you should love, holding deep in your
　　　　memory
　　He was the one who brought home in fetters the Spartans' young
　　　　ravens.'
SAUSAGE-SELLER.　*That* was a deed which Paphlagon ventured
　　when utterly drunk!

'Kekrops' son, ill-advised, why thinkest thou this a great exploit?
Even a woman can carry a load which a man places on her.
War, though, is not for a woman—she'd shit if she entered a battle.'*
PAPHLAGON. Mark thou the Pylos which god prophesied stood
  forth before Pylos.
'Pylos stands before Pylos'*—
DEMOS [*also chanting*].   But what does he mean, 'before Pylos'?
SAUSAGE-SELLER. Pylos means *piles* of people who'll lose their
  access to bath tubs.*   1060
DEMOS [*restoring speech*]. You mean I won't be able to bathe today?
SAUSAGE-SELLER. That's right, since *he* will steal our bath tubs too.
  But here's an oracle now about the fleet.
  You ought to give it extremely close attention.
DEMOS. I'm doing so now. Read out and let me know
  How all my sailors will receive their pay.*
SAUSAGE-SELLER [*chanting again*]. 'Scion of Aigeus, beware of the
  tricks of the mongrel fox-dog,
  Treacherous, swift of foot, all cunning and foxy and wily.'
  Knows't thou the meaning of this?
DEMOS [*chanting*].   It's Philostratos, 'fox-dog', the
  pimp!*
SAUSAGE-SELLER [*speaking*]. That's wrong. He means whenever
  this man requests   1070
  Swift ships whose task will be collecting tribute,*
  Loxias lays it down you must refuse.
DEMOS. Then how's a trireme 'fox-dog'?
SAUSAGE-SELLER.   Isn't it clear?
  A trireme and a dog both move at speed.
DEMOS. Then why was 'fox' as well attached to 'dog'?
SAUSAGE-SELLER. He thought of soldiers being like little foxes:
  They eat the grapes from farms when on campaign.
DEMOS. Okay, but where's the pay for these little foxes?
SAUSAGE-SELLER. I'll guarantee it's paid—within three days.*

[*From 1080 to 1095 the chanted oracular metre, and the pseudo-oracular
  tone, is again maintained unbroken.*]

Hark now again to an oracle, this from the great son of Leto: 1080
Shun Kyllene he warns you, in case you submit to deception.*

DEMOS. Kyllene? What for?

SAUSAGE-SELLER.   There's a clue from the god in the name:
  Kyllene means 'bent', like the crooked hand of this man.

PAPHLAGON. *That's* not the right explanation. For Kyllene is
      a riddle
  Phoibos employs to refer to the hand of but one—Diopeithes!*
  [*To* DEMOS] Hark now, I have a winged oracle here that directly
      concerns you,
  Promising you'll be an eagle and rule all the earth as its king.

SAUSAGE-SELLER. *I've* got a better one still—you will rule all the
      Red Sea as well,
  Holding your trials in Ekbatana while licking some very nice
      cakes.*

PAPHLAGON. *I* had a dream apparition, in which our Athena
      herself   1090
  Poured with a ladle all over the folk wealth-and-health in
      abundance.

SAUSAGE-SELLER. *I* had a dream of my own, in which our Athena
      herself
  Came from her shrine on the Akropolis with an owl on her
      helmet.
  Then with an oil-flask she poured in abundance all over your head
  Streams of ambrosial liquid—but garlic-brine sauce over *him*!*

DEMOS. Hurrah! Hurrah!
  [*In normal speech*] It's turned out, then, that no one's wiser than
      Glanis.*
  [*To* SAUSAGE-SELLER] I'll now entrust myself into your care:
  Please guide me in old age—re-educate me.*

PAPHLAGON [*to* DEMOS]. No don't, I beg; please wait a little
      longer.   1100
  I'll give you barley grain and a daily allowance.

DEMOS. I loathe this talk of barley grain. Too often
  I've been deceived by you and by Thouphanes.*

PAPHLAGON. I'll give you groats already prepared for baking.

SAUSAGE-SELLER. But *I'll* give barley cakes all thoroughly
      kneaded,
  Roast fish as well: your task is just to eat them.

DEMOS. Well both of you must hurry and keep your word.
  Whichever of you turns out to treat me better

Will have from me the reins of the Pnyx to hold.

PAPHLAGON. I'll run inside first.

SAUSAGE-SELLER [*jostling*]. No you won't! I'll beat you to it. 1110

[*The two rivals rush into* DEMOS*'s house, the* SAUSAGE-SELLER *getting through the door first. In the following lyric exchanges,* DEMOS *sings in the same rhythms as the* CHORUS.]

CHORUS.　　O Demos, the power you have
　　　　　　Is exceptional: all men
　　　　　　Fear you just as much as they would
　　　　　　The reign of a tyrant.*
　　　　　　But you're far too easily swayed:
　　　　　　You seem to enjoy being flattered,
　　　　　　And being hoodwinked as well.
　　　　　　You listen to every speaker
　　　　　　With mouth agape; but your mind
　　　　　　Isn't really at home.　　　　　　1120

DEMOS.　　There's no mind beneath *your* hair*
　　　　　　If you think I've lost my wits
　　　　　　When I'm actually just pretending
　　　　　　I'm quite as gormless as this.
　　　　　　I derive great pleasure in fact
　　　　　　From being spoon-fed every day,
　　　　　　And I'm happy to nurture a leader
　　　　　　Who steals his way to the top.
　　　　　　But after he's filled his boots,
　　　　　　I smash him to pieces!　　　　　　1130

CHORUS.　　In that case all seems well,
　　　　　　If shrewdness is yours indeed
　　　　　　And part of your temperament
　　　　　　In such far-reaching ways,
　　　　　　And if you deliberately rear
　　　　　　These men like public victims
　　　　　　On the Pnyx, and when it happens
　　　　　　That you're lacking tasty food,
　　　　　　Then whichever of these is fattest
　　　　　　You sacrifice and eat!　　　　　　1140

DEMOS.   Consider how skilful I am
               In the way that I outwit them
               When they think that *they're* being clever
               And making a fool of me.
               I constantly monitor them,
               Even though they think I can't see;
               Their thefts don't escape my notice.
               Then I make them vomit back up
               All the money they've stolen from me,
               With my votes down their throat!*   1150

[PAPHLAGON *and the* SAUSAGE-SELLER *reappear from the house door,
still jostling one another and both carrying food baskets which they place
on the ground.*]

PAPHLAGON. Get out of my way!

SAUSAGE-SELLER.   Get lost yourself, you louse!

PAPHLAGON. It's been so long, O Demos, that I've been ready
      And full of desire to give you a better life.

SAUSAGE-SELLER. But *I've* been ready ten times as long. Twelve times!
      A thousand times! For ever and ever and ever!

DEMOS. The pair of you have let me down so often
      You make me want to puke—for ever and ever!

SAUSAGE-SELLER. D'you know what you need to do?

DEMOS.   I'm sure you'll
      tell me!

SAUSAGE-SELLER. Make him and me run a race from a starting line,
      To test us both on equal terms.

DEMOS.   I will!   1160
      On your marks.

PAPHLAGON and SAUSAGE-SELLER. We're ready.

DEMOS.   You're off!

SAUSAGE-SELLER.   Keep out
      of my lane!

[PAPHLAGON *and the* SAUSAGE-SELLER *race into the house, once again
competing to get through the door first. After only a short pause they run
back out, one carrying a stool, the other a table.*]

DEMOS. Will I find great happiness brought to me today

By my lovers? I'll certainly play quite hard to get!*
PAPHLAGON. Look, I've come first, with a stool for you to sit on.
SAUSAGE-SELLER. But you haven't brought a table—I'm *firster*
   with that.

[DEMOS *sits on the stool provided and with the table in front of him.*
PAPHLAGON *and the* SAUSAGE-SELLER *now open their baskets and
produce various foods, which* DEMOS *inspects in turn and piles up on
the table.*]

PAPHLAGON. Look, here's a little barley cake for you;
   I kneaded it with the grain I brought from Pylos.
SAUSAGE-SELLER. But *I've* got crusts of bread all ready for
   sopping,
   Prepared, no less, by Athena's ivory hand.*
DEMOS. I now realize, O mistress, the size of your fingers!   1170
PAPHLAGON. Pea-soup I've got for you too—such a lovely colour.
   It was ladled out by Pallas the Pylos-fighter.*
SAUSAGE-SELLER. Athena clearly looks after you, O Demos:
   Over you she holds a protective . . . potful of broth!
DEMOS. D'you think this city would still be so secure
   If she didn't protect us well with such a pot?
PAPHLAGON. Athena, Scourge of Armies, brings you sliced fish.
SAUSAGE-SELLER. But Athena, Scion of Zeus, gives you broth-
   boiled meat
   And a portion of gut, cow's stomach, and belly of pork.
DEMOS. Well, nice of her to remember the peplos we gave
   her.*   1180
PAPHLAGON. Athena, fearsome-crested, urges you
   To taste this cake as fuel to power our rowers.
SAUSAGE-SELLER. Here, take these things as well.
DEMOS.   What use should I make
   Of these intestines?
SAUSAGE-SELLER.   The goddess explicitly meant
   They belong inside the *ribs* of all our triremes.*
   She clearly watches over the city's fleet.
   And take this wine to drink, mixed three and two.*
DEMOS [*tasting*]. How lovely it is! The mixture's nice and strong.
SAUSAGE-SELLER. Athena *Tri*togenes had *tried* it first!*

PAPHLAGON. Here, take a slice of rich honey-cake from me.   1190
SAUSAGE-SELLER. I'll give you the whole of this cake, not just a
   slice.
PAPHLAGON. But you won't have any hare-meat to give like me.*
SAUSAGE-SELLER [*aside*]. Oh no, I need some hare-meat—where
   will I get it?
   It's time, my heart, to discover a sneaky ploy.
PAPHLAGON. Do you see this meat, you wretch?
SAUSAGE-SELLER.   I couldn't care less,
   Since I see some men approaching me over there,
   Ambassadors carrying purses full of silver.
PAPHLAGON. Where, where? [*Drops the meat*]
SAUSAGE-SELLER [*picks it up*].   Forget it, they're nothing to do
   with you.
   D'you see, dear Demos, the hare-meat I've got for you?
PAPHLAGON. Outrageous, you filched what really belonged to me. 1200
SAUSAGE-SELLER. You did the same with the prisoners brought
   from Pylos!
DEMOS [*to* SAUSAGE-SELLER]. How on earth did you think of such
   an ingenious theft?
SAUSAGE-SELLER [*paratragically*]. The thought was that of the
   goddess, the theft was mine.
PAPHLAGON. But *I* ran all the risk and roasted the meat.
DEMOS [*to* PAPHLAGON]. Away! The thanks are for him who serves
   the food.
PAPHLAGON. I'm doomed! My shamelessness will be outstripped.
SAUSAGE-SELLER. Why not decide now, Demos, which of us
   Has shown the most concern for you and your stomach?
DEMOS. What test could I employ to choose between you
   If I want spectators to think my judgement's clever?   1210
SAUSAGE-SELLER. I'll tell you which. Just quietly take my basket
   And check exactly what its contents are,
   Then the same with *his*. You're bound to judge correctly.

[DEMOS *follows the* SAUSAGE-SELLER'*s advice and examines each of the
                           baskets in turn.*]

DEMOS. Right then, what have we here?
SAUSAGE-SELLER.   You see, old Daddy,

It's empty. I served you everything I had.

DEMOS. This basket has the people's interests at heart.

SAUSAGE-SELLER. Now come and inspect the basket of Paphlagon.
You see?

DEMOS. Good heavens, it's stuffed with lots of goodies!
A huge amount of the cake he kept for himself.
The slice he cut for me was a tiny bit.   1220

SAUSAGE-SELLER. But this isn't new—he's always done this to you.
He'd let you have a fraction of what he took,
But stash away the most for just himself.

DEMOS [*to* PAPHLAGON]. Scumbag! Is this the way you robbed and
tricked me?
[*Grandiloquently*] Yet I enwreathed thy head and gave thee gifts.*

PAPHLAGON. But I only stole for the good of the city itself.

DEMOS. Take off the wreath at once: I want to give it
To *him*.

SAUSAGE-SELLER.   Remove it quickly, whipping boy!

PAPHLAGON. I won't! I've got an oracle issued at Delphi
Which names the only person who'll ever defeat me.   1230

SAUSAGE-SELLER. The name must be my own, it's all too clear.

PAPHLAGON [*solemnly*]. I want indeed to put you to the test*
To see if you match the prophecies from the god.
And here's the first enquiry I shall make:
Whose school did you attend when still a boy?

SAUSAGE-SELLER. I was beaten into shape in the slaughter house.

PAPHLAGON. What's this! The oracle doth my mind perturb!
Very well.
Which tricky moves did you learn in wrestling school?

SAUSAGE-SELLER. I learnt to steal and perjure in barefaced fashion.

PAPHLAGON. O Phoibos Apollo, Lykian god, what wilt thou!*   1240
What trade did you have when you came to manhood's stage?

SAUSAGE-SELLER. I sold sausages for my trade—and was fucked
a little.*

PAPHLAGON. I'm doomed! There is no place for me in the world!
One slender hope remains to buoy me up.
So tell me this: was it actually in the market
Or at the city gates you sold your meat?

SAUSAGE-SELLER. At the city gates, where pickled fish is sold.

PAPHLAGON. Alas, what the god foretold has been fulfilled!

Wheel back inside this godforsaken man.*

[*Removing garland*] O garland, now depart, farewell! 'Tis not   1250
    By choice I leave thee. Another's wilt thou be:
    In theft he'll ne'er outdo me, only in fortune.*

SAUSAGE-SELLER [*taking garland*]. Zeus, god of Hellenes, the prize
    of victory's thine!

SLAVE^A [*appearing at door*]. All hail, great victor!* Don't forget one
    thing:
    It was *I* made you a man. Now grant a favour:
    Let me be Phanos, bringing court cases for you.*

DEMOS. But I still don't know your name.

SAUSAGE-SELLER.   Agorakritos: *
    The Agora brought me up on a diet of quarrels.

DEMOS. To Agorakritos I then entrust myself,
    And Paphlagon I'm handing over to you.   1260

SAUSAGE-SELLER. I promise, Demos, I'll be your faithful servant.
    You'll soon agree you've never seen anyone else
    Who's done more public good for the city of Gawpers.*

[DEMOS *and the* SAUSAGE-SELLER, *the latter now in control of the
    humiliated* PAPHLAGON, *exit into* DEMOS'*s house.*]

[SECOND PARABASIS: 1264–1315]

CHORUS.   What finer way to start or end our song   *Strophe*
        Than for us, as riders of swift steeds,
        To sing *nothing* about Lysistratos
        And decline to make homeless Thoumantis
        The object of a wilful attack?
        The latter, O dear Apollo, is always   1270
        Starving, as with tears profuse
        He clutches your quiver and prays
        At sacred Delphi to escape his wretched poverty?*

LEADER. Reviling the wicked should never arouse resentment
    among our audience.
    It's a way of honouring decent men, if you think about it
    carefully.
    Now, if the person I have in mind—and someone who merits
    outright abuse—

Were in the public eye himself, I wouldn't have needed to name
    a friend.
As it is, I must. You're all aware who Arignotos is—well all
Who know what music is and how the old tunes ought to be
    performed.*
Now, Arignotos has a brother, but someone not akin in
    type.   1280
Ariphrades this is; he's vile. In fact, being vile is what he *wants*.
But vileness isn't enough for him—if it were, I'd hardly have
    noticed him—
Not even hyper-vileness, no: he's ventured even further still.
His very own tongue he stains and taints with pleasures of the
    filthiest kind:
He visits whore-houses and cleans the plates by licking up the
    abominable dew,
Befouling all his facial hair and stirring the pots on the women's
    hearths,
Producing work like Polymnestos and sharing time with
    Oionichos.*
If anyone doesn't feel sheer disgust at the thought of what this
    man is like,
They can never expect to drink with me and put their lips to
    a cup we share!

CHORUS.   So often I've pondered in dead of   *Antistrophe* 1290
             night
        And puzzled about the source from which
        Kleonymos easily feeds himself.
        They say that once when chewing upon
        The food of propertied men
        He wouldn't remove his snout from the grain bin.*
        They had to entreat him with one voice,
        'We beg you, O master, by your knees,
        Please leave and spare our table!'

LEADER. It's said some triremes came together to hold a meeting
    among themselves.   1300
    And one of the ships, an older female, delivered a speech to the
    rest of them:

'Well, haven't you heard the latest news, you maidens, about the
city's affairs?

They say a certain man requests a hundred of us to sail to
Carthage—

A nasty man what's more, like wine that's turned all sour:
Hyperbolos!'*

The ships were all agreed that this was a terrible thing they
couldn't accept.

A younger one, who'd never been near a man, was next to speak to
them:

'Apollo avert this plague of a man! He'll never control *this* ship at
least.

If need be, I'll let wood-worm rot me and live as a spinster into
old age.'

'He won't control me either', declared another—Nauphante,
Nauson's daughter;*

Of that I'm as sure as I am that all my timbers are made of finest
pine!   1310

If Athens approves Hyperbolos' plan, I propose we need to seek
sanctuary:

We could sail to Theseus' shrine for refuge or enter the Awesome
Goddesses' precinct.*

He won't hold *us* under his command while showing contempt for
the city's needs.

If he wants some ships to set afloat, and to sail to perdition along
with them,

Let him take the *vessels* in which he used ... to sell his lamps in the
marketplace!

[*The* SAUSAGE-SELLER *re-enters from the house of* DEMOS. *From 1316
to 1334 the lines are chanted in a recitative metre which suits the ostensible
solemnity of the occasion.*]

SAUSAGE-SELLER. Keep ritual silence, seal all mouths, no calling
witnesses here!

Close up the courtrooms now, the ones in which the city delights.*

To cap its new good luck, the audience ought to sing in triumph.

LEADER. O shaft of light for sacred Athens, protector of all the
islands,

What tidings these you bring to prompt the fumes of
    sacrifice? 1320
SAUSAGE-SELLER. I've boiled the dross from Demos for you,
    transforming him into beauty.
LEADER. And where is he now, O you whose mind produces
    stupendous ideas?
SAUSAGE-SELLER. He lives in Athens of ancient times, a city that's
    violet-wreathed.*
LEADER. How may we see him? What dress does he wear? What
    sort of man is he now?
SAUSAGE-SELLER. He's the same as when he dined with Aristeides
    and Miltiades.
    You'll see him soon: I hear the gates of the Propylaia open.*

[*During the following lines the house door slowly opens and the transformed figure of* DEMOS, *now to be imagined on the Akropolis, steps out:
he is wearing old-fashioned but luxurious dress, including a golden brooch
in his hair.*]

    Cry out with joy at the apparition of Athens of ancient times,
    A city of wonder, renowned in song, which glorious Demos
    inhabits.
LEADER. O Athens, gleaming, violet-wreathed, an object of great
    envy,*
    Put on display for us the monarch of Greece and of this
    land. 1330
SAUSAGE-SELLER. Behold him with his cicada-brooch, aglow in
    ancient dress.*
    He smells no more of voting-shells but of peace, he's sleek with
    myrrh.*
LEADER. Hail, king of the Greeks! We share in celebrating the joy
    you bring.
    Your condition is worthy of Athens itself and the trophy on
    Marathon plain.*

[*As* DEMOS *steps forward, the dialogue switches back from recitative
to speech.*]

DEMOS. My dearest friend, come here, Agorakritos.
    You've done me such good by boiling me down.

SAUSAGE-SELLER.   What, me?
But you've no idea, old chap, what you used to be like,
Or your former ways. Otherwise, you'd think me a god!
DEMOS. What sort of things did I do? And what was I like?
SAUSAGE-SELLER. Well, first, when any Assembly speaker
    said,   1340
'I'm your passionate lover, Demos, and full of affection,*
I care for you and alone protect your interests'—
Whenever a speaker began with words like these,
You flapped like a cock and pranced like a calf.
DEMOS.   What, me?
SAUSAGE-SELLER. Such speakers thoroughly fooled you and got
    what they wanted.
DEMOS. You mean I was totally clueless about these things?
SAUSAGE-SELLER. Your ears, by Zeus, would spread themselves
    wide open,
And close as easily too, as a parasol does.*
DEMOS. Had I really become as stupid and senile as that?
SAUSAGE-SELLER. You certainly had. And if two orators
    clashed,   1350
The one proposing to build more ships, the other
That the money be spent on increasing state pay, the second
Would race ahead of the first when it came to the vote.
But why are you hanging your head? You mustn't waver.
DEMOS. I feel ashamed of all my previous faults.
SAUSAGE-SELLER. But you're not to blame yourself, you mustn't
    think that;
It's the fault of those who tricked you. Look, just tell me:
If a mischievous advocate should say to you,
'You jurymen will have no grain to eat
Unless you vote for conviction in this case',   1360
Tell me how you'll treat this sort of advocate.*
DEMOS. I'll lift him up and hurl him into the pit,
After hooking onto his throat . . . Hyperbolos!*
SAUSAGE-SELLER. That's better: you've given a highly sensible
    answer.
What other policies too will you adopt?
DEMOS. To start with, those who row on the city's triremes
Will get their pay in full from me when they dock.*

SAUSAGE-SELLER. That's nice for lots of smoothly worn-down
    buttocks!
DEMOS. And another thing: no one on the hoplite lists
    Will get his name transferred by devious means.*   1370
    Everyone will stay on the list where he first appeared.
SAUSAGE-SELLER. A bite for Kleonymos' hand...where he holds
    his shield!*
DEMOS. And the Agora will be barred to beardless youths.
SAUSAGE-SELLER. Then where will Kleisthenes and Straton live?*
DEMOS. It's the adolescents I mean in the perfume shops,
    Who sit around and prattle pretentiously:
    'Phaiax is smart—how deftly he won acquittal!
    He's so stylistical, emphatical too,
    Aphoristical and clear and caustical,
    Contemptical of noisy publical heckles.'*   1380
SAUSAGE-SELLER. Be obscenical to such linguistical tosh!*
DEMOS. My plan is rather to force every one of them
    To spend time hunting and leave the Assembly alone.
SAUSAGE-SELLER. On the terms we've agreed you can have this
    folding stool
    And a boy with full-grown balls to carry it round.
    If you want, treat the boy himself as a folding stool!*

[*A slave* BOY *carrying an old-fashioned folding chair comes out of the
    house and takes up his position in attendance on* DEMOS.]

DEMOS. How blessed I am, restored to ancient ways!
SAUSAGE-SELLER. And what will you say when I also hand to you
    A thirty-year peace? [*Calling*] Here, quick, Peace Treaties, enter.*

[*Enter* PEACE TREATIES *in the form of two naked females personifying
    a thirty-year peace between Athens and Sparta.*]

DEMOS. O Zeus supreme, how gorgeous they are! By heaven,   1390
[*Gesturing sexually*] Any chance of *treating* them to a *piece* of myself?
    Where on earth did you get them?
SAUSAGE-SELLER.   You won't be surprised to hear
    That Paphlagon hid them away, to keep them from you.
    I'm handing them over to you to take to the country
    When you now return.*

DEMOS.   And Paphlagon himself,
  Who behaved so badly—what are your plans for him?
SAUSAGE-SELLER. Nothing much, except he'll have my former
    trade.
  He'll sell sausages all on his own at the city gates,
  Mixing bits of dog and donkey meat together.
  He'll wrangle drunkenly with prostitutes   1400
  And drink the dirty water from the baths.
DEMOS. A great idea—the place where he belongs,
  Having shouting matches with whores and bath attendants!
  I invite you, in return, to the Prytaneion,
  To occupy the seat that outcast had.
  So follow now and wear this frog-green dress.* [*Hands it to him*]
  Let Paphlagon be taken to ply his trade,
  So the visitors whom he harmed can see him punished.

[DEMOS *and the* SAUSAGE-SELLER *exit by one* eisodos. SLAVE[A] *appears
from the house with the disgraced* PAPHLAGON, *now costumed in the former garb of the* SAUSAGE-SELLER, *and leads him off on the opposite side.
The* CHORUS *makes its exit in suitably equestrian style.*]

WASPS

INTRODUCTION

THE five surviving Aristophanic plays from the 420s all involve a combination of the same two fundamental elements: on the one hand, a plot constructed around a peculiar entanglement between the contrasting realms of domestic and public life; on the other, an eccentric old male protagonist who is the chief reason for the entanglement in question.[1] In *Acharnians* (425), Dikaiopolis enacts the wish-fulfilment of a 'private' peace, including a market set up outside his own house, while the city as a whole continues at war. In *Knights* (424), city and household are allegorically superimposed, with the political roles of people and demagogues played out in the relationship between the seemingly gullible Demos and his slaves. In *Clouds* (423), the naive Strepsiades finds his way into the 'school' of Sokrates in the (ultimately forlorn) hope of acquiring immoral rhetorical skills that would enable him to defeat the legal prosecutions which are looming up as a result of his (son's) unpaid debts. In *Peace* (421), Trygaios visits the world of the gods in order to 'excavate' the peace that he has long yearned for, and in the process he finds a new symbolic bride for himself.

Wasps (422) fits into this sequence with its own outré permutation of the comic resources provided by the domestic/public contrast and the antics of an unruly old man. Taking a figure, Philokleon, who is both near-senile and yet addicted to playing a supposedly important role, qua juror, in the city's democratic institutions, the play confines him to a domesticity which he at first resists, somewhat like a trapped animal (as well as like a failed emulator of Odysseus),[2] but to which he eventually submits once the world inside his house is reconfigured into a miniature version of the public realm—i.e. a private court where he can supposedly exercise all his judicial powers without any interference from others. *Wasps* has two further, interlocking features

---

[1] Two later surviving plays, *Birds* and *Women at the Thesmophoria*, also have an elderly male protagonist who becomes embroiled in an absurd scenario, as well as one more, *Wealth*, where the protagonist is an old man but of a relatively sober character. (The 'age' of Dionysos in *Frogs* is never indicated, but he has something in common with Aristophanes' 'old men' protagonists.)

[2] For Philokleon's pseudo-Odyssean ruse of hanging underneath the family's donkey, see 179–89; the chorus will later think of Odyssean ingenuity at 351.

which lend its plot-structure a distinctive shape and ethos. One of
these is the prominence of the old man's son, Bdelykleon, who, unlike
Strepsiades' son in *Clouds*, is active and even (partly) in control of
things for much of the drama. The other is the abrupt though not
entirely unanticipated shift of direction which occurs when, after
Philokleon's spell as juror inside his own house has collapsed in the,
for him, traumatic acquittal of a defendant, his son attempts to re-
educate him, though with ill-fated results (unlike Dikaiopolis's triumphant party-going in *Acharnians*), for a luxurious lifestyle that
centres on attendance at drinking parties with members of the city's
supposed elite. In a sense, then, Philokleon 'fails' twice over: first as
juror, whether we think in terms of his abandonment of his original
addiction or of his unintended vote for acquittal; and then as symposiast, when he shows himself incapable of social finesse and even turns
into an aggressive criminal contemptuous of the legal system he used
to serve.[3] Yet, unlike Strepsiades in *Clouds*, whose own failure is hardly
redeemed by an ambiguous ending in which he tries to destroy Sokrates
and his school,[4] Philokleon ends *Wasps* as a crazily rejuvenated figure
whose energies express themselves in an irrepressible whirligig of
drunken dancing—a kind of comically life-affirming gesture that somehow overrides all the twists and turns of what has preceded.

The dramatic trajectory of *Wasps*—from a subdued opening scene
with somnolent slaves guarding a locked house (bizarrely draped with
netting) in the middle of the night, to the wildly exuberant choreography (which, alas, we can only imagine) of the finale—is, as so often
with Aristophanes, irreducibly outlandish. The play is a vehicle for
multiple modes of comedy and has several paradoxes built into it. In
the broadest terms, *Wasps* both is and is not a 'political' play: it contains some ostensibly detailed treatment, principally in the agon
(526–724), of the putative workings of Athens' law-courts within the
system of democracy, but at the same time it focuses that treatment
through the lens of a character so deludedly obsessive as to leave us
with a highly unstable sense of how the elaborate judicial machinery

---

[3] Philokleon's drunken antics take on, however, an ironic *resemblance* to the more
rowdy and disruptive behaviour of some wealthy symposiasts: this irony is proleptically
signalled at 1253–63 (n.b. 1256), and subsequently underlined by Philokleon's insouci-
ance in his reactions to those who seek reparation from him.

[4] For my own reading of the end of *Clouds*, against the grain of much critical opinion,
see *Aristophanes: Frogs and Other Plays*, 17–19.

of Athens really operated at this date. More specifically, *Wasps* both is and is not a play about the leading politician Kleon, who had been at the (allegorical) centre of *Knights*: we are told near the outset (62–3), in a passage I shall return to, that Kleon will not be the work's satirical target, and yet the two main characters are called Kleon-lover (Philokleon) and Kleon-loather (Bdelykleon)—a piece of nomenclature which nicely captures the idea, anticipated in the dream at 39–41, that Kleon is a divisive, polarizing force in the city—and when the domestic court is set up in their house the only case brought before it involves two dogs, one of whom is a blatant allegory of Kleon himself.[5] But paradoxes and anomalies abound in other thematic aspects of the play as well. One of these is incorporated in the double-sided conception of Philokleon's and Bdelykleon's family. While the father, like all his elderly friends in the chorus, notionally belongs to a class of poorer citizens for whom the jurors' three-obol daily fee is essential income in hard times (Philokleon stresses how much the money matters to *everyone* in his household, 606–7), the son seems to belong to a different socio-economic as well as cultural world, familiar with the lifestyle of an Athenian elite and anxious to introduce his father to that world. Although one could concoct a sociological hypothesis to make vaguely conceivable sense of this disparity in relation to contemporary Athens, it is much more straightforward to regard it as a piquant detail whose raison d'être is the productive comic tension, not to say contradiction, which it creates.[6]

Something comparable is true of a more diffuse anomaly in the ideas that underpin the scenario of *Wasps*. Whether we think of the protagonist himself or of the larger group to which he belongs, as represented by the chorus, we are confronted by a janus-faced image that combines pathetic senility with fanatical vindictiveness. The paradoxical syndrome of obsessive commitment to jury service on the part of older Athenians is individualized in Philokleon's case as both a weird 'disease' (71 ff.) and a quasi-erotic obsession (97–9), whereas

---

[5] The other dog allegorizes Laches, a contemporary general, though the supposed prosecution of Laches by Kleon is probably fictitious: see my notes on lines 240 and 836–8 of the play.

[6] The relationship in *Clouds* between the rustic Strepsiades and his son, Pheidippides, the latter expensively addicted to horses, is partially similar; it comes about via Strepsiades' improbable marriage to a supposed member of the aristocratic Alkmaionid family: see *Clouds* 41–74, with my brief discussion in *Frogs and Other Plays*, 7–8.

the chorus manifests it as a collective phenomenon, the behaviour of a whole tranche of the population. There was a very basic demographic justification for the collective aspect of this picture in the facts of the judicial system. As *Wasps* itself mentions (662), six thousand Athenians, a far from negligible portion (perhaps between 15 and 20 percent)[7] of the total number of male citizens at this date, were selected annually (by lot, from volunteers) for the roster of jurors or 'dikasts'. Both the size of the jurors' roster and the provision of daily state-pay, first proposed by Perikles in the middle of the fifth century, were designed to maximize the democratic rationale of the system, i.e. the representative participation of the citizen body, the demos, as a whole. But it is extremely likely that by the time of *Wasps* almost a decade of war against Sparta had produced, or accentuated, a preponderance of jurors who were both elderly, i.e. past the age of normal military service, and drawn from the less affluent sections of the population.[8] *Wasps* converts these socio-economic factors into a running caricature of jurors as decrepit old men, badly dependent on obtaining their three-obol fee for subsistence purposes.

But that, as already stressed, is only one half of a compound picture. The other half makes the jurors aggressively vindictive towards defendants, as symbolized by their instrument of fiery anger, their wasp 'sting' (223–7, 403 ff.). On one level, this amounts to the preposterous notion that jurors have an automatic, overwhelming desire to convict defendants: even without anything like statistics for Athenian courts, we know of enough cases of acquittal to recognize a distorted stereotype at work here, a comic exaggeration of just one of the ways in which a jury can behave. In fact, *Wasps* itself repeatedly betrays the distortion in passing: at 157 Philokleon suggests that if he is prevented from getting to court that day, a particular defendant will be acquitted (the logic is nonsense, of course); at 277–80 the chorus states that Philokleon is by far the most 'acrid', i.e. implacable, of jurors, indeed 'the only one unpersuadable' by defendants; at 281–3,

---

[7] Most modern estimates of the size of the Athenian citizen body at this date vary between twenty and forty thousand. The figure of twenty thousand used by Bdelykleon at *Wasps* 709 seems to represent the size of the general citizen body other than the wealthy; on this passage, see my text below.

[8] This would have included some Athenians who had been displaced from their rural properties and needed income while living in the city: this is implied in the case of the chorus of farmers in *Peace* at 348–52.

the chorus refers (admittedly as to a traumatic exception) to a recent acquittal; and at 558 Philokleon mentions the kind of defendant who tries to bribe him before his trial but 'wouldn't have known I existed at all if not for his prior acquittal'. So the supposed propensity of jurors to convict is transparently comic in terms of general judicial psychology: it serves to heighten the impression of Philokleon's manic mentality as an individual, as well as to fit with the colourful theatricalization of the chorus as wasps.

There is, however, a further dimension to the idea of dikastic vin-dictiveness, namely its alignment with the proposition that jurors are not independent agents but pawns of those powerful figures, espe-cially Kleon and his henchmen, who use the courts to pursue their political enmities and exploit a repertoire of populist rhetoric to keep juries on their side. If there is an intelligible critique of the Athenian courts threaded through the fabric of *Wasps*, it is a political, not a purely legal or institutional, critique. But is this really a sustainable way of reading the play?

I have already suggested that *Wasps* both is and is not a play about Kleon: although the politician lurks round the edges of the work's field of vision almost throughout, his relationship to the judicial sys-tem never comes into clear and steady focus. When prevented by his son from leaving the house, Philokleon calls out to Kleon, as well as his fellow jurors, to come to his aid (197; cf. the chorus's similar reac-tion at 409). The absurdity of that plea, as though a politician could intervene in a domestic dispute, is nonetheless compatible with a feel-ing that many jurors might regard Kleon as a defender of the demo-cratic values which underpin the city's courts. When the chorus later enters, falteringly making its way towards the courts, its leader speaks as though Kleon has both a protective and a controlling relationship towards their group:

> LEADER. So yesterday our kinsman Kleon gave orders not to be late.
> He urged us bring a stock of anger to last for three whole days,
> Enough with which to punish Laches for all those crimes of his.
>
> (242–4)

Once again, sense and nonsense are intertwined. The description of Kleon as kinsman or guardian strengthens the humorous subtext, especially strong in Philokleon's own case, that jury service somehow detaches individuals from their households and attaches them to an alternative, politically defined 'family'. At the same time, the notion that Kleon regulates the time at which jurors turn up at court is flagrantly ludicrous, as is the linked suggestion that he controls jurors as though they were soldiers under his command (with 'anger' substituted for the food rations that troops were instructed to bring with them for the first three days of a campaign); and the comic thrust of the lines is all the more hyperbolic if, as I mentioned earlier, the 'trial' of Laches is a piece of pure fiction.

But satirical hyperbole, as so often, cuts two ways: while it draws attention to its conspicuous overstatement, and therefore makes space for appreciation of the gap between satire and reality, it can also be read as employing exaggeration to hammer home its essential points. In the case of Kleon and the jurors, matters are further complicated by the question of comic perspective: when Philokleon and the chorus appeal to Kleon or talk of his dominance over them, is the audience invited to hear these things as reflecting more on Kleon's political behaviour or on the jurors' own naive perceptions and impulses? The constant operations of fantasy in Old Comedy make such questions impossible to answer in any meaningful way, but the questions nevertheless provide a partial critical framework for analysis of Aristophanes' work. In the case of *Wasps*, the issue of comic perspective becomes all the more pertinent when we reach the set-piece agon between father and son at 526–724. What we are given here is a clash of ideas involving a radical divergence between Philokleon's perspective as individual juror and Bdelykleon's perspective as 'external' observer of the system. For basic orientation, it will be worthwhile to summarize the main claims and counter-claims advanced in the two halves of the agon.

PHILOKLEON

548–58: Jurors possess power and even a kind of 'kingship'; they are supplicated outside court by important men (who are on trial for stealing from public funds).

560–75: Jurors have the satisfaction of listening to the varied ploys adopted by defendants, including their use of humour and their fulsome appeals for pity.

578–87: Among the further delights of the juror's life are opportunities to see boys' genitals (during citizenship reviews) or to reverse the stipulations people have made in their wills. Juries' decisions are not subject to higher review.

590–602: The courts deal with important democratic business; juries are wooed by politicians; even Kleon and his henchmen protect jurors.

605–18: The juror's three-obol fee makes Philokleon popular with his wife and daughter; it gives him a buffer against the domestic control exercised by his son.

619–30: Juries are as powerful as Zeus himself! The rich fear their 'thunder'.

BDELYKLEON

655–79: The city's annual revenue is some two thousand talents; the annual total paid out in jurors' fees is no more than one hundred and fifty talents. The rest of the revenue goes to corrupt politicians: it is these people, not jurors, who are bribed by the allies.

682–95: Jurors are enslaved to the city's office-holders; although elderly jurors once fought, as soldiers and sailors, to build up the city's empire, they are now the dupes of young office-holders who manipulate the system and keep juries in the dark.

698–712: The city's revenue from its thousand tribute-paying allied states is enough to support twenty thousand citizens in the lap of luxury; instead, Athens' leaders keep the people poor in order to manage them for their own ends.

715–24: As a sop to the people, the politicians sometimes promise grain doles, though they do not deliver them; Bdelykleon, by contrast, wants to provide his father with a comfortable way of life.

When the arguments are schematized like this, it is immediately obvious that the two characters see things from such different angles that, to a considerable extent, they are simply speaking past one another. Philokleon is preoccupied with the subjective experience of attending court, enjoying the emotional drama of the court room, and savouring (above all) the precarious psychology of defendants. Bdelykleon, on the other hand, presents a fundamentally economic argument to the effect that the costs of the jury system represent only a small fraction of the city's total revenue and that in principle the majority of ordinary, i.e. non-wealthy, citizens (he gives the figure of twenty thousand) could benefit to a much greater extent if Athens' economy were properly organized for their benefit. In effect, Philokleon extrapolates from his subjective gratification to a claim of 'power' for jurors in general (though that claim of power could in principle be more seriously stated),[9] while Bdelykleon uses a general analysis of Athens' economy, and the way it supposedly functions in the interests of populist politicians, to convince his father that he is actually being denied a truly pleasurable life (which his son, however, is offering to provide for him away from the courts) and is being cheaply exploited by the existing system.

There is, as always with Aristophanes, more than one way of deciphering the clash of ideas presented in the agon of *Wasps*, with its concomitant discrepancy between first-person and third-person points of view. But it is important to recognize not only the asymmetry noted above but also the comically visible fallacies and shortcomings of *both* sides of the argument, not just Philokleon's. The latter's absurd arbitrariness (not to mention his paratragic antics in brandishing a sword)[10] is blatant. He magnifies the significance of small details such as having his hand shaken by an imploring defendant outside the courtroom; he dwells on (far-fetched) incidentals such as pieces of declamation or musical performances by actors or musicians who happen to be on trial; he drools over the thought of seeing male adolescents' genitals; and he deludes himself that jurors matter enough for Kleon and his henchmen to take direct personal care of them (596–600). Less immediately obvious (to us, at any rate), but no less telling however, are the ruses employed by Bdelykleon. Three points are worth highlighting in this regard. First, Bdelykleon fiddles some of his figures: his claim that there are a thousand allied cities (707), whose tribute could easily pay for twenty thousand Athenians to live lives of subsidized luxury, is grossly exaggerated; there were, in fact, fewer than four hundred, and this huge discrepancy must have been immediately glaring to many in the play's first audience. Secondly, both in that same specific passage and in his entire line of argument that the jury-serving class is somehow cheated out of the profits of empire, Bdelykleon totally ignores the major costs, not least of the war with Sparta (not even mentioned in this

---

[9] For the fundamental principle, see, for instance, pseudo-Aristotle, *Constitution of the Athenians* 9.1: 'If the people controls the vote [sc. in the courts], it controls the constitution.'

[10] Philokleon requests the sword at 522–3, anticipating the possibility of a 'heroic' (e.g. Ajax-like) suicide in the event of defeat; he probably brandishes it throughout the agon, eventually dropping it at 714. This is a very good example of the kind of detail which would have been conspicuous in performance but which modern readers need to make a special effort to build into their visualized appreciation of Aristophanes' work.

context), which the city had to meet from its revenues: on this key point there is no room for uncertainty, since we know that Athens' finances had been coming under major strain for some years before *Wasps* and would continue to do so in subsequent years.[11] Finally, and relatedly, Bdelykleon manages to turn the idea of financial corruption on the part of individual (demagogic) politicians into a ludicrously all-devouring phenomenon, insinuating, with more bluster than logic, that the revenue not spent on jury pay is somehow swallowed in massive bribes paid to such people.[12] That, in its way, is every bit as wild and fanciful as some of the things Philokleon says. Indeed, part of the comic impact of the agon stems from the way in which it shows how unreliable arguments can issue from the mouth not only of a patently deranged old man but also, despite his air of rhetorical and economic professionalism, from that of his 'somewhat haughty-snorty' son (as Xanthias originally called Bdelykleon, with a wonderful nonce word, at 135).[13]

The dramatic point of the agon is not, of course, an abstract debate of political principles, but a means by which Bdelykleon can undermine and loosen his father's obsession with jury service. The agon turns out, in fact, to be the first part of a two-stage process of dissuasion. The second stage, which is a piece of improvisation by Bdelykleon (see 764–6, with the chance incident that supplies the actual material of the trial at 835 ff.), is enacted by the domestic trial scene, whose humour, not least the elaborate charade with would-be courtroom furniture and other paraphernalia, is mostly too transparent (rather on the lines of children's make-believe with household objects) to require much explication. Aristophanes employs here one of his favourite comic techniques, the collapse of the political and

---

[11] Thucydides 2.13.2–5 makes Perikles explain the healthy state of Athenian finances, including special reserves, at the start of the war, but at 3.19.1 he attests a growing shortage of funds, and the need for a property tax (cf. n. on *K*. 924), as early as 428–7. The major tribute reassessment of 425–4 (see n. on *K*. 312–13) was itself necessitated by the mounting costs of war. A decade after *Wasps*, in the aftermath of the Sicilian expedition of 415–413, Thucydides 7.28.4 describes the city as practically bankrupt.

[12] At 666–71 Bdelykleon swerves from claiming that most of the city's revenue is pocketed by demagogic politicians (666) to the very different claim that such people take huge bribes by threatening allied cities in order to extract their tribute from them (669–71).

[13] We need, as readers, to keep that description of Bdelykleon in mind throughout, since it may well have been translated into the general inflection of voice and comportment with which a professional actor would have played the role.

civic into the domestic and personal: subtle variations on this technique are found in, for example, the equivalence of Dikaiopolis's 'private' peace in *Acharnians* to a personal supply of exceptional wine, the
emphasis on food-preparation in the household of Demos in *Knights*,
Trygaios's marriage to Harvest in *Peace*, the women's sex-strike in
Lysistrata, Chremes' conversion of household utensils into elements
of the Panathenaic procession in *Assembly-Women* (730 ff.), and
Chremylos's installation of recovered Wealth into his own family in
Wealth. The domestic court is organized by Bdelykleon in a manner
which picks up from the agon by appealing principally to Philokleon's
desire for personal gratification: physical comfort and convenience is
the keynote (771–8, 807–14), together with a continuing guarantee of
a three-obol fee (784–5, an ironic detail given that the money will
implicitly come from the family's existing resources). But the canine
mock-trial which comes about when Xanthias reports the theft of a
piece of cheese by one of the household dogs also looks back to the
agon and to the emphasis placed there by Bdelykleon on the self-
interested use of the judicial system by politicians, even if the encoded
prosecution of Laches by Kleon is probably, as mentioned earlier, a
historical fiction. So the domestic trial borrows, in a sense, from the
agon's clash between the respectively subjective and political considerations advanced by father and son, but turns some of its abstract,
argumentative components into the stuff of physical, even panto-
mimish, action.

Because the trial scene is arranged for Philokleon's immediate
benefit, to reduce the supposed trauma of his enforced withdrawal
from real jury service, things proceed initially as though the old
man now has the best of both worlds: he gets his gratification (now
ludicrously encapsulated in the opportunity to sup soup, as well as
urinate, while he listens to a case) but he is no longer being exploited
by corrupt politicians, since everything, he thinks (as he always
did), is under his direct control. But the double irony of his comic
psychology is that while he continues to manifest a gullible parti-
sanship in his prejudicial acceptance of everything alleged by the
prosecuting Dog (alias Kleon), his very gullibility is open to crafty
manipulation by his own son and proves his ultimate downfall when
he is tricked into voting for acquittal after all—a fact which makes
him collapse in melodramatic despair (995 ff.) though it also complements the play's various hints, noted earlier, that Athenian juries

do not in reality bear out the stereotype of convicting almost all defendants.[14]

Philokleon's unwitting acquittal of the thieving dog, Labes, ends his resistance to his son's wish to remove him from the grubby life of a poor juror and to introduce him to the supposedly superior social and cultural world of those who attend drinking parties and, in a nice metatheatrical touch, the theatre itself (1005)! Philokleon now submits tamely (1008). This is a pivotal plot-juncture of a kind unmatched in any other surviving play by Aristophanes. The subsequent scenes of the comedy, after the immediately following second parabasis, will see the 'liberation' of Philokleon from his former ways and his transmutation into a rampantly lawless individual who promiscuously indulges his appetites (for alcohol, sex, and food) at the expense of others. While other Aristophanic comedies feature hedonistically 'rejuvenated' old men (Dikaiopolis in *Acharnians*, Trygaios in *Peace*, Peisetairos in *Birds* all fall into this category), no other protagonist follows a trajectory where it is actually his defeat which produces the opportunity for an explosion of quasi-youthful energy and self-gratification. This twist in the plot is also, therefore, a sort of turning of the tables on that 'haughty-snorty' son of his: it is Bdelykleon, in the final analysis, who gets far more than he had bargained for by setting out to make his father a reformed character.

The differences between Philokleon and Bdelykleon, salient since the outset of the play, are freshly exhibited in the latter's re-education of the former for a symposium they are to attend together by means of a sympotic 'rehearsal' at 1122–1264.[15] It is a reasonable assumption that most of Aristophanes' audience were sufficiently au fait with the protocols and expectations of symposia to appreciate Philokleon's combination of ignorance and ineptitude. But that does not make the rehearsal scene an entirely one-dimensional or one-sided piece of comedy; things can be laughed at from, so to speak, more than one angle. The comic material unfolds in a series of thematically marked

---

[14] This stereotype will be reasserted shortly afterwards by the chorus, in the second parabasis (1113), as their modus operandi as jurors.

[15] Aristophanes had already staged a sympotic contrast between father and son in Strepsiades' narrative at *Clouds* 1353–76: there the two characters, when drinking together after dinner, disagree over whether to sing or recite poetry (including the choice of poets) and end up coming to blows. For an example of a 'rehearsal' scene as a comic technique from later in Aristophanes' career, see the women's planning for their infiltration of the Assembly at *Assembly-Women* 116 ff.

stages: first, the attempt to overcome Philokleon's stubborn reluctance to abandon his sordid old cloak and to wear a fancy 'Persian' garment (which turns out to be ludicrously large for him) as well as some smart shoes (1122–67); second, a short passage concerned with bodily comportment, more specifically with the idea of walking with a self-important strut (1168–73);[16] third, the social skill of contributing to a high-class group of symposiasts by telling impressive anecdotes, whether about oneself or others (1174–1207); fourth, the essential business of reclining on a couch with style and in such a way as to display a well-honed physique (1208–18); finally, and now with the make-believe of a symposium at which none other than Kleon and his cronies are guests, how to engage in the practice of not just singing poems and drinking songs but being adept, in particular, at taking one's turn with knowledgeable flair as the moment to sing circulates round the room (1219–49).

That overview of the rehearsal's structure foregrounds the multiplicity of factors—the social codes of clothing, the 'styling' of the body, the use of speech habits which help define one's membership of a group, and the related importance attaching to sympotic sharing of poetry—which shape the scene's humorous travesty of the culture of drinking parties. But it also draws attention to the scope for comic instability and ambiguity: at every stage, Philokleon himself is woefully clumsy or uncouth in ways which confirm, despite his son's efforts, a lack of fitness to participate in gatherings of those who purport to be socially superior; it is also the case, however, that this same disparity opens up some of the pretensions of self-regarding symposiasts to a degree of ridicule in their own right. This kind of comic ambiguity is not something, it goes without saying, that can be calibrated or neatly resolved into a clear-cut reading of the scene. Everything depends on point of view, but Aristophanic comedy often makes more than one point of view available at the same time. Interpretation is made all the more difficult by the fact that the rehearsal scene depends heavily on visual elements whose staging we can discern in outline but have no hope of reconstructing in detail.

The following observations are nonetheless worth briefly making in order to illustrate what has just been said. In the lengthy 're-dressing'

---

[16] Compare Bdelykleon's earlier mockery (and mimicry) of an individual's physical pretentiousness at 687–8.

of Philokleon, the new garment Bdelykleon wants him to wear is ostentatiously exotic, a so-called 'Persian' cloak with some sort of tufted woollen fringe. We cannot identify the garment type for certain, but we can be sure that it would have been available only to a few wealthy Athenians (cf. the absurd exorbitance of its supposed cost, 1146–7) with a taste for showy luxury, and this itself must have struck most spectators as excessively flaunting dress for a symposium: Philokleon's own gibes about it (seven of them between 1137 and 1156) are capable of simultaneously displaying his own coarseness and striking a chord with those who can see the Persian cloak as an affected choice. Similarly, when Bdelykleon demonstrates a swanky walk for his father to adopt, he himself uses language which gives away the posturing pretentiousness of such behaviour and Philokleon is able to cap things with some kind of parodic buttock-waggling (and probably 'feminized')[17] strut: once again, the humour is not directed simply at the old man's vulgarity but at the acute disparity between two social and cultural extremes. That principle applies to some extent to the whole scene, but it is given a special twist when we reach the singing section of the rehearsal. Here, not only are Kleon and his political set, formerly idolized by Philokleon, turned ironically into an object of the old man's hostility and cynicism, but this is overlaid with the further irony that Philokleon actually succeeds in displaying something of the improvisatory ability suitable for an adept symposiast: the problem turns out to be not his ability as such but his derogatory intentions, an omen of his readiness to disrupt the desired harmony of a symposium. The anomalous depiction of Philokleon as putting his knowledge of songs to perversely boorish purposes brings the comic ambiguities of the whole scene to a climax.

The points I have drawn attention to in the sympotic rehearsal are characteristic of the paradoxical mixture of crudity and sophistication in Aristophanic humour and of the playwright's penchant for shifting constantly between different comic registers. Aristophanes' audience is never allowed for very long to adopt a settled viewpoint on what they see and hear; the plays will catch out anyone who thinks that what is being exposed to mockery is easy to identify. That general observation makes it appropriate to conclude this introduction to

---

[17] The first part of the verb used by Philokleon at 1173 occurs in fr. 113 *PMG* of the archaic poet Anakreon with reference, it seems, to the sexy walk of courtesans.

Wasps by looking at a series of passages in the play which, in a spirit of metatheatricality, overtly reflect certain aspects of the elusiveness of Aristophanic comedy. The three passages in question are the preliminary piece of audience-address by the slaves (who also physically interact with the spectators) at 54–87; the section of the parabasis, the 'anapaests', at 1015–59, which contains a piece of authorial self-justification in relation to the poet's career to date; and the short final section of the second parabasis at 1284–91 which offers a vignette of Aristophanes' relationship to Kleon. It is important, however, not to lose sight of the fact that these passages, like similar material in other works, are themselves part of the fabric of the play; they cannot be treated as though they somehow offer a sober commentary on it. What, then, do they contribute to *Wasps*?

In the first passage, which exemplifies a technique found also in *Knights*, *Peace*, and *Birds* for informing the audience of the initial dramatic scenario, Xanthias prefaces his explanation of the source of the plot with 'some words of warning':[18]

> XANTHIAS. You mustn't expect from us any grand pretensions,
>   But you won't get stale Megarian clichés either.
>   There's no room in our repertoire for slaves
>   Who chuck the audience nuts they carry with them,
>   Nor for Herakles being cheated out of dinner,   60
>   Nor for pouring scorn again on...Euripides!
>   And even if Kleon has had some lucky success,
>   We won't mince him again into garlic paste.
>   We've got, instead, a subtle little plot:
>   It's not too clever, of course, for people like *you*,
>   But it's more sophisticated than vulgar laughs.

We have already seen that a key detail of this passage—the seeming denial that the play will target Kleon—is partly disingenuous, though it is given extra edge by the fact that even before this Kleon has been grotesquely allegorized as a female inn-keeper and whale in one of the slaves' dreams at 31–41. A further layer of the humour of this point will emerge later with the revelation of the main characters' pro and contra Kleon names, an announcement held back to the very end of Xanthias's speech (133–5). At the same time, the inclusion of Euripides' name in a list of old comic routines and clichés of the kind

---

[18] See my notes on the passage for further information.

that could be pejoratively called 'Megarian comedy' is a joke in its own right, as well as a way of exploiting the reputation which Aristophanes may already have acquired for extracting comic material from Euripidean tragedy.[19] But what is most telling about the passage is the, so to speak, serpentine movement of thought from the opening modesty of 'You mustn't expect from us any grand pretensions' to the promise of a 'subtle little plot' with its own claim to comic sophistication—and all this couched in the witty metonymic pretence, conveyed by the repeated first-person plurals, that the characters (or even the actors) are themselves authors of the play.

Aristophanes is not, however, espousing modesty. Xanthias's artfully contrived suggestion, mixed in with flattery of the audience's 'cleverness', that *Wasps* will not have 'grand pretensions' yet will offer a superior standard of comic theatre, finds a further resonance when we reach the play's parabasis and the chorus's extended transmission of a message from poet to spectators (1015–59). That message is embedded in the terms of a complaint that the audience (treated as a fixed entity, though multiple dramatic performances are involved) has done the playwright wrong, i.e., by not always appreciating his work or awarding it first prize, even though he has been an exceptional benefactor of theirs. In providing, with poetically rich supporting imagery, a selection of highlights from Aristophanes' career, the chorus emphasizes the 'Heraklean' courage with which the poet has satirically attacked, and continues (1037) to attack, 'the greatest targets' (1030), above all 'the jag-toothed monster' who is patently Kleon.[20] But this authorial self-image stands in a somewhat ironic relationship to the claim in line 63 that the play is not going to target Kleon again: as I suggested earlier, *Wasps* seems to want to be a play that both is and is not 'about' Kleon—to have its comic cake and eat it. Furthermore, the parabasis gives a double twist to two other ideas in Xanthias's words at 56–66: by depicting the playwright himself as Herakles, but a full-blown monster-slaying hero not a vulgar sub-comic

[19] The well-known fr. 342 of Kratinos, which calls an intellectually pretentious spectator a 'Euripid-aristophanizer', is very likely to be earlier in date than *Wasps*. In addition to *Acharnians* 393–488, Aristophanes may have included Euripidean material in some of the lost plays of the mid-420s.

[20] Aristophanes largely reused this passage, *Wasps* 1030–5, at *Peace* 752–8; in that later context, he created a nice contrast between his own Heraklean persona and the (supposedly) stale versions of Herakles as a comic character employed by his rivals (*Peace* 741–2), the latter a fuller version of the motif at *Wasps* 60.

Herakles 'cheated out of his dinner', how could it not appear to claim 'grand pretensions' for his work? Yet far from providing a transparent profession of Aristophanes' political commitments, this stance is blatantly a tissue of comic self-aggrandizement, made all the more fantastic by the fact that in *Wasps* itself the supposedly monstrous, Kerberos-like beast that is Kleon has already been reduced, in the earlier trial scene, to the status of a domestic dog seeking scraps in a kitchen.

After the lines about Kleon, the chorus's parabatic report of the poet's message to his audience continues with a passage on an unidentifiable play from the preceding year (1037–42) and then brings Aristophanes' complaint to a head with criticism of the spectators for failing to appreciate the sophisticated comic originality of *Clouds*, which had been placed only third at the Dionysia of 423. The parabasis of *Wasps* here overlaps with the partly revised parabasis of *Clouds* itself, as found in the transmitted text of that play.[21] In both places we find strong boasts for the originality and sophistication of *Clouds* combined with partial criticism of the theatre audience: partial, because Aristophanes distinguishes the minority of 'clever' spectators who *did* supposedly appreciate his own comic ingenuity from the rest who did not. When we bring this consideration together, once more, with Xanthias's words at *Wasps* 56–66, what we have looks rather like a teasing game with the audience. Spectators are ostensibly invited to disown the low, vulgar tastes of *some* of their number—as though Aristophanes' plays themselves were not saturated with vulgarity—and to self-identify as theatrical connoisseurs who know how to relish the sophistication of Aristophanic comedy. But if they are to do that, they will need, among other things, to remain alert to the ruses and ambiguities, the incongruities and ironies, with which the playwright makes his characters and choruses speak about his work.

The last of the trio of passages in *Wasps* where we encounter Aristophanic comedy commenting on itself is in the second parabasis at 1284–91. The chorus, here ventriloquizing the poet in the first person, refer to an earlier incident when Kleon had subjected Aristophanes to violent verbal attack, and in a context, perhaps in the

---

[21] For brief discussion of the revised parabasis of *Clouds*, see *Frogs and Other Plays*, 15–16, where I draw attention to the ambiguous way in which that play applies value-terms of 'cleverness', etc., both to the poet and to derided intellectuals like Sokrates.

Council chamber, where some public spectators were present. The compressed reference is probably to the controversial aftermath of *Babylonians* in 426.[22] But any suggestion that the playwright had made concessions to the politician has proved to be a hoax:

> I played the monkey a little,
> And in due course the vine-pole fooled the vine.
>
> (1290–1)

Far from being a Herakles-like hero taking on Kleon the monster, Aristophanes depicts himself here as a comic monkey reliant on duplicity: he was even able, it seems, to exercise some tricky humour when originally under attack, and, as time has proved (with plays including *Knights* and *Wasps* itself), he has very much had the last laugh. We cannot hope to penetrate this allusive account in order to reach any hard facts about Aristophanes' dealings with Kleon, but what stands out, as in Xanthias's prologue speech and in the authorial apologia of the main parabasis, is at least to some degree a celebration of comic elusiveness. In both practice and self-presentation, Aristophanic comedy makes numerous claims for its theatrical artifice, and part of that artifice is a refusal to be finally pinned down. Modern readers of *Wasps*, and of the plays in general, had better cultivate 'clever' habits of reading if they are not to be fooled themselves.

---

[22] See my note on *Wasps* 1284–91 for further information.

WASPS

Speaking Characters

SOSIAS: slave of BDELYKLEON and PHILOKLEON
XANTHIAS: likewise
BDELYKLEON: son of PHILOKLEON; his name means 'Kleon-loather'
PHILOKLEON: an elderly Athenian; his name means 'Kleon-lover'
BOY: one of the CHORUS's CHILDREN
DOG: allegorical representation of the politician Kleon
MAN: an Athenian assaulted by PHILOKLEON
MYRTIA: an Athenian woman, a market bread-seller
ACCUSER: an elderly Athenian
CHORUS: of elderly Athenian jurymen
LEADER: of the CHORUS

Silent Characters

CHILDREN: of the CHORUS
MIDAS: another slave of PHILOKLEON
PHRYX: likewise
MASYNTIAS: likewise
LABES: a dog (allegorical representation of the general Laches)
PUPPIES: of LABES
DARDANIS: a pipe-girl
MEN: other Athenians assaulted by PHILOKLEON
CHAIREPHON: an Athenian, witness to the assault on MYRTIA
WITNESS: to the assault on the ACCUSER
SONS OF KARKINOS: a trio of theatrical dancers
KARKINOS: an Athenian tragic playwright

[*The stage building, with a single door, represents the house of* PHILOK-
LEON *and* BDELYKLEON. *The door has a large bar across it, and there is
netting over the windows (and, at least by implication, over the interior
courtyard as well). A number of other objects are visible, including a
mortar, some stones, and harvest branches hanging next to the door. It is
night: a figure, who will turn out to be* BDELYKLEON, *is lying asleep on
the roof. In front of the house are two slaves on guard duty: both are
having difficulty staying awake, but* SOSIAS *has just woken and seen*
XANTHIAS *asleep.*]

SOSIAS. Hey there! What's wrong with you, damned Xanthias?
XANTHIAS [*waking abruptly*]. I'm learning to drop my guard on
    nighttime watch.
SOSIAS. Then you're storing up big trouble your ribs will pay for.
    Do you know what a monstrous brute we're guarding here?
XANTHIAS. Of course, but I'd like a little carefree break.
SOSIAS. Go ahead, then, take the risk. As it happens, I feel
    A lovely slumber trickle down *my* eyes too. [*Starts to drowse*]
XANTHIAS [*stirring*]. Are you mad—or in a Korybantic trance?*
SOSIAS. No, in the grip of sleep from Sabazios.
XANTHIAS. Then you worship the same Sabazios as me.   10
    Just now, in fact, I felt a sudden attack
    By a drowsy Persian sleep against my eyelids.*
    What's more, I had an amazing dream just now.
SOSIAS. Me too! I've never had anything like it before.
    But you describe yours first.
XANTHIAS.   I saw an eagle
    Swoop down, an enormous bird, to the Agora.
    It used its claws to snatch a serpent up,
    A serpent of bronze, which it carried aloft to the sky.
    Then the serpent became a shield—and Kleonymos dropped it!*
SOSIAS. That makes Kleonymos quite a riddle himself.   20
XANTHIAS. How come?
SOSIAS.   At a drinking party someone might say: *
    'On earth and in the sky and on the sea
    The very same beast discards a serpent...or shield'.
XANTHIAS. Oh no, what terrible thing will happen to me
    After having a dream like this?
SOSIAS.   Don't give it a thought.

There's nothing that's dreadful here, I swear there isn't.

XANTHIAS. It's surely bad if a man discards his gear!
But tell me your dream now.

SOSIAS.   It's quite portentous:
It's about the city as ship of state, no less.

XANTHIAS [*wittily*]. Then tell me quickly the *hull* of what it's
about!   30

SOSIAS. I'd just nodded off when I dreamt that on the Pnyx
An Assembly took place of sheep all sitting together.
They were carrying sticks and wearing shabby old cloaks.
Then I dreamt this crowd of sheep was being harangued
By an inn-keeper woman who took the form of a whale
And had the voice of a sow that's set on fire.

XANTHIAS. Ugh!

SOSIAS.   What's the matter?

XANTHIAS.   Please stop, don't tell me more:
Your dream has a nasty stench of putrid pig-hide!

SOSIAS. Then the filthy whale picked up some weighing scales
And put beef-fat in separate pans.

XANTHIAS.   Alarming!   40
It clearly wants to divide the *meat* of our city.*

SOSIAS. I dreamt Theoros was there right next to the whale:
He was seated on the ground with a raven's head.
Then Alkibiades said to me with a lisp:
'D'you thee Theoloth? Thuch a *craven* toady.'*

XANTHIAS. Alkibiades' lisping words hit on the truth!

SOSIAS. But isn't it weird—Theoros in raven shape?

XANTHIAS. Makes perfect sense.

SOSIAS.   How come?

XANTHIAS.   Well don't you see?
He suddenly switched from human to raven form.
The meaning stares you in the face: it shows   50
He's *ravin'* mad and won't be round much longer!*

SOSIAS [*wryly*]. You're surely worth a two-obol fee from me
For reading dreams with expertise like this.*

XANTHIAS [*changing tone*]. Well, let me explain the plot to these
spectators.
I should preface it, though, with just a word of warning.
[*To audience*] You mustn't expect from us any grand pretensions,

But you won't get stale Megarian clichés either.*
There's no room in our repertoire for slaves
Who chuck the audience nuts they carry with them,
Nor for Herakles being cheated out of dinner,   60
Nor for pouring scorn again on...Euripides!
And even if Kleon has had some lucky success,
We won't mince him again into garlic paste.*
We've got, instead, a subtle little plot:
It's not too clever, of course, for people like *you*,
But it's more sophisticated than vulgar laughs.
The situation's this: we've got a master—
[*Pointing*] That great big fellow you see asleep on the roof—
Who's put us both in charge of guarding his father.
He's locked him inside, to stop him leaving the house.   70
The father's ill, but his illness is rather weird:*
You won't recognize or work out what it is
Unless we help you. Go on, if you like, try guessing.

[SOSIAS *approaches the audience and, in a spirit of lively interaction with
the spectators, purports to relay specific guesses to* XANTHIAS.]

SOSIAS. Amynias, Pronapes' son,* suggests
    He's got an addiction to gambling.
XANTHIAS.   Terrible guess!
    He's assuming an illness that's just the same as his own.
SOSIAS. Well at least he's right the illness involves addiction.
    But Sosias here suggests to Derkylos*
    That the father's addicted to drink.
XANTHIAS.   That's certainly false:
[*Ironically*] It's only *superior* men with that disease.   80
SOSIAS. Nikostratos* of Skambonidai suggests
    He's addicted to sacrifice or hosting guests.
XANTHIAS. By the dog, Nikostratos, we don't want that:
    Philoxenos, guest-hoster, is quite an arsehole!*
    Your guesses are all far out; you'll never get it.
    If you really want to know, then please keep quiet.
    I'll tell you now what our master's illness is:
    He's an addict of *jury service*—yes, wildly so!
    He's in love with judging cases; he's wracked with grief

If he fails to find a seat on the very front bench.   90
He never gets even a soupçon of sleep at night,
Or if he gets just a morsel, his mind flies off
To the courts and spends the night by the water clock.*
Because he's so used to clutching his voting pebble
He wakes every day with three fingers stuck together,
[*Gesturing*] As if he were holding incense for sacrifice.*
If he comes across graffiti on a door
Calling Pyrilampes' son 'the handsome Demos',
He'll go and scrawl 'the handsome voting funnel'!*
When his cock was crowing as sunset came, he claimed   100
It was waking him late because of receiving a bribe
From one of the magistrates who were facing review.*
As soon as dinner's finished he shouts for his boots,
Then he's straight to the courts to wait there early and snooze:
He clings to the queuing marker just like a limpet.*
He always peevishly votes for the harshest fines,
Then comes back into the house like a bumble bee
With masses of wax caked under his finger nails.*
Neurotic he might run out of voting pebbles,
He keeps a private beach inside his house!   110
That's how demented he is. Reproaching him
Only heightens his passion. That's why we're guarding him
And have barricaded the door to lock him in.
His son's concerned about his father's sickness.
He tried at first to reason gently with him
And persuade him not to wear his shabby old cloak
Nor leave the house; but persuasion simply failed.
He tried a purificatory bath—no change.*
He next exposed him to Korybantic rites,
But his father rushed to court with his tambourine!*   120
And when those rites provided no relief,
He sailed with him to Aigina and made quite sure
He lay at night in Asklepios' healing shrine.*
Yet the very next dawn the old man popped up at court!
He tried to escape from the house through the drains, no less,
As well as through chinks in the walls; we needed rags
To block every one of them up and keep them sealed.
But he hammered pegs in the wall, then like a jackdaw

He tried to climb to the top and jump right over. 130
We've now hung netting around the courtyard too
And are keeping watch on the house by day and night.
The old man's name, by the way: Philokleon.
Yes it is, by Zeus! And his son's Bdelykleon,
A man whose character's somewhat haughty-snorty.

[BDELYKLEON *suddenly wakes up on the roof, aware that his father is making his latest attempt to escape. He jumps up and calls urgently to the slaves below; his movements show that he is observing events down inside the courtyard of the house.*]

BDELYKLEON. Are you sleeping, Xanthias and Sosias?
SOSIAS. Oh no!
XANTHIAS.   What's wrong?
SOSIAS.   Bdelykleon's woken up!
BDELYKLEON. Quick, one of you two must run to the back of the house.
My father's managed to get inside the kitchen.
He's on all fours and scurrying like a mouse. 140
Make sure he can't slip down the basin outlet.
The other one stay by the door.
XANTHIAS.   Okay then, master.

[*As* SOSIAS *exits round the side of the house and* XANTHIAS *stays by the door,* BDELYKLEON's *attention is attracted by a noise in the middle of the roof: in what follows, a trap door opens and* PHILOKLEON's *head sticks out.*]

BDELYKLEON. O lord Poseidon, what noise is the chimney making?
[*Peering inside*] Who on earth are you?
PHILOKLEON [*popping up*].   I'm smoke that's leaving the house.
BDELYKLEON. You're smoke? Let's see: what wood produced you?
PHILOKLEON.   Fig wood.*
BDELYKLEON. Not half, the most acrid smoke that stings your eyes!
Get out of here! Where's the lid for the chimney vent?

Back down with you! Let me put on this log as well.
[BDELYKLEON *pushes* PHILOKLEON *back down through the trap door,*
closes it, then takes a piece of wood and puts it on top of the door to weigh
it down.]

Now try to find some other deceptive scheme!
[*Mock-ruefully*] But no man's so ill-fated as myself: 150
   My name will now be changed to Smoky's son.

[*The voice of* PHILOKLEON *is heard shouting from inside the house.*]

PHILOKLEON. Hoy, slave!
XANTHIAS.   He's pushing the door.
BDELYKLEON.   Then press it harder.
   Use all the strength you've got. I'm coming down now.
   Keep a special eye on the latch and the bar as well.
   Watch out in case he gnaws right through the bolt.*

[BDELYKLEON *disappears from the roof to make his way down to the*
front of the house. Almost immediately, PHILOKLEON *appears at a raised*
window.]

PHILOKLEON. Won't you let me out, scumbags, to get to court?
   If you don't, Drakontides will be acquitted.*
XANTHIAS. Would you mind about that?
PHILOKLEON.   I would: the god Apollo
   Prophesied when I asked a question once at Delphi
   That *any* acquittal of mine would finish me off!   160
XANTHIAS. Apollo preserve us! An oracle like no other!
PHILOKLEON. I beg you, let me out, or I'll split apart.
XANTHIAS. It's totally out of the question, Philokleon.
PHILOKLEON. Then I'll use my teeth to nibble right through this net.
XANTHIAS. But you haven't got any teeth left!
PHILOKLEON.   O woe is me!
   I wish I could kill you! But how? [*Melodramatically*] I need a sword
   At once—or a tablet to vote for your execution!*

[BDELYKLEON *now reappears from round the side of the house and sees*
his father at the window.]

BDELYKLEON. This fellow has set his sights on causing big trouble.

PHILOKLEON. Not so, by Zeus! I want to sell our donkey,
 Pack-saddles and all. I'd like to take it to market: 170
 Today's new moon.

BDELYKLEON.   But couldn't I take it myself
 And have it sold?

PHILOKLEON.   You wouldn't do such a good job.

BDELYKLEON. I'd do it far better!

PHILOKLEON [*slyly*].   Well take the donkey out then.
  [*Leaves window*]

XANTHIAS. What a cunning ploy that was, a piece of guile,
 To make you let him outside.

BDELYKLEON.   But I wasn't fooled.
 I was quite aware of the crafty plan he was trying.
 I think I'll go in and bring the donkey out
 To stop the old man peeping outside again.

[BDELYKLEON *unbars and unlocks the door, goes inside, then re-emerges with a 'pantomime' donkey beneath which is suspended...*
      PHILOKLEON.]

Little donkey, why these tears? Because you'll be sold?
Move faster. Why are you groaning, unless you've got   180
An Odysseus under here.*

XANTHIAS [*checking*].   He certainly does!
 There's someone lurking here beneath its belly.

BDELYKLEON. I don't believe it!

XANTHIAS [*pointing*].   Him!

BDELYKLEON.   What have we here?
 Who on earth can you possibly be, old fellow?

PHILOKLEON.   I'm No-man.*

BDELYKLEON. No-man? Where from?

PHILOKLEON.   From Ithaka—Runaway's son.

BDELYKLEON. Well No-man has no hope of having success!
[*To* XANTHIAS] Quick, pull him out from there. The filthy wretch,
 To have slipped right under. [*Ironically*] I think he looks quite like
 A donkey's little foal—or a hanger-on!*

PHILOKLEON [*resisting*]. If you don't leave me alone, we'll end up
 fighting.   190

XANTHIAS. Fight with us both, what for?
PHILOKLEON.   A donkey's shadow.*
BDELYKLEON. You're a rotten sod with all your devious tricks.
PHILOKLEON. Me rotten? By Zeus, I'm not. But don't you know
    I'm now in peak condition. You'll see, if you eat
    An underbelly slice of a well-aged juror.

[XANTHIAS *pulls* PHILOKLEON *out from under the donkey and, with*
BDELYKLEON*'s help, starts to push the struggling old man and the animal*
through the house door. Once PHILOKLEON *is back inside, the door will*
be barricaded again.]

BDELYKLEON. Get the donkey and yourself back into the house.
PHILOKLEON. My fellow jurors and Kleon, I need your help!
BDELYKLEON. You can scream away inside, behind locked doors.
[*To* XANTHIAS] Make sure you pile up stones against the door.
    And fix the bolt inside the bar again.   200
    Then quickly take that great big mortar there
    And roll it against the bar.
XANTHIAS [*looking up*].   What the hell was that?
    A piece of dirt just hit me—but where was it from?
BDELYKLEON. Perhaps a mouse up there somehow dislodged it.

[*In what follows, there are signs of furtive movement in the eaves of the*
roof and PHILOKLEON *once more sticks out his head.*]

XANTHIAS. A mouse? Not at all. What's slipping out here
    From right beneath the tiles is . . . a juryman roof-pest!
BDELYKLEON. Oh no, not more! He's turned into a sparrow.
    He'll escape by wing. [*Flustered*] The netting, the netting, is
      needed!
[*Shouting up*] Shoo! Shoo! Get back! I'd find it easier work
    To serve on the siege of Skione than guard my father.*   210

    [*After a few moments,* PHILOKLEON *disappears back inside.*]

XANTHIAS. Well, now that we've managed to scare him back inside,
    And there's no more chance he could slip his way through
      the net,

Can we not allow ourselves a smidgen of sleep?
BDELYKLEON. Do you need to ask, you dolt! It won't be long
  Before his fellow jurors come to fetch him.
XANTHIAS. Not long? But dawn is still a little way off.
BDELYKLEON. Too true—which means they've got up late today!
  They always come to fetch him in dead of night.
  They carry lanterns and hum away with songs,
  Archaic-honeyed-exotic-Phrynichan lyrics.*   220
  They summon him with their singing.
XANTHIAS.   If need be
  We'll drive them off by pelting them with stones.
BDELYKLEON. That's not a good idea! If anyone angers
  Old men like this, they're like a nest of wasps.
  They've actually got a sting fixed on their rump.
  It's very sharp for stinging, and with loud shrieks
  They pounce and strike like jumping sparks from fire.
XANTHIAS. No need to worry. Provided I've got some stones,
  I'll scatter a nest of jurors and make them flee!

[BDELYKLEON *and* XANTHIAS *sit down in front of the house; they are
soon visibly asleep. After a short pause, the* CHORUS *enters from one side:
contrary to* BDELYKLEON*'s preceding description, the immediate impression they create is of stumbling, ineffectual decrepitude. The old jurors,
swathed in cloaks at this stage and using walking sticks, are accompanied
by a number of* CHILDREN *carrying lamps for them. The* LEADER *chants
in recitative.*]

[PARODOS: 230–333]

LEADER. Keep going, advance with all your vigour. Hey Komias,
      you're sluggish.   230
  How things have changed: you used to be as supple as dog-lead
      leather,
  Yet now Charinades is better than you at keeping pace.
  O Strymodoros from Konthyle, the best of all us jurors,
  Is Euergides among us here or Chabes from Phlya deme?*
  We've only got the rump of those—oh shiver me ancient
      timbers!—
  Who were young with us, when in those days, at far Byzantion,*

You and I did sentry duty together. When on our night patrol,
We sneaked into that bread-seller's shop and stole her mortar
   from her,
Then broke it up to light a fire and boiled some greens for grub.
Let's quicken our step, my men: today it's Laches for the
   chop!* 240
Everyone's aware he's stashed away a hive of stolen money.
So yesterday our kinsman Kleon gave orders not to be late.
He urged us bring a stock of anger to last for three whole days,*
Enough with which to punish Laches for all those crimes of his.
Let's press ahead before day breaks, all you my old coevals,
And as we walk let's use our lamps to check in all directions,
In case we stub our feet on stones and hurt ourselves quite badly.
BOY. Watch out, dear father, lots of mud; be careful where you step.
LEADER. Pick up some twigs from on the ground and push the
   lamp wick up.
BOY. No need for that; I'll do the same by poking with this finger. 250
LEADER. Who taught you such bad habits as pushing wicks with
   just your finger,
Especially when the oil's in short supply, you stupid child! [*Strikes
him*]
It isn't *you* who feels the pinch, when oil is so expensive.
BOY. If any of you should use your fists to chide us once again,
We'll snuff the lamps out all at once and then return back home.
And if we do, you'll be deprived of light and have to tramp
Just like a francolin through mud and spray it all around.
LEADER. Don't answer back—I'm used to punishing bigger folk
   than you!
I get the sense I'm walking through thick sludge here underfoot.
I'm sure within the next four days at most we'll find that Zeus 260
Is bound to send a lot more rain and make things even worse.
I know that's so from the fungus here that's growing in our lamps:
This always means that heavy rain is heading soon our way.
On the other hand, there are plenty crops still in their growing
   season
Which need more rain as well as wind from the north to help
   them on.

Lead on then, boy, lead on. 290*

[*As the* CHORUS *proceeds, it engages in a sung exchange with the* BOY
*which starts in a mostly colloquial register but goes on, anomalously, to
incorporate some elements of 'high' lyric.*]

BOY.	Will you grant me a favour, father,	*Strophe*
	If I make a request for something?	
CHORUS.	Of course, my child. But tell me,	
	What would you like me to buy you?	
	A treat perhaps? No doubt you'll say	
	Some knucklebone dice, my son.	
BOY.	Not that but figs instead, dear Daddy.	
	I'd much prefer—	
CHORUS.	But out of the question!	
	I don't care if you hang yourselves!	
BOY.	Then I won't escort you in future.	
CHORUS.	From my measly juror's pay I need*	300
	To purchase groats for three, and firewood and savouries.	
	Yet *you* are asking for figs!	

BOY.	Tell me, father, what will happen	*Antistrophe*
	If the Archon doesn't summon	
	The court today—how will we	
	Afford the food for lunch?	
	Do you have any hope for us	
	'Beyond the sacred Hellespont'?*	
CHORUS.	Alas for woe, alas for woe!	
	I certainly know no means at all	
	To pay for dinner for us.	310
BOY	'Why gave you birth, O wretched mother, to me'?*	
CHORUS.	To give *me* the problem of feeding you!	
BOY.	A useless ornament you've proved, my dear little food bag!	
	Nothing left for us both but to grieve.	

[*The metre now returns to recitative.*]

LEADER. I wonder why our fellow juror who lives in this house
here   266*
   Has not appeared. Is something wrong? He usually joins our
   group.

He was never a slowcoach in the past; he used to be at the front
And while he led us he'd sing some lyrics from plays by
    Phrynichos.*
He's nothing if not a lover of song. Let's stop here now, my
    men,   270
And sing in order to call him out, in the hope that hearing my
    tune
The pleasure he takes in the sound we make will bring him
    creeping out.

CHORUS.   Why no sign of him outside the door?   *Strophe*
            Can't the old man even hear us?
            Surely he can't have lost
            His boots? Or has he stubbed
            His toe somewhere in the dark,
            Then found his ankle swelling
            The way that old men's ankles do?
            Perhaps his groin would swell as well.
            He always was the most acrid in our group,*
            The only one unpersuadable: when defendants
               pleaded,
            He'd lower head and shoulders like this
            And say, 'You're trying to boil a stone!'   280

            Perhaps it's because of yesterday,   *Antistrophe*
            When someone somehow slipped through our fingers
            By fooling us with all his claims
            To be a lover of Athens
            And the first informer in Samos.*
            Perhaps that acquittal has made him sick
            And he's lying in bed with a fever.
            For that's the kind of man he is.
            Please get out of bed, good fellow, and don't
            Let it gnaw or anger you. A beefy figure is coming,
            One of those who betrayed our interests in Thrace:*
            You've got to boil him into a stew!

[PHILOKLEON *now appears at a window. He sings a monody in a manner which is parodically reminiscent of certain figures from Euripidean
tragedy.*]

PHILOKLEON. My friends, I've been pining away　317*
　　　　　　So long through this gap in the wall,
　　　　　　Straining so hard to hear you.
　　　　　　But since my plight makes me unable
　　　　　　To sing myself, what am I to do?
　　　　　　I'm under guard at the hands of these people,
　　　　　　Because I've never lost my desire
　　　　　　To go with you to the voting urns　320
　　　　　　And carry out something wicked!

　　　　　　O Zeus, god of mighty thunder,
　　　　　　Turn me instantly into smoke,
　　　　　　Or Proxenides, or the son of Baloney,*
　　　　　　That utter pseud and liar.
　　　　　　Bring yourself, O lord, to do me this favour
　　　　　　With a heart of pity. Or with thunderbolt,
　　　　　　Red-hot, reduce me quickly to cinders,
　　　　　　Then lift me up, blow off the ashes,　330
　　　　　　And dip me in hot brine-sauce!
　　　　　　Or else transform me into the stone
　　　　　　On which they count the voting-shells.*

CHORUS.　Who is the one who confines you like this　　*Strophe*
　　　　　　And bars the door? Don't hesitate to tell your faithful
　　　　　　　friends.
PHILOKLEON. My very own son! But don't shout out. He happens
　　　　　　to be
　　　　　　This person sleeping here in front. So lower the pitch.
CHORUS.　What motivation, O wretched one, makes him want to
　　　　　　do this to you?
　　　　　　What pretext has he?
PHILOKLEON. He's keeping me, friends, from jury service—and
　　　　　　wicked deeds!　340
　　　　　　He'd like to give me a pampered life. But *I* don't want
　　　　　　it at all!
CHORUS.　Does he dare, this revolting man, to make
　　　　　　Such outrageous claims, this Demagogue-Kleon,*
　　　　　　Just because you speak the truth about
　　　　　　Subversive youngsters like himself?

                    This fellow would never have dared
                    To say such things
                    If he weren't a conspirator.*

LEADER. Well now's the time for you to find a clever solution for
     this,
   A means of getting you down from there without this man's
     attention.
PHILOKLEON. What means could there be? Please help me find it.
     I'm ready to take any risk.
   I'm raring to see the court agenda while clutching my voting-
     shell.
LEADER. Do you know of a chink in the wall through which you
     could burrow your way from inside,   350
   Then slip out here, disguised in rags, like resourceful Odysseus
     himself?*
PHILOKLEON. Every route is blocked—not even enough of a chink
     for a gnat to get through!
   You need to find some other trick: I can't trickle out like fig-juice!*
LEADER. You surely remember when on campaign you stole some
     skewers for meat,
   Then rapidly scaled back down the wall, when Naxos had been
     captured?*
PHILOKLEON. I certainly do. But what's your point? Things then
     were not like this.
   I was in my prime, adept at theft, in full control of myself.
                    I was under no guard but easily able
                    To make a fearless escape. But now
                    There are serried ranks of hoplite troops   360
                    Overseeing all possible routes of escape.
                    There are two of them here, keeping watch at the door,
                    As though I were a weasel that's stolen meat—
                    And they're the ones who've got the skewers!*

CHORUS.   It's an urgent matter for you to devise   *Antistrophe*
            A clever ruse as fast as you can—it's *dawn*, my little
                    bee!
PHILOKLEON. In that case, best for me to gnaw my way through
                    the net.

May Artemis, huntress with nets, pardon me for the
damage! [*Gnaws*]

CHORUS.   This action befits a man who battles his way to safety.
Apply your jaw with vigour!   370

PHILOKLEON. I've gnawed my way right through. But don't shout
out at all.
We need to be alert; Bdelykleon must not be woken.

CHORUS.   Have no fear at all, old chap.
If he wakes and starts to complain,
I'll make him suffer heartache
And run for fear of his life. He'll learn
Not to trample down
The decrees of the goddesses twain!*

[PHILOKLEON *now brandishes a rope at the window and starts to calculate how to get himself down by means of it.*]

LEADER. Attach the rope to something inside and let it hang down
through the window,
Then lower yourself, after filling your soul with the courage of
Diopeithes!*   380

PHILOKLEON. But what if this pair of men wake up and try to haul
me up
And pull me back inside the house, what then? What's your advice?

LEADER. We'll summon up all our oak-hard spirit and come to your
defence,
So they won't be able to lock you inside. That's how we'll help you
out.

PHILOKLEON. Then I'll put my trust in you and do it. But if the
plan goes wrong,
Lament me well and take my body for burial under the courts.

LEADER. It won't go wrong; don't be afraid. So come, friend, lower
yourself:
Don't hesitate, just offer a prayer to your ancestral gods.

PHILOKLEON. O Lykos master, whose hero's shrine's my
neighbour, you share my pleasures.*
We both enjoy defendants' tears and all their lamentations.   390
That's why you took up residence where you'd hear these
courtroom sounds;

You alone, of all known heroes, chose to sit by someone weeping.
Take pity on me and keep me safe, for I live next door to you.
I promise I'll never defile your shrine...by pissing or crapping
   nearby.*

[*As* PHILOKLEON *starts to lower himself from the window with his rope,*
BDELYKLEON *wakes up with a jolt; he and* XANTHIAS *continue the
recitative metre already in use.*]

BDELYKLEON. Hey you, wake up.
XANTHIAS.   What's wrong?
BDELYKLEON.   I thought a voice
   was ringing round me.
   It's surely not the old man sneaking out again?
XANTHIAS.   This time
   He's coming down a rope.
BDELYKLEON [*jumping up*].   You swine! What's this? You won't
   get down.
[*To* XANTHIAS] Climb up there quickly, block his way, and hit him
   with those boughs:
   We need to make his ship reverse when he's struck by harvest
   branches.*

[XANTHIAS *grabs the harvest branches from next to the house door and
starts to shimmy up the rope from the bottom, waving the branches at*
PHILOKLEON, *dangling above him. Meanwhile* BDELYKLEON *unlocks
the door and rushes inside, appearing shortly afterwards at the window,
where he hauls his father back up on the rope.*]

PHILOKLEON. Won't you bring me help, all you whose cases are
   due to be heard this year?   400
   Come, Smikythion and Teisiades and Chremon and
   Pheredeipnos!*
   When if not now will you come to my aid, before I'm pulled inside?

[*Having pulled his father inside,* BDELYKLEON *takes him back down: the
two of them appear in the doorway before the end of the following song, in
the course of which the members of the* CHORUS *remove their cloaks
(which the* CHILDREN *duly carry off stage) to reveal their wasp costume,
including prosthetic stings, underneath.*]

CHORUS.   Tell me, why delay to rouse the usual bile
                We feel when anyone angers our wasps' nest?
                Now, yes now, is the perfect moment
                To reveal the quick-tempered sting with which we punish
                And stretch it taut to maximum length.
                Here, take these cloaks at once, you children.
                Run off, cry out, and carry this news to Kleon.
                Urge him to come in person   410
                To confront a man who hates our city*
                And is ripe to be destroyed because
                He advances a new proposal—
                That law-courts be abolished!

BDELYKLEON. Please listen, gentlemen, to what I have to say. Don't
    keep on shouting.
LEADER. We'll shout to the very heavens above!
BDELYKLEON.   But I still won't let
    him out of my hands.
LEADER. This situation's quite outrageous—a blatant case of
    tyrannous plans!*
CHORUS [*singing*]. We call on you, city, and loathsome Theoros,
                And all other patrons of ours who are toadies!*
XANTHIAS. In Herakles' name, they've got real stings! Can you see
    the size of them, my master?   420
BDELYKLEON. Yes, these they used to destroy Philippos in court,
    the son of Gorgias.*
LEADER. You too we'll destroy with these! [*To* CHORUS] Now every
    one of you face this way to attack,
    Extend your sting to maximum length, then charge with all your
        force towards him,
    Keep tightly packed in ordered ranks, each one of you full of
        angry might:
    He needs to learn, yes, once and for all, what kind of hive he's
        roused to anger.
XANTHIAS. This situation's worrying now, by Zeus, if we face a
    fight with them:
    I'm certainly feeling scared myself at the sight of the spike at the
        tip of their stings.
CHORUS [*singing*]. Release the man at once; otherwise, I promise,

You'll wish you had a tortoise shell.

PHILOKLEON. Attack with venom, my fellow jurors, you wasps with
hearts so full of wrath. 430

Let some of you fly with passionate rage and stick your stings
right up their anus,

While others must swarm all over them and sting their eyes and
hands as well.

[*The* CHORUS *moves in choreographed patterns partly evocative of military action, partly of a wasp attack. In what follows, several slaves rush
out of the house to help* BDELYKLEON *and* XANTHIAS.]

BDELYKLEON. Come quickly, Midas and Phryx, I need immediate
help—Masyntias too:

Take tight control of my father, don't let anyone else get hold on him;

If you fail in this you'll find yourselves in heavy fetters and
starved of food.

Don't be alarmed by all their noise: I know hot air when I hear its
sound!

[*Two of the slaves take control of the struggling* PHILOKLEON, *while the
third helps ward off the wasp attack.* BDELYKLEON *and* XANTHIAS *exit
into the house to fetch further equipment (see 456).*]

LEADER. Release this man or else you'll find our sting deposited in
your flesh.

PHILOKLEON. Lord Kekrops, hero, whose lower parts resemble
snakey Drakontides,*

Please intervene to stop me being subdued like this by barbarous
men,

The very people I taught in the past...to weep until their eyes
were dry. 440

LEADER. Old age, alas, is a time of life when terrible sufferings
multiply!

It's patent here for all to see: this pair of slaves are even willing

To knock about their ancient master. They don't recall with
gratitude

The rustic jerkins and belted tunics he went to the trouble of
buying for them,

And the leather caps as well. He even cared for their feet in winter
time
To stop them always feeling the cold. Yet now they don't show any
respect,
No sign at all of it in their eyes, in gratitude for those boots of yore.
PHILOKLEON [*to* MIDAS]. Well won't you take your hands off me
and let me go, you monstrous beast!
Don't you remember the time I caught you stealing grapes from
the family vines,
How I tied you up to that olive tree and flayed the skin clean off
your back?   450
I made you such a fine example, but what did I get? No word of
thanks.
Please let me go, the pair of you, before my son dashes back out here.
LEADER [*to the slaves*]. We'll make you pay for this behaviour, a
mighty punishment's heading your way.
It will hit you soon and then you'll know the temperament of men
like us
Who are quick to anger and keen on justice, whose eyes look
daggers all the time.

[*As the* CHORUS *now moves into attack,* BDELYKLEON *and* XANTHIAS
*re-emerge from the house with sticks and a source of smoke: a pantomime
fight ensues.*]

BDELYKLEON. Hit harder and harder, Xanthias, to drive these
wasps away from the house.
XANTHIAS. That's what I'm doing.
BDELYKLEON.   And you, Masyntias, repel them
with plenty of smoke.
XANTHIAS. Shoo, shoo!
BDELYKLEON.   To hell with you!
XANTHIAS.   Get out of here!
BDELYKLEON.   Keep
hitting them with the stick.
And you, Masyntias, keep smoking them . . . with Aischines' hot air!*

[*The* CHORUS *is quickly defeated and re-assumes something of the appearance of pathetic decrepitude which it had shown at its first entrance.*]

BDELYKLEON. I always knew that we were bound to scare you off
        before too long.   460
PHILOKLEON. By Zeus, you wouldn't so easily have managed to
        make this narrow escape
    If only these men had fed themselves...on the bitter lyrics of
        Philokles!*
CHORUS [*singing*]. Well, isn't it now self-evident
                    To poor men like us that tyranny
                    Has stealthily caught me in a trap?
[*To* BDELYKLEON] You good-for-nothing, you long-haired
        Amynias type!*
                    You're stopping us keeping the city's laws,
                    Without the slightest justification
                    Or any appealing argument,
                    Just seizing autocratic power.   470
BDELYKLEON. Now's the time to put aside this fighting and this
        deafening clamour
    And start a calm exchange of views, in the hope we might achieve
        a truce.
CHORUS.   What, talk to *you*, a people-hater,*
                    A person who lusts for exclusive power,
                    Who liaises with Brasidas and wears
                    Wool-fringed Spartan dress, and keeps
                    His facial hair untrimmed!*
BDELYKLEON. I realize now it would have been better for me to
        abandon all care for my father
    Than fight a naval battle with so many problems as these every
        day of my life.
LEADER. You've only had a preliminary taste, an hors d'oeuvre
        even, of what you face.   480
    (Well that's our choice of culinary terms to say the quarrel has
        hardly started!)
    You've scarcely felt our pain as yet, but just you wait till an
        advocate*
    Exposes you to a torrent of charges and calls you all conspirators.
BDELYKLEON. I wish, by all the gods, you'd just give up this hostile
        stance of yours.
    Or is it decided we'll spend all day in flaying the skin off each
        other's backs?

CHORUS [*singing*]. I'll never give up, I won't, so long as my strength
  holds up—
              Not when someone's set on tyranny over us.
BDELYKLEON. It's tyranny and conspiracy that you seem to find on
      every side,
  No matter how large or small the matter a prosecutor brings to court.
  I hadn't heard anyone use this word, this 'tyranny', not for fifty
      years.   490
  Yet now it's become more commonplace than the cheapest
      salt-fish anyone buys;
  The word's on everyone's lips these days, it's tossed around in the
      Agora.
  If someone goes to buy some perch and has no interest in buying
      sprats,
  The vendor of sprats on the neighbouring stall takes notice at
      once and then exclaims:
  'The way this fellow goes shopping for fish is proof he's aiming at
      tyranny!'
  If somebody buying whitebait asks the vendor to throw in an
      onion too,
  It makes the woman who's selling veg look quite askance and say
      to him:
  'You want an onion—tell me why. Could it be to establish a
      tyranny?
  Or is it your view that Athens produces foods like that for just
      yourself?'
XANTHIAS. It happened to me just yesterday, when I entered a
      brothel towards midday   500
  And told the whore to mount and ride me: she flew into an
      immediate rage
  And asked if my aim was to re-establish the tyranny of Hippias!*
BDELYKLEON. This is the stuff these people like to hear. And that's
      why in my case,
  Because I want to free my father from all the things that spoil his
      life—
  The early mornings, legal abuses, and general hardship to weigh
      him down—
  And want him instead to live a life of luxury just as Morychos
      does,*

I face these accusations of conspiracy and a tyrant's plans.

PHILOKLEON. They're right, by Zeus, to make these charges! Not
    even birds' milk could ever tempt me*
To give up the life I already lead, the one you want to take from me.
I don't like fancy fish like skate or eels; I'd really rather have   510
A tasty little trial served up in court, well cooked into a stew.

BDELYKLEON. Of course you would: you've learned the habit of
    taking pleasure in things like that.
But if you can bear to hold your tongue and understand my point
    of view,
I think I'll change your mind and show you're going astray in all
    your ways.

PHILOKLEON. What, going astray by jury service?

BDELYKLEON.   Yes, turned into
    a laughing stock
Unwittingly at the hands of men you almost worship like the gods.
You just can't see you're like a slave.

PHILOKLEON.   A slave! Stop all this stuff and
    nonsense.
I myself am ruler of all.

BDELYKLEON.   Not so, you're subject to others' instructions
While *thinking* it's you who wields the power. Let's see, then,
    father, please explain
The status you claim accrues to you as one who profits from all of
    Greece.   520

PHILOKLEON. I certainly will. And I want these men to arbitrate.

BDELYKLEON.   I'll
    agree to that.
But what if you fail to—what's the phrase? Abide by the formal
    adjudication?   524*

PHILOKLEON. May I never again put my lips to a cup of
    undiluted . . . juror's pay!*   525

BDELYKLEON [*to slaves*]. It's fine for you all to release him now.

PHILOKLEON.   And
    give me a sword to keep by me here.*   522
If I lose this argument with you, I undertake to fall on my sword!

[*One of the slaves brings out a sword for* PHILOKLEON, *who may brandish it at various points in what follows; the other slaves exit, taking with*

them the various objects previously used, while the main characters and
CHORUS *prepare to embark on the formal debate.*]

[AGON: 526–724]

CHORUS.   Now the one who's on our side   *Strophe*
            Must deliver a speech with novel ideas.
[*To* PHILOKLEON] Make sure you're seen—
BDELYKLEON [*cutting in*]. Let one of the slaves bring out at once
    my basket from the house.

[*One of the slaves returns with a basket from which* BDELYKLEON *will
    soon produce a wax tablet and stylus for note-taking.*]

    But what impression should he create, if he follows your
        advice?   530

CHORUS.   —not to follow this young man's style
            In the way you speak. You can see yourself
            How great the contest,
            With everything at stake,
            Since this man here, though god forbid it,
            Intends to win the argument and—
BDELYKLEON [*cutting in*]. For every single point he makes, I'll keep
    a memo here.
PHILOKLEON [*to* CHORUS]. But what will happen if this man here
    should win the argument?
CHORUS.   No longer will a crowd of old men   540
            Have even the slightest usefulness.
            The butts of jeering in the streets,
            We'll find ourselves called olive-branch-bearers*
            And husks of affidavits.

LEADER. Come, you whose task is now to make the case about our
    kingship,
    Embark with boldness on your speech and test your verbal art.
PHILOKLEON. And straightaway, from the starting-line, I'll aim to
    demonstrate
    That the power we hold is just as great as any other kingship.
    What creature can be found whose life's more blissful than a
        juror's,   550

More pampered or impressive, even when the juror's old?
When off to court first thing each day, there greet me at the
    entrance
Important men of towering height; as soon as I approach,
I receive a grasp from a delicate hand that has thieved from public
    funds.
With lowered heads they start to plead, in a voice that drips with
    pathos:
'I beg you, father, take pity on me, if you've been a thief yourself
When holding office or in the army when buying food for mess-
    mates.'
Yet he wouldn't have known I existed at all if not for his prior
    acquittal!

BDELYKLEON [*writing*]. Let me take a note of this point he makes
    about people who entreat him.

PHILOKLEON. After being entreated like this and having my anger
    wiped away,   560
Once inside court I quite ignore the things I said I'd do;
I simply enjoy the sounds they make to win themselves acquittal.
Let's see, a juror's able to hear every possible kind of appeal.
Defendants may describe with tears the impoverished life they've
    led;
They pile their problems up so high, they almost equal mine!
Some tell us stories, while others narrate funny tales that come
    from Aisop.*
And others again tell jokes to make me laugh and drop my anger.
If we're not persuaded by all this stuff, they drag their children
    forward,*
Both daughters and sons led by the hand. And *I* sit back and listen,
While the children huddle together and bleat, then the father, for
    their sake,   570
Implores me in fear, as if I'm a god, to conclude his review with
    acquittal:*
'If the sound of a lamb can give you joy, please pity the voice of
    my child!'
He adds that if I'm fond of piglets, his daughter's voice should
    sway me.*
When we hear such things, we slacken the strings on the
    instrument of our anger.

Do we not, then, wield a mighty power and show contempt for
    wealth?

BDELYKLEON [*writing*]. I'm noting down your second point, the
    contempt you show for wealth.

And tell me the benefits you receive from supposedly ruling
    Greece.

PHILOKLEON. When citizen boys are up for review, their genitals
    get displayed.*

And if Oiagros faces a charge, we're not prepared to acquit him
Until he selects the finest speech from *Niobe* and recites it.*   580
If an *aulos*-player should win his case, the price we expect from
    him
Is to wear his mouth-strap and pipe a tune as we jurors leave the
    court.
If a father's died and specified who his heiress daughter should
    marry,
We're free to tell the text of the will we don't give a damn for its
    contents,
Still less for the fancy casing placed officiously round the seal:
We give the woman instead to who persuades us with entreaties.*
We do these things without review; no one can match this power.*

BDELYKLEON [*ironically*]. That all sounds rather grandiose. I'm
    sure this makes you happy.

But you're wrong to break an heiress's seal and open up her
    status.

PHILOKLEON. What's more, when some great case gets stuck in
    Council or Assembly,   590
They'll vote to make the suspects face a trial before a jury.
Euathlos then and big fat Hanger-onymos, shield-discarder,*
Proclaim they'll never betray us folk but always fight for the
    masses.
And in the Assembly no one wins a vote for any proposal
Without suggesting the courts should close for the day after just
    one trial.*
We alone are left unharmed by Kleon, the conquer-by-shrieking
    hero:*
He holds us safely in his hand and scares away the flies,
While *you* never took such care as this to cherish your own father.
Theoros, who's a man to match Euphemides himself,*

Has sponge and basin at the ready to waterproof our boots.   600
Consider how great these benefits are from which you want to
      exclude me.
And yet you said you'd show my life is fit for a slave and a drudge!
BDELYKLEON. Have your fill of words! And once you stop, I'll show
      the world that you
Are an arsehole that resists all washing, despite pretence of power.
PHILOKLEON. The most delightful thing of all I've only just
      remembered.
   It's when I get back home with my pay and the family all come
      running
   To welcome me for my money's sake. Then first my daughter
      takes me
   And gives me a wash, rubs oil on my feet, then bends to give a
      kiss
   While Daddying me and with her tongue fishing out my three-
      obol fee!*
   My sweet little wife fawns over me and brings a barley-cake,   610
   Then comes and sits right next to me and urges, 'Here now, eat
      this,
   And pop this too inside your mouth'. I glow with this attention,
   Which means I don't depend on *you* or the steward to serve
      my meals
   While cursing and grumbling. And even if he's slow to prepare
      my food,
   My state pay keeps me safe from trouble, defends me from
      aggression.
   If *you* don't pour me wine to drink, I've brought this 'donkey'
      home:*
   [*Gesturing*] It's full of wine and I tip it to pour; then opening wide
      its mouth
   It brays aloud at *your* wine-cup before giving a soldier's fart!
   Is this not mighty power I wield? Am I not as great as Zeus?   620
            I'm spoken of in terms like him:
            When we jurors start to make a clamour,
            Every passer-by is heard to comment,
            'What thunderous noise that courtroom makes,
            O Zeus the king!' At my lightning bolts
            The rich, for all their haughtiness,

                    Cry out in shock—and shit themselves!
[*To* BDELYKLEON] And you yourself are afraid of me,
                    I swear by Demeter you're full of fear.
                    But damn me if I'm afraid of you!   630

CHORUS.   Never before have I heard a speech   *Antistrophe*
                    From one who spoke so lucidly
                    Or with such intelligence.
PHILOKLEON. Too true! Yet *he* believed he'd somehow win without
    resistance.
    He knew that in a full debate I'm a far superior speaker.
CHORUS.   He's covered every angle,
                    Omitting nothing that matters.
                    As I listened I swelled with pride
                    And felt I was judging a case
                    In the isles of the blest,*   640
                    So great was my joy at his words.
PHILOKLEON. Just look at how he's fidgeting now and lacks all
    self-composure.
[*To* BDELYKLEON] I promise I'll make you look today like a dog that
    fears a whipping.
CHORUS [*to* BDELYKLEON]. You need to devise every possible kind
                    Of artful cunning, to win acquittal.
                    Assuaging my anger to softness
                    Is a task that's hard to accomplish—
                    Unless the speaker's on my side.

[BDELYKLEON *now steps forward to put his case; his comportment is that
        of an accomplished forensic speaker.*]

LEADER. If you fail to deliver an adequate speech, you'll need a
    special millstone
    To give you even the slightest chance of grinding down my fury.
BDELYKLEON. It's a challenge requiring insight far beyond the
    wine–song's reach*   650
    To heal a very old disease which breeds inside the city.
    But, father of all, O son of Kronos*—
PHILOKLEON.   Give up paternal appeals!
    Unless you soon explain to me how come I'm like a slave,

[*Waving his sword*] Your death is certain—even if I'm banned from
    sacrifice.*

BDELYKLEON. Please listen, dear old Daddy, and relax that angry
    face.

To start with, roughly calculate—on hands, no abacus needed—
The total amount of tribute paid to Athens from our allies.
Then add to that the taxes and the many one-percent levies,
Plus further income from the courts, from markets, mines, and
    harbours.
The sum arising from these things is near two thousand
    talents.*   660
Subtract from that the pay that in a year the jurors get,
Six thousand men—'and never more inhabited the land'.
The annual jurors' pay adds up to a hundred and fifty talents.*

PHILOKLEON. But that's not even a tenth of all the revenues of
    our city!

BDELYKLEON. It certainly isn't.

PHILOKLEON.   Then where does all the rest of the
    money end up?

BDELYKLEON. With those who always say 'I'll never betray the
    Athenian riffraff,

I'll always fight on behalf of the masses'.* Yet *you* prefer, dear
    father,
To let these people rule over you; you swallow the nonsense they
    feed you.
These men consume enormous bribes, some fifty talents a time;
They take them from the allied cities with bullying threats like
    these: 670
'You'll pay your tribute, otherwise a storm will sink your city.'
Yet *you're* content to nibble the meagre scraps produced by empire.
As soon as allies realize most citizens are trash
Who scrape a living on jury pay, no dainties for *them* to eat,
They think of you as worthless votes but bribe the politicians*
With fish, wine, blankets, cheese, and honey, with sesame-cakes
    and cushions,
With bowls, cloaks, garlands, necklaces, with cups—with wealth-
    and-health.
Of all the people whom you rule, 'after many campaigns on land
    and sea',*

No one gives *you* so much as a head of garlic for boiled fish!
PHILOKLEON. But I myself sent a slave to buy three cloves from
    Eucharides.*   680
You haven't explained my servitude—I find your failure grating.
BDELYKLEON. Well isn't it massive servitude when all these
    office-holders
Together with their hangers-on receive abundant pay,
While you're content to get three obols from funds that *you*
    brought in
By rowing, and fighting, and manning the sieges, with endless toil
    for the city?
Moreover, you always follow commands—this really makes me
    choke—
When a youngster makes his way into court, some arsehole,
    Chaireas' son,*
[*Aping*] And poses like this, while swaying his body in such a foppish
    manner,
And tells you to turn up in good time for a trial, 'Since any of you
Who arrive too late for the start of the case will not receive three
    obols'.   690
Yet he himself gets an advocate's fee, a drachma, even if late.
He enters into a special arrangement with one of the other
    officials,
Then if a defendant offers a bribe, the pair of them in cahoots
Adopt a pretence but pull and push together, like working a saw.
But *you* just gawp at the court paymaster; the whole thing's lost
    on you.
PHILOKLEON. They treat me like that? Is it really so? You're
    churning my deepest feelings,
And starting to make me change my mind. You're having a weird
    effect.
BDELYKLEON. Consider then this: you could be rich, and all other
    citizens too,
Yet those who make their populist claims have run big rings
    around you.
It's you who rule so many cities from Pontos to Sardinia,*   700
Yet the only benefit you derive is this measly pittance you're paid;
And even this they give you in dribbles, providing bare
    subsistence.

Their real desire is to keep you poor, and I'll tell you why that's so.
It's to make you like an obedient dog, so when your owner whistles
To set you on some foe of his, you pounce with nasty growls.
If they really wished to give the people a livelihood, it's easy.
A thousand cities, that's how many, bring tribute now to Athens.*
If each of these were given the task of feeding twenty men,
Then twenty thousand Athenian folk could live in lavish style,
Hare-meat to eat, garlands to wear, and plentiful beestings to
drink, 710
Enjoying the kind of rewards this land and our Marathon trophy
warrants.
But as things stand, like olive-pickers you follow the person who
pays you.

PHILOKLEON. Oh no, what's wrong! A kind of numbness spreads
across my hand.
I can no longer grip this sword at all—I feel myself enfeebled.
[*Drops sword*]

BDELYKLEON. But when these men themselves are worried, they
bribe you with Euboia*
And promise to give out doles of grain—yes, fifty measures a
time.
And yet they never deliver the goods! You recently got *five*
measures
In crumbs of barley—even for that, your citizenship was queried.
So these are the reasons I kept you locked up.
I only wanted to feed you myself 720
And to stop their claptrap fooling you.
And now I'm simply prepared to provide
Anything that you want—
Except paymaster's milk to drink!

[*Despite his son's words and gestures of help,* PHILOKLEON *has slumped
into a kind of stunned stupor, perhaps parodically reminiscent of a grief-
stricken figure in tragedy. The* CHORUS *too has been visibly softened by*
BDELYKLEON's *arguments; in what follows it abandons all its previous
signs of aggression.*]

LEADER. What a sage, whoever it was who said, 'Before you've
heard both sides,

Don't judge a case'. [*To* BDELYKLEON] It's now apparent that *you*
  have won this contest.

It's time to let my anger slacken, put down my walking stick.

[*To* PHILOKLEON] Come now, you fellow member of our aged
  brotherhood—

CHORUS [*joining in*]. Please, please do what he says, don't   *Strophe*
      be unreasonable
        Or obstinate or obdurate.   730
        How I wish I had a guardian or kinsman
        Who could reproach me in such ways!
        But *you* have one of the gods right here before you:
        He's on your side and clearly trying to do you good.
        You should actively welcome his help.

BDELYKLEON. I'll look after him and supply him with all
        That an old man needs: that's porridge to sup,
        A soft cloak to wear, a sheepskin blanket,
        A whore who'll rub his prick for him
        And his rump as well.   740
        But the fact he just won't speak a word
        Is filling me with misgivings.

CHORUS. He's reproached himself for all the ways   *Antistrophe*
        In which he went quite crazy. It's just struck home,
        He recognizes as bad mistakes
        The many times he spurned your advice.
        Perhaps he now accepts your claims
        And in future he'll be transformed in mind and heart
        Because he's convinced by you.

[PHILOKLEON *now (partially) adopts the melodramatic language and
        attitude of a tragic character in crisis.*]

PHILOKLEON. Alas, alas, oh woe is me!
BDELYKLEON. But what do you mean by these cries?
PHILOKLEON. Don't promise me these new things.   750
        It's those others I long for, that place I pine to be,
        Where the herald says, 'Who's not voted? Come
          forward now.'

Would I could linger by the voting funnels
And be the last to cast my vote!
Hasten now, my soul! Where are you, soul?
Give way, shadowy grove*—[*Angrily*] In Herakles'
    name,
May I no longer serve on a jury
And convict the thieving...Kleon!*

[*After an exceptionally long stretch of recitative and song, the metre now
returns to unaccompanied speech as* BDELYKLEON *initiates a more 'normal' conversation with his father, who has evidently abandoned plans to
fall on his sword.*]

BDELYKLEON. By all the gods, dear father, take my advice.   760
PHILOKLEON. What advice is that? There's one thing out of the
    question.
BDELYKLEON. One thing? What's that?
PHILOKLEON.   To give up being a juror.
    I'd rather submit to Hades than be persuaded.
BDELYKLEON. Well, look: since this is what gives you so much
    pleasure,
    Stop going off there to court, stay here at home,
    And be the juror in trials of household slaves.
PHILOKLEON. What trials? Such nonsense!
BDELYKLEON.   Just like the ones in court.
[*Improvising*] If a slave-girl leaves the house for an assignation,
    You can vote for a fine...[*with innuendo*] and ram the penalty
        home.
    That's the sort of thing you always do in the courts.   770
    Just think how nice it will be on a sunny morning
    To hold a trial at home and enjoy the heat.
    But when it snows, you can sit by the fire and judge.
    If it rains, you'll stay indoors. If you wake at noon,
    No magistrate will bar you at the gate.
PHILOKLEON. I like the sound of this.
BDELYKLEON.   And if a speaker
    Goes on at length, you won't be stuck there hungry,
    Just biting your lips and angry with the defendant.
PHILOKLEON. But how can I hope to make such good decisions,

The way I've always done, if I'm chewing food? 780

BDELYKLEON. You'll make much *better* decisions: they always say
When witnesses lie in court the jurors find
They can only work things out by chewing them over!

PHILOKLEON. You're starting to win me round. There's one more
thing—
Who'll give me my daily pay?

BDELYKLEON. I will.

PHILOKLEON. That's good.
It means the money will just be paid to me.
I suffered a nasty trick from Lysistratos,*
That jester. He took the drachma for him and me
And went to get small change at one of the fish stalls,
Then put three shiny mullet-scales into my hand. 790
I popped them into my mouth; I thought they were obols.*
The smell made me feel quite sick and I spat them out!
I started to grab him.

BDELYKLEON. But what did he say?

PHILOKLEON. Just listen!
He claimed I had a stomach as strong as a cock's:
'You're quick to consume your money', he dared to say.

BDELYKLEON. So you see there'll be an advantage this way
as well.

PHILOKLEON. And a big one too! Go ahead, carry out your plan.

BDELYKLEON. Wait here a moment; I'll soon bring out some
things. [*Into house*]

PHILOKLEON [*musing*]. Well just consider, the oracle's being
fulfilled.
I'd heard the day would come when people of Athens 800
Would judge lawsuits inside their very own homes
And in the porch of his house every single man
Would build for himself a teeny weeny court,
Just the size of Hekate's shrine outside the door.*

[BDELYKLEON *returns: assisted by slaves, he brings out various pieces of
furniture, including a bench, together with a wax tablet, chamber-pot,
brazier, cooking-pot (of soup), two cups, and a caged cock. In the course
of what follows, everything is arranged to form a makeshift domestic
substitute for a courtroom.*]

BDELYKLEON. Right then. What else could you want? Here's
    everything
    That I mentioned before—and plenty more besides.
    This chamber pot, in case you need to piss,
    Will hang right by you here, attached to this peg.
PHILOKLEON. A clever idea—just what an old man needs:
    You've found the perfect cure for my bladder problems!   810
BDELYKLEON. You've also got this fire, plus a pot of soup.
    You can sup from it when you want.
PHILOKLEON.   That's handy too.
    I'll even get my fee if I have a fever
    While staying at home and slurping lentil soup.
    But what's the point of the bird you've brought outside?
BDELYKLEON. If you fall asleep midway through the defence,
    This cock will wake you up by singing here.
PHILOKLEON. There's just one thing I'm missing still—
BDELYKLEON.   What's that?
PHILOKLEON. If only you could fetch the shrine of Lykos.
BDELYKLEON [*improvising*]. Look, this is the shrine and here's the
    master himself.   820
PHILOKLEON [*deceived*]. Oh, master and hero, I'd failed to notice
    you there.
BDELYKLEON. He's surely just as big as Kleonymos is.
PHILOKLEON. It's true, although a hero, he's got no weapons.*
BDELYKLEON. The sooner you seat yourself, the sooner I'll call
    Your first case.
PHILOKLEON [*sitting down*]. Call it then—I've been sitting for
    ages.
BDELYKLEON [*musing*]. Let's see, which case should I introduce for
    him first?
    What crime has anyone in the house committed?
    The Thracian maid burnt a pot just the other day—
PHILOKLEON [*agitated*]. Wait a moment there, you nearly finished
    me off!
    Are you going to call a case when the court lacks railings   830
    Which mark a sacred space in the eyes of us jurors?
BDELYKLEON. You're right, they're missing.
PHILOKLEON.   I'll dash inside myself
    And fetch them out; I'll be back in just a moment. [*Exits*]

BDELYKLEON. What next! His love of the courtroom's quite
   obsessive.

[*Just a moment after* PHILOKLEON *has entered the house,* XANTHIAS
   comes out of the door, shouting over his shoulder as he does so.]

XANTHIAS. To hell with it! Why keep this kind of dog?
BDELYKLEON. What's going on here?
XANTHIAS.   It's Labes, that dog of ours—
   A moment ago he darted into the kitchen
   And snatched and devoured a chunk of Sicilian cheese.*
BDELYKLEON. Then this can be the very first crime to be tried
   In my father's court. You can lead the prosecution.   840
XANTHIAS. That's not for me. Our other dog insists
   It will prosecute, if someone brings the charge.
BDELYKLEON. Right, bring both dogs out here.
XANTHIAS.   I'll do it at once.

[*No sooner has* XANTHIAS *gone back into the house than* PHILOKLEON
   emerges with a pig-pen as a substitute for the courtroom railings.]

BDELYKLEON. What's *this*!
PHILOKLEON.   Our hearth-side pig-pen from the house.
BDELYKLEON [*ironically*]. You mean you've pillaged our sacred
   hearth?
PHILOKLEON.   I haven't:
   I want my verdict to get to the *hearth* of the matter!
   Bring in the case at once—I'm itching to punish.
BDELYKLEON. But I need to fetch the legal documentation. [*Exits*]
PHILOKLEON. You're wasting time; I can't take more delay.
   I'm keen to plough my verdict in the wax.*   850

[BDELYKLEON *returns with objects which supposedly represent the kinds
of notices that were posted outside the courts showing details of pending trials.*]

BDELYKLEON. Here they are.
PHILOKLEON.   Then call the case.
BDELYKLEON.   I will.
PHILOKLEON.   Who's first

For trial today?

BDELYKLEON.　Oh damn! I'm so annoyed:
I've forgotten to bring the voting urns out here. [*Starts to exit*]

PHILOKLEON.　Hey, where are you going?

BDELYKLEON.　　　　　　　　　　　　　I'm fetching the urns.

PHILOKLEON.　　　　　　　　　　　　　　　　　　Don't
　　bother:
I've already got these cups that came with the soup.

BDELYKLEON.　That's perfect then. We've both got all we need—
　Oh, one thing's missing: I mean the water clock.* [*Turns again*]

PHILOKLEON [*points to chamber pot*].　But what have we here if not a
　　water clock?

BDELYKLEON.　Well improvised—that's native Athenian wit!
[*Calling*] We need a slave to bring us out some fire,　　　　　　860
　　Some myrtle wreaths, and a bit of incense as well:
　　We have to start by praying to the gods.

[*As one of the household slaves brings out the required objects, among them
the wreaths which* BDELYKLEON *and* PHILOKLEON *then place on their
heads, the* CHORUS *steps forward to join in the prayers, which are accompanied by ritual actions, including the burning of incense, on the part of*
BDELYKLEON, *whose words are also sung.*]

CHORUS.　　To cement your reconciliation
　　　　　　And join in these prayers of yours
　　　　　　We too will pronounce fair words for you,
　　　　　　Since you've nobly ended the strife of war
　　　　　　And reached a firm agreement.

BDELYKLEON.　Let ritual silence now descend on all!　　　　*Strophe*

CHORUS.　　O Phoibos Apollo, Pythian god, grant us a propitious
　　　　　　　　outcome
　　　　　　To the business here contrived　　　　　　　　870
　　　　　　By this man in front of the house,
　　　　　　And be a guide to us all
　　　　　　Now we've ceased our wandering ways,
　　　　　　O Paian, healer!*

BDELYKLEON.　O lord and master, my neighbour Aguieus, guardian
　　　　　　of my porch,*

Receive this novel rite, O lord, invented for my father's
    sake,
And put a stop to his bitter, oak-hard temperament
By mixing a little honey-sweetness into his dear old
    heart.
May he now show everyone
A gentle side, and give defendants   880
More sympathy than plaintiffs.
May he weep for those who entreat him.
May he cease his peevishness
And remove from his anger
Its prickly nettle sting!

CHORUS. We share these prayers and add our own   *Antistrophe*
    refrain
To this new beginning, for the sake of all you've said.
We've been well-disposed to you
Ever since we realized
That you love the people far more
Than other young men do.   890

[*The prayers complete, the* CHORUS *steps back to the side of the* orchêstra
and the fantastical scenario of the domestic courtroom is resumed, with
BDELYKLEON *playing the roles of both court official and presiding*
magistrate.]

BDELYKLEON. Any juror still outside should enter now:
    There'll be no admission as soon as the speeches start.
PHILOKLEON. What defendant have we here? Conviction's certain!
BDELYKLEON [*formally*]. Now hear the charge: a dog from
    Kydathenaion*
Is prosecuting Labes, deme Aixone,
For eating all alone the piece of cheese
From Sicily. Punishment asked: a fig-wood collar.*
PHILOKLEON. No, worse—let him die like a dog, once he's convicted!
BDELYKLEON. The defendant himself, Labes, now comes before you.

[XANTHIAS *enters from the house door, bringing out* LABES, *an actor*
wearing a canine mask and costume; XANTHIAS *then goes back inside.*]

PHILOKLEON. Oh, what a disgusting beast! Such a thieving
    look!   900
  He clearly thinks his simpering smile will fool me!
  Where's the prosecuting Kydathenaion dog?

[XANTHIAS *comes out again, this time bringing* DOG, *whose canine mask
and costume are notably nasty.*]

DOG. Woof woof!
BDELYKLEON.   Here he is.
XANTHIAS.   This one's another filcher;
  He's good at snarling and licking the pots quite clean.*
BDELYKLEON [*to* XANTHIAS]. Keep quiet, sit down. And you, Dog,
    bring your case.
PHILOKLEON. Well now, I'll pour some soup and take a slurp.
DOG. You've heard the charge I've brought before the court,
  O men of the jury, against this dog. He's done
  A terrible thing to me and the 'yo-ho' rowers.*
  After scurrying into a corner, he made the cheese   910
  A Sicilian feast for himself, growing fat in the dark—
PHILOKLEON. In the name of Zeus, that's all too clear! Just now
  He belched a nasty whiff of cheese at me,
  This repulsive beast!
DOG.   —and refusing to give me a share.
  Yet who will ever be able to do you good
  Unless he tosses a morsel to me, your guard-dog?*
PHILOKLEON. He refused to share with me as well, the people.
  The man's hot-headed—as hot as my lentil soup!
BDELYKLEON. By the gods, don't reach a premature judgement,
    father,
  Before you've even heard both sides.
PHILOKLEON.   What nonsense!   920
  The matter's as plain as day. Screams in your face.
DOG. You mustn't acquit him, jurors: of all your dogs
  He's a man with totally selfish eating habits.
  He sailed his way right round the kitchen mortar
  And has eaten all the cheese rind from the cities.
PHILOKLEON. But *I* don't even get the smallest scraping!
DOG. So punish this dog—remember, there's no room

In a single bush for a pair of thieving magpies*—
So my own loud barks don't prove a waste of time.
Otherwise, I'll cease to bark at all in future.   930

[BDELYKLEON, *unnoticed by* PHILOKLEON, *now moves from his previous position to get ready to call the 'witnesses', who consist of objects either brought on stage earlier (see at 805) or now carried out by household slaves.*]

PHILOKLEON. Appalling!
  What terrible misdemeanours he alleged.
  It's an outright case of theft. [*To caged cock*] Don't you agree,
  My cock? By Zeus, he's winking his eye at me!
  Where's the magistrate gone? I need my chamber-pot.
BDELYKLEON. Just take it yourself. I'm calling the witnesses in.

[PHILOKLEON *gets up, takes the chamber pot off its peg, and, with the trial proceeding, starts to urinate into it.*]

[*Formally*] As Labes' witnesses I call: a dish,
  A pestle, cheese-grater, brazier, and pot,
  And all the other equipment burnt in cooking.
[*To* PHILOKLEON] Have you still not finished your piss and sat back
  down?   940
PHILOKLEON. The defendant won't just piss—he'll *shit* himself!
BDELYKLEON. Won't you stop this harsh and peevish state of mind
  Towards defendants? Don't get your teeth into them.
[*To* LABES] Mount the stand, defend yourself.

[LABES *steps up but then adopts a mute posture.*]

                                        But why this silence?
PHILOKLEON. It's perfectly plain he has nothing at all to say!
BDELYKLEON. That's not the case. I think he's been afflicted
  In the way Thucydides was when once on trial:
  He was suddenly dumbstruck, just couldn't open his mouth.*
[*To* LABES] Move out of the way; I'll make the defence myself.
[*Rhetorically*] O men of the jury, it's hard to put the case   950
  On behalf of a slandered dog; even so, I'll try.

He's a *good* dog, one who drives off all the wolves.
PHILOKLEON. You mean a thief and conspirator, that's what he is!
BDELYKLEON. Not at all, he's the best of all the dogs at present,
  Well capable of controlling lots of sheep.*
PHILOKLEON. What's the benefit of *that*, if he eats our cheese?
BDELYKLEON. You ask? He fights for you and guards the door,
  And is best in other ways too. If he happened to steal,
  Show mercy—he doesn't know how to play the lyre.*
PHILOKLEON. I wish he didn't know even how to write,*   960
  Then he couldn't have falsified official accounts.
BDELYKLEON. But listen, I beg, to what the witnesses say.
  Mount the platform now, cheese-grater, and speak up loud.
  Since you were in charge of supplies, please answer clearly:
  Did you grate the cheese you received for all the soldiers?
[*As if listening*] It says that it did.
PHILOKLEON.   I bet, but it's telling a lie!
BDELYKLEON. I beg you, please show pity to those who suffer.
  For Labes here eats all the scraps of offal,
  The fish bones too. He's always on the move.
  But this other dog does nothing but guard the house: 970
  He stays at home, and whatever's brought inside
  He asks for a share for himself. Otherwise, he bites!
PHILOKLEON. Oh no, I'm starting to soften: what's making this
    happen?
  I'm overcome by weakness; I'm being convinced.
BDELYKLEON. I beg you all, take pity—and you, dear father!
  Don't ruin this dog. Someone, bring forward his children.*

[LABES' 'PUPPIES' *are now brought out in some form or other and* BDE-
LYKLEON *treats them in the way the children of defendants were sometimes produced in court to arouse sympathy. In what follows, it becomes
increasingly clear that* PHILOKLEON *himself is starting, against his normal habits, to shed tears of pity for the defendant.*]

  Mount the rostrum now, poor things. Be sure to whimper
  While you beg and beseech the jury and cry your eyes out.
PHILOKLEON [*to* BDELYKLEON]. Get down, get down, get down,
    get down!
BDELYKLEON.   I will.

Though shouts of 'get off the platform' have often deceived 980
Defendants in the past. But I'll still get down.
PHILOKLEON. To hell with it! This soup's not good for me.
My tears have washed away my stern resolve,
All because I'm full of this steaming lentil soup.
BDELYKLEON. So you mean he's not acquitted?
PHILOKLEON [*evasively*]. It's hard to tell.
BDELYKLEON. Please, dearest father, choose the kinder option.

[BDELYKLEON *now goes up to his father, puts a voting pebble in his hand,
and starts to steer him towards the voting urns, eventually tricking him
about which urn is which.*]

Here, take this pebble and, shutting your eyes, rush past
The first of the urns, then vote for acquittal, dear father.
PHILOKLEON [*resisting*]. I won't! 'I don't know how to play the
lyre.'*
BDELYKLEON. Look, let me lead you here by the shortest route. 990
This urn is the first.
PHILOKLEON. This one? Then here's my vote! [*Inserts pebble*]
BDELYKLEON [*aside*]. I've fooled him into voting for acquittal!
[*To* PHILOKLEON] Let me now tip out the votes.
PHILOKLEON. Well, what's the
outcome?
BDELYKLEON [*feigning a count*]. We'll soon find out...O Labes,
you're acquitted!

[PHILOKLEON *melodramatically collapses in a faint of horror at the
result. In what follows, one of the slaves fetches water which is splashed on*
PHILOKLEON *to revive him.*]

What's wrong, what's wrong with you, father? Bring some water!
[*Helping*] Get up on your feet.
PHILOKLEON. You've got to tell me this:
Was he really acquitted?
BDELYKLEON. He was.
PHILOKLEON. My life is worthless!
BDELYKLEON. You mustn't be so dismayed—come on, stand up.
PHILOKLEON. Well how I can live with a thing like this on my
conscience?

I let a defendant go free. My prospects are bleak.   1000
I beseech you, venerable gods, show mercy to me!
I didn't intend it. It's not what I normally do.
BDELYKLEON. No need to feel upset. I'll care for you, father.
   Wherever I go, I'll take you round with me:
   To dinners, to drinking parties, [*gesturing to audience*]...even the
      theatre.*
   In future you'll live a life that's full of pleasure;
   Hyperbolos won't make a fool of you.*
   Let's go inside.
PHILOKLEON [*submissively*]. Very well, if that's what you want.

[BDELYKLEON *lifts his father to his feet and the two of them exit into the
house, followed by various slaves who remove the paraphernalia used
for the trial scene. The* CHORUS *then moves into position to deliver the
parabasis.*]

[PARABASIS: 1009–1121]

CHORUS.   We wish you both well, wherever you go!
[*To audience*] But meanwhile *you*,   1010
              O thousands too many to count,*
              Should listen to all the good things we'll say
              Ensuring our words don't fall in vain
              On stony ground:
              That's the mark of stupid spectators,
              And not what's expected of *you*.

LEADER. Now pay attention to us, great throngs, if you'd like to
      hear something candid.
   Our poet desires to make a complaint about people who watch his
      plays:
   He says he's been wronged, even though he'd earlier done them
      all much good.
   To begin with, he gave some secret help to a number of other
      poets
   And emulating Eurykles' prophetic-minded voice
   He entered the bellies of others and poured out streams of comic
      language.*   1020
   After that, he openly started to take a risk with work of his own,*

Becoming the charioteer of his personal Muses, not those of others.

After great success and winning acclaim more than anyone else
    had done,

He states that he never got carried away by these things or inflated
    with pride.

He didn't cruise round the wrestling schools in the hope of
    picking up boys,

And if a resentful lover insisted his former beloved be mocked,

The poet would never oblige such things but maintained a sense
    of fairness:

It wasn't his wish to make his Muses a group of go-betweens.*

What's more, when he started to stage his plays, he didn't attack
    common folk.*

With a temper worthy of Herakles, he tackled the greatest
    targets,   1030

Taking stand with boldness, right from the start, against the
    jag-toothed monster,

Whose eyes flashed fearsome beams of light like those of Kynna
    the whore,

While round him licked a hundred heads of revolting hangers-on,

And he had the voice of a mountain torrent that threatens wrack
    and ruin,

Plus the stench of a seal, with Lamia's unwashed balls and a
    camel's arsehole.*

Yet this monstrous sight never frightened him into taking bribes
    for silence;

He's kept on waging war for you.* And another target of his

Are the symptoms of sickness, the shivers and fevers, he launched
    an attack on last year,

Those people who strangled their fathers at night and choked
    their grandfathers too,

And lay on their beds in the middle of night making plans against
    innocent people,   1040

Contriving all manner of legal threats, with concocted witness
    statements,

So that numerous citizens leapt up in fear and rushed for the
    magistrate's help.*

Yet though you'd discovered this poet could serve as defender and
    purge of this land,

You betrayed him last year when he sowed in his work the most
 brilliant, novel ideas,
Whose value you totally failed to grasp and prevented from
 bearing their fruit.*
Even so, with numerous libations he swears by the god Dionysos*
That no finer comic creation has ever been heard than that last
 play of his.
So it's shame on those of you who failed to appreciate its merits,
But our poet himself's no less esteemed in sophisticated circles
Just because in overtaking his rivals his poetic chariot crashed!   1050
> In future when you're judging poets,
> We beg you, try to recognize
> The ones who strive to innovate:
> You need to cherish and nurture them
> And take good care of their ideas
> By storing them in special chests
> With sweetest-smelling citrons.
> If you act like this, then all year round
> You'll find your clothes
> Will have the fragrance of cleverness.

CHORUS.   Alas, so long since we were lusty dancers, *Strophe*   1060
            Lusty too on the battlefield,
[*Gesturing*] And with this *sting* the lustiest of men.
            But that was then, ah then! Now all
            Is vanished, and whiter far than a swan
            Are these wispy hairs on our heads.
            And yet from these feeble remnants
            I need to recover some youthful vigour.
            I think that even my old age counts for more
            Than the fancy long hair of many young men,
            With the sodomized poses they strike!   1070

LEADER. As you contemplate this body of mine, if any of you
  spectators wonder,
    Observing how the shape of my waist has been given a thoroughly
     wasp-like form,
    What's the special point of the sting we carry attached to our
     rump behind us here,

The explanation is easy to state, 'however uncultured one may
   have once been'.*
Who *are* we, then, this group whose buttocks are marked by such
   a prominent trait?
We're the only truly Attic men—autochthonous right to the core—*
The manliest breed, the ones on whom the city relied to the
   greatest extent
To fight its battles when in the past the Persians came to invade
   the land,
Filling all the city with clouds of smoke and burning everything
   as they went,
Their purpose to use such violent means to attack and destroy our
   nests, no less.   1080
We swarmed at speed and without delay, 'equipped with spear,
   equipped with shield',
We carried the fight right back to them, our bellies primed with
   vinegar wine,
Our ranks packed tight together, man next to man, each biting his
   lips in anger.
The masses of arrows they fired at us filled up the sky like banks
   of cloud,
But nevertheless we pushed them back, with the gods' support, as
   evening came;
The omens were good—an owl had flown across our army before
   the battle.
We chased them away and speared them like tuna, with thrusts at
   their baggily trousered legs;
They fled in haste, all covered in stings, including their jaws and
   eyebrows too.*
To this very day, in every place across the whole barbarian world,
There's nothing that's said to be feistier than...a good and
   proper Attic wasp!   1090

CHORUS.   How mighty I was in those days, so that   *Antistrophe*
                 everyone feared me.
             I imposed myself upon
             My foes when I sailed out in triremes.
             Our generation lacked a concern
             For learning to give a persuasive speech

Or using legal threats for blackmail.
Our only concern was who would be
The finest rower. So since we captured
Numerous cities from Persian rule, it's our
    achievement
That so much tribute is brought to Athens—
Though stolen by young politicians!*   1100

LEADER. No matter which way you look at us, you'll find that we're
    in all respects
Remarkably wasp-like in our habits, in every aspect of our lives.
To start with, there's no other creature which, when its anger's
    been provoked,
Flies into a sharper rage or surpasses me in peevishness.
Furthermore, we plan our affairs in a manner that's just the same
    as wasps.
We huddle together in separate swarms, the way that wasps
    construct their nests:
Some of us sit at the Archon's court, and others at where the
    Eleven preside,
Others again in the Odeion, yet others right up against the walls,*
All crammed together in tight-knit groups and nodding their
    heads towards the ground   1110
Like tiny grubs that, as they grow, keep wriggling round inside
    their cells.
As regards the way of life we lead, we show ourselves resourceful
    too:
We stick our stings into every man and earn a living by doing so.
Yet even so there sit among us some lazy drones who are not like us:
They have no sting of their own but wait in the hive while *we* do
    all the work
Then simply devour what we bring back, but have no share in the
    trouble it costs.
The greatest grief for us is when somebody who's never fought
    for the city
Gulps down a juror's pay although they've never defended this
    land of ours
By pulling an oar or wielding a spear or earning themselves large
    blisters too!

I propose such things should change in future, so here's a simple
suggestion from me: 1120
No citizen who's *without* a sting should ever receive the three-
obol fee!*

[*As the* CHORUS *moves back to the sides of the* orchêstra, PHILOKLEON
and BDELYKLEON *enter from the house, evidently locked in argument:*
BDELYKLEON *is trying to persuade his father to exchange his shabby old
cloak for a larger, more luxurious garment, which is carried at first,
together with a pair of fine shoes, by one of the household slaves.*]

PHILOKLEON. As long as I live, I'll never be stripped of this cloak.*
It saved my life on its own when I fought in the ranks
And a great cold wind from the north made war against me.
BDELYKLEON. You seem to have no interest in being pampered.
PHILOKLEON. No I don't: that sort of thing doesn't suit me at all.
I gorged myself on roasted small fry once,
But it cost three obols to take my cloak to the cleaner's!
BDELYKLEON. Won't you simply give it a try, since you've now
agreed
To allow me a chance to make your life much nicer?   1130
PHILOKLEON. Well what do you want me to do?
BDELYKLEON.   Give up this cloak
And put on this finer one to look more stylish.

[*In what follows,* PHILOKLEON *reluctantly removes his old cloak and
suspiciously inspects the much larger, heavier one which his son wants him
to wear, before eventually, and after a physical struggle, allowing it to be
draped round him.*]

PHILOKLEON. What's the point of breeding children and bringing
them up
When this son of mine now wants to choke me to death?
BDELYKLEON. Here, drape yourself with this one. Just stop
gabbling.
PHILOKLEON. What the hell's this thing, in the name of all the
gods!
BDELYKLEON. It's called a Persian cloak or a tufted robe.
PHILOKLEON. It looks to me more like a rustic blanket!

BDELYKLEON. That's not surprising: you've never visited Sardis.*
　　If you had, you'd recognize this. As it is, you don't.   1140
PHILOKLEON. I certainly don't! But I think it looks the same
　　As the tasselled military bag that Morychos carries.*
BDELYKLEON. Not at all—these things are woven in Ekbatana.
PHILOKLEON. Are there sausages made of wool in Ekbatana?*
BDELYKLEON. Don't be absurd! Barbarians weave such stuff
　　At huge expense. This very cloak, in fact,
　　Consumed at least a talent's worth of wool.*
PHILOKLEON. That's a price that sounds more like a kind of *fleecing*
　　Than a tufted robe!
BDELYKLEON.　　　　Look, please stop making this hard:
　　Stand still while we get you dressed.
PHILOKLEON.　　　　　　　　　　What the heck is this?   1150
　　This nasty thing gave a big hot belch in my face.
BDELYKLEON. Just drape it round you.
PHILOKLEON.　　　　　　　No!
BDELYKLEON.　　　　　　　　　　I beg you, please.
PHILOKLEON. I'd prefer to be covered up with a baking lid!
BDELYKLEON. Look, let me wrap it round. Come on, like this.
PHILOKLEON [*now re-dressed*]. Make sure you keep a
　　meat-hook ready.
BDELYKLEON.　　　What for?
PHILOKLEON. To pull me out before I'm cooked to shreds!
BDELYKLEON. Right, now take off these old appalling boots;
　　Slip on instead these dapper Spartan ones.*

[BDELYKEON *forces his father, once again with something of a struggle, to
　　remove his existing boots and replace them with a more stylish pair.*]

PHILOKLEON. You think I'd bring myself to wear on my feet
　　Such hostile leather that comes from the city's foes?   1160
BDELYKLEON. Just put in your foot, old chap, and push down
　　firmly
　　Inside this Spartan shoe.
PHILOKLEON.　　　　　　You're doing me wrong
　　By making me place my foot onto enemy ground!
BDELYKLEON. Look, there. Now the other foot too.
PHILOKLEON.　　　　　　　　　　　No, not this one—

This foot has a specially anti-Spartan toe!

BDELYKLEON. You've got no choice.

PHILOKLEON.   What a wretched state I'm in:
On top of old age, I'll never have more chilblains.

BDELYKLEON. Hurry up and fasten the shoes. Then like the rich
[*Demonstrating*] Step forward in this way with a swanky swagger.

PHILOKLEON. Right then. Observe my posture and try to
    guess   1170
Which one of the rich my style of walk resembles. [*Struts*]

BDELYKLEON. You resemble a boil that's dressed in a garlic
    poultice!

PHILOKLEON. But I'm trying to do the slinky buttock walk.

BDELYKLEON [*moving on*]. Now then, will you know how to tell
    impressive stories
When you mix with erudite, highly discerning men?

PHILOKLEON. Of course.

BDELYKLEON.   Then give me one.

PHILOKLEON.   I can give you lots.
For one, how Lamia farted when caught in a trap;
For another, how Kardopion once took his mother—*

BDELYKLEON. Not made-up tales but stories of human events,
Our favourite kinds, and fit for homely settings.   1180

PHILOKLEON. I know a story that has a homely setting,
It's 'Once upon a time, a mouse and a weasel—'

BDELYKLEON. You stupid oaf! [*Checking himself*]—as once
    Theogenes said*
To the dung-collector, when locked in a slanging match.
Will you talk about mice and weasels among real men?

PHILOKLEON. What kind of stories then?

BDELYKLEON.   Imposing ones.
How you went as envoy with Androkles and Kleisthenes.*

PHILOKLEON. What, *me* on a state delegation! My only trip
Was to Paros, and that for merely two obols' pay.*

BDELYKLEON. Well you ought to recount for instance the
    memorable fight   1190
When Ephoudion beat Askondas in pankration,*
Even though he was old and grey, but still possessed
A muscular flank, strong hands, as well as a torso
As good as armour.

PHILOKLEON.   Stop, stop! Don't talk such nonsense.
No one can fight pankration using armour.*
BDELYKLEON [*persisting*]. That's how sophisticated people speak.
But tell me this as well: suppose you're drinking
With foreign guests, what's the manliest feat you could tell
From all the things you did in your youthful days?
PHILOKLEON. I've got it, I've got it—the bravest of all my
          deeds,   1200
When I managed to filch vine-poles from Ergasion.*
BDELYKLEON. You'll finish me off! Vine-poles! You need to narrate
How you hunted a boar or hare, or perhaps how you ran
In a race with torches—select a *macho* deed.
PHILOKLEON. I know the most macho thing I ever did do:
When still a big lad I caught the runner Phaÿllos* . . .
And convicted him of slander by just two votes!
BDELYKLEON. Enough of that. Now recline over here and learn
The convivial manners required at drinking parties.

[BDELYKLEON *points his father to a couch that the household slaves have
brought out on his instructions.* PHILOKLEON *starts by throwing himself
clumsily onto it.*]

PHILOKLEON. Well tell me how I ought to recline.
BDELYKLEON.   With *style*.   1210
PHILOKLEON. You mean like this?
BDELYKLEON.   Not at all.
PHILOKLEON.   Then how do you mean?
BDELYKLEON. Extend your legs and, showing a well-honed body,
Spread out yourself at ease on the blanketed couch.
Next, make some laudatory comment about the bronzes,
Gaze at the ceiling, admire the tapestry hangings.*
[*As if instructing slaves*] Bring water for hands. Now bring the tables
          of food.
We dine—wash our hands again—then pour libations.
PHILOKLEON. By all the gods, are we dreaming we're at a banquet?
BDELYKLEON. The female piper has started to play. The guests
Are Theoros, Aischines, Phanos, Kleon,   1220
And a foreigner at your head, Akestor's son.*
In this company, take your turn at singing with skill.

PHILOKLEON. I know the old songs as well as our ancestors did.

BDELYKLEON. We'll soon find out. I'll play the part of Kleon:
I start the Harmodios song, then you take over.*
[*Singing*] 'Never before had Athens possessed a man—'

PHILOKLEON [*likewise*]. '—Who was such a scoundrel or thief.'

BDELYKLEON. You can't do that! You'll be shouted down and
crushed.
Kleon will vow to break you into pieces
And drive you out of this land.

PHILOKLEON.   Well if he does   1230
I'll answer his threats with another song of my own.
[*Singing*] 'O you who set your heart on great power,
You will yet overturn the city, which hangs in the
balance.'*

BDELYKLEON. But suppose Theoros, reclining next to your feet,
Takes Kleon's right hand and starts to sing as follows:
'Learn the wisdom of Admetos, befriend good men'.*
What snatch will you sing in reply?

PHILOKLEON.   In my finest voice: 1240
'One cannot behave like a fox
Nor be friend to both sides'.*

BDELYKLEON. Then Aischines, Braggart's son, will take his turn.
He's sophisticated and cultured. He'll start to sing:
'Abundant wealth and livelihood
Kleitagora and I
Possess among the Thessalians—'

PHILOKLEON. 'Abundantly you and I exchanged our bluster.'*

BDELYKLEON. You seem to be very well versed in drinking songs!
Well, let's be off to dinner at Philoktemon's.*   1250
I'll call a slave. Right, Goldy, pack our food.*
We intend to get really drunk—it's been too long.

PHILOKLEON. No we mustn't. It's bad to drink. And lots of wine
Leads to smashing of doors, fist fights, and throwing things
round,
Then having to pay for the damage while quite hung over.*

BDELYKLEON. No, not if you mix with men of *superior* status.
They'll know how to mollify any victim of yours,
Or you yourself can tell a witty story—
An amusing Aisop's tale or a Sybarite fable*—

From things you learnt at the party. And that allows you   1260
  To turn things into a joke; no charges are brought.
PHILOKLEON. Then I really must acquire a stock of stories
  If it means I won't have to pay for misdemeanours!
BDELYKLEON. Right then, let's go. No need for further delay.

[*Accompanied by* XANTHIAS, *who has just come out of the house with a
basket of food,* PHILOKLEON *and* BDELYKLEON *set off down one of the
eisodoi.*]

[SECOND PARABASIS: 1265–91]

CHORUS.   I've often thought of myself as being   *Strophe**
             A naturally rather clever type
             With no oafish traits of any kind.
             But I can't compete with Amynias,
             The son of Braggart, a hair-bun type.
             I remember seeing him seize the chance,
             Instead of his own starvation diet,
             To dine at the house of Leogoras.
             His hunger's as great as Antiphon's.   1270
             When he went as envoy to Pharsalos
             He kept the exclusive company
             Of Thessaly's poor, the Penniless ones,
             Since he himself is really a pauper
             Of a quite unparalleled sort.*

LEADER. O fortunate Automenes, we congratulate you profusely!
  The sons you begot possess exceptional skills.
  One is a friend to all, a man of the greatest talent,
  The finest of *kithara*-singers, whose art is full of beauty.
  Another's an actor, a fearsomely talented one.
  And then there's Ariphrades, who's highly clever as well.   1280
  His father once swore that without any formal instruction,
  And prompted by nothing besides his natural gifts,
  He frequented brothels to practise... his oral artistry.*

...*

There are those who said I'd accepted terms of peace
After Kleon attacked me, tried to shake me up,

And shredded me with slander; then when I was flayed
The watching crowd were amused to hear my screams.
Their only interest in me was to ascertain
If I'd toss out a witticism when under pressure.
Aware of this, I played the monkey a little,   1290
And in due course the vine-pole fooled the vine.*

[XANTHIAS *now reappears, holding his ribs and back in a way which
makes it evident that he is in pain.*]

XANTHIAS. How lucky you tortoises are to have your shell!
How really savvy to have your back roofed over
With a set of tiles, to keep your ribs protected,
Whereas *I've* been beaten to pulp and am covered in bruises.
LEADER. What's wrong then, boy? And 'boy' is rightly the word
For a slave who's beaten, no matter how old he is.
XANTHIAS. The old man proved to be the most pernicious
And the most intoxicated of all the guests.   1300
Hippyllos was there, Antiphon and Lykon too,
Lysistratos, Thouphrastos, Phrynichos' set.*
But *he* was the most outrageous of all the guests.
As soon as he'd stuffed himself with food and drink,
He leapt to his feet then pranced and farted and scoffed,
Like a little donkey that's feasted on roasted barley.
He kept on calling for me then thrashed me badly.
When Lysistratos saw his actions, he framed a likeness:
'You resemble, old chap, a Phrygian nouveau riche,
Or a donkey that's romped to eat a pile of bran.'   1310
But the old man likened *him* in turn, with a yell,
To a locust that's lost the flimsy wings of its cloak,
And to Sthenelos shorn of all his theatrical props.*
The other guests applauded, except Thouphrastos.
He pulled a long face, as though a superior wit,
And the old man asked Thouphrastos, 'Tell me then
Why you preeningly take yourself to be so subtle,
While smarmily buttering up whoever's in favour?'
He delivered insults like this around the room,
Making boorish gibes and adding all sorts of remarks   1320
That were crudely out of keeping with what was wanted.
Once thoroughly drunk, he left and headed for home,

Dealing blows to every person who got in his way.
[*Pointing*] Look, here he comes, though he's almost falling over.
I'll get out of here before I'm beaten again.

[XANTHIAS *hastily exits into the house as* PHILOKLEON *staggers into the* orchêstra, *wildly brandishing a torch, pulling after him the naked* DARDANIS, *and threatening an imagined crowd in the street. Shortly afterwards, a group of irate* MEN *will briefly appear. in pursuit of* PHILOKLEON.]

PHILOKLEON [*half-singing*]. Out of here! Get out of my path!
          It will end in tears for all
          Who try to pursue me here.
          If you don't all scarper,
          You wretches, I'll use this torch   1330
          To turn you into fried fish.
MAN. You'll pay a heavy price for this tomorrow
    To all of us, no matter how young you are.
    We'll return together to issue a legal summons.
PHILOKLEON [*half-singing*]. Ha! ha! ha! ha! 'To issue a summons'!
          You're out-of-date. Don't you realize
          I can't even stand the slightest mention
          Of legal trials? Ugh! Loathsome things!
          I like my new life! Damn voting funnels!*
          Skedaddle! I see no jurors round here!   1340

[*The* MEN *beat a hasty retreat in the face of* PHILOKLEON'*s aggression. The latter now turns his attention to the pipe-girl: he finds somewhere to seat himself and tries to manoeuvre* DARDANIS *onto his knees.*]

Come up here now, my dainty little cockchafer:
[*Offering his phallus*] Take a good firm grip of this rope to help you
    do so.
  Hold tight! But careful—the rope is starting to rot,
  Though it doesn't at all complain when it gets some rubbing.
  You see how smart I was to smuggle you out
  When about to give the drinkers a Lesbian job.*
  For that, you owe this prick of mine a favour.
  But I know you won't apply your hands to the task;

Your open mouth will cheat and laugh at this thing,
The way you've done to so many others before.   1350
But if you decide to be a good woman instead,
I'll buy your freedom, as soon as my son has died,
And keep you as a mistress, my darling piglet.*
At the present time I don't control my money;
I'm still too young and don't yet have my freedom.
My son keeps constant watch on me; he's peevish,
A totally scrimping, cheese-paring person as well.
So he's very afraid in case I get corrupted—
It's because he's got no other father than me!
[*Pointing*] But here he comes himself; he's running towards us.   1360
   Quick, take this torch from me and stand right here;
   I want to give him a really vigorous ribbing
   The way he did to me before the Mysteries.*

[BDELYKLEON *comes running on stage in belated pursuit of his father,
who steadies himself for an exchange of abuse, while* DARDANIS *stands
holding the torch above her head.*]

BDELYKLEON. Hey there, I've found you! You crazy pussy-rubber!
   This lust of yours will put you in your coffin!
   I swear you won't escape unscathed for this.
PHILOKLEON [*jeeringly*]. Perhaps you'd like to taste a spicy
      courtcase!
BDELYKLEON. How dare you scoff like this after stealing the
      pipe-girl
   From the other guests!
PHILOKLEON.   The pipe-girl? What do you mean?
   Such nonsense! Have you cracked your head right open?   1370

[*The two characters attend closely to* DARDANIS's *features:* BDE-
LYKLEON *draws attention to her female anatomy, including the representation of her pubic hair, while* PHILOKLEON *maintains the pretence
that she is a torch.*]

BDELYKLEON. Look, this is the girl right here, she's Dardanis!
PHILOKLEON. No, this is a torch in the Agora for the gods.
BDELYKLEON. A torch?

PHILOKLEON.   Of course. Can't you see the split in the wood?

BDELYKLEON.   But what's this black patch here right in her middle?

PHILOKLEON.   It's the pitch, of course, that comes from a burning
torch.

BDELYKLEON.   And isn't this part at the back the woman's *arse*?

PHILOKLEON.   No, that's a bulging knot in the wood of the torch.

BDELYKLEON.   A bulging knot? What nonsense! [*To* DARDANIS] Get
over here. [*Grabs her*]

PHILOKLEON.   Hey! What are you going to do?

BDELYKLEON.   I'll take this girl
Away from you. And I know you're so decrepit   1380
There's nothing you're able to do.

PHILOKLEON.   But listen to me.
At Olympia, when I served as the city's envoy,
Ephoudion beat Askondas in pankration
Even though he was old.* With a single blow of his fist
The old man knocked the younger man flat out.
[*Gesturing*] So beware in case you get a black eye yourself!

BDELYKLEON.   Well you've certainly learnt what I said about telling
stories!

[*From the same* eisodos *by which* PHILOKLEON *returned from the symposium, the bread-seller* MYRTIA *enters, carrying an empty bread tray
and accompanied by* CHAIREPHON, *a pale-faced individual.*]

MYRTIA [*to* CHAIREPHON].   Please come over here, I beg you, stand
beside me.
[*Pointing*] Here's the very man, the one who assaulted me
By hitting me with his torch and making me drop   1390
Ten obols' worth of bread, four loaves as well.

BDELYKLEON [*to* PHILOKLEON].   You see what you've done? We're
facing legal trouble
Because of your drunkenness.

PHILOKLEON.   No need to worry:
A few smart words will soon resolve this business.
I'm confident how to reach agreement with her.*

MYRTIA [*to* PHILOKLEON].   By the goddesses twain, you won't
slight Myrtia,*
The daughter of Agkylion and Sostrate,

Not after you've ruined my merchandise like this.

PHILOKLEON. Just listen, woman; I'd like to tell you a story.
It's highly amusing.

MYRTIA.   Don't try that on with me!   1400

PHILOKLEON. Aisop was walking home from dinner one evening.*
A crude and drunken bitch was barking at him.
He turned to her and said: 'You bitch, you bitch,
If you'd only stop the noise from your filthy tongue
And buy some wheat, I think you'd show good sense.'

MYRTIA. You dare to make fun of me? I'll issue a summons
To the market officials for damage to merchandise.*
I've Chairephon right here to be my witness.*

PHILOKLEON. Please don't—just listen, to see if you like what I say.
Lasos and Simonides were once competing.*   1410
Then Lasos said: 'I really couldn't care less!'

MYRTIA. I don't believe it!

[MYRTIA *turns in disgust and exits, followed by* CHAIREPHON, *who
clings closely to her; as they depart,* PHILOKLEON *calls his final insult at
them.*]

PHILOKLEON.   And you there, Chairephon,
Do you act as a woman's witness? You resemble
A sallow Ino who clutches Euripides' feet!*

BDELYKLEON [*pointing*]. Here's someone else approaching now, it
seems,
To deliver a summons to you; they've brought a witness.

[*From the same* eisodos *used by* MYRTIA *enters the* ACCUSER, *an old
man nursing his injuries and accompanied by his* WITNESS.]

ACCUSER. I'm in distress. [*To* PHILOKLEON] I'm accusing you, old
man,
Of *hybris*.

BDELYKLEON.   *Hybris*? No, no! Don't bring a charge.*
I'll pay you recompense on his behalf:
Just stipulate what you want; I'll be so grateful.   1420

PHILOKLEON. I'll reach an agreement with him on my own behalf.
I admit I struck him hard and beat him up.

[*To* ACCUSER] Step over here. Are you happy to let me choose
  The amount I ought to pay to put things right,
  Then we'll be friends? Or would you prefer to decide?
ACCUSER. I'll let you choose. I'd rather avoid the courts.
PHILOKLEON. A man from Sybaris once had a chariot crash;*
  He was thrown right onto his head and broke it badly.
  He was totally clueless in all equestrian matters.
  A friend of his stood there and said to him: 1430
  'Each man should stick to whatever he knows about.'
  So run along to Pittalos for some treatment.*
ACCUSER. This is more of the same and just as bad as before!
[*To* BDELYKLEON] And *you* should remember as well the answer
    he gave.

[*The* ACCUSER *and his* WITNESS *now start to leave, but* PHILOKLEON
        has not finished with them yet.]

PHILOKLEON. Please listen, don't hurry away. A Sybarite woman
  Once smashed a storage pot. [*Strikes him*]
ACCUSER.   I call for a witness!
PHILOKLEON. The pot then called on a man to serve as witness.
  The Sybarite woman declared: 'In Persephone's name,
  If rather than calling a witness you'd promptly bought
  A bandage to mend the pot, you'd have more sense.'   1440
ACCUSER. Keep up your nasty *hybris*—I'll see you in court! [*Exits*
    with WITNESS]
BDELYKLEON. In Demeter's name, you're staying out here no longer.

[BDELYKLEON *gets hold of his father in order to force him into the house.*
   DARDANIS *takes the opportunity to slip away by an* eisodos.]

  I'm going to lift you up and—
PHILOKLEON.   What are you doing?
BDELYKLEON. I'm taking you straight inside. Otherwise we'll find
  There aren't enough witnesses left for your accusers!
PHILOKLEON [*struggling*]. The Delphians once charged Aisop—
BDELYKLEON.   I
  couldn't care less!
PHILOKLEON. —with stealing a bowl that belonged to Apollo himself.

Aisop then told the story of the dung-beetle*—

BDELYKLEON. Enough! Dung-beetles will be the final straw!

[BDELYKLEON *finally manages to drag his father back inside the house.*]

CHORUS.   I envy the positive fortune   *Strophe* 1450
             Of this old man, so much transformed
             From his harshness of temper and way of life.
             Once his lessons have reached a further stage
             He'll take a great step forward
             To a life of voluptuous softness.
             But perhaps he's reached his limit:
             No easy thing to leave behind
             One's own inveterate nature.
             Yet many succeed in doing that:
             Exposed to the views of others   1460
             They undergo a character change.

             Heaps of praise will be earned from me   *Antistrophe*
             As well as from all who have good sense
             By the one who's shown such filial love
             And such an abundance of wisdom too—
             The son of Philokleon!
             I've never encountered one so benign
             And nobody's cast of mind has ever
             Sent me so crazy or wild with delight.
             Did not each one of his arguments   1470
             Command conviction? His only wish
             Is to elevate his progenitor's life
             To a grander level of social style!

[XANTHIAS *comes rushing out of the house in evident panic.*]

XANTHIAS. By Dionysos, we're in a hopeless mess
    Inflicted on the house by some god or other!
    Having got more drunk than he'd been for a very long time,
    When the old man heard an *aulos* he went euphoric
    And spent the whole night long performing dances,
    The ancient type that Thespis put on the stage.*

He says he'll outdance the current tragic dancers   1480
And make it clear how primitive they are!

[*The voice of* PHILOKLEON *is now heard from inside the house, chanting
to the accompaniment of the* aulos *in quasi-tragic recitative, to whose
rhythms* XANTHIAS*'s utterances will also be assimilated. At 1484 the
house door opens and the old man rushes out to perform a wild dance routine, while* XANTHIAS *stands to one side and supplies a commentary.*]

PHILOKLEON. Who keeps watch here at the courtyard doors?
XANTHIAS. Here comes the very trouble I meant!
PHILOKLEON. Let these locks be released, now the time has come
            For the start of my dance—
XANTHIAS. The start of madness, I think you mean!
PHILOKLEON. —as I twist my flanks in a show of strength.
            My nostrils snort with heavy breathing,
            My backbone cracks!
XANTHIAS.   You're quite deranged!
PHILOKLEON. Phrynichos cowers just like a cock*—   1490
XANTHIAS. You'll soon be pelted with stones!*
PHILOKLEON. —and kicks his leg sky high.
            My arsehole gapes—
XANTHIAS.   Better watch out there!
PHILOKLEON. —as in each of my hip-joints
            The socket smoothly rotates. [*Stops his wild gyrations*]

[*Speaking*] Well wasn't that good?
XANTHIAS.   No it wasn't, it's all insane.
PHILOKLEON. Let me make a public announcement and issue a
    challenge.
[*To audience*] Any tragic performer who claims to be a fine
    dancer
    Should come on stage to compete in dance with me.
    Does anyone take the challenge?
XANTHIAS [*pointing*].   Just that one person.   1500

[*A figure steps forward from the audience and starts to do some preliminary dance exercises. In the course of what follows, two further* SONS OF
    KARKINOS *will emerge from the audience and do likewise.*]

PHILOKLEON. Well, who's this wretch?

XANTHIAS. He's one of Karkinos' sons,*
The middle of three.

PHILOKLEON. I'll eat him up for dinner!
I'll finish him off with a dance that will give him a drubbing.
What a lousy sense of rhythm he's got.

XANTHIAS. Watch out,
There's another Karkinite dancer coming alone,
The first one's brother.

PHILOKLEON. Then more for me to devour!

XANTHIAS. Not much of a dinner with just three *crabs* to eat!*
Yet another of Karkinos' sons is stepping forward.

PHILOKLEON. What's crawling forward? A lobster or a spider?

XANTHIAS. A miniature crab, the so-called 'look-out' type—   1510
The smallest son, the one who's a tragic poet.*

PHILOKLEON. O Karkinos, how blessed with offspring you are!
As they flutter around, they're like a crowd of wrens.
I'd better square up to them. [*To* XANTHIAS] But you get mixing
Brine sauce to eat with these crabs, if I'm the winner!

[PHILOKLEON *moves into the centre of the* orchêstra. *In the course of the* CHORUS's *final song, which is delivered from the edge of the performance space,* PHILOKLEON *and the* SONS OF KARKINOS *vigorously compete with dance-moves. At 1531 a further figure, purporting to be* KARKINOS *himself, comes forward to join in the concluding whirligig.*]

LEADER. Very well, let's all move back just a little, to allow enough
     space for these dancers.
So we're not in the way while they spin themselves like tops in
     front of us here.

CHORUS. Come, illustrious children of your saltwater father,
Leap along the sand   1520
And the shore of the unharvested briny, O brothers of shrimps!
Whirl wildly your flashing feet, let one of you do
The Phrynichean kick, so that
The spectators may gasp at the sight of a leg in the air.
Rotate yourself, move round in circles, and slap your belly!
Hurl your legs sky-high; practise spinning-top moves.   1530
Here's your father himself, your sea-ruling lord, advancing,

Taking real delight in his trio of frolicking sons.
Lead us out, if you please, from the stage with your dance,   1535
Since no one has done such a thing before,
Using solo dancers to lead off a wine-song chorus.*

[*Exit all with general dancing and merriment.*]

PEACE

INTRODUCTION

ARISTOPHANES' *Peace* was staged at the City Dionysia in Spring 421. The historian Thucydides tells us (5.20.1) that it was immediately after this same festival that the Athenians and Spartans concluded a fifty-year peace treaty (the so-called Peace of Nikias) which brought to a halt the ten-year-old conflict that acquired the name of the Archidamian War but which turned out, after the rapid unravelling of the treaty, to be only the first decade of the much longer conflict that has come to be known as the Peloponnesian War.[1] Aristophanes' play was produced, then, at a time when the hope of peace, after protracted and difficult negotiations between the two sides during the preceding winter, must have seemed a real, if not quite certain, prospect to many Athenians. It would be fascinating to know, though we never will, exactly how Aristophanes conceived of the play when he was originally awarded a place at the festival by the eponymous Archon in mid- to late summer 422, and whether or how far he adapted his conception over the following months of composition, revision, and rehearsal.[2] Prior to the deaths of the Athenian general Kleon and the Spartan general Brasidas in battle outside the northern city of Amphipolis in late summer 422, Aristophanes may well have considered the idea of peace to be something that could still be treated within the realms of comic fantasy, just as he had treated it in *Acharnians* in 425. But the deaths of Kleon and Brasidas are presented in *Peace*, through the allegory of War's loss of a pair of pestles with which to mash up Greece into mincemeat (or, strictly speaking, garlic paste) in his mortar (269–86), as having radically changed things—a perception which matches the statement of Thucydides (5.16.1) that this was one of the factors which made majority opinion in both Athens and Sparta turn markedly towards a desire for peace during the winter of 422–421.

Whatever the detailed correlation between the composition of *Peace* and the politico-military chronology of 422–421, Aristophanes

---

[1] In *Peace* itself, Trygaios speaks at one point (990) as though the war had so far lasted for 'thirteen' years; see the note on that line.

[2] On the official process whereby playwrights were selected for each festival, see the general Introduction, 'Old Comedy and Dionysiac Festivity'.

must eventually have known that at the time of its staging the play would at least resonate sentimentally with a substantial body of opinion at Athens. In a certain sense this makes *Peace* almost the polar opposite of *Acharnians*, which depicts a solitary figure making a 'magical' private peace in a context where, so it seems at any rate, most Athenians are happy to support the continuation of war. If the Dikaiopolis of *Acharnians* is solitary and (perforce) selfish, the Trygaios of *Peace* is someone who acts on behalf of the whole class of people to which he belongs—i.e. smallholder peasant farmers—and which he takes to be yearning for the peace that will allow them to 're-turn to the land' and enjoy its fruits in abundance. What is more, Trygaios even takes into account, however vaguely, the interests of peasant farmers on *both* sides of the conflict between Athens and Sparta, so that one can say, with just a little exaggeration, that if Dikaipolis is almost solipsistic in the pursuit of his desires, Trygaios is panhellenically altruistic in the motivation which drives his actions.[3] That difference is naturally mirrored in the two protagonists' con-trasting relationships with their respective choruses. Whereas Dikaiopolis comes under aggressive attack from the bellicose Acharnian charcoal-burners (who only turn into his admirers, later in the play, when they have softened into a more anonymized group of observers), Trygaios actually summons a panhellenic chorus of farmers, merchants, and others to join him in the shared enterprise of digging Peace out of her Cave. And with the exception of some short-lived difficulties at *Peace* 464–99 (where elements of the chorus momentarily represent pockets of resistance to peace in different parts of the Greek world) protagonist and chorus are in harmony throughout.

Despite those major differences, one should not lose sight of some significant points of resemblance between Trygaios and Dikaiopolis. Both, after all, are representatives of the same (comically simplified) rustic type, smallholder farmers attached to the wholesome pleasures of country life and equally disillusioned with the impact of war on that form of existence. One can even locate a curious affinity between

---

[3] Trygaios's reference to Spartan farmers at 625 depends on a basic distinction between (corrupt) political leaders and (suffering) rural inhabitants which does not fit the complex socio-economic situation of Sparta and its subject populations in the Peloponnese. But this does not undermine the panhellenic thrust of Trygaios's action: see esp. 59, 93, 105–8, 292, 302.

their manifestations of a comic psychology which combines positive and negative strands in their attitudes to Sparta. To defend his private peace before the hostile chorus, Dikaiopolis feels impelled to declare that he 'hates' the Spartans just as much as the Acharnians do, and even hopes that an earthquake will destroy the houses of Sparta, since he too has had his vines chopped down during the enemy's invasions of Attika (509–12); but he nonetheless thinks that the Spartans cannot be entirely blamed for the war and offers his own (fanciful) account, centring on the Megarian decree (which he ascribes to a personal grudge on Perikles' part), of how hostilities between the two powers had come to a head. In *Peace*, we get an alternative but equally fanciful account, from the god Hermes (605 ff.) rather than the protagonist himself, of how Perikles had used the Megarian decree to distract attention from suspicions over his possible implication in a financial scandal regarding the finances of the Parthenon.[4] But shortly after Hermes has given that account and then counterbalanced it by apportioning some blame for the war to the Spartan leadership as well, Trygaios expresses momentary (and purely vindictive) pleasure at the thought of the sufferings that the war had supposedly brought to Spartan farmers: they deserved to suffer, he says, because when invading Attika the Spartans had chopped down a particularly precious fig-tree of his, one that he had planted himself and nurtured 'with loving care' (628–9). So Dikaiopolis hates the Spartans but thinks they cannot be entirely blamed for the war; Trygaios too implicitly accepts the latter proposition, yet he is spurred to voice his relish at the sufferings of Spartan 'farmers', notwithstanding the panhellenic concern for Greek farmers in general that he had displayed at the outset of his quest for peace. Both characters have personal grievances for which they viscerally detest the Spartans while at the same time recognizing responsibility for war on the part of certain Athenian politicians. For closely related reasons—a strong, earthy attachment to their rural homes and lives—they want peace more than anything.

In sharp contrast to *Acharnians*, however, in which Dikaiopolis's private peace is capriciously enabled via the peculiar figure of Amphitheos, Trygaios's achievement of peace is the result of a

---

[4] For the differences between the treatment of the Megarian decree in the two plays, see my notes on *Acharnians* 530–4 and *Peace* 609.

venture of extravagantly mythologized comic heroism that extends across the entire play. In this respect *Peace* employs a paradigm (of both protagonist and plot) which has most in common, among Aristophanes' surviving plays, with *Birds*, where Peisetairos similarly finds a point of entry to the world of myth and even, in the ne plus ultra of comic self-transformation, ends up replacing Zeus himself and ruling the whole world as tyrant of his new city in the sky.[5] For reasons already touched on, Trygaios's venture has none of the magnified self-centredness of Peisetairos's, but it does share with it a parodic, indeed absurdist, twist on the role of animals in myth. In Peisetairos's case, this element is supplied by the metamorphosed figure of Tereus-turned-hoopoe, who opens up a channel from the world of humans to that of birds. In Trygaios's case, the equivalent plot-device is the conspicuously double-sided replacement of Pegasos—the winged, immortal horse on which the hero Bellerophon attempted to ride up to Olympos—with the most disgusting creature imaginable, a giant dung-beetle fed on copious quantities of human faeces. Although the dung-beetle as a story-motif has a good Aisopic pedigree, as the audience is reminded at 129–30, it is hard to think of anything in the extant plays which more blatantly exemplifies the quintessentially Aristophanic fusion of gross vulgarity with sophisticated manipulation of the phenomena of 'high culture', in the present instance not just an old piece of myth but more specifically its recent treatment by the tragedian Euripides.[6] This combination allows the play to start with a section of in-your-face scatological (and sexual) humour that exploits the two-slave routine already developed in *Knights* and *Wasps*, as well as incorporating a crude side-swipe at Aristophanes' bête noire, Kleon (47–8, embedded within a miniature parody of intellectual pretentiousness on the part of imaginary spectators).[7] But further moments of scatology (137–9, 151–72, 176) are placed within a theatrical framework dominated by the paratragic

---

[5] In a more muted vein, Aristophanes' last surviving play, *Wealth*, also depends on the protagonist's discovery of a mythologized solution (the restoration of sight to 'blind' Wealth) to the problems of the human world.

[6] See notes on lines 76–7, 136, 155, 722.

[7] This metatheatrical joke about the attempts of spectators to make sense of comic obscurity can be compared with a passage in Samuel Beckett's *Endgame* where Hamm wryly imagines an observer of the play over-confidently detecting meaning in it: 'Ah, good, now I see what it is…' (*Samuel Beckett: The Complete Dramatic Works* [London, 1986], 108).

use of the theatrical machine or crane (*mêchanê*) to represent Trygaios's journey from earth to sky in his self-declared role as a quasi-Euripidean hero.[8]

Although one of Trygaios's slaves thinks his master is merely mad (54 ff., a motif initially reminiscent of *Wasps* 71), the role of a would-be Euripidean Bellerophon is here identified with a desire to confront Zeus and challenge his treatment of mankind (58–9, 105–6). As already mentioned, this is in fact understood by Trygaios himself as a heroic undertaking motivated by a sort of panhellenic altruism:

> My flight's on behalf of all the Greeks.
> I've contrived an unprecedented venture.
>
> (93–4)

Exactly how far Aristophanes takes his cue from, and how far parodically distorts, Euripides' hero and play, we cannot now be sure. Bellerophon's motive for attempting to fly up to Olympos in the Euripidean version may have involved a challenge to Zeus's standards of justice, but the question is complicated, in the parlous state of our evidence, by the fact that at one point in the play the hero seemingly expressed atheistic sentiments, albeit in relation to a traditional account of what the gods were like.[9] It is certainly part-and-parcel of the comedy of Trygaios's action that he has chosen an ill-fated hero, and a mission unfulfilled, to emulate; on this level, the slave is absolutely right: he is comic craziness incarnate. But it is the other side of the parodic coin that Trygaios *does* succeed in reaching Olympos: the dung-beetle (or 'hippo-beetle', as he wittily calls it at 181) accomplishes what divine Pegasos could not. The comic hero outdoes the tragic hero; Aristophanes trumps Euripides.

But if comedy, by its own standards of course, can outdo the model that it borrows from tragedy, we need the whole of *Peace*, not just Trygaios's arrival on Olympos, to see how this works out as an

---

[8] On the *mêchanê*, see the general Introduction, 'Stage Directions'. Aristophanes had earlier used it in *Clouds* (219 ff.) to satirize the idea of a 'higher' world of intellectual thought inhabited by Sokrates.

[9] See Euripides fr. 286 (to be attributed, on this hypothesis, to Bellerophon himself), which starts with an emphatic denial, on the basis of the unpunished evil of some human behaviour, that the (traditional) gods actually exist. Some scholars think that the Euripidean plot made Bellerophon's journey a matter of trying to confirm the non-existence of the gods by flying up to their supposed home, before he was refuted by being struck down by Zeus.

authentically comic triumph. Simply getting up to the world of the gods is only a start. As soon as Trygaios arrives, he finds himself, as he seems to expect (178–9), in an environment not unlike the one he has left behind, where people occupy houses and answer the door to visitors. Encountering a very abusive Hermes as doorkeeper hardly fazes Trygaios; he knows this god's soft spot and has brought a gift of meat with which to mollify and bribe him (192).[10] But one thing takes Trygaios (and us) totally by surprise: the gods have actually 'moved out' of their normal dwellings, leaving Hermes behind to protect their belongings (from whom, one could idly ask!) while allowing War and his assistant Uproar to live there as lodgers (107–209). This twist in the plot makes a big difference to the scenario. It exculpates Zeus and the other Olympians from direct responsibility for war,[11] while allegorizing a situation in which it is humans themselves who have chosen war over peace (211–19). War himself is a nasty 'chef' who wants to pound everything in his mortar, but to do so he needs, as earlier mentioned, a human 'pestle' (236–88). The loss of War's previous pestles, the recently deceased generals Kleon and Brasidas, creates a window of opportunity to restore peace; and having learnt from Hermes that Peace, now treated as a goddess (or, at least, a divine personification),[12] has been buried by War in a cave, Trygaios decides to seize his chance by organizing a collective endeavour of 'excavation'.

The choral entry (parodos) in an Aristophanic comedy is always an event of heightened and carefully focused theatricality; the combined resources of choreography, costume, music, and language come together to define a special juncture in the unfolding action. The tone of a chorus's arrival on the scene can range from the parodically sombre (the pathetically stumbling old jurors in *Wasps*) or the ether-

[10] For an interesting comparandum to the treatment of Hermes in this scene, see his other appearance in the extant plays at *Wealth* 1097–1170: in a radical role-reversal, Hermes there knocks on a door rather than answering one, and has to beg a human for help rather than providing it himself; but the information he brings about Zeus's anger (1107–9) is a detail common to the two scenes.

[11] In a typical Aristophanic anomaly, Hermes later claims (371–2) that Zeus has decreed the penalty of death for any human who tries to dig Peace out of the cave. It would be pointless to rationalize this detail, which is in any case overriden by the extended process of bribing Hermes to be on Trygaios's side after all (374–425).

[12] Peace is already mythologically personified as early as Hesiod, *Theogony* 902, *Works and Days* 228, and in Aristophanes' time there may have been at least one altar of Peace in Attika. A public cult of Peace was instituted at Athens about 375 (Isocrates, *Antidosis* 109–10).

eally lyrical (*Clouds*) to the physically aggressive (the stone-throwing crowd in *Acharnians*, the attack of the cavalry in *Knights*). In *Peace*, there is a synergy between protagonist and chorus of a kind unique in the surviving plays. Trygaios, with a reality-defying confidence characteristic of the genre (how are all these Greeks supposed to get to Olympos!), specifically summons a panhellenic throng to bring the equipment—shovels, crowbars, ropes: an unusual amount of paraphernalia for a chorus—needed to carry out the grand communal enterprise of excavating Peace from her cave (292–9). Admittedly, it proves necessary, before the task can be properly completed, to weed out opponents of peace who are obstructing the work (464 ff.), though we cannot be sure whether this was visibly enacted, i.e. by the removal of mute figures who represent the recalcitrant groups, or (more probably) is to be treated as an entirely verbal matter of symbolic expulsion.[13] Once that is done, the chorus's purer identity as 'farmers' is established (508 ff.) and everyone is, literally, pulling in the same direction, as the song-and-dance routine of vigorously heaving Peace into view with ropes (attached to the theatrical 'trolley', *ekkuklêma*) reaches its climax at 519. Later on, it is a further consequence of the harmony between protagonist, chorus, and (once he has been bribed) Hermes that the play has no need for a full formal agon or set-piece contest. Instead, there will be a half-agon (582–656), which provides the vehicle for Hermes' colourful explanation, mentioned earlier, of how war broke out in the first place. This is a prime instance of the flexibility and adaptability built into Aristophanes' use of the traditional formal structures of Old Comedy.[14]

When Peace is excavated from her cave, she comes into view in the shape of a statue (its properties totally undecipherable from the text)[15] which will remain on stage for the remainder of the play—even during the period, coinciding with the parabasis, when Trygaios is

---

[13] It would be easy to imagine a difference between the removal of the only individual named, Lamachos (though he was actually a signatory to the peace treaty of 421), at 473, and the various groups (Boiotians, Argives, etc.) identified at 466–502. But the text gives no real encouragement to posit a concrete use of stage action in either case.

[14] For the formal structure of an agon, and the use of a half-agon in several plays, see the general Introduction, 'Formality and Performance'.

[15] The statue of Peace was apparently the object of some mockery by two of Aristophanes' rivals, Eupolis (fr. 62) and Plato comicus (fr. 86): we have limited scope to guess exactly what they targeted about it; might it have been the rather inert presence of the statue in the second half of the play (see my text below)?

supposedly making his way back from Olympos to earth (725–8 and 819 ff.). She is accompanied by two personified figures played by mute actors (probably males wearing padded body stockings, rather than actual females): Harvest (whose Greek name associates her with the fruitfulness of late summer and early autumn) and Festivity (whose identity represents the holding of festivals and the attendance of individuals and groups at panhellenic religious occasions of various kinds). Peace, Harvest, and Festivity are between them both symbols and embodiments of a supposedly recovered world of hedonism, abundance, and carefreeness, with the accent strongly placed on the enjoyment of life in the countryside: the motif of 'back to the land/ fields', which signifies above all the return of peasant farmers to their smallholdings, is particularly prominent at 552–85, and will be resoundingly echoed in the play's conclusion at 1320 and 1331.[16] Although it would be misguided to labour the point, the statuesque representation of Peace suits the idea of a stable set of conditions— including possibilities of trade (see esp. 999 ff.) and safe travel (cf. the anticipation of this at 341–2)—across the whole Greek world, while the use of actors for her two companions serves to evoke active human engagement in the pleasures of sensuality and celebration. Of the triad, Peace alone is called 'goddess' (308, 315, etc.). Whether we think of the other two figures as aspects or consequences of peace (or both), their embodied form makes them available, as we discover in the post-parabatic scenes in the second half of the play (see below), for some earthily physical interaction with the protagonist.

I mentioned at the start of this introduction that negotiations for a real peace treaty between Athens and Sparta were proceeding throughout the period when Aristophanes was preparing his comedy for performance. Whatever speculative hypotheses one might adopt about the ways in which those negotiations could have influenced the play's composition and rehearsal, it is important to notice that Aristophanes has incorporated only minimal allusions to actual military and political details of the sort that necessarily dominated the

---

[16] The idea of 'back to the land' had a special resonance for an Athenian audience because of the Spartan invasions, and the consequent (partial) evacuation of Attika, which had marked the early years of the war; see the Introduction to *Acharnians*. Although the invasions had ceased in 425, some disruption of normal rural patterns continued, hence a 'return to the fields' is still in the future at *Knights* 805 (though fulfilled in fantasy at the end of the play, 1394).

process of peace-making. The details that do occur in the play, all confirmed by Thucydides, amount to no more than the following: the significance of the deaths of Kleon and Brasidas allegorized by War's loss of his two pestles at 269–86 (see above); an ironic reference at 478–80 to the continuing pressure on Sparta to recover the citizens of hers which Athens had captured on Sphakteria in 425; the recognition of resistance to a peace treaty on the part of Boiotia, Megara, and (from a different standpoint) Argos, as flagged up in lines 466–502; and Hermes' suggestion at 506–7 that if Athens wants peace it should be prepared to scale down its ambitions to a land-based empire. Since Aristophanes could not have been sure, at any rate until very close to the time of his play's performance, that a peace-deal would be successfully struck, one might suppose that it was inevitable that he would avoid including much specific material that was closely tied to contemporary developments and that changing events could have proved 'wrong'. That might be true, as far as it goes, but it does limited justice to the positive way in which the play appropriates and internalizes the making of peace as something that happens inside its own comic world. As *Acharnians* demonstrates (and as *Lysistrata*, in a very different spirit, will later do as well), Aristophanes did not need the existence of a real peace process in order to manufacture a comic version of peace. He may well, of course, have intended and expected his play to chime with the increasingly pro-peace mood at Athens as described by Thucydides. But *Peace*, like all of Aristophanes' plays, constructs a comic universe of its own, and the satisfaction it offers its audience (who are drawn into that universe, metatheatrically, at several points)[17] is of an imagined recovery of peace that is the achievement not of politicians but of an ordinary Attic vine-dresser (see 190) who transforms himself into a non-tragic avatar of a Euripidean hero and, with the help of Hermes, organizes the farmers of Greece under his own leadership.

The fantasy is carried further still, since Harvest is to be no less than a new bride for a rejuvenated Trygaios (whose original family can be conveniently forgotten about). This is a self-decreed and self-authorized action, unprepared for and simply announced to the slave

---

[17] In addition to the substantial interplay with the audience in its opening scene (9–14, 20–3, 43–77), *Peace* contains a considerable number of metatheatrical moments: for the most explicit (though others too can be detected), see 244–5, 263–6, 276–9, 543 ff., 658–9, 821–3, 877 ff., 962–7, 1115–16, 1365–7.

at 842–4. The closest parallel here is with Peisetairos and his allegorical bride Princess, symbol of Zeus's power itself, at the end of *Birds*: in both cases we have a play which ends with a comically transmuted version of a wedding procession celebrating the protagonist's ultimate achievement of his goals. Although Trygaios's marriage is associated with the recovery of agricultural fertility in general (see 1322–7), there is nothing didactically solemn about this; on the contrary, the spirit of it is lustily down-to-earth and openly bawdy. In fact, Harvest as well as Festivity is made into a lewdly sexualized figure almost as soon as Trygaios has returned to Athens.[18] When Trygaios's slave is first made aware of the two females who have accompanied his master on his return, his immediate perception of them, which Trygaios only casually qualifies, is as a pair of prostitutes (848–50). This gives us a clue as to their theatrical presentation, which must have involved some (no doubt absurdly rather than realistically) accentuated depiction of female anatomical features, and perhaps some sexually provocative body language on their part as well. The slave feels free, at any rate, to extract from Trygaios's reference to Harvest's previous diet on Olympos an opportunity for an obscene double entendre at 855.

We are certainly not dealing here with what could be narrowly categorized as the coarseness of 'slave humour', since just after this, while his bride is being washed offstage, Trygaios pictures the pleasures of his marriage to Harvest in ribald terms (863) of precisely the same kind that Dikaiopolis uses at *Acharnians* 1199 while fondling the breasts of two prostitutes. He also resorts to sexual slang to encourage the chorus to anticipate similar pleasures for themselves after their return to the countryside (867). When Trygaios's slave brings Harvest back out of the house, he continues to talk about her in the same crudely sexualized manner as before, now drawing attention to the figure's buttocks and making a phallic reference, no doubt with a suitable gesture, at 868–70. He returns to the image of a prostitute in the case of Festivity as well, when Trygaios prepares to hand over the latter to the Council. Indeed, the humour becomes free-wheeling and

---

[18] There is no real textual hint of a sexualized presentation when the two figures first appear at 520 ff., though Trygaios's praise of Festivity's face and aura (524–6) has mildly erotic overtones. But it is not hard to imagine various ways in which the scope for sexual humour about them was left latent until 847 ff. (or, alternatively, was anticipated in visual terms without any verbal reference at 520 ff.).

detached from the premises of the plot when the slave suggests that Festivity may actually be a woman they had drunkenly whored with some years ago—and Trygaios ostensibly confirms that she *is* (875)! At this point, in fact, the sexual emphasis of the scene is ratcheted up even further, and Trygaios himself gets carried away into imagining Festivity as, first, the object of group sex by the Council (888–90), and, then, engaged in a series of 'athletic' competitions which are all too evidently the metaphorical medium for a sequence of vigorous sexual manoeuvres (894–904). Whatever larger social ideas and values Harvest and Festivity might be associated with in the abstract, the all-too-corporeal thematics of the second half of the play turn them indelibly into comic icons of sexual pleasure, very much in the same way in which the military-political idea of Reconciliation in *Lysistrata* is reductively objectified as territory to be taken possession of by the fantasies of male lust.[19]

In contrast to Harvest and Festivity, Peace herself might be thought to be treated in what is, by the standards of Old Comedy, an unusually decorous manner. It is certainly true that, unlike her companions, she is not herself the object of any sexual or any other kind of demeaning humour; the (reverse) comparison with adulterous women at 979 ff. can hardly count as an exception. But it is also the case that the statue is little more than an inert presence for most of the second half of the play—a background reminder of the protagonist's achievement on his trip to Olympos. It matters most at the point (from 922 ff.) at which it is dedicated and installed, with animal sacrifice, as an object of cult. When Trygaios and the chorus join in prayer to Peace at 974–1016, they must orientate themselves appropriately towards the statue. But the prayer itself digresses into a series of jokes, and drifts into an imagined scenario of Schadenfreude.[20] Once the prayer is complete, the statue as such goes virtually unmentioned for the remainder of the play and presumably makes little or no difference to anything that happens on-stage, even in the parodic scene of sacrificial ritual (1017–1126) which follows the prayer.

---

[19] See *Lysistrata* 1115–74, where the men's libido is manipulated for 'political' purposes by Lysistrata herself: as often in Old Comedy, the passage can be read as exposing some of the absurdities of male desire rather than endorsing it.

[20] The miniature scenario imagined at 999–1015 involves the same kind of comic technique ('just imagine if…wouldn't it be hilarious!') found also at *Acharnians* 1153–73.

   That scene is dominated by two main kinds of thematic material,
which become ludicrously entangled with one another: the first is
Trygaios and his slave's excited absorption in the process of cooking
food for a post-sacrificial meal; the other is the exclusion (from what
is supposed, notionally, to be a collective celebration) of a detested
individual, the seer and oracle-expert Hierokles, who is known to be
an opponent of peace with Sparta. Both kinds of material are familiar
components of Aristophanes' repertoire. Food complements sex as a
domain of sensual pleasure in which the protagonist can satisfy his
appetites with an aplomb and abandon made possible by his own
achievements, while unwanted 'intruder' types of various sorts are
similarly driven from the stage in the second half of *Acharnians*, *Birds*,
and *Wealth*. The symbolism of food is widespread in Aristophanes, but
one might think here of particular affinities of comic ethos with the
scene in *Acharnians* (1085–1143) where Dikaiopolis prepares his
food-basket of delicacies for a party while simultaneously making
mockery of the warmongering general Lamachos, and also with the
on-stage cookery of Peisetairos in *Birds* (1578 ff.), who, after an earlier
sacrifice that was interrupted by several intruders (848–1057), is preparing some fine bird-meat when the food-loving figure of Herakles
turns up as part of a divine embassy. In Trygaios's case, the cooking
scene becomes knitted together with a lengthy exchange between
himself and Hierokles in the hexameter rhythms and the portentously
prophetic language of oracles. Aristophanes had earlier produced a
protracted parody of oracles in the competition between Sausage-
Seller and Paphlagon at *Knights* 1015–95, and there are other passages in a similar vein of humour in *Birds* (in a scene with another
unwanted oracle-collector at 959–91) and *Lysistrata* (where the heroine
herself purports to cite oracles at 770–6). Hierokles switches into the
hexameter at *Peace* 1063 but is immediately matched by Trygaios,
who can even *laugh* in the same metre (1066)! What unfolds here is a
piece of virtuosic writing on Aristophanes' part—a set of pseudo-
oracular exchanges in which Hierokles' coded images (the Spartans
as 'cruel-eyed monkeys' and 'fox-cubs') and allegorical warnings
('*Never* success will be yours in making a crab's walk go straight',
'*Never* at all will you make the rough hedgehog transform into
smoothness') are rebutted by Trygaios's accusations of charlatanry,
his wittily devious adaptations of Homer, and his sarcastic reversals
of Hierokles' own words. And the whole sequence is accompanied by

a physical confrontation over the sacrificial cooking: at 1100 Hierokles makes a move to grab some food, but then decides to behave like a willing participant, until he is eventually repelled with violence (1119–26).

Hierokles is not the only unwelcome visitor in the later scenes of *Peace*; there are also the arms-makers/sellers who had been cursed much earlier as hostile to peace (447–9, cf. 549) and who now appear at 1210 ff. to complain that their businesses have been ruined by Trygaios. One thing worth noticing here is the marked shift of comic technique and register for Trygaios's treatment of these people from his encounter with Hierokles. With the latter, the humour primarily depends, as we have seen, on the verbal ingenuity of the quasi-oracular exchanges through which the protagonist matches and then outdoes the seer's hieratic pomposity; it appeals to an ear for linguistically intricate wit, as does the later scene with the sons of Lamachos and Kleonymos (1270–1304), where Trygaios manipulates their rehearsal of poetry by Homer and Archilochos in order to make sure that the entertainment at this wedding will be suitably pro-peace and anti-war. But with the arms-dealers, everything revolves around a visual charade with the now unsaleable weapons they bring with them, for which Trygaios mockingly suggests alternative uses: horse-hair helmet crests as tablecloths, an upturned breastplate as a kind of chamber pot (on which Trygaios duly sits to demonstrate his idea scatologically, while also working in some byplay with rowing: 1228–39), part of a trumpet as rustic weighing-scales, and spears as vine-poles. The scene literally dismantles the equipment of war, appealing no doubt especially to those Athenian citizens who had seen and survived military service and could viscerally relish the thought of escaping from its physical demands.[21]

The post-parabatic scenes in *Peace* are characterized, then, as in most other Aristophanic plays, by a loosely connected episodic sequence set within a rather minimal framework of dramatic action. The latter consists partly of preparations for Trygaios's wedding—initiated at 842–4, imminent at 1192–6, and in full swing at the end of the play—and partly of the sacrificial dedication of Peace's cult-statue

---

[21] *Peace* contains numerous appeals to the mentality of (reluctant/weary) citizen soldiers in the form of references to escaping the rigours and problems of military service: see e.g. 293, 303, 311–12, 336, 347–56, 438, 528–9, 553, 1127–30, 1172–90, 1330.

which is interrupted, as already discussed, by the unwanted objections of Hierokles. The various comings and goings framed by those events are unified not by tight dramatic structure but by general thematic association with the comically schematic peace-war antithesis that governs the whole play. Fully in keeping with this is the second parabasis at 1127–90, which combines gently parodic evocation of a world of rural simplicity and contentment (peasant farmers who enjoy relaxing in one another's company with wholesome food and plenty of wine) with a soldier's-eye view of military officers as cowards beneath the uniforms in which they flaunt themselves. When all is said and done, there is nothing left for the second half of the play to accomplish other than the translation of peace into the exclusive enjoyment of sensual pleasure on the part of Trygaios and his fellow farmers. If this was designed to resonate with the Athenian mood of the time (though it is just worth remembering that the play was not awarded the first prize), it did so in a way which steered safely clear of the unresolved issues affecting any prospect of a lasting rapprochement with Sparta. Aristophanes was both professionally and temperamentally too shrewd to make his work a hostage to uncertain and constantly changing events outside the theatre, let alone to offer his play as some kind of 'manifesto' for the imminent Peace of Nikias. And it is just as well that he was, since disappointment lay in store for anyone celebrating an anticipated future of peace in the spring of 421. The treaty about to be signed with Sparta was to prove short-lived (indeed, Thucydides observed that what it brought about did not deserve to be called 'peace' at all: 5.26.2), and if Trygaios's marriage can be imagined as having avoided the same fate, that was only because it belonged to the parallel universe of reality-defying comedy.

PEACE

Speaking Characters

SLAVE[A]: of TRYGAIOS
SLAVE[B]: of TRYGAIOS
TRYGAIOS: an elderly Attic peasant farmer
DAUGHTERS: (at least) two small children of TRYGAIOS
HERMES: acting as Zeus's doorkeeper
WAR: an anthropomorphized personification
UPROAR: companion of WAR
CHORUS: of peasant farmers (and others)
LEADER: of the CHORUS
HIEROKLES: an oracle-collector and supposed religious expert
SICKLE-MAKER: a blacksmith specializing in farming equipment
ARMS-SELLER: a profiteer from war
BOY[A]: son of the Athenian general Lamachos
BOY[B]: son of the Athenian politician Kleonymos

Silent Characters

PEACE: a personificatory 'goddess' (represented by a statue)
HARVEST: female personification of agricultural fertility
FESTIVITY: a kindred personification
POTTER: accompanying the SICKLE-MAKER
HELMET-MAKER: companion of the ARMS-SELLER
SPEAR-MAKER: likewise

[The stage building has two doors. SLAVE[B] *enters with a kneading-trough and a sack from door A, which in the first part of the play represents* TRY-GAIOS'*s house; he takes material from the sack and starts kneading it into large cakes, though trying to hold his nose as he does so. Soon afterwards,* SLAVE[A] *sticks his head out of the same door and urgently takes delivery of the cakes his companion has kneaded.]*

SLAVE[A]. It's urgent, be quick—a cake for the dung-beetle, please.
SLAVE[B]. Take this one then. You can let the vile beast have it.
[*Sarcastically*] I hope it's the nicest cake he'll ever consume!

*[*SLAVE[A] *grabs the cake and goes back inside, but after only a short pause reappears with similar urgency.]*

SLAVE[A]. I need another cake now, this time from ass-dung.
SLAVE[B]. Here's another, but where's the one you took just now?
    Did he not devour it?
SLAVE[A].   He snatched it out of my hands,
    Rolled it round on his legs, then gulped it in one piece.
    Get kneading lots of thick ones quick as you can. [*Exits again*]
SLAVE[B] [*to audience*]. You dung-collectors, help me, by the gods,*
    If you don't want to see me choke to death with the smell!   10
SLAVE[A] [*reappearing*]. Another, another one, quick—this time from
    a rent boy:
    He says he'd like a well-squeezed one.
SLAVE[B].   Here then. [SLAVE[A] *exits
    again*]
[*To audience*] There's one accusation, men, from which I'm safe:
    No one could say I'm eating the food I'm kneading!*
SLAVE[A] [*reappearing*]. It's so disgusting! But pass me another two
    now,
    Then knead some more.
SLAVE[B].   By Apollo, that's out of the question—
    I'm now in danger of drowning in this sludge.
SLAVE[A]. I'll take the sludge and carry it in with me.

*[*SLAVE[A] *picks up the kneading-trough and takes it back inside.]*

SLAVE[B]. Damnation on this stuff—and on you too!

[*To audience*] If anyone out there knows, please tell me where   20
  I can buy a replacement nose that's got no nostrils.
  I've never been given a job that turns your stomach
  Like kneading cakes to be dung-beetle food.
  A pig or a dog will wallow wherever there's shit,
  Exactly as it comes. [*Gesturing at door A*] But this beast's choosy:
  It adopts a haughty manner, refusing to eat
  Any cake that's not been kneaded all day long
  And made a nice round shape a woman would give it.
  I'll take a look to see if he's finished his meal;
  I'll open this door just slightly, in case he sees me. [*Peeks inside*] 30
  Go on, keep gnashing away, and don't stop eating
  Till you've managed to stuff yourself to bursting point.
[*Imitating*] Look at how he's all hunched up while eating, the
       wretch,
  Just like a wrestler, and how he grinds his molars,
  And all the time he twists his head and legs
  Like this, the way that people making cables
  For merchant ships are constantly crossing their hands.
SLAVE^A [*returning*]. What a filthy, smelly, and gluttonous ogre he is!
  Whichever god has inflicted this thing upon us,
  I'm certain it can't be Aphrodite's work.   40
SLAVE^B. And it's not the Graces' either.
SLAVE^A.   Then whose?
SLAVE^B.   It's like
  A lightning strike from Zeus who hurls...the shit!*
SLAVE^A [*pointing at audience*]. By now there'll be a spectator sitting
       there,
  A showy young man, who asks, 'What's it all about?
  What's the point of the *beetle*?' Then someone else replies,
  An Ionian fellow who's sitting right next to him:
[*Knowingly*] 'I suspect it's all an allegory aimed at Kleon:
  He's on a diet in Hades of liquid faeces.'*
[*Waving his phallus*] I'll go inside and give the beetle a drink. [*Exits*]
SLAVE^B. Meanwhile I'd better explain the plot to the boys,*   50
  To the mannikins too, as well as the real men here,
  And I mustn't forget the men of the highest rank,
  Especially the ones who think they're *hyper*-manly!
[*Drawing breath*] My master's mad—in a way that's rather novel:*

Not the way that *you're* all mad; it's much more novel.
From dawn to dusk he gazes at the sky,
[*Imitating*] His mouth agape like this, abusing Zeus
    By calling: 'Zeus, what plans do you have for us?
    Lay down your broom! Don't sweep up all of Greece!'
Aha! Aha! [*Turning towards house*]   60
Keep silent—I think I hear a voice inside.
TRYGAIOS [*inside*]. O Zeus, what wilt thou do to all our people?
    Take care not to knock the stuffing from all Greek cities!
SLAVE[B]. That's it, the very affliction I described.
    You're hearing a perfect example of how he raves.
    As for what he said when he had his first attack,
    I'll tell you: he stood on this spot and said to himself,
    'If only I could go straight up to Zeus!'
    Then he made for himself a set of light little ladders
    And kept on trying to clamber up to the sky,   70
    Till he tumbled down and fell very hard on his head.
    Then yesterday, after buggering off somewhere,
    He brought back home a huge Aitnaian dung-beetle*
    And made me groom it in full equestrian manner.
    He stroked it himself, the way that one would with a foal,
    Saying, 'Sweet little Pegasos, noble wingéd creature,
    Be sure to take me and fly right up to Zeus.'*
    I'd better peep round the door and check things now. [*He does so*]
    Oh no! It's trouble! Come quickly, quickly, neighbours!
    My master's starting to rise up into the air;   80
    He's sitting astride the beetle as if on a horse.

[TRYGAIOS, *hoisted by the theatrical crane, appears above the stage
building 'riding' a giant winged dung-beetle. Lines 82–101 are chanted in
recitative metre.*]

TRYGAIOS.   Steady there, steady! Gently, my beetle-nag!
             Don't rush ahead with excessive spirit.
             Rely from the start on your mighty strength
             Till your sweat starts to pour and you loosen up
             Your sinewy joints with a whirl of your wings.
             Don't breathe foul air in my face, I beg you;
             If you do, you'll have to stay on the ground

Inside this house of mine.

SLAVE^B.   My lord and master, you've lost your wits!   90
TRYGAIOS.   Keep quiet! Keep quiet!
SLAVE^B.   Why vainly thrash around in the air?
TRYGAIOS.   My flight's on behalf of all the Greeks.
I've contrived an unprecedented venture.
SLAVE^B.   What's the point of your flight? Why this folly and
frenzy?
TRYGAIOS.   Avoid ill-omened speech. Don't utter
Any negative word. Proclaim my deed.
Tell all mankind to hold their tongues,
To block up their privies and filthy alleys*
With newly constructed brick walls—   100
And to shut up their arseholes as well!

[*The scene now switches back to spoken dialogue.*]

SLAVE^B.   I refuse to hold my tongue unless you say
Where you mean to fly?
TRYGAIOS.   Where else do you think if not
Up to Zeus in the sky above?
SLAVE^B.   But *why* do that?
TRYGAIOS.   I intend to ask him in person what plans he harbours
For the whole of this land of Greece and all its people.
SLAVE^B.   And if he won't give you an answer?
TRYGAIOS.   I'll take him to court
For being to blame for betraying Greece to the Persians.*
SLAVE^B.   By Dionysos, you won't, if it's up to me.
TRYGAIOS.   But there's really no alternative.   110
SLAVE^B [*calling into house*].   Help! Help!
Come out here, children, your father's leaving home,
Abandoning you by secretly flying to heaven.
Come, plead with your father, poor wretches, to change his plans.

[*Enter from the house two small* DAUGHTERS *of Trygaios; their words
could easily be divided between them.*]

DAUGHTER [*singing*].   O father, O father, is it verily true,
The rumour that reaches this homestead of ours,

That you'll leave me behind and amidst the birds
Will end forlorn—and come a right cropper?
[*Chanting*] Are they verily so, these things? If you love me, father, do
  answer.
TRYGAIOS. You can form your own view, my daughters. The truth
  is, I find you a burden
Every time you entreat me for bread, with affectionate use of
  'Daddy',   120
Yet I'm totally skint, not a scrap of cash to be found in the house.*
If this venture succeeds and I come back home, you will have in
  good time
A big special loaf—and as relish a slap from the back of my hand!

[*The exchange now switches to spoken dialogue, much of which carries
        parody of the formal style of (Euripidean) tragedy.*]

DAUGHTER. What means of transport have you for this journey?
  No ship, forsooth, will carry you on this path.
TRYGAIOS. A wingéd foal will take me, no seacraft.
DAUGHTER. What fancy makes you yoke a large dung-beetle
  And ride it up to the gods, O sweetest Daddy?
TRYGAIOS. I found the information in Aisop's fables:
  It's the only creature with wings who's reached the gods.*   130
DAUGHTER. I can't believe this story at all, dear father—
  That such a malodorous beast ever went to the gods.
TRYGAIOS. It went there once from hatred of the eagle.
  It spilt the eagle's eggs to gain revenge.
DAUGHTER. Why didn't you yoke winged Pegasos, then, instead,
  So the gods would find the sight of you more *tragic*?*
TRYGAIOS. O pitiful child, I'd then need double rations.
  As things are now, the food I eat myself
  Will serve in turn as dung to feed the beetle!
DAUGHTER. But what if the beetle falls to the ocean's depths?   140
  How can something with wings like those expect to escape?
TRYGAIOS. That's precisely why I've brought a rudder with me.
    [*Brandishes it*]
  Instead of a beetle I'll have a water boatman!*
DAUGHTER. What *harbour* will receive you from your voyage?
TRYGAIOS. At Peiraieus, of course, there's Beetle Harbour.*

DAUGHTER [*pointing*]. Watch out you don't slip off and plunge from
    there:
  If you do, you'll find that you've become a cripple,
  Supplying Euripides with a tragic plot!*
TRYGAIOS. You can leave all that to me. Farewell to you!

[*The* DAUGHTERS, *as well as* SLAVE[B], *now go back inside the house. As
they do so, the theatrical crane starts to swing* TRYGAIOS *a little higher:
during the following lines, he will gradually be hoisted, not without some
turbulence, right over the stage building, and eventually (by line 177)
swung down into the* orchêstra, *which will at that point represent the
summit of Olympos.*]

  All you for whom I undertake these toils,   150
  Don't fart or shit for all the next three days:
  If this beetle gets a whiff while in the air,
  He'll throw me off head first and rush to the source.

[*To beetle, chanting*] Come now, my Pegasos, onwards and upwards,
          And make your golden bridle's chains*
          Rattle loud with a flick of your gleaming ears.
  [*Alarmed*] What now? What now? Why are you bending
          Your nostrils towards the filthy alleys?*
          Steer yourself with boldness away from earth,
          Then stretching out your wings for sprinting   160
          Head straight for the palace of Zeus himself,
          Holding up your snout away from all crap
          And away from all trace of human food.
  [*Looking down*] Hey you, the man who's having a shit
          At Peiraieus, in the brothel quarter!
          You'll be my ruin, you really will,
          Unless you bury your shit with soil
          And plant some thyme to grow on top
          And pour on scented oil as well.
          If I fall from here, the fine for my death   170
          Will be five talents for Chios to pay*
          All because of that arsehole of yours.

[*Speaking*] I'm really frightened, no time for joking now.
  Hey, crane-operator, take special care with me.*
  I can feel some wind that's churning up my guts:

If you don't watch out, I'll start to feed the beetle!

[*The crane now deposits* TRYGAIOS *in the* orchêstra: *he dismounts, carrying a bag, and starts to look around. At some point, and without* TRYGAIOS's *awareness (cf. 720–1), the dung-beetle will be swung back away behind the stage building.*]

Well I think I'm in the vicinity of the gods.
In fact, I can see the house of Zeus himself.

[TRYGAIOS *approaches door B, which represents Zeus's house, and starts to knock. The door is promptly answered by* HERMES.]

[*Calling*] Who's in charge of Zeus's door? Open up there, please.
HERMES [*opening*]. I can't have heard a *human*— [*seeing beetle*] lord
    Herakles!   180
What monstrous thing is this?
TRYGAIOS.   A hippo-beetle.
HERMES. What a foul, outrageous, shameless fellow you are!
    You're foul, entirely foul, extremely foul!
How did you get here, you foulest of the foul?
I need to know your name. Well?
TRYGAIOS [*facetiously*].   Call me Foulest.
HERMES. Your father's name?
TRYGAIOS.   My father? Foulest too.
HERMES. What place are you from? Just tell me.
TRYGAIOS.   Also Foulest.
HERMES. I swear by Earth you're looking death in the face
    If you don't reveal your name to me at once.
TRYGAIOS. Trygaios, deme Athmonon; skilful vine-dresser.*   190
    I'm not a litigious type; I don't like trouble.
HERMES. But why have you come?
TRYGAIOS [*opening his bag*].   To bring you this present of meat.
HERMES [*melting*]. Poor thing, so *pleased* you got here.
TRYGAIOS.   Ah, greedy one,*
    You no longer seem to find me utterly foul!
But come, please call Zeus out for me.
HERMES.   Ha ha!
No chance you'll find the gods anywhere round here.
They've gone—they moved out only yesterday.
TRYGAIOS. Where on earth have they gone?

HERMES.   'On *earth*'!
TRYGAIOS.   Where then?
HERMES.   Very
    far.
They've moved right up underneath the curve of the sky.
TRYGAIOS. How come, then, *you* remained here on your own?   200
HERMES. To protect the gods' utensils left behind:
    Small pots and wooden things and storage jars.
TRYGAIOS. But what's the reason the gods decided to move?
HERMES. They were furious with the Greeks. So in this place
    Where they used to live they've settled War instead:
    He's got carte blanche to do what he wants to you.
    They've moved themselves to the highest point they could,
    So they won't any longer be able to see you fighting
    And won't be aware at all if you plead with them.
TRYGAIOS. But why treat us like this? You must explain.   210
HERMES. Because you opted for war even though the gods
    Often tried to offer you peace. Whenever the Spartans
    Got a slight advantage, they'd start to talk like this:
[*Imitating*] 'By the Twain, we'll make this laddie from Attika pay!'*
    Whenever, in turn, you Attic-ish folk did well
    And the Spartans came to make some peace proposal,
    You'd say at once: 'There's a trap being laid for us here,
    By Athena there is!' 'By Zeus, they can't be trusted!
    But they'll soon come back if we take possession of Pylos.'*
TRYGAIOS. That's the typical way we speak, I can't deny it.   220
HERMES. That's why I doubt you'll ever set eyes again
    On Peace herself.
TRYGAIOS.   Why, where's she vanished to?
HERMES. She's been hidden inside a big deep cave by War.
TRYGAIOS. What kind of cave?
HERMES.   Right down in here.

[HERMES *opens door A to reveal a large pile of stones just inside it: the door remains open, representing the cave entrance, until* PEACE *is eventually hauled out (see 431 ff.).*]

                              You see
What a pile of stones he then heaped up on top

To ensure you'd never again get hold of Peace.
TRYGAIOS. But what's War planning to do with all us Greeks?
HERMES. Don't know, except one thing: just yesterday evening
  He brought a really enormous mortar home.
TRYGAIOS. What sort of use will he make of this mortar of his?   230
HERMES. He's planning to pound the cities of Greece inside it.
  [*Loud noises heard*]
  I'm off. Unless I'm mistaken, he's coming out now:
  I can hear his clamour inside. [*Exits into door B*]
TRYGAIOS.   Oh dear, I'm worried!
  I ought to run off before he comes. I too
  Heard the sound of a mortar fit for military conflict.

[*Before* TRYGAIOS *can leave the scene, the figure of* WAR, *costumed as a comically hideous cross between a warrior and a cook, comes storming out from door B: he carries a giant mortar and a variety of ingredients to mash up in it.* TRYGAIOS *observes events, cowering, from a position over to the side of the* orchêstra; WAR *remains unaware of his presence throughout what follows.*]

WAR. O mortals, mortals, mortals with abject lives,
  Any moment now I'll batter you round the head!
TRYGAIOS. O lord Apollo, just look at the size of the mortar!
  What a monstrous thing! And that look on the face of War!
  Is this the figure we always try to avoid,   240
  The dire, shield-shaking one who...sends shit down our legs?
WAR [*brandishing leeks*]. Alas Prasiai, three times, nay five times
    woeful,*
  Nay many times more, you face destruction today! [*Puts leeks into
    mortar*]
TRYGAIOS [*to audience*]. There's nothing yet, men of Athens, that
    matters to *us*.
  The trouble he's mentioned belongs to Sparta alone.
WAR [*taking garlic*]. O Megara, Megara, how you'll now be crushed!
  I'll pound every bit of you down into garlic paste.* [*Puts garlic
    into mortar*]
TRYGAIOS. Good gracious me! What he's put in the mortar now
  Means lots of pungent tears for Megarian folk.
WAR [*taking cheese*]. Alas for Sicily, doom awaits you too!*   250

TRYGAIOS. What a land will now be grated to miserable shreds!

WAR. Let me pour some honey from Attika into the mix. [*Does so*]

TRYGAIOS [*to* WAR]. Hey there, I suggest you use some *different* honey.
Please spare the Attic kind—it's very expensive.

WAR [*calling in*]. Where's Uproar, slave!

UPROAR [*entering from door B*].   Well, what do you want?

WAR.   To
    thrash you!
    Are you standing idle? Try my fist in your face! [*Strikes him*]

UPROAR. What a pungent taste! That stung me. Surely, master,
    You didn't rub garlic onto your knuckles, did you?

WAR. Go and fetch me a pestle.

UPROAR.   I'm sorry, we don't have one:
    We only moved in here just yesterday.   260

WAR. Go quick as you can and fetch me one from Athens.

UPROAR. I'll go at once—to avoid a further beating. [*Exits to one side*]

TRYGAIOS [*to audience*]. Well, what are we going to do, you poor
        little people?
    You can see how great a danger's threatening us.
    If he comes back here with the pestle he's gone to fetch,
    The whole of Greece will be mashed down into chaos.
    May he drop down dead, Dionysos, and never come back!

UPROAR [*returning*]. I'm back.

WAR.   But where's the pestle?

UPROAR [*nervously*].   Um, er, you see,
    The Athenians have lost that pestle of theirs—
    The leather-seller, who used to stir up Greece.*   270

TRYGAIOS. And a good thing too, our mistress queen Athena!
    The death of that man was timely for the city,
    Before we found ourselves in garlic paste!

WAR [*to* UPROAR]. Then go and fetch a different pestle from Sparta,
    And quickly!

UPROAR.   Will do, master.

WAR.   Get back soon!

[UPROAR *exits this time by the opposite* eisodos *from his previous trip.*]

TRYGAIOS [*to audience*]. Well, gentlemen, what now? The danger's
        urgent!
    If any of you are initiates of the cult

In Samothrace, it's now the time to pray*
That this messenger's feet will turn in another direction!
UPROAR [*returning*]. I'm really in trouble, yes trouble, yes very big
    trouble.   280
WAR. Have you still not brought what I wanted?
UPROAR.   That's because
The Spartans too have lost the pestle they had.
WAR. What's that, you rogue?
UPROAR.   They lent it to other people
For use in Thrace, but then it wasn't returned.*
TRYGAIOS. And an excellent outcome too, ye Dioskouroi!*
    Perhaps there's still some hope. Take courage, mortals!
WAR [*to* UPROAR]. Take all this stuff of mine inside the house.
    I'll come in myself and make my very own pestle.

[WAR *and* UPROAR *exit through door B.* TRYGAIOS *moves back towards
centre-stage.*]

TRYGAIOS. Well here's a familiar thing. It's like the song
    Which Datis sang at midday, having a wank: 290
    'What pleasure! I joy myself! It's sheer delight!'*
[*With expansive gestures*] This is now the perfect time, O men of
    Greece,
    For to you escape from all the trouble of war
    And rescue Peace, the friend of all, from the cave,
    Before some other 'pestle' blocks our way.
    Come, all you farmers, merchants, builders as well,
    And other craftsmen, metics, and foreigners too,*
    And all who inhabit the islands: come, great throngs,
    Pick up at once your shovels, crowbars, ropes:
    It's now our chance to seize a moment of fortune.   300

[*The* CHORUS *enters, carrying the kind of equipment indicated in line
299; the exchange between the* CHORUS LEADER *and* TRYGAIOS *is in
chanted recitative.*]

[PARODOS: 301–44]

LEADER. Come eagerly in this direction, each one of you join our
    rescue mission.

O men from every part of Greece, it's time, if ever, to act together,
Escaping from our armies' ranks and lousy officers dressed in
    scarlet.
The light of this special day has dawned, a Lamachos-hating day
    indeed.*
[*To* TRYGAIOS] So tell us what we need to do and put yourself in
    charge of our work.
Rely on me for the present task; I'm sure my stamina won't run out
Before with bars and other tools we pull back up into the daylight
The goddess who stands as greatest of all, the one who loves our
    grapevines most.

TRYGAIOS. Then lower your voices straightaway. If not, you'll find
    in all your glee
Your noisy shouts will rouse up War and bring him out in a fiery
    state.   310

LEADER. We're full of glee because we heard the public summons
    you issued before.
It was so much better than being required to go on campaign with
    three days' food.*

TRYGAIOS. Better beware old Kerberos who's now in Hades down
    below,*
In case he starts to splutter and shout, the way he did when still
    alive,
And comes to block the task we face of pulling the goddess out of
    the cave.

LEADER. There's no one at all who'll ever succeed in taking the
    goddess away from me
As soon as she's safely back in my hands; I assure you of that—
    hurrah! hurrah!

TRYGAIOS. You'll be the death of me, you men, unless you stop this
    shouting at once.
If not, then War will rush out here and trample all before him.

LEADER. Well let him churn up everything, and trample and
    confound.   320
No way we'll cease to show delight and celebrate on this special
    day.

[*The choreographed movements of the* CHORUS *have been building in
eager expressiveness and now start to turn into highly animated dancing.*]

TRYGAIOS. Are you out of your minds? What's wrong with you,
men? I beg you to stop, in the name of the gods.
You'll ruin this beautiful chance we have if you start to perform
such vigorous dance.

LEADER. It's not myself who wants to dance, it's all this pleasure
that's welling up here:
My legs themselves are starting to dance—they're independent of
my control!

TRYGAIOS. Don't take a single further step—please stop, please
stop your dance at once.

LEADER. Look, there you are: I've actually stopped.

TRYGAIOS.   You say you
have, but you actually haven't!

LEADER. Allow me to dance one final move, and then I won't dance
any more at all.

TRYGAIOS. Very well, just finish this final part, then stop your
dancing once and for all.

LEADER. We'll stop there now, there'll be no more, assuming this is
what you want.   330

TRYGAIOS. But look, it's clear you still haven't stopped.

LEADER.   I need to let
my right leg here
Have one more kick, and then it's done; that's all I ask before we
finish.

TRYGAIOS. I'll grant that wish, but on condition you cease to cause
me further trouble.

LEADER. My left leg too can't help itself; it needs to have one final
skip.
I'm full of pleasure, I'm jumping for joy, I'm farting away and
laughing aloud
For losing the burden of military service—far better than losing
old age itself!

TRYGAIOS. Hold back for now your celebrations; what's going to
happen is not yet clear.
Once Peace is in our hands again, then that's the time to celebrate
And shout with joy and laugh aloud.
For then you'll all be wholly free   340
To sail, stay home, to screw, to sleep,
To go on trips to festivals,

     To feast, to party, in Sybarite style,*
     And scream with ecstasy!

[*The* CHORUS, *reacting to the preceding words, now breaks into full song.*]

CHORUS.   If only I live to see that day arrive!   *Strophe*
          I've endured so much in the past
          Of the hardships of military beds
          Which Phormion had for his lot.*
          You'd no longer find me an acrid, peevish juror,*
          Nor showing my previous harshness of temperament,
          But instead you'd see me soften   350
          And grow much younger again
          Once relieved from all my hardships.
          We've spent too much time already
          Worn out, ground down,
          Going endlessly back and forth
          To and from the Lykeion, 'equipped with spear,
            equipped with shield'.*
[*To* TRYGAIOS] But whatever action of ours
          Will please you most, do tell us:
          For you're our supreme commander,
          Elected by our good fortune.   360

[TRYGAIOS *now moves closer to door A and starts to contemplate the clearance of the entrance to the cave. But almost immediately* HERMES *reappears from door B.*]

TRYGAIOS. Let me see, then, where will we put the stones we
    remove?
HERMES. You foul, audacious man, just what are you up to?
TRYGAIOS. Oh, nothing too bad—as Killikon explained.*
HERMES. You're done for, wretched thing!
TRYGAIOS [*facetiously*].   Have I drawn first lot?*
  Because you're Hermes I know you like such things.
HERMES. You're done for, thoroughly done for!
TRYGAIOS.   When will I die?
HERMES. You'll die on the spot!
TRYGAIOS.   But I haven't yet bought provisions:

I've got no groats or cheese to prepare for death.*
HERMES. You're as good as pulverized!
TRYGAIOS.   But in that case
How could I have failed to see how lucky I am?   370
HERMES. Don't you know that Zeus has ordered immediate death
For anyone trying to dig up Peace?
TRYGAIOS.   You mean
My death's completely inevitable?
HERMES.   That's right.
TRYGAIOS. Then lend me, please, three drachmas to buy a piglet:
I need to be initiated first.*
HERMES. O Zeus of thunder and lightning—
TRYGAIOS.   No, by the gods,
Please don't denounce me to Zeus, I beg you, master.
HERMES. I can't keep silent.
TRYGAIOS.   You *can*—for the sake of the meat
Which I brought as a gift for you when I came up here.*
HERMES. It can't be done, I'll be pulped at the hands of Zeus   380
[*Stiltedly*] If I don't make attestation of these things.
TRYGAIOS. Please don't make attestation, dearest Hermes!
[*To* CHORUS] What's wrong with you, men? Are you standing
          dumbstruck there?
Speak up, you oafs, to prevent his 'attestation'!

CHORUS.   You mustn't, O master Hermes, mustn't,   *Antistrophe*
              mustn't,
              If your memory tells you that once
              You received a piglet from me
              Which provided a lovely meal—
              You mustn't dismiss that now at our time of need.
TRYGAIOS. Don't you hear, O lord and master, these fawning words?
CHORUS.   Don't turn your anger against us   390
              As we plead with you like this,
              Don't stop us recovering Peace.
              Show special favour to us,
              Most philanthropic,
              Most benevolent of gods,
              If you loathe Peisander's helmet-crests and supercilious
                looks.*

And in return with sacrifices
And grandiose processions
We'll glorify you, O master,
Throughout the rest of time.

TRYGAIOS. Show pity, I beg, for these plaintive cries of theirs.   400
   They honour you more than ever they did before.
HERMES. That's because they're *thieves* more than ever they were
   before!*
TRYGAIOS [*confidentially*]. I'll also inform you of something big and
   bad,
   A conspiracy being set up against the gods.
HERMES. Right, give the information. You *might* persuade me.
TRYGAIOS. It's the moon and the mischievous sun who lie behind
   it.
   For a very long time they've been forming a plot against you
   To betray and abandon Greece to the Persians, no less.*
HERMES. But what's their reason for this?
TRYGAIOS.   Because, by Zeus,
   We Greeks sacrifice to *you*, while all the Persians   410
   Sacrifice to the sun and moon. So it's not surprising
   They'd like us Greeks wiped out from the face of the earth,
   Then the sun and moon would monopolize religion.
HERMES. That's why, of course, they've been filching days from the
   year
   And been naughtily nibbling round their celestial cycles.*
TRYGAIOS. That's right, by Zeus! So please, dear Hermes, help us
   With willing support, and join in pulling out Peace.
   If you do, we'll hold the Panathenaia for *you*
   And convert all other rites into your worship:
   The Mysteries, Dipolieia, Adonia too.*   420
   All other Greek cities, once freed from problems of war,
   Will worship Hermes as Warder-off-of-evils.
   You'll have lots of other rewards as well; for starters,
   I'd like you to have this bowl as a gift from me.

[TRYGAIOS *takes a gold bowl from his bag and hands it to* HERMES, *who
instantly starts to melt at the sight. Shortly afterwards,* TRYGAIOS *will
take a wineskin from his bag as well.*]

HERMES. Oh dear, I'm always moved to pity by...gold.

[*The following four lines are chanted in recitative metres.*]

TRYGAIOS [*to* CHORUS]. The task is now for *you*, my men: come,
    take your shovels and set to work;
  Get into the cave without delay and start to pull the stones away.
LEADER. We'll undertake the task. [*To* HERMES] But you, O
    cleverest one of all the gods,
  Stand over us and give instructions with all the expertise that's
    yours.
  You'll find that we're equipped to do whatever you say and carry
    it out.   430

[*The* CHORUS *moves into position to clear the entrance to the cave and
prepare to pull out* PEACE*; they attach their ropes to the wheeled platform* (ekkuklêma) *on which the statue of the goddess will later emerge
(500 ff.).*]

TRYGAIOS [*to* HERMES]. Right, take the bowl I gave you and hold
    it up
  To allow us to pray to the gods then tackle the work.
HERMES [*priest-like*]. Libation, libation!
                    Ritual silence, ritual silence!
TRYGAIOS. Let us pour libations and pray that this present day
  May inaugurate good times for all the Greeks.
  Whoever is eager to help in pulling these ropes,
  May he never pick up a shield to fight in war.
LEADER. We'd add, may he live the rest of his life in peace
  With a prostitute in his arms...and a fire to poke.*   440
TRYGAIOS. But whoever desires continuation of war—
LEADER. May he be condemned, we pray, lord Dionysos,
  To pulling out arrow-heads from both his elbows.
TRYGAIOS. If a would-be officer wants to block your return
  To the light of day, O mistress Peace: in battle—
LEADER. May he suffer the very same fate as Kleonymos did!*
TRYGAIOS. If a maker of spears or a merchant of military shields
  Wants war to continue in order to make more profit—
LEADER. May kidnappers seize him and feed him on dry barley!

TRYGAIOS. If any aspiring general won't assist us,   450
   Or a slave is prepared to desert to the enemy side—
LEADER. May he first be whipped, then stretched out on the rack!
TRYGAIOS. May the rest of us prosper! Strike a refrain, 'all hail'!
LEADER. No *striking*—blows aren't wanted. Just 'all hail'!
TRYGAIOS. All hail! All hail! I say. Nothing but all hail!
   Hail Hermes, Graces, Seasons, Aphrodite, Desire—
LEADER. Not Ares.
TRYGAIOS.   No!
LEADER.   Whatever his title.
TRYGAIOS.   No!
HERMES. Everyone must strain to the limit and pull the ropes.

[*The* CHORUS *sets to work pulling the ropes, the whole action choreo-graphed in enhancement of the sung exchanges that follow.* TRYGAIOS *lends a helping hand but takes overall responsibility for monitoring progress of the task.*]

CHORUS. Heave away there!   *Strophe*
HERMES. Heave indeed!   460
CHORUS. Heave away there!
HERMES. Heave still more!
CHORUS. Heave away! Heave away!
TRYGAIOS. The men are not pulling with equal effort.
   [*Pointing*] You there, start helping! You're showing
      disdain!
   You'll pay for this, Boiotians!*
CHORUS. Heave away there!
HERMES. Keep heaving away!
CHORUS [*to* TRYGAIOS *and* HERMES]. Come on, you two must
      join us in pulling.
TRYGAIOS. But aren't I pulling and holding on tight,   470
   And bending my back and trying my best?
CHORUS. Then why are we not succeeding?

[*As the pulling continues,* TRYGAIOS *and* HERMES *comment on the action as though it reflected the behaviour of particular groups and individuals in relation to the war; their comments extend imaginatively beyond what is actually visible on-stage.*]

TRYGAIOS. O Lamachos, you're wrong to obstruct our work.*
    The last thing we need around is a bogey like you.
HERMES. These Argives here have long been failing to pull;
    They've been aiming derision at all those toiling away,
    And claiming food for pay from both sides at once.*
TRYGAIOS. But the Spartans, my friend, are pulling with manly
      might.
HERMES. The only Spartans really keen to pull
    Are the ones being held in prison, and they're chained up!*   480
TRYGAIOS. The Megarians too are useless; but still, they're tugging
    As hard as they can, and baring their teeth like dogs—
HERMES. Because, by Zeus, they've almost starved to death!*
LEADER. We're achieving nothing, my men. With concerted effort
    We must all grip tight on the ropes for a further attempt.

CHORUS.	Heave away there!	*Antistrophe*
HERMES.	Heave indeed!	
CHORUS.	Heave away there!	
HERMES.	Heave, by Zeus!	
CHORUS.	We're moving it slightly.	490
HERMES.	But isn't it shocking and wrong	
	That some are straining, while others are pulling	
	against them?	
	You'll be thrashed for this, you Argives!	
CHORUS.	Heave away there!	
HERMES.	Keep heaving away!	
CHORUS.	There are people among us who don't wish us well.	
HERMES.	Then all of you who crave for peace	
	Must pull the ropes with all your might.	
CHORUS.	But some here want to stop us.	

[HERMES *continues a 'historical' commentary on the action. At 509 ff.*
the ekkuklêma *carrying (the statue of)* PEACE, *flanked by her two at-*
tendants, HARVEST *and* FESTIVITY, *starts to emerge from door A, until*
by line 519 it has become fully visible.]

HERMES. You men of Megara, get the hell out of here!   500
    The goddess detests you because of the things that you did:
    It was you, at the start, who smeared her body with garlic!*
    And I've got some advice for you Athenians too:

Stop pulling the ropes from the angle you're currently using;
You're acting as though you were jurors sitting in judgement.
If you really desire to pull out the goddess from here,
Then take a step back and stick to command of the sea,*

LEADER [*chanting*]. Come, men, let us the farmers hold the ropes
    all on our own.

HERMES. It's clear you're having more success by acting in this
    fashion.

LEADER. He says we're having more success; come, every man,
    keep striving.   510

HERMES. The farmers, no one else, are making progress with their
    pulling.

LEADER. Try harder now, even harder, all!

HERMES. And look, you've almost done it.

LEADER. No time to slacken; we must exert ourselves with manly
    strength.

HERMES. This is it, this is it!

CHORUS [*singing*]. Then heave and heave, each one of you.
                Then heave and heave and heave and heave and heave!
                Then heave and heave and heave and heave, each one!

[*Now that the statue of* PEACE *has been pulled from the cave, the* CHORUS
detaches the ropes from the ekkuklêma.]

TRYGAIOS [*formally*]. O grape-giving mistress, suitable language
    fails me.   520
    I need my words to have unlimited scope,
    Like a boundless wine-jar—nothing like that in my house!
    Hail to you, Harvest! You too, Festivity!
    What a beautiful face you have, Festivity.
    How lovely your breath, how it gives the heart deep pleasure
    With its scent of a perfumed life away from the army!

HERMES. And quite unlike the smell of a soldier's back-pack?

TRYGAIOS. I detest that hateful part of a hateful life!
    It reeks of oniony indigestion belches.*
    But *here* wafts ripeness, feasts, Dionysiac cheer,   530
    Pipes, tragic dancers, Sophokles' songs, and thrushes,
    The versicles of Euripides—

HERMES.   How dare you

Defame this goddess like that! She takes no pleasure
In a poet who writes in the style of litigious wrangling.*
TRYGAIOS [*persisting*]. There are scents of ivy, wine-straining,
    bleating lambs,
The bosoms of women in and out of the kitchen,
A female slave who's drunk, a wine-jug spilt,
And lots of other good things.
HERMES [*as if pointing down to earth*]. And look here now
How all Greek cities are gabbling one to another,
Now they've reconciled themselves and are happily
    laughing—   540
TRYGAIOS. Even though they've got black-eyes of a terrible kind
And are using cupping-glasses to try to heal them.
HERMES [*gesturing*]. Now, look over here at all the play's spectators.
You can tell their crafts from the looks on their faces.
TRYGAIOS.   Ugh!
HERMES. Do you see that maker of helmet-crests over there?
He's tearing out his hair.
TRYGAIOS.   But that maker of mattocks
Just gave a contemptuous fart at the nearby sword-smith.
HERMES. Can you see the delight on the face of that sickle-maker
And the way he gave the finger to that spear-maker?*
TRYGAIOS. Come, make an announcement that farmers are free to
    go home.   550
HERMES [*formally*]. Attend to this, you people: the farmers can
    leave
And take their farming equipment back to the fields,
[*Chanting*] Returning there without your spears, without your
    swords and javelins too,
Since everything round here abounds with a state of nice old
    mellow peace.
Each one of you should cheer with thanks, then back to the fields
    to do your work.
LEADER [*chanting*]. O day of peace, for whose appearance good
    people and farmers have yearned so long,
Now I've seen your arrival with happy eyes I want to salute my
    vines again.
And as for the fig-trees I planted once, so long ago in my younger
    years,

I'm full of desire to greet them all after such a lengthy passage of
    time.

TRYGAIOS. Now then, my men, let's first of all devote a prayer to
    this goddess Peace,   560
    Since she's the one who's rescued us from helmet-crests and
    Gorgon shields.*
    And once that's done, let's scurry back home to occupy our
    country farms,
    Though not before we've bought some good salt-fish to take along
    with us.

HERMES. In Poseidon's name, what a gorgeous sight these serried
    ranks of farmers make,
    All packed together and coruscating, like barley-cakes amidst a
    feast.

TRYGAIOS. You're right, by Zeus! Their clod-breaking mallets are
    gleaming just as brightly as weapons,
    While three-pronged forks reflect the brilliant light of the sun in
    all directions.
    Equipment like this will make a fine job of clearing the soil
    between their plants.
    The sight is making me full of desire to get myself to the
    countryside
    And to work with a mattock to turn the soil of that farmlet of
    mine I've missed so long.   570
[*To* CHORUS] It's time, you men, to call to mind
            The way of life we used to lead,
            The one that Peace bestowed on us,
            Including cakes of rich dried fruit,
            And juicy figs and myrtle berries,
            And the taste of sweet wine-must to drink,
            And a patch of violets next to the well,
            And the olive trees we've pined to see.
            For every one of these reasons, now   580
            Proclaim this goddess with fervour.

[HALF-AGON: 582–656]

CHORUS.   Hail! Hail! O dearest goddess, how happy we   *Epode**
          are to see you!
          I was overwhelmed with longing for you;

I was pierced with desire
To return to the countryside.
…*

You were the greatest boon for us, our longed-for
    darling,
For all of us who practised
The farming life. You alone
Brought benefit to us.   590
Abundance was ours to enjoy,
When we had you before, of things that were sweet,
Without expense, and delicious.
For rural folk you were porridge and safety!*
So our dear little vines
And our new little fig-trees
And all our other plants as well
Will laugh with delight to have got you back.   600

LEADER. But where was this goddess concealed from us for such an
    extended stretch of time?
    We'd like you please to explain this to us, O most benevolent of
    the gods.

[*In much of what follows,* HERMES *can be seen to be addressing not just
    the* CHORUS *but the theatre audience itself.*]

HERMES [*formally*]. You farmers whose minds are exceedingly
    shrewd, pay close attention to what I say,
    If you'd like to hear precisely how this goddess Peace was lost
    from your world.
    It all began when a scandal occurred involving the sculptor
    Pheidias,
    And that in turn made Perikles afraid that he'd be implicated.*
    He feared the temperaments of you Athenians, with your vicious
    ways,
    So before he suffered a nasty fate of his own he set the city
    aflame
    By tossing a tiny spark of fire—the Megarian decree, I mean.*
    He blew and blew to make the fire so large that from its clouds of
    smoke   610

The whole of Greece had streaming eyes—the Spartans there,
    Athenians here.
As soon as the conflagration spread and the vines were forced to
    crackle with flames,
While wine-jars smashed into each other, each blow returned with
    an angry kick,*
There was no one left who could stop the war, and this goddess
    began to be lost from sight.

TRYGAIOS. In Apollo's name, I'd never heard this same account
    from anyone else!
And nor had I heard of the special link between Pheidias and the
    goddess herself.

LEADER. And I hadn't either, until just now. [*Naively*] But that
    explains her beautiful face,
If *she* was related to Pheidias. Many things for sure escape our
    notice.

HERMES. There's more to tell. When all the cities that Athens
    controlled became aware
Of how you were locked in bitter dispute, with factions snarling at
    each other,   620
They plotted against you in every way, afraid you'd raise their
    tribute higher,
And started to bribe with hefty sums important Spartans to back
    their cause.
These Spartans, greedy for filthy lucre, and always given to
    cheating others,*
Threw out this goddess in shameful fashion and snatched the
    chance of war instead.
But gains those Spartans won for themselves brought suffering on
    their farming folk:
The warships sent in turn from Athens to take reprisals over there
Consumed the figs of innocent men, instead of the leaders who
    bore the blame.*

TRYGAIOS. But rightly so, since Spartans came and chopped to
    pieces a fig-tree of mine!
I'd planted that tree with my very own hands and nurtured its
    growth with loving care.

LEADER. By Zeus, old chap, quite right indeed! I suffered some
    damage myself at their hands.   630

They smashed a storage chest of mine when wrecking my
    property with their stones.

HERMES. When all the working folk of Athens moved off the land
    into the city,*

They failed to understand just how they too were being cruelly
    duped.

No longer with their vines to tend and hungry for dried figs to eat,

They felt dependent on their leaders. The latter understood too
    well

The poor were weak from going hungry and badly lacked the
    grain they needed.

With noisy cries like verbal pitchforks they turfed this goddess
    out of here,

Even though she often showed herself because of her longing for
    this land.*

Meanwhile they used extortion on those allies who possessed
    great wealth

By making constant accusations of secretly favouring Brasidas.*
    640

In such a case you all behaved like dogs and tore the accused to
    pieces.

Because the city was apprehensive and always hunched in a state
    of fear,

Every scrap of slander tossed its way got swallowed down with
    great delight.

When people in the allied states saw how you thrashed the likes of
    them,

They tried to stuff gold into the mouths of those responsible for
    such things,

Thereby enriching politicians, while Greece itself grew destitute

Though you were kept quite in the dark. The man who caused
    this situation

Was a leather-seller.

TRYGAIOS.   Stop at once! Don't speak his name, O
    Hermes master.

Just leave that terrible man to lie where he is, far down beneath
    the earth.

No longer is he one of ours, he's one of yours in the land of the
    dead.*   650

So whatever you choose to say about him,
No matter how rotten he was while alive,
A loudmouth and blackmailer too,
An implement for stirring and churning—
Well, every one of these insults now
Refers to one of *yours*.

[TRYGAIOS *now turns to the statue of* PEACE, *with which he and* HERMES *start to interact physically as though it were animate. The dialogue switches back from recitative to speech*.]

But tell me, mistress, why this silence of yours.
HERMES. She won't reply in front of these spectators.
   She feels great anger for what they made her suffer.
TRYGAIOS. Then let her whisper a little just into your ear.*   660
HERMES [*to* PEACE]. Well tell me what you think of them, O
   dearest.
   Come, combat-loathing female like no other!
[*Puts ear to statue*] I'm listening now. [*Pause*] Is *that* your grievance?
   Got it.
[*To audience*] You people, hear the reproach she brings against you.
   She says she freely came here after Pylos,
   With a basket full of peace for the city's sake,
   But was spurned three times by your Assembly votes.*
TRYGAIOS [*to* PEACE]. We made a bad mistake, but please
   forgive us:
   Our minds were tangled up in strips of leather!*
HERMES. Oh, listen to the question she just asked: 670
   Who here in Athens was most averse to her,
   And who was her friend and wanted the war to end?
TRYGAIOS. Most well-disposed to her by far ... Kleonymos!
HERMES. What kind of person was he in military matters,
   Kleonymos?
TRYGAIOS.   Oh, dauntless in spirit—except:
   He's turned out not to be his father's son.
   Whenever he went to serve on an expedition,
   He dropped his weapons and proved an utter ... bastard!*
HERMES. Oh, here's another question she asked just now:
   Which politician now commands the Pnyx?   680

TRYGAIOS. Hyperbolos controls that place right now.

[*At the mention of Hyperbolos, the head of* PEACE *is seen to start turning
(under the mechanical control of someone hidden either behind or inside
the statue).*]

[*To* PEACE] But what are you doing? Why turn your head like this?
HERMES. She's turning away in disgust at the people of Athens
    For putting their trust in such a degenerate leader.
TRYGAIOS. Don't worry, we'll soon discard him. At the moment
    Because the people felt naked without a steward
    It's girded its loins with him for just a while.
HERMES. But how, she asks, will this be good for the city?
TRYGAIOS. We'll make far better decisions.
HERMES.   I don't see why.
TRYGAIOS. Because Hyperbolos is a maker of lamps.   690
    In our past affairs we always groped in the dark,
    But now his lamps will make us more enlightened!*
HERMES. She's got some further questions—odd ones!
TRYGAIOS.   What?
HERMES. There are many that reach right back to when she left.
    And first, she's asked how Sophokles is faring.
TRYGAIOS. He's prospering, but one thing's strange.
HERMES.   What's that?
TRYGAIOS. He's changed from Sophokles into . . . Simonides!
HERMES. Simonides! How's that?
TRYGAIOS.   Though old and frail
    For the sake of lucre 'he'd put to sea on a mat'!*
HERMES. And next: is skilful Kratinos living?
TRYGAIOS.   He perished   700
    When the Spartans invaded.
HERMES.   What happened?
TRYGAIOS.   You want to know?
    He passed out when he just couldn't take the sight
    Of a big full jar of wine being smashed to pieces.*
    There are too many things besides that have happened at Athens,
    So we'll never let go of you ever again, O mistress.
HERMES. Well, on that understanding, now take Harvest
    To be your very own wife. In the countryside

You'll live with her and beget a family of . . . grapes!

TRYGAIOS. Come here, my darling, let me give you a kiss.
[*Suggestively*]. D'you think it would do me harm, after all this
 time,   710
 O Hermes master, to . . . go all the way with Harvest?

HERMES. Not as long as you settle your guts with a herbal drink.*
 As soon as you can, you should take Festivity here
 And return her to the Council, where she belonged.

TRYGAIOS. O fortunate Council, to have Festivity back!
 What copious broth you'll sup for three whole days,
 And how much sausage and meat you'll eat as well!*
 It's time, dear Hermes, to say farewell.

HERMES.   You too,
 My man, farewell. Make sure you remember me.

TRYGAIOS [*looking round*]. O beetle, let's fly homeward, homeward
 now.   720

HERMES. He's no longer here, old fellow.

TRYGAIOS.   But where's he gone?

HERMES. He's yoked to Zeus's lightning chariot now.*

TRYGAIOS. What source of food will the poor thing get from there?

HERMES. Ambrosia—that's what Ganymede excretes.*

TRYGAIOS. Well how will I get back down to earth?

HERMES.   Don't worry:
 Go past the goddess here.*

TRYGAIOS.   This way then, girls,
 Just follow me quickly. Lots of people on earth
 Are waiting for you with longing . . . and big erections.

[TRYGAIOS, *together with* HARVEST *and* FESTIVITY, *exits by door A,*
HERMES *by door B. The statue of* PEACE *remains on-stage. As the*
CHORUS *members assemble for the parabasis, they put aside the shovels,*
ropes, etc. which they earlier brought with them: these objects are now re-
moved by stagehands.]

[PARABASIS: 729–818]

LEADER. Safe journey to you. But now it's time for us to give our
 equipment
 To these attendants for keeping safe. We know there's always
 a risk   730

From thieves who lurk around this place, just waiting to make
  some mischief.
[*To stagehands*] Take special care of all these things. And now it's up
  to us
To tell the spectators our path of words and all our deepest
  thoughts.
The theatre-stewards would be in order to strike any comic poet
Who stepped before you in anapaest verse in order to praise
  himself.*
But if it's right, O daughter of Zeus, to honour a special person,
The one who's become the best and most renowned of comic
  poets,
Our chorus-trainer declares that *he* deserves the greatest
  praise.*
He single-handedly put a stop, for a start, to those of his rivals
Who constantly mocked the wearers of rags, making comic war
  on lice!   740
And as for versions of Herakles presented as glutton or starving,
He was first to expel such trash from the stage. He also dispensed
  with slave roles
Of kinds that others resorted to—those slaves who howl with
  pain,
So a fellow-slave can mock their blows, then pose the following
  question:
'You wretched thing, what was done to your hide? It surely wasn't
  a *whip*
That attacked your ribs with military force and cut its way
  through your back?'
By doing away with all such rubbish, all cheap and vulgar
  joking,*
Our poet created a mighty art and built a towering structure
With splendid language, lofty thoughts, and jokes in no way
  vulgar.   750
He didn't make fun of ordinary folk or minor men and women.
With a temper worthy of Herakles, he tackled the greatest targets,
And waded through the stench of hides and the filthy mud of
  threats.
[*As the poet*] Above all else I took up the fight against the jag-toothed
  monster,

Whose eyes flashed fearsome beams of light like those of Kynna
    the whore,
While round him licked a hundred heads of revolting hangers-on,
And he had the voice of a mountain torrent that threatens wrack
    and ruin,
Plus the stench of a seal, with Lamia's unwashed balls and a
    camel's arsehole.
Yet this monstrous sight never made me afraid, but fighting on
    your behalf,
And for all the islands as well, I stood my ground.* For all these
    reasons   760
It's right for you to return the favour and never forget my deeds.
When I had success in the past, I didn't go round the wrestling
    schools*
And try to pick up boys; I packed my theatrical stuff and left,
Having caused little pain but a great deal of joy, and satisfied
    comedy's needs.

        So everyone should be on my side,
        That's all the men and all the boys,*
        And the bald are also recommended
        To show support for my victory:
        If I win, then everyone will say,
        At every dinner and drinking party,   770
        'Serve the *bald* man first, give the *bald* man nibbles,
        And pay attention to every need
        Of a man who has the same forehead*
        As the noblest of all poets.'

CHORUS.   Muse, spurning the subject of war   *Strophe*
        Consort along with me,
        Your friend, in the present dance,
        Celebrating weddings of gods,
        The feasts of men,
        And banquets to honour the blesséd:*   780
        These are your age-old themes.
        If Karkinos approaches you
        To beg you come and join his sons
        In a dance performance,
        Don't listen to him

Or collaborate,
But count them all
As home-bred quails, stump-necked dancers,
Dwarfish creatures, snippets of goat-dung, artifice-
    delvers.   790
Their father said the play he'd surprisingly written
Disappeared one evening—a mouse the weasel killed!*

Such are the public songs   *Antistrophe*
Of the fair-tressed Graces
The skilful poet should sing
When in the season of spring
The swallow cries out,   800
Taking pleasure in its own voice,*
And a chorus is denied to Morsimos
And Melanthios as well,*
Whom I once heard intoning
In a gratingly piercing voice,
When a chorus of tragic dancers
Was granted to him and his brother,
The two of them forming a pair
Of gourmet Gorgons, skate-spearing Harpies,   810
Foul scarers of hags, with goat-stinking armpits,
    defilers of fish.*
Spit down on them a great big gob of phlegm,
O goddess Muse, and revel in the festival with me.

[*As the* CHORUS *moves back to the side of the* orchêstra, TRYGAIOS,
HARVEST, *and* FESTIVITY *reappear from one of the* eisodoi. TRYGAIOS
   rubs his legs like someone who has walked a very long way.]

TRYGAIOS. What a difficult task it was to visit the gods.
  I can hardly stand, my legs are so worn out.   820
[*To audience*] You all looked tiny from high up there; in fact
  From up in the sky I thought you seemed quite nasty,
  But close up here you're... even nastier still!

[SLAVE[B] *enters from door A, which now reverts to representing the house
      of* TRYGAIOS.]

SLAVE^B. You're back then, master?

TRYGAIOS [*facetiously*]. Someone told me I am!

SLAVE^B. And how did it go?

TRYGAIOS. I've made my legs very sore
By going so far.

SLAVE^B. I'd like to know—

TRYGAIOS. Well what?

SLAVE^B. Was there anyone else you saw apart from yourself
Who drifted around in the air?

TRYGAIOS. Not really, unless
You count the souls of a few dithyrambic poets.*

SLAVE^B. And what were they doing?

TRYGAIOS. Just flying around to gather   830
Their bright-and-breezy-windy-floaty preludes.

SLAVE^B. So isn't it true, as people claim, that we all
End up in the air and turn into stars after death?*

TRYGAIOS. It certainly is.

SLAVE^B. And who's a star right now?

TRYGAIOS. Well Ion of Chios is one. He once composed
A poem about the dawn, so up in the sky
They all decided to call him the Morning Star.*

SLAVE^B. And who are those stars which shoot across the sky
With a scurrying trace of fire?

TRYGAIOS. They're some of the rich
Who have turned into stars and are walking home from
dinner   840
With brightly burning lanterns in their hands.
[*Pointing to* HARVEST] But take this woman inside my house at once,
Then wash the bathtub out and heat the water,
And lay out the nuptial bed for me and her.
Once you've done all that, come back out here to me.
[*Pointing to* FESTIVITY] Meanwhile I'll give this other one back to
the Council.

SLAVE^B. But where did you get these women?

TRYGAIOS. From the sky, of course.

SLAVE^B. I'll never spend even a pittance to honour the gods
If they're brothel-keepers the way that humans are!

TRYGAIOS. They're not, but others up there make money like
that.*   850

SLAVE^B [*to* HARVEST]. Right, in we go. [*To* TRYGAIOS] Oh, tell me,
  shall I give her
  Some food to eat?

TRYGAIOS.   No, nothing. She'll simply refuse
  Either bread or barley-cake, because she's used
  To licking ambrosia up in the world of the gods.*

SLAVE^B [*lewdly*]. Then let's make sure she does some licking here too!

[SLAVE^B *leads* HARVEST *into door A. The choral song that follows is
interspersed with recitative from* TRYGAIOS *and the* CHORUS LEADER.]

CHORUS.   What felicity this elderly fellow,   *Strophe*
            If our senses don't deceive us,
            Is enjoying here and now!

TRYGAIOS.   But what will you say when you see me dressed in the
                gleaming clothes of a bridegroom?

CHORUS.   We'll envy you, old man,   860
            When you've been rejuvenated
            And anointed well with perfume.

TRYGAIOS.   I think so too. But what will you say when I bed her and
                hold her tits?

LEADER.   You'll certainly seem a happier man than Karkinos'
                whirling sons.*

TRYGAIOS.   And quite right too, since I mounted on the vehicle of
                my beetle
            And saved the people of Greece, to ensure that in the
                countryside
            They're able, all, to screw and sleep secure.

[SLAVE^B *comes back out of the house as previously instructed.*]

SLAVE^B.   The girl's been washed—her buttocks are looking
                lovely.
            The flat cake's baked, the sesame cake's being kneaded,
            The rest is ready. We just now need...your prick!   870

TRYGAIOS.   Right then, let's take Festivity here at once
            And return her to the Council.

SLAVE^B.   What's that name?
            Is this the same Festivity I remember,

When we used to shag our tipsy way to Brauron?*
TRYGAIOS.   You bet! It was hard to get her back.
SLAVE[B].   O master,
    She's got the arse for a good quadrennial hump!

[*As* TRYGAIOS *turns towards the Council seats in the auditorium,* SLAVE[B]
starts to run his hands round the body of FESTIVITY *while making
indecent movements with his phallus.*]

TRYGAIOS [*to audience*]. Right, which of you can be trusted? Can
    anyone be?
    Who'll take this woman and keep her safe for the Council?
    [*To* SLAVE[B]] Hey, what's this poking around?
SLAVE[B].   Er, just preparing
    To stake a tent at the Isthmian games with . . . my prick.*   880
TRYGAIOS [*to audience*]. No volunteer to guard her? [*To* FESTIVITY]
    Come over here:
    I'll take you myself and deposit you with the Council.

[TRYGAIOS *takes* FESTIVITY *by the hand, as though intending to take
her to the section of the auditorium where current members of the Council
are seated.*]

SLAVE[B] [*pointing*]. That man is nodding.
TRYGAIOS.   Who's that?
SLAVE[B].   Ariphrades.
    He implores you to hand her to him.
TRYGAIOS.   I know what he wants:
    He'll get on his knees and lap up all her broth!*
    [*To* FESTIVITY] Right, first of all remove this dress of yours.*

[FESTIVITY *removes a garment to reveal some exaggerated anatomical
features.*]

Behold Festivity, Council and Prytaneis!*
Consider how many good things I'm bringing for you.
You'll be able at once to lift her legs up high,
Then onwards and upwards with lots of pumping joy.   890
[*Pointing to her pubes*] And here, you see, is an oven for you.

SLAVE[B].   How lovely!
   That explains the smoky stain. This was the place
   Where before the war the Council kept its pot-stands.*
TRYGAIOS. And now you've got her back, you'll also be able
   To hold a fine athletic contest tomorrow:
   To wrestle her on the ground, get on all fours,
   And—once you're thoroughly oiled for the pankration—
   To strike, to gouge, with your fists... and your prick as well.
   In two days' time you can also hold horse-races,
   To find who rides the best in the jockey position,   900
   And chariots turned right over on top of each other
   Will puff and pant as they rub their flanks together,
   While others will lie, their foreskins pulled right back,
   Like charioteers collapsed at the bend in the course.*
   Come, Prytaneis, receive Festivity here.

[TRYGAIOS *now guides* FESTIVITY *to the Council seats, where she may remain till the end of the play. He briefly interacts with a (supposed) member of the Council in the audience.*]

   Observe how keen this Prytanis was to take her!
   You'd never have been so keen with normal business.
   You would have held out your hand—but just for bribes!

CHORUS.   A citizen like this   *Antistrophe*
           Brings benefits to all,   910
           Such qualities are his.
TRYGAIOS. When you gather your grapes, you'll know still more
           what a splendid fellow I am.*
CHORUS.   It's clear to us already:
           You've turned into a saviour
           For all mankind.
TRYGAIOS. Then what will you say when you drain to the bottom a
           flagon of fine new wine?
LEADER.   Apart from the gods we'll always deem you first in our
           rank of honour.
TRYGAIOS. Quite right, since I, Trygaios of Athmonon, deserve
           great thanks.*
           I've freed from terrible toils of war the masses of
           ordinary people   920

And all the farming folk, while putting a stop to
   Hyperbolos!*

SLAVE[B]. Very well, what's next for you and me to do?
TRYGAIOS [*pointing to* PEACE]. We must dedicate this statue, of
   course—with pots.
LEADER. With *pots*! As if it were any old wretched herm?*
TRYGAIOS. Well what should we use? A fatted bull, perhaps?
LEADER. A bull! Not at all. No *bullying* warfare here!
TRYGAIOS. Then perhaps a big fat pig?
LEADER.   No, no!
TRYGAIOS.   Why not?
LEADER. We need to avoid Theagenes' swinishness.*
TRYGAIOS. Well which other option is yours?
LEADER.   A bleater, I think.
TRYGAIOS. A bleater?
LEADER.   That's right!
TRYGAIOS.   But that's an Ionic word.   930
LEADER. That's why I chose it—so at Assembly meetings
   If anyone argues for war, then all the people
   Will bleat their terror in true Ionic manner*—
TRYGAIOS. Good idea!
LEADER.   —and be averse to all aggression.
   We'll be like lambs in our treatment of one another
   And very much milder towards the allied cities.
TRYGAIOS [*to* SLAVE[B]]. Right then, go and fetch the sheep without
   delay.
   And I'll get ready the altar for sacrifice.

[SLAVE[B] *exits into* TRYGAIOS*'s house; he will return, around line 950,
with the required sheep.* TRYGAIOS *himself arranges an altar, perhaps
using the one that stands in the middle of the* orchêstra, *and gathers together various objects required for animal sacrifice, some of them perhaps
makeshift alternatives to the real thing.*]

CHORUS.   How everything here, god willing and with   *Strophe*
       good fortune,
      Fulfils this man's intentions. Each element   940
      Coincides opportunely with every other.

TRYGAIOS.   It's clearly as you say. Here's the altar ready outside!
CHORUS.   Proceed with urgency while a vigorous wind
            From the gods prevails against the war:
            Now visibly some deity
            Transforms all things for the best.
TRYGAIOS.   The ritual basket is ready and waiting, with barley,
               garland, and knife.
            Here's the fire as well, so the only thing we lack is the
               sheep itself.
CHORUS.   You'd better both move with speed.   950
            If Chairis sets eyes on you
            He'll approach uninvited to play his pipes.
            And then, I have no doubt,
            As he puffs and toils
            You'll be forced to give him some meat.*

TRYGAIOS [*to* SLAVE^B]. Very well, take this basket here and the ritual
      water
   And circle the altar quickly from left to right.
SLAVE^B.   There you are—what's next? I've finished the ritual
      circuit.
TRYGAIOS. Right then, let me dip this fire-brand into the water.

[TRYGAIOS *dips the brand into the water and sprinkles some water over
the sheep. In what follows, various standard procedures of sacrifice are
                    followed (or parodied).*]

[*To the sheep*] Come on then, bob your head!* [*To* SLAVE^B] You, pass
      some barley.
   Now give me the bowl of water and wash your hands.   960
   And throw the spectators some barley as well.
SLAVE^B.   It's done.
TRYGAIOS. Have you done it already?
SLAVE^B.   By Hermes, I certainly have.
   Of all the many spectators watching us here
   Every single one is holding his very own piece.
TRYGAIOS. But the wives didn't get it.
SLAVE^B.   Don't worry, they'll get it
      this evening—

[*Suggestively*] Their husbands will give it to them!* Let's start the
    prayer.
TRYGAIOS [*formally*]. Who's here in attendance? [*Looking round*]
    But where is a group of good men?
SLAVE[B] [*pointing to* CHORUS]. Let me sprinkle these people; they're
    surely a group of good men.

[SLAVE[B] *takes the ritual water, of which there is an unusually large vessel,
and sprinkles it liberally over the* CHORUS, *who, after some physical byplay, end up standing round the altar as participants.*]

TRYGAIOS. You think they're good?
SLAVE[B].   Well isn't it clear that they
    are?   970
We've thoroughly doused them in water from head to foot
But they're nonetheless happy to stand their ground right
    here.
Let's start the prayer at once.
TRYGAIOS.   Very well, let's pray.
               [*Intoning*] Most magisterial queen and goddess,
               Our lady Peace,
               Mistress of choruses, mistress of marriage,
               Receive this sacrifice of ours.
CHORUS.   Receive it, do, O venerable goddess,
         We beg you by Zeus. And don't behave
         As adulterous women behave: 980
         They stick their heads round the door of the
            house
         And take a peek into the street,
         But if somebody takes note of them
         They retreat back inside,
         Though as soon as he's gone, they peek out again.*
         Please don't keep acting like this.
TRYGAIOS.   Instead, you should show the whole of yourself
         In dignified fashion to us your lovers.*
         We've worn ourselves out with longing for you
         For all of thirteen years.*   990
         Put an end to the tumult of war
         Then we'll call you Lysimache!*

Put an end as well to all the suspicions,
So subtly over-contrived,
Which we mutter against one another.
Blend all us Greeks,
As we once used to be,
In an essence of friendship, and mix our minds
In a milder spirit of sympathy.
Allow our market to teem with goods:
From Megara bring us heads of garlic,   1000
Early cucumbers, apples, pomegranates,
Fancy cloaks for slaves to wear.*
From Boiotian traders we'd like to see
Geese, ducks, wood-pigeons, and wrens,
As well as baskets of Kopaïc eels.*
Then may we all crowd round these baskets
And buying our food get into a jostle
With Morychos, Teleas, Glauketes,*
And numerous other gluttons. And next
May Melanthios come to the market too late,   1010
When the eels are all sold: let him ululate,
Then sing a solo from his *Medea*,
'I'm doomed, I'm doomed, now quite bereft
Of a female embedded in beetroot'.*
May all the bystanders feel glee!

Grant all these prayers of ours, O venerable goddess.
[*To* SLAVE^B] Take hold of this knife and like a master chef
    Cut the throat of the sheep.
SLAVE^B.   It's not allowed.
TRYGAIOS.   Why not?
SLAVE^B. Since Peace, of course, enjoys no violent killing:
    Her altar knows no blood.   1020
TRYGAIOS.   Then take it inside,
    Do the sacrifice there, and bring the thigh-bones out.
    That way, the *chorêgos* keeps his sheep for the feast.*

[SLAVE^B *goes back into the house with the sheep and the knife. In what
follows,* TRYGAIOS *arranges firewood on the altar and sets light
to it.*]

CHORUS. Well *you* should stay outside, old man;   *Antistrophe*
    there's lots to do.
  You must quickly arrange the firewood here
  And put everything else in order as well.

TRYGAIOS. Don't you think I'm handling the brushwood like a
    professional seer?*

CHORUS. You certainly are! You've overlooked no task
  Of an expert in these matters. You're fully aware
  Of all that falls within the scope of one
  Esteemed for sagacity
  And resourceful boldness.   1030

TRYGAIOS. The firewood's burning—that's worrying Stilbides!*
  I'll fetch the table myself; no need for a slave. [*Exits
    through door A*]

CHORUS. Who could fail to feel admiration
  For a man of such attributes,
  Who endured so many ordeals
  To save the sacred city?
  He'll never cease to be
  An object of envy to all.

[*During the last part of the preceding song,* TRYGAIOS *has reappeared with a table and several other objects.* SLAVE[B] *now comes back out of the house carrying the sheep's thigh-bones, wrapped in fat for burning as a sacrificial offering.*]

SLAVE[B]. All's done. Take the thighs and put them on the fire.
  [*Hands them over*]
  I'll fetch the entrails and sacrificial cakes. [*Exits*]   1040

TRYGAIOS. I've got everything under control. Get a move on
  there!

[SLAVE[B] *returns with the animal's innards (on a spit) and the sacrificial cakes.*]

SLAVE[B]. There you are, I'm back. You can't complain I'm slow.

TRYGAIOS. Right, roast the innards nicely. [*Looking to side*] I see
  some fellow
  Approaching here: he's wearing a laurel garland.

[HIEROKLES, *garlanded and draped with sheepskin fleeces (cf. 1122),
enters from one of the wings and makes his way with a look of suspicion
towards the sacrifice; the other characters size him up from a
distance.*]

SLAVE[B]. Who on earth can he be?
TRYGAIOS.   A charlatan, I'd say.
SLAVE[B]. A seer perhaps?
TRYGAIOS.   God, no! It's Hierokles,
  It really is—the oracle-monger from Oreus.*
SLAVE[B]. Well what will he have to say?
TRYGAIOS.   It's all too clear
  He'll try to block the peace we've now agreed.
SLAVE[B]. He surely won't—it's the smell that's drawing him
    here.   1050
TRYGAIOS. Let's pretend we haven't seen him.
SLAVE[B].   Good idea!

[TRYGAIOS *and* SLAVE[B] *busy themselves with the burning of the sacrificial meat, at first trying studiously to ignore* HIEROKLES.]

HIEROKLES. Just what's this sacrifice, and for which of the gods?
TRYGAIOS [*to* SLAVE[B]]. Keep roasting in silence, and don't disturb
    the loin.
HIEROKLES. Won't you say which god it is?
TRYGAIOS.   This tail is doing
  Just *nicely*.
SLAVE[B].   Nicely indeed, O lady Peace!
HIEROKLES [*butting in*]. Cut the first fruits from the meat and give
    them to me.*
TRYGAIOS. It's better to roast them first.
HIEROKLES.   But these bits here
  Are roasted already.
TRYGAIOS.   Stop meddling, whoever you are!
[*To* SLAVE[B]] Now slice.
HIEROKLES.   You've got a table?
TRYGAIOS.   And bring the wine.
HIEROKLES. The tongue gets kept aside.*
TRYGAIOS.   We haven't forgotten.   1060

You know what we'd like you to do?

HIEROKLES.   Just tell me.

TRYGAIOS.   Keep quiet!

We're making a sacrifice to Peace, the goddess.

[HIEROKLES, *in keeping with his status as an oracle-collector, now starts to chant in quasi-oracular hexameters;* TRYGAIOS *mockingly responds in the same rhythm and the scene remains in hexameters, a sustained parody of high-flown tone, until line 1114. The sacrificial action continues throughout.*]

HIEROKLES. *Wretched* and childish mortals,—

TRYGAIOS.   May you damn
   yourself with these words!

HIEROKLES. Full of your foolish thoughts, unaware of the mind of
   the gods,

   Treaties you've made with those who resemble cruel-eyed
   monkeys.*

TRYGAIOS. Ha! Ha! Ha!

HIEROKLES.   Why laugh?

TRYGAIOS.   How I like your 'cruel-eyed
   monkeys'!

HIEROKLES. Timorous gulls you've become, placing all your trust
   in fox-cubs;

   Guileful they are in their souls, and guileful in mind.

TRYGAIOS.   How I wish
   Heat like this fire here before me inflamed your lungs, you great
   sham!

HIEROKLES. *If* divine nymphs didn't fool the oracular mind of
   great Bakis,*   1070

   If Bakis fooled not mortals, and *if* nymphs, yea, fooled not
   Bakis—

TRYGAIOS. Death and damnation on you, if you just don't stop
   Bakis-izing!

HIEROKLES. Sanction divine was not given to loose Peace out of her
   bindings,

   Not till—

TRYGAIOS [*to* SLAVE^B]. Please make sure that this meat's well
   seasoned with salt.

HIEROKLES. Ever the fortunate gods up above find this action
    displeasing,
  Ceasing from tumult of battle until wolf and sheep should be
    wedded.
TRYGAIOS. *How*, cursed fool, could it be that a wolf ever wedded a
    sheep?
HIEROKLES. Just as a stinking beetle makes foulest farts when
    escaping,
  Just as a polecat's haste for her birth-pangs leads to blind
    offspring,*
  So, on the very same grounds, it was not yet time to make peace.
TRYGAIOS. *What* was it time, then, to do? To continue fighting the
    war?   1080
  Should we have left it to luck to decide which side came to grief,
  Spurning the chance to make peace and enjoy joint rule over Greece?
HIEROKLES. *Never* success will be yours in making a crab's walk go
    straight.
TRYGAIOS. *Never* oh never again will you dine in the grand
    Prytaneion.*
  Nor will you write mantic verses that postdate events they predict.
HIEROKLES. *Never* at all will you make the rough hedgehog
    transform into smoothness.
TRYGAIOS. *Can* we envisage a day when you no longer trick all of
    Athens?
HIEROKLES. Tell me which oracle warrants this burning of thighs to
    the gods?
TRYGAIOS. None but the finest of all, as composed by the great
    poet Homer:
  'Thus when they'd thrust far away the hostile cloudbank of
    war,   1090
  Peace was the goddess they chose and set up with sacrifice
    splendid.
  Then, when the thigh-bones were burnt and they'd tasted the
    entrails as well,
  Lavish libations they poured from their cups, and I led them the
    way.
  No one, however, gave bright cup of wine to an oracle-monger.'*
HIEROKLES. None of these things I accept; never came they from
    lips of the Sibyl.*

TRYGAIOS. Shrewd though, by Zeus, were the words of the brilliant
　　Homer himself:
　　'Lacking all kinship and law and a hearth is that man whose heart
　　　longs for
　　War of the bitterest kind which consumeth the life of his people.'*
HIEROKLES. Mark thou with care lest thy mind is deceived by a
　　devious swindle
　　Wrought by a kite which then seizes—
TRYGAIOS [*to* SLAVE^B]. 　　　　　　　　You there, better be on
　　your guard now: 　　　　　　　　　　　　　　　　　　　　1100
　　Threats are conveyed by this oracle's words to these entrails
　　　of ours.
　　Pour then libations of wine and bring me some entrails to sample.

[SLAVE^B *follows the instructions just given. In what follows,* HIEROKLES
*decides to join in the peace sacrifice after all, picking up a cup and at-
tempting to get a portion of both wine and meat.*]

HIEROKLES. *Since* you seem set on your plans, I had better look
　　after myself.
TRYGAIOS [*formally*]. Libation! Libation!
HIEROKLES. Wine for me too please dispense, and allow me a
　　portion of entrails.
TRYGAIOS. 'Ever the fortunate gods up above find this action
　　displeasing.'*
　　First must we pour for ourselves, while *you* can just push off
　　elsewhere.
　　[*Praying*] Stay, mistress Peace, with us now, here abide for the rest of
　　our lives.
HIEROKLES. *Give* me the tongue.
TRYGAIOS. 　　　　　　　　　You the tongue? You can take your
　　own tongue somewhere else.
　　Further libation!
SLAVE^B. 　　　　　And here is some meat to go with your libation. 1110
HIEROKLES. *Still* am I entrails denied?
TRYGAIOS. 　　　　　　　　　　　　That's because there's a
　　strong prohibition:
　　Meat we're forbidden to offer 'until wolf and sheep should be
　　wedded'.*

HIEROKLES. *Please*, by your knees I beseech you.
TRYGAIOS.   Beseeching is
        wasting your time.
    Never, you see, 'will you make the rough hedgehog transform into
        smoothness.'*

[*The metre now changes back to that of normal spoken dialogue. In what
follows,* TRYGAIOS *turns to address the audience with a broad gesture, but
is immediately required, with* SLAVE^B*'s help, to use physical force against*
                              HIEROKLES.]

    Come now, spectators, share these entrails here
    With us.
HIEROKLES.   And me?
TRYGAIOS.   You can go and eat the Sibyl!*
HIEROKLES. I swear by Earth you two won't eat them all!
    I'll snatch some from you—it's here for all to share. [*Makes a
        grab*]
TRYGAIOS [*to* SLAVE^B]. Come, batter this Bakis.* [*Strikes him*]
HIEROKLES.   I call for witnesses!
TRYGAIOS. I call a witness that you're a glutton and fraud!   1120
[*To* SLAVE^B] Keep hitting the charlatan hard with this piece of wood.
SLAVE^B. No, you do that, while I peel off these fleeces
    He's managed to get for himself by sheer deceit.*
    Let go of these fleeces, you expert in sacrifice!
TRYGAIOS [*striking*]. Yes, do what he says! [*Starts pulling*]

[*Under attack from both characters,* HIEROKLES *abandons his fleeces but
    struggles free and runs off by the same* eisodos *by which he entered.*]

                                    What a raven that was from
        Oreus!
[*Calling*] Fly away as fast as you can to Elymnion!*

[TRYGAIOS *and* SLAVE^B *now exit into the house, taking the sacrificial
                    meat with them.*]

            [SECOND PARABASIS: 1127–90]
CHORUS.   What delight, what delight,   *Strophe*

To be free of my helmet
And rations of cheese and onions!*
I take no pleasure in battles, 1130
I'd much rather sit by the fire
Quaffing wine with some fellows,
My closest friends, and burning
Some logs that are ready and waiting,
All dried out nicely in summer
On top of my pile of lumber,
And toasting some chickpeas
And roasting sweet acorns
And stealing a kiss with the Thracian maid
While my wife takes her bath!

LEADER. *Nothing* can be as nice as when the farmer's seeds have all
been sown, 1140
Zeus sends down light showers, and then a neighbour comes
along to say:
'Tell me, at this quiet time what shall we do, Komarchides?'*
'Drink our fill, that's my desire, while Zeus is doing his work so
well.
Hey there, wife, let's have some nuts—get toasting plenty on the
fire;
Mix some roasted wheat in too, and fetch some dried figs from the
store.
Let the slave-girl Syra go and summon back Manes from the
fields:*
Out of the question to spend a day like this with work on pruning
vines;
Breaking clods is also out—the ground is far too soaked for
that.'
'*I'll* supply a thrush', he says, 'and a pair of chaffinches from my
house.*
Beestings too I've got at home, as well as four pieces of tender
hare, 1150
All provided that wasn't the weasel that helped herself to those
things last night:*
Noisy commotion I heard from her with something, I'm sure,
inside the house.

Bring us, slave, three pieces of hare, and leave the last for my
    father to eat.
Go and request Aischinades to supply some flowering myrtle
    wreaths.
Let the slave who runs that errand invite Charinades as well:*
            Quaffing with us is what he needs,
            All the while that on our ploughlands
            Zeus himself takes care of things.

CHORUS.   When the cicada sings   *Antistrophe*
            Its lovely melodious tune,   1160
            I take delight in inspecting
            My Lemnian vines,
            To check if they're ripe so soon—
            It's a plant which tends
            To bear fruit early. I also love
            To see the wild fig swelling:
            Then when it's ripe
            I can't stop eating the fruit.
            I cry 'What a gorgeous season!'
            And grind some thyme for a posset.
            And then I grow so plump   1170
            While summer's at its height.

LEADER. Better by far to live like that than face a godforsaken
    officer
Wearing his triple helmet-crests as well as a dazzling scarlet cloak
Dyed, he claims, with dye from Sardis—only the best for him, it
    seems.*
If, however, he has to fight while wearing this scarlet cloak of his,
Then he shows his own true colours and turns himself a shade
    of . . . brown.
He's the first to turn on his heels and flee, just like a tawny
    horse-cock,*
Shaking his crests, while *I* stand firm like someone guarding
    hunting-nets.
Just as bad is how these people behave at home in shocking ways,
Messing around with campaign lists, inserting names, deleting
    others.*   1180

Say that tomorrow an expedition that's been announced is due to
leave:
Here's a fellow who's not had time to buy provisions; he wasn't
informed.*
Just by chance he's standing by the board in front of Pandion's
statue:*
There he sees his name! Dismayed, his face contorted, he scuttles
along.
That's the way they treat us country folk, far more than urban
folk;
Shield-discarding cowards they are, whom gods as well as men
detest!
Held to account they need to be.* I'll make them pay, if god is
willing.

> Many the wrongs they've done to me,
> Men who strut like lions at home,
> But *foxes* once it comes to the fight!   1190

[TRYGAIOS, *wearing a celebratory wreath, comes back out of his house,*
followed by SLAVE[A] *and* SLAVE[B], *who follow his instructions and between*
them bring out tables, a brazier, a cooking-pot, and various items of food
to be prepared for the wedding feast.]

TRYGAIOS [*pointing at audience?*]. Well I never!
What a crowd of guests has arrived for my wedding dinner!
[*To* SLAVE[A]] Here, use this band from my helmet to clean the
tables;
I've certainly got no further use for this.
Then pile the tables with fine milk-cakes and thrushes
And lots of pieces of hare-meat, bread-rolls too.

[*As* TRYGAIOS *starts to oversee the cooking of food by* SLAVE[B], *enter from*
one of the wings a SICKLE-MAKER, *carrying sickles and other objects,*
and a POTTER *who carries a number of wine-jars.*]

SICKLE-MAKER. Now, where will I find Trygaios.
TRYGAIOS.   I'm boiling
thrushes.
SICKLE-MAKER. O dearest friend, Trygaios, how many good things

You've done for us by making peace! In the past
No one would buy a sickle for even a pittance,   1200
But now I can sell each one for fifty drachmas
And this man sells three-drachma jars for farms.
So come, Trygaios, accept some sickles for free
And whichever pots you'd like. Take these as well. [*Hands him gifts*]
From the profits we made from all the goods we sold
We're bringing these things as wedding gifts for you.
TRYGAIOS. Right, leave these things with me and go inside
To join the meal at once. [*Gesturing*] I can see over here
A seller of weapons approaching in great vexation.

[*As the* SICKLE-MAKER *and* POTTER *deposit their various gifts with*
TRYGAIOS *and proceed into his house, there enter from one of the* eisodoi
an ARMS-SELLER, HELMET-MAKER, *and* SPEAR-MAKER, *between*
them carrying a range of military equipment.]

ARMS-SELLER. You've destroyed me root and branch, Trygaios,
    damn you!   1210
TRYGAIOS [*pointing to helmet-crests*]. What's wrong, poor wretch?
    Do you feel a bit *crest-fallen*?
ARMS-SELLER. You've destroyed the whole of my trade and
    livelihood,
    And the same is true for these other two men as well.
TRYGAIOS. How much do you want for these helmet-crests of
    yours?
ARMS-SELLER. How much will you offer?
TRYGAIOS.   How much? I'm rather
    embarrassed.
    But since there's plenty of workmanship in the base,
    I'll give three measures of figs for the pair of crests.
    I'll use one of them to wipe the table clean.
ARMS-SELLER. Then go in your house and bring me out the figs:
    This swap is better than nothing at all, old chap. [*Gives him
    crests*]   1220
TRYGAIOS [*inspecting*]. Away, away from my house with this rotten
    rubbish!
    They're shedding their horsehair—utterly trashy, these crests!

They're not even worth the price of a single fig.

ARMS-SELLER. But what will I do with this ample ten-mina
 breastplate?*

It's beautifully fitted together. I can't discard it.

TRYGAIOS. This needn't result in a loss of income for you.

 You can sell me this for the price you paid yourself.

[*Sits on it*] It's perfectly shaped to use for doing a crap—

ARMS-SELLER. Stop treating me and my goods with such
 contempt!

TRYGAIOS [*miming*]. With three stones here to wipe with: isn't that
 neat?*   1230

ARMS-SELLER. But how will you manage to wipe? Don't be so
 stupid!

TRYGAIOS [*inserting his arms*]. With one hand here inserted through
 the... oar-hole

And the other one here.

ARMS-SELLER.   Both sides at once?

TRYGAIOS.   That's right!

[*As if rowing*] I mustn't be caught taking pay without pulling my
 oar.*

ARMS-SELLER. So you mean to sit and shit on a ten-mina corslet?

TRYGAIOS. That's certainly right, by Zeus, you miserable clod!

 D'you think I'd sell my arse for a thousand drachmas?

ARMS-SELLER. Then bring me out the money.

TRYGAIOS [*standing up*].   I'm sorry, my friend,

 It's chafing my rump. Take it back—I don't want to buy it.

ARMS-SELLER. Well what am I going to do with this trumpet
 here?   1240

 It cost me sixty drachmas to buy it myself.

TRYGAIOS [*demonstrating*]. You could pour some lead inside this
 hollow part here,

Then stick inside a longish rod right here,

And you'll find you've got a knock-down kottabos stand!*

ARMS-SELLER. You're making fun of me.

TRYGAIOS.   I've another suggestion.

 First, pour in the lead, the way I said before;

[*Miming*] Then using some little cords attach a scale-pan

From this other end—and there'll you have what's needed

To weigh out figs for your slaves in the countryside.

ARMS-SELLER [*melodramatically*]. O pestilential spirit, you ruined
    my life   1250
  When I paid as much as a mina for these scabbards.*
  What hope have I now? Who'll buy these things from me?
TRYGAIOS. You should go and find an Egyptian buyer for these:
  They're perfect for measuring radish-juice for purges.*
ARMS-SELLER. O helmet-maker, what miserable fate is ours!
TRYGAIOS. Well *he's* not suffered a thing.
ARMS-SELLER.   But what's the need
  For helmets now? Nobody has use for them.

[TRYGAIOS *approaches the* HELMET-MAKER *and pulls his large ears.*]

TRYGAIOS. If he learns to give them handles just like these,
  He'll sell them far more easily than now.
ARMS-SELLER. Let's go, spear-maker.
TRYGAIOS.   No, no, you mustn't go
    yet: 1260
  I'll buy these spears of his for myself, I will.
ARMS-SELLER. What price will you pay?
TRYGAIOS.   If you saw them down the
    middle,
  I'll convert them into vine-poles—a drachma per hundred.*
ARMS-SELLER. He's treating us with contempt. Let's go, old chaps.

[*Exit* ARMS-SELLER, HELMET-MAKER, *and* SPEAR-MAKER. *As they
    depart from the* eisodos *from which they earlier entered, two
    children,* BOY[A] *and* BOY[B], *come out of door A.*]

TRYGAIOS. By Zeus, here come some children out of my house:
  They belong to the guests and are coming outside to piss
  And then rehearse, I imagine, the songs that they'll sing.
[*To* BOY[A]] Whatever the song you're meaning to sing, my boy,
  Come and stand right by me here and rehearse it first.

[*While* BOY[B] *hangs around in the background,* BOY[A] *stands by* TRYGAIOS
*and starts to chant in the dactylic hexameters of epic; as in the earlier case
of oracles (1063 ff.),* TRYGAIOS *assimilates his response to the rhythm of
    the poetry quoted.*]

BOY^A [*chanting*]. 'First let us sing of the warriors youthful who—'*

TRYGAIOS. Stop
    this at once! 1270
  Songs of a warrior class are the last thing we want here, you
    wretch,
  Not now peace is restored. What a clueless, accursed thing you are!

BOY^A. '*Then* when the armies approached and came face-to-face
    with each other,
  Shield clashed on shield with the thunderous thud of their oxhide
    and bosses.'*

TRYGAIOS. *Shields*, did you say? I forbid you to make any mention
  of war shields.

BOY^A. 'Then there arose lamentations and desperate prayers from
  the soldiers.'*

TRYGAIOS. Soldiers lamenting, was that? You'll soon get a beating, I
  swear it,
  Singing of lamentations—and bossed lamentations at that!

BOY^A. *What*, then, should furnish my song? Please tell me the
  things you enjoy.

TRYGAIOS. 'Thus did they feast on the meat of the cattle'—and
  things of that sort. 1280
  'Breakfast they placed on the tables and loveliest foods to be
    tasted.'

BOY^A. 'Thus did they feast on the meat of the cattle, untying their
  horses,
  Horses now covered in sweat, since sated with warfare they were.'*

[*For the next two lines,* TRYGAIOS *returns to the metre of ordinary speech,
before* BOY^A's *singing pulls him back into epic hexameters.*]

TRYGAIOS. Good! They were sated with war, then started to eat.
  Sing all about that, how they ate even though they were sated!

BOY^A. 'After a pause they prepared for the hard stuff—'

TRYGAIOS. And gladly,
  I warrant!

BOY^A. 'Forth from the ramparts they poured, and immense was the
  cry that arose.'*

[TRYGAIOS *again reverts to the iambic metre of ordinary speech.*]

TRYGAIOS. Oh damn you, boy, with all this talk of battles.
    You sing about nothing but war. So *whose* son are you?
BOY^A. You're asking *me*?
TRYGAIOS.   Yes, you!
BOY^A.   I'm Lamachos' son.*   1290
TRYGAIOS. Ugh!
[*Chanting parodically*] Puzzled I was, as I listened, concerning whose
    son you might be:
    Only a war-yearning, war-grieving father was yours, I surmised.
[*Speaking*] Get out of here! Go and sing for spear-bearing men!

[BOY^A *runs off down one of the* eisodoi, *while* TRYGAIOS *turns his atten-
    tion to* BOY^B, *who is on the point of going back into the house.*]

TRYGAIOS. I need to find Kleonymos' son instead.*
[*To* BOY^B] Stay here a moment and sing for me. I'm sure
    Your song won't be about strife—your father shirks it!
BOY^B [*chanting*]. 'One of the Thracians now proudly possesses that
    shield that was mine,
                A splendid object I left, unwillingly, by a bush.'
TRYGAIOS [*chanting*]. Tell me, my little willy, is this song about your
    own father?   1300
BOY^B. 'Thus did I keep my life safe—'
TRYGAIOS.   '—but exposed your own
    parents to shame!'*
[*Speaking*] Let's go inside. I've got no doubt at all
    That the song you sang just now about the shield
    Is one you'll remember well, in view of your father. [*Exit* BOY^B]

[TRYGAIOS *now turns to the* CHORUS, *whom he invites to the feast in
    facetiously colourful terms and recitative metre.*]

    It's now the task for all of you, while remaining in this place,
    To crush this food inside your mouths; no resting on your oars.
                Attack the task with manly vigour
    And grind away with both your jaws. There's no use here, you
        wretches,   1310
    For teeth that look all gleaming white, unless they do some
        chewing! [*Exits*]

LEADER. We'll take good care of all these things; it's good of you to
    tell us.

[*To* CHORUS] Come you, who were short of food before, get stuck
    into this hare-meat.

            It isn't every day, for sure,

  We come across cakes that lack a home and offer no resistance!

  Get munching away: if you don't, I swear, you'll soon be full of
    regret.

[TRYGAIOS *reappears in the doorway of his house, now wearing the special cloak of a bridegroom; the following lines start with recitative (up to
1330), then break into an exchange of full song with the* CHORUS.]

TRYGAIOS [*solemnly*]. Keep ritual silence in this place while the
    bride's escorted here.

Bring torches too and let the throng rejoice and shout their
    cheers.

Let all of you go back to the fields, and take your equipment with
    you.   1320

But first you must dance and pour libations and banish
    Hyperbolos,*

            And pray to all the gods above
            To grant the Greeks abundant wealth
            And bumper crops of barley grain
            For all alike, and much wine too,
            And figs to nibble,
            And healthy offspring born to our wives
            And a chance to recover the good things we lost
            And replenish our stocks of them once more,
            But abolish the weapons of war.   1330

[TRYGAIOS *now steps out of the doorway, together with* HARVEST, *costumed as a bride. In what follows, bride and bridegroom process across the*
orchêstra, *with the* CHORUS *(which splits into two groups for part of the
procession) accompanying them and, at 1344, lifting* TRYGAIOS *onto
their shoulders.*]

[*Singing*]   Come with me, wife, to the country
               And prepare to lie beside me

In all your gorgeous beauty.

CHORUS. Hail Hymen, Hail Hymenaios!*
Hail Hymen, Hail Hymenaios!

[*To* TRYGAIOS] Happiest of men, how right it is
That prosperity is yours.
Hail Hymen, Hail Hymenaios!
Hail Hymen, Hail Hymenaios!

CHORUS^A. What shall we do with her? 1340
CHORUS^B. What shall we do with her?
CHORUS^A. Gather her fruit!*
CHORUS^B. Gather her fruit!
CHORUS^A. Let's lift and carry the bridegroom,
Those of us standing at the front,
Let's do this now, my men!

CHORUS. Hail Hymen, Hail Hymenaios!
Hail Hymen, Hail Hymenaios!
...* 1350
Hail Hymen, Hail Hymenaios!
Hail Hymen, Hail Hymenaios!

TRYGAIOS. You'll all live happily now,
Your existence free from trouble,
With lots of time to gather your figs.

CHORUS. Hail Hymen, Hail Hymenaios!
Hail Hymen, Hail Hymenaios!
His organ's big and thick,
And her . . . fig's extremely nice. 1360

TRYGAIOS. Just wait till you're eating your fruit
And washing it down with wine!

CHORUS. Hail Hymen, Hail Hymenaios!
Hail Hymen, Hail Hymenaios!

[*To audience*] Farewell, farewell now, men!
If you follow along with me,
You too can eat some cakes! [*Exit all in high spirits.*]

EXPLANATORY NOTES

The Explanatory Notes are designed to provide concise explanations of historical, literary, and other details which might puzzle a modern reader. Fuller
information about most points can be found in the commentaries cited in the
Bibliography. The following abbreviations are occasionally used in the notes:

IEG *Iambi et Elegi Graeci*, ed. M. L. West, 2nd edn., 2 vols. (Oxford,
   1989–92)
OCD⁴ *The Oxford Classical Dictionary*, ed. S. Hornblower and
   A. Spawforth, 4th edn. (Oxford, 2012)
PMG *Poetae Melici Graeci*, ed. D. L. Page (Oxford, 1962)

THE fragments of comic and tragic poets are cited according to the numbering
in the following editions:

Poetae Comici Graeci, ed. R. Kassel and C. Austin (Berlin, 1984–)
Tragicorum Graecorum Fragmenta, ed. B. Snell et al. (Göttingen, 1971–2004)

Aristophanes' play titles are abbreviated as follows:

A.	Acharnians
AW	Assembly-Women
B.	Birds
C.	Clouds
F.	Frogs
K.	Knights
L.	Lysistrata
P.	Peace
W.	Wasps
We.	Wealth
WT	Women at the Thesmophoria

ACHARNIANS

6–8 *Kleon . . . Hellas*: we do not know the details of this supposed clash between
 Kleon (see Index of Names) and the Knights, who formed one of the richest classes of Athenians and provided the city's cavalry corps; cf. 301. If it
 was historical (though some think it might only have been a scene in comedy, perhaps in Aristophanes' *Babylonians*: see n. on 378), it is more likely
 to have involved the exposure of an act of financial corruption than the
 judicial imposition of a fine on Kleon. The sum of money in the Greek,
 five talents (one talent = 6,000 drachmas; cf. n. on 67), is extremely high
 (a single talent would be much more than the total wealth of most individual citizens: see *B.* 154); see the same amount at *K.* 829, with the even
 bigger sums at e.g. *K.* 438, *W.* 669. For the metaphor 'vomit', cf. *K.* 1148

and the related image at *K*. 404. The quotation in line 8 is a half-line from Euripides' *Telephos* (fr. 720); see n. on 430.

11 *Theognis*: a minor tragic poet; cf. 140 and *WT* 170. Dikaiopolis describes waiting for the start of a tragedy in the theatre; he was hoping for a revival of a play by the long-dead Aischylos (*c.*525–456): such revivals did sometimes take place, but Dikaiopolis's hope probably sounds naive (cf. Strepsiades' old-fashioned taste for Aischylos at *C*. 1365–6).

13–14 *Moschos…Dexitheos*: unknown musicians; we cannot explain Dikaiopolis's preference between them. Boiotian here refers to a traditional melody.

16 *Chairis*: consistently treated in Aristophanes as an embarrassingly bad pipe-player; see 866, *P*. 950–5, *B*. 858. The traditional tune mentioned here is the same one as at *K*. 1279. Dikaiopolis implies that Chairis gyrated while playing.

22 *crimson rope*: used to encourage people in the Agora to attend the Assembly; fines may have been imposed on those stained by the dye on the rope, though the whole arrangement is uncertain. The rope was later used to keep people *out* of the Assembly: see *AW* 379.

23 *Prytaneis*: see Index of Names.

27 '*O city! O city!*': a (mock-)solemn exclamation; compare 75 and *We*. 601. The same words occur in Sophokles, *Oedipus Tyrannus* 629, but that does not make the present passage a quotation.

32–3 *gazing…urban life*: from the Pnyx one could look out northwards beyond the city walls, in the direction of the Attic countryside. Dikaiopolis, as a displaced farmer (cf. my Introduction to the play), contrasts the traditional ways of his rural deme with the highly commercial life of the urban centre of Athens.

38 *To barrack…*: see e.g. *AW* 248 ff., together with the highly evocative picture at Plato, *Republic* 6.492b–c, for heckling and noisy abuse in the Athenian Assembly.

43 *sacred ground*: meetings of the Assembly were preceded by a ritual purification of the location.

46 *Amphitheos*: this real but very rare name means lit. 'god on both sides'. The genealogy that follows is a jumble of mythological and contemporary Athenian names; Triptolemos and Keleos were legendary kings of Eleusis involved in dealings with Demeter (see Index of Names) which led to the founding of the Eleusinian Mysteries (n. on 747), while Phainarete was, among other things, the name of Sokrates' mother. There is no reason to suppose that the audience was expected to identify Amphitheos as a real person.

61 *Persian king*: both Athens and Sparta had intermittently sought Persian assistance since the start of the war; cf. Thucydides 2.7, with 4.50 for (ineffectual) dealings with Persia in the winter of 425–424. But as line 67 shows, there is no direct reference to current negotiations. Cf. *K*. 478–9.

63 *peacocks*: at least one contemporary aristocrat was known to keep peacocks in an aviary; but the bird is also a symbol of strutting pretentiousness. Cf. *B.* 102, 269.

64 *Persian posers*: the Greek uses an exclamation, 'O Ekbatana'; for this city, the Persian king's summer residence, cf. *K.* 1089, *W.* 1143–4.

67 *Euthymenes*: eponymous Archon (Index of Names) in 437/6, i.e. eleven years previously; the ambassadors' absence has been preposterously long. Two drachmas is a very high rate of daily pay: cf. 160 and compare nn. on 159–60, 162–3.

68–70 *Kaÿstrian…cushioned*: part of the ambassadors' supposed journey to distant Susa (n. 80–2) follows the river Kaÿster, NE of Ephesos; the type of luxurious carriage envisaged had some association with aristocratic Persian women.

72 *walls*: Dikaiopolis speaks either as a country-dweller forced into temporary accommodation in the city (cf. *K.* 792–3) or, more likely, as someone doing garrison duty on the city walls (see Thucydides 2.13.6–7).

75 *unmixed*: denoting excess and decadence; Greeks themselves standardly drank wine mixed with water. Cf. 1229, *K.* 85, 354.

79 *For us…*: Dikaiopolis assimilates Athenian politicians, in standard comic fashion, to a stereotype of passive homosexual behaviour which equates them with male prostitutes; cf. n. on *K.* 426.

80–2 *palace…Mountains*: the king of Persia's palace was at Susa; the idea of Golden Mountains plays on a standard Greek association of the Persians with gold (cf. 102–3, 113), but there may also be an innuendo that the mountains are the colour of faeces.

87 *oven-baked oxen*: attested, in fact, as a Persian practice at Herodotos 1.133.1.

89 *Kleonymos*: see Index of Names.

92 *Eye*: the title of an important Persian official; cf. Aischylos, *Persians* 979, Herodotos 1.114.2. The made-up Greek name Pseudartabas suggests 'false measure'; it plays on the real Persian name Artabazos (cf. Thucydides 1.129.1).

95 *warship*: Greek warships (triremes: n. on 162–3) sometimes had large painted eyes on their prows.

97 *leather flap*: the visual point is uncertain; it may refer to swathing round Pseudartabas's mouth. Leather flaps were fitted round the lower oar-ports on a trireme; Dikaiopolis is therefore combining images from two different parts of a warship.

100 *iarta…satra*: scholars have attempted to reconstruct elements of genuine Old Persian in this line, but it will evidently have sounded gibberish to most of Aristophanes' audience.

104 *Ionee*: the term Ionian (see n. on *P.* 46–8) was applied by the Persians to Greeks in general.

112 *Sardis*: the former capital of Lydia and at this date a regional centre of the Persian empire; cf. *W.* 1139, *P.* 1174.

113 *nods*: the Greek head-movement for 'no' was (and is) an upward or 'backward' nod.

118 *Kleisthenes*: see Index of Names. One known Sibyrtios owned a wrestling-school; the patronymic may therefore be ironic for the allegedly effeminate Kleisthenes.

119–20 '*O you...o ape*': Dikaiopolis distorts two quotations, from Euripides (fr. 858) and Archilochos (fr. 187 *IEG*), to make a gibe at Kleisthenes' allegedly pathic sexual nature.

122 *Straton*: an associate of Kleisthenes; they are paired again at *K.* 1374.

125 *Prytaneion*: see Index of Names.

134 *Theoros...Sitalkes*: Theoros is probably the associate of Kleon's mentioned at *K.* 608, *C.* 400, *W.* (esp.) 42–51, 1220–42. Sitalkes was a Thracian king with whom Athens had had an alliance, 431–428; see under Thrace in the Index of Names.

140 *Theognis*: cf. 11.

143–4 *lover...handsome*: 'lover' echoes a metaphor fashionable in Athenian politics; see n. on *K.* 732. But Sitalkes (next n.) goes further: he behaves like a homosexual suitor writing graffiti about his beloved; such graffiti survive on many Greek drinking cups in the form 'X is beautiful/handsome (*kalos*)'. Cf. *W.* 97–9.

145–7 *son...homeland*: Sitalkes' son, Sadokos, made an honorary Athenian citizen in 431, speaks like a true-born, not an adopted, Athenian. The Apatouria was a festival at which new citizens were introduced; cf. *WT* 558.

150 *locusts*: for their status as an agricultural pest, cf. *B.* 588.

156 *Odomantian*: the Odomantians were, as it happens, a Thracian tribe *outside* Sitalkes' kingdom; see Thucydides 2.101.3.

158 *pricks*: the Odomantians' phalluses may have been represented as circumcised, even though this was not a Thracian practice; alternatively, they are (perceived by Dikaiopolis as) aggressively erect. Some Greeks perceived circumcision as ugly (cf. Herodotos 2.37.2) and perhaps sexually enfeebling; cf. *K.* 964.

159–60 *These men...Boiotia*: the proposed rate of pay for the mercenaries is very high (cf. next n.); for Boiotia, see Index of Names.

162–3 *rowers...city-saving*: even the best rowers (the top deck) on Athens' triremes (warships with a triple bank of oarsmen) might be paid only one drachma a day for service; see Thucydides 6.31.3, and cf. the lower rate at *W.* 1189. Athens' fleet was the most important part of its military resources; many of the rowers were poorer citizens and hence the crews could easily be thought of as representing the people in general. Cf. *K.* 1065–6, 1366–7, *W.* 909.

166 *fighting cocks*: an established Greek 'sport'; the birds were fed garlic with the aim of making them more aggressive (cf. *K.* 493–7).

171 *omen...rain*: an Assembly meeting could be ended by an 'omen' such as an earthquake (Thucydides 5.45.4) or perhaps by extreme weather events (cf. the ambiguous implications of *C.* 581–7); but the present passage is, of course, an absurd parody of such procedures.

174 *garlic paste*: made from garlic, cheese, honey, leeks, and oil; cf. *K.* 771, *W.* 63, *P.* 242–54.

181 *Marathon veterans*: a comic sobriquet for reactionary old Athenians (cf. *C.* 986); any real survivors from the battle of Marathon (Index of Names) would have been at least nonagenarians by the date of this play.

183 *vines*: Spartan invasions during the early years of the Peloponnesian War had ravaged vineyards in N Attika as well as other rural property; cf. 512, and see the Introduction to the play.

187 *vintages*: the Greek for peace treaty (*spondai*) means lit. 'libations (of wine)'; treaties of different duration are thus comically reified as vintages.

190 *pitch*: used to waterproof wine-jars and occasionally added to wine, but also applied to ships' timbers.

196–7 *ambrosia...rations*: ambrosia (*K.* 1095, *P.* 724, 854) and nectar were the gods' food and drink; soldiers called up for service were sometimes required to bring three days' rations with them (cf. *P.* 312, 1182, and the joke at *W.* 243).

202 *Rural Dionysia*: celebrated in various demes of Attika during (approximately) December.

214 *Phaÿllos*: a famous athlete of half a century earlier; cf. *W.* 1206 for similar humour.

225 *he's made*: the object of the Chorus's pursuit tacitly slips from Amphitheos, who carried the peace treaty, to Dikaiopolis, its proponent and beneficiary.

242 *basket-girl*: girls from (normally) leading families ceremonially carried baskets on their heads in sacrificial processions at various Athenian festivals; cf. *B.* 1551, *L.* 646, 1193, *AW* 732.

257 *crowds*: Dikaiopolis fantasizes that his procession is part of a full deme festival, packed with onlookers, rather than a private event.

261 *phallic song*: Aristotle, in *Poetics* ch. 4 (1449a11–12), identified phallic songs as the cultural starting-point of comic drama; see the general Introduction, 'Aristophanes' Career in Context'.

268 *sixth year*: since the outbreak of the war in 431; cf. 890.

270 *Lamachos-types*: Lamachos's name is pluralized to play on its etymology (lit. 'very warlike'), as again at 1071; see Index of Names and my Introduction to the play.

301 *Knights*: see n. on 6–8 with the Introduction to *Knights*. The passage is usually taken as looking ahead to that play itself, though this is not a necessary

inference and it would certainly have been difficult for the original audience to understand it that way.

308 *Can't be trusted . . .* : a standard Athenian stereotype of the Spartans as perfidious; cf. *P.* 217–18, 623, 1063–8, *L.* 169, 629, 1270, with Thucydides 5.105.4.

318 *butcher's block*: this idea, physically enacted at 366 ff., is the literalization of a metaphor in Euripides' *Telephos* (nn. on 331 and 430), where Telephos refers hypothetically (and hyperbolically) to a situation in which someone is holding an axe above his neck (fr. 706).

331 *child*: the scene which follows is a parody of a scene from Euripides' *Telephos* (n. on 430) in which the eponymous hero threatened the baby Orestes; Aristophanes parodies the scene again at *WT* 689–764, where the kidnapped 'baby' turns out to be a wineskin. Note that in Euripides' play the scene in question is *later* than the speech parodied in Dikaiopolis's speech at 497 ff.

348–9 *Parnes . . . demesmen*: part of the Acharnai deme was adjacent to the mountain range of Parnes (cf. *C.* 323) at the NW border of Attika.

357 *'And yet . . .'*: the line may be a quotation from tragedy.

377–8 *Kleon . . . comedy*: Dikaiopolis suddenly speaks in the voice of Aristophanes himself; the reference is to Kleon's political harassment of the playwright after the staging of *Babylonians* in the previous year (see my Introduction to the play).

388–90 *Hieronymos . . . Hades*: Hieronymos is probably the dithyrambic poet mocked as hirsute at *C.* 349; the helmet of Hades (see Index of Names), a magical mythological device which conferred invisibility (e.g. Homer, *Iliad* 5.845), is here apparently a hyperbole for Hieronymos's thick head of hair.

391 *Sisyphean*: Sisyphos was a notorious mythological trickster, capable even of cheating death (though eventually given a symbolic punishment in Hades of attempting eternally to push a boulder uphill), and sometimes regarded as the father of Odysseus.

396 *Not at home . . .* : the Slave's speech reflects a supposedly Euripidean penchant for paradox; for related humour, see *F.* 1477–8.

405 *if . . . before*: a humorous adaptation of an old and standard formula in prayers to the gods; for a famous instance, see Sappho's *Hymn to Aphrodite* (fr. 1), line 5.

406 *Cholleidai*: the location of this deme is disputed but was probably in N Attika; its combination with a name derived from a unique Pindaric adj. (*Pythian* 8.22) is itself a piquant piece of comedy.

408 *trolley*: the *ekkuklêma*, a device for presenting interior scenes on stage in tragedy; compare the emergence of Peace's statue from the cave at *P.* 509 ff., Agathon's entrance and exit at *WT* 96 and 265, and see the general Introduction, 'Stage Directions'. There is a further parodic reference to the device at *K.* 1249.

411 *lame*: for this exaggerated notion of a Euripidean liking for crippled heroes, cf. *P.* 146–8, *F.* 846.

418–19 *Oineus...role*: Euripides speaks of Oineus as simultaneously a mythological figure and a theatrical role. Oineus was originally king of Kalydon but later expelled and maltreated by his brother, before being assisted to take revenge by his grandson Diomedes: the full plot of Euripides' play is uncertain.

421–2 *Blind...Phoinix*: Euripides' version of Phoinix's story diverged from the famous one at Homer, *Iliad* 9.447–84, by having him blinded and exiled by his father Amyntor on a false accusation of rape.

424 *Philoktetes*: Euripides' version of the story (now best known from Sophokles' *Philoktetes*) of the crippled hero abandoned by the Greeks on the island of Lemnos was staged in 431.

427 *Bellerophon*: a Korinthian hero who attempted to fly up to Olympos on the winged horse Pegasos but was fatally wounded when Zeus threw him from the horse; see nn. on *K.* 1249, *W.* 751–7, *P.* 76–7. Bellerophon's 'lameness' may allude to the fact that in Euripides' play he was carried on stage with his legs broken (cf. *P.* 146–7) or possibly to the hero's miserable state, after a period of wandering, at the start of the play.

430 *Telephos*: king of Mysia who was wounded by Achilles' spear (during an abortive first Greek expedition against Troy) and came to Greece disguised as a beggar to seek a cure, as an oracle had advised him, from the one who had wounded him. Cf. nn. on 8 and 331, with further nn. below. Euripides' play had been staged as long ago as 438; Aristophanes' audience can hardly have had intimate familiarity with its text. But it continued to exercise fascination for Aristophanes in later plays too: see nn. on *K.* 813, 1240, *WT* 466 (with *Frogs and Other Plays*, pp. 94–5), *F.* 855.

433–4 *Thyestes...Ino*: Euripides wrote more than one play which dealt with the story of Thyestes, who seduced his brother Atreus's wife and was later tricked by Atreus into eating the cooked flesh of his own children; he also spent time (twice) in exile, a possible context for the wearing of rags. In Euripides' *Ino*, the eponymous heroine, first wife of the Thessalian king Athamas, was disguised in rags to conceal her identity from Athamas's second wife, Themisto. Cf. n. on *W.* 1414.

439 *cap*: Telephos's felt cap must have been a highly incongruous piece of costume for an Athenian tragedy.

440–1 *I need...appear*: a slightly altered quotation from Euripides' *Telephos* (fr. 698).

440–4 *I need*: Dikaiopolis makes his point with a kind of twisted metatheatricality, treating himself as both character and performer and likewise with the chorus. See my Introduction to the play. For the obscene gesture referred to, see n. on *P.* 549.

446 *'And for Telephos...'*: Euripides fr. 707, possibly from the speech (n. on 430) where the disguised Telephos himself was deceiving the Greeks.

453 *basket*: the Euripidean Telephos used a damaged wicker basket for his beggar's possessions.

457 *mother*: Euripides' mother was the target of recurrent comic jibes, including the suggestion that she had been a vegetable-seller in the market; see 478, *K*. 19, *WT* 387, *F*. 840.

461 *defects*: perhaps delivered aside; in any case, a vague insult which should not be interpreted as some deep Aristophanic critique of Euripidean tragedy.

463 *pot*: probably the vessel in which the Euripidean Telephos kept ointment for his wound.

470 *plays*: it may be that Euripides hands Dikaiopolis, as metaphorical leaves, some of the papyrus rolls on which his plays are written.

472 *'Though...'*: the line is Euripidean (fr. 568.2), though there is uncertainty about its source.

478 *maternal*: see n. on 457.

480–8 *O heart...heart*: an elaborately parodic play on traditional poetic forms of self-address; see e.g. *Odyssey* 20.18–21, with Euripidean examples at *Medea* 1242–50, *Iphigeneia in Tauris* 344, *Orestes* 466.

497–9 *Please...city*: 497–8 are adapted from Euripides' *Telephos* (fr. 703). 'Wine-song', here and in 500 (cf. 886, with *W*. 650, 1537), is a comic term for comedy itself; it is etymologically related to the protagonist's name Trygaios in *Peace* (n. on *P*. 190).

500–1 *right*: the same vocabulary recurs in the parabasis at 645, 655, 661; see my Introduction to the play.

502–3 *Kleon...visitors*: see n. on 377–8. *Babylonians* had been produced at the City Dionysia, when many visitors, including allied ambassadors (bringing payment of their cities' annual tribute: cf. 643), were present in Athens; *Acharnians* itself was produced at the Lenaia: for the two festivals, see the general Introduction, 'Old Comedy and Dionysiac Festivity'.

508 *metics*: resident aliens; cf. *K*. 347, *P*. 297.

510–11 *god...earthquake*: there was a temple of Poseidon, god of earthquakes, at Tainaron, the central southern tip of the Peloponnese; cf. *F*. 187. Sparta had suffered a notoriously bad earthquake in 465 (Thucydides 1.101.2), and various parts of Greece had experienced earthquakes in the summer (426) prior to *Acharnians* (Thucydides 3.87.4, 89.1).

512 *vines*: see n. on 183.

515–22 *Some men...resold*: for comparison of people to coinage (517–18), compare the elaborate analogy at *F*. 720–6. We have no independent evidence for this emergent economic conflict between Athens and Megara (see Index of Names) in the lead-up to the Megarian decree (n. on 530–4), though we know from Thucydides 1.67.4 that there were numerous complaints on the Megarian side. Among the types of goods mentioned as Megarian specialities, cf. *P.* 1002 for clothing; piglets will be important in the Megarian scene at 729 ff.; for Megarian garlic, see 761–3 with n. on *P.* 247.

524–7 *young men … Aspasia*: the present passage might have reminded anyone familiar with the work of Herodotos of his account (1.1–5) of the antecedents of the Persian Wars in the supposed history of thefts of women between Greeks and barbarians. Aspasia was the mistress of Perikles; her assimilation here to a 'madam' is wildly scurrilous. The Megarian 'theft' in question may be a comically grotesque distortion of the harbouring of runaway slaves of which the Athenians complain at Thucydides 1.139.2.

530–4 *Perikles … mainland*: the Megarian decree (highlighted at Thucydides 1.67.2 and 139, but without explanation of its origins) was probably passed some time in 433–432; its banning of the Megarians from Athens and its imperial markets is here exaggerated into a world-wide ban that uses the language of a drinking song by Timokreon of Rhodes (731 *PMG*, also perhaps echoed at *K.* 610). How much Perikles had to do with the passing of the Megarian decree, we do not know; but he was chiefly responsible for persuading the Athenians not to revoke it (Thucydides 1.140.3–5). Cf. *P.* 608–11 for a different comic perspective on the decree.

540 *Someone …* : adapted from a line in Euripides' *Telephos* (fr. 708).

541–3 *Well suppose … think so*: the counterfactual scenario owes something to Euripides' *Telephos*; the second half of 541 has been speculatively assigned as Euripides fr. **708a, and line 543 quotes fr. 709. Seriphos is a tiny island in the Cyclades; though a member of the Athenian empire, it is chosen for its nugatory status (cf. the same nuance at Plato, *Republic* 1.329e–30a).

546–51 *clamour … black eyes*: a vivid evocation of preparations for a major naval expedition; a trierarch was a citizen required (as a public service) to pay for the maintenance of a trireme (cf. *K.* 912–18); the echoing porticoes may allude to the barley-market stoa (n. on *K.* 857); in addition to the sale/stocking of provisions, line 551 seems to envisage drinking parties (hence the pipe-girls: cf. e.g. *W.* 1219) which degenerate into brawls.

556 *Telephos*: Dikaiopolis returns to his role as would-be disguised Telephos; the end of his speech quotes Euripides fr. 710.

568 *tribesman*: a member of the same official Athenian 'tribe' (one of ten), Oe, to which the deme Acharnai belonged.

574 *Gorgon*: for the head of a Gorgon (Index of Names) as an emblem on a shield, cf. *P.* 561, *L.* 560.

577 *Besmirching …* : another quotation from Euripides' *Telephos* (fr. 712); the following line has also been speculatively assigned to the play (fr. **712a).

592 *foreskin*: Dikaiopolis ironically suggests that Lamachos should use his masculine prowess to overcome him like a homoerotic suitor seeking maximum arousal.

593 *general*: Lamachos was possibly not a serving general at the date of this play; he may be self-regardingly speaking as someone who has held that office in the past.

598 *three cuckoos*: Dikaiopolis implies that the Assembly meeting at which Lamachos was elected may have been thinly attended (cf. 19–22).

601 *younger men*: Lamachos was probably 40 or more in 425, but could still be treated as relatively young in comparison to Dikaiopolis and the chorus.

602–6 *Thrace...Sicily*: on Thrace, see 136 ff., with the Index of Names; Teisamenos, Phainippos, Geres, and Theodoros cannot be securely identified; the Chaonians (cf. *K.* 78) were a non-Greek tribe in NW Greece (see Thucydides 2.80–2 for their cooperation with Sparta earlier in the war); Athens was engaged in a number of military and diplomatic activities in Sicily at this date (see Thucydides 3.86, 90, 115, with n. on *W.* 240).

609 *Marilades*: an invented name, based on the word for coal-dust (cf. 350). The Greek has three more invented names in 612.

614 *Koisyra*: the name belonged to one or more women in the aristocratic family of the Alkmaionidai; cf. *C.* 48. It is unclear whether 'the son of Koisyra' is an identifiable individual (some have suspected it means Alkibiades: n. on 716) or just a stereotype. Dikaiopolis is in any case disparaging elite Athenians who obtain paid work as ambassadors but are dissolute in their personal lives.

620 *Peloponnesian foes*: i.e. Sparta (Index of Names).

627 *anapaests*: the first part of the parabasis is often composed in the anapaestic metre; cf. *K.* 504, *P.* 735, *B.* 684. See the general Introduction, 'Formality and Performance'. It is uncertain whether the reference to the chorus's shedding of their cloaks is to be taken literally or as a conventional motif.

628–9 *trainer...skilful*: although the chorus-trainer (*didaskalos*), i.e. producer/director, of *Acharnians* was Kallistratos, not Aristophanes himself, the whole of the present passage refers to the latter, since it treats the *didaskalos* as equivalent to the playwright (633), as was more often than not the case in practice; cf. n. on *P.* 737–8, and see the general Introduction, 'Aristophanes' Career in Context'. The Greek verb for 'step forward' here is cognate with the noun *parabasis*; cf. *K.* 508, *P.* 735, *WT* 785.

637–9 *'violet-wreathed' ... 'gleaming'*: both epithets were applied to Athens by Pindar fr. 76; for the second, see also Pindar, *Isthmian* 2.20. The implication is not necessarily that political speakers quoted Pindar but that they resorted to equivalently extravagant eulogy of the city in pursuit of their aims. For Athens as 'violet-wreathed', cf. *K.* 1323; for the combination of 'violet-wreathed' with 'gleaming', see *K.* 1329.

642 *democracy*: the reference, as throughout 630–42, is to *Babylonians* (n. on 377–8) but the exact point at issue remains uncertain; see my Introduction to the play.

643 *tribute...what's right*: for tribute, see 505–6; for the self-image of the poet as telling 'what's right', cf. 500–1, 655, and *K.* 510.

652–4 *Spartans...poet*: Aigina had been incorporated into the Athenian empire in 458–457. We do not know for certain the connection between Aristophanes and Aigina, but the likely implication is that he possessed property there, possibly as one of the settlers installed by Athens after it took over the island in 431 (Thucydides 2.27). Thucydides 1.139.1 (cf. 1.67.2) records a Spartan demand regarding Aigina just before the outbreak of war in 431; the present passage cannot be reliably taken as evidence for a specific recurrence of the issue, which may therefore be a partial fiction.

660 *against me*: the Chorus Leader, like Dikaiopolis at 377–82 and 502–3, now momentarily speaks in the voice of Aristophanes himself, and probably with an allusion to the same events (Kleon's reaction to *Babylonians*) as in those two earlier passages. Lines 659–63 are partly adapted from Euripides fr. 918 (possibly, though not certainly, from *Telephos*).

681 *pipes*: i.e. reed pipes, *auloi*; see n. on *K*. 9.

685 *advocate*: the term denotes a publicly appointed, state-paid prosecutor in certain kinds of trial; cf. 705–15, *K*. 1361, *W*. 482, 691.

688 *Tithonos*: a Trojan figure of myth; the goddess Dawn fell in love with him and obtained for him immortality from Zeus but forgot to request agelessness, with the result that he grew ever older and more decrepit.

702 *Marpsias*: we know hardly anything about him; he here presumably represents the same class of orators/advocates as those at 685 and 703–18.

703 *Thucydides... Kephisodemos' son*: Thucydides son of Melesias had been a political rival of Perikles (Index of Names); he was ostracized *c.*443 and, if the present passage is reliable, had been subsequently prosecuted in old age, a trial at which he may have suffered an embarrassing incapacity to defend himself (see *W*. 947–8). Kephisodemos' son is Euathlos (n. 710).

709 *Artachaias*: the Greek text is corrupt at this point; my translation follows an emendation of E. K. Borthwick's which introduces a reference to the giant Persian Artachaias mentioned at Herodotos 7.117.

710–12 *Euathlos... father's kin*: Euathlos was a minor political figure, possibly an associate of Kleon's (cf. *W*. 592), who is here cast in the role of a state advocate (n. on 685). The suggestion that his father was Skythian (cf. 704–5), 'barbarians' to the north of Greece associated with military archery (and cf. the Prytaneis' armed slave attendants earlier involved at 39/40), must be a satirical distortion of some point about the family.

716 *Kleinias' son*: Alkibiades, a flamboyant aristocratic figure with a controversial political career ahead of him (*OCD*⁴), at this date aged around 25 but apparently already known as a public speaker; for his lisp, see *W*. 44–6.

723 *market officials*: minor magistrates (five of them for the central Agora), elected annually by lot, with responsibilities for maintaining trading standards and related matters; cf. *W*. 1407.

725–6 *Informers... grass*: informer (Greek *sykophantês*) is a pejorative stereotype of someone who actively seeks opportunities to exploit the legal system maliciously and for private gain, including blackmail (*W*. 1096, *P*. 653); as well as the later scenes at 818 ff., 910 ff., see *B*. 1410 ff., *AW* 439–40, *We*. 850 ff.

739 *piglets*: what follows involves not just the absurdity of animal 'disguise' but also a vein of sexual humour which depends on the fact, probably signalled by the actors with gestural innuendo, that the term 'piglet' could be used as slang for female genitalia. See n. on 782 and cf. *W*. 573, 1353.

747 *Mystery rites*: i.e. the Eleusinian Mysteries (n. on *W*. 1363); initiands sacrificed piglets at a certain point in the festival (cf. 784–5, with *P*. 374–5, *F*. 338).

755–6 *Commissioners...city*: Megara (Index of Names) had an oligarchic regime at this date; Commissioners represent some kind of ruling council.

762–3 *mice...garlic*: the analogy depends on the way in which large numbers of field mice can destroy grain crops; for Megarian garlic, cf. 521 and n. on *P*. 247. Since the outbreak of war Megara had been subject to a partial blockade, as well as invasions, by Athens.

772 *thyme-flavoured salt*: cf. 1099.

774 *Diokles*: a legendary king of Eleusis who later became a cult-hero at Megara.

782 *pussy*: the Greek has the primary obscenity *kusthos* ('cunt'); cf. 789, with other Aristophanic occurrences at *L*. 1158, *F*. 430. See n. on 739 for the innuendo that underlies this aspect of the scene.

785 *tail*: it was important that an animal be wholly intact for sacrifice; cf. the animal's tail at *P*. 1054. But there is also a further sexual double entendre on 'tail' as slang for penis (cf. *WT* 239).

808 *gorge*: the Greek puns, perhaps with deliberate feebleness, on the place-name Tragasai (in the Troad) and a verb meaning 'eat' (used in the following line by the Megarian).

821 *our woes...began*: see Dikaiopolis's account of the origins of the Megarian decree at 519–35.

826 *no wick*: Dikaiopolis makes a sarcastic pun on a verb which means lit. 'bring to light' but can also refer to a procedure of legal denunciation. Cf. 917.

835 *bread into salt*: the meaning of the Megarian's parting line has never been satisfactorily explained.

839 *Ktesias*: possibly a fictional figure, to be understood etymologically ('acquisitive'); but the name was real and there may be a topical reference now lost on us.

843–7 *Prepis...Hyperbolos*: the Chorus imagine Dikaiopolis's agora without the kinds of unpleasant characters one might bump into (literally) in the real Agora of Athens. Prepis cannot be securely identified; for Kleonymos and Hyperbolos, see Index of Names.

848–52 *Kratinos*: see Index of Names; Artemon was a figure (real or fictitious) mocked as a social upstart in the work of the sixth century poet Anakreon.

854–5 *Pauson...Lysistratos*: Pauson may be the satirical(?) painter known from e.g. Aristotle, *Poetics* 2.1448a6, and mocked as hungry (i.e. a social parasite) at *WT* 949–52, *We*. 602; Lysistratos is also cast as some kind of joker at *W*. 787–8 and 1308–10, in the latter as a member of a socially select set, despite the present jibe (and probably likewise, by association with Thoumantis, at *K*. 1266) against his supposed poverty.

866 *Chairis*: see n. on 16.

867 *Iolaos*: a nephew and associate of Herakles, the recipient of hero-cult in Boiotia.

880 *Kopais*: a lake in Boiotia noted for its gourmet eels.

886 *wine-song*: see n. on 497–9.

887 *Morychos*: a wealthy Athenian who acquired a comic reputation as a gourmand; see *W*. 506, 1142, *P*. 1008–9.

890 *sixth year*: see n. on 268.

894 *beetroot*: compare eel in beetroot in another parodic passage at *P*. 1014.

901 *Phaleron*: the old harbour of Athens, pre-dating the building of the Peiraieus (Index of Names) in the 480s; small fish like whitebait (cf. 640) or sprats were a common and cheap food for Athenians (cf. *K*. 644–79).

905 *twins*: Amphion and Zethos, mythical founders of Thebes.

908 *Nikarchos*: perhaps a real contemporary but otherwise unknown to us.

917 *lamp-wick*: Dikaiopolis's gibe involves a similar pun to that at 826.

920–5 *cockroach…boat*: the term translated as 'cockroach' (certainly one of the word's later meanings) may at this date have designated the type of insect known as a pond-skater or water skater; it is possible that it could also denote a kind of boat. Nikarchos's scenario is in any case a preposterous fantasy.

938–9 *mixing-bowl…cup*: the metaphors ironically characterize the Informer's maliciousness in a cluster of social, legal, and political terms.

942 *head down*: it is possible that there is a visual allusion to the myth, depicted in Greek art, in which Herakles hung two of the Kerkopes (a band of thieving dwarfs) upside down from a shoulder-pole.

961–2 *Choes…eel*: the Choes ('Wine-jugs') was the second day of the Dionysiac festival of the Anthesteria (late February); cf. 1076. For Kopaïc eels, see n. on 880.

964–5 *fearsome…crests*: for Lamachos's shield, see 574; the description mixes Homeric and tragic language, with a particular adaptation of the image of Tydeus at Aeschylus, *Seven against Thebes* 384.

967 *salt-fish*: cheaply available from vendors at the city gates of Athens (*K*. 1247); cf. 1101, *W*. 491.

968 *market officials*: see n. on 723.

970 *on the wings*: there is some reason to suppose that Dikaiopolis is quoting the words of a popular song.

976 *own accord*: a motif of utopian Golden Age narratives; see the canonical version at Hesiod, *Works and Days* 117–18.

977–9 *Never again... drinking party*: this whole passage pictures War as an unruly, inebriated guest at a symposium (compare *W*. 1253–4). Harmodios (cf. 1093, *K*. 786, *W*. 1225), with Aristogeiton, was one of the so-called 'tyrannicides' (cf. Thucydides 1.20.2, 6.54–9) who assassinated Hipparchos, brother of the tyrant Hippias (n. on *K*. 449), in 514; the pair were glorified as Athenian heroes in drinking songs: for an example focusing on Harmodios alone, see 894 *PMG*.

984–5 *vine-poles... vines*: a further allusion to the Spartan invasions of Attika; see n. on 183. For vine-poles, cf. *W*. 1201, *P*. 1263.

989–92 *Reconciliation... blossoms*: the Chorus picture Reconciliation (i.e. an end to war) as a young woman: cf. her personified embodiment at *L*. 1114 ff., with the same idea in the form of plural Peace Treaties at *K*. 1389 ff. For Kypris (Aphrodite) and the Graces, see Index of Names; 992 refers to a contemporary wall painting of Eros, personification of sexual desire and a traditional companion of Aphrodite.

994 *make it*: the sexual slang is a metaphor for the new vigour with which the Chorus imagine returning to the countryside and replanting the land after the Spartan invasions (n. on 183); a similar fusion of agriculture and sex plays a large thematic part in *Peace*.

999 *rub*: after exercising and/or bathing.

1001–2 *wine-jugs... Ktesiphon*: the Herald announces a drinking contest as part of the Choes (n. on 961–2). Ktesiphon is unidentifiable: the joke may allude to his drinking habits and/or the size of his belly.

1023 *Phyle*: an Athenian deme in the extreme NW of Attika on the border with Boiotia; a location vulnerable to raids.

1024 *white*: as opposed to black for mourning; Dikaiopolis is sceptical about Derketes' real condition.

1028 *Derketes*: a man of this name from Phyle is known from inscriptional evidence, but it is hazardous to guess whether, or in what way, Aristophanes expected his audience to identify this figure as a real individual.

1030 *public doctor*: some doctors were paid an annual fee by the city for the retention of their services.

1032 *Pittalos*: a doctor mentioned in similar terms at *W*. 1432; cf. 1222.

1071 *Lamachos-es*: in the Greek, Lamachos's name is again pluralized as at 270.

1075 *passes*: the roads into Attika from the north, used by enemy invasions and raids.

1076 *Choes and Chutroi*: the second and third days of the Anthesteria; cf. n. on 961–2. The dramatic time-scheme implied by the reference is loose.

1082 *monster... feathers*: the text and meaning of this line are uncertain; there is a reference in the Greek to Geryon, a three-bodied monster killed by Herakles.

1086 *basket*: for the practice of taking a contribution of food to a dinner and drinking party, compare *W*. 1251.

1090–3 *couches…Harmodios*: with this picture of the resources for a lavish symposium (preceded by a meal), cf. *W.* 1208 ff.; for Harmodios, see n. on 977–9.

1099 *thyme-flavoured salt*: cf. 772; for onions as soldiers' food, see *K.* 600, *P.* 529, 1129.

1101 *salt-fish*: see n. on 967.

1102 *fig leaf full of beef-fat*: see n. on *K.* 954.

1120 *cowardice*: in a judicial context, the category of cowardice probably covered various derelictions and evasions of military duty; cf. *K.* 368. Lamachus's words may allude to the practice of predicting the future with mirrors (catoptromancy).

1134–5 *fit this tight…get tight*: the Greek verb for wearing a breastplate also has a slang sense of 'get drunk'; the pun is here reinforced, like many other details in the passage, by stage action. Cf. n. on *P.* 1286–7.

1150 *Antimachos*: both his identity and the description of him as 'poetaster' are uncertain; the lampoon is ostensibly motivated by resentment about his behaviour as *chorêgos* (financial sponsor) at the Lenaia (cf. 504) in the previous year (426), though whether that was the occasion of the staging of one of Aristophanes' own plays remains uncertain. For the normal expectation that a *chorêgos* would fund a 'cast party' after the performance, cf. *P.* 1022.

1167–71 *Orestes…Kratinos*: Orestes is used as the nickname of a notorious/imaginary mugger; cf. *B.* 712, with *B.* 1491 for fusion with the mythological figure of the same name. On Kratinos, see Index of Names.

1182 *braggart-buzzard*: see 579 for this invented compound.

1188 *drove…spear*: another line from Euripides' *Telephos* (n. on 430), fr. 705a; few spectators are likely to have recalled Euripides' play well enough to detect the latent irony that Lamachos is now being partly modelled on the same tragic character whose persona Dikaiopolis himself had earlier adopted.

1203 *first to drink*: i.e. to win the competition announced at 1000–2.

1210–11 *charge…Choes*: Dikaiopolis puns on Lamachos's use of a poetic word for a military encounter by reusing the word in a very different sense; for the Choes, see nn. on 961–2, 1076.

1222 *Pittalos*: see n. on 1032.

1224–5 *judges…wineskin*: the judges of the theatrical contest (addressed in similarly metatheatrical fashion at e.g. *B.* 1102 ff., *AW* 1154 ff.) were seated near the front of the audience; the King Archon (Index of Names) was responsible for the organization of the Lenaia festival. Dikaiopolis wants to claim the wineskin promised as a prize at 1001–2.

1227 *All hail*: a traditional cry for victorious athletes and the like; cf. *K.* 1254. At *B.* 1764 it is chanted in celebration of Peisetairos's marriage, which marks his victory over Zeus.

1229 *unmixed*: see n. on 75; cf. *K.* 85 ff.

KNIGHTS

8 *Paphlagonian*: Paphlagonia was a region south of the Black Sea from which Greeks sometimes acquired slaves; but the play will also encourage a phonic association with the verb *paphlazo*, 'boil noisily' hence 'bluster, splutter', etc. (see 919, *P.* 314), a motif suitable for the satire of Kleon as an exceptionally vociferous orator. Cf. *C.* 581.

9 *auloi*: plural of *aulos*, the double-reed pipe, which was the musical instrument used, among other things, to accompany the lyric sections of comedy (and tragedy) itself.

16 '*If only…*': a quotation from Euripides, *Hippolytos* 345, where Phaidra is afraid of telling the Nurse her secret passion for Hippolytos.

19 *chopping herbs*: an allusion to the satirical topos of Euripides' mother as a market gardener; see n. on *A.* 457.

31 *supplicate*: for slaves seeking religious sanctuary, see n. on 1312.

32 *gods exist*: atheism was an intellectual position available, if rare, at this date; see *C.* 247, 1233, with the statement of atheism by Bellerophon in Euripides fr. 286 (cf. Introduction to *Peace*, n.9).

42 *Pnyx*: see Index of Names.

44 *tanner*: the politician Kleon owned a tanning business; Aristophanes reductively converts this into an image of Kleon himself as a low-grade worker; cf. *C.* 581.

50–1 *single… pay*: the same populist measure of proposing that the courts should close early on particular days, after hearing just one trial, is hypothesized at *W.* 595. Three obols (cf. 255), i.e. half a drachma, was the amount paid to a juror for a day's jury service, having been raised from two obols on the proposal of Kleon in 425, the year before *Knights*; cf. 800 and numerous references in *Wasps* (n. on *W.* 788–91).

55 *Pylos*: a site in the SW Peloponnese occupied by the Athenians in 425 under the leadership of the general Demosthenes (with whom Slave[A] here momentarily identifies); from there, with the involvement of Kleon as a replacement for the general Nikias (see 358) and supposedly taking credit for a plan already made by Demosthenes (see Thucydides 4.29), the Athenians had captured a group of Spartan soldiers on the nearby island of Sphakteria, a success for which Kleon managed to win great acclaim. See further references at e.g. 392–4, 469, 742–3, 1201, with my Introduction to the play.

60 *politicians*: one of numerous points of cross-over between the allegorical domestic scenario and its underlying political reference.

61 *oracles*: see 109 ff., 961 ff., with my Introduction to the play; for the hold which oracles had on Athenian minds in this period, see Thucydides 2.8.2 and 21.2, 3.104.1.

67 *Hylas*: apparently used here as a special slave name; in mythology, Hylas was companion (and beloved) of Herakles on the voyage of the Argonauts.

78–9 *Chaonians...Klopidai*: the three place names all involve puns. On the Chaonians, here with a play on a Greek word for 'gaping', see n. on *A*. 602–6; Aitolia (in SW central Greece) plays on the language of 'demanding' (i.e. bribes: cf. 66); and Klopidai (a small deme in NE Attika) puns on the vocabulary of theft.

84 *Themistokles*: major Athenian politician of the era of the Persian Wars, a proponent of building up the city's navy and with it the Peiraieus harbour (see 815 with Index of Names), as well as responsible for the strategy which won the battle of Salamis in 480 (n. on 781–5). But he was ostracized *c*.470 and ended his life in Persia, where a legendary account held that he committed suicide by drinking (supposedly poisonous) bull's blood. Cf. 812–18, 884.

85 *unmixed wine*: cf. 354, with n. on *A*. 75; toasting a 'good spirit', with a small amount of unmixed wine, was a ritual often followed at the start of a symposium (cf. 106, *W*. 525, *P*. 300), but drinking unwatered wine was more generally associated with slaves and alcoholics.

98 *recline*: for reclining as the usual practice at symposia, see esp. *W*. 1208 ff.

103 *confiscated goods*: confiscated from perpetrators of crimes against the state and then resold; cf. *W*. 659. The implication here is either that Paphlagon has siphoned off such revenues or that he was entitled to some of the confiscated goods as a prosecutor in such cases.

107 *Pramnian*: a traditional term for some fine Greek wines, but it is not a place name.

118 *read*: note that in what follows the slave reads *silently*, contrary to the still common claim that Greeks at this date always read out loud.

123 *Bakis*: an oracular authority of uncertain origin, though sometimes located in Boiotia; cf. 1003–4, *P*. 1070–2, 1119, and e.g. Herodotos 8.20.

129–30 *flax...leader*: Eukrates (named at 254; see n. there), a shadowy figure who seems to have been briefly prominent as a 'leader of the people' after the death of Perikles in 429; flax-production must have been his family business, just as tanning was for Kleon (n. on 44), but he may have been the same Eukrates who was general in 432–431.

132 *seller of sheep*: Lysikles, mentioned again at 765; he was general in 428–427 and died in service in Karia (Thucydides 3.19, see n. on 173–4).

137 *torrent*: cf. the same image for Kleon's supposedly brash style of rhetoric at *A*. 381.

165–7 *Pnyx...Prytaneion*: see Index of Names for both terms. The comic imputation is that those who enjoy state hospitality in the Prytaneion (a leitmotif of the play: 280, 535, 574–5, 709, 766, 1404) debase themselves sexually in order to benefit their political careers; cf. n. on 426 below.

173–4 *Karia...Carthage*: Karia, in SW Asia Minor, included coastal, tribute-paying cities of the Athenian empire (Thucydides 2.9) and non-Greeks in the hinterland who could be militarily problematic (Thucydides 3.19 on the death of Lysikles; see n. on 132); Carthage, on the coast of N Africa, was on the horizon of Athenian imperial expansionism (see 1303–4).

188–9 *education… badly*: the Sausage-Seller implies that he has had no formal education, which started, where reasonably well-to-do Athenians were concerned (and presumably, therefore, most members of the theatre audience), with basic literacy, before proceeding to the study of poetry and music (as well as gymnastics); cf. Plato, *Protagoras* 325d–6d. Compare the related, though less drastic, educational shortcomings alleged against Kleon at 985–96, and note the reference to basic literacy at *W.* 960.

212 *steward*: i.e. a domestic overseer, part of the allegory of Demos as a householder; cf. 426, 947–9, and *P.* 686 for the same metaphorical idea.

221 *Dimwit*: Slave^A ironically invents a suitably uneducated deity for the Sausage-Seller to worship.

225 *thousand*: the size of the enlarged cavalry corps which Athens had established some time prior to the Peloponnesian War; for the figure, see Thucydides 2.13.8 (one thousand plus two hundred mounted archers as adjuncts).

230–2 *mask… likeness*: an elaborate bit of humour; there was probably no standard practice of recognizable portrait masks, but the double-layered joke is that while the mask-makers were supposedly afraid of Kleon they have produced something which, in comic reality, no doubt looked highly grotesque.

238 *Chalkis*: in W Euboia, the city was at this date a member of the Athenian empire; it had long been renowned for its metalwork.

242–3 *Simon… Panaitios*: Simon may be the equestrian expert mentioned at the start of Xenophon's treatise *On Horsemanship* (1.1); Panaitios too may have been a real cavalry officer, though it is implausible that most of Aristophanes' audience could have been fully familiar with both individuals or made much of this passing reference to them.

248 *farmer… Charybdis*: tax-farmers became a byword for extortion; it is unlikely that Kleon actually held such a position. For the mythical Charybdis, a deadly whirlpool, see Homer, *Odyssey* 12.104 ff.

254 *Eukrates*: see n. on 129–30; the reference in this line has never been satisfactorily explained, but it may allude to a further commercial business in which Eukrates had some involvement.

255 *three-obol fee*: see n. on 50–1, with *Wasps* for sustained satire on Kleon's political manipulation of the Athenian court system.

259 *up for review*: magistrates had to face an official audit and review at the end of their term of office; cf. 825, *W.* 102, 571, 587, *P.* 1187.

264 *Chersonese*: probably the Gallipoli peninsula on the N side of the Hellespont; but it is unclear what kind of legal scenario is envisaged in this passage.

267–8 *honour… war*: the Chorus's response suggests that we are to take Paphlagon as resorting to a barefaced lie, though it is not inconceivable that the real Kleon was prepared to try to court the cavalry for certain purposes; the military allusion is possibly to the cavalry's part in a victory over Korinthian forces during the previous summer (n. on 599).

280–3 *Prytaneion... Perikles*: see Index of Names on both names; cf. n. on 165–7. Kleon had been awarded special dining privileges as a result of his part in capturing the Spartans on Sphakteria in the preceding summer (n. on 55).

297–8 *Hermes... perjure*: a bronze statue of Hermes Agoraios (god of the marketplace and commerce) stood in the Athenian Agora; since Hermes was also a god of trickery and deceit, the Sausage-Seller's oath is appropriate. For theft compounded by perjury, compare 428 and 1239.

301–2 *tithe... sacred tripe*: a tithe (to the treasury of Athena) was levied on goods in certain legal situations; the application of this principle to tripe is self-evidently ludicrous. For the Prytaneis, see Index of Names.

312–13 *tunny... tribute*: in tunny/tuna fishing (cf. *W.* 1087) a lookout positioned on the rocks called to those waiting on the shore below, ready to catch the shoals of fish in a large net (seine); cf. *W.* 1087. Kleon may have been involved in a major reassessment, which we know that Athens had recently undertaken, of the tribute paid by its allied cities: see n. 30 to my Introduction to the play, and cf. 1071.

327 *Hippodamos's son*: Archeptolemos (see 794), son of the town-planner Hippodamos of Miletos, who had designed the layout of the residential quarter of Athens' Peiraieus harbour. Archeptolemos, who had probably been made an Athenian citizen, must have been out of tune with Kleon's style of democratic populism: he became a member of the oligarchic coup of the Four Hundred in 411 and was subsequently executed by the restored democracy.

347 *metic*: a resident alien; cf. *A.* 508, *P.* 297. For Paphlagon's sneer at amateurish delusions about ability at public speaking, note the similar gibe on the part of Kleon at Thucydides 3.38.6.

354–5 *unmixed... Pylos*: for unmixed wine, see n. on 85; on Pylos, see n. on 55.

358 *Nikias*: the Athenian general who was attacked by Kleon and stood down in favour of him in the debate over Pylos (n. on 55); see Thucydides 4.27–8. Some scholars think that Slave^B in the opening scene of *Knights* represents Nikias, but the arguments for this are thin.

361 *Miletos*: on the SW coast of Asia Minor and known for its fine bass, this Ionian city was a member of the Athenian empire; cf. 932. We do not know what lies behind Paphlagon's admission of hypocrisy or duplicity towards Miletos.

362 *leases*: Athens leased its silver mines in SE Attika to private individuals; cf. *W.* 659. The Sausage-Seller anticipates getting rich on the profits of such a lease.

367 *stocks*: various forms of stocks or pillories were used to imprison/punish certain classes of criminals in Athens; in some cases, the person would be

on public display (Demosthenes 24.114). Cf. 705, 1049, with other references at e.g. *C.* 592, *L.* 680–1, *WT* 931.

368 *cowardice*: see n. on *A.* 1129.

375–83 *hammer...pimples*: the imagery relates to the practice of holding open an animal's mouth with a wooden peg so that its tongue can be inspected for disease; the shift from mouth to anus hints at the stereotype of politicians as willing to prostitute themselves in pursuit of power (see n. on 426).

390 *coward*: cf. *A.* 664.

392–4 *reaping...gain*: a further, elaborately metaphorical reference to the way Kleon had appropriated the chief credit for the capture of Spartan troops on Sphakteria, who were now imprisoned at Athens: Thucydides 4.41.1; see n. on 55.

400–1 *Kratinos...Morsimos*: the chorus momentarily blurs its dramatic identity with the metatheatrical persona of a group of performers. For Kratinos, here implied to be incontinent in bed, see Index of Names; Morsimos (cf. *P.* 802, *F.* 151), son of Philokles (n. on *W.* 462), was a minor tragedian, an easy butt of a passing joke.

404 *throw up*: the physical metaphor for relinquishing bribes is related to the one used at 1148 and *A.* 6.

407 *Oulios*: probably the son of the famous statesman Kimon (cf. *L.* 1143–4); as an official (corn-controller) responsible for the city's grain supply, he may have clashed in some way with Kleon.

410 *Agoraios*: lit. 'of the Agora'; invoked again at 500. The Athenian Agora (see Index of Names) is here symbolic of both political (see 165) and commercial life (e.g. 636, 1258).

416 *dog-faced baboon*: the Greek term 'dog-headed' was used for the hamadryas baboon (e.g. Plato, *Theaetetus* 161c).

426 *steward*: for the metaphor, see n. on 212. The line encapsulates the cynical popular idea (alluded to at Plato, *Symposium* 192a) that young men improved their chances of a political career by making themselves sexually available to older men; cf. nn. on 165–7 and 375–83, with 879–80 and *AW* 111–13. For a more general idea on the same lines, see n. on *A.* 79.

438 *Potidaia*: this city on the W arm of the Chalcidic peninsula had surrendered to Athens after a two-year siege in 430–429 (Thucydides 2.70); it is hard to make realistic sense of the idea that the historical Kleon had profited on a large scale from this event, so we are probably dealing with a comically exaggerated illustration of the uses of political slander (a speciality of Paphlagon/Kleon himself: see 7, 45, 63, etc.).

443 *hundred-talent*: this and the following figures are ludicrously off the scale; cf. nn. on 829, 834–5.

447 *polluted*: an allusion to the sacrilegious killing of the supporters of Kylon (after his failed attempt to become tyrant of Athens) on the Akropolis in the 630s or 620s (Thucydides 1.126); those responsible, especially the

Alkmaionidai, were placed under a perpetual curse. This curse continued to be available for political manipulation by opponents (see Thucydides 1.127 for its use against Perikles).

449 *Hippias*: tyrant of Athens 527–510; his wife was called Myrsine (Thucydides 6.55.1), here distorted to Byrsine (lit. a leather thong, whip, etc.). The gibe imputes descent (quite absurdly for the historical Kleon) from a member of a bodyguard consisting of foreign mercenaries.

465-7 [n.b. line 464, 'But can't you…', is here transposed to between 467 and 468] *Argos…Sparta*: Athens was at this date wooing Argos (see Index of Names), whose thirty-year treaty with Sparta was due to expire in 421; the charge of duplicity against Paphlagon satirizes the political brandishing of conspiracy theories and is especially absurd given Kleon's actual aggressiveness towards Sparta.

469 *prisoners*: i.e. the Spartans captured on Sphakteria (n. on 55); cf. 394 and *P*. 479–80.

478–9 *Persian king… Boiotian*: on Greek negotiations with Persia, see n. on *A*. 61. Negotiations with certain pro-Athenian rebels in Boiotia (see Index of Names) were afoot around this time: Thucydides 4.76.

494 *fighting cock*: see n. on *A*. 166.

500 *Zeus Agoraios*: see n. on 410.

504 *anapaest section*: see n. on *A*. 627.

507–8 *tried / To make us*: the theatrical status of the choral parabasis is comically blurred by the suggestion that it is 'really' members of the cavalry appearing in public to testify on the poet's behalf; similar language to express the idea of a chorus being compelled to deliver a parabasis is found in one of Aristophanes' rivals (Plato comicus fr. 99).

510 *speak what's right*: cf. the similar sentiment, together with the bizarre supporting 'testimony' from the king of Persia, at *A*. 645.

511 *Typhos*: a hundred-headed monster (Typhoios) at Hesiod, *Theogony* 820 ff.; cf. *C*. 336, together with the description of Kleon at *W*. 1033.

513 *requested a chorus*: on the official process referred to here, see the general Introduction, 'Old Comedy and Dionysiac Festivity', with n. on *A*. 628–9 and the entries on individual plays in the Chronology for Aristophanes' use of independent theatrical producers for several works prior to *Knights*.

520 *Magnes*: not only one of the earliest poets of Old Comedy (he was already active in the 470s) but one of the most successful; he won no fewer than eleven victories. It is possible, though not certain, that the following lines allude to plays entitled *Lyre-Players*, *Birds*, *Lydians*, *Fig-Flies*, *Frogs*.

526–30 *Kratinos… 'hymns'*: Kratinos (see Index of Names) is treated ironically as a figure from the past when he was actually competing against *Knights* itself! The phrases in 529–30, in a parodic lyric style (Kratinos fr. 70), come from a comedy called either *Eumenides* or *Euneidai*.

534 *Konnos*: a successful musician who had, among other things, supposedly taught Sokrates (Plato, *Euthydemos* 272c) but who had also become something of a figure of comic ridicule; cf. n. on *W.* 675.

535 *Prytaneion*: see n. on 165–7; the joke here is that Kratinos is an alcoholic who would be interested in free drink, not food. Kratinos appears to have responded to this jibe the following year (Dionysia, 423) with a play called 'Wine-Bottle', *Pytine*, which won first prize when Aristophanes' *Clouds* came third and in which Kratinos ironically incorporated a depiction of himself as a drunkard.

537 *Krates*: active in the third quarter of the fifth century; according to Aristotle, *Poetics* 5.1449b7–9, he pioneered a less satirical style of comedy.

542–4 *rower...steer*: an elaborate metaphor from the hierarchical organization of roles on a trireme (n. on *A.* 162–3); it seems to imply that in his early career Aristophanes had served a gradual theatrical apprenticeship in the staging of his plays.

550 *Lenaia...forehead*: for the Lenaia festival, cf. the general Introduction, 'Old Comedy and Dionysiac Festivity'; 'forehead' is apparently an allusion to Aristophanes' premature baldness, which is also referred to at *P.* 767–74 and was mentioned by his rival Eupolis (fr. 89).

551–64 *Poseidon...present situation*: on Poseidon, see Index of Names (with *W.* 652 for the Titan Kronos); his double connection with horses and the sea allows celebration here of both the city's cavalry and navy (and with no suggestion of holding back from the war effort, 579). Phormion (cf. *P.* 348), probably dead by this date, had been a successful Athenian general prior to, and in the early years of, the Peloponnesian War, not least in command of fleets.

566 *peplos*: the special robe for the statue of Athena in the Parthenon (n. on 1169) which was carried to the temple in a ritual procession during the Great Panathenaia festival every four years, as depicted on the E frieze of the Parthenon itself. Cf. 1180 and *B.* 827.

574–5 *Kleainetos...grub*: Kleainetos was the father of Kleon; he was wealthy enough (presumably from the family tannery) to be a *chorêgos*, i.e. a financial sponsor (n. on *P.* 1022), of a festival chorus (in dithyramb) at the City Dionysia of 460–459. These lines refer to honorific awards of *prohedria* (front seats in the theatre and at other public events: see 702–4) and state hospitality in the Prytaneion (n. on 165–7), insinuating that Kleon exercises influence over such awards.

580 *long hair*: for this fashionable trait of the cavalry (which will have been incorporated in the chorus's masks), most of whom were younger men (see 731), cf. *C.* 14; note the later allusion at 1121. The cavalry class was wealthy but the text and meaning of the last part of this line are uncertain.

581–9 *Pallas...Nike*: Pallas (again at 1172) is a cult title of Athena, here invoked as goddess of the Akropolis ('citadel'), at whose W end there stood an altar (later a temple) of Nike, goddess/personification of victory; the statue of Athena in the Parthenon (n. on 1169) also held a miniature Nike in her right hand.

599 *Once they leapt...*: the reference is to a campaign against Korinthian territory in summer 425; the cavalry played a decisive part in the Athenian victory (Thucydides 4.42–4). Equestrian transport ships were used by Athens for the first time in the Peloponnesian War: Thucydides 2.56.2. In the next line, the horses behave like rowers or soldiers required to take their own (initial) provisions on campaign with them; for onions and garlic in this context, cf. *A.* 550, 1099, *P.* 529, 1129.

603 *branded*: in the case of horses, brand marks of various kinds were used to signal fine pedigree.

608–10 *Theoros...cavalry*: Theoros is probably the associate of Kleon's mentioned in other plays too; see n. on *A.* 134. His remark parodically combines allusion to two drinking songs: 892 *PMG*, where a crab speaks, and Timokreon of Rhodes 731.2 *PMG* (see n. on *A.* 530–4), where the same phrase 'Neither on land nor in the sea' occurs.

629 *huge persuasiveness*: the same Greek term is applied to the historical Kleon, together with an indication of his aggressive political style, at Thucydides 3.36.6 and 4.21.3.

639 *to the right*: an indication that the Sausage-Seller takes the fart as a favourable omen—an appropriate one for his chances in a contest of shamelessness and vulgarity.

641 *gate*: a gate in the wooden fence (see 675) that enclosed the Council chamber; there was a similar arrangement in the law-courts (see *W.* 775).

645 *small fry*: for various references to small fry (sprats, whitebait, etc.) as plentiful and cheap food in Attika, see *A.* 640, 901–2, *K.* 644–79, *W.* 493–6, 679.

656 *sacrifice*: the implication is that most of the meat would be distributed to individual citizens.

665 *Prytaneis...removed*: the same procedural arrangements as in the Assembly; see *A.* 54.

668–9 *Spartans...peace*: for the Spartans' peace overtures after their loss of Pylos and of troops on Sphakteria, see Thucydides 4.41.4; Kleon probably led the rejection of such approaches (cf. 795–6, and note the statement of Thucydides 5.16.1), which would make Paphlagon's behaviour here comically disingenuous.

675 *fence*: see n. on 641.

702 *seating*: i.e. *prohedria* (n. on 574–5) awarded to Kleon for his success at Pylos (n. 55). It is an intriguing thought that Kleon might actually have been sitting in the front row at the performance of *Knights* itself!

705 *stocks*: see n. on 367.

729 *harvest branch*: branches of olive or laurel, decorated with wool and foodstuffs, were attached to or near the door of Athenian houses in the autumn; cf. *W.* 399, *We.* 1054.

732 *lover*: the erotic metaphor was part of real Athenian rhetoric; at Thucydides
2.43.1 Perikles generalizes the metaphor as something desirable for all
citizens in relation to the city. See 1163, 1341, and cf. *A*. 142, together with
W. 411 and 473 for the other side of the coin (accusing individuals of
'hating' the city); cf. Plato, *Gorgias* 481d–e. In the background of the present passage is the realistic idea of rival homosexual lovers becoming
involved in violent feuding: see Lysias speech 3 (*Against Simon*) for a case
in point.

735 *superior people*: see n. on 227. This particular gambit of the Sausage-
Seller's is out of line with the calculated vulgarity that he otherwise
exploits to outdo Paphlagon.

739 *lamp-sellers*: an allusion to Hyperbolos (cf. 1315); see the Index of Names.

742–3 *Pylos...Spartans*: see n. on 55.

762 *dolphin-weights...ship*: dolphin-weights were large metal objects which
could be dropped (from a yard-arm) onto an enemy vessel in order to damage it; cf. Thucydides 7.41.2. The second half of the line probably refers to
having a small craft ready for abandoning ship in an emergency.

765 *finest man...*: for Lysikles, see n. on 132. Kynna (see *W*. 1032 = *P*. 755)
and Salabaccho (cf. *WT* 805, a similar joke to the present one) were courtesans or prostitutes; as often in Aristophanes, a speaker is made to utter
self-damning words as if inadvertently.

772 *Kerameikos*: an area outside the city walls to the NW and the location of
Athens' largest cemetery; cf. *B*. 395, *F*. 129.

781–5 *Marathon...Salamis*: the two battles of the Persian Wars in which the
Athenians played the largest part, the first (in 490) an infantry victory on
the plain of Marathon (see 1334 with Index of Names), the second (in 480)
a sea-battle around the island of Salamis off the W coast of Attika. Both
were frequently recalled as among the city's supreme achievements.

786 *Harmodios*: see n. on *A*. 977–9.

792–3 *shantytowns...seven*: see Thucydides 2.17 and 52 for the squalid makeshift living conditions of the (poorer) rural population displaced into the
city during the early years of the war.

794–5 *Archeptolemos...peace*: on Archeptolemos, here serving as a go-between
for the Spartans, see n. on 327; Athens repeatedly rebuffed peace overtures from Sparta after the capture of the latter's troops on Sphakteria
(Thucydides 4.41.4).

798–800 *jury service...juror*: a fantasized extension of the power of the Athenian
legal system (and by implication the city's empire) over all Greece, including—rather preposterously—remote Arcadia in the central Peloponnese.
For the current daily juror's stipend of three obols, see n. on 50–1.

803–4 *blinded...jury pay*: the suggestion that war served to obscure
Paphlagon/Kleon's nefariousness is the same claim as made by Thucydides
5.16.1; for jury pay as an essential element of the workings of Athenian
democracy, see my Introduction to the play.

805–7 *If ever . . . state pay*: for the note of uncertainty about the duration of the war, cf. 579; for 'porridge', cf. *P.* 595. On the idea of peace as making possible a return to the countryside, see the play's nostalgic/idealized outcome at 1394, together with my Introduction to *Peace*.

809 *dreams*: dreams, like oracles, might be put to prophetic purposes; see 1090–5.

813 *'O city of Argos . . .'*: a quotation from Euripides' *Telephos* (fr. 713); cf. n. on 1240, with n. on *A.* 430 for further information about this lost play. The utterance is clearly an expression of outrage (used again at *We.* 601) but its original context is uncertain.

812–15 *Themistokles . . . Peiraieus*: see n. on 84.

818 *Creating factions*: for Paphlagon-Kleon as a divisive force, compare the symbolic dream at *W.* 39–41.

825 *under review*: see n. on 259; Paphlagon is accused here of taking bribes in order not to cause trouble for the magistrates in question, who are described here with a botanical metaphor.

829 *thirty thousand drachmas*: i.e. five talents; cf. the same amount at *A.* 6, with the even larger sums of money in the exchange of accusations and threats at 438–45.

834–5 *Mytilene . . . minas*: we know from Thucydides 3.36–50 that Kleon had argued for the harshest treatment of Mytilene (on the island of Lesbos) after its revolt from Athens in 428–7; the Sausage-Seller's present suggestion is therefore probably ironic. Forty minas = 4,000 drachmas, a much smaller amount than in 829.

846 *shields . . . from Pylos*: the shields from the Spartans captured on Sphakteria (n. on 55) which were put on display in Athens.

855 *toy with ostracism*: the Greek involves a pun on a children's game with potsherds, which were also the physical means of voting in cases of ostracism (see *OCD*[4]), a procedure for selecting a politician to be exiled for ten years.

857 *barley-market stoa*: Athens' main grain market, probably in the Peiraieus; cf. *AW* 686, with an allusion at *A.* 548.

877 *I put a stop . . .*: if there is anything historical behind this, Kleon may have prosecuted Grypos (though the name is uncertain) under a law which disbarred male prostitutes from exercising citizenship; a prominent case from the fourth century involving this law is preserved in Aischines' speech *Against Timarchos*.

880 *turned into public speakers*: see n. on 426.

884–5 *Themistokles . . . Peiraieus*: see n. on 84.

895 *silphium*: a pungent, fennel-type herb, imported from Kyrene in N Africa and much used in Greek cooking.

899 *Koprian*: Kopros was a deme in W Attika, close to Eleusis; it carries with it here a pun on *kopros*, 'shit'.

901 *with light-brown hair*: the Greek has the name Pyrrandros (here a purely fictive figure), the first part of which is the same colour term used in the preceding line for a scatological joke (cf. *F.* 308 for a similar joke).

912–18 *warship...sails*: Paphlagon threatens the Sausage-Seller with the expensive duties of a trierarch (see n. on *A*. 546–51); this involved a level of expenditure which only the richest four hundred or so Athenians could afford.

924 *property tax*: a special levy (*eisphora*) on the rich to support the costs of war; there had been a major imposition of such a tax in 428–7 during the siege of Mytilene (n. on 834–5). See Thucydides 3.19.1.

929–30 *squid...fire*: compare the similar scenario imagined at *A*. 1156–60; such passages belong to a deliberately 'naive' style of comic Schadenfreude.

932 *Miletos*: see n. on 361; 'profit' here is a euphemism for a bribe.

947 *ring*: a household steward (n. on 212) might wear a signet ring which allowed him to exercise his master's financial authority in certain contexts.

954 *masses*: the Greek word for animal fat differs only in its accent from the word *dêmos* for the people or masses (as in the verb for making a political speech in 956); cf. the similar pun at *W*. 40–1. For the food in question, cf. *A*. 1102.

958 *Kleonymos*: see Index of Names. The imagery of the present passage plays both on Kleonymos's comic reputation for greed and on the similarity between his name and Kleon's, but it may also suggest a political link between the two men (cf. n. on *W*. 592): we know that two years prior to *Knights* Kleonymos had proposed a decree tightening up tribute collection in the allied cities, a proposal that must have been close to Kleon's heart (n. on 312–13).

964 *foreskin*: for circumcision (here as a symbol of being unmanned), see n. on *A*. 158.

969 *in pursuit*: the Greek has an untranslatable pun on 'pursuing' people in a war-chariot and 'prosecuting' defendants in court (compare the related joke at *W*. 1207–8), together with a name, Smikythe, which appears to be that of a woman but may be a swipe at a putatively effeminate man of a similar name.

976 *Kleon*: this is the play's only named reference to the politician, as opposed to his allegorical representation as Paphlagon.

989–96 *Dorian...tune*: the passage plays on the term 'Dorian (mode)' and an invented word, *dôrodokisti*, lit. 'in the mode of bribery'.

1003 *Bakis*: see n. on 123.

1013 *eagle in the clouds*: cf. 1087, with the same motif in the oracle at *B*. 978.

1015–20 *Erechtheus...downfall*: Erechtheus (cf. 1022, 1030) is here thought of as a legendary early king of Athens and ancestor of all Athenians; 'jag-toothed' (cf. *W*. 1031 = *P*. 754) is a Homeric epithet for dogs. The oracle's claim to come from Apollo at Delphi comically contradicts line 1004.

1024 *your dog*: for Kleon as guard-dog, cf. *W*. 902–30; for Phoibos as a title of Apollo's, see Index of Names. Throughout this passage the need to interpret oracles, and the possibility of conflicting interpretations, reflects actual practice; cf. the famous example at Herodotos 7.142–3 (with n. on 1040).

1030 *Kerberos...slaves*: for Kleon as Kerberos, the guard-dog of the underworld, see *P.* 313 and Eupolis fr. 236, with *F.* 111, 467 for the myth of Herakles' capture of the hound. If 'trader of slaves' is more than a crude insult, it might allude to Kleon's involvement in a plan to enslave the women and children of Mytilene (n. on 834–5) in 427; see Thucydides 3.36.2.

1034 *islands*: shorthand here for Athens' allies; licking pots is also a canine metaphor for peculation at *W.* 904, in a scene where Kleon and one of his political opponents are both allegorized as dogs.

1040 *made of wood*: an echo of the Delphic oracle issued to Athens before the battle of Salamis in 480 (Herodotos 7.141–3) and understood by some Athenians to be a coded reference to the ships of their fleet.

1044 *leonine traits*: the Greek makes a pun on the proper name Antileon, whose etymology is taken as meaning 'in the place of a lion'.

1047 *Loxias*: a further title of Apollo's; cf. 1072.

1049 *pillory*: see n. on 367.

1055–7 *Kekrops...battle*: Kekrops was a legendary early king of Athens and a cult-hero for one of the Athenian tribes (cf. *W.* 438); lines 1056–7 incorporate a quotation from an early Greek epic, *The Little Iliad* (fr. 2), where a Trojan girl is depreciating the fact that Ajax carried the dead body of Achilles off the battlefield.

1059 *Pylos...Pylos*: an old piece of verse about different places called Pylos in the Peloponnese; Paphlagon desperately tries to appropriate it as a reminder of his own success at Pylos in the previous year (n. on 55).

1060 *bath tubs*: the Greek term (*puelos*) involves phonetic word-play with Pylos.

1066 *receive their pay*: part of the pay of rowers could be withheld till the end of an expedition, and presumably was not always paid promptly even then; cf. 1366–7 with Thucydides 8.45.2. On rowers as representative of the demos, see n. on *A.* 162–3.

1067–9 *Aigeus...pimp*: Aigeus, father of Theseus (1312), was, like Kekrops (1055), a legendary Athenian king and tribal hero. Philostratos is also mentioned, together with his nickname 'fox-dog', at *L.* 957. Demos naively forgets that the oracles are supposed to be warning him about Paphlagon.

1071 *tribute*: see n. on 312–13.

1078–9 *pay...three days*: Athenian infantry (hoplites) were paid for service, though they may not always have been paid promptly; the 'three days' boast may play on the promise made by Kleon that he would capture Sphakteria (n. on 55) within twenty days (Thucydides 4.28.4).

1080–1 *Leto...Kyllene*: Leto was mother of Apollo; Kyllene, a harbour in the NW Peloponnese, is chosen entirely to allow play with the adj. *kullos*, 'crooked'.

1085 *Diopeithes*: the main thing known about this figure is his religious conservatism, which may have involved proposing a decree against atheism in the 430s; his name allows a purely verbal pun at *W*. 380. He was probably himself a collector of oracles (cf. *B*. 988), though we cannot be sure about the comic point of the present mention.

1088–9 *Red Sea... Ekbatana*: the former denotes the whole Persian Gulf and the waters beyond (cf. *B*. 145), the latter was the summer residence of the king of Persia (cf. *W*. 1143–4). The fantasy is of an Athenian empire spreading ever eastwards and paying for a life of luxury for the people of Athens.

1095 *ambrosial... sauce*: in early Greek poetry, ambrosia (n. on *A*. 196–7) can be both a food and a drink of the gods, but it is also sometimes applied externally to humans as a divine preservative; for garlic-brine sauce, cf. 199.

1097 *Glanis*: see 1004.

1099 *Please guide...*: adapted from a line in Sophokles' (lost) *Peleus* (fr. 487.2).

1103 *Thouphanes*: evidently a political ally of Kleon's but otherwise unknown. For false demagogic promises of grain distributions, cf. *W*. 716–17.

1114 *tyrant*: the immediate point should be the tyranny of the majority within Athens, but there may also be overtones of the idea attributed in Thucydides to both Perikles (2.63.2) and Kleon (3.37.2) that the Athenian empire involved a kind of tyranny over the city's allies.

1121 *hair*: see n. on 580.

1148–50 *vomit.... throat*: for 'vomiting' up corruptly acquired money, see *A*. 6; the metaphor in 1150 pictures a judicial voting funnel (*W*. 99, 754, 1339) being used as an emetic probe down the throat. Cf. also 404.

1163 *lovers... hard to get*: for the erotic imagery, see n. on 732.

1169 *ivory hand*: i.e. part of the chryselephantine (gold-and-ivory) statue of Athena made by Pheidias for the Parthenon; cf. n. on *P*. 605–6.

1172 *Pylos-fighter*: Paphlagon misuses a poetic epithet (*Pulaimachos*) meaning 'fighting at the gates' as though it meant 'fighting at Pylos', the scene of his military triumph (n. on 55). For Pallas, see n. on 581–9.

1180 *peplos*: see n. on 566.

1184–5 *intestines... ribs*: the Greek involves a pun on a word for part of the internal structure of a warship.

1187 *three and two*: three parts water to two parts wine; this is stronger than the common ratio of three parts water to one of wine.

1189 *Tritogenes*: an old cult title (often Tritogeneia) of Athena's, though of uncertain origin and meaning. In the Greek, the verb in this line is a unique word meaning (roughly) 'add three parts'.

1192 *hare-meat*: cf. e.g. *A*. 1005, 1110–12, *W*. 710, *P*. 1150–3, 1313.

1225 *Yet I...*: the line, in Doric dialect, may be adapted from Eupolis's comedy *Helots*.

1232 *I want...*: the following passage contains several paratragic features; it is partly redolent of (which does not mean derived from) Oedipus's fateful interrogation of the herdsman at Sophokles, *Oedipus Tyrannus* 1121–85.

1240 *O Phoibos...*: the line is from Euripides' *Telephos* (fr. 700); cf. n. on 813. 'Lykian' is a cult title of Apollo's but of obscure origin and meaning.

1242 *was fucked*: in mundane terms, as though the Sausage-Seller engaged in a little prostitution on the side; but with the added irony that he has, from a cynical point of view, one of the prime 'qualifications' to be a politician (n. on 426).

1248–9 *Alas...godforsaken man*: line 1248 is taken from an unknown context in Sophokles (fr. 885a), and line 1249 is an adaptation of a line from Euripides' *Bellerophon* (n. on *A*. 427), fr. 311, where the verb has been changed (from 'carry' to 'wheel') to parody tragedy's use of the *ekkuklêma* or trolley (for the staging of interior scenes: see n. on *A*. 408). But it seems unlikely that the *ekkuklêma* was actually employed here.

1251–2 *Another's...fortune*: parodically adapted from Euripides, *Alcestis* 181–2, spoken by Alcestis on the point of death.

1254 *All hail*: see n. on *A*. 1227.

1256 *Phanos*: an associate of Kleon's mentioned again at *W*. 1220 but otherwise unknown; the suggestion is that he brings prosecutions in Kleon's political interests.

1257 *Agorakritos*: a real but rare Greek name, lit. 'judged/approved by a public meeting', but treated by the Sausage-Seller as though it meant 'quarrelling in the Agora'.

1263 *Gawpers*: for the motif of gawping democratic audiences, see 651, 755, 824, 1032, as well as *A*. 635. The whole of 1261–3 ironically echoes earlier statements by Paphlagon.

1264–73 *What finer...poverty*: the strophe is a comic version of *praeteritio* (i.e. drawing attention to something one purports to pass over); it also echoes and parodies a passage of Pindar (fr. 89a). For Lysistratos, see n. on *A*. 854–5; Thoumantis was mocked as thin by another comic poet (Hermippos fr. 36) but we cannot know what lies behind the (no doubt exaggerated) gibes of homelessness and poverty.

1278–9 *Arignotos...music*: Arignotos appears to have been a successful professional performer on the *kithara* (concert lyre); cf. *W*. 1277–8.

1281–7 *Ariphrades...Oionichos*: Ariphrades is elaborately ridiculed for a supposed fetish for cunnilingus, as again at *W*. 1280–3 and *P*. 883–5; if he was the comic poet mentioned later at Aristotle, *Poetics* 22.1458b31, then Aristophanes may have had ulterior motives for satirizing him. 1287 certainly alludes, however obscurely, to musico-poetic activities: Polymnestos was an archaic singer and Oionichos was some kind of musician.

1293–6 *Kleonymos...grain bin*: the antistrophe provides the reverse of the strophe's theme of 'starving' characters, picturing Kleonymos (see Index of Names) as a threat to his host's entire stock of food.

1300–4 *triremes...Hyperbolos*: the city's warships are personified, in keeping with their grammatical gender, as a group of females; note that Aristophanes wrote a play, *Holkades* ('Merchant Ships': see *Frogs and Other Plays*, p. 247), whose chorus probably consisted of personified ships. On Carthage, see n. on 173–4; on Hyperbolos, see Index of Names.

1309 *Nauphante*: this female name, like that of the father, incorporates the noun *naus* ('ship').

1312 *Theseus...Awesome Goddesses*: the shrine of Theseus (a legendary king of Athens) was somewhere east of the Akropolis (and self-evidently not to be 'sailed' to!); it was a place of sanctuary for runaway slaves (cf. 30–1). The Awesome Goddesses are elsewhere sometimes known as the Eumenides: their precinct, at the E end of the Areopagos hill, was also a place of sanctuary: cf. *WT* 224 and Thucydides 1.126.11.

1316–17 *witnesses...courtooms*: Athenian courts were closed during festivals; see e.g. pseudo-Xenophon, *Constitution of the Athenians* 3.8. For the idea of Athenians as addicted to their judicial system, cf. *B.* 40–1.

1323 *violet-wreathed*: see n. on *A.* 637–9.

1325–6 *Aristeides...Propylaia*: Aristeides (nicknamed 'the Just') and Miltiades were prominent Athenian political and military figures in the era of the Persian Wars; Aristeides was involved in the establishment in the 470s of the system of tribute which Athens imposed on its allies, while Miltiades had been the leading general in the battle of Marathon (see 781 with the Index of Names). Both became, in time, bywords for a supposedly higher standard of political life in a past age: see Isokrates, *On the Peace* 75, Demosthenes, *Third Olynthiac* 26. The Propylaia is the formal entrance to the Akropolis at its W end; cf. *L.* 265.

1329 *gleaming*: cf. *A.* 639.

1331 *cicada-brooch*: a golden hair-brooch, used to fix in place a kind of 'hair bun' (cf. *W.* 1267); this was an older fashion (n.b. of the wealthy) mentioned at Thucydides 1.6.3 and mocked as absurdly out-of-date at *C.* 984.

1332 *voting-shells*: see n. on *W.* 333.

1334 *Marathon*: see nn. on 781–5 and 1325–6.

1341 *passionate lover*: see n. on 732.

1348 *parasol*: cf. Prometheus's parasol at *B.* 1508 and the reference to women's parasols at *WT* 823.

1361 *advocate*: a public, state-paid prosecutor in certain sorts of trials; cf. *A.* 685, 705–15, *W.* 482, 691.

1362–3 *pit...Hyperbolos*: the 'pit' was a place outside the city walls where the corpses of executed criminals were thrown (for a famous reference to it, see Plato, *Republic* 4.439e). It lent itself to vehement curses: cf. *C.* 1450, *F.* 574, *We.* 431, 1109. On Hyperbolos, see Index of Names.

1366–7 *row...dock*: cf. n. on 1065–6.

1369–70 *lists...transferred*: the reference is probably not to lists (posted in the Agora) of citizens called up for hoplite (infantry) service on individual expeditions, though those lists too could be improperly manipulated

(*P.* 1180–1, and cf. *A.* 1065), but to the full lists held by individual demes of all eligible citizens, ordered according to yearly age-groups.

1372 *Kleonymos*: see Index of Names.

1374 *Kleisthenes and Straton*: also coupled for the purposes of a joke about their supposed beardlessness (*alias* effeminacy) at *A.* 118–22.

1377–80 *Phaiax...publical*: Phaiax, a contemporary political figure, is praised by young men who are addicted to rhetorical neologisms (with the Greek *-ikos* suffix).

1381 *obscenical*: the Greek refers to the kind of finger gesture also mentioned at *A.* 444, *P.* 549.

1384–6 *folding stool*: an old-fashioned appurtenance of the lifestyle of some wealthy Athenians, here setting up, of course, an easy sexual joke.

1389 *thirty-year*: cf. *A.* 194.

1394–5 *country...return*: see n. on 805–7.

1406 *frog-green*: we cannot say why this particular kind of garment is chosen here.

WASPS

8 *Korybantic*: a type of ritual in which ecstatic music and dance were used as a quasi-medical cure for various mental disturbances (cf. 119); I take the present context to allude to a trance-like state that might be engendered by the ritual.

9–12 *Sabazios...Persian*: Sabazios was a Phrygian god (cf. *B.* 875) whose cult, recently introduced into Athens, involved ecstatic music (cf. *L.* 388) but also, perhaps, trance-like states. Xanthias's association of Sabazios with Persia is probably meant to be humorously imprecise.

17–19 *serpent...Kleonymos*: the joke hinges on the fact that the same Greek word can mean both 'serpent' and 'shield'; for Kleonymos, see Index of Names.

21 *drinking party*: posing riddles was one of many word games that might be played at Greek symposia.

40–1 *beef-fat...city*: for the Greek pun here, see n. on *K.* 954.

42–5: *Theoros...toady*: for Theoros, see 418, 599, 1220 ff., with n. on *A.* 134. Alkibiades (n. on *A.* 716) is exploited here for the comic value of his lisp, which seems to have been a real trait and which, among other things, turns the Greek *korax* (raven) into *kolax* (flatterer), the latter indicating the idea of Theoros as a hanger-on of Kleon's, i.e. a member of his inner political circle. Cf. n. on 592.

51 *ravin' mad*: the Greek plays on a colloquial expression, lit. 'to the ravens', used to dismiss or curse someone.

53 *reading dreams*: dream-interpretation was a very old but contested Greek practice; cf. the exchange between Penelope and (disguised) Odysseus at Homer, *Odyssey* 19.535, 555, 560–9. There were 'professional' dream-interpreters in classical Athens: e.g. Theophrastus, *Characters* 16.11. For two obols as a sum of money, compare 1189.

56–7 *grand... Megarian*: Aristophanes does in fact claim that his comic artistry was 'grand', lit. 'big', at *P.* 749–50. 'Megarian comedy' (see Index of
Names under Megara) became an Athenian byword for a crude style of
entertainment; this was a dismissive response to Megarian claims to have
been the original inventors of comic drama (see Aristotle, *Poetics*
4.1448a31–4). The three examples in lines 58–63 are meant to illustrate
stale comic routines, but the introduction of Euripides' name is a surprise:
mockery of Euripides was an Aristophanic speciality (cf. *A.* 395 ff.), not
the same kind of commonplace as the burlesque figure of a gluttonous
Herakles (cf. *P.* 741, *B.* 1583 ff., *L.* 928).

62–3 *Kleon... garlic paste*: it is doubtful whether line 62 refers to any particular
event; the main point (similar to that at *C.* 549–50) is that the play will not
repeat the major satirical onslaught against Kleon in *Knights*. For garlic
paste, see n. on *A.* 67.

71 *unwell... weird*: compare the similar point in the prologue at *P.* 54.

74 *Amynias*: mocked again at 466 and 1267–74; the various gibes against his
supposed vices supply no reliable information. We cannot, of course,
assume that any of the named individuals in this passage were actually
present in the theatre (though generals had special seats at the front: cf.
Nikostratos in 81): if the slaves can pretend to hear suggestions, they can
equally pretend who is making them!

78 *Sosias... Derkylos*: neither figure can be identified with confidence.

81 *Nikostratos*: probably the serving general mentioned at Thucydides 4.129–
30; Skambonidai was one of the central urban demes of Athens.

84 *Philoxenos*: he cannot be identified with confidence, but his name (a common
one) is the same as the adj. in 82 which literally means 'lover of guests'.

93 *water clock*: used for the timing of litigants' speeches; cf. 857.

94–6 *pebble... incense*: jurors voted by dropping a pebble (or sometimes a shell:
cf. 333) into one of two urns (cf. 109, 987 ff.); the grip is compared to the
action of pinching some incense between three fingers.

97–9 *graffiti... handsome*: for homoerotic graffiti, see n. on *A.* 143–4. In the
Greek, the word for voting funnel (placed in the top of a voting urn),
kêmos, is only one letter different from *dêmos*. Pyrilampes was, among
other things, stepfather of the philosopher Plato; for his son Demos, cf.
Plato, *Gorgias* 481d–e.

102 *review*: see n. on *K.* 259; cf. 587.

105 *queueing*: because of uncertainty over the number of trials held on any
particular day, and the number of jurors who attended for duty (it was not
obligatory), individuals were not guaranteed assignment to a court.

108 *wax*: in cases where jurors had to choose between alternative penalties
for a convicted defendant, they scratched a mark on a wax tablet (making
a longer mark for the prosecution's proposal); cf. 167, 850.

118 *purificatory bath*: a domestic version of a religious ritual.

119–20 *Korybantic...rites*: see n. on 8.

122–3 *Aigina...Asklepios*: one of several shrines of Asklepios, god of healing, was on the island of Aigina; the Asklepian rites involved sleeping overnight in the sanctuary (cf. *We.* 659 ff.).

145 *Fig wood*: there is a pun on the word *sukophantês*, lit. 'fig-revealer', which is the standard term for an informer (n. on *A.* 725–6); cf. 897. Philokleon is symbolically associated with abuse of the legal system. For 'acrid' in 146 as a metaphor for judicial harshness, cf. 277, with *P.* 348.

152–4 *pushing...bolt*: the fact that house doors opened inwards and were locked on the inside is inverted for obvious comic purposes.

157 *Drakontides*: we do not know which of several contemporary Athenians of this name is meant, nor whether a real trial is being referred to; see the further reference at 438.

167 *tablet*: see n. on 108. The mention of a sword in 166 lays a kind of comic seed for a later part of the play: see 522–3.

181 *Odysseus*: he escaped from the Cyclops' cave by hanging undetected beneath a ram (*Odyssey* 9.431–5).

184 *No-man*: the false name adopted by Odysseus as part of his deception of the Cyclops (*Odyssey* 9.366).

189 *donkey...hanger-on*: the same Greek word can mean both donkey and the witness who accompanied someone delivering a summons (cf. 1408 ff.).

191 *donkey's shadow*: a proverbial expression for something nugatory.

210 *Skione*: this city on the W arm of the Chalcidic peninsula had seceded from the Athenian empire in 423 and was currently under siege; cf. n. 33 to the Introduction to *Knights*.

220 *Phrynichan*: Phrynichos was one of the earliest Athenian tragic playwrights, active *c.*510–475; see 269, 1490, 1524, and cf. *B.* 748–51, *F.* 910, 1299. It is hard to know how much accurate knowledge survived at this date of his choral lyrics. In the Greek, the whole of line 220 is a single compound word.

230–4 *Komias...Chabes*: most of the names in these lines seem to have been rare and probably sounded eccentric. Konthyle and Phlya were both small rural demes.

236 *Byzantion*: the allusion is probably to the capture of this city (at the SW end of the Bosporos) from the Persians in 478; in a realistic context, this would imply an age of about 80 for the jurors.

240 *Laches*: an Athenian general who served in Sicily during 427–425 and who will be allegorized as Labes the dog in the mock-trial at 894 ff.; whether he was threatened with prosecution by Kleon at this date is extremely doubtful; see n. on 836–8.

243 *three whole days*: a play on the instructions given to soldiers about to go on campaign; see n. on *A.* 196–7.

290: in the edition of the Greek text followed here, lines 290–316 have been moved to between 265 and 266 in order to correct what seems to have been a textual corruption at some point in the transmission of the play.

300 *juror's pay*: three obols for each day of service; see n. on *K*. 50–1.

308 '*Beyond…Hellespont*': an adaptation of Pindar fr. 189, chosen so as to produce not only a clash of stylistic registers but also an allusion to Athens' importing of grain from the Black Sea region.

312 '*Why gave you…?*': a quotation from Euripides' lost play *Theseus* (fr. 385), here serving a characteristically paratragic function.

266: for the reordering of lines, see n. on 290.

269 *Phrynichos*: see n. on 220.

277 *most acrid*: see n. on 145.

283 *Samos*: this island's revolt from the Athenian empire in 440 had been a major event; the idea of a defendant in 422 appealing to his pro-Athenian actions in the distant past may be meant to sound far-fetched (and/or to make the jurors seem gullible).

289 *Thrace*: Athens was at this date facing considerable problems in this northern region (see Index of Names), including the revolts of several allied cities, as a result of the activities of the Spartan commander Brasidas (n. on 475).

317: for the re-ordering of lines, see n. on 290.

326 *Proxenides…Baloney*: the first is treated again as a braggart at *B*. 1126; the 'son of Baloney' is the Aischines of 459, where the present association with smoke is confirmed.

333 *voting-shells*: an alternative to pebbles (n. on 94–6); cf. 349 and *K*. 1332.

342b *Demagogue-Kleon*: the chorus distorts Bdelykleon's name (which they technically do not know) and at the same time, by dramatic irony, allow a sneer at Kleon himself, even though he is their great patron (242); cf. the similarly paradoxical humour at 759.

345b *conspirator*: for this motif, see 483 ff., 507, 953, together with my Introduction to *Knights*.

351 *Odysseus*: he once entered Troy disguised as a beggar (*Odyssey* 4.244 ff.), as well as using a drain on another occasion to get into the city (Sophokles fr. 367); the chorus's mythical analogue for someone trying to *escape* is deliciously quirky. For Philokleon's own earlier attempt to emulate a different ruse of Odysseus's, see 179–89.

353 *fig-juice*: the Greek literally denotes cheese curdled with fig-juice; the noun in question puns on the word for 'chink'.

355 *Naxos*: this Cycladic island had revolted from the Delian League (the incipient Athenian empire) as early as 467; the historical allusion is another marker of the jurors' age and the long reach of their memories (cf. n. on 236).

363–4 *weasel…skewers*: weasels could be found in some Athenian houses; they killed rodents (cf. 1182 and *P*. 792) but might also 'steal' meat (*P*. 1151), a fact which became a metaphor for certain sorts of excuses (*P.* 795, *WT* 558–9).

378 *goddesses twain*: Demeter (see Index of Names) and her daughter Persephone; cf. 1396.

380 *Diopeithes*: see n. on *K.* 1085.

389 *Lykos*: an Athenian cult-hero with a shrine next to one of the courts in Athens. Cf. 819–23.

394 *defile*: for the idea of such casual desecration of sanctuaries, see *F.* 366.

399 *harvest branches*: see n. on *K.* 729.

401 *Smikythion...*: the first two names are real, the others not; it is doubtful whether any identifiable individuals are meant.

411 *hates our city*: such language is the other side of the coin from 'love of the city', for which see n. on *K.* 732 and my Introduction to that play.

417 *tyrannous*: an extreme version of the accusation of political conspiracy; cf. 464, 487–502.

418–19 *Theoros...toadies*: see n. on 42–5.

421 *Philippos...Gorgias*: the specific reference is unknown; Philippos was probably not the literal son, but rather a follower, of the Sicilian rhetorician Gorgias (cf. *B.* 1701–3 for their further association as practitioners of forensic rhetoric).

438 *Kekrops...Drakontides*: for Kekrops, who was sometimes depicted as serpentine below the waist and is here invoked as a cult-hero, see n. on *K.* 1055–7; for Drakontides (the first part of whose name means 'serpent'), see n. on 157 above.

459 *Aischines*: cf. 326, 1220 (which points to a political connection with Kleon), 1243; but we know nothing else for sure about him.

462 *Philokles*: a contemporary Athenian tragedian, nephew of the great Aischylos and father of Morsimos and Melanthios (nn. on *K.* 400–1, *P.* 803–4); he is the subject of jokes both artistic and personal at *B.* 281, 1295, *WT* 168.

466 *Amynias*: see n. on 74.

473 *people-hater*: see n. on 411.

475–7 *Brasidas...untrimmed*: Brasidas was the leading Spartan commander at this date, currently active in the region of Thrace (n. on 289); cf. n. on *P.* 282–4. Spartans were associated with a rougher style of dress and longer beards and moustaches than those of Athenians.

482 *advocate*: see n. on 687–90.

502 *Hippias*: son of Peisistratos, brother of Hipparchos (n. on *A.* 977–9), and tyrant of Athens *c.*527–10; cf. *L.* 619, 1153. The name Hippias, lit. 'Horseman', picks up the sexual imagery (cf. *P.* 900) of the previous line.

506 *Morychos*: see n. on *A.* 887.

508 *birds' milk*: for this proverbial (and imaginary) luxury, cf. *B.* 734, 1673.

524: in the text followed here, lines 522–3 are transposed to follow 524–5.

525 *put my lips to...pay*: Philokleon replaces the unmixed wine drunk at the start of a symposium (to toast a 'good spirit': n. on *K.* 85) with the state pay he receives as a juror (300, etc.).

522 *sword*: see n. 10 to my Introduction to the play; cf. Philokleon's previous thoughts of a sword at 166.

543 *olive-branch-bearers*: a group of older men chosen to carry olive branches in the Panathenaic procession (cf. n. on *P.* 418–20).

566 *Aisop*: a legendary figure, reputedly a Samian slave of the sixth century BC, to whom a body of well-known fables was traditionally ascribed; see also nn. on 1401, 1446–8, *P.* 129.

568 *children*: for a famous reference to the practice of bringing one's children into court for melodramatic appeals to the jurors' pity, see Plato, *Apology* 34c. Cf. 976.

571 *review*: implying a scenario where a magistrate under annual review (n. on *K.* 259) has had charges brought against him in court.

573 *piglets*: the word has an obscene slang usage, activated here (as at 1353), for which see n. on *A.* 739.

578 *review*: a process (*dokimasia*) by which 18-year-old Athenian males had their citizenship credentials checked; the precise details at this date are not certain, but clearly at least some cases might involve the courts.

579–80 *Oiagros...Niobe*: Oiagros was presumably a tragic actor but is otherwise unknown; various playwrights wrote plays about Niobe (for Aischylos', cf. *F.* 912, 920), an archetypal tragic figure whose children were killed by Artemis and Apollo and who was herself turned into stone (see Homer, *Iliad* 24.602–17 for her already paradigmatic story).

583–6 *father...entreaties*: an Athenian who died without male offspring but with an unmarried daughter could specify in his will who should marry the latter and inherit his property (cf. the joke at *B.* 1653–4); such cases often involved family disputes. The reference to the will's seal sets up a sexual double entendre in 589.

587 *without review*: unlike magistrates; cf. 102, 571, with n. on *K.* 259.

592 *Euathlos...*: for this figure, see n. on *A.* 710–12; 'Hanger-onymos' is a distortion of Kleonymos (see Index of Names) which changes the first part of the name to *kolax* (see n. on 42–5) and probably conveys a suggestion of his political connection with Kleon (n. on *K.* 958).

595 *just one trial*: see n. on *K.* 50–1.

596 *shrieking*: for the satire of Kleon's voice, see the Introduction to *Knights*.

599 *Theoros...Euphemides*: for Theoros, see n. on 42–5; we know nothing of Euphemides, but the humour must involve inadvertent bathos on Philokleon's part (compare e.g. *K.* 765).

607–9 *daughter...fee*: Athenians sometimes carried small coins in their mouths; cf. 788–92, *B.* 503, *AW* 818; whether the image in these lines has incestuous overtones is hard to say with confidence. For a related father-daughter relationship, cf. *P.* 119–23.

617 *'donkey'*: the word here denotes a kind of wine-jug; it is probably imaginary and metaphorical, though it is not inconceivable that Philokleon somehow produces one at this point.

640 *isles of the blest*: the traditional designation of a special location where, in stark contrast to Hades, a privileged few live in perpetual bliss after death; for one early image, see Hesiod, *Works and Days* 167–73.

650 *wine-song*: see n. on *A.* 497–9.

652 *Kronos*: Titan father of several Olympian gods (cf. *K.* 561), including, as here, Zeus (though Philokleon, in keeping with 621–5, absurdly thinks he is being addressed himself).

654 *banned from sacrifice*: i.e. as religiously polluted on account of murder.

660 *two thousand talents*: the figure Bdelykleon gives must reckon with the considerably increased tribute assessments of 425–4 (n. on *K.* 312–13). The sources listed in the Greek of 659 include various kinds of prosecutors' legal fees, mine leases (n. on *K.* 362), and the proceeds of sales of confiscated property (n. on *K.* 103).

661–3 *subtract...talents*: Bdelykleon's calculation presupposes that all 6,000 jurors on the annual roster were paid for service on three hundred days per year; this is likely to be an over-estimate. The unidentifiable quotation in 662 is partly in epic diction.

666–7 *'never betray...masses'*: Bdelykleon sarcastically echoes his father's words in 593.

675 *worthless votes*: the Greek literally means 'a vote of/for Konnos', but the reference here to Konnos (n. on *K.* 534) is opaque.

678 *'after many campaigns...'*: an unidentifiable poetic quotation.

680 *Eucharides*: since we know nothing else about this person, we cannot be sure whether he was an actual garlic-seller or if there is an ironic point to the humour.

687 *Chaireas' son*: we know nothing of either Chaireas or his son, but the latter is depicted here as a state-paid advocate involved in certain public trials, including the prosecution of magistrates accused of malfeasance in office (cf. n. on 571).

700 *Pontos*: the Black Sea.

707 *thousand*: a gross exaggeration; the current number was fewer than four hundred.

715 *Euboia*: this island, the largest in the W Aegean, is thought of here as either a source of grain or a location for the settlement of Athenian colonists, or perhaps both.

751–7 *It's those others...shadowy grove*: the passage includes a mish-mash of tragic language and motifs; see e.g. Sophokles, *Ajax* 1218, Euripides, *Alkestis* 866, *Hippolytos* 219, 230. 'Give way, shadowy grove' is a quotation from Euripides, *Bellerophon* fr. 308, where the hero is starting his flight on Pegasos (see n. on *A*. 427).

759 *Kleon*: for the comic paradox of this reference in Philokleon's mouth, see n. on 342b.

787 *Lysistratos*: see n. on *A*. 854–5.

788–91 *drachma... obols*: a drachma coin might sometimes be given to a pair of jurors for them to divide (three obols each: e.g. 684, with n. on *K*. 50–1); Philokleon puts what he takes to be small coins into his mouth (n. on 607–9).

799–804 *oracle... door*: for (parodic) oracles involving Athenian jurors, cf. *K*. 798 and 1089; but this one mocks the idea of jury service as the most important thing in life for some Athenians. Hekate was a goddess with magical and underworld associations: for her shrines, cf. *F*. 366, *We*. 594–7.

819–23 *Lykos... weapons*: for Lykos, see n. on 389. The nature and staging of the present joke are wholly uncertain; 'weapons' may involve a play on the slang use of this word to refer to male genitalia, as well as alluding to Kleonymos's supposed cowardice (see Index of Names).

836–8 *Labes... Sicilian*: the allegory encodes the figure of Laches and his previous command in Sicily (known for its cheese-production: cf. *P*. 250); see n. on 240. But the trial is almost certainly a fiction: for legal reasons, Laches could not have been prosecuted for Sicilian misconduct as late as 422, though his enemies, including Kleon, could have continued to make general political capital out of claims of such misconduct.

850 *wax*: see n. on 108.

857 *water clock*: see n. on 93.

869–74 *Phoibos... Paian*: see the entry for Apollo in Index of Names.

875 *Aguieus*: a title of Apollo associated with sacred pillars that stood by the doors of some houses; cf. *WT* 489.

895 *Kydathenaion*: an urban deme to which Kleon (as well as Aristophanes himself) belonged; the replacement of Kleon's name with the similarly disyllabic *kuôn*, 'dog', serves to nail the allegorical point.

897 *fig-wood*: a pun on the word for a malicious prosecutor; see n. on 145.

904 *licking*: the same metaphor for peculation as at *K*. 1034.

909 *'yo-ho' rowers*: a reference to the cries used by the crews of triremes; for the idea of these crews as representative of the Athenian *dêmos*, see n. on *A*. 162–3.

916 *guard-dog*: cf. *K*. 1023–4.

928 *thieving magpies*: the Greek has simply 'thieves' but is a distortion of a proverb 'a single bush does not feed two robins'.

947–8 *Thucydides... dumbstruck*: for Thucydides son of Melesias, see n. on *A*. 743–5.

955 *sheep*: see the imagery of 32–4.

959 *play the lyre*: part of a standard musical education for those affluent enough to afford it (see Plato, *Protagoras* 325d–6c); Bdelykleon is therefore claiming that the dog comes from a socially poor background. With the reference to basic literacy in the following line, compare *K.* 188–91.

960 *how to write*: see n. on *K.* 160.

976 *children*: see n. on 568.

989 *play the lyre*: Philokleon ironically echoes his son's words at 959.

1005 *the theatre*: the Greek here can be understood in more ways than one, but it best lends itself to the (metatheatrical) suggestion that father and son could attend the theatre together.

1007 *Hyperbolos*: see Index of Names.

1011 *thousands*: the text hyperbolically says 'tens of thousands'; on the size of the theatre audience, see the general Introduction, 'Stage Directions'.

1018–20 *help... language*: ostensibly a claim that at the start of his career Aristophanes served a kind of apprenticeship by contributing secretly to plays by other comic poets. Eurykles denotes a type of prophetic spirit that seems to speak from inside the body of a person.

1021 *openly started*: with *Banqueters* in 427; see the Chronology.

1025–8 *cruise... go-betweens*: the (semi-humorous) idea that Aristophanes could have exploited his theatrical renown to impress young men for sexual ends is reworked at *P.* 762–3; the second scenario, i.e. using comic satire at the request of the (older) lover in a homoerotic relationship who wants revenge against his former (younger) beloved, is unique to this passage.

1029 *started to stage*: although this might refer to *Knights*, the first play for whose staging Aristophanes took full responsibility as chorus-trainer and producer (*didaskalos*), it may be an alternative way of referring to the start of Aristophanes' career as a writer of plays, since the vocabulary of 'producing' plays is sometimes interchangeable with that of composing them; see n. on *A.* 628–9. Note also that lines 1029–37 are substantially recycled at *P.* 751–60.

1030–5 *Herakles... Lamia*: Aristophanes pictures his role as comic satirist in quasi-heroic terms equivalent to Herakles' labours; the 'jag-toothed monster' is Kleon (see n. on *K.* 1015–20) and the hundred heads of hangers-on (n. on 42–5) are reminiscent of the mythological monster Typhos (n. on *K.* 511). For Kynna, see *K.* 765. Lamia was a mythological bogey figure, sometimes used to frighten children; she is here androgynous and is mentioned again at 1177.

1037 *waging war*: a parodic echo of the 'fighting' rhetoric of populist politicians, as at 593 and e.g. *K.* 767. In one of Aristophanes' rivals, Plato comicus fr. 115, an unknown speaker (and probably not the poet himself) claims to have been the first person to have 'waged war against Kleon'.

1037–42 *another target... magistrate*: the reference is to a play by Aristophanes staged at Lenaia 423, but we do not know which one; its subject-matter evidently included the nastiness of 'informers' (n. on *A.* 725–6) who terrorized innocent citizens.

1044–5 *betrayed... failed*: the reference is now to *Clouds*, which was placed in third and last place at Dionysia 423; the play's bad reception is interestingly attributed not directly to the judges but to the inadequate appreciation of its comic originality and cleverness on the part of a majority of spectators.

1046 *libations... Dionysos*: libations make an oath more formal; Dionysos (see Index of Names) is, as god of theatre in Athens, an appropriate oath for a playwright. The same oath occurs, also in authorial boasts about the quality of Aristophanes' work, at *C.* 519.

1074 *'however uncultured...'*: a quotation from Euripides' lost *Stheneboia* (fr. 663), here used as a playful tag; the original states 'Love teaches [i.e. inspires] a poet, no matter how uncultured he previously was'.

1076 *autochthonous*: the chorus adapts the standard mythologized Athenian boast that the inhabitants of Attika could trace their ancestry back to Erichthonios, who had been born from the earth (the literal meaning of 'autochthonous').

1078–88 *Persians... fled*: an impressionistic encapsulation of the Persian Wars; 1079 recalls the burning of Athens in 480, while, out of chronological sequence, 1084–8 probably evokes the battle of Marathon in 490. With the tuna metaphor in 1087 compare Aeschylus, *Persians* 424–6 on the battle of Salamis. The quotation in 1081 is from the minor tragedian Achaios (fr. 29) and recurs at *P.* 356.

1097–1100 *captured... politicians*: a simplified précis of the historical process by which, in 478–477, after the second Persian invasion of Greece, Athens led the creation of a new federation, the Delian League, to which many Greek cities of Asia Minor and the Aegean contributed either tribute or ships. The organization soon effectively turned into an Athenian empire, and the charge against politicians of profiting corruptly from its financial system had already been brought by Bdelykleon at 656–71.

1108–9 *Archon's court... walls*: the reference is to four of the city's court buildings; the locations of all but the second are uncertain. The Odeion was a multi-purpose building on the SE slope of the Akropolis. The Eleven were magistrates responsible for the prisons and judicial executions.

1120–1 *I propose...*: for this way of ending a parabasis with a comically simplistic proposal, compare *A.* 717–18.

1122 *this cloak*: we were originally told about the disagreement over Philokleon's clothing at 116.

1139 *Sardis*: see n. on *A.* 112; of Athenians, the only ones likely to visit Sardis in this period would be high-ranking ambassadors, so the humour anticipates 1186–9.

1142 *Morychos*: see n. on *A.* 887; the point of the present joke is uncertain.

1143–4 *Ekbatana*: see n. on *K*. 1088–9.

1147 *talent*: a preposterous sum in the context; cf. n. on *A*. 6–8.

1158 *Spartan*: the term denotes a style of male footwear, not the actual place of origin, though this elementary point is lost on Philokleon.

1177–8 *Lamia…Kardopion*: for Lamia, see n. on 1030–5; Kardopion must have been another base figure of folklore, but we know no more than that.

1183 *Theogenes*: we do not know which bearer of this common Athenian name is meant, nor what anecdote Bdelykleon is using as a cover for his own outburst of abuse. For dung-collectors, see *P*. 9.

1187 *Androkles and Kleisthenes*: Androkles is probably the democratic politician who was later murdered by the oligarchs in 411 (Thucydides 8.65.2); for Kleisthenes, see Index of Names.

1189 *Paros…pay*: Philokleon apparently implies that he had simply served as a rower in an Athenian expedition (imaginary/unknown) to the Cycladic island of Paros; for rowers' pay, cf. n. on *A*. 162–3.

1191 *pankration*: a kind of all-in wrestling; cf. *P*. 897–8. Ephoudion won the event at the Olympic games of 464; Askondas is otherwise unknown.

1194–5 *armour…armour*: in the Greek, the humour revolves around the fact that the same noun can mean either 'torso' or 'breastplate'.

1201 *Ergasion*: presumably just a token name (its etymology = 'industrious') of a putative Athenian peasant farmer; for vine-poles, cf. the proverbial reference at 1291 and see *A*. 984, *P*. 1263.

1207 *Phaÿllos*: see n. on *A*. 214; the Greek verb in the next line puns, as does *K*. 969, on the two senses of 'chasing' and 'prosecuting in court'.

1214–15 *bronzes…hangings*: Bdelyklon imagines a drinking party in the house of someone affluent enough to have bronzeware (including weapons) and tapestries on display, and in a room whose ceiling is also noteworthy (e.g. coffered). For the protocols of the symposium in what follows, see *OCD*⁴, s.v. symposium, together with the various features dramatized in both Plato's and Xenophon's *Symposium*.

1220–1 *Theoros…Akestor*: the group must represent part of Kleon's clique. For Theoros, see n. on 42–5, for Aischines, n. on 459; Phanos is mentioned also at *K*. 1256 but is otherwise unknown; Akestor was a minor tragic poet (*B*. 31 refers to him) but we know nothing about his son. 'At your head' refers to the fact that the guests are reclining on couches around the four sides of the room; cf. 'next to your feet', 1236.

1225 *Harmodios song*: see n. on *A*. 977–9. It was a standard sympotic practice for the guests to take turns in singing (parts of) a song. Kleon starts a song intended to praise Harmodios; Philokleon twists it, with an invented verse of his own, into a comment on Kleon himself.

1232–3 *'O you…balance'*: an adaptation of part of a song by the archaic poet Alkaios (fr. 141.3–4 *PLF*), probably aimed at his political enemy Pittakos, who at one stage was the tyrant of Mytilene on the island of Lesbos.

1239 *'Learn the wisdom...'*: the first line of a drinking song, 897 *PMG*, possibly by the fifth-century poetess Praxilla of Sikyon (cf. 749 *PMG*); Admetos was a mythological Thessalian king whose wife was brought back from the dead by his friend Herakles (as dramatized in Euripides' *Alkestis*).

1241–2 *'One cannot...'*: an otherwise unknown drinking song, 912(a) *PMG*.

1245–8 *'Abundantly...bluster'*: Aischines starts with the drinking song 912(b) *PMG* (in which the identity of Kleitagora is now uncertain, but she may have been a courtesan); Philokleon's response is probably meant to be an improvised invention.

1250 *Philoktemon*: almost certainly here just a token 'speaking name' (its literal meaning is 'wealth-loving'), not a reference to a real individual.

1251 *Goldy*: most easily understood as a nickname for Xanthias (whose name literally means 'blond-haired'). For the practice of taking a contribution of food to a dinner/drinking party, see *A*. 1086, 1096.

1253–5 *wine...hung over*: for this image of a symposium turned violent, cf. the (allegorical) description at *A*. 978–83.

1259 *Sybarite*: named after the Greek colony of Sybaris (later replaced by Thurii) in S Italy, which became a byword for self-indulgent luxury (see *P*. 343); Sybarite tales were a class of entertaining anecdotes (see Philokleon's version of them at 1427 ff.).

1265 *Strophe*: note that the antistrophe is lost in the lacuna after line 1283.

1267–74 *Amynias...unparalleled*: for Amynias, see n. on 74; the present song ironically combines the idea of his social-climbing with the (supposedly) underlying fact of his acute poverty. 'Hair-bun type' refers to a once fashionable hair style of wealthy Athenians: see n. on *K*. 1331. Leogoras was known for his luxurious lifestyle; cf. *C*. 109 (the breeding of pheasants). There is no way of knowing which of many contemporary Athenians called Antiphon is meant here (cf. n. on 1301–2). The 'Penniless ones' (Penestai) were a Thessalian serf class.

1275–83 *Automenes...artistry*: the passage focuses on the musico-theatrical talents of the sons of Automenes (otherwise unknown) as a way of building up to mockery of Ariphrades' supposed liking for cunnilingus. For Ariphrades and the first brother mentioned here, Arignotos, see *K*. 1278–87, with nn. on that passage; the second brother referred to, an actor, is not known from elsewhere.

1283/4: a lacuna at this point means we have lost the text of the antistrophe.

1284–91 *There are those...fooled the vine*: the chorus, speaking in the first-person voice of the poet himself, recalls the political attack on Aristophanes by Kleon after *Babylonians* in 426 (see n. on *A*. 378, with my Introduction to *Acharnians*); this is in line with the boasts earlier in the play (1030 ff.) about the poet's comic targeting of Kleon himself, especially in *Knights*. The present passage seems to describe an occasion, probably in the Council (cf. *A*. 379–82), when Aristophanes was thought to have reached some kind of accommodation which his continuing satire of Kleon and others has supposedly circumvented. 'The vine-pole fooled the vine' was a proverbial expression for going back on a promise or the like.

1301–2 *Hippyllos… Phrynichos*: almost certainly these figures were all real individuals, between them forming a putative social/political circle, but we cannot identify any of them for certain. Antiphon is no doubt the same man as at 1270, and Lysistratos the same as at 787. Lykon is probably the figure who, with his son Autolykos, was widely mocked by other comic poets of this period; he is also a guest in Xenophon's *Symposium*. Phrynichos (not the early tragic playwright mentioned at 220, etc.) might be the man who, a decade later, became a member of the oligarchic coup of the Four Hundred (Thucydides 8.68.3).

1308–13 *Lysistratos… Sthenelos*: Lysistratos initiates the party game of witty 'likenesses'; cf. 1413–14, with Xenophon, *Symposium* 6.8–10. Apart from the image of a rich Phrygian ex-slave, the comparisons are hard to decipher, including the one involving Sthenelos, a minor tragic poet later criticized at Aristotle, *Poetics* 22.1458a20–1 for banality of style.

1339 *voting funnels*: see 99 and 754.

1346 *Lesbian job*: i.e. fellatio; in ancient texts, the sexual associations of women from Lesbos more often related to the services of prostitutes than to the idea of female homosexuality; cf. *F.* 1308, *AW* 920.

1353 *piglet*: see n. on 573 for this sexual euphemism. In the present passage, Philokleon absurdly inverts the normal psychological and financial dynamics of a father-son relationship.

1363 *Mysteries*: i.e. the Eleusinian Mysteries, an initiatory cult of Demeter and Persephone at Eleusis in NW Attika; cf. *A.* 747, *P.* 375, 420. The Mysteries involved various moments of ritualized abuse (here, by implication, within families), though there is considerable uncertainty about how the following lines reflect (and/or distort) such practices.

1382–4 *Olympia… old*: Philokleon ludicrously recycles material from the earlier rehearsal at 1187–94.

1394–5 *smart words… agreement*: Philokleon's perverted application of the practice he heard about at 1256 ff.

1396 *goddesses twain*: for the deities in question, see n. on 378; this form of oath was a linguistic peculiarity of women, hence the comic nature of the woman's error at *AW* 155–9. Myrtia cites her parents in the following line to emphasize her respectability, but Agkylion, a rare name, is probably amusing for its literal sense of 'crooked'.

1401 *Aisop*: a (perverse) echo of Bdelykleon's advice at 1259; cf. also 566.

1407 *market officials*: see n. on *A.* 723.

1408 *Chairephon*: probably the Chairephon who was a close friend of the philosopher Sokrates (see *C.* 104, 144, etc., *B.* 1553–64), but why he is chosen as a witness to accompany Myrtia remains comically opaque.

1410 *Lasos and Simonides*: Lasos of Hermione and Simonides of Ceos were lyric poets of the sixth century; for Simonides, cf. *P*. 697–9, *C*. 1356–62, *B*. 919.

1413–14 *You resemble... Euripides*: Philokleon echoes the game of likenesses from 1308 ff. Ino was the subject of a complex myth treated in three plays by Euripides (*Ino* and two plays called *Phrixos*). In one of these plots, it seems she supplicated someone by the knees, conceivably when in disguise (cf. n. on *A*. 433–4), though Philokleon replaces the character's name with the playwright's. Chairephon's sallowness was a running joke: see *C*. 503–4 (corpse-like appearance), *B*. 1296, 1564 (his nickname 'bat'). But the present image remains puzzlingly convoluted.

1418 *hybris*: a category of crime which covered forms of both physical and verbal aggression; the nub of the matter here is outrageous public debasement of a fellow citizen.

1427 *Sybaris*: see n. on 1259.

1432 *Pittalos*: see n. on *A*. 1032.

1446–8 *Delphians... dung-beetle*: the reference—employed perversely by Philokleon—is to a biographical legend about how the Delphians falsely accused Aisop by planting a sacred bowl among his belongings; Aisop defended himself with a fable about how the lowly dung-beetle, with justice on its side, defeated the eagle (see n. on *P*. 129–30). With 'I couldn't care less', Bdelykleon turns his father's earlier words (1411) against him.

1479 *Thespis*: the (perhaps legendary) founder of Athenian tragedy as a dramatic genre; he was supposedly active *c*.530.

1490 *Phrynichos*: see n. on 220.

1491 *pelted*: an apotropaic action used against those perceived as mad; cf. *B*. 524–5.

1501 *Karkinos*: a tragic poet (cf. *C*. 1261), though also a figure with serious military experience (he was general in 432–431: Thucydides 2.23.2), whose theatrical career stretched back to the 440s; he and his sons (who are probably impersonated, not actually performing in the present passage) are mocked again at *P*. 781–95 and 864.

1507 *crabs*: crab is the literal meaning of the name Karkinos.

1511 *tragic poet*: Xenokles, the butt of jokes at *WT* 169, 440–3, *F*. 86.

1537 *wine-song*: cf. 650 with n. on *A*. 497–9.

PEACE

9 *dung-collectors*: cf. *W*. 1184.

14 *eating*: i.e. as if he were a slave pilfering some of the food he is supposed to be preparing for his master's household.

42 *Zeus... shit*: in the Greek, a phrase meaning 'Zeus the descender' (alluding to thunderbolts) allows the noun for 'shit' to be heard by slurring the sounds of the two words together.

46–8 *Ionian…faeces*: 'Ionian' means speaking the Ionic dialect (n. on 929–33) used (especially) in the Greek cities of the central W coast of Asia Minor; the term sometimes connoted sensuous luxury (cf. *WT* 163) but the hypothetical spectator is imagined as an intellectually over-confident interpreter. 'Liquid faeces' is a medical term, here euphemistic for an eternal punishment in Hades. Kleon (Index of Names) had been killed in battle the previous year (422) at Amphipolis; see Thucydides 5.10.9–11.

50 *boys*: for the presence of boys in the theatre audience, see 766 and *C.* 539; cf. Eupolis fr. 261 and, at a later date, Plato, *Laws* 2.658d (comedy a favourite entertainment for older boys).

54 *insane…novel*: compare the similar gambit in the slave's prologue at *W.* 71.

73 *Aitnaian*: from mount Aitna (Etna) in Sicily, a source of a reputedly large species of dung-beetle.

76–7 *Pegasos…Zeus*: line 76 is partly parodic of Bellerophon's address to Pegasos in Euripides' *Bellerophon* (fr. 306); see n. on *A.* 427. Pegasos was the immortal winged horse on which Bellerophon attempted to fly up to Olympos to remonstrate with Zeus; he was fatally wounded when Zeus threw him from the horse (which ultimately served Zeus himself: cf. 722). For further evocations of Euripides' play in the present passage, see 135–6, 146–8.

99 *alleys*: i.e. backstreets where people might sometimes defecate; Athens had no public toilets at this date. For matters of sanitation, cf. the implications of *A.* 1170.

108 *Persians*: the reference here is a vague one to the idea that the Persians still represented a major military threat to Greece, especially as both sides in the Peloponnesian War periodically sought assistance from them; cf. 408 and n. on *A.* 61.

120–1 *Daddy…cash*: compare Philokleon's relationship to his daughter at *W.* 607–9.

129–30 *Aisop…gods*: in an Aisopic fable (n. on *W.* 566) a dispute between a dung-beetle and an eagle leads the latter to fly up to Zeus and nest in his lap, but the eagle's eggs are broken when the dung-beetle annoys Zeus and makes him jump up. Cf. *W.* 1448.

136 *tragic*: a further allusion to Euripides' *Bellerophon*, as again at 146–8; see n. on 76–7.

143 *water boatman*: the Greek depends on the fact that the word *kantharos*, 'dung-beetle', can also mean a kind of boat (here also described in the Greek as 'made in Naxos', probably with reference to specialist ship-building).

145 *Beetle Harbour*: the largest of the three harbours that formed Peiraieus (Index of Names, with n. on *K.* 84), but the name was a homonym of *kantharos* (n. on 143) and was not derived from the term for a dung-beetle.

146–8 *plunge…tragic plot*: for Bellerophon's fall, see n. on 76–7, with n. on *A.* 411 for the idea that Euripides had a general liking for crippled heroes.

155 *golden bridle*: the term is a parodic echo of Bellerophon's address to Pegasos in Euripides fr. 307.

158 *filthy alleys*: as at 99.

171 *Chios*: this island in the E Aegean was one of Athens' allies. If an Athenian was murdered in an allied city, the city was fined five talents (for the amount, cf. n. on *A.* 6–8), but it is uncertain why Chios is picked out here: is Trygaios envisaging falling out of the sky and landing on the island?

174 *crane-operator*: on the stage crane, *mêchanê*, see the general Introduction, 'Stage Directions'.

190 *Trygaios...*: the name Trygaios is not found outside this play; it is derived from a verb meaning 'gather fruit', including grapes (see 912, 1339), and therefore has an etymological connection with the term *trygôdia*, 'wine-song', used as a comic substitute for 'comedy' itself in several passages (n. on *A.* 497–9). Athmonon was a deme in mid-Attika, NE of the city. For the viticulture motif, see 308, 520, 557, 597, 1162, with e.g. *A.* 183, 232, 512.

193 *greedy*: in comedy, at least, Hermes could be depicted as excessively eager for food and other gifts from humans; cf. *We.* 1120–42.

214 '*By the Twain...*': this Spartan oath (by Kastor and Pollux: n. on 285) is used frequently by the Spartans in *Lysistrata*, e.g. 81, 983, 1105; 'laddie from Attika' translates a diminutive which is unique to this line. In 215, Hermes himself uses a jocular, invented term for Athenians.

216–19 *Spartans...Pylos*: see n. on *K.* 55, with n. on *K.* 668–9 for Spartan peace overtures after their loss of troops at Pylos; cf. 665–7. For the Spartans as untrustworthy (in Athenian eyes), cf. 623 and 1063–8, with n. on *A.* 308.

242 *Prasiai*: on the E coast of the Peloponnese, this town had been sacked by Athens early in the war (Thucydides 2.56.6); its name is chosen here as a pun on *prason*, 'leek'.

247 *garlic paste*: see n. on *A.* 174 for this food; garlic (cf. 502 and 1000) was a Megarian speciality (*A.* 521, 761–3, with Index of Names under Megara).

250 *Sicily*: known, among other things, for its cheese-production; cf. *W.* 838.

270 *leather-seller*: for this caricature of Kleon (Index of Names), see 648–50 with n. on *K.* 44; for Kleon as a 'stirrer' of things, see 654 with the Introduction to *Knights*.

278 *Samothrace*: an island in the NE Aegean which was home to an important mystery cult whose initiates had special prayers for times of acute danger.

282–4 *pestle...returned*: a reference to the leading Spartan commander Brasidas (cf. 640, *W.* 475), who had been killed the previous year in the same battle as Kleon (n. on 46–8); the implication that Brasidas, like Kleon, was a leading opponent of peace coincides with the view of Thucydides 5.16.1.

285 *Dioskouroi*: Kastor and Pollux, twin sons of Zeus and Leda; cf. 214.

290–1 *Datis...joy myself*: probably a reference to one of the commanders of the Persian invasion defeated at the battle of Marathon (Herodotos 6.94.2), though we cannot be sure what popular humour underlies the reference. The second of the three verbs in 291 is comically ungrammatical in Greek.

297 *metics*: resident aliens (here, not just of Athens); they were often liable to military service in the cities where they resided.

303–4 *officers… Lamachos*: for officers in scarlet cloaks, see 1172–8; for Lamachos, cf. 473, 1290, with the Index of Names and Introduction to *Acharnians*.

312 *three days' food*: for this requirement on those called up for military service, see n. on *A*. 196–7; cf. 367–8, 1182.

313 *Kerberos*: another reference to the recently dead Kleon (nn. on 46–8 and 270); he had already been figured as Kerberos, guard-dog of the underworld, at *K*. 1030, on account of his supposedly barking voice and brash rhetoric, as well as his claim to be a guard-dog of the city (see *K*. 1023–4, *W*. 916).

343 *Sybarite*: see n. on *W*. 1259.

347b *Phormion*: for this former Athenian general, see n. on *K*. 551–64.

348 *acrid, peevish juror*: the chorus is characterized as conforming to the same stereotype as Philokleon (and the jurors in general) in *Wasps*: see esp. *W*. 106, 145, 277, 883, 942.

356 *Lykeion*: a gymnasium and training ground to the E of the city; for the quotation, see n. on *W*. 1078–88.

363 *Killikon*: a semi-proverbial criminal, perhaps from Miletos, who was seemingly associated in folklore with obfuscating his deeds with disingenuous language.

364 *first lot*: Trygaios speaks as though he were one of a number of people condemned to death and the order of their executions was to be determined by lot (a process with which Hermes was associated, hence the next line).

367–8 *provisions… death*: Trygaios facetiously takes 'death' to mean being called up for military service; see n. on 312.

375 *initiated*: i.e. into the Eleusinian Mysteries (cf. 420); initiands sacrificed piglets (nn. on *A*. 747, *W*. 1363).

378–9 *meat… gift*: a reference back to 192–3.

395 *Peisander*: a prominent politician here treated as a proponent of bellicose policies; he is later satirized for cowardice at *B*. 1556 and for using the war to enrich himself at *L*. 490–2. A decade after *Peace* he became one of the leaders of the 411 oligarchic coup at Athens (Thucydides 8.49 ff.).

402 *thieves*: Hermes himself was sometimes considered the god of thieves; cf. *We*. 1139–41, with e.g. Homer, *Odyssey* 19.395–8.

408 *Persians*: here and in 411 the Greek says 'the barbarians', but this would most readily have been understood with reference to the Persians (compare the same point at *L*. 1133), for whose sacrifices to sun and moon see Herodotos 1.131.2; for 'betraying' Greece in this context, cf. 108.

414–15 *days… cycles*: an allusion to occasional adjustments in the solar and lunar elements of the Athenian calendar (compare *C.* 615–26), absurdly taken by Hermes as the work of the sun and moon themselves.

418–20 *Panathenaia… Adonia*: the Panathenaia was a major festival in honour of Athena (Index of Names), the Dipolieia a festival of Zeus held on the Akropolis (*C.* 984); for the Eleusinian Mysteries, see n. on *W.* 1363; for the Adonia, a women's vegetation cult in honour of the originally Semitic deity Adonis, see *L.* 389–96.

440 *fire to poke*: probably a sexual double entendre. Compare the imagery of 891.

446 *Kleonymos*: see Index of Names for this politician; cf. 673–8 and 1295.

466 *Boiotians*: their opposition to the Peace of Nikias, concluded shortly after the performance of *Peace* (see the Introduction to the play), is noted at Thucydides 5.17.2.

473 *Lamachos*: see n. on 303–4; but Lamachos was in fact a signatory to the Peace of Nikias (Thucydides 5.19.2, cf. 24.1).

475–7 *Argives… both sides*: Argos (see Index of Names, and cf. 493) had been neutral in the Archidamian War and had its own reasons for not wanting a stable peace between Athens and Sparta (see Thucydides 5.27.2–28.3).

479–80 *Spartans… chained*: the Spartans captured on Sphakteria in 425 (n. on *K.* 55) and kept prisoners at Athens (*K.* 469).

481–3 *Megarians… starved*: despite the present passage, Thucydides 5.17.2 tells us that Megara (see Index of Names) was opposed to the Peace of Nikias; for the Megarians' wartime 'starvation', see *A.* 535, 729 ff.

500–2 *Megara… garlic*: a reference to the Megarian decree in the antecedents of the war; see n. on 609, with n. on 247 for Megarian garlic.

507 *step back… sea*: i.e. the Athenians should not make excessive demands on land territory in the negotiations for peace; cf. Thucydides 5.17.2.

528–9 *I detest… oniony*: line 528 is adapted from Euripides fr. 727 (possibly from *Telephos*: cf. n. on *A.* 430); for onions as soldiers' meagre fare, cf. 1129 and *A.* 1099–1100.

530–4 *ripeness… wrangling*: Trygaios's compound evocation of peacetime good living incorporates tragedy as part of Dionysiac festivity; cf. the general Introduction, 'Old Comedy and Dionysiac Festivity'. For Sophokles, the great tragic playwright, cf. 695–9; for thrushes as gourmet food (Athenians ate a wide variety of birds), cf. 1149, 1195, with *C.* 339. Euripides is also characterized as a poet who reduced the style of tragedy to a less elevated level, including that of quasi-forensic rhetoric, at *F.* 937–79.

549 *gave the finger*: the same obscene gesture as referred to at *A.* 444, *K.* 1381, *C.* 652–4.

561 *Gorgon shields*: cf. Lamachos's shield, with its Gorgon emblem, at *A.* 574, 964–5, 1095, etc.; see also *L.* 560.

582 ff. *Epode*: this lyric section forms a triad with the strophe and antistrophe at 345 ff. and 385 ff.

586: we can tell on metrical grounds that a line has dropped out of the text here.

595 *porridge*: cf. *K*. 806, also associated with the pleasures of rural life under peace.

605–6 *Pheidias...Perikles*: Pheidias sculpted the colossal gold-and-ivory statue of Athena for the Parthenon (see n. on *K*. 1169); he was convicted of embezzlement at some point around 438. His close association with Perikles (see Index of Names) may have tarnished the latter as well, though we have no reliable details; the connection to the outbreak of war is, to put it mildly, far-fetched.

609 *Megarian decree*: an economic embargo on Megarian goods in the late 430s; see note on *A*. 530–4, where it is given a different but equally fanciful 'explanation' (a series of tit-for-tat events between Athens and Megara, though also, as here, supposedly involving personal motives on Perikles' part).

613 *wine-jars smashed*: the image combines (i) the destruction of wine-jars in war (see 700–3) with (ii) an allegory of the combatants themselves as wine-jars smashing aggressively against one another.

623 *cheating others*: another reference (n. on 216–19) to Spartans as perfidious.

619–27 *cities...leaders*: a highly compressed and tendentious sequence of claims, (i) that Athens' allied/subject cities bribed Sparta to go to war (in order to allow the cities opportunities for revolt from Athens), (ii) that Spartan leaders sought profit for themselves, and (iii) that it was peasant farmers who suffered from Athenian raids on Peloponnesian (coastal) territory (for which see e.g. Thucydides 2.25, 3.16.2).

632 *moved off the land*: for the displacement of the rural population in the early years of the war, and the Spartan invasions of Attika alluded to in the preceding lines, see the Introduction to *Acharnians*.

638 *showed herself*: i.e. in the form of spurned opportunities for peace; see 215–19.

640 *Brasidas*: see n. on 282–4; cf. the similar reference to him at *W*. 475. For secret plotting between Athenian allies and Brasidas, see Thucydides 4.108.3.

648–50 *leather-seller...dead*: see 270 for Kleon as leather-seller, with 47–8 and 313 for other references to his death. 650 alludes to the longstanding role of Hermes as escort of the souls of the dead to Hades.

660 *whisper*: compare Strepsiades' behaviour with the herm that stands outside his house at *C*. 1478–83.

665–7 *Pylos...Assembly*: see n. on 216–19; Thucydides 4.41.4 stresses the plurality of Spartan offers in this context.

669 *leather*: see n. on 648–50.

673–8 *Kleonymos...bastard*: see Index of Names; there is a pun in the Greek on words meaning 'throwing away' and 'illegitimate'.

681–92 *Hyperbolos… lamps*: for the politician Hyperbolos, see Index of Names and cf. 921, 1319; for the term 'steward' at 686 as a domestic metaphor for a democratic leader's relationship to the people, see n. on *K*. 212.

695–9 *Sophokles… mat*: Sophokles, the tragic playwright (cf. 531), was about 75 at the date of *Peace*; he is compared to the archaic lyric poet Simonides (n. on *W*. 1410) apparently for reasons of financial greed or avarice (for which Simonides had a popular reputation) but on the basis of something now unknown to us. 'Putting to sea on a mat' was a proverbial expression for risky ventures.

700–3 *Kratinos… wine*: for the comic poet Kratinos, see Index of Names; he had at least a humorous reputation, exploited in his own play *Wine-Flask* (423), for being a tippler. His supposed death in the present passage may well be a fiction, since he had certainly outlived the Spartan invasions of the early 420s. For smashed wine-jars, see 613.

712 *herbal drink*: i.e. to settle the stomach after over-indulgence; Hermes answers Trygaios's question as though it referred to food and drink rather than sex.

710–13 *Festivity… meat*: the Council (see Index of Names) was responsible, among much else, for administering certain festivals; in the references to lavish food consumption—a standard feature of festivity—some scholars detect sexual double entendres.

722 *He's yoked…*: the line is from Euripides' *Bellerophon* (fr. 312); cf. n. on 76–7, with Hesiod, *Theogony* 285–6, for the role of Pegasos in Zeus's service.

724 *Ganymede excretes*: Ganymede, the beautiful Trojan prince chosen by Zeus as his cup-bearer (and, as sometimes supposed, his catamite); the joke here obviously implies that Ganymede has fed on the food of the gods, ambrosia (cf. 854, with n. on *A*. 196–7). The scatological humour overlaps with the earlier joke at 11–12 about the dung-beetle's food from the excrement of a young male prostitute.

726 *past the goddess*: i.e. through door A, behind the statue of Peace on the *ekkuklēma*; the door's previous identity as a cave is ignored or cancelled for the sake of theatrical humour, since Trygaios lacks any 'plausible' means of getting back to earth.

734–5 *theatre-stewards… anapaest verse*: the stewards had some powers to enforce good order in the theatre, but the application of those powers to boastful poets is transparently ironic; for 'anapaest verse', see n. on *A*. 627. For mock-modesty as a parabatic gambit, cf. *A*. 629. 'Step forward' is the verb cognate with *parabasis*.

737–8 *poets… chorus-trainer*: the terms poet and chorus-trainer are here synonymous; see n. on *A*. 628–9.

739–48 *put a stop… vulgar joking*: an expanded version of the type of claims made at *W*. 57–61; but here as there the claims are at least partly disingenuous, given Aristophanes' own willingness to exploit the whole spectrum of humour from 'high' to 'low' (see e.g. the opening of *Knights* for humour extracted from the physical beating of slaves). To address a textual problem in this passage, I have diverged from Olson's edition by following those scholars who reverse the order of lines 742 and 743.

751–60 *didn't make fun . . . stood my ground*: this passage is largely repeated from *W*. 1029–37; see the notes there for individual details.

762 *wrestling schools*: see n. on *W*. 1025–8.

766 *boys*: see n. on 51.

767–73 *bald . . . forehead*: for this oddly autobiographical allusion to the poet's premature hair loss, see n. on *K*. 550.

775–80 *Muse . . . blesséd*: the passage is based on part of the *Oresteia* by the archaic lyric poet Stesichoros; the lofty lyric tone is used as a foil to the following mockery.

782–92 *Karkinos . . . weasel*: for the tragic poet Karkinos and his dancer sons, mentioned again at 864, see the closing scene of *Wasps* (1501–37); the point of the gibe about a missing or lost play is now indecipherable. For weasels (and excuses), see n. on *W*. 363–4.

796–801 *songs . . . voice*: the passage contains further borrowings from Stesichoros (n. on 775–80).

803–4 *Morsimos . . . Melanthios*: brothers, and both tragic playwrights; for Morsimos, see n. on *K*. 400–1, and for Melanthios see the further references at 1010–14 and *B*. 151.

810–11 *Gorgons . . . fish*: the brothers are pictured, in comically mythologized imagery, as swooping on and terrorizing the female fish-sellers (hence 'skate') in the market (cf. Melanthios again in a market scene at 1009–15). For the Gorgons, see the Index of Names; the Harpies were winged demons whose deeds relevantly included an episode in which they snatched the food of a Thracian king.

829 *dithyrambic*: dithyramb was a genre of choral poetry in honour of Dionysos; its (comic) associations with airy/cloudy language are elaborately developed in the scene with Kinesias at *B*. 1372–1409.

833 *stars*: although there were various Greek beliefs, both mythological and philosophical, about a possible destiny in the upper air for the soul after death, a specifically astral version of such ideas is not well attested elsewhere at this date.

835–7 *Ion . . . Morning Star*: Ion of Chios (*c*.480–425) wrote poetry and prose in multiple genres; the poem referred to here was a dithyramb (n. on 829) which called the Morning Star 'air-roaming'.

850 *others up there*: in response to Slave[B]'s perception of Harvest and Festivity as looking like prostitutes, Trygaios exculpates the gods from pimping but makes a throwaway remark whose humorous implications are unclear (the pimps up there are not themselves gods? or *some* gods are pimps?).

854 *ambrosia*: cf. 724 with n. on *A*. 196–7.

864 *Karkinos*: see the earlier reference at 782–92.

874 *Brauron*: a region on the E coast of Attika associated with an important quadrennial cult of Artemis (see *L.* 644–5); Slave^B apparently recalls the company of a prostitute called Festivity who had accompanied them on the procession from Athens to Brauron.

880 *Isthmian games*: a biennial festival held near the isthmus of Korinth; it was common for visitors to occupy tents for the duration of a festival.

883–5 *Ariphrades…broth*: a euphemistic joke about this character's supposed fetish for cunnilingus; see n. on *K.* 1281.

886 *this dress*: the transmitted text has 'this equipment', which is hard to make sense of. Festivity, like Harvest (and also like e.g. the naked Reconciliation at *L.* 1115 ff.), will almost certainly have been played by a male actor in drag.

887 *Prytaneis*: the steering committee of the Council; see Index of Names. In addition to the present passage, the special area of theatre seating reserved for members of the Council is alluded to at *B.* 794.

893 *pot-stands*: stands for cooking pots; the visual 'pun' (with Festivity's legs and pubic hair matching the legs and dark-stained top of a pot-stand) presumably made more effective comic sense than it does in purely verbal terms. Cf. the obscene humour at *W.* 1374–5.

896–904 *wrestle…course*: an elaborate (con)fusion of imagery from athletics, including equestrian events, and sex. For the pankration, see n. on *W.* 1191; for the 'jockey position', cf. *W.* 501.

912 *gather your grapes*: the Greek verb is the etymological root of Trygaios's own name (nn. 190, 1339).

919 *Athmonon*: see n. on 190.

921 *Hyperbolos*: the politician (see 681–92) is here treated as a comic metonymy for war.

923–4 *dedicate…herm*: dedication turns the statue into a recognized sacred object; 'with pots' refers to a basic ritual (cf. *We.* 1197–8) sometimes used to dedicate smaller statues like household herms (i.e. symbolic icons of Hermes: cf. *C.* 1478, with the famous reference at Thucydides 6.27.1).

928 *Theagenes*: this was a common name, as was Theogenes (n. on *W.* 1183), which some editors prefer to read here. Either way, we cannot know which individual is meant. For 'swinishness', cf. Kleon's at *K.* 986.

929–33 *bleater…Ionic*: the word for sheep is used by the chorus-leader in the form found in the Ionic dialect (n. on 46–8); there is a pun in 933 on a similar-sounding exclamation of woe.

951–5 *Chairis…meat*: for Chairis the piper, see n. on *A.* 16; he is treated here as a scrounger like the priest Hierokles at 1045 ff. or e.g. the poet at *B.* 905 ff.

959 *bob your head*: this alludes to the belief, sometimes called a 'comedy of innocence' by modern scholars, that an animal for sacrifice needed to signal a kind of consent to its own killing.

966–7 *wives…husbands*: the sexual point depends on a Greek word for barley which is also slang for 'penis'. The passage contributes to the uncertainty of our evidence for whether some women attended the theatre in this period: it can be interpreted, with more or less equal justification, as implying *either* that there were no women in the theatre *or* that there was a section for them near the back (and therefore out of reach of the barley thrown into the audience). See the general Introduction, 'Stage Directions'.

980–5 *adulterous...peek out*: a similar vignette occurs at *WT* 797–9; both passages presuppose that 'respectable' (younger) women were not expected to be seen at their house doors, but the later text helps confirm that 'adulterous' at 980 represents the men's sexist prejudice more than the intended behaviour of the women as imagined.

988 *lovers*: Trygaios implies, somewhat ironically, that Peace should behave not as an adulterous wife but something more like a grand courtesan.

990 *thirteen*: an approximate figure; with the normal Greek practice of inclusive counting, this takes one back to (early) 433, which predates the official outbreak of war but can be roughly correlated with one of the antecedents of war, the Athenian decision to make an alliance with Kerkyra, in its dispute with Korinth, in the summer of 433 (Thucydides 1.44–5). Contrast the chronology of *A*. 268, *K*. 793.

992 *Lysimache*: lit. 'breaker up of war', a real female name (cf. *L*. 554) which we know was held at this date by an Athenian priestess of Athena Polias, though that fact has no bearing on this passage as such.

1000–2 *garlic...cloaks*: for Megarian garlic, see n. on 247; for Megarian clothing, cf. *A*. 519.

1003–5 *Boiotian...eels*: see the Boiotian scene at *A*. 860–958.

1008 *Morychos...*: all three figures were probably wealthy and of some social standing; for Morychos, see n. on *A*. 887, for Teleas, see *B*. 168, 1025, and for Glauketes, *WT* 1033.

1010–14 *Melanthios...beetroot*: for Melanthios, tragic poet, see n. on 803–4; we do not know the exact relationship of the parodic tragic language in 1013–14 to Melanthios's own work, though we may be dealing with distortion of something said by Jason after Medea had killed his new wife. In the comic scenario, the 'female' is, of course, the eel Melanthios has failed to buy; for eel served in beetroot, cf. *A*. 894.

1022 *chorêgos*: a wealthy citizen (or, at the Lenaia, it could be a metic) selected to pay for the staging of a play, as well as for providing a feast afterwards (cf. *A*. 1150–5).

1026 *seer*: an expert, among other things, in observing burnt offerings as a form of divination.

1031 *Stilbides*: a leading contemporary seer.

1047 *Oreus*: the same place as Hestiaia in N Euboia. We know from an official inscription that Hierokles had been involved in religious rituals (with oracular backing) relating to an Athenian settlement on Euboia in 446; he may himself have been granted land on the island. For oracle-mongers, cf. the scene at *B*. 959–91.

1056 *first fruits*: a portion of the meat notionally for a god but sometimes put aside as a perquisite for a religious official; cf. nn. on 1060 and 1122–3.

1060 *the tongue*: cf. *B*. 1704–5, *We*. 1110, and Homer, *Odyssey* 3.332; the principle is the same as at 1056.

1065 *cruel-eyed monkeys*: the adjective is applied in early Greek epic to lions, hence the incongruity of the phrase; Hierokles is alluding to the idea of the Spartans as untrustworthy (see 216–19, 623, and n. on *A*. 308). For monkeys as tricksters, cf. *A*. 907, *K*. 887.

1070 *Bakis*: for this oracular authority, see n. on *K*. 123.

1078 *blind offspring*: an allusion to an old proverb, warning against haste, that 'an eager bitch gives birth to blind offspring'.

1084 *Prytaneion*: see Index of Names for the civic honour of dining in this building.

1090–4 *Thus... oracle-monger*: a mélange of partly Homeric phrases, including a whole line (1092) which occurs in both the *Iliad* and *Odyssey*; but the sentiment in 1091 is comically unhomeric.

1095 *Sibyl*: in origin a legendary prophetess; the term was by this date generically applicable to several oracular sources. Cf. 1116.

1097–8 *Lacking...people*: a quotation of Homer, *Iliad* 9.63–4, spoken by Nestor; in context, the lines refer not to war in general but to strife within a community.

1106 *Ever...*: Trygaios quotes back Hierokles' words at him from 1075.

1112 *until wolf and sheep*: another sarcastic echo, this one from 1076.

1114 *will you make...*: see Hierokles' words at 1086.

1116 *Sibyl*: see 1095.

1119 *Bakis*: an echo of 1070–2.

1122–3 *fleeces...deceit*: the accusation is that Hierokles had improperly obtained animal fleeces as priestly perks (n. on 1056) at previous sacrifices.

1125–6 *Oreus...Elymnion*: for Oreus, see n. on 1047; Elymnion was also on Euboia, though its exact location is uncertain, as is the point of Trygaios's reference to it here.

1129 *onions*: see n. on 528–9.

1142 *Komarchides*: the name is not elsewhere attested for classical Athens but suits the chorus-leader, since it can be interpreted as 'Son of revel-leader', the *kom-* element being the same as in the term 'comedy' itself (cf. the general Introduction, 'Old Comedy and Dionysiac Festivity', on the practice of the *kômos* as revel).

1146 *Syra...Manes*: typical slave-names, the first indicating Syrian origins, the second Phrygian.

1149 *thrush*: see n. on 530–4 and cf. 1195 ff.

1151 *weasel*: see n. on *W*. 363–4.

1154–5 *Aeschinades… Charinades*: both are real Athenian names, though both seem to have been rare; for the second, cf. *W.* 232.

1172–4 *officer… Sardis*: for the triple crests, cf. n. on *A.* 965, and for dye from Sardis see n. on *A.* 112, with the earlier reference to officers in scarlet cloaks at line 303.

1177 *tawny horse-cock*: a phrase from a lost play by Aischylos (fr. 134) applied to an officer also at *B.* 700 and mocked further at *F.* 932–5; the horse-cock was a hybrid creature depicted in archaic Greek art.

1180 *campaign lists*: i.e. of troops called up for individual campaigns; for the suggestion of corruption in the compiling and alteration of such lists, see n. on *K.* 1369–70.

1182 *provisions*: soldiers normally had to provide their own for the start of a campaign; see n. on 312.

1183 *Pandion*: one of Athens' ten tribal heroes, whose statues stood in the Agora (see Index of Names); the lists of levied troops were posted on notice-boards in front of these statues.

1187 *Held to account*: a reference to the process whereby military officials, like magistrates (n. on *K.* 259), had to submit to a review at the end of their term of office and could be charged with misconduct of various kinds.

1224 *ten-mina*: one mina = 100 drachmas, making the breastplate absurdly expensive.

1230 *stones… to wipe with*: a standard toilet practice; cf. *We.* 818.

1234 *pay*: the meaning of the line is very uncertain; for rowers' pay, see n. on *A.* 162–3.

1244 *kottabos*: a game played at symposia in which wine lees were thrown at a target, which had to be knocked down in the form of the game referred to here.

1251 *mina*: see n. on 1224.

1253–4 *Egyptian… purges*: Egyptians were believed to use medicinal purges on a regular basis; cf. Herodotos 2.77.2.

1263 *vine-poles*: cf. *A.* 984, *W.* 1201.

1270 *First let us…*: the opening line of an epic poem, *Epigoni* (authorship uncertain), concerning an attack on Thebes by the sons of the earlier attack by the famous Seven against Thebes (part of the feud between the sons of the dead Oidipous).

1273–4 *Then when… bosses*: mostly an amalgam, as at 1090–4, of Homeric language.

1276 *Then there arose…*: a line from the *Iliad* (4.450 = 8.64).

1280–3 *Thus did they… they were*: 1280–1 are in epic style but not from a known source; 1282–3 closely resemble two lines from the later compilation, *The Contest of Homer and Hesiod* (§9 West), where they represent a line of Hesiod to which Homer has to supply a suitable continuation.

1286–7 *After... arose*: 1286 has no known source; it contains a Greek verb which literally means 'put on a breastplate' but also has a slang sense of 'drink heavily' (hence Trygaios's interpretation); see the similar humour at *A*. 1132–5. The second half of 1287 corresponds with *Iliad* 16.267.

1290 *Lamachos*: see n. on 303–4.

1295 *Kleonymos*: see 446, 673–8, and Index of Names for this supposedly cowardly politican, here ironically enlisted on the side of peace.

1298–1301 *Thracians... shame*: 1298–9 are the start of a famous poem by Archilochos (fr. 5.1–2 *IEG*) about discarding his shield in battle; for Thrace, see Index of Names. The start of 1301 adapts line 3 of the same poem, which Trygaios completes with a further gibe at Kleonymos.

1321 *Hyperbolos*: a final sneer at this politician; see 681–92, 921, with the Index of Names.

1334 *Hail Hymen*: for this traditional wedding refrain, cf. *B*. 1736 ff. Hymen/ Hymenaios is the personification of the wedding-song itself (which was of great antiquity, as we can see from Homer, *Iliad* 18.493).

1339 *gather her fruit*: the Greek verb here is the root of Trygaios's own name (n. 190).

1350 ... : several verses are probably missing at this point.

INDEX OF NAMES

Listed here are those proper names (excluding the purely fictional) of people, places, and institutions which are not fully glossed in the Explanatory Notes. Further information about many of these items can be found in *OCD*[4]. References are selective; capitals within entries indicate cross-references. For abbreviations of play-titles see p. 299.

ATTIKA (adj. Attic), the entire geographical territory of the Athenian polis, comprising both the city proper and the territory of the demes; Athenians thought of themselves as the original (autochthonous) inhabitants of the place (*W.* 1076, cf. *P.* 214–15); its characteristic products included honey (*P.* 252–4)

BOIOTIA, region of central Greece bordering ATTIKA to the NW, it included the city of Thebes (*A.* 862, 911) and was on the SPARTAN side in the Peloponnesian War (*A.* 920, 1023, 1077, *P.* 466, cf. *K.* 478–9); eels from its lake Kopaïs were renowned as a culinary delicacy (*A.* 880 ff., *P.* 1003–5)

COUNCIL (*Boulê*), of 500, responsible for important administrative aspects of Athenian democracy (*A.* 124, 379, *K.* 363, 475 ff., 625 ff.), including preparation of the ASSEMBLY's agenda (cf. *A.* 60, *W.* 590); the PRYTANEIS were its standing committee; members of the Council had a privileged seating area in the theatre (*P.* 871 ff.)

DELPHI, site of the famous oracle of APOLLO

DEMETER, sister of ZEUS and mother of Persephone, goddess of corn and fertility whose cults included the Eleusinian Mysteries (*A.* 747, *W.* 1363, *P.* 375)

DIONYSOS, son of ZEUS and Semele, god of wine (*A.* 195 ff., *W.* 1474 ff.) and of the dramatic festivals at which comedy itself was performed (cf. *A.* 1087, *W.* 1046); his other festivals (cf. *P.* 530) included the Rural Dionysia (*A.* 237 ff.) and the Anthesteria (*A.* 961–2)

EURIPIDES, tragic playwright (*c*.485–406), whose mother was satirically treated as a vegetable-seller (*A.* 457, *K.* 19); his style was thought partly notable for its pointedly rhetorical elements (*P.* 532–4); *A.* 395 ff. makes fun of his supposed penchant for 'beggar' heroes, and *P.* 124 ff. of his treatment of Bellerophon's flight on Pegasos

GORGONS, a trio of female mythological monsters, one of them Medusa (who was decapitated by the hero Perseus); a Gorgon's fearsome head, thought capable of turning viewers to stone, was sometimes used as an intimidating symbol on military shields (*A.* 574, 964, etc., *P.* 561)

GRACES, a trio of divine females, personifications of beauty, including the alluring charm of poetic song (*P.* 797), often associated with APHRODITE (*A.* 989, *P.* 40–1, 456)

HADES, the underworld, synonymous with death (*W.* 763), a place, for some, of grim punishments (*P.* 48); its entrance was guarded by the three-headed dog Kerberos (*K.* 1030, *P.* 313)

HERAKLES, human son of ZEUS, though deified after death (hence the frequency of oaths in his name), the ne plus ultra of physical heroism, his twelve 'labours' included confronting various monsters (*W*. 1030 ff., *P*. 752 ff.); but he also acquired a distinctively comic persona as a gourmand (*W*. 60, *P*. 741)

HERMES, traditionally a messenger god as well as escort of the dead to HADES (*P*. 650); he is sometimes a god of trade (*A*. 816, *K*. 297) and he serves comically as doorkeeper to Zeus (*P*. 180 ff.); symbolic icons ('herms') of the god stood outside many Athenian houses (*P*. 924)

HYPERBOLOS, an Athenian political leader, satirically thought of as a populist (*W*. 1007), whose family wealth was in lamp-making (*K*. 739, 1315, *P*. 690); he came into prominence in the mid-420s (*A*. 846), became the leading demagogue after the death of KLEON (*P*. 681), and was associated, like the latter, with an aggressive war policy (*P*. 921, 1321) as well as ambitious imperialism (*K*. 1303–4)

KLEISTHENES, an Athenian who in reality must have been of some social and even political prominence (*W*. 1187) but was repeatedly satirized by Aristophanes as effeminate and notorious for passive homosexual proclivities (*A*. 118, *K*. 1374, cf. his later appearance at *WT* 574 ff.)

KLEON, the most prominent Athenian politician of the 420s (died 422: *P*. 47–8) after the death of PERIKLES; his family wealth came from the tanning industry (*K*. 44 ff., 136, etc.); he used his political power to challenge Aristophanes after the latter's *Babylonians* (*A*. 377–82, 502–3, 659–60, *W*. 1284–91); Aristophanes' satirical portrait of him as demagogue is polarized around persecution of the rich (including supposed hostility to the Knights: *A*. 6–8, 300–1, and a recurrent theme in *Knights* itself) and populist appeal to poorer Athenians

KLEONYMOS, an Athenian politician, probably an associate of KLEON's (*K*. 958, *W*. 592), and known to have proposed a tightening of the collection of tribute from Athens' allies in 426; mocked for gluttony/obesity (*A*. 89, cf. 843, *K*. 956–8, 1290–9, *W*. 16) and for a supposed act of military cowardice (*K*. 1372, *W*. 15–23, 592, 822–3, *P*. 446, 673–8, 1294–1304)

KRATINOS, the most successful comic poet of the generation before Aristophanes'; as a rival of Aristophanes in the 420s, he is treated ironically as in his dotage (*K*. 526–36) and subjected to a range of personal abuse (*A*. 849–51, 1171, *K*. 400); a reference to his death (*P*. 700–3) may be a humorous fiction

KYPRIS, a poetic title of APHRODITE'S

LAMACHOS, one of Athens' most experienced military leaders, more than once an elected general (*A*. 593), whose name etymologically means 'very warlike' (cf. *A*. 270, *P*. 304) and therefore makes him a comically convenient stereotype of a warmongering officer (*A*. 561 ff., *P*. 473–4, 1290–3)

MARATHON, remote NE region of ATTIKA, site of the famous Athenian victory over the invading Persian army in 490 (*A.* 181, 697–8, *K.* 781, 1334, *W.* 711, cf. *P.* 290–1)

MEGARA, a city situated W of Athens towards the middle of the isthmus of Korinth, it was the object of a commercial ban by Athens, the 'Megarian decree' (*A.* 515–39, *P.* 609), shortly before the Peloponnesian War; known for its garlic (*A.* 761–3, *P.* 246–9, 1000) and pork farming (*A.* 521, 739 ff.); the Athenians used 'Megarian comedy' as a disparaging term for low-grade farce (*A.* 738–9, *W.* 57)

MUSES, traditionally nine daughters of ZEUS and Memory, personifications of poetic and artistic inspiration, their metaphorical 'personalities' adaptable to the identity of particular voices, including those of comic choruses (*A.* 665 ff., *P.* 775 ff., 813) and the comic poet himself (*W.* 1022–8)

PEIRAIEUS, the main harbour complex of Athens (*P.* 145), built up (to replace the older Phaleron, *A.* 991) on the advice of Themistokles in the 480s in association with a policy of expanding the city's naval power (*K.* 814–16, 885, Thucydides 1.93.3–7); its residential quarter had a reputation for its 'red light' district (*P.* 145)

PERIKLES, major Athenian politician (*c.*495–429), pre-eminent during the heyday of the city's imperial dominance of Greece (see Chronology under 462, 455, 451), and instrumental in determining Athens' policy at the outbreak of the Peloponnesian War (*A.* 530 ff., *P.* 605 ff.); he became the subject of posthumous nostalgia (cf. *K.* 283)

PERSIANS, imperial Near Eastern power since the mid-sixth century, ruled by kingship (*A.* 61–2), defeated by the Athenians at the battles of MARATHON and Salamis (*K.* 785); both sides in the Peloponnesian War were periodically involved in negotiating with the Persians for financial help (*A.* 61 ff., 613, 647, *K.* 478, cf. *P.* 108); the king of Persia's palace was at Susa (*A.* 80), his summer residence at Ekbatana (*K.* 1089, *W.* 1143–4, with n. on *A.* 64), and one of the empire's administrative centres at Sardis, a byword for luxury (*A.* 112, *W.* 1137–9, *P.* 1172)

PHOIBOS, lit. 'radiant', an archaic title of APOLLO's

PNYX, Athenian hill W of the Akropolis, meeting-place of the ASSEMBLY (*A.* 20, *K.* 42, 165, 749 ff., *W.* 31, *P.* 680)

POSEIDON, son of Kronos (*K.* 561) and brother of ZEUS, god of the sea (*K.* 554–60), horses (*K.* 561–3, 609–10), and earthquakes (*A.* 510–11); his shrines included one at Sounion, the southern tip of ATTIKA, and Geraistos, in S Euboia (*K.* 560–1)

PRYTANEION, a building on the N or E side of the Akropolis where the privilege of dining at the city's expense was awarded to certain individuals, including the descendants of Harmodios and Aristogeiton (cf. n. on *A.* 977–9), KLEON in 425–4 (*K.* 280–3, 709, etc.), visiting ambassadors (*A.* 125), and some religious officials (*P.* 1084)

PRYTANEIS (singular Prytanis), members of the standing committee of the COUNCIL (*K.* 300, 665 ff., *P.* 887, 905), responsible for presiding at its meetings and those of the ASSEMBLY (*A.* 23 ff.); each Athenian tribe's fifty representatives on the Council served for a prytany (a tenth of the official year)

SPARTA, most powerful city in the Peloponnese (cf. *A.* 620, 623), head of a military league at war with the Athenian empire 431–404, the so-called Peloponnesian War (for its origins, cf. the comic accounts at *A.* 509 ff., *P.* 604 ff.); stereotypically thought of by Athenians as incorrigibly perfidious (e.g. *A.* 308, *P.* 1065)

THRACE, the broad region to the N of the Aegean, including Greek cities belonging to the Athenian empire (*W.* 289); a traditional interface between Greeks and non-Greeks (cf. *P.* 1298); its non-Greek peoples were a prime source of Athenian slaves (*A.* 273, *W.* 828, *P.* 1138), but Athens also sought alliances with certain Thracian tribes (*A.* 136 ff., 602), partly with a view to obtaining the provision of light-armed troops (*A.* 148 ff.)

ZEUS, son of Kronos (*W.* 652), 'king' (*W.* 625) of the gods on mount Olympos (*P.* 177 ff.), father of APHRODITE, APOLLO, ATHENA, etc.; originally a sky- and weather-god (*W.* 260–1, 322 ff., 624, *P.* 42, 376, 1141); supremely powerful (*A.* 435), hence oaths are sworn ubiquitously in his name; traditionally god of friendship (*A.* 730); lover of the Trojan boy Ganymede (*P.* 724); he is sometimes conceived of as hostile to humans (*P.* 57–63, 371–2); Zeus Agoraios (*K.* 410, 500) can be loosely understood as an 'avatar' of Olympian Zeus

*The
Oxford
World's
Classics
Website*

www.oxfordworldsclassics.com

- Browse the full range of Oxford World's Classics online

- Sign up for our monthly e-alert to receive information on new titles

- Read extracts from the Introductions

- Listen to our editors and translators talk about the world's greatest literature with our Oxford World's Classics audio guides

- Join the conversation, follow us on Twitter at OWC_Oxford

- Teachers and lecturers can order inspection copies quickly and simply via our website

www.oxfordworldsclassics.com

American Literature

British and Irish Literature

Children's Literature

Classics and Ancient Literature

Colonial Literature

Eastern Literature

European Literature

Gothic Literature

History

Medieval Literature

Oxford English Drama

Philosophy

Poetry

Politics

Religion

The Oxford Shakespeare

A complete list of Oxford World's Classics, including Authors in Context, Oxford English Drama, and the Oxford Shakespeare, is available in the UK from the Marketing Services Department, Oxford University Press, Great Clarendon Street, Oxford OX2 6DP, or visit the website at www.oup.com/uk/worldsclassics.

In the USA, visit www.oup.com/us/owc for a complete title list.

Oxford World's Classics are available from all good bookshops.

Classical Literary Criticism
The First Philosophers: The Presocratics
  and the Sophists
Greek Lyric Poetry
Myths from Mesopotamia

APOLLODORUS   The Library of Greek Mythology

APOLLONIUS OF RHODES   Jason and the Golden Fleece

APULEIUS   The Golden Ass

ARISTOPHANES   Birds and Other Plays

ARISTOTLE   The Nicomachean Ethics
     Politics

ARRIAN   Alexander the Great

BOETHIUS   The Consolation of Philosophy

CAESAR   The Civil War
     The Gallic War

CATULLUS   The Poems of Catullus

CICERO   Defence Speeches
     The Nature of the Gods
     On Obligations
     Political Speeches
     The Republic and The Laws

EURIPIDES   Bacchae and Other Plays
     Heracles and Other Plays
     Medea and Other Plays
     Orestes and Other Plays
     The Trojan Women and Other Plays

HERODOTUS   The Histories

HOMER   The Iliad
     The Odyssey